Macroeconomics

www.oup.com/uk/bw3/

Macroeconomics

A European Text · THIRD EDITION

Michael Burda and Charles Wyplosz

OXFORD
UNIVERSITY PRESS
2001

For Maike, Maxwell, Robert, and Henry
A la Dame de Taulignan et ses enfants

OXFORD

UNIVERSITY PRESS

Great Clarendon Street, Oxford OX2 6DP

Oxford University Press is a department of the University of Oxford.
It furthers the University's objective of excellence in research, scholarship,
and education by publishing worldwide in

Oxford New York

Athens Auckland Bangkok Bogotá Buenos Aires Cape Town
Chennai Dar es Salaam Delhi Florence Hong Kong Istanbul Karachi
Kolkata Kuala Lumpur Madrid Melbourne Mexico City Mumbai Nairobi
Paris São Paulo Singapore Taipei Tokyo Toronto Warsaw

with associated companies in Berlin Ibadan

Oxford is a registered trade mark of Oxford University Press
in the UK and in certain other countries

Published in the United States
by Oxford University Press Inc., New York

A catalogue record for this book is available from the British Library

Library of Congress Cataloging in Publication Data
Data available

ISBN 0 19 877650 0

Typeset in 8.8/12.5pt ITC Stone Serif by Graphicraft Limited, Hong Kong
Printed in Italy on acid-free paper by
LEGOPrint S.p.A., Trento, Italy

Foreword to the Third Edition

A great deal has occurred since the second edition was published. First and foremost, the euro has arrived. Second, unemployment has receded throughout Europe, and has done so quite spectacularly in some countries. Third, the field of macroeconomics continues to move forward, and has expanded and improved our understanding of the way the economy works. Finally, most closely related to our enterprise, a number of new textbooks with an international outlook have been published. Along with friendly comments and suggestions from colleagues and students, this healthy dose of competition and criticism has redoubled our efforts to better the offerings from the other side of the Atlantic. The result? A new textbook with the best features of the second edition, but with a number of innovations: eight chapters are either new or have been thoroughly rewritten, while many others have been subjected to critical revision.

The euro is here

It is natural to expect a European text to put the euro at the forefront in all its manifestations, and we have done just that! This major step in Europe's process of widening and deepening has inspired a number of profound changes, as well as some minor touch-ups:

- The chapter on monetary policy (Chapter 9) has been completely rewritten. It now explains the objectives and procedures of the European Central Bank, without forgetting the Grand Old Lady of Threadneedle Street (the Bank of England), which has rejuvenated herself and seems to have a new lease of life.

- In the past, we had always quoted the exchange rate (as on the continent) using 'European' terms (e.g. DM per US$1 from the German perspective), despite the fact that the UK uses the British terms (e.g. US$ per £1 from the British perspective). As in much of the technical economics literature, we had used European terms, with a certain sense of uneasiness. Now, with the euro also widely quoted in British terms, the temptation was irresistible to adopt British terms, treating sterling and euro in the same way. Furthermore, we are able to accommodate the natural expectation of students and common usage in practical affairs that a 'higher' exchange rate is an *appreciation*. The cost of the change is that most of us have trained ourselves—and our students along the way—to think about currencies in European terms. The change will be unsettling at first; much like the old lady struggling with euros, seasoned teachers will have to adjust, but better sooner than later.

- Chapter 21 of the second edition which dealt with the fixed exchange rate systems in Europe, like the EMS itself, is gone. Key features of EMU in the context of global economic architecture are introduced in Chapter 20.

New knowledge

New research and new events continuously challenge and reshape our field, and teachers must continuously adapt. The third edition reflects many of these changes and provides teachers with an up-to-date treatment of modern macroeconomics and major trends in Europe.

The success achieved in several countries in bringing unemployment down is a blessing for society and provides economists with a sharpened understanding of labour markets. Some ideas were proved wrong, others have been vindicated. Our labour market chapter, now Chapter 4, has well withstood this test. While its structure survives, many details and all data have been updated with important new examples.

- Chapter 17, on the supply side, has been overhauled fundamentally. It now focuses on the principles behind supply-side policies, providing an overview of market failures as the basis for government intervention. It includes many ideas from the political economy approach which has been developed over the last decade and includes some new data on successes with labour market reform in countries like Denmark, the Netherlands, and Spain.

- A new chapter (Chapter 18) has been introduced to deal with the 'new economy' and many aspects of endogenous growth theory which, many adopters felt had not been given adequate space.

- Chapter 19, which deals with markets for financial assets and foreign exchange in particular, unifies two different chapters in the second edition, with less attention to institutional details. It should help students see the commonality between domestic and exchange markets, and thus better grasp the links between these markets.

- Chapter 20 now combines an analysis of EMU and the debate on the new architecture of the international monetary system, again bringing under one house the material that used to be spread into two chapters. Our aim here is to streamline the book.

Improvements

Over the years, many users of *Macroeconomics: A European Text* have expressed dissatisfaction with two chapters. They could not be wrong, we thought, and have taken advantage of this edition to offer what we hope is a much improved treatment.

- Chapter 3, on economic growth, was originally structured along the lines of the Solow decomposition. The new version is designed to lead the student to think of the growth phenomenon in a systematic way: why do economies seem to grow forever? The chapter then introduces the production function, adding factors of production one by one, concluding that it does not add up to an explanation of trend growth in GDP per capita. It then brings exogenous technological change, and shows that this does the trick. It concludes with a brief presentation of endogenous growth theory, which is further developed in Chapter 18. Thus, this chapter is essentially new and should prove to be considerably easier to digest.

- Chapter 12, on inflation, used to be built around the Phillips curve, presented as a key empirical result in search for a theoretical interpretation. We now turn things around. We first develop the theory of wage and price setting—the battle of the mark-ups. We then justify the Phillips curve, moving carefully from price levels to inflation. It should be easier to teach and to study.

Data, examples, and exercises

Most tables and figures have been updated, thus providing teachers with data that will better speak to the students' own experience. Many old examples have been replaced with new ones that refer to recent events that should be familiar to nowadays students. The book reflects the last few years, not the previous decade.

Most of the exercises have been replaced by newer ones. We provide short answers to the even-numbered exercises at the end of the book, and answers to odd-numbered exercises will be available on the text's website described below in more detail. The idea is to encourage students to train themselves, while attaching some cost to jumping too fast to the solution. The first—small—hurdle is to search the end of the book, the second hurdle is to hook on to the web.

Book structure, length, and level

The order of chapters has been changed slightly. We retain the logic of the first edition, which has since been adopted by most major textbooks: start with the long run, the real side, and then look at the shorter run, the nominal side, before providing an integrated treatment. In the third edition, we have pushed the logic further to its natural conclusion, starting with growth and the labour market rather than intertemporal constraints and demand behaviour. Thus we first provide a complete treatment of aggregate supply before tuning to demand. As a result the book has become more streamlined and 'linear' in topic development.

Every single sentence in the whole book has been written with a view to improving conciseness and ease of reading. No page has been left unturned. A number of tables, figures, and boxes which had cluttered the text have been eliminated. We also agonized on how to treat the mathematical appendices. Some teachers reported that they and their students had no use for them. Others thought that they were a key strength of our text: 'soft' treatment in the text, formal development at the end of the most challenging chapters. In the end, we kept most appendices on the grounds that if they help some they belong in there. All in all, we provide a shorter text, with no loss in content.

We also agonized on the level of treatment of the material. Our most successful competitors offer an easier treatment, sweeping under the rug the more challenging parts. Most of our adopters have urged us to keep our 'market niche', and so we have done. At the same time, we have a taken a hard look at every single difficulty and, whenever possible without altering the text's rigour and completeness, we have sanded down the rough edges.

Website

Last but not least, the brave new world of the Internet is here. Students are learning as much from the web as from books, if not more. This edition makes full use of this exciting technological advance. Our publisher, Oxford University Press has set up a website dedicated to the text: http://www.oup.com/uk/bw3/. This website includes three main features:

- A remarkably user-friendly study companion developed by Professor Irwin Collier (Free University Berlin). It includes PowerPoint slideshows designed both for teachers who wish to use them in class, chapter by chapter, and for students who want to see the course shown to them as in the classroom.

- Solutions to the odd-numbered exercise are presented here along with details, as well as more difficult material that was removed from the text. We intend to post new data and examples as important events occur. We also intend to add new exercises with their solutions.

- A user's corner will also be set up in the hope that teachers and students will join us in making this website lively. We look forward to ideas, comments, hints, exercises, exam samples, etc.

Table of Contents

The eight chapters indicated in colour have been completely restructured or are new.

Acknowledgements for the Second Edition

The second edition owes a great deal to the many colleagues who have taken the time to let us know of their reactions. We have not always followed their suggestions, but we have certainly listened very carefully.

Major changes have been undertaken following extensive exchanges with Jean-Pierre Danthine (University of Lausanne), Antonio Fatas (INSEAD), Michael Funke (Hamburg University), Alistair Milne (University of Surrey), and Anders Vredin (Stockholm School of Economics).

Very useful comments and suggestions which have also shaped the revisions were provided by Hans Aage (Roskilde University), Roger Backhouse (University of Birmingham), Antonio Barbosa (Universidade Nova de Lisboa), Guiseppe Bertola (Universita Turin), Mark de Broeck (KU Leuven), Manuel Correla de Pinho (University of Porto), Stefan Gerlach (BIS), Nathalie Gilson (Facultés Catholiques de Mons), Francis X. Hof (Technische Universität Wien), Jesper Jespersen (Roskilde University), Thorolfur Matthiasson (University of Iceland), Andrew Oswald (Oxford), and Heiki Taimio (University of Joensuu). In addition, we have used some exercises generously offered to us by Morten Skak (Odense University).

The following have generously helped with data collection: Benoit Coeuré (INSEE), Francesco Papadia (Bank of Italy), Pierre Sicsic (Banque de France), Jorg Elmeskov (OECD). Institutional (not proprietary) information on the Bundesbank was provided by Karen Cabos and Otmar Issing.

Our publisher has shown understanding as successive deadlines were transgressed; we appreciate the trust and encouragement from Andrew Schuller and Tracy Mawson. Graduate students Antje Mertens, Stefan Profit, Manfred Königstein, and especially Mark Weder should be thanked for their careful reading of draft chapters as well as constructive comments. Michaela Kleber and Gitte Aabo also provided useful comments at the development stages of the second edition.

A number of research assistants have helped us update the data and produce new tables and figures; we acknowledge the dedicated efforts of Matthas Almus, Ulrike Handtke, Matthew Hansen, and Astrid Knott. Finally, we are indebted to our secretaries Brigitte Pernet in Fontainebleau, Laurence Péricard in Geneva, and especially Claudia Keidel in Berlin.

Acknowledgements for the Third Edition

The third edition of *Macroeconomics: A European Text* owes a great deal to colleagues who shared their views with us on previous editions. First and foremost, our thanks go numerous anonymous referees who sent detailed comments on our proposed restructuring and on the first drafts of the new chapters. They will find that many of their suggestions were taken to heart. The book has benefited enormously from Bud Collier's probing and persistent questions. We are also grateful for constructive criticism and suggestions offered by António Pinto Barbosa, Ingo Barens, Jan Bentzen, Barbara Dluhosch, Michael Funke, Lauri Luiker, Pierre Pestieau, Pedro Vaz Pinto, Andras Simonovits, Stan Standaert, and Heikki Taimio. Thanks also to Silvia Strub, who reminded us that much domestic unpaid work is simply forgotten.

We are grateful to Anja Heinze and Bianca Brandeburg who performed stellar research assistantship with the updating of figures and tables under severe time pressure. In the critical final weeks, we benefited from extra help from Frank Tiefenbeck, Almut Balleer, and Tom Krüger. Claudia Keidel was an enormous help in processing the manuscript in all its forms from beginning to end.

Our publisher has been a supportive partner in this enterprise. Tim Barton, with the assistance of Charlotte Lang, has thought through the various strategic decisions with us and organized a very efficient review process. Matthew Cotton organized the production of the book, showing admirable patience when we were late. Edwin Pritchard performed excellent copy-editing.

Contents

Detailed Contents

Part II The Real Macroeconomy 41

3 Economic Growth 43

4 Labour Markets and Unemployment 69

Part IV   Macroeconomic Equilibrium   221

10   Output, Employment, and Prices   223

Part VI	**Macroeconomic Policy**	**361**

15	**Fiscal Policy, Debt, and Seigniorage**	**363**

Part VII   Asset Markets and International Financial Architecture   461

19   Asset Markets and Macroeconomics   463

List of Figures

List of Tables

List of Boxes

Introduction to Macroeconomics

This part sets the scene. Chapter 1 explains the object and methods of macroeconomics, its history and usefulness, and its controversies. It provides a large number of essential definitions and offers a preview of what is to follow. Chapter 2 presents the national income accounts, a good way to describe the inner relationships of the economy's activity, as well as the balance of payments, which summarizes an economy's dealings with the rest of the world.

What is Macroeconomics?

1.1   Overview

Not a day passes when we don't hear about unemployment, inflation, economic growth, stock markets, interest rates, or foreign exchange rates. We hear and read so much about these phenomena because, directly or indirectly, they affect our well-being. It is perhaps mostly for this reason that macroeconomics, the study of economy-wide phenomena, is so exciting. More than just headlines, however, macroeconomics is a fascinating intellectual adventure. The breadth of issues it covers is evidence enough of its inherent complexity, yet, simple economic reasoning can take us a long way. And it is often surprising how well a few simple ideas fit complex situations.

Macroeconomics can also be useful. The economic well-being of poor and wealthy households alike is affected by movements in interest rates or the rate of inflation. Businesses stand to gain or lose considerable amounts of money when their economic environment changes, regardless of how well they manage their affairs. Being prepared for such changes in fortunes can have considerable value and makes us all better citizens able to grasp the challenges that our societies face. Macroeconomics is relevant to voters who wonder what their governments are up to, or to consumers who care about interest and exchange rates. It is useful to governments as it may help avoid some of the miseries that have plagued mankind, such as deep recessions and hyperinflations which can tear at a society's social fabric.

1.1.1 Income and Economic Growth

The most frequently used measure of a nation's economic well-being is its output and income, the **gross domestic product (GDP)**. Figure 1.1(*a*) displays the evolution of GDP for France, Germany, and the UK since 1870. A positive long-run general tendency or **trend** dominates shorter-run fluctuations. The trend rate of growth has been fairly stable, perhaps with an increase after the Second World War. Another way of looking at this is to plot the GDP on a logarithmic scale, as in panel (*b*). With such a scale the slope of

the curve is a direct measure of the growth rate: a constant annual growth rate would yield a straight line.[1] In the long run, on average, we are not far from it.

For the large majority of countries, this trend growth in total output reflects remarkable increases in living standards. Table 1.1 shows that per capita or average income has increased by a factor of 5 in Belgium since 1900, by a factor of 6.5 in Sweden, and by a factor of 17 in Japan. In contrast, real income per capita rose by only 120% over the same period in Bangladesh. Some countries have faced serious setbacks, such as wars and famines, while others have grown rapidly.

Economic growth is one of the most exciting issues in macroeconomics. There are many reasons for economies to grow, and they are reviewed in Chapter 3. One of them is population increase, since more people can produce more output. Another is the accumulation of means of production: plant and equipment, roads, communication networks, and other forms of infrastructure make workers more productive. Most important is the development and harnessing of knowledge to economic ends. The sharp acceleration of scientific discoveries towards the end of the eighteenth century is thought to have triggered the industrial revolution, and some believe we are now witnessing the onset of a new wave of advances related to information and telecommunications technology.

A second important message from Figure 1.1 is that the real output tends to fluctuate around its trend. This is made more apparent in Figure 1.2, which shows the quarter-by-quarter evolution of the British GDP. These sustained periods of ups and downs are called **business cycles**. One important challenge of macroeconomics is to explain these deviations of GDP from its underlying trend: why they occur and persist over a few years, and what can be done, if anything, to avoid the disruptions that are associated with them. This is the common thread of Parts III, IV, and V of this book.

---

[1] For mathematically inclined readers, if $x(t)$ grows at the constant rate g, $(1/x)\,\mathrm{d}x/\mathrm{d}t = g$, so that $x(t) = A\exp(gt)$ or $\ln x(t) = \ln A + gt$, where A is a constant and t stands for time.

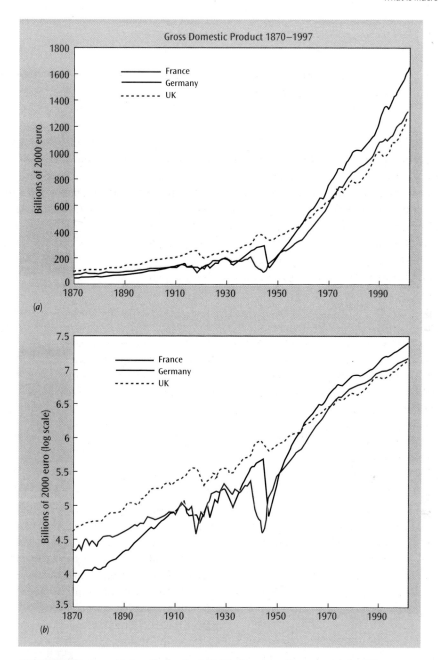

Fig. 1.1 **Gross Domestic Product (GDP), Germany, France, and the UK, 1870–2001**

The movements of real product and income exhibit a powerful growth trend. Growth tends to be exponential; that is, annual percentage increases are reasonably stable in the long run, which does not preclude important year-to-year variations. When the data are displayed on a logarithmic scale instead (part *b*), the slope of the curve measures the annual rate of growth.

Source: Maddison (1995); OECD.

Table 1.1	Real Income per Capita (GDP in €, 2000)

	1900	1913	1929	1950	1987	1992	1999	Av. Growth rate
Austria	3,345	4,022	4,291	4,301	17,813	20,260	25,325	2.1
Belgium	4,307	4,875	5,839	6,309	17,766	20,635	25,866	1.8
Canada	3,663	5,618	6,658	9,891	25,735	25,599	25,216	2.0
Denmark	3,509	4,550	5,902	7,891	20,157	21,117	25,758	2.0
Finland	2,075	2,624	3,377	5,288	19,247	18,336	22,727	2.4
France	3,242	3,918	5,326	5,959	19,197	21,040	25,216	2.1
Germany	3,157	3,864	4,362	5,081	20,187	22,996	24,567	2.1
Italy	2,721	3,592	4,232	4,706	18,283	20,522	23,160	2.2
Japan	1,372	1,611	2,354	2,261	19,766	23,974	25,325	3.0
Netherlands	4,348	4,862	6,834	7,201	18,633	20,915	25,000	1.8
Sweden	3,003	3,631	4,542	7,897	20,925	20,893	22,403	2.1
Switzerland	4,208	5,012	7,440	10,649	24,124	24,785	29,329	2.0
UK	5,669	6,210	6,483	8,451	18,595	19,551	23,593	1.5
USA	5,898	7,642	9,946	13,568	27,453	28,828	36,688	1.9
Bangladesh	707	752	754	671	760	914	1,591	0.8
Argentina	2,601	3,586	4,125	4,688	6,690	5,499	10,823	1.5

Sources: Maddison (1991); Summers and Heston, Penn World Tables Mark 5.6a, http://www.odci.gov/cia/publications/factbook/

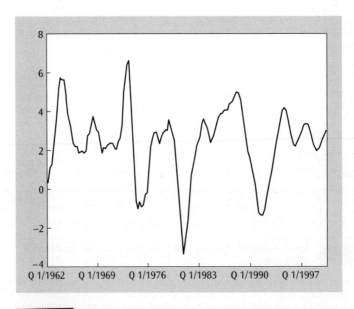

Fig. 1.2	Quarterly Gross Domestic Product, UK, 1962: 1–1999: 2

With quarterly data, fluctuations of economic activity around trend become more apparent.
Sources: IMF; OECD.

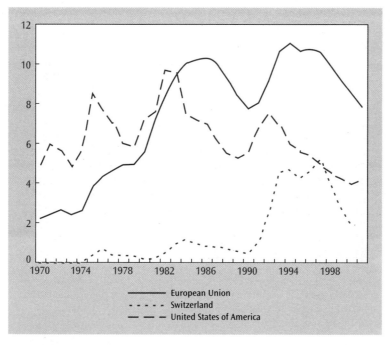

Fig. 1.3 **Unemployment Rates in the European Union, Switzerland, and the USA, 1970–2001**

The experience with unemployment (measured as the proportion of workers who do not have a job but look for one) is varied across countries. In the USA, the unemployment rate fluctuates according to business cycles. In the European Union, there has been a marked trend increase, signalling a key specificity of the continent. Not all countries of Europe, however, have suffered from massive unemployment, as Switzerland shows.

1.1.2 Unemployment

One important phenomenon associated with cyclical fluctuations is **unemployment**, the fact that people seeking jobs cannot get them, even when the economy is growing rapidly. The **unemployment rate** is the ratio of the number of unemployed workers to the size of the **labour force**. The labour force consists of those who are either working or are actively looking for a job. In comparison with the total population, it leaves out young people who are not yet working, the old who are retired, and those who do not wish to work—or have given up hope of working.

There are many reasons why we are concerned about unemployment. It represents a loss of output and income as workers stay idle. Even with well-developed and efficient unemployment assistance programmes, unemployed workers may experience emotional stress and their skills may deteriorate. Even if they are not measurable, the social and psychological costs of unemployment are high for the affected individuals and for society as a whole. On that criterion, Europe has not done well over the last decades, as Figure 1.3 shows. The rate of unemployment has grown inexorably to reach double-digit numbers. In the USA, in contrast, unemployment has closely followed the business cycles, rising in periods of slowdown, declining when growth returned. At the same time, not all European countries have shared this misery, as the case of Switzerland shows. Chapter 4 presents the many reasons behind these contrasted experiences.

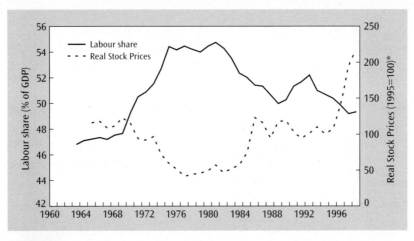

Fig. 1.4 **Labour Share of Income in Manufacturing and Stock Prices, Four Countries, 1960–1999**

Labour and capital share the fruits of the economic activity of a nation. The labour share is the fraction accruing to workers in the form of wages and other compensation. The valuation of firm assets reflected in stock prices is negatively associated with the labour share.
Sources: OECD; IMF; US Department of Labor.

1.1.3 Factors of Production and Income Distribution

GDP is created by work effort combined with equipment. (Land and other inputs also matter, but in a much smaller proportion.) **Labour** and **capital** are the technical names given to these two main **factors of production**, or inputs. The distribution of total income between these two factors of production is often a political issue, with important economic aspects. Understandably, wage-earners wish to enlarge their share of the pie. Figure 1.4 shows the share of income in manufacturing that goes to labour, the **labour share**. It also plots the evolution of the stock market **index** over time. An index is a number whose value does not have a meaning per se, but is set to take a simple value (e.g. 1 or 100) on a particular date for easy comparison. In stock markets, companies are traded and valued on the basis of their profitability. The figure shows an inverse relationship between the labour share and the stock price index. When the share of income going to labour is high, less is available for the firms' owners, and stock prices are depressed. In Chapter 6 we will see that depressed stock prices may adversely affect the accumulation of productive equipment and, ultimately, the growth and size of the economic pie itself.

1.1.4 Inflation

The **inflation rate** measures the rate of change of the average level of prices. Inflation is usually quoted in percentages per year, even when it is measured more frequently, such as every quarter or every month. Most of the time, inflation is low or moderate at rates ranging from just above 0% to 4%. In the 1970s many European countries experienced double-digit inflation, with rates rising to 10%, 20%, or more. In a number of countries, for example in Latin America or in the transition countries of Eastern Europe, inflation rates of several hundred per cent were quite common in the 1980s. When inflation is very high it is usually measured on a monthly basis; the term **hyperinflation** describes situations when this monthly inflation rate exceeds 50%. A sign of exceptional economic distress, hyperinflation has been observed in Central Europe in the early 1920s, in Latin America in the 1980s, and in many countries born out of the collapse of the Soviet Union in the early 1990s.

In normal times, inflation is related to the business cycle. Figure 1.5 shows how the rate of inflation changes when the rate of capacity utilization varies. The rate of **capacity utilization** is a measure of how fully companies employ their plant and equipment,

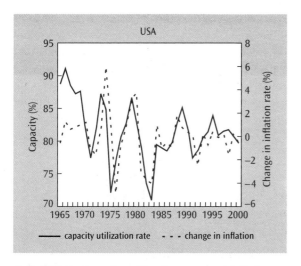

Fig. 1.5   **Capacity Utilization Rates and Inflation, USA, 1965–2000**

When measures of the utilization of capacity indicate a high level of activity in factories, the rate of inflation tends to increase. Conversely, low levels of activity are accompanied by falling inflation.

Sources: IMF; OECD *Main Economic Indicators*.

economy: the former concerns the production and consumption of goods and services, and the incomes associated with productive activities; the latter deals with trade in assets, i.e. monetary and financial instruments. Chapter 10 draws the first linkages between real and monetary spheres of the macro-economy, while Chapter 11 directly addresses the short-run determination of output, interest rates, and exchange rates. Chapters 12 and 13 bring together the issues of inflation and exchange rates.

1.1.6 Openness

Every country engages in trade, exporting and importing goods and services to and from other partner countries. An increasing number of countries— sometimes called emerging market countries—are also linked together through trade in financial assets. One measure of a country's openness, or exposure to the influences of the rest of the world, is the ratio of its exports to its GDP. Table 1.2 shows that openness has

and it serves as a good indicator of cyclical conditions. The inflation rate is generally **procyclical**: it rises in periods of high growth and declines in periods of slow growth. In contrast, the behaviour of unemployment is **countercyclical**. The behaviour of inflation is investigated in Parts IV and V of this book.

1.1.5 Financial Markets and the Real Economy

Financial markets play a central role in modern economies. They trade in currencies, stocks, and bonds. In conjunction with banks, financial markets collect resources from households in the form of savings and lend them out. One specific feature of these markets is the extreme volatility of their prices.

Physical investment, the accumulation of productive capital, is related to financial conditions. It is one channel through which financial markets affect the **real economy**. The other channel is consumption. Stocks—shares in corporations—represent one form of private wealth. When share prices rise, people feel richer and consume more. The real economy is contrasted with the financial or **monetary**

Table 1.2   **Openness (Ratio of Exports to GDP, %)**

	1960	1997
European Union	6.1	9.9
United States	5.2	12.1
Japan	10.7	11.1
Belgium	38.3	72.9
Denmark	32.7	36.0
Germany	19.0	27.8
Hungary	—	45.5
Ireland	30.6	79.7
Netherlands	46.3	56.0
Poland	—	25.7
Portugal	16.0	31.4
Russian Federation	—	23.7
Spain	8.9	28.4
Sweden	22.7	43.8
Switzerland	27.7	39.9
Ukraine	—	40.6
United Kingdom	20.9	28.7

Source: World Bank and European Commission.

considerably increased over the past decades, as part of the process of globalization. Smaller countries tend to be more open than larger countries, and indeed the USA and Japan are fairly closed by international standards. This is also the case of the European Union vis-à-vis the rest of the world, even though considerable trade integration has taken place among its member countries as the table well illustrates.

As a consequence, no one country is free from influences of events that occur elsewhere, sometimes far away. For example, the financial crisis that started in Thailand in June 1997 spread to the rest of South-East Asia, then moved on to Russia, affecting Hungary and Poland along the way, before hitting Brazil. Chapters 19 and 20 look at these issues.

1.2   Macroeconomics as a Discipline

1.2.1 The Genesis of Macroeconomics

Why do we observe cyclical fluctuations in the level of activity, for example the movements of GDP around its trend? Why is unemployment generally countercyclical while changes in inflation seem to be procyclical? It is only relatively recently that economics has concerned itself with such questions. For a long time it was believed that, as a good approximation at least, properly functioning markets would deliver the best possible outcome, and that there was no point in looking into their aggregate behaviour. This principle was called 'laissez-faire'. Laissez-faire was opposed by proponents of **interventionism**, who advocated government support for particular markets and industries, including subsidies and protection from foreign competition.

This does not mean that the business cycle was ignored. In fact, a number of cycles were studied and identified, from inventory cycles of one or two years' duration to the long-wave cycles lasting half a century. Such cycles were seen as the cumulative outcomes of disturbances such as discoveries, inventions, exceptionally good or bad crops, wrong bets by firms on goods that customers want to buy, or even changing tastes of consumers at home and abroad. Inflation was seen as the consequence of rapidly growing money stocks, first because of gold discoveries in the 19th century, afterwards because of reckless paper money creation by central banks. As will be seen in Chapter 14, much of this wisdom remains valid today. Yet the Great Depression of the 1930s, which spread worldwide sending millions into unemployment and misery, seemed too severe to be simply bad luck. Reflecting upon the Great Depression in 1936, British economist John Maynard Keynes published *The General Theory of Employment, Interest and Money*, a book that launched the study of macroeconomics. Keynes stressed the role of aggregate demand in macroeconomic fluctuations. His followers later persuaded policy-makers to engage in **aggregate demand management**, that is, to manipulate government demand in order to smooth out fluctuations, mainly to avoid protracted recessions.

An evaluation of the success of demand management policies—which is the subject of Chapters 15 and 16—is not conclusive. There have been both benefits and costs. Since the Second World War, the amplitude of the business cycle seems to have diminished considerably, as can be seen in Figure 1.1. While earlier generations assumed that favourable periods of growth were inevitably followed by periods of declining activity, today we worry mostly about slowdowns of growth. At the same time, economists have also begun to think hard about the supply side—meaning the productive capacity of an economy—and more efficient utilization of labour and capital resources. This applies especially to unemployment, which is a big problem in Europe. These topics are the subject of Chapter 17.

Another remarkable change in the behaviour of the post-war economy concerns the general **price level**, or the cost of goods in terms of money. Up until the Second World War, prices were as likely to rise as they were to fall, as can be seen from Figure 1.6. Apart from war periods, the price level was trendless. Over long periods, say twenty or fifty

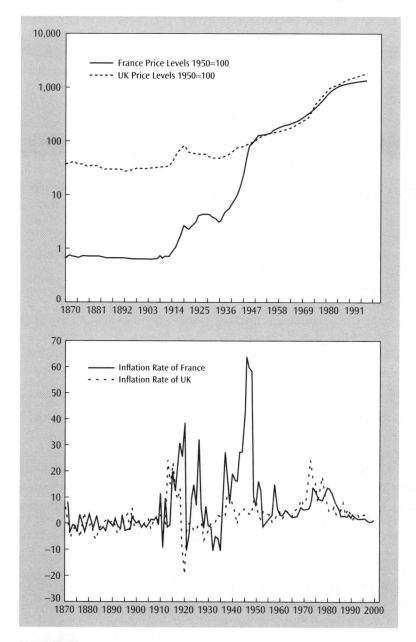

Fig. 1.6   **Price Levels and Inflation Rates, France and the UK, 1870–2000**

Until the outbreak of the First World War, the price level was stable, and inflation was close to zero on average. Since the Second World War, the price level has risen secularly, average inflation has been positive, high in the late 1970s and much of the 1980s, declining over the 1990s.

Source: Maddison (1991), OECD.

years, the cost of living, a measure of the average price level, was essentially constant. One interpretation of the post-war era—a controversial one, as we shall see—is that macroeconomics has led to more stable growth rates at the cost of inflation. In the mid-1980s, concern with high inflation has triggered a change of heart. In particular, most central banks have given up Keynesian policies and refocused their energy on keeping inflation low.

1.2.2 Macroeconomics and Microeconomics

The macroeconomy is just the sum of hundreds or thousands of markets, each of which is explained by microeconomic principles. Microeconomics is devoted to the study of prices of individual goods and of the markets where these goods are produced and sold. Why do we need two separate disciplines? To a great extent they are linked. Microeconomics is dedicated to the analysis of market behaviour of individuals. Macroeconomics is concerned with collective behaviour, the outcome of individual decisions taken without full knowledge of what others do. Keynes stressed the notion of **coordination failures**, which arise in decentralized markets as illustrated in the following example.

A consumer wants to purchase a car, but his income is insufficient for him to do so. A car manufacturer could actually hire him to build cars, and with his salary he would then be able to buy one. That one sale, however, would not suffice to pay his salary, so other buyers would need to be found. In order to generate sufficient demand for his employment, several other individuals would need to be hired, perhaps in different industries. For this scheme to work, a considerable amount of coordination among producers and consumers would be required. The laissez-faire principle is that prices and markets fulfil this coordinating role. Keynes's view was that sometimes they fail to do so. Then, there may be many consumers wishing to buy goods and willing to work to produce them, and many firms that would benefit from hiring them if only they could be persuaded that their sales would increase. But this potential may not be realized and we have both recession (fewer sales) and unemployment

(fewer jobs). Even if market forces tend to correct this imbalance (which they eventually do), the period of time necessary may be long enough to involve significant social costs.

Macroeconomics started with the idea that prices and markets do not continuously resolve all the coordination requirements of a modern economy. As microeconomics has moved in this direction too, the sharp distinction between the two fields has been eroded. Modern macroeconomics starts from sound microeconomic principles, and we follow this approach in the early chapters. We then focus on market failures to study business cycles and what can be done about them.

1.2.3 Macroeconomics and Economic Policy

Early macroeconomists argued that governments have the means and the duty to correct market failures. The experiences of the past decades have shown that governments too may fail. Indeed, one major dividing line among macroeconomists is between those who most fear market failures and those who most fear government failures. Yet, in nearly every country, governments are held responsible for the good health of the macroeconomy. At election times incumbent governments are judged, first among many other issues, on their economic performance. This is largely a consequence of the **Keynesian revolution**. It explains why the study of macroeconomics is so intertwined with policy and indeed with politics. Part V is devoted to these issues.

1.2.4 Demand and Supply Sides

In its most concentrated form, macroeconomics boils down to separating events into two categories: those that affect the demand for goods and services, and those that affect the supply of those goods and services. The **demand side** relates to spending decisions by **economic agents**—households, firms, and government agencies—both at home and abroad. The principle of aggregate demand management policies is that the government can take actions to offset or smooth out those of private agents—firms and households—in order to dampen or eliminate fluctuations in total spending. The idea is to take the edge off recessions as well as booms. Two traditional demand management instruments are fiscal and monetary policy. **Fiscal policy** manipulates government expenditures or taxes in an attempt to affect the volume of national spending. This subject is studied in detail in Chapter 15. **Monetary policy** is directed at influencing interest and exchange rates, and more generally conditions in financial markets. Chapters 8 and 9 provide an in-depth analysis.

The **supply side** relates to the productive potential of the economy. The choice of hours worked by households, the productivity of their labour, and in general the efficiency with which resources are allocated in generating a nation's output, all influence an economy's aggregate supply. Accordingly, supply-side policies represent the government's effort to increase the economy's overall efficiency. In part, this effort is about cutting down government-induced inefficiencies, which were introduced before the importance of the supply side was understood, or as the result of successful lobbying by interest groups. Unemployment policy—designed to fight the scourge of market economies—occupies a key role in the supply side. Chapter 17 explores these issues and shows how the government can improve or worsen the economic climate.

1.3   The Methodology of Macroeconomics

1.3.1 What is to be Explained?

Macroeconomics is concerned with aggregate activity, the level of unemployment, interest rates, inflation, wages, the exchange rate, and the balance of payments with other countries. Before commencing such an analysis, it is essential to be clear about what we want to explain and what we take as given. This distinction is represented in Figure 1.7. The variables to be explained using economic principles are called **endogenous** variables. The other variables—those we do not try to explain—are called **exogenous** variables. Examples of variables considered exogenous are policy instruments (the tools of fiscal and monetary policies), economic conditions abroad (foreign levels of activity and interest rates), the price of oil, and sometimes even domestic social conditions such as business optimism or trade union militancy.

The distinction between endogenous and exogenous variables is somewhat arbitrary. Many exogenous variables are not strictly independent of the endogenous variables. For example, fiscal and monetary policy decisions are often responses to the course of inflation or unemployment. While it is convenient to take policy variables as exogenous, it is sometimes illuminating to endogenize them. Chapter 16 takes some steps in this direction.

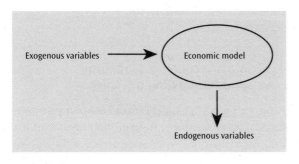

Fig. 1.7   **Endogenous and Exogenous Variables**

Endogenous variables are the object of analysis in an economic model. Exogenous variables are determined outside the economic model. The weather, political decisions, and the onset of time are examples of variables usually considered exogenous.

1.3.2 Theory and Realism

Macroeconomics proceeds by making simplifying assumptions. We never literally believe in our assumptions, but we need them in order to see through the vast complexity of an economy. This is why the distinction between endogenous and exogenous variables is artificial. Truly exogenous variables are few: two examples are climatic conditions (and even these may be affected by economic events, such as the greenhouse effect) and scientific discoveries and inventions (which also may result from economic decisions). The task of systematically linking the behaviour of endogenous variables to changes in exogenous variables is accomplished by specifying relationships between all the variables of interest.

All these relationships, when brought together, constitute a *theory*. Almost by definition, theory departs from realism. If the real world could be understood without simplifying assumptions, theories would be unnecessary. The problem is not with economics, it is with the world's inherent complexity. Progress is made by weeding out those assumptions and theories that lead us to false conclusions. As time passes, some theories prove to be unfounded, while others gain acceptability. This process is long and complex, and far from complete. Because macroeconomics is a young discipline, a number of controversies continue to dominate, and this aspect is discussed in Section 1.4 below.

1.3.3 **Positive and Normative Analysis**

Macroeconomic analysis and policy are closely linked. Because a number of exogenous variables are under the control of government, it makes sense to ask what is good and what is bad policy. At its best, macroeconomics can explain the economy; for example, it can link particular events to exogenous events or policy decisions. This is **positive economics**: it refrains from value judgements. **Normative economics** takes a further step and passes judgement or makes policy recommendations. In so doing, it must specify what criteria are used in arriving at particular conclusions. This inevitably implies a value judgement. Economists generally like to make policy recommendations. As long as they reveal their criteria, this is part of their professional activity. In this text however we will generally refrain from normative economics.[2] We believe and hope that many readers will make use

of their newly acquired knowledge to indulge in the normative side of macroeconomics: this is what makes it fun.

1.3.4 **Testing Theories: The Role of Data**

The generally accepted way of evaluating theories is to submit them to scientific tests. In macroeconomics, this means looking at the facts, i.e. at data. This is easier said than done, and there are a number of unusual difficulties. First, data correspond to sometimes elusive concepts, as Chapter 2 illustrates. Second, constructing aggregate data implies enquiring into the behaviour of millions of individuals, who sometimes have good or bad reasons to misrepresent the truth. Third, economics shares the predicament common to other social sciences that experimentation is not really possible—when observed, people often change their behaviour. Not only is it possibly immoral—no macroeconomist would wish to start a hyperinflation just to test a theory—but more importantly, many important variables simply are not observable. This is the case of expectations, for example. Macroeconomists are forced to conduct empirical tests with the data that they have. They develop statistical techniques, often sophisticated ones, to deal with observation and measurement errors. They refine the techniques they use to gather and analyse data. This allows the elimination of some theories and the modification of others. The surviving theories will be those that withstand the test of time in this scientific process.

1.3.5 **Macroeconomic Modelling and Forecasting**

Economists are always being asked to make forecasts. Governments, international organizations, and large financial institutions frequently employ large teams of economists to prepare forecasts. If macroeconomics were to be judged by the performance of forecasts, the verdict would not be unkind. The respectable track record of forecasters has however been sullied by some large historical errors. Box 1.1 illustrates this fact by examining the accuracy of forecasts for the year 1998.

---

[2] It is a fact that 'social conscience' motivates many to study economics. Much like medical doctors who want to cure the sick, economists are often eager to provide relief to the disadvantaged and suffering.

Box 1.1 **Forecasting the Year 1998**

Table 1.3 shows how forecasts evolve over time. It presents the forecasts for GDP growth and inflation presented by the OECD every six months in its publication, *Economic Outlook*. In most countries, growth turned out to be stronger and inflation lower than first expected at end 1996. The main reason is that oil prices declined sharply in 1997 (oil shocks are studied in Chapter 12. This was a counter-oil shock that was followed by sharp increases in oil prices during the course of 2000.) Note that the forecasters gradually realized what was happening but, as late as December 1997, they were still too conservative in their revisions, by a large margin in the case of the USA. This is a common feature, forecasters often tend to underestimate large changes. On the other side, the outcome for Japan and Korea was much worse than expected, even by the end of 1997. The explanation is the huge financial crisis that hit Asia. It started in June 1997 in Thailand, then spread in the region and finally hit Korea in December, probably after the OECD had produced its forecast. This is another lesson: crises do occur and are hard to predict. And, maybe, the OECD was trying to be optimistic while the whole world was waiting to see how Korea would emerge from its crisis.

Table 1.3 **Forecasting the Year 1998**

	France	Germany	Japan	Korea	UK	USA
GDP growth rate						
Forecast (December 1996)	2.6	2.6	3.7	n.a.	3.0	2.0
Forecast (June 1997)	2.8	2.8	2.9	6.5	2.7	2.0
Forecast (December 1997)	2.9	3.0	1.7	5.5	2.2	2.7
Actual Outcome	3.2	2.1	−2.5	−6.7	2.6	4.4
Inflation rate						
Forecast (December 1996)	1.4	1.3	0.0	n.a.	1.9	2.1
Forecast (June 1997)	1.4	1.8	1.0	4.9	2.3	2.4
Forecast (December 1997)	1.3	1.2	0.8	2.8	2.4	1.9
Actual Outcome	0.8	0.9	0.6	7.5	3.4	1.6

Source: OECD Economic Outlook.

There are several reasons why economic forecasting is inherently difficult. First and foremost, even an excellent understanding of an economy's structure—how its endogenous variables interact—does not preclude misjudging changes in exogenous variables. A good example of this was the oil price increases of 1973 and 2000, or the Gulf War of 1991. Second, expectations—which are volatile in nature—wield an important influence over the economy. Governments sometimes react to their own forecasts by implementing policies designed to prevent those forecasts from happening. Political changes occur quickly and can disrupt the economic environment. Finally, it takes time—often several months—to know what has really happened at any given point, so forecasts are always based on provisional information which becomes more precise only with time.

Most forecasts are generated by computer-based models. These models resemble those that we present in this book. They are made of hundreds, sometimes thousands, of equations. Constructing these equations is a long and difficult task. The exogenous variables must be guessed by forecasters before they can ask their computers for an answer. This introduces many margins of error. The models can never be fully reliable, and the exogenous vari-

ables may be difficult to pinpoint. For these reasons, the forecasters themselves take their results with a grain of salt, and often, when the outcome is not completely satisfactory, 'drop in' their own subjective factor to the results.

1.4 Preview of the Book

1.4.1 Structure

The book proceeds in steps. Parts I–IV build up an understanding of the measurement and the behaviour of the underlying economy. Part I is concerned mostly with defining terms and constructing a macroeconomic vocabulary. Part II elaborates the behaviour of the real economy. It focuses on the motivations of consumers and producers, abstracting from the influences of money and financial aspects of the economy. Part III studies money and its central role in macroeconomics, as well as the financial system that creates it. Part IV studies macroeconomic equilibrium in the short, medium, and long run. Part IV examines inflation and its evolution, and pins down its determinants over a longer horizon. It introduces a framework for thinking about inflation and the business cycle. Part V then uses this framework to explore policy issues facing governments: fiscal policy, demand management, and supply policy. The focus then shifts in Part VI to more specialized topics, financial markets and foreign exchange rates, as well the world international financial system.

1.4.2 **Controversies and Consensus**

Economists often make a bad name for themselves by quarrelling in public. This is intellectually healthy, but highly misleading to outside observers, whose opinions are often based on accounts in the popular press. Disagreements bear on what most outsiders will see as finer points, if not outright hair-splitting. It is unfortunate that some of these disagreements have important policy implications. We present some—but by no means all—of the

disagreements along the way, leaving readers free to judge for themselves. Yet we do not dwell upon them. Because there is so much that is not controversial, it is best first to understand the broad areas of consensus.

Almost from the beginning, macroeconomics has been divided into two main schools of thought. Keynesians (and their neo-Keynesian heirs) and monetarists (and neo-monetarists)[3] continue to pursue the old debate between laissez-faire and interventionism. Keynesians are often characterized by the view that markets are imperfect and that governments can and should conduct active policy interventions. Monetarists see politics and the power of bureaucracies as barriers to government attempts to deal successfully with market failures, which they see as of lesser importance. Given these premises, each school uses theories and data to build and support its case.

1.4.3 **Rigour and Intuition**

The only possible scientific approach to the complexities of the real world is the rigour of reasoning. However, to be useful, macroeconomics must be

---

[3] These are not exclusive labels. In the USA, where most of the debate takes place, reference is sometimes made to saltwater and fresh-water macroeconomists. Salt-water economists defend the Keynesian legacy from universities located on the two seaboards (Harvard, MIT, Yale, Stanford, Berkeley). Freshwater economists, most often associated with the Monetarist legacy, hail from universities located near the Great Lakes, e.g. Chicago, Rochester, or Minnesota. In Europe, these controversies are less evident: national traditions tend to make British or French economists more Keynesian and German or Swedish economists more Monetarist. But in each instance, there are as many exceptions as examples of the rule.

versatile and easily put to work when we want to understand particular events. This is why a great deal of macroeconomics simply amounts to accumulating intuition about particular phenomena. Our objective is, therefore, to leave readers with an intuitive understanding of how the economy functions. We do this by trying to draw robust yet simple conclusions from the various and often intricate principles presented. Such intuition is never completely rigorous, but can be useful in practice. Rigour plays its crucial role in reminding us when intuition is correct, and when it should be used with caution.

1.4.4 **Data and Institutions**

Macroeconomics is fascinating because it tells us a great deal about the world in which we live. It is not merely a set of abstract principles with interesting logical properties. Many assumptions and results will look odd at first sight, yet they capture key aspects of the real world. This is why at each important step we pause to look at facts. Facts can be data or particular episodes. Studying them carefully shows how theories work and shape our understanding of macroeconomic phenomena. It broadens our knowledge of important events that have shaped the lives of millions of people.

On the other hand, a graph or a table is no substitute for more rigorous analysis of the data. Merely demonstrating that two economic variables move closely together is a far cry from proving that one causes the other. Our motive in using data to illustrate economic phenomena is to give readers a feel for economics itself. At the end of each chapter we give a list of suggested reading—which is by no means meant to be exhaustive—for those who want to learn more about the theory and practice of macroeconomics.

Finally, good economic theories must be valid under different conditions. At the same time, the response of different countries to exogenous economic stimuli are often shaped by their particular economic and political institutions. These include their form of government, the existence of labour unions and employers' associations, and differing

regulations. The interplay of macroeconomic principles and institutions is an essential part of a proper understanding of the field, and this is why we spend a lot of time reviewing them. The economics of these institutions is, however, far beyond the level of this textbook.

1.4.5 **Europe**

Our textbook bears the subtitle 'A European Text'. Does this mean that we think that macroeconomics in Europe is fundamentally different from macroeconomics elsewhere, say in the USA, Japan, or Latin America? Most certainly not! On the contrary, we take the view that macroeconomics is sufficiently *global* in scope to apply to economies around the world. This includes the transforming economies of Central and Eastern Europe as well as the newly emerging economies of southern and eastern Asia. On the other hand, we do wish to send a more subtle signal: we believe strongly that European economies have important distinguishing features that make them hard to study through the lens of, say, the leading textbooks from North America.

There is much in Europe that warrants such a European emphasis. Rather than a collection of states under a federal government, Europe is a mosaic of nation-states, each with a sovereign macroeconomic policy-maker, but also with distinct preferences and endowments. Surely, the completion of the Single European Market, the creation of a monetary union, the continuing accession of new countries to the European Union to include the ex-communist economies in the heart of Europe, will increase the pressure towards integration, raising specific new challenges along the way. In addition, to varying degrees, European countries share a common view of the relationship between market forces and social justice. The attachment to fairness and economic solidarity is deeply ingrained in Europe's traditions and history, which explain why our labour markets differ so much from the US markets. This observation alone warrants a markedly different look, even if the theory is the same.

Key Concepts

- macroeconomics
- gross domestic product (GDP)
- trend
- economic growth
- business cycle
- unemployment
- labour force
- unemployment rate
- correlation coefficient
- labour
- capital
- factors of production
- labour share
- index number
- inflation
- hyperinflation
- capacity utilization
- procyclical and countercyclical
- investment ratio
- real economy
- laissez-faire versus interventionism
- aggregate demand management
- price level
- coordination failure
- Keynesian revolution
- misery index
- demand side
- economic agents
- fiscal policy
- monetary policy
- supply side
- endogenous
- exogenous
- normative and positive economics

Suggested Further Reading

On economics as a science, and the process of scientific discovery, see:

Friedman, Milton (1953), 'The Methodology of Positive Economics', in his *Essays in Positive Economics*, University of Chicago Press.

Kuhn, Thomas S. (1982), *The Structure of Scientific Revolutions*, University of Chicago Press.

On the state of macroeconomics and its controversies, see:

Dornbusch, Rudi (2000), *Keys to Prosperity*, MIT Press.

Greenwald, Bruce C., and Stiglitz, Joseph E. (1988), 'Examining Alternative Macro-economic Theories', *Brookings Papers on Economic Activity*, 1: 207–70.

Solow, Robert M. (1980), 'On Theories of Unemployment', *American Economic Review*, 70: 1–11.

Teranishi, Juro and Yukat Kosai (eds.) (1993), *The Japanese Experience of Economic Reforms*, St Martin's Press.

The symposium 'Forecasts for the Future of Economics', *Journal of Economic Perspectives*, Winter 2000.

Media

Students will greatly benefit from reading daily the economic section of their newspaper. Some publications with high-quality analyses (but not free of prejudices) are (in English): the *Financial Times* and *The Economist*. There is also a wealth of information on the web, see our site for directions.

Data are produced by national statistical institutes and central banks. Some international institutions produce comparable data and are of easy access: the IMF's *International Financial Statistics* and its biannual survey *World Economic Outlook*, the OECD's biannual *Economic Outlook*, the World Bank's *World Development Report* and *Global Economic Prospects*, the European Commission's *European Economy*, and the EBRD's annual *Transition Report*. All maintain websites, more or less generous in allowing access to their publications.

Macroeconomic Accounts

Facts and theories meet in analysis. The combination of the two is essential if economics is to progress, since it is neither a pure subject, like mathematics, of which one does not ask that the theories should be applicable to actual phenomena, nor is it a collection of facts, like the objects on a junk heap, of which one does not ask how they are related.

– Richard Stone

2.1 Overview

This chapter provides the background, a description of the macroeconomy and a definition of the more frequently used concepts. It takes as its departure point the national income accounts which are summarized with a number of **accounting identities**—how magnitudes relate to each other *by definition*—which play a central role throughout the study of macroeconomics.

While chapters which follow will explain behavioural relationships among these magnitudes, here we only describe them. The distinction between description (this chapter) and analysis (the rest of the book) can be illustrated by an example from biology. That living organisms consist of a collection of different cells is a biological description; how these cells function and affect each other constitutes the analysis. In a similar way, decomposing the gross domestic product into its components, or looking at the external accounts, sets up the picture that subsequent chapters will animate. It is an unavoidable step, and it is essential to be clear about these definitions which may be trickier than meets the eye.

2.2 Gross Domestic Product

2.2.1 Three Definitions of Gross Domestic Product

The **gross domestic product (GDP)** is defined for a particular geographic area—usually a country, but possibly a region or a city, or a group of countries such as the European Union (EU). It is also defined over a time interval, usually a year or a quarter; this is because the GDP is a **flow variable**, much like the amount of water flowing down a river. Flow variables differ from **stock variables**, such as the amount of water retained by a dam, which are always defined at a particular point in time.[1]

A country's GDP is a measure of its productive activity. A first definition is the sum of all final sales of goods and services:

Definition 1:
GDP = Σ net final sales within a geographic location during a period of time.

This definition specifically refers to **final sales**, i.e. goods and services sold to the consumer or firm that will ultimately use them. For example, the purchase of a loaf of bread or a motor car by a household is a final sale. In contrast, a car sold to a dealer which is subsequently resold during the measurement period, or a car bought by a firm to be used as part of its own production process, are not final but **intermediate sales**. Intermediate sales are excluded from GDP to avoid double counting, for example the car bought and later sold again by a dealer. For that reason, GDP

---

[1] Another example of a stock variable is a company's *balance sheet*, which measures its financial state at a single point in time, say 31 December; in contrast, an *income statement* records the profit or loss attributed to the firm over a time period, say 1 January to 31 December, and is a flow variable.

should never be confused with total sales, or turnover. In contrast, exports are counted as final sales regardless of how the foreigners use them, because they leave the national economy.

Our second definition of GDP recognizes that each final sale of a good or service represents the ultimate step that validates all the efforts that have gone into producing and making it available to the buyer. It encapsulates a chain of economic activities which are each seen as commercial **value added**:

Definition 2:
GDP = Σ value added created within a given
 geographic location during a period of time.

A firm creates value added by transforming raw materials and unfinished goods into products it can sell in the market place. The firm's value added is the difference between its sales (turnover) and the costs of raw materials, unfinished goods, and imports from abroad. If the firm produces intermediate goods, its sales are costs to its customers who themselves are producers. This value added is not counted twice as it is deducted from those customers' own sales. When the final consumer purchases a good or a service in the market, the price includes all the value added created at each stage in the production process, hence the consistency between Definitions 1 and 2. Box 2.1 illustrates how productive activities contribute to a country's total value added.

The value added produced within an economy is the source of income for the factors of production employed by the firm. In the course of their economic activities wage-earners, stockholders, and other factors of production are all compensated for their contribution to increasing the value of goods and services. Without value added it would not be possible to pay wages, salaries, interest, and profits. The third and final definition of GDP is therefore implied by the second one:

Definition 3:
GDP = Σ factor incomes earned from economic
 activities within a geographic location
 during a period of time.

The GDP includes all incomes earned within a country's borders—by residents and non-residents alike. Because one person's spending must be someone else's income, the third definition of GDP is also consistent with the first.

GDP statistics are quoted daily in the financial and political press. The GDP is generally considered to be the most important indicator of an economy's health, and its evolution is closely watched by managers, economists, and politicians. Yet the definition of GDP contains a fair amount of arbitrariness, and it is open to debate whether every positive movement in GDP constitutes an improvement in national well-being. More details on this controversial issue are provided in Box 2.2.

Box 2.1 Value Added: An Example

Suppose a keg of beer was produced and sold for final consumption at the price of €100. What steps were involved? A brewery bought barley from a farmer, paying €10, energy with a value of €20, and a keg at a cost of €5. (For simplicity, the intermediate inputs of the farmer, energy producer, and keg manufacturer are ignored.) The beer is actually sold to a wholesaler for €80, so the brewery's own contribution to value added per keg is €45, which is used to cover labour costs of €35 (wages and salaries as well as social security contributions) and €5 in taxes. The remaining €5 are the brewer's profits. The wholesaler sells the keg for €90 to the retailer, so his value added is €10; by selling the keg for €100, the

retailer also generates €10 of value added. Summing up, the final price can be broken down into value added at each stage of production and delivery of the final good:

Value added contributed by the:

	€
Farmer	10
Energy producer	20
Keg manufacturer	5
Brewery	45
Wholesaler	10
Retailer	10
Sum	100

Box 2.2   **What GDP Measures**

The GDP concerns only recorded market transactions. This leaves out many activities which are not carried out through legal channels or which do not reach the market place, like growing vegetables in the garden. Furthermore, since goods and services are measured by their sale prices, two identical goods may enter the GDP differently if one of them is sold at a discount. Finally, it is not a measure of happiness: painful expenses (having a tooth removed, for example) enter the GDP in the same way as pleasurable ones. When someone dies, GDP rises: the funeral service, the hospital expenses, and the execution of the will by lawyers and bankers all represent additional final sales of goods and services. Pollution and other forms of environmental damage are ignored in the GDP, since they are not traded in the market.

Services enter the GDP exactly like goods. Services include medical doctors' fees or an estate agent's commission when an existing house is sold. In the latter case, if the house's value has increased since it was purchased, the previous owner enjoys a capital gain, but this form of income does not enter GDP. Used-goods sales, such as cars or antique furniture, do not enter the GDP either. Such transactions represent a transfer of ownership rather than production; these goods entered GDP when first sold, but the fees of the dealers represent a service which is accounted for. Sales by retailers from inventory accumulated in earlier periods actually reduce GDP, as they represent a depletion of stocks.

Public services are part of GDP, even if they are not really sold. Their price is simply measured by their cost of production. For example, public education enters GDP as the sum of teachers' salaries, operating costs such as electricity or heating costs, and equipment including rents. Similarly, the national defence enters the GDP as total expenditure on armed forces.

A related measure is **Gross National Product** (GNP). Unlike the location-based GDP, the GNP is *ownership* based. It is the value added that is generated by all factors of production, owned by residents both at home and abroad. It includes value added or income earned abroad and repatriated by residents. For example, an Italian living in Como and commuting to work in Lugano in Switzerland contributes to the Italian GNP and to the Swiss GDP, but not to the Italian GDP or Swiss GNP. We follow the standard practice of only considering the GDP.

2.2.2 Real versus Nominal, Deflators versus Price Indices

Real and nominal GDP

Now that we understand how GDP data are constructed, we can see how the national income statisticians add up apples and oranges. The solution is to use prices to convert volumes (the numbers of apples and oranges) into values (sales of apples and oranges).

Suppose an economy produces these two goods and requires no imports. Multiplying the quantities of apples and oranges sold, Q^a and Q^o, by their respective prices, P^a and P^o, yields the **nominal GDP**, or GDP at current prices:

(**2.1**) $\text{GDP} = P^a Q^a + P^o Q^o.$

If the price of oranges increases from one year to the next, the GDP rises even if the volume of final sales remains unchanged. An increase in nominal GDP can result from either higher prices or more output. To separate the effects of output and price movements, we distinguish between nominal and **real GDP**. Increases in real GDP correspond to increases in physical output, the number of apples and oranges produced and sold. Whereas nominal GDP is computed as in (2.1) using the actual selling prices, real GDP is computed by using prices observed in some predetermined base year.[2] In our example, if prices of apples and oranges were P_0^a and P_0^o in the base year, the real GDP in year t, when net final sales of apples and oranges are Q_t^a and Q_t^o, is:

(**2.2**) $\text{Real GDP}t = P_0^a Q_t^a + P_0^o Q_t^o.$

This distinction is very general and applies to all macroeconomic variables: nominal variables represent values at current prices; real variables represent volumes at constant prices. As an example, Table 2.1

---

[2] Problems arise when new goods are introduced, or existing goods improve in quality. National income accountants have devised procedures to deal with such effects.

Table 2.1	Growth Rates of Nominal GDP, Real GDP, and GDP Deflator: Euro Area 1975–1999 (% per annum)		
	Nominal GDP	**Real GDP**	**GDP deflator**
1990	7.7	3.0	4.7
1991	8.8	1.6	7.2
1992	4.3	1.1	3.2
1993	0.3	−0.5	0.8
1994	5.0	3.0	2.0
1995	3.9	2.4	1.5
1996	5.1	1.8	3.3
1997	5.4	2.7	2.7
1998	4.6	2.9	1.7
1999	4.6	2.1	2.5

Source: Eurostat.

reports growth rates of nominal and real GDP for the Euro-zone.

Price deflators and indices

The distinction between nominal and real GDP can be used as a measure of the general price level, or the price of goods in terms of money. The **GDP deflator**, one way of measuring the price level, is defined as the ratio of nominal to real GDP:

(2.3) GDP Deflator = Nominal GDP/Real GDP.

The rate of increase in the GDP deflator can be approximated by the formula:

(2.4) GDP deflator inflation = nominal GDP growth
− rate real GDP
growth rate.

For example, Table 2.1 shows that in 1999 the nominal GDP of the Euro-zone rose by 4.6% while the real GDP increased only by 2.1%. On average, therefore, prices rose by roughly 2.5%.[3]

In the chosen base year, nominal and real GDP coincide and the GDP deflator equals 1.0. (Some-times it is multiplied by 100 for ease of comparison over the years.) It can be thought of as an average of all prices of final goods in terms of money, where each price is implicitly weighted by the proportion of the corresponding good in the GDP. As these proportions change over the years, so do the weights.

An alternative measure of inflation is based on an average of prices with fixed weights, called a **price index**. A basket of goods is selected and the amount of each good, or category of goods, in the basket is used to weight the corresponding prices. An example is the **consumer price index (CPI)**. This is based on a basket of goods consumed by an 'average citizen'. Box 2.3 presents some frequently used deflators and indices. Figure 2.1 shows the growth rates of the GDP deflator and of the CPI in Italy. Differences between the two measures of inflation are usually not very important but they can be significant—for example, when the price of imports changed sharply as in 1981 and 1986.

2.2.3 Measuring and Interpreting GDP

GDPs are difficult to measure, they are meant to cover the whole economy. The task is generally carried out by official statistical offices which draw

---

[3] To see why this formula is an approximation, suppose real GDP increased at rate g and inflation at rate π. The rate of nominal growth must be $(1 + g)(1 + \pi) - 1 = g + \pi + g\pi$. For g and π small, $g\pi \cong 0$, so the rate of growth of nominal GDP is approximately $g + \pi$.

Box 2.3 **Price Deflators and Price Indices**

The price index closest to the GDP deflator is the producer price index (PPI), with fixed weights corresponding to a basket representative of national production. Similarly, the CPI is closely tracked by the consumption deflator, the ratio of nominal and real aggregate consumption. Indices such as the CPI and the PPI are examples of a fixed-weight, or **Laspeyres index**. The consumption deflator, which is based on the actual share of goods in the corresponding year's consumption, is called a variable weight or **Paasche index**. The CPI and the consumption deflator include goods and services produced abroad and imported, while the PPI and the GDP deflator do not, but these latter measures include goods and services locally produced and exported. Figure 2.1 suggests a growing divergence between the PPI and the CPI in Italy over the 1980s. The reason is that imported goods prices increased by less than those of domestically produced goods.

Other frequently used deflators are related to exports, imports, investment goods, and government purchases. The wholesale price index (WPI) measures the average price of goods at the wholesale stage, and various commodity price indices track the evolution of raw materials prices. The dizzying diversity of indices and deflators simply reflects the fact that there is no absolute 'average' price. Different price levels are used for different purposes. For example, wage-earners wish to tie their wages to their cost of living; in this case, the relevant index is the CPI or the consumption deflator. In the case of Italy, linking wages to the CPI rather than to the PPI resulted in higher profits for firms whose incomes are better described by the PPI. Because the CPI and other Laspeyres indices are easy to compute, they tend to be used most often in practice.

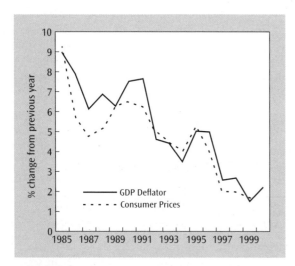

Fig. 2.1 **GDP Deflator and the Consumer Price Index Inflation Rates: Italy**

Both the GDP deflator and the consumer price index (CPI) measure the price level, or the price of goods in terms of money. They are used to compute the inflation rate.
The figure shows that both inflation rates tend to move together over time, with occasional exceptions when the difference in the underlying 'baskets' makes a difference. In 1986, world oil prices went down sharply. Since gas and heating oil are part of household consumption, inflation measured by the CPI declined. Oil being imported (so it does not create value added in Italy) has only a small impact on the GDP deflator.
Sources: OECD *Economic Outlook*, Dec. 2000.

on various sources of information. One natural source is the tax authorities. Firms report sales (first definition of GDP), individuals report incomes (third definition), and in most countries (all EU countries, but not the USA) value added taxes (VAT) are collected by intermediate and final sellers who then report their value added as they pay the tax (second definition).

The fact that GDP figures are collected through tax returns immediately raises the suspicion that individuals and firms may be less than candid about their finances to the fiscal authorities. Such unreported incomes form what is referred to as the **underground economy**. Box 2.4 presents estimates of how large it could be. It also alerts us to the importance of **unpaid work**.

Another shortcoming associated with the magnitude of the task is the time it takes to get reasonably accurate numbers. Furthermore, data from tax returns are processed with considerable delay. Usually at the end of the first month of each quarter, figures for the preceding quarter are released. Box 2.5 explains how such flash estimates are produced and updated several times over the following years. The inaccuracy of these estimates is unsettling because they are frequently used by governments when setting

Box 2.4   The Underground Economy and Unpaid Work

Who hasn't taken advantage of a carpenter's, car mechanic's, or painter's offer to do some work 'without a receipt'? Agents engage in the underground, or informal economy for straightforward reasons. First, they want to avoid taxes (the value added tax, employment and social security charges, profit taxes). Another reason is that criminal activities, such as drug-dealing, prostitution, or racketeering, are obviously better kept underground.

How large is the underground economy? By definition, its size is unknown, but national income statisticians often attempt to guess its importance. They use various approaches such as measuring electricity consumption which is higher in economies where unreported market activity is more significant,[4] or looking at the amount of large-denomination currency in circulation since underground transactions do not use bank accounts and profits are held in large bills.

Table 2.2   Estimates of the Size of the Underground Economy (% of GDP)

Africa		Central Europe	
Nigeria, Egypt	68–76	Hungary, Bulgaria, Poland	20–28
Tunisia, Morocco	39–45	Czech Republic, Romania, Slovakia	9–16
Latin America		**Former Soviet Union**	
Mexico, Peru	40–60	Belarus, Georgia, Ukraine	28–43
Chile, Brazil, Venezuela	25–35	Baltic States, Russia	20–27
Asia		**OECD**	
Thailand	70	Belgium, Greece, Italy, Spain, Portugal	24–30
Philippines, Malaysia, Korea	38–50	All others	13–23
Hong Kong, Singapore	13	Austria, Japan, USA, Switzerland	8–10

Source: Schneider and Enste (2000).

Another serious limit to GDP measures is unpaid work. Fixing the house, typically by men, and caring for the family and cleaning around, typically by women, take up much time and effort. Wealthier people hire help for these chores, in which case it becomes part of GDP (if reported to the tax authorities). Most people do it themselves, and it is unrecorded. Table 2.3 presents estimates for the Netherlands of the size of this 'lost output'. The first part shows that women perform much unpaid work. The second part shows that unpaid work represents a sizeable part of official GDP. The estimates depend on which salary we impute to this activity, the lowest figure corresponds to the minimum wage, the highest to the average wage.

Table 2.3   Unpaid Work: The Netherlands in 1990

Hours per week	Average paid work	Average unpaid work
Men	32.6	17.5
Women	9.4	39.8
% of GDP		36–58

Source: Marga Bruyn-Hundt, *The Economics of Unpaid Work*, Thesis Publishers, Amsterdam (1996).

---

[4] More generally, the sale of intermediate inputs related to final production is often used to indicate underground economy activities. For example, a wide discrepancy exists between the purchase of construction materials and reported construction activity.

Box 2.5   How National Accounts Estimates Vary over Time

Because governments, firms, and investors require timely information about the economy, national statistical institutes in advanced economies have devised ways of quickly producing preliminary estimates of GDP. The procedure is based on the knowledge that the value added of, for example, the 100 largest corporations represents a given proportion of GDP. If the proportion were 10%, as these firms fill in VAT tax reports or respond to specially designed questionnaires, multiplying by 10 their combined value added provides a rough early estimate of GDP. A few months later, revised estimates can be based on data provided by a larger sample of firms. Waiting still longer will allow the incorporation of estimates based on an early and partial analysis of tax returns. Detailed analysis of all tax returns data—using procedures to reconcile differences between measures based on the three definitions—lead to a final figure. Table 2.4 shows successive estimates of 1986 French GDP. The first estimate, published six months after year end, fell short of the latest figure by more than 1%! This may not seem like much, but it amounts to a full 15% difference for the actual growth rate recorded that year (7.5%).

Table 2.4   Various Estimates of French GDP for 1986

Date of publication	GDP (bns of current FF)	% difference from previous year	% difference from June 1987
June 1987	5015.9	—	—
Sept. 1988	5034.9	+0.4	0.4
Sept. 1988	5052.5	+0.3	0.7
June 1990	5069.3	+0.3	1.1

Source: Bulletin Trimestriel de la Banque de France, various issues.

policy, by investors assessing the value of their assets, and by firms deciding on hiring or firing workers and on acquiring equipment. This is why other indicators are often used to supplement the GDP figures.[5] It is also why analysts tend to concentrate on growth *rates* rather than *levels*. As long as the distortions do not change much over time, measured GDP growth rates are fairly accurate.

It is tempting to compare GDPs across countries. Most often we look at GDP per capita, or the average income earned within a country's boundaries. Such data must be regarded with caution, however. First, GDP is a measure of *income*, not wealth. Income is a flow, while wealth is the stock of assets accumulated over longer periods of time. For example, the average income earned in the UK is lower than that of Abu Dhabi; yet average British wealth is likely to be much higher, as Britain has been accumulating wealth for centuries, in the form of private assets (e.g. houses, factories, jewels, stocks) and national assets (e.g. the London Bridge, the paintings in the British Museum, the roads and telecommunication networks, and much more). The second caveat is that in developing countries a large number of transactions are not recorded. They belong to what is sometimes called the informal economy. For example, much food can be produced within the extended family (a non-market activity), or exchanged for other food (a non-reported market activity). Very low reported per capita income levels in LDCs underestimate true value added and income. Finally, GDPs are measured in the country's local monetary unit, or currency and are then converted into a common currency using the exchange rate. But local costs are often much lower in poor countries, for reasons presented in Chapter 7. To correct for this effect, we use GDP figures corrected for purchasing power.

[5] Ch. 14 provides a description of the most frequently used indicators.

2.3   Flows of Incomes and Expenditures

2.3.1 The Circular Flow Diagram

Each individual's expenditure necessarily contributes to some other individual's income. The simplified **circular flow** diagram represented in Figure 2.2 is

based on this simple truth and goes a long way in tracking the functioning of an economy. Based on the first and third definitions of GDP, it shows how income from sales goes from firms to individuals and back to the market place. The GDP appears in

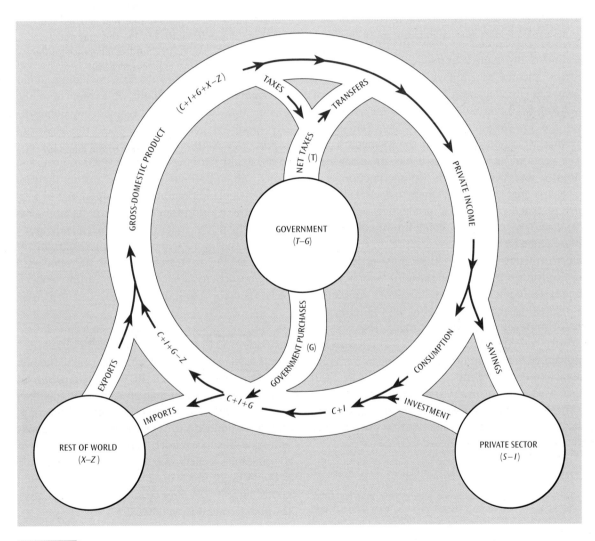

Fig. 2.2   **The Circular Flow Diagram**

The lower left part of the wheel represents sales of domestically produced goods and services, the sum of consumption spending (*C*), investment spending (*I*), government purchases (*G*), and exports (*X*) less imports (*Z*). In the upper left part of the wheel this is interpreted as income to residents. This income is taxed by the government, which also pays out various transfers. What is left, private income, may be saved (*S*) or spent (*C*). The private sector borrows to invest in productive equipment (*I*). The balance *S − I* is the private sector's net saving behaviour. The balance *T − G* is the public sector budget surplus. *X − Z* represent the country's net exports.

the left part of the figure. It represents the final net sales of firms.[6]

What do firms do with their receipts? To find out we move clockwise. The government, represented by the circle inside the circular flow, takes (in the form of taxes) and gives (in the form of various transfers). It always takes more than it gives! The difference between taxes and transfers is called **net taxes** and is represented by T. What is left of GDP after these taxes and transfers is **private income**.

Once they have paid wages and salaries, other production costs and taxes,[7] firms can either save their income or distribute it to their owners. Households receive income as employees or as shareholders. They can either spend it on *consumption* or save it. Merging firms and households into the private sector, the flow diagram shows how aggregate private savings (S) are deposited with the financial sector. The financial sector includes banks, financial institutions, and stock markets whose function is to collect savings and channel them to firms seeking to invest, that is to purchase productive equipment. This activity, called **financial intermediation**, is represented by the right-lower circle. In the aggregate, the private sector uses its **savings**—what it does not consume—to finance the acquisition of new productive equipment by firms. Productive equipment is referred to as physical **capital**, and purchases of new equipment is called **investment**. The excess of private saving over investment ($S - I$) is called net private saving. It can be positive or negative. Firms and households spend their income—part of it borrowed—to consume (C) and to invest (I).[8]

To private sector expenditures on goods and services ($C + I$) the government adds its own demand (G). Governments purchase goods (roads, military equipment, newly built buildings, and stationery for the bureaucracy) and services (of civil servants and other employees). In addition, governments distribute various subsidies to firms and households, and pay interest on the public debt. Total national spending, sometimes called **absorption**, is the sum ($C + I + G$) of private and public spending on goods and services. Part of absorption includes the purchase of imported goods and services (Z). This is shown as the branch going into the left-most circle which represents the rest of the world; it should not be thought of merely as merchandise purchases, but as covering all kinds of services, including labour and capital services. Similarly, while some domestic income thus leaks abroad, foreigners buy domestically produced goods and services, the country's exports (X). Netting these two flows with the rest of the world gives net exports ($X - Z$). Net exports, which can be positive or negative, further increase the total demand for domestic production.

The sum of absorption and net exports represents the total final sales that occur within the geographic area, in other words the GDP. The circular flow of income is closed. This circularity is the essence of economic activity: we (collectively) earn to (collectively) spend.

2.3.2 Summary of the Flow Diagram

The flow diagram can be summarized using the first and third definitions of GDP, which is represented by the symbol Y. As net final sales, the GDP is broken down into four main categories: sales of consumption goods and services (C), sales of investment goods and additions to stocks (I), sales to the government (G), and sales to the rest of the world (X). Since part of domestic income leaks abroad to pay for imported goods, imports (Z) must be subtracted, which gives the first decomposition of GDP:

(2.5) $$Y = C + I + G + X - Z.$$

The flow diagram also shows that GDP can be viewed as net incomes earned by factors of production. What do they do with this income? The three possibilities are given by the right-hand side of the flow diagram: they pay taxes net of transfers (T),

---

[6] Technically it also includes the 'sales' of households' labour and capital abroad, as well as the 'sales' of the self-employed.

[7] The other production costs are mainly land and buildings, financial costs (borrowing from banks and bondholders), and raw materials and intermediate goods which, for the country as a whole, are imported.

[8] It is important to stress the difference of this terminology from that often used in the business or popular press, in which 'investment' includes the acquisition of existing assets or financial instruments. Although these assets are often issued by firms to finance the purchase of productive equipment, their simple acquisition or sale does not give rise to what is called 'investment' in economics, i.e. the creation of new productive capacity.

Table 2.5	Components of GDP: Expenditure (average of Quarterly Data 1970–1998, as % of GDP)		
	Consumption (C)	Investment (I)	Government purchases (G)
Australia	57.8	23.5	18.7
Germany	56.2	24.4	19.4
France	59.9	22.2	17.7
UK	62.2	17.0	20.8
Italy	62.0	22.0	16.0
Japan	57.9	32.7	9.4
Canada	57.8	22.4	19.7
Switzerland	60.1	26.2	13.7
USA	64.9	14.7	20.4

Source: IMF.

they save (S), and they consume (C). Hence the second decomposition:

$$(2.6) \qquad Y = C + S + T.$$

Table 2.5 presents the components of the first decomposition as a percentage of GDP for a few countries. Consumption typically amounts to 50–65% of GDP. The 'size of government' is often measured by the share of its expenditures, the sum of purchases and transfers, or the share of gross taxes. It varies considerably, even among advanced economies. When total spending is considered, adding transfers to expenditures, the government often 'captures' more than half of GDP: many goods and services that are privately produced elsewhere are delivered freely as public goods in northern Europe; these include medical services, schools, child care, and public transport. The investment rate—the ratio of investment to GDP—varies between 15% and 25%. Because investment corresponds to the accumulation of productive equipment, it matters for future economic growth. Note that governments too invest in infrastructure equipment (roads, bridges, public utilities).

The flows of incomes and spending captured by the diagram make up what is sometimes called the real side of an economy. Parts of these flows leak out

to the financial side in the form of corporate and household savings; others leak out to the government; others to foreigners as net exports. Over time, they accumulate into stocks of assets or liabilities. How the financial side of the economy functions, and how the real and financial sides are linked, is studied in Part III of this book.

2.3.3 **More Detail**

While GDP represents the collective income earned within a nation's boundaries, not all of it ends up in the hands of individuals. What households actually receive to spend or save is called **personal disposable income**. Table 2.6 shows that some 30–40% of GDP does not reach individual households. It either goes to the government (net taxes) or is saved by firms (retained earnings).

Figure 2.3 starts with GDP and, moving right, decomposes it by its ultimate recipient. The first item is **depreciation**: in the process of producing GDP, productive equipment is subjected to wear and tear and obsolescence. Properly measured, this depreciation should be subtracted from GDP to give a clearer picture of the output that is actually available as income. Subtracting depreciation from GDP gives us the **net domestic national product**

	GDP	Households' disposable income	
		Level	% of GDP
Germany	2052.4	1211.8	**59.0**
France	1406.5	846.3	**60.2**
Sweden	246.1	118.7	**48.2**
Switzerland	260.2	140.1	**53.9**
United States of America	10730.3	7093.0	**66.1**
United Kingdom	1548.6	917.0	**59.2**

Table 2.6   GDP and Households' Disposable Income 2000 (€ bn)

Source: OECD, Economic Outlook; ECB.

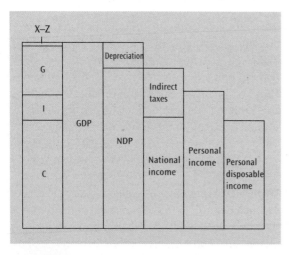

Fig. 2.3   From Expenditure to Income to Personal Disposable Income

Depreciation is stripped away from GDP to obtain the net national product (NDP). Indirect taxes are removed from, and firm subsidies added to, NDP, to give the national income (NI). After this, national income is distributed: firms' savings (retained earnings), corporate taxes, and contributions to social security are subtracted from national income, and what remains is paid to households as various forms of income. The government also transfers income to households (social security, unemployment insurance, etc.). This results in personal income (PI). After income taxes and some miscellaneous fees, we are left with personal disposable income (PDI), that is, resources available to households for spending or saving.

(NDP).[9] Moving further to the right, national income is what is left for firms once indirect taxes are paid out. Indirect taxes vary from country to country, and include the value added tax (VAT) and excise taxes (on petrol, tobacco, alcohol). They are collected by sellers on behalf of the government.

After indirect taxes, firms dispose of the value added they generate in four ways. First, they pay wages and salaries and other compensation to their employees. This includes contributions to social insurance. Second, they pay interest to bondholders and banks. Third, they pay corporate or business income taxes. What remains is profits to the firms' owners, or shareholders. These profits are either distributed as dividends or held back as retained earnings, sometimes called net corporate saving.[10]

To summarize, what is not paid as corporate taxes or saved by firms accrues to households as employees, owners, or rentiers. When government transfers (e.g. unemployment benefits, disability

---

[9]   In practice, financial accounting of depreciation is determined by tax regulations. Firms are allowed to subtract from their revenues a given proportion of the book value of equipment for computing taxable profits. It may under- or overstate actual economic depreciation by a wide margin.

[10]   Adding net corporate savings to depreciation gives gross corporate savings. It represents the resources that firms set aside to strengthen their financial position, and to replace used equipment.

payments, health care reimbursements, family allowances) are added to labour incomes and distributed profits, the result is personal income. Households cannot freely dispose of their personal income: they must first pay personal income taxes, as well as non-tax payments like parking fines and other governmental fees. What is left for consumption and saving is personal disposable income.

2.3.4 A Key Accounting Identity

The two decompositions of GDP, (2.5) and (2.6), are accounting identities: they hold by definition. Therefore it is always the case that:

$$C + S + T = C + I + G + X - Z.$$

Consumption C appears on both sides of this equality and can be eliminated. When this is done and terms are rearranged, the two accounting identities yield a third one:

(2.7) $(S - I) + (T - G) = (X - Z).$

Parentheses highlight the fact that the corresponding expressions appear in Figure 2.2 as net flows to the private sector (household and business), government, and the rest of the world, respectively. Each of the three net flows can be thought of as a form of saving, a leakage out of (if positive), or an injection into (if negative) the flow of income and expenditure. If $S > I$, the private sector as a whole is a net saver. If $S < I$, the private sector is a net borrower. Similarly, if $T > G$ the government is saving, and if $G > T$ it is borrowing by issuing public debt to domestic or foreign residents. The identity shows how these leakages are linked, *by definition*. Section 2.4 explains why and how.

Table 2.7 presents the accounting identity (2.7) for several countries in 1999. In the USA the private sector is dissaving, spending more than it earns, by a large amount. The public sector's surplus is too small to compensate, so the country as a whole is running an external deficit. The situation is exactly the opposite in Japan. The private sector's massive surplus swamps the public sector's deficit, leaving the country with an external surplus. The European Union as a whole is behaving more like Japan, but the internal imbalances are smaller and nearly cancel each other

Table 2.7	The Accounting Identity in 1999 (% of GDP)		
	S − I	**T − G**	**CA**
USA	−4.7	1.0	−3.7
Japan	10.3	−7.6	2.7
European Union	2.8	−2.5	0.3
Belgium	4.2	−1.0	3.2
Denmark	−3.2	2.9	−0.3
France	4.6	−2.2	2.4
Germany	−1.6	1.6	0.0
Italy	2.9	−2.3	0.6
Netherlands	4.2	−0.6	3.6
Spain	0.3	−1.4	−1.1
Sweden	−0.6	2.3	1.7
UK	−2.2	0.7	−1.5

Source: OECD Economic Outlook Dec. 1999.

to deliver near-external balance. Its individual member countries display different and varied situations.

2.3.5 Identities versus Economics

The identity (2.7) implies that all goods and services produced must be purchased, or that the demand for goods and services must equal the supply. For example, if private savings in a country exceed private investment $(S > I)$, either net exports must be positive or the government budget must be in deficit, or both. Without knowing more, it is impossible to know whether (1) the government deficit is at the origin of positive net private savings, (2) an export boom is generating income that is simply saved by residents, or (3) a fall in domestic investment spending induces a domestic recession which reduces both imports and tax revenues, leading to current account surplus and/or budget deficit. This is the difference between measuring data and interpreting them. This is also the difference between accounting and economics. The identity (2.7) is not only a requirement that accounts be correctly measured: we will later see that it can also be seen as a market equilibrium condition which implies that some adjustment mechanism is at work.

2.4 Balance of Payments

The **balance of payments** records all transactions between a country and the rest of the world. The presentation in Table 2.8 separates out international transactions on goods and services (upper part) from financial transactions (lower part). The balance of payments obeys the following simple rule: transactions involving *outflows of our money* are recorded as deficit (−) items; items leading to *inflows of our money* are considered as surplus (+) items. The rest will become clear as we move along.

Table 2.8 Balance of Payments

1. Exports of Goods	
2. Imports of Goods	
3. **Merchandise Trade Balance = (1) − (2)**	
4. Exports of Services	
5. Imports of Services	
6. Net Royalties	
7. Net Investment Income	
8. **Invisible Balance = (4) − (5) + (6) + (7)**	
9.	**Balance on Goods and Services = (3) + (8)**
10. Net Foreign Workers' Remittances	
11. Net International Aid	
12. **Unilateral Transfers = (10) + (11)**	
13.	**Current Account Balance (*CA*) = (3) + (8) + (12)**
14. Gross Inward Direct Investment	
15. Gross Outward Direct Investment	
16. Gross Inward Portfolio Investment	
17. Gross Outward Portfolio Investment	
18. **Long-Term Capital Account Balance = (14) − (15) + (16) − (17)**	
19. Short-Term Inward Capital Flows	
20. Short-Term Outward Capital Flows	
21. **Short-Term Capital Account Balance = (19) − (20)**	
22.	**Capital Account Balance (*KA*) = (18) + (21)**
23. Errors and Omissions	
24.	**Overall Balance = (13) + (22)**
25. **Balance on Official Intervention Account (net sales of foreign exchange) (*OFF*)**	

Memo: Balance of Payments: $CA + KA + OFF = 0$.

	Euro area	USA	Sweden	Mexico	Turkey
Table 2.9	**Balance of Payments, Various Countries, 1998 ($US bn)**				
Trade balance	137.17	−244.97	17.54	−7.74	−14.33
Balance on Goods and Services	−10.66	71.00	−9.53	−14.06	10.47
Unilateral transfers	−51.19	−46.59	−3.44	6.01	5.73
Current account	75.32	−220.56	4.57	−15.79	1.87
Long-term financial account	−226.38	35.48	−19.94	10.76	−5.82
Short-term financial account	226.02	181.72	26.32	6.54	6.58
Errors and omissions	−98.83	10.09	−8.57	1.67	−2.20
Overall Balance	−23.87	6.73	2.38	3.19	0.43
Change in official reserves	23.87	−6.73	−2.38	−3.19	−0.43

Source: IMF.

2.4.1 Commercial Transactions

The first accounts to consider in Table 2.8 record exports and imports of goods, imports entered with a minus sign. The net result is the **merchandise trade balance**. The balance of trade on goods and services is equal to the merchandise trade balance plus the balance on **invisibles**, which include investment income, royalties, and other services. The most important item is undoubtedly the **current account**. It is obtained by adding to the balance of goods and services the balance of unilateral transfers, that is payments not related to commercial or financial transactions (public transfers, foreign aid, payments to and from the EU budget, and what guest workers remit to their home countries). All current account items may be broadly interpreted as transactions describing sales and purchases of goods and services, including the services of foreign workers, capital, and know-how, or the goodwill of countries receiving aid. This is how to interpret net exports $(X - Z)$ in the previous sections.

The importance of the current account is best seen by returning to the GDP decomposition (2.5) which can be rewritten as:

(2.8) $CA = Y - (C + I + G) = Y - A,$

where $A = C + I + G$ is referred to as absorption, or total domestic spending on goods and services, both domestic and foreign, by households, firms, and government agencies. By definition, the current account is the excess of income (GDP) over spending. It signals whether the country is a net borrower or a net lender. When a country earns more than it spends $(CA = Y - A > 0)$, it is a net lender vis-à-vis the rest of the world. Conversely, a country running a current account deficit spends more than it earns $(CA < 0$ and $A > Y)$ and must match the difference by borrowing abroad.

Table 2.9 provides a few examples. Turkey is one country whose citizens work as guest workers abroad. This explains its positive transfers balance, as is the case for Mexico. Sweden is in the opposite situation with its many foreign workers who live there and send money back home. This is also the case of the EU and the USA.

2.4.2 Financial Transactions

The rest of the balance of payments describes financial transactions. As any exercise in accounting, all items in the balance of payments must add up to zero. This is not only accounting, this is a consequence of (2.8): current account surpluses must be matched by net financial outflows because the country is lending to the rest of the world, or, put differently, is acquiring assets abroad. Current account deficits imply borrowing from abroad, so financial capital is flowing into the country. Accordingly, the remainder of the balance of payments, representing financial transactions, must be equal to, and of opposite sign to, the current account. The remaining question is: who does the balancing act?

The answer is found by noting two main distinctions among financial transactions. The first concerns private and official accounts. The balance of purchases of foreign assets by private domestic residents is called the **financial account**, it is part of the balancing act. The official account captures the fact that the monetary authorities also contribute to the balancing process. If this account is in deficit, it means residents have sent more money abroad than they received, through either commercial transactions—the current account—or financial transactions—the financial account—or any combination of both. This was the case of the Euro-zone in 1998, as can be seen in Table 2.9. In that case the monetary authorities absorb the difference, bringing domestic money back home; hence the positive entry in the table. But be careful, this means that the monetary authorities have spent some of their **foreign exchange reserves** (foreign currencies that they hold) to buy back the domestic currency.[11] Such actions are called **foreign exchange market interventions**. When a monetary authority buys back its own currency, it spends some of its foreign exchange reserves. The distinction between private and official financing is further taken up in Section 2.4.4.

The second distinction is between long-term and short-term financial transactions. Long-term accounts concern the sales or purchases of assets of more than one year to maturity. Examples are foreign direct investment, acquisition of foreign companies, portfolio investment, or the establishment of subsidiaries abroad. Short-term transactions involving assets of less than one year of maturity—including bank accounts—are often associated with 'hot money', motivated by the expectation of quick returns rather than by long-term business strategies.

2.4.3 Errors and Omissions

There is a final item in Table 2.9, 'Errors and Omissions', which requires some explanation. By definition, the total of the balance of payments should be zero:

$$\textbf{(2.9)} \qquad \underset{\substack{\text{current} \\ \text{account}}}{CA} + \underset{\substack{\text{financial} \\ \text{account}}}{FA} + \underset{\substack{\text{official} \\ \text{interventions}}}{OFF} = 0.$$

While accounting guarantees the consistency of current and financial accounts in theory, the nature of data gathering for payments statistics virtually guarantees discrepancies. Trade data originate with customs authorities. Financial data come from the banking system, since international transactions are mediated by financial organizations. Official interventions, of course, are known by the monetary authorities, which are often responsible for collecting the data and producing the balance of payments accounts. In practice, relationship (2.9) never holds when data are actually collected, hence the need for an additional account called 'Errors and Omissions': this balancing item is necessary to arrive at zero at the bottom of the table. While there are genuine mistakes—the sheer volume of data to be treated is an invitation for errors—there may be fewer innocent 'omissions'.[12] Table 2.9 shows some that deficits on errors and omissions can be very sizeable. Large negative numbers might reflect smuggling or savings illegally exported to escape taxation.

2.4.4 The Meaning of the Accounts

A current account imbalance must be matched one-for-one by either the private financial account or official interventions by the monetary authorities.

---

[11] Note that this follows the rule of thumb mentioned above for thinking about the sign of an entry in the balance of payments: ask yourself whether it means that domestic money comes in (a plus) or goes out (a minus).

[12] Normally, the sum of the current accounts of all countries in the world should equal zero. In fact, it is systematically negative, as receipts are 'omitted' more often than expenditures.

What difference does it make? A country running a current account surplus is receiving more payments from abroad than it disburses. If the private financial account is in balance, more domestic money must be flowing in than is leaving the country. This is possible only if someone makes up the difference. In fact, the imbalance between inflows and outflows translates into excess demand for the domestic currency on exchange markets worldwide. This demand tends to appreciate, or increase the value of, the domestic currency.[13] If the monetary authorities want to avoid such an appreciation, they must relieve the pressure by selling the 'missing' domestic currency—hence a minus entry in the official financial account (OFF) in (2.9)—against foreign currencies. The country's current account surplus takes the form of an acquisition of foreign exchange reserves. This can be thought of as an official loan to foreign monetary authorities.

Suppose the central bank refused to intervene (OFF = 0). In this case the domestic currency would be in short supply on world markets and would tend to appreciate in value. The exchange rate appreciation works towards reducing the current account surplus as domestic goods become more expensive and foreign goods become cheaper, and prompts capital outflows as residents find it profitable to acquire cheap foreign assets. In the accounting identity (2.9), either the current account surplus disappears or the private financial account is negative, or both. Similarly, a current account deficit can be financed privately (a positive financial account), publicly (a sales of foreign exchange reserves), or both.

The monetary authorities determine if, and to what extent, a current account imbalance translates into a change in the exchange rate. At one extreme, the monetary authorities may be committed to maintaining a fixed exchange rate and they *must* intervene. If they do so, they must purchase or sell foreign exchange to whatever extent necessary. At the other extreme, the monetary authorities never intervene and the exchange rate is determined solely by the market. This is why the sum of the current and financial accounts (including errors and omissions) attracts special attention: it is the negative of the interventions by the monetary authorities and reveals their behaviour. It is called the **official account**, and most often somewhat improperly the balance of payments (BoP):[14] ignoring errors and omissions,

$$(2.10) \qquad BoP = CA + KA = -OFF.$$

A balance of payments surplus means that the authorities have acquired foreign exchange reserves. Put differently, they have sold the domestic currency to match an excess demand for the domestic currency, thus preventing or reducing pressure for an exchange rate appreciation (OFF < O). A balance of payments deficit corresponds to a loss of reserves as the monetary authorities buy back the domestic currency to prevent a depreciation (OFF > O).

Summary

1. The gross domestic product (GDP) can be defined in three equivalent ways: as the flow of final sales, the flow of factor incomes, or the flow of value added.

2. Because nominal GDP measures final sales at market prices, an increase in the price level leads to an increase in GDP even if quantities sold are constant. Real GDP is computed by pricing current output with constant prices, corresponding to a chosen base year.

---

[13] Later chapters develop this in greater detail. A currency *appreciates* when its value in terms of other currencies increases. Conversely, if its value decreases, we speak of a *depreciation*.

[14] Strictly speaking, this is incorrect because the balance of payments represents the whole document. The official balance is its bottom line and the one that attracts the most attention.

3. The GDP deflator is the ratio of nominal to real GDP. It is one measure of the price level. Inflation is approximately equal to the difference between the nominal and real GDP growth rates. Price indices, also used to compute inflation rates, use constant-weights baskets of goods and services.

4. Measurement of GDP is imperfect, costly, and time-consuming. A large amount of economic activity is unmeasured, such as household services and the underground economy. Yet year-on-year comparisons, such as annual growth rates, are less affected by measurement problems.

5. GDP is equal to the sum of consumption, investment, government spending, and the current account ($Y = C + I + G + CA$). At the same time, GDP is equal to consumption, plus private sector savings, plus net taxes (gross taxes less public transfers received by the private sector) ($Y = C + S + T$). It follows as an identity that the current account surplus is equal to the surplus of the government plus the surplus of the private sector ($CA = (T - G) + (S - I)$).

6. The balance of payments is a record of current account transactions and their financial counterparts, the financial account. The current account is the sum of the merchandise, invisibles, and transfer accounts; any surplus or deficit must be matched by an equal and opposite sum of private long-term capital, short-term financial, errors and omissions, and official intervention accounts.

7. When the monetary authorities undertake to maintain the value of their country's exchange rate, they must intervene on exchange rate markets to match any possible balance of payments imbalance. Conversely, the exchange rate floats freely when the monetary authorities refrain from intervening; then all adjustment for balance of payments equilibrium occurs within the private sector, as a result of changes in the market-determined exchange rate.

Key Concepts

- accounting identities
- gross domestic product (GDP)
- flows and stocks
- final sales
- intermediate sales
- factors of production
- value added
- underground economy
- unpaid work
- nominal and real GDP
- GDP deflator
- consumer price index (CPI)
- gross national product (GNP)
- circular flow
- net taxes
- private income
- consumption
- financial intermediation
- physical capital
- investment
- saving, net private saving
- absorption
- net exports
- real and financial sides of the economy
- depreciation
- net national product
- personal disposable income
- current account
- balance of payments
- merchandise trade balance
- invisibles
- financial account, private versus official, short-term versus long-term
- foreign exchange market intervention
- foreign exchange reserves

Exercises

1. You are given the following data:

GDP	5000
depreciation	500
before-tax corporate profits	1000
social security contributions	700
transfers to households and firms	1000
net interest to foreigners	200
proprietary income	70
net corporate saving	600
indirect taxes	1000
subsidies to enterprises	400
fines and fees	100
net remittances to rest of world	500
corporate taxes	100
consolidated government deficit	100
personal taxes	1500
household savings	200
investment expenditure	1200

Compute: NDP, national income, personal income, personal disposable income, consumption, government purchases, GDP, the current account balance. State your assumptions clearly.

2. What happens to GDP when the owner of a small firm marries her secretary and stops paying for his work, which he continues to perform?

3. 'Services do not contribute to GDP as much as industry because industry produces tangible goods.' Comment.

4. I bought my house for €80,000. I have just sold it for €110,000, and the estate agent received a 10% commission from the buyer. What is the effect on GDP?

5. Suppose you have the following data on prices and quantities:

Prices (€)

	Apples	Pears	Petrol
1993	1.0	2.0	5.0
1994	1.0	3.0	6.0

Quantities

	Apples	Pears	Petrol
1993	300	100	50
1994	400	150	40

(*a*) If the economy produced all three (and only these three) goods, compute the nominal GDP in both periods, and real GDP at 1993 prices. What is the rate of inflation in 1994, as measured by the change in the GDP deflator?

(*b*) Suppose a CPI is constructed using weights corresponding to quantities produced in 1993. What is the rate of inflation measured by the CPI?

6. Over the past five years taxes were about 60% of GDP in Sweden. Yet disposable income over the past five years also amounted to 60% of GDP. How can these numbers be reconciled?

7. How would the following transactions be recorded in the French balance of payments?
   - A French resident buys a Volkswagen produced in Wolfsburg, Germany.
   - A French resident purchases a house in Switzerland.
   - A French national living in Switzerland buys a house in Switzerland.
   - A French resident builds a house in Italy, paying Italian residents to do the job.
   - A German banker sends his daughter at the Sorbonne a wire transfer in French francs.
   - The same German banker wires money to his bank account in Paris.
   - A Tunisian worker in Marseilles sends money to his family in Tunis.
   - Peugeot SA, a French concern, pays dividends to a resident of Finland.
   - Profits of Owen Corning, a US company, are reinvested in capacity expansion of a factory in Fontainebleau, France.
   - Banque de France sells pesetas to prevent the price of pesetas in francs from rising above its maximum allowable rate in Paris.
   - A French resident of Colmar, a town in Alsace near the German border, smuggles home a stereo purchased in Freiburg (Germany).

8. 'Commuters reduce the GDP because they send home a large fraction of their earnings.' Comment.

9. 'Legalizing drugs would increase the GDP and tax receipts, but worsen the balance of payments.' Comment.

Suggested Further Reading

Internationally standardized macroeconomic data are published by:

The International Monetary Fund in *International Financial Statistics* (monthly), and *World Economic Outlook* (twice a year).(www.imf.org)

The Organization for Economic Cooperation and Development (OECD) in *National Income Accounts*, *Main Economic Indicators*, and *Employment Outlook* (annual with monthly updates), and *OECD Economic Outlook* (twice a year). The OECD also publishes a yearly *Country Report* on each of its member countries—the major industrialized countries.

The United Nations in its *Annual Yearbook*.

On Europe, the European Commission publishes *Eurostat* and a bimonthly review, *European Economy*.

The World Bank specializes in less developed countries and publishes annually, among others, the *World Development Indicators* (www.worldbank.org).

The European Bank for Reconstruction and Development publishes data on the transition economies in its annual Transition Report (www.ebrd.com). Data for these countries are also available in *Economic Survey of Europe*, a publication of the UN Economic Commission for Europe (www.unece.org).

Each country has its own reporting system, with the central bank often publishing balance of payments data. The list of central bank websites is available from www.bis.org.

The methodology to track down the underground economy—along with lots of numbers—is presented in:

Schneider, Friedrich, and Dominink Enste (2000) 'Shadow Economies: Size, Causes, and Consequences', *Journal of Economic Literature* 38: 77–114.

The Real Macroeconomy

Part II focuses exclusively on the real side of the macroeconomy, the demand for and production of goods and services, leaving aside the monetary sphere, the nominal side. It is concerned with the behaviour of households, firms, and the government, and studies how these interact in various markets. We start with the phenomenon of growth, the most fundamental of all economic issues which is what makes countries rich or poor. It will anchor our understanding of the long run. Then, we look at a very special market, the labour market: the supply of labour by households, the demand by firms, and how to think about unemployment. We next move to spending decisions by households, firms, and governments: why are they constrained by resources, and how to make the best of these? The last chapter introduces the real exchange rate, which defines a country's competitiveness as well as its terms of trade.

Economic Growth

The consequences for human welfare involved in questions like these are simply staggering: Once one starts to think about them, it is hard to think about anything else.

– R. E. Lucas, Jr

3.1   Overview

Economic growth looks like an almost immutable law of nature. Over decades and centuries, more goods are produced and standards of living improve. Despite setbacks arising from wars, natural disasters, or epidemics, **economic growth** has been responsible for staggering changes in the way we live. The upper part of Table 3.1 shows the evolution of GDP per capita, the usual measure of standard of living, in Western Europe and China over the past six centuries. On this measure, standards of living increased by a factor of 33 in Western Europe compared with 4.7 in China, the most advanced economy at the outset of this period. Such enormous changes are the result of seemingly very small,

Table 3.1   The Growth Phenomenon

(a) GDP per catpita in Western Europe and China, 1400–1989 (1985 $US)

	1400	1820	1950	1989
Western Europe[a]	430	1,034	4,902	14,413
China	500	500	454	2,361

(b) Average Annual Real GDP Growth Rates, 1820–1997

	1820–70	1870–1913	1913–50	1950–73	1973–97	Overall growth 1820–1997
Belgium	2.2	2.0	1.0	4.1	2.2	2.1
Denmark	1.9	2.7	2.5	3.8	2.1	2.5
Finland	1.6	2.7	2.7	4.9	2.6	2.7
France	1.2	1.5	1.1	5.0	2.3	1.9
Germany	1.6	2.8	1.3	5.9	2.6	2.5
Italy	1.2	1.9	1.5	5.6	2.5	2.2
Netherlands	1.8	2.3	2.4	4.7	2.4	2.5
Norway	1.8	2.1	2.9	4.1	3.6	2.6
Sweden	1.6	2.2	2.7	4.0	1.7	2.3
Switzerland	n.a.	2.1	2.6	4.5	1.4	n.a.
United Kingdom	2.0	1.9	1.3	3.0	2.1	2.0
Japan	0.3	2.3	2.2	9.3	3.5	2.8
United States	4.5	3.9	2.8	3.6	2.8	3.6

Source: Maddison 1991, IMF.

annual steps. For example, the advanced economies grow by roughly 2–4% per year. These apparently limited advances should not be taken lightly: a 2% difference compounds into 49% after twenty years, and 170% after half a century.

The lower part of Table 3.1 presents more detailed information covering nearly two centuries. It is well worth looking carefully at it for it raises a host of intriguing questions. Is economic growth a universal phenomenon? Why are national growth rates so similar? Why do some countries exhibit periods of spectacular growth, as Japan in 1950–73, the USA in 1820–70, or much of Europe after the Second World War? Why do nations sometimes experience long periods of stagnation, as did China until the last two decades of the twentieth century? Is there a tendency for growth rates to converge, so that periods of above-average growth compensate for periods of below-average growth? What does this imply for levels of GDP per capita? These questions are among the most important ones in economics, for growth determines the wealth and poverty of nations.

We will see that there are four main reasons why economies grow. First, **savings** are channelled into productive investment which adds to the stock of productive equipment. More equipment enables workers to produce more. Second, the **population** often tends to grow, which means that more workers are potentially available for market production. In Europe, indigenous population growth has given way to immigration and the entry of a higher proportion of women into the labour force. The third reason is **technological progress**: as knowledge accumulates and techniques improve, workers and the machines they work with become more productive. Finally, advances in productivity are influenced by a host of factors, including rewards to innovation, quality of education, or the size of a country. These four explanations are not mutually exclusive. In this chapter, each source of growth will be considered, step by step, using a framework known as the **Solow growth model**,[1] which incorporates the first three explanations. Because it is such an extensive topic, discussion of the fourth source of growth will be postponed until Chapter 18.

| 3.2 | **Stylized Facts and Steady States** |

3.2.1 **Five Stylized Facts**

The most remarkable aspect of the growth phenomenon is that real GDP, the volume of goods and services produced, seems to grow endlessly. Think of an economy producing an output (the real GDP) by combining inputs: labour, equipment also called physical capital, to which land could be added for agricultural production. Growth theory—the study of economic growth across nations and over time —asks whether we produce more because we use more inputs, or whether the inputs become more productive over time, or both. It also asks what is the contribution of each factor. In 1961, the British economist Nicholas Kaldor identified several **stylized facts**.[2] Stylized facts are empirical regularities which

may not be rigorously exact everywhere and all the time but seem to well encapsulate some important features. Such stylized facts help us organize our ideas, much like a detective looks for clues before undertaking a thorough investigation.

Stylized Fact No. 1: Output per capita and capital intensity keep increasing

Labour input measured in man-hours (L) grows more slowly than capital (K) and output (Y). This means that the production process becomes increasingly more capital-intensive or, equivalently that the ratio of capital to labour (K/L) increases secularly. It also means that the ratio of output to labour (Y/L) rises. Because output per hour of work is closely related to income per capita, economic growth is desirable, since it implies a continuing increase in standards of living. Figure 3.1 presents the evolution of the

---

[1] Robert Solow, MIT economist and Nobel Prize winner, pioneered the study of economic growth in the 1950s.
[2] Kaldor (1961: 177–222).

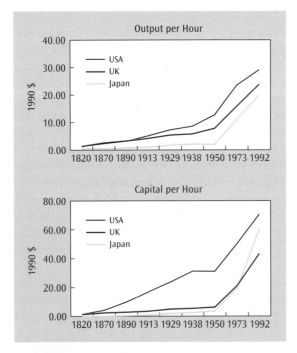

Table 3.2 **Capital–Output Ratios (K/Y), 1913–1992**

	1913	1950	1973	1992
France	1.6	1.7	1.8	2.3
Germany	2.3	2.1	2.4	2.3
Japan	1.0	1.8	1.7	3.0
UK	1.0	1.1	1.7	1.8
USA	2.9	2.3	2.1	2.4

Source: Maddison (1995).

Fig. 3.1 **The Output–Labour and Capital–Labour Ratios in Three Countries**

Output–labour and capital–labour ratios are continuously increasing. Growth accelerated in the USA in the early twentieth century, after 1950 in Japan and the UK.
Source: Maddison (1995).

output–labour and capital–labour ratios for three countries.

Stylized Fact No. 2: the capital–output ratio is trendless

As they grow secularly, the capital stock and output tend to track each other. As a consequence, the ratio of capital to output (K/Y) shows no systematic trend. This is apparent from Figure 3.1, but Table 3.2 shows that it is only approximately true. Yet, even if the capital–output ratio is not exactly constant, it does not display the steady, unrelenting increases seen in Stylized Fact No. 1.

Stylized Fact No. 3: hourly wages keep rising

The trend increase in the ratios of output and capital to labour (Y/L and K/L) means that an hour of work uses ever more equipment to produce ever more output. As workers become productive, they are entitled

to higher hourly wages (this link will be shown more formally in the next chapter). And, indeed, hourly real wages grow secularly, which means ever increasing living standards for workers.

Stylized Fact No. 4: the rate of profit is trendless

The absence of a clear trend for the capital–output ratio (K/Y) implies that the same amount of equipment delivers about the same amount of output. It is to be expected therefore that the rate of profit does not exhibit a trend either (this is the same logic as in the previous stylized fact, to be confirmed in subsequent chapters). Income from owning capital increases only because the stock of capital itself increases.

Stylized Fact No. 5: the relative shares of GDP going to labour and capital are trendless

It has already been shown that total incomes deriving from labour and capital have increased secularly. It turns out that they also tend to increase at about the same rate, so that the distribution of total income (GDP) between capital and labour has been relatively stable.

3.2.2 Steady States

Why should we care about stylized facts if they are not really true? Because they approximate the important concept of steady state. As we study growth, we track down moving targets, variables that keep increasing all the time, going towards infinity! To make any progress we need to be on firmer ground. To that effect, we try to identify some variables which are stable even if the economy grows all the time. For example the GDP is increasing, but could it be that its growth rate is constant? The answer is yes and no. We have noted in Chapter 1 the important phenomenon of business cycles, periods of fast growth followed by periods of slow growth. Here we are not interested in business cycles, in fact we wish to overlook shorter-term fluctuations—compare Figures 1.1 and 1.2—to concentrate on the long run.

This is why it is convenient to *imagine* how things would look if there were no business cycles. Such a situation is called a **steady state**. It never happens, much as the stylized facts are never exactly observed. We never reach the long run: looking at today ten years ago, we thought of it as the long run, but now that we are there, we can see all the details that were indistinguishable back then. Still, when we consider GDPs that double up every ten to twenty years, a temporary boom or recession, which shifts today's GDP by one or two percentage points, amounts to little in the greater order of things, the powerful phenomenon of continuous long-run growth. Steady states—and stylized facts—are not just convenient ways of making our lives simpler, they are essential tools to distinguish the wood from the trees.

3.3   Capital Accumulation

This first of our three explanations focuses on savings and investment. To keep things simple, we start by assuming that the size of the population, the labour force, and the numbers of hours worked remain constant. The story to be told is easily observed in Figure 2.2, the circular flow diagram. Households and firms save part of their income. Savings flow into the financial system (banks, stock markets, etc.), where they are channelled to borrowers, firms and households. Here, the relevant part is that which goes to firms which want to invest, i.e. to increase their productive capacity by purchasing capital goods. This, in turn, raises output, hence future savings and investment, and so on. But this simplicity conceals some issues which turn out to be interesting and important: is this **accumulation** process never-ending? Does more saving necessarily mean faster growth? And since saving can be thought of as deferred consumption, is it a good idea?

3.3.1 The Aggregate Production Function

To answer these questions, we need a number of tools. The first, and most important tool we will use, is the **aggregate production function**. It describes how an economy's capital stock K and employed labour L produce the total output of an economy, or its GDP:

(3.1) $$Y = F(K, L).$$
$$+ \quad +$$

The production function is meant to capture the simple fact that goods and services are produced using (at least) two *factors of production*, equipment and manpower. The production function is a powerful short-cut widely used in microeconomics to study the output of individual firms; here instead we use it to study the output of the entire economy. Box 3.1 provides an example of a production function. The total stock of capital, which includes plants and machinery as well as roads and railroads, electricity and telephone networks, is represented by K; the symbol L stands for the total number of hours worked, or man-hours. Thus L combines the numbers of workers (N) and the average hours (h) that they work per year ($L = Nh$).[3] The *plus* ('+') signs

---

[3] Since output and labour inputs are flows, they could also be measured per quarter or per month, but should be measured over the same time interval. Note that capital is a stock, usually measured at the beginning of the current, or end of the last period. The important distinction between stocks and flows was introduced in Chapter 1.

Box 3.1 **For the Mathematically Minded: The Cobb–Douglas Production Function**

The various properties of the production function can be easily (for the happy few at ease with calculus?) established by using a special form, the Cobb–Douglas production function:

(B3.1) $$Y = K^{\alpha}L^{(1-\alpha)}$$

where α is a constant parameter which represents the technology in use, which can take values between 0 and 1. We can now reproduce formally all the results in the text.

Diminishing marginal productivity

The marginal productivity of capital is $\partial F/\partial K = \alpha K^{\alpha-1}L^{(1-\alpha)}$. Since $\alpha < 1$, we see that this expression is a decreasing

function of K. The same applies to the marginal productivity of labour $\partial F/\partial L = (1-\alpha)K^{\alpha-1}L^{-\alpha}$.

Constant Returns

The Cobb–Douglas function has the constant returns to scale property:

$$F(tK, tL) = (tK)^{\alpha}(tL)^{1-\alpha} = t^{\alpha+(1-)-\alpha}K^{\alpha-1}L^{-\alpha}$$
$$= tK^{\alpha-1}L^{-\alpha} = tF(K, L)$$

The intensive form

We divide both sides of (B3.1) by L to get:

(B3.2) $$y = \frac{Y}{L} = K^{\alpha}L^{-\alpha} = \left(\frac{K}{L}\right)^{\alpha} = k^{\alpha}$$

which is indeed well represented by Figure 3.3.

---

shown underneath the production function in (3.1) signify that output rises with either more capital or more labour.[4] How this happens is related to two basic assumptions which are central to understanding production and growth.

Diminishing marginal productivity

Consider a country with workers and a stock of capital. Then imagine that one machine is added and the capital stock rises by the amount ΔK, with the number of workers constant. Output will also rise, by ΔY. The ratio $\Delta Y/\Delta K$, the amount of new output per unit of incremental capital, is called the economy's **marginal productivity**. Now, imagine that we continue again and again to add capital, while continuing to hold labour input constant. Do we expect to always see output increase by the same amount? It turns out generally not to be the case. As more and more equipment is brought into the production process, it works with less and less of the given labour input. This is the principle of **diminishing marginal productivity**. It is represented in Figure 3.2 which describes how output rises with capital, holding the use of labour unchanged. The

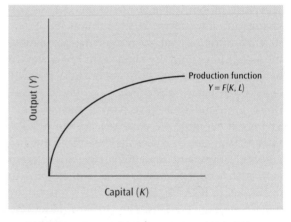

Fig. 3.2 **The Production Function: Diminishing Marginal Productivity**

Holding labour input L (the number of hours worked) unchanged, adding to the capital stock K (available productive equipment) allows an economy to produce more, but in smaller and smaller increments.

flattening of the curve illustrates the assumption. In fact the slope of the curve is equal to the economy's marginal productivity.

It turns out that the principle of diminishing marginal productivity applies also to the labour input. Increasing the employment of man-hours will raise output; but output from additional man-hours

---

[4] Formally, it means that the two derivatives $F_K(K, L) = \partial F/\partial K$ and $F_L(K, L) = \partial F/\partial L$ are positive.

declines as more and more labour is being applied to a fixed stock of capital.

Returns to scale

Output increases when either input capital or labour increases. But what happens if *both* capital and labour increase in the same proportion? Suppose, for example, that the inputs of capital and labour were both doubled. If output doubles as a result, the production function is said to have **constant returns to scale**. If output more than doubles, we observe **increasing returns to scale. Decreasing returns** is the case when output increases by less than 100%. It is believed that decreasing returns to scale are unlikely. Increasing returns, in contrast, cannot be ruled out, but we will ignore this possibility until Section 3.6, and later in Chapter 18. In fact, the evidence points in the direction of constant returns to scale.

With constant returns we can think of the link between inputs and output—the production function—as a zoom: as long as we scale up the inputs, so does the output. It should be intuitive that, under this condition, an attractive property of the production function emerges: output per hour of work—the **output–labour ratio** (Y/L)—depends only on capital per hour of work—**the capital–labour ratio** (K/L). This permits a great simplification as the production function can be written in the following *intensive form*:[5]

(3.2) $y = f(k)$ where $y = Y/L$ and $k = K/L$.

The intensive form representation is convenient for three reasons. First, it allows us to track per capita values of output and the capital stock (y and k) which, according to Stylized Fact No. 1, grow secularly together. Second, as long as average hours worked per person do not change, output per hour and GDP per capita increase at the same rate: total

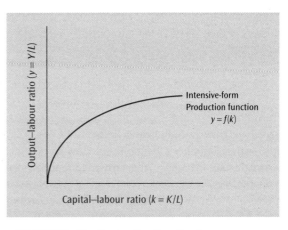

Fig. 3.3 **The Production Function in Intensive Form**

The production function shows that the output–labour ratio y grows with the capital–labour ratio k. Its slope is the marginal productivity of labour since with constant returns to scale $\Delta Y/\Delta K = \Delta y/\Delta k$. The principle of declining marginal productivity implies that the curve becomes flatter as k increases.

hours worked $L = Nh$ grows at the same rate as the number of workers N when the number of hours worked per person h remains constant. Consequently, the intensive form which describes output per hour Y/L allows us to study the rate of growth of output per capita Y/N, the standards of living. We will freely use these two expressions as equivalent. Third, income per capita does not depend on the absolute size of the economy, but what the average person has to work with. Put differently, the size of a country does not matter for its growth performance. The intensive-form production function is depicted in Figure 3.3. Because of diminishing marginal productivity, the curve becomes flatter as the capital–labour ratio increases.

3.3.2 **Savings and Capital Accumulation**

The national accounts of Chapter 2, more precisely identity (2.7), captures all potential sources that can be tapped to finance private investment, i.e. additions to the capital stock. Investment (I) can be financed either by private savings by firms or households (S), by government savings (the consolidated

---

[5] Formally, things are a bit harder. The definition of constant returns is that if we blow up K and L by a factor t, Y is blown up by the same factor, i.e. $tY = F(tK, tL)$ for all $t > 0$. In the text we use the case where $t = 2$, we double all inputs and produce twice as much. Now we can choose any value for t, for instance $t = 1/L$. This gives $y = F(k, 1)$, which we rename as $f(k)$ to recognize that $F(k, 1)$ only depends on k. The intensive production function $f(k)$ is so called because it expresses output produced per unit of labour (y) as a function of the capital intensity of production (k).

budget surplus, or $T - G$), or the net savings of foreigners (which is the current account deficit, $Z - X$):

(3.3) $\qquad I = S + (T - G) + (Z - X)$

For the time being we will assume that the government does not run any deficit or surplus so $T = G$ and, similarly, that the current account is balanced, so $Z = X$. Then $I = S$, increases in the stock of capital are entirely financed by domestic saving. This is the first explanation of the growth phenomenon: we save, we invest, we grow. To make things more precise, we now assume that a constant fraction s of GDP is saved to finance investment:

(3.4) $\quad I = sY$ and therefore $\quad I/L = s(Y/L) = sy = sf(k)$

3.3.3 Depreciation and the Steady State

New capital is accumulated through investment, but the old capital **depreciates:** some of it wears out, some becomes obsolescent. The proportion δ of capital thus routinely lost is called the **depreciation rate.** The depreciation rate for the overall economy is fairly stable and will be taken as constant: the more capital is in place, the more proportionally depreciates. Depreciation is represented in Figure 3.4 as the **depreciation line**, with a slope δ.

If investment exceeds depreciation, the capital stock rises. It could even shrink if investment were to be smaller than depreciation, a phenomenon not uncommon in declining industries. The net effect of gross investment and depreciation on the capital stock can be expressed in the following way:

(3.5) $\Delta K = sY - \delta K$ or equivalently, in intensive form:

$\Delta k = sy - \delta k,$

where the Greek letter Δ stands for a change over some period of time.

Let us take stock of our results up until now. The production function (3.2) relates the output to inputs, capital and labour. Its intensive form, presented in Figure 3.3 and Figure 3.4, relates the output–labour ratio to the capital–labour ratio. According to (3.5), capital accumulation is also driven by the output–labour ratio. Since, for the moment, population and hours per worker are held constant, saving is a fixed fraction of output (sY)

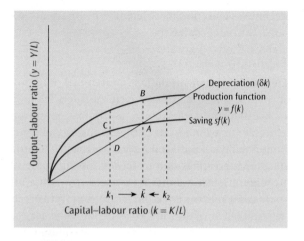

Fig. 3.4   **The Steady State**

The capital–labour ratio stops changing when investment is equal to depreciation. This occurs at point A, the intersection between the saving schedule $sf(k)$ and the depreciation line δk. The corresponding output–labour ratio is determined by the production function $f(k)$ at point B. When away from point A, the economy moves towards its steady state. Starting with below the steady-state at k_1, investment (point C) exceeds depreciation (point D) and the capital–output ratio will increase until it reaches its steady-state level $\bar{k}$.

and therefore of output per capita ($sY/L = sy = sf(k)$). Depreciation is proportional to the per head capital stock and given by δk. Putting the two processes together, we find that, at any moment of time, capital accumulation is driven by the existing, previously accumulated stock of capital:

(3.6) $\qquad \Delta k = sf(k) - \delta k$

In Figure 3.4, Δk is the vertical distance between the savings investment schedule $sf(k)$ and the depreciation line δk, so we can see where the economy is heading. When $\Delta k > 0$, the capital stock per capita is rising and the economy is growing, since more output can be produced; when $\Delta k < 0$, the capital stock per capita is falling and the output per capita is declining. This is like filling up a bathtub with a leak, where investment plays the role of the tap and depreciation the role of the leak. At the intersection A of the saving-investment schedule and the depreciation line, investment and depreciation are equal, so the capital–labour ratio (point B) no longer changes. The newly accumulated capital stock exactly compensates the older one that is lost to depreciation—the water flows into the bathtub at the same speed as it leaks out. This is the steady state, where the capital–output ratio is neither rising nor falling.

The analysis predicts that the economy will automatically gravitate to its steady state and then stay there. Suppose the economy is to the left of the steady-state capital–output ratio $\bar{k}$, say at the level k_1.[6] Figure 3.4 shows that investment $sf(k_1)$ at point *C* exceeds depreciation δk_1 at point *D*. As can be seen from (3.6), the distance *CD* represents the increase in the capital–labour ratio, which now rises towards its steady-state level $\bar{k}$.

Could it pass beyond $\bar{k}$, going all way to say, k_2? Suppose that it did. Then investment $sf(k_2)$ is less than depreciation δk_2, the capital–labour ratio must decline, and we move leftward towards $\bar{k}$, the economy's stable resting point. Later we shall see that the stability of capital and output per capita carries over when we account for population growth.

3.3.4 **The Role of Savings**

The last section established that the more a country saves, the more it invests; the more it invests, the higher is its capital–output ratio; and the larger its capital–output ratio, the higher its output–labour ratio. Since the output–labour ratio is per capita income, we find that countries with high savings and investment rates should have high per capita incomes. Is this true? Figure 3.5 looks at the whole world and indeed detects such a link. The poor countries of Africa typically invest little, in contrast with the richer countries of Europe and Asia.

Yet, the link is not strong enough to explain even most of the differences between countries; much more must be going on. Indeed, we soon proceed to put more flesh on the bones we just pieced together. But one aspect should be recognized immediately: savings and investment in the Solow model affect the steady-state *level* of output, but not the steady-state *growth rate*. To see this consider Figure 3.6, which shows the effect of an increase in the savings

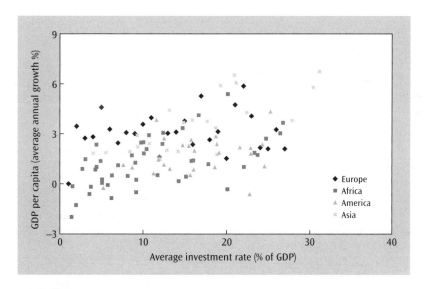

Fig. 3.5   **Investment and Growth Rates, 122 Countries, 1950–1992**

For a sample of 124 countries over the period 1950–88, the correlation coefficient between the investment rate (the ratio of investment to GDP) and GDP per capita is 0.57.
Source: Summers and Heston (1991) and update (http://www.nber.org/data_index.html)

---

[6] Note that we represent steady-state values with a bar.

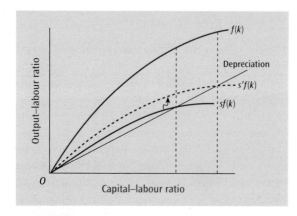

Fig. 3.6   **An Increase in the Savings Rate**

An increase in the savings rate raises capital intensity (k) and
the output/labour ratio (y).

rate from s to s'. The savings function shifts upwards,
but the production function remains unchanged.
The steady-state output–labour and capital–labour
ratios are both higher, indicating more capital-
intensive production. Adjustment to the new steady
state will not be immediate, meaning higher growth
for some time. But once the steady state has been
reached, there is no further growth effect. We still
need a story to explain growth in per capita output:
this is the story told in Sections 3.4 and 3.5.

The result that increased savings does not affect
long-run growth may come as a surprise. Why can't
higher savings allow capital and output to grow forever? Initially, the capital stock rises, but once more
capital is in place, more capital depreciates and thus
needs to be replaced. So we need more investment
to keep the capital stock constant. Yet the resources
for that increased investment are not there because
the marginal productivity of capital decreases. As
a result, further additions to the capital–labour
ratio yield smaller and smaller increases in income,
and therefore in savings. Depreciation, however,
rises proportionately. Put simply, the decreasing
marginal productivity principle implies that saving
more and more pays off less and less. The last section
of this chapter confirms that the outcome is very
different when the marginal productivity of capital
is not decreasing.

3.3.5 The Golden Rule

Figure 3.5 seems to convey an important message: to
become richer, you need to save more. But is being
richer *always* necessarily better? Besides the philo-
sophical doubts one might have about growth—
which are not the subject of this chapter—this
question is well posed if more savings are necessary
for increasing GDP per capita. Savings represent a
sacrifice; from the perspective of the household, it is
income which is not spent on consumption. Once
we remember that savings come at the expense of
consumption, we need to ask whether it is worth it.
Savings are income put aside for later consumption;
it is consumption that brings economic satisfaction. So when we ask what is the best that can be
achieved, we ought to be aiming for the highest
possible level of per capita consumption.

To see this more concretely, note that in the
steady-state $\bar{k}$, savings equal depreciation, so steady-
state consumption $\bar{c}$ (the part of income that is not
saved) is:

(3.7) $$\bar{c} = \bar{y} - s\bar{y} = f(\bar{k}) - \delta\bar{k}$$

In Figure 3.7, consumption is given by the vertical
distance between the production function and the
depreciation line.[7] If we could choose the saving
rate, we could effectively pick any point of intersection of the savings schedule with the depreciation
line, and therefore any level of consumption we
so desired. The figure shows that the highest consumption level is achieved where the slope of the
production function is parallel to the depreciation
line.[8] The corresponding optimal steady-state capital–
output ratio is $\bar{k}'$. Since the slope of the production
function schedule is the marginal productivity of
capital (*MPK*), the most desired situation can be
characterized by the following condition:

(3.8) $$MPK = \delta.$$

This condition is called the **golden rule**, and can
be thought of as a recipe for achieving the best use

---

[7] Note that everything, including consumption and saving, is
measured as a ratio to the labour input, man-hours. As already
noted, if he number of hours worked does not change, the ratios
move exactly as per capita consumption, saving, output, etc.

[8] An exercise asks to prove this assertion.

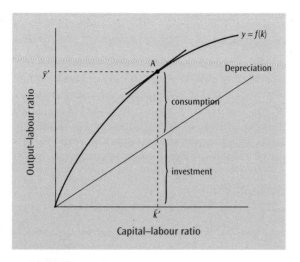

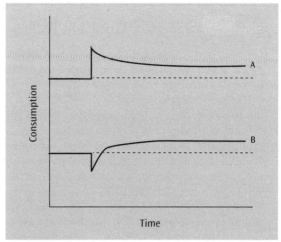

Fig. 3.7 **The Golden Rule**

Steady-state consumption $\bar{c}$ (as a ratio to labour) is the vertical distance between the production function and the depreciation line δk. It is at a maximum at point A corresponding to $\bar{k}'$, where the slope of the production function, the marginal productivity of capital, is equal to δ, the slope of the depreciation line.

Fig. 3.8 **Raising Steady-State Consumption**

In a dynamically inefficient economy, it is possible to permanently raise consumption by reducing saving. In a dynamically efficient economy, higher future consumption requires early sacrifices.

of existing technological capabilities. What are the consequences of 'disobeying' it? If the capital–labour ratio exceeds $\bar{k}'$, too much capital has been accumulated. This represents a situation of **dynamic inefficiency**: by reducing savings today, an economy can consume more both today *and* in the future. This looks like a free lunch, and indeed, it is one. Dynamically inefficient economies simply invest too much and consume too little. To the left of $\bar{k}'$, in contrast, steady-state income and consumption may be raised by saving more, but only in the long run. The economy is called **dynamically efficient** because there is no free lunch readily available. Indeed, moving towards $\bar{k}'$ from a position on the left requires the current generation to give up some consumption—that is, save now—so that future generations can enjoy more consumption which results from more capital and income. The difference between dynamically efficient and inefficient savings rates is illustrated in Figure 3.8 which shows how we move from one steady state to another one with higher consumption.

Dynamic inefficiency arises when savings are too high. We must keep saving a lot forever to make up

for the depreciation of an excessive amount of capital. Dynamic inefficiency may have characterized the centrally planned economies of Central and Eastern Europe. We say 'may' because the proof that an economy is inefficient lies in showing that its marginal productivity of capital is lower than the depreciation rate, and neither of these is easily measurable. What we do know is that Communist leaders were rather proud of their economies' high investment rates, which were in fact considerably higher than in the capitalist West. Yet it is also well documented that overall standards of living were considerably lower, and consumer goods in notoriously short supply. Box 3.2 presents the case of Poland.

In dynamically efficient countries, future generations would benefit from raising saving today, but those currently alive would lose. Should governments do something about it? Since it would represent a transfer of revenues from current to future generations, there is no simple answer, it is truly a deep political choice with no solution since future generations don't vote today. Anyway, can it be done? Savings depend on a host of factors such as taxation, the existence of health and retirement

Box 3.2 **Dynamic Inefficiency in Poland?**

The upper part of Figure 3.9 compares centrally planned Poland with Italy, one of the countries with the highest saving rates in Europe. The first graph shows the increase in GDP per capita between 1980 and 1990 (the GDP measure is adjusted for purchasing power to take into account different price systems): while Italy's income grew by 63%, Poland's only increased by 36%, about half. The second graph shows the average proportion of GDP dedicated to saving over the same period. Clearly, Poland saved a lot, and received little for it in terms of income growth. And, as the lower part of the figure shows, the situation was reversed after 1991, when Poland dropped central planning: from 1991 to 1997, its per capita GDP increased by 40%, while it grew by 17% in Italy, with the same saving rate. However, our theory predicts that savings affect the steady-state level of GDP per capita, not its growth rate. If we look at GDP per capita, in 1980 it stood at $3250 in Poland, and at $5790 in Italy, with the difference only deepening thereafter. Is this proof of dynamic efficiency, i.e. that a significant part of savings was used merely to keep up an excessively large stock of capital? Anecdotal evidence would suggest so. Stories about centrally planned economies are replete with examples of wasted resources: never installed equipment rusting in backyards, recent machinery prematurely discarded because of lack of parts, tools ill-adapted to factory needs, etc. One important factor behind this wastage was that factory managers were rewarded for spending on equipment and their promised plans, not for the actual output. An alternative interpretation is that the investment was in poor quality equipment, which could not match western technology. No matter how we look at it, savings were not put to their best use in centrally planned Poland.

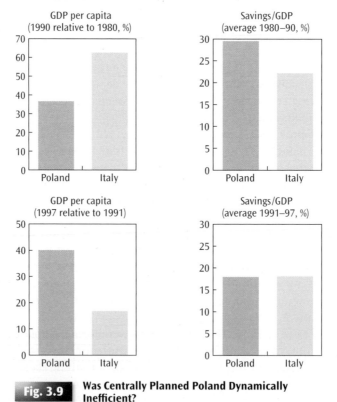

Fig. 3.9 **Was Centrally Planned Poland Dynamically Inefficient?**

Despite a higher rate of saving, Polish per capita GDP grew only about half as fast Italy's over the period 1980–90. Afterwards, during the transition period, Poland grew much faster, with about the same saving rate as Italy.
Source: OECD.

systems, cultural aspects affecting family links. Most importantly, perhaps, saving and investment are influenced by political conditions. Political instability and especially wars, civil or otherwise, can lead to destruction and theft of capital, and hardly encourage thrifty behaviour. Indeed, in many of the poorest countries in the world property rights are under threat or non-existent.

3.4   Population Growth

We have found that, when decreasing marginal productivity sets in, capital accumulation cannot sustain permanent growth. The result that output and the capital stock are constant grossly violates the evidence, so we must be missing some crucial ingredients. This section takes a first step and shows that growth can be permanent once we introduce population growth.

Labour input grows either when more people are at work, or when each worker works more hours. In the next chapter, we will see that the number of hours worked per person has declined secularly over the past century and a half. At the same time, the number of workers has been rising, as illustrated in Figure 3.10, either because of natural demographic forces (the balance between births and deaths) or immigration. Overall, the balance of effects is ambiguous. In order to make the general point, we will simply assume that the number of man-hours is growing and look at the data afterwards.

Fortunately, the reasoning of Section 3.3 remains valid: the economy will gravitate to its steady state, at which the capital–labour and output–labour ratios (K/L and Y/L) stabilize. With L growing at the rate n, this means that output Y and capital K will grow at the same rate. The increase in the labour input is a source of growth. Quite simply, if income per capita is to remain unchanged in the steady state, income must grow at the same rate as the number of people.

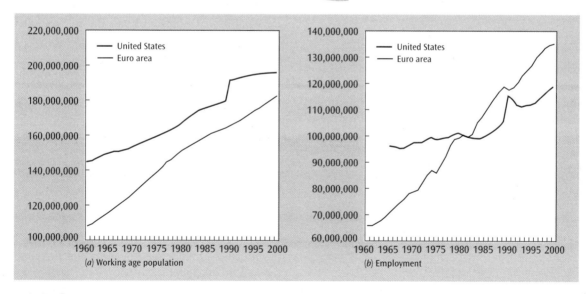

(a) Working age population

(b) Employment

Fig. 3.10   **Population Growth**

Population of working age (between 15 and 64) has been growing both in the USA and Europe (the data refer to EU11, i.e. the European Union less Denmark, Greece, Sweden and the UK). Employment has also been growing, albeit less fast in Europe. Note the jump in Europe in 1991, the year after German unification.
Source: OECD, *Economic Outlook*.

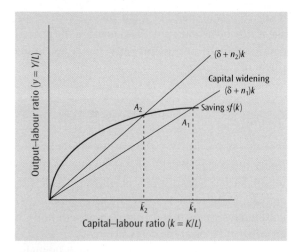

Y-axis: Output–labour ratio ($y = Y/L$)
X-axis: Capital–labour ratio ($k = K/L$)

Labels in figure: $(\delta + n_2)k$, Capital widening $(\delta + n_1)k$, Saving $sf(k)$, A_2, A_1, $\bar{k}_2$, $\bar{k}_1$

Fig. 3.11 **The Steady State with Population Growth**

The capital–labour ratio remains unchanged when investment is equal to $(\delta + n_1)k$.

This occurs at point A_1, the intersection between the saving schedule $sf(k)$ and the capital widening line $(\delta + n_1)k$. An increase in the rate of growth of the population from n_1 to n_2 is shown as a counter-clockwise rotation of the capital widening line. The new steady-state capital output ratio declines from $\bar{k}_1$ to $\bar{k}_2$.

The role of saving and capital accumulation remains the same as in the previous section, only the details change. For the capital–labour ratio to remain unchanged in the steady state, investment must not only compensate for capital depreciation, but also for labour growth, providing new workers with the same equipment as their elders. The capital accumulation condition (3.6) now becomes:[9]

(3.9) $$\Delta k = sf(k) - (\delta + n)k$$

Figure 3.11 summarizes the Solow model with population growth. The only difference with Figure 3.4 is that the depreciation line δk has been replaced by the **capital widening** line $(\delta + n)k$. The term 'capital widening' captures the notion that

the capital stock must now also increase to equip the newly arrived workers. The steady state is at point A_1, the intersection of the saving-investment schedule and the capital widening line where $\Delta k = 0$.

The role of population growth is best illustrated by asking what is the effect of an increase in the rate of population growth, from n_1 to n_2. In Figure 3.11 the capital widening line becomes steeper and the new steady state at point A_2 is characterized by a lower capital–labour ratio $\bar{k}_2$. Thus the higher is the rate of population growth, the lower is the sustainable steady-state capital–labour ratio. Since the output–labour ratio is $f(\bar{k})$ we find that it also declines with population growth. Put differently, the Solow model implies that, *all other things being equal*, countries with rapidly growing population will tend to be poorer than countries with lower population growth. More investment is needed to keep the capital–labour ratio steady when more workers are arriving each year. Investment which is forthcoming at the constant savings rate will be insufficient to do the job; capital intensity must decline, and so will the output–labour ratio. Box 3.3 examines whether it is indeed the case that population growth lowers GDP per capita. The complete story turns out to be somewhat more complicated, but the Solow model is a good starting point for organizing our thoughts on this issue.

Since a growing population increases continuously the number of people who are able to consume, it requires that we modify the golden rule. Following the same reasoning as before, we note that steady-state investment per man-hour is $(\delta + n)\bar{k}$, so consumption per man-hour $\bar{c}$ is given by $f(\bar{k}) - (\delta + n)\bar{k}$. Proceeding as before, it is easy to see that consumption is at a maximum when:

(3.10) $$MPK = \delta + n.$$

The modified golden rule equalizes the marginal productivity of capital with the *sum* of the depreciation rate δ and the population growth rate n. When the population is growing, the marginal product of capital must be higher; the principle of diminishing marginal productivity implies that the capital–labour must be lower. Consequently, output per head is also lower.

[9] To formally establish this result, start again with investment $I = sY$ and note that $\Delta K = I - \delta K$, as before. Then compute $\Delta k = \Delta(K/L)$, noting that $\Delta(K/L) = (\Delta K/K)/(K/L) - (\Delta L/L)/(K/L)$ by the law of differentiation.

Box 3.3   **Population Growth and GDP per capita**

Figure 3.12 plots GDP per capita in 1992 and the average rate of population growth over the period 1960–92. The figure could be seen as confirming the negative relationship predicted by the Solow growth model. Taken at face value, this result would support the hypothesis —associated with English economist and philosopher Thomas Malthus—that population growth impoverishes nations. Malthus's reasoning was not based on the Solow model, however. He thought that a fixed land area could not feed a constantly increasing population and that population growth would result in starvation. He ignored technological change, in this case the green revolution which significantly raised agricultural output over the decades. As we confirm in Section 3.5, technological change can alter the outlook radically.

But the Malthusian view is sometimes taken seriously in some countries which attempt to limit demographic growth, the most spectacular example being China's one-child-only policy. Several European countries, in contrast, view demography as a source of growth. Anyway, what should one make of the evidence displayed in Figure 3.12? Probably that one should exercise care interpreting such diagrams. The figure can also be read as saying that as people become richer, they have fewer children. There exists a great deal of evidence in favour of this alternative interpretation.

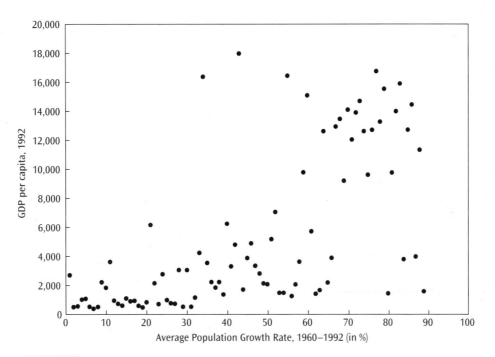

Fig. 3.12   **Population Growth and GDP per capita**

The figure, which reports on 107 countries, indicates a weak but discernible negative association between GDP per capita and the rate of population growth.
Source: Summers and Heston (1992).

3.5   Technological Progress

Having taken population growth into account, we have found one good reason why output—and the capital stock—can grow permanently. Yet the picture remains incomplete: in the steady state, the capital–labour and output–labour ratios are constant, which means that the standards of living are not rising. This is grossly inconsistent with Kaldor's first stylized fact and the data reported in Table 3.1. What other sources of growth are there? An obvious candidate is technological progress. It stands to reason that over time, increased knowledge and better, more sophisticated techniques make workers and the equipment they work with more productive.

It turns out that with a slight alteration, our framework readily shows how technological progress works. To do so, we need to extend the aggregate production function introduced in (3.1) to allow for the same quantity of equipment and labour to yield more output. The most convenient way to do this is to introduce a measure of the state of technology, A:

(3.11) $Y = F(A, K, L)$.

                   +   +   +

Along with the production function itself, A captures the state of technology. When it increases, even if K and L remain unchanged, Y rises. It should be emphasized that A is *not* a factor of production, it is not paid for, each firm just benefits from it. We will assume that A increases regularly at a constant rate a, without trying to explain so far precisely how and why. Technological progress, which is the increase in A, is therefore exogenous.

In order to connect immediately to previous results in this chapter, we take two steps. First we modify (3.11) in the following way:

(3.12) $Y = F(K, AL)$

and we refer to AL as **effective labour**, to capture the idea that, with the same equipment, one hour of work today produces more output than before because A is higher. Effective labour grows for two reasons: more labour L, and greater effectiveness A: the rate of growth of AL is $a + n$.

Next, we redefine y and k as ratios to effective labour: $y = Y/AL$, $k = K/AL$. Once this is done, we recover the now-familiar production function in intensive form, $y = f(k)$. Not surprisingly, the ratio of capital to effective labour k accumulates as follows:

(3.13) $\Delta k = sf(k) - (\delta + a + n)k$

The reasoning is the same as when we introduced population growth. The ratio $k = K/AL$ rises with K and declines with A and L. So k will increase if saving $sf(k)$, and hence investment, exceeds capital accumulation needed to make up for depreciation δ, population growth n, and increased effectiveness a. From there on, it is a simple matter to modify Figure 3.11 to Figure 3.13. The steady state is now characterized by constant ratios of capital and output to effective labour ($y = Y/AL$ and $k = K/AL$). As a consequence both output Y and capital K will grow at the rate $a + n$, the sum of technological progress and population growth.

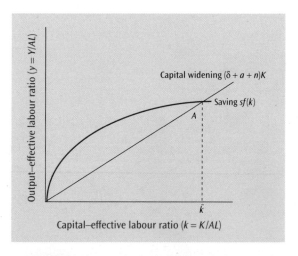

Fig. 3.13   **The Steady State with Population Growth and Technological Progress**

In an economy with both population growth and technological progress, inputs and output, as well as the intensive form production function, are measured in units per effective labour input. The slope of the capital accumulation line is now $\delta + a + n$, where a is the rate of technological progress. The steady state occurs when investment is equal to $(\delta + a + n)k$. This occurs at point A, the intersection between the saving schedule $sf(k)$ and the capital widening line $(\delta + a + n)k$. At the steady-state $\bar{k}$, output and capital increase at rate $a + n$, while GDP per capita increases at rate a.

An increase in the rate of technological progress a steepens the capital accumulation line and reduces the ratios of capital and output to effective labour. Does this mean that technological change reduces capital and output per capita? Intuition says that it should not be the case, and it is not. While more progress means a decline in y and k, recall that these are measured not in labour units, but in effective units, Y/AL and K/AL. In the steady state, these ratios are constant, but if we look at the more meaningful ratios per hour (or per capita if we ignore changes in hours worked) $Y/L = Ay$ and $K/L = Ak$, we do find that they increase, both at the rate a, the rate of technological progress.[10] Figure 3.14 shows this evolution which nicely matches Kaldor's first and second stylized facts. Finally, we now have an account of the continuous increase in standards of living.

Finally, how is the golden rule affected? Redefining c as the ratio of total consumption to effective labour C/AL, in the steady state the following modified version of (3.7) will hold:

$$\bar{c} = f(\bar{k}) - (\delta + a + n)\bar{k}$$

Now the golden rule requires that the marginal productivity of capital be the sum of the rates of depreciation, of technological change and of population growth:

(3.14) $MPK = \delta + a + n.$

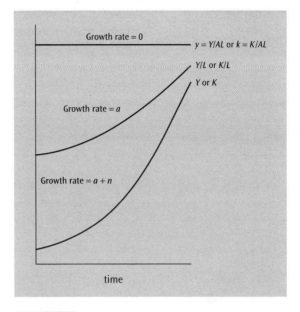

Fig. 3.14   **Growth Rates along the Steady State**

While output and capital measured in effective labour units (Y/AL and K/AL) are constant in the steady state, output–labour and capital–labour ratios (Y/L and K/L) grow at the rate of technological progress a, and output and the capital stock (Y and K) grow at the rate $a + n$, the sum of the rates of population growth and technological progress.

3.6   Putting It All Together: Growth Accounting

In its fully developed form, the Solow model identifies three sources of GDP growth: capital accumulation, population growth, and technological progress. Because of diminishing marginal productivity, capital accumulation alone cannot sustain growth. Population growth explains GDP growth, but not the continuous increase of standards of living which is so striking in most parts of the world. Technological progress, therefore, is the key to better economic conditions.

How big is it? Unfortunately, it is very difficult to measure technological progress. Computers, for instance, probably raise growth, but by how much? Some people believe that the 'new economy', borne by the information technology revolution, is going to push standards of living faster than ever; others are sceptical that the effect is any bigger than the other big discoveries which mark economic history. Box 3.4 provides some details on this exciting debate.

One approach to put numbers on technological progress is to start with the things we know and can measure: GDP growth, capital accumulation, and man-hours worked. Going back to (3.11), we can measure Y and two of its inputs, K and L. The

---

[10] If we define e.g. y as $y = Y/AL$, the rate of growth of y is: $\Delta y/y = \Delta Y/Y - \Delta A/A - \Delta L/L$. Along the steady state, $\Delta y/y = 0$, so with $a = \Delta A/A$ and $n = \Delta L/L$, we have $\Delta Y/Y = a + n$, or $\Delta(Y/L)/(Y/L) = a$.

The New Economy: Another Industrial Revolution?

The fantastic changes brought about by innovations in computer technology, and the associated wonders of IT (information technology) such as the internet and conspicuous use of electronic equipment, have led many observers to conclude that a new industrial revolution is upon us, of the dimensions of the fantastic acceleration of growth that started towards the end of the nineteenth century. Figure 3.15 reports estimates of increases in A (multifactor productivity) in the USA, computed as annual averages over four periods. A difference of 1% per year cumulates to 28% after 25 years. The figure shows a formidable acceleration in the period 1913–72, and again over 1995–9, hence the case for a second industrial revolution.

In reviewing this evolution, however, Gordon (2000) notes that what is really extraordinary is the collapse of productivity growth in the period 1972–95. In his view, we are now only recovering from this unusual period of decline, related to the two oil shocks and associated increases in inflation and unemployment. To buttress his case, Gordon lists the great inventions that brought the first industrial revolution—the discovery of electricity, the combustion engine (cars, planes, tools), electronics (including radio, telephones, television) and sanitation

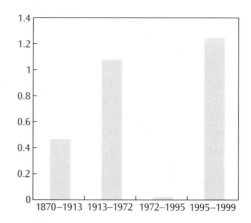

Fig. 3.15 **Multifactor Productivity in the USA (average annual growth, %)**

The average annual increase in A (multifactor productivity) has accelerated sharply after 1913, came to a near stop over 1972–95, and seems to have vigorously bounced back at the end of the 1990s.
Source: Gordon 2000.

(including the discovery of germs and bacteria)—and claims that computers (already invented in 1950) pale in comparison. Time will tell.

remaining input A, sometimes called **multifactor (or total factor) productivity**, has to be deduced. In practice, once we know how much GDP has increased, and how much of this increase is explained by capital and hours worked, we can interpret what is left over as the increase in A, i.e. $a = \Delta A/A$. This unexplained part of output growth is called the **Solow residual** and it is computed as follows:

$$\text{Solow residual} = \frac{\Delta Y}{Y} - \text{contributions of capital}$$

accumulation and man-hours worked.

The contributions of factor inputs, capital and labour depend on their growth and income shares in GDP.[11]

[11] The formula is $\frac{\Delta Y}{Y} = (1-\alpha)\frac{\Delta K}{K} - \alpha\frac{\Delta L}{L} + \text{residual}$, where Y is real GDP, α is the share of labour in GDP and $(1-\alpha)$ is the share of capital. It uses the assumption, standard from microeconomics, that each factor receives a reward equal to its marginal productivity.

Capital accumulation

Table 3.3 shows that, typically capital has been growing at about 2% per year over most of the twentieth century in the developed countries. Capital accumulation accelerated sharply in the 1950s and 1960s as part of the post-war reconstruction. The table also shows that Japan has continued to accumulate capital fast well into the 1980s; the reason is that Japan was much poorer than Europe and the USA at the beginning of the twentieth century. These periods of temporarily rapid capital accumulation fit well the description of catch-up, when the capital stock is below its steady-state level.

Labour input

The most appropriate measure of labour input is total number of hours worked. For several reasons, growth in population or the number of employees does not necessarily translate into increased

Table 3.3	Productive Capital Stock, 1913–1987 (average annual growth rates)		
	1913–50	**1950–73**	**1973–87**
France	1.2	6.4	3.7
Germany	1.1	7.7	2.7
Netherlands	2.4	6.9	2.2
UK	1.6	5.7	2.3
Japan	3.6	10.2	6.7
USA	1.7	3.8	2.6

Source: Maddison (1991).

Table 3.4	Population, Employment, and Hours Worked, 1900–1997 (average annual growth rates)		
Country	**Population**	**Employment**	**Hours worked per person**
France	0.4	0.1	−0.5
Germany	0.7	0.7	−0.6
Netherlands	1.1	1.4	−0.7[a]
UK	0.4	0.5	−0.5
Japan	1.1	1.0	−0.4[a]
USA	1.3	1.6	−0.3

[a] 1900–1995.
Source: Maddison (1989), OECD *Annual Labour Force Statistics-Database*, OECD *Employment Outlook*, *Statistical Yearbook of the Netherlands 1998*.

man-hours. Even if unemployment is ignored, the number of employed people at work differs from the size of the population, and the relationship between employment and hours worked is constantly changing. People live longer, study longer, and retire earlier. At the same time, women have increased their labour force participation over the past three decades.[12] Table 3.4 shows that these effects have roughly cancelled each other out as employment and population size have increased by similar amounts in our sample of developed countries.

Second, employment and the number of hours worked may grow at different rates. Table 3.4 documents the sharp decline in the number of hours worked per person in the developed world, as people put in shorter days, shorter weeks, and fewer weeks per year. Indeed, the number of man-hours has grown much more slowly than population and employment, even declining in Austria, Belgium, France, and the UK. Overall, European labour input

[12] Chapter 4 explores these various issues in more details.

Table 3.5	The Solow Decomposition, 1913–1987[a] (average annual growth rates)		
Country	**GNP**	**Contribution of inputs**	**Residual**
France	2.6	1.1	1.5
Germany	2.8	1.4	1.4
Netherlands	3.0	2.0	1.0
UK	1.9	1.2	0.7
Japan	4.7	3.0	1.7
USA	3.0	2.0	1.0

[a] An adjustment is made to account for the modernization of productive capital.
Source: Authors' calculation from data in Maddison (1991).

has increased between nil and 0.3%, while immigration lifted it well above 1% in North America and Australia. The dramatic decline in hours worked per person (an average annual reduction of 0.6% per year means a total reduction of 68% over the period 1900–86) is a central feature of the growth process. As societies have become richer, demand for leisure has increased. In the UK, for example, the average number of hours worked per year has declined from 2725 in 1900 to 1720 in 1999.

The Solow residual

Table 3.5 presents the Solow decomposition. As already suspected, labour and capital growth can account for only one-half to two-thirds of total economic growth. The rest is the **Solow residual**, and confirms the importance of technological progress. A puzzling observation is the apparent slowdown in technological change during the 1970s and the 1980s, which contrasts with reports of an acceleration since the late 1990s.

3.7 Endogenous Growth: A Primer

According to the Solow growth model, technological change is the engine that pushes the output–labour ratio—or GDP per capita—ever higher. But what generates technological change? So far, we have assumed that it is *exogenous*, rising at a rate *a*. Is it as simple as that? Could it not be that technological progress itself is driven by man-made decisions? For example, technological progress seems likely to depend on investment in education and science, on research and development (R&D) and on millions of discoveries, small and large. Opening up this box makes the rate of growth *endogenous*. This is the exciting task assigned to Chapter 18. Here, for the sake of completeness, we briefly sketch the theory

of endogenous growth, leaving out most of the substantial issues for later.

In a nutshell, the Solow growth model predicts that the capital–output ratio converges to a predetermined steady-state level. What drives this result is the principle of declining marginal productivity, which is represented in Figure 3.13 by the flattening of the aggregate production function schedule. But if marginal productivity does not decline, the schedule no longer becomes flatter. In fact, it becomes a straight line, conveying the fact that output increases at the same rate when new capital is accumulated. The same property also applies to the saving schedule since savings are a constant

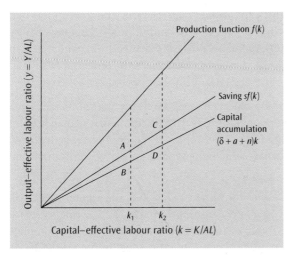

 Fig. 3.16   Endogenous Growth with Non-Declining Marginal Productivity

Here we look at the case of constant marginal productivity of capital: the production function is now represented by a straight line. If saving is large enough to exceed depreciation and the need for capital widening, the capital stock will increase without bound. For example, starting from k_1, *AB* represents new capital being installed, which takes the economy to k_2. There *CD* corresponds to a further increase in the capital stock. And so on.

proportion of output. Figure 3.16 shows how things radically change. If the capital–labour ratio is initially at k_1, investment corresponds to point *A* and the ratio of capital to effective labour ratio $k = K/AL$

increases by the distance *AB*. As this ratio grows to reach the level k_2, saving is determined by point *C* and the capital-effective labour ratio keeps rising even faster as indicated by the distance *CD*. There is no end to this process.

What is happening? Because the marginal productivity of capital does not decline, more of it produces more income and therefore more saving. Growth of the income-effective labour and capital-effective labour ratios never ends.[13] This contrasts sharply with the case of declining marginal productivity, in which a unique steady state is always reached with $y = K/AL$ constant and GDP per capita Y/L grows at constant rate a. Now y itself is rising secularly, and Y/L rises even faster.[14] Another implication of non-declining marginal productivity of capital is that an increase in the saving rate makes the saving schedule rotate upward, leading to faster accumulation of the capital stock and permanent growth in GDP per capita.

We have thus found an example whereby growth can be determined endogenously. In the absence of diminishing returns, policies which accelerate growth become feasible, because these effects are permanent. Among other things, it may pay handsomely to subsidize education, research and development, other innovative activities, and even certain types of investment spending. This and related aspects of economic growth are the subject of Chapter 18.

Summary

1. Growth theory is concerned with the study of the steady state, a situation where output and capital grow at the same pace and remain in constant proportion to labour in effective terms. This approach reflects key stylized facts.

2. The aggregate production function shows that output grows when more inputs (capital and labour) are used, and when technological progress increases the effectiveness of those inputs.

3. The stock of capital is accumulated through investment, and investment is financed by savings. If, as seems reasonable, savings represent a stable proportion of output, the steady-state capital

---

[13] Formally, if the production function in intensive form is $y = Ak$, then $\Delta k = sAk - (\delta + a + n)k$, which implies a permanent growth rate of k given by $\Delta k/k = sA - (\delta + a + n)k$.

[14] Note that in this case we need the saving line to be above the capital accumulation line. If the configuration were the opposite, the capital-effective labour ratio would instead shrink to zero over time.

stock is determined by the net effect of savings and capital depreciation. The assumption that the marginal productivity of capital is declining implies that output, and therefore savings, grow less than proportionately to the stock of capital, in contrast to depreciation, which rises in proportion to capital. Eventually, the size of the capital stock exhausts the potential of savings to raise it further.

4. In the absence of population growth and technological change, the steady state is characterized by zero output and capital growth. Adding population growth provides a first explanation of secular output growth, but standards of living (output per capita) still do not increase. It is only when we allow for technological progress that permanent growth in per capita output and capital is possible.

5. Savings represent deferred consumption: less is consumed today, but the capital stock will increase in the future, which will raise income and consumption. The golden rule looks for the situation in which consumption is as high as possible in all periods. In the complete Solow model, it occurs where the marginal productivity of capital is equal to the rate of depreciation (replacing worn out capital) *plus* the rate of population growth (providing new workers with equipment) *plus* the rate of technological change (adjusting capital to enhanced labour effectiveness): $MPK = \delta + n + a$.

6. An economy is dynamically efficient when steady-state consumption can be raised in the future only at the expense of lower consumption today. An economy is dynamically inefficient when both current and future steady state consumption can both be raised. In the former case, the capital stock is lower than the golden-rule level, calling for additional accumulation. In the latter case, the capital stock is above the golden-rule level.

7. In the Solow model, saving does not affect the steady-state growth rate, but only the level of output per capita.

8. Removing the assumption of diminishing marginal productivity allows output to grow forever, even in the absence of population growth and technological change. It implies that changes in saving and/or productivity can have permanent growth-enhancing effects. This is the basis for the theory of endogenous growth.

Key Concepts

- economic growth
- technological progress
- steady state
- aggregate production function
- diminishing marginal productivity
- returns to scale (constant, increasing, decreasing)
- output–labour ratio
- capital–labour ratio
- depreciation rate
- capital widening
- capital accumulation
- multifactor (or total factor) productivity
- Solow decomposition, Solow residual
- stylized facts
- golden rule
- dynamic inefficiency/efficiency
- endogenous growth

Exercises

1. Draw intensive-form production functions $f(k)$ with decreasing, constant, and increasing returns to scale.

2. Can we have a steady state with zero capital accumulation?

3. Suppose K/Y is constant at 2. (*a*) Assume first that there is no population growth and no technological progress. What is the steady-state saving–output ratio consistent with a rate of depreciation of 5%? (*b*) Now allow for population growth and technological progress. What is the steady-state saving–output ratio consistent with a rate of depreciation of 5% and 3% real growth?

4. Consider a country with zero technological progress and $K/L = 3$. Its population grows at the rate of 2% per year. What is the steady-state rate of growth of its GDP per capita if the saving rate is 20%? If it is 30%? How do your answers change if depreciation occurs at a rate of 0.05% per year?

5. Suppose the aggregate production function is given by $Y = \sqrt{KL}$. Does it have increasing, decreasing, or constant returns to scale? Are the marginal products of capital and labour declining?

6. Why is the golden rule in Figure 3.7 achieved at $\bar{k}'$? To establish this result, imagine that you start to the left of $\bar{k}'$ and explain why moving to the right increases consumption. Similarly show that consumption decreases when moving rightwards from a position to the right of $\bar{k}'$.

7. The golden rule (3.14) is MPK $= \delta + a + n$. In comparison with the no-technological change case, we find that we need a higher marginal productivity of labour. With diminishing marginal productivity, this means a lower capital stock. Is that not surprising? How can you explain away this apparent paradox?

8. How can the Solow model explain that nowadays workers use a vast array of highly efficient equipment such as powerful machinery or computers?

9. Draw a graph showing the evolution of Y/L in the catch-up phase and then in the ensuing steady state when the economy starts from a capital-effective labour ratio below its steady-state level. Draw a picture showing investment (not the capital stock).

Suggested Further Reading

Two classics are:

Maddison, Angus (1982), *Phases of Economic Development*, Oxford University Press.
Solow, Robert M. (1970), *Growth Theory: An Exposition*, Oxford University Press.

Surveys are:

Solow, Robert M. (1994), 'Perspectives on Growth Theory', *Journal of Economic Perspectives*, 8: 45–54.
'Symposium on New Growth Theory' in the *Journal of Economic Perspectives*, 8(1): 3–72, 1994 (articles by Paul Romer, Gene Grossman and Elhanan Helpman, Robert Solow, Howard Pack).

On Europe, see:

Crafts, Nicholas, and Tonniolo, Gianni (eds.) (1996), *Economic Growth in Europe Since 1945*, Cambridge University Press.

Appendix: The Modified Solow Growth Model, Conditional Convergence, and the Golden Rule

The Basic Model and Equilibrium

The following is a brief mathematical exposition of the most commonly studied version of the growth model analysed in the text. Advanced textbooks, such as Barro and Sala-i-Martin (1995), provide details.

Production is given by the constant returns to scale production function

(A3.1)
$$Y = F(K, AL),$$

with the characteristics discussed in Box 3.2. Technical progress, or growth in A, is labour-augmenting; it increases effectiveness of labour input. It grows at constant rate a. By the constant returns to scale property, we can write

(A3.2)
$$y = f(k),$$

where $y = Y/AL$ and $k = K/AL$. Notice that the intensive form is defined in terms of capital per *effective* unit of labour. (Sometimes the term 'efficiency units' of labour is used.) The source of growth in this model is increases in k over time, given by

(A3.3)
$$\frac{dk}{dt} = \frac{(1/AL)dK}{dt} - \frac{(K/AL^2)dL}{dt} - \frac{(K/A^2L)dA}{dt}$$

$$= \left[\frac{(1/K)dK}{dt} - \frac{(1/L)dL}{dt} - \frac{(1/A)dA}{dt} \right] k$$

$$= \left[\frac{(1/K)dK}{dt} - n - a \right] k;$$

or, in terms of growth rates, the growth rate of the capital stock in per capita effective labour terms is the gross growth rate of the capital stock minus the growth rate of the labour force (n), minus the rate of exogenous technical progress (a):

(A3.4)
$$\frac{(1/k)dk}{dt} = \frac{(1/K)dK}{dt} - n - a.$$

In the Solow model, the capital stock increases because households save a constant fraction s of their income Y; it decreases at the same time by depreciation at rate δ, so

$$\frac{dK}{dt} = sF(K, AL) - \delta K,$$

or, dividing by AL and substituting,

(A3.5)
$$\frac{(1/AL)dK}{dt} = \frac{k(1/K)dK}{dt} = sf(k) - \delta k.$$

Now substitute (A3.5) into (A3.3) to obtain

(A 3.6)
$$\frac{dk}{dt} = \left[\frac{sf(k)}{k} - a - \delta - n \right] k = sf(k) - (a + \delta + n)k.$$

This equation is sometimes called the fundamental equation of the Solow growth model. It completely describes the dynamics of the capital stock, and thereby of output as well.

The steady-state equilibrium in the Solow growth model is characterized by $dk/dt = 0$. Define $\bar{k}$ as the value of k that solves this condition, and let $\bar{y}$ be the output per efficiency unit of labour which corresponds to $\bar{k}$; that is, $\bar{y} = f(\bar{k})$. Then

(A3.7)
$$sf(\bar{k}) = (a + \delta + n)\bar{k}.$$

The equilibrium is shown as the intersection of the savings curve $sf(\bar{k})$ and the investment requirement line (the ray given by $(a + \delta + n)k$) at point E in Figure A3.1. As long as the economy lies to the left of point E, positive capital accumulation and growth will take place (per efficiency unit of labour), whereas an economy lying to the right of point E will have falling k and y.

Convergence near the steady state

We now use the Solow model to study the approximate growth behaviour of the economy in the neighbourhood of the steady state. The growth rate of y, $(1/y)dy/dt$, can be written as

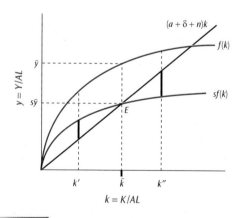

Fig. A3.1 The Modified Solow Growth Model

$$\frac{(1/y)dy}{dt} = \frac{d \ln y}{dt} = \frac{d \ln(f(k))}{dt} = (1/y)f'(k)\frac{dk}{dt}$$

$$= \left(\frac{1}{y}\right)f'(k)[sf(k) - (a + \delta + n)k].$$

Assuming that $f(k)$ can be inverted, we can write k as a function of y, $k = k(y)$, so

(A3.8) $$(1/y)\frac{dy}{dt} = G(y),$$

where the function

$$G(y) \equiv sf'(k(y)) - (a + \delta + n)\frac{f'(k(y))k(y)}{y}.$$

By definition of this function, $G(\bar{y}) = 0$. Take a first-order Taylor approximation around $G(\bar{y})$ to obtain

$$\frac{d \ln y}{dt} = G'(\bar{y})(y - \bar{y})$$

$$= \left[sf''k' - (\alpha + \delta + n)\left(f''k'k + f'k' - \frac{f'k}{y^*}\right)\right]\frac{y - \bar{y}}{\bar{y}}.$$

Since $k'(y) = 1/f'(y)$ and $(y - \bar{y})/\bar{y} \approx \ln y - \ln \bar{y}$, we can rewrite

$$\frac{d \ln y}{dt}$$

$$= \left[\frac{sf'' - (\alpha + \delta + n)(f''k + f' - f'^2k/\bar{y})}{f'}\right](\ln y - \ln \bar{y}),$$

or, defining $\alpha_K = f'k/y$ as the income share of capital in national output at the steady state $\bar{y}$,

$$\frac{d \ln y}{dt} = \left\{\frac{f''}{f'}[s\bar{y} - (a + \delta + n)\bar{k}]\right.$$

$$\left. - (1 - \alpha_K)(a + \delta + n)\right\}(\ln y - \ln \bar{y}).$$

Using (A3.7), this last expression can be rewritten as

(A3.9) $$\frac{d \ln y}{dt} = \lambda(\ln \bar{y} - \ln y),$$

where $\lambda \equiv (1 - \alpha_K)(a + \delta + n)$. The parameter λ, which is positive, can be thought of as the 'speed of convergence', or the rate at which the gap $\ln \bar{y} - \ln y$ is closed; when $\bar{y} > y$, y is growing. The solution of the differential equation (A3.9) is

$$\ln y(t) = \ln y(0)e^{-\lambda t} + \ln \bar{y}(1 - e^{-\lambda t}),$$

where $y(0)$ is the initial per capita GDP level and $\bar{y}$ is as before the corresponding steady-state value. Using the fact that $(y - \bar{y})/\bar{y} \approx \ln y - \ln \bar{y}$, this can be approximated by

(A3.10) $$y(t) = y(0)e^{-\lambda t} + \bar{y}(1 - e^{-\lambda t}).$$

Note that $y(t)$ is a weighted average of the initial condition $y(0)$ and the steady-state $y(\infty) = \bar{y}$.

Golden Rule Per Capita Capital Stock, Savings Rate, and Output

At each instant, effective per capita consumption is c, which in a closed economy without a government is given by $f(k) - (a + \delta + n)k$, or that output which is not diverted to capital formation. To find the characteristics of the steady-state path with the highest per capita consumption level, it is necessary to find the value $\bar{k}'$ that solves the following problem:

$$\max_{k} c = f(k) - (a + \delta + n)k,$$

subject to a side condition that k is non-negative.[15] The first-order condition for an optimum is

(A3.11) $$f'(\bar{k}) = (a + \delta + n).$$

(The second-order condition for a maximum, is fulfilled as long as $f'' < 0$, which is assumed.) The intuition of (A3.11) is that consumption is maximized when the marginal consumption made possible by a higher level of capital intensity (the left-hand side) is equal to the 'cost' or the steady-state investment necessary to maintain that intensity (the right-hand side) or the sum of the growth rate of technical efficiency (A), the depreciation rate, and the population growth rate.

From (A3.7), the savings rate corresponding to $\bar{k}'$ can be found to be

(A3.12) $$\bar{s}' = \frac{f'(\bar{k}')\bar{k}'}{f(\bar{k}')}.$$

Equation (A3.12) implies that per capita steady-state consumption is maximized when the savings rate is equal to the income share of capital, assuming that labour and capital are traded under conditions of perfect competition and receive their marginal products.[16] Finally, output is given by

(A3.13) $$\bar{y}' = f(\bar{k}') = \frac{(a + \delta + n)\bar{k}'}{\bar{s}'}.$$

---

[15] Technical note: usually this problem, as well as those involving the uniqueness of the equilibrium, can be ruled out by the conditions $\lim_{k \to 0} f'(k) = \infty$, $\lim_{k \to \infty} f'(k) = 0$, as well as $k(0) = 0$.

[16] To see this, note that $s = F_K(K/AL, 1)(K/AL)/F(K/AL, 1) = F_K(K/AL, 1)K/F(K, AL) = F_K(K, AL)K/F(K, AL)$. The last step follows from the fact that F is homogeneous of degree 1, and that first partial derivatives of F are therefore homogeneous of degree 0.

Labour Markets and Unemployment

4

Labour is the source of all value.

– Karl Marx

In our present day complicated economic life we are likely to be confused by the many industrial operations and money transactions. But net income remains exactly what it was to primitive Robinson Crusoe on his island—the enjoyment from eating the berries we pick, so to speak, less the discomfort or the labour of picking them.

– Irving Fisher

4.1   Overview

In the last chapter, output was a function of an economy's **endowment** of factors of production: its capital, labour, and technical sophistication. The evolution of the capital stock and of technology were examined in some detail, but the supply of labour was taken as given, regardless of the wage or other variables. Even in storybooks, life is not so simple. In the famous novel by Daniel Defoe, the shipwrecked castaway Robinson Crusoe was blessed with a stock of capital (coconut trees) to produce output (coconuts), but needed to expend time and effort to gather and transport the fruits that he would eventually consume. Like most people, Crusoe had to choose whether or not he would work, and how much effort he would put into it. Presumably, the rewards to work played a role in his decision.

Marx may be out of favour these days, but had a point when he viewed labour as the most important factor of production. Virtually everything stems directly or indirectly from labour. Raw materials are brought forth from the earth by human hands; equipment used in this and other forms of economic activity is made using labour and previously manufactured equipment, itself the output of labourers and capital in a more distant past. Even the knowledge embodied in people—human capital—comes from our own efforts at mastering skills and techniques, as well as the time our teachers spent trying to educate us.

In order to introduce the labour market into the macroeconomy, we study the decisions of households and firms to supply and demand hours of work. Households work so that they can consume, but they also want to spend some of their time *not* working and enjoying **leisure** or free time. The *supply* of labour

is seen as a trade-off between consumption and leisure. At the same time, someone must be willing to employ and pay for the hours of work that workers want to supply at the going wage; labour must also be *demanded*. For firms to demand labour, it must have some value to them in production. How the markets value labour and how demand and supply interact is the subject matter of this chapter. Most importantly, we will learn how **unemployment** emerges—when labour goes unutilized in an economy.

We begin by studying the behaviour of a representative household that can choose its working time. Next, we look at demand for labour by a representative firm. This naturally leads to the standard confrontation of demand and supply. Yet we will see that labour is not a standard 'commodity'. Workers are not identical, and the quality of labour services is difficult to ascertain and harder to monitor. Unlike machines or raw materials, workers can decide whether they would like to work for a particular employer and under which conditions to render labour services. In fact, the employment relationship involves explicit and implicit contractual arrangements which are highly specific to both firm and employee. The functioning of labour markets is also influenced by country-specific institutions, such as labour law or collective bargaining, and is the object of complex legal and customary rules. Finally, the labour market is a dynamic market, with suppliers of labour entering and exiting unemployment at a remarkable rate. We show how these interactions help understand the concept of equilibrium unemployment, which may differ from actual unemployment observed at a particular point in time.

4.2 | Demand and Supply in the Labour Market

4.2.1 Labour Supply and the Consumption–Leisure Trade-off

In modern societies, consuming requires income. Earning income most often means working, or supplying labour to firms in return for a wage or salary. But labour has a cost, too: every hour of work means an hour less of free time. Because households value both consumption and leisure, they balance the two the best they can, given the possibilities available to them. This trade-off is known as the **consumption–leisure trade-off**. In a parable which should be familiar, we consider the choice of Robinson Crusoe, who was forced to make do with the limited resources of his island.[1]

We see Crusoe as consuming all that he earns from work, the coconuts that he picks up, leaving aside saving and investment which are treated in Chapters 5 and 6. Crusoe's preferences with regard to consumption and leisure are summarized by indifference curves in Figure 4.1. Each indifference curve shows combinations of consumption and leisure which make Crusoe equally happy. Higher indifference curves correspond to higher levels of utility or happiness. The steepness of each curve at any given point shows how readily Crusoe substitutes consumption for leisure, holding his level of satisfaction constant. The shape of Crusoe's indifference curves tells us that the greater his consumption relative to its leisure, the more of that consumption he is willing to give up for an additional unit of leisure, or the higher is the **marginal rate of substitution** of consumption for leisure. It is an important principle in economics that the more scarce a good becomes relative to others, the more of those other goods one is willing to give up for it.

Crusoe is limited by natural circumstances in the total amount of time, denoted $\bar{\ell}$, available over any given period (a day, a month, a year, or more). All scarce resources have a price, and time is no exception. The price of an hour of leisure is its opportunity cost: how much could one otherwise earn in that hour by working in the market? For this reason, the price of leisure is called the **real (consumption) wage**. In practice, it is measured as the ratio of nominal wages (W) to the consumer price index (P). With $\bar{\ell}$ hours at his disposal and facing an hourly real wage $w = W/P$, the value of Crusoe's total time endowment valued in terms of consumption is $\bar{\ell}w$. This endowment can be allocated between C units of consumption and ℓ hours of leisure, with value ℓw, according to the following equation:[2]

$$(4.1) \qquad \bar{\ell}w = \ell w + C.$$

Equation (4.1) can be thought of as a time budget line, since it stipulates various combinations of leisure and consumption which are possible without

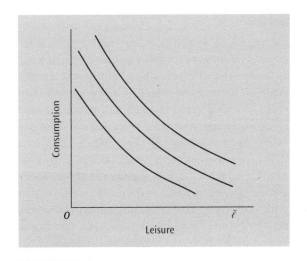

Fig. 4.1 | **Household Preferences**

An indifference curve shows how readily a household substitutes consumption C for leisure ℓ, holding utility constant. Higher curves correspond to higher levels of utility.

---

[1] The use of this character, based on the classic novel by Daniel Defoe (1660–1731), is traditional in economics and will recur in Ch. 5, in which goods are distinguished by the point in time that they are consumed.

[2] The nominal budget constraint is $\bar{\ell}W = \ell W + PC$. To write it in terms of consumption goods as in (4.1), we simply divide by P, the price of consumption goods.

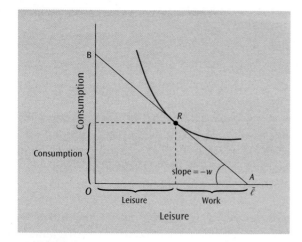

Fig. 4.2 **The Household Budget Line and Optimal Choice**

The household has a total of $\bar{\ell}$ hours at its disposal (measured by the distance OA) for either leisure or work. For every unit of leisure that it gives up, it can earn w consumption goods. The real wage w determines the slope of the budget line AB. Given the budget line, the highest possible utility is achieved at point R, where an indifference curve is tangent to the budget line.

additional resources.[3] It is depicted in Figure 4.2 as the negatively sloped line AB. The horizontal distance OA is equal to $\bar{\ell}$, Crusoe's endowment of time, or the fixed number of hours at his disposal. The distance OB measures the value of that endowment in terms of consumption goods. It is the total amount of consumption attainable when leisure is zero—when Crusoe is working all the time.[4]

The negative slope of the budget line ($-w$) measures the trade-off of consumption for leisure offered by the market: how much consumption must be given up to get an additional unit of leisure, or how much consumption can be 'purchased' with an additional hour of work. It explains why the real wage is often referred to as the **relative price** of leisure in terms of consumption. If the real wage changes, the budget line rotates around point A, which measures his fixed time endowment $\bar{\ell}$.

Optimal choice and the individual labour supply schedule

Crusoe maximizes his utility by choosing the highest possible indifference curve without violating his budget line. This is achieved at point R in Figure 4.2, where the indifference curve is tangent to the budget line. At this point, the marginal rate of substitution of consumption for leisure is equal to the market wage w. Given the terms of trade offered by the market, he cannot make himself any better off (reach a higher indifference curve) by further swapping leisure for consumption. This property is a defining characteristic of an optimum.

An important question is the influence of the real wage on household behaviour. How does Crusoe react to an increase in the real wage depicted in the upper panel of Figure 4.3? At any level of leisure and labour supplied, a higher wage increases the amount of consumption that can be afforded (i.e. OB increases) and the budget line rotates clockwise. This change has two effects. First, the relative attractiveness of leisure declines, since its relative price has risen. This alone would encourage Crusoe to take less leisure, work harder, and consume more. This is the **substitution effect**. At the same time, Crusoe's labour is better paid so that, holding leisure constant, he earns and consumes more. His reaction to this increase in income should be to work a bit less and enjoy both more consumption *and* more leisure. This incentive to work less is called the **income effect**.

So, will he work more (substitution) or less (income)? This question cannot be answered unambiguously without knowing more about Crusoe's preferences. In Figure 4.3, the substitution effect dominates, so the net effect is positive: an increase in the wage leads to a decline in leisure and an increase in labour supply. This is depicted in the lower panel of Figure 4.3 as an upward-sloping **household labour supply curve**.

In practice, the response to rising wages varies widely across individuals, depending on tastes, family circumstances, age, etc. It also depends on

---

[3] Alternatively, the budget constraint can be expressed in terms of 'cash flow': when Crusoe takes ℓ hours of leisure, he works $\bar{\ell} - \ell$ hours and earns $w(\bar{\ell} - \ell)$ coconuts. Since Crusoe does not save, this income $w(\bar{\ell} - \ell)$ is spent on consumption; so $w(\bar{\ell} - \ell) = C$, which is simply a rearranged version of equation (4.1).

[4] If Crusoe possessed some initial wealth to begin with, the budget line would be shifted upwards (vertically) by that amount. This represents the consumption he could attain without having to work at all.

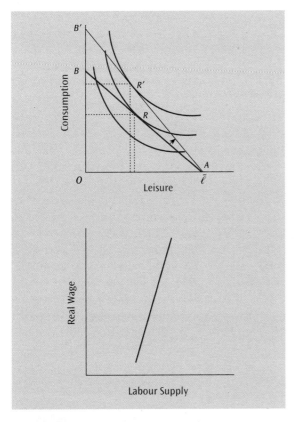

sex. For men, the average work-week, the retirement age, and the **labour force participation rate** have fallen secularly since 1900.[6] In contrast, labour force participation and hours per week of women have risen. One possible interpretation is that the income effect of higher wages dominates for men, whereas the substitution effect dominates for women. Another interpretation is that customs and sociological factors change, and that services such as child care and schooling have made it possible for more women to take up paid jobs.

The aggregate labour supply curve

We have studied a representative household's decision to work. The next step economists usually take is to add up the supplies of individual households across the economy, while noting the special aspects of labour and labour markets. In many instances, individuals cannot vary the hours of work that they supply; at best, they can choose between working or not working at all. Most labour contracts specify a standard working time (length of the work-week, days of leave per year). It is a matter of 'take it or leave it'. Sometimes workers are better off not working at all. In cases such as these, small wage increases may not be sufficient to motivate households to take up jobs, although large ones might.[7] Anyhow, the aggregate labour supply remains the sum of many individual decisions (to work or not work, and how many hours to work). While individual labour supply is measured in hours during some period of time (for example, per year as in Table 4.1), aggregate supply is measured in **man-hours**, the total amount of hours supplied by all workers during that same period (men and women, of course).[8] When wages rise, even if those who already work do not modify their supply of labour (the benchmark case), others who had preferred not to work may now

| **Fig. 4.3** | **Reaction of the Household to a Wage Increase: Labour Supply** |

When the real wage increases, the budget line rotates around point A (the endowment of time remains unchanged) and becomes steeper, because a unit of leisure is exchanged for more units of consumption. This allows both consumption and leisure to increase at the same time (income effect). Because leisure is more expensive, however, some is given up (substitution effect). In the case depicted here, the substitution effect dominates.

the time horizon under consideration.[5] In the short run, most individuals do not seem to react much to changes in the real wage. In the long run, the labour supply decreases as the income effect dominates. Indeed, Table 4.1 shows that, over the last 100 years, real wages have increased by five- to fifteen-fold, while working hours have declined by one-half. Labour supply behaviour also varies according to

---

[5] For details the reader is invited to look at the WebAppendix.

[6] The labour force participation rate is defined as the proportion of working-age people either working or registered as unemployed.
[7] These important cases are taken up in detail in Chapters 14 and 17.
[8] Aggregate employment is sometimes measured as the number of people who have a job. Generally, we will use the first definition (man-hours), and make explicit mention when referring to the number of employed workers. Under any definition, when more workers enter the labour force, the labour supply curve shifts to the right independently of the wage level.

Table 4.1	Annual Total Hours Worked and Average Wages, 1870–1992				
	1870	**1913**	**1938**	**1973**	**1992**
Annual hours worked per Person					
France	2945	2588	1848	1771	1542
Germany	2941	2584	2316	1804	1563
UK	2984	2624	2267	1688	1491
USA	2964	2605	2062	1717	1589
Sweden	2945	2588	2204	1571	1515
Real Wage (index: 1870 = 100)					
France	100	205	335	1048	1417
Germany	100	185	285	944	1178
UK	100	157	256	439	640
USA	100	189	325	596	659
Sweden	100	270	521	1228	1493

Source: Hours worked are from Maddison (1991); wages are from Mitchell (1978, 1983) and OECD, *Main Economic Indicators* and *Economic Outlook*; German wage data from 1913–38 are approximated using average labour productivity growth.

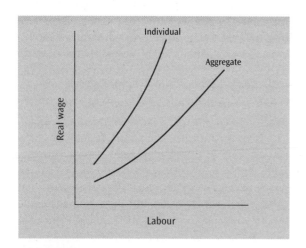

Fig. 4.4   Individual and Aggregate Labour Supply

The aggregate labour supply curve is less steep than that of individual households for two important reasons. First it represents the summation of a great number of upwardly sloped individual supply curves. Second, new workers choose to enter the labour force as wages rise.

decide to join the labour force. Figure 4.4 shows how it is then possible for a steep or even vertical (inelastic) individual supply curve to coexist with a flatter aggregate supply curve.

4.2.2 Labour Demand, Productivity, and Real Wages

Labour demand and the extended production function

Firms use both capital and labour to produce goods and services. As discussed in Chapter 3, the capital stock at any particular point in time is best thought of as given; from month to month firms vary their output by adjusting employment of labour (man-hours). The link between output Y and employment L holding capital constant is captured by the production function shown in Figure 4.5. The slope of the production function measures the **marginal productivity of labour** (MPL), the quantity of additional output which results from one more unit of input (an hour). The shape of the curve reflects the

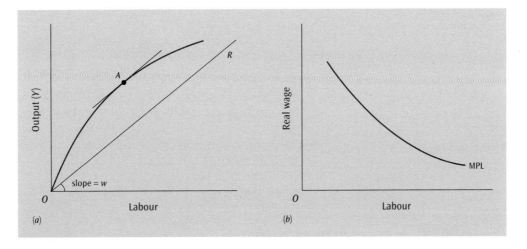

Fig. 4.5   **The Production Function and the Labour Demand Curve**

When labour input increases, output increases, but at a declining rate. This additional output is the marginal productivity of labour (MPL). In panel (*a*), the ray *OR* represents the labour cost of producing when the hourly real wage is *w*. The vertical distance between the production function and the cost line represents the firm's profit. The firm maximizes its profit at point *A*, where the curve is parallel to *OR*, i.e. where MPL = *w*. Its demand for labour is given in panel (*b*) by the declining marginal product of labour (MPL) curve.

principle of decreasing marginal productivity: all else held constant, the MPL in a representative firm is declining as the amount of labour employed increases.

In deciding how much labour to employ, the representative firm seeks the highest possible profit given the cost of labour, the real hourly wage *w*. The capital stock is assumed fixed. The line *OR* represents the total cost of labour to the firm at different levels of employment. Because *L* hours of work cost *wL*., its slope is −*w*. For each level of employment, profit is measured as the vertical distance between the curve depicting the production function and the labour cost line *OR*. Profit is at a maximum at point *A*, where the production function is parallel to *OR*. At this point, the MPL, the slope of the production function, is equal to the real wage, the slope of *OR*. If the MPL exceeds the real wage, hiring one more hour of work raises revenues by MPL and raises costs only by *w*, implying an increase in profits. The firm would therefore hire the extra hour, and will continue to hire extra hours until the MPL has declined to the point where it is equal to the real wage. In the opposite case, in which the real wage exceeds the

MPL, the firm can increase its profit by reducing its demand for labour. Because it is optimal to set labour such that MPL = *w*, the MPL schedule in panel (*b*) of Figure 4.5 is also the firm's **labour demand curve**.

Shifts in the demand for labour

Now consider the effects of an increase in the capital stock *K*, which until now was assumed constant. Panel (*a*) of Figure 4.6 shows that this raises MPL— the production function becomes steeper at every level of production. The labour demand curve shifts out in panel (*b*). A technological improvement that shifts out the production function by making the labour more productive brings about a similar effect. This helps account for the fact that wages have grown secularly over time. Similarly, a decline in the capital stock, brought about by war, natural disasters or technical obsolescence, will cause the labour demand curve to shift down to the left. In the case of *labour-saving* technical change, it is possible for the demand for labour to decline, even as total output is increasing. Box 4.1 explains the important phenomenon of technical change in more detail.

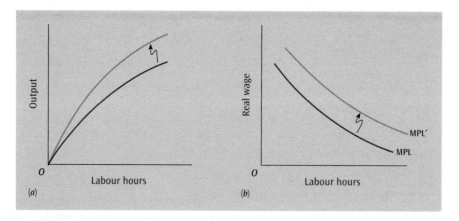

Fig. 4.6   **An Increase in Labour Productivity**

Labour can become more productive either because more capital is put in place, or because technological progress makes labour more productive using the existing stock of equipment. In panel (*a*), at any level of labour input, more output is produced and the production function is everywhere steeper. The MPL increases and the demand for labour schedule shifts up in panel (*b*).

Box 4.1   **Technical Change and Unemployment**

What is the effect of technological progress on jobs? It is often believed that technology kills jobs by making people less important for the production of goods and services. Don't computers reduce the need for secretaries? Isn't the internet replacing mail and jobs in the post office? It would be hard to deny that technological advances kill some jobs, and even whole professions. From the dawn of the industrial revolution in the early 19th century, the Luddites in Britain or the 'soyeux' in France agitated against mechanized weaving machines and went as far as to incite mobs to destroy them in large numbers. And indeed, weaving cloth by hand has disappeared as a trade, as have many other technically backward activities. Nevertheless, *overall* productivity of labour has increased roughly tenfold in the nations of Western Europe in the past 120 years, and if anything, unemployment is somewhat lower now than it was a century and a half ago, so the story must be more complicated than technology killing jobs.

True, technological progress means that more can be produced with fewer man-hours, i.e. labour productivity (Y/L) rises. Yet employment L must not necessarily decline, because output Y can, and usually does rise as a result. And if output rises as fast as labour productivity, employment must have increased (since $L = Y/(Y/L)$). In the end, the key question is: How are increases in labour productivity split between Y and L? A correct answer requires much more knowledge about the macroeconomy, in order to trace all the effects that affect the net outcome. That is the task of macroeconomics.

We note first that higher productivity of labour leads to higher real wages w. For demand for labour to decline and unemployment *in the aggregate* to rise, it must be that real wage rises faster than productivity. In fact, there are two good reasons why the effect should be one-for-one: first, it implies a constant share of labour in income (wL/Y), one of the stylized facts presented in Chapter 3.

At the same time, labour supply is at work. Table 4.1 suggests that over the long haul, increasing wages leads to a voluntary *decline* in hours supplied by individuals. But this still does not tell us what happens to the number of people at work, since L is measured in man-hours: if hours worked per person decline, there is no need for employment to decline. This is indeed what has happened.

So what about the disappearance of some jobs, and the decline of whole regions? Here we face the 'fallacy of composition': what applies to a particular industry will generally not apply to the economy as a whole. The demand for secretaries may have fallen, but who builds and maintains the computers that make secretaries redundant? New jobs replace old jobs. Of course, these are not the same people. At the aggregate level, old skills are replaced by new skills, but some individuals must be retrained, which takes time, and some are sidelined. That some people become unemployed does not mean that total employment declines. Economic progress may be painful for some, but it is by no means a systematic job-killer. And it is the most important way of bringing about increases in the standards of living.

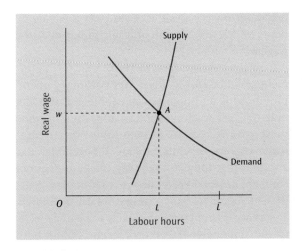

Fig. 4.7   **Equilibrium in the Labour Market**

Labour market equilibrium occurs at point *A* where demand and supply are equal. The real wage *w* clears the market at employment level *L*. Since total labour endowment is given by $\bar{L}$, the distance $(\bar{L} - L)$ is voluntary unemployment.

4.2.3 Labour Market Equilibrium

We now have the building blocks for understanding the labour market: a supply curve derived from household behaviour, and a demand curve derived

from firm behaviour. The interaction of supply and demand for labour is depicted in Figure 4.7. Equilibrium occurs at the intersection of the two curves (point *A*). At wage *w* the market clears (there is no excess demand or supply): *L* is the number of hours firms want to hire and households want to work. Both the real wage rate and employment are endogenously determined in the labour market.

This simple characterization of the labour market is an important part of an economist's toolkit, and its predictions serve as the benchmark for the rest of the chapter. Figure 4.8 provides two examples of its usefulness. Panel (*a*) shows the outcome of an increase in labour productivity resulting from capital accumulation or technological advances. The labour demand curve shifts outward; the supply curve remains unaffected. The result is an unambiguous increase in real wages. In the figure, employment increases, but if the labour supply curve is vertical, employment remains unchanged and labour income *wL* would rise proportionally with the real wage. If the supply curve is backward-bending, employment (man-hours) would even decline, as Table 4.1 suggests has been the case over the past century. The second panel of Figure 4.8 shows that

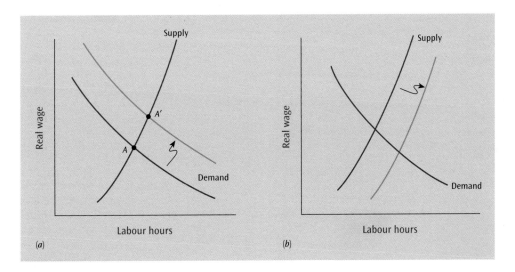

Fig. 4.8   **Shifting Labour Demand and Supply**

When labour demand increases (panel (*a*)), for example because of additional capital or technological progress, the real wage and the employment level both increase. When labour supply increases instead (panel (*b*))—because of new entries into the labour force, for example—employment rises but the real wage declines.

an exogenous increase in the supply of labour leads to an increase in employment, but also to a reduction in real wages.

4.2.4 The Interpretation of Unemployment

While the supply-and-demand apparatus allows us to evaluate the effect of various changes on equilibrium employment and real wages, it is disappointing in one crucial respect. At point A in Figure 4.7, labour supplied is equal to labour demand and denoted by L. Any unemployed labour—literally, labour not employed—reflects the voluntary decisions of households and firms. If total potential labour supply is $\bar{\ell}$, unemployment (measured as hours of work not employed) is measured as $\bar{\ell} - L$. Since point A is on the labour supply curve, it reflects the optimal behaviour of households. The standard interpretation of Figure 4.7 is that the equilibrium real wage w is too low to persuade all workers to give up leisure: some may wish to work only part-time, others may

not want to work at all. In Figure 4.7, there are no hours which are involuntarily unemployed at the wage w.

It might be disturbing to think that unemployment could be chosen freely. Yet **voluntary unemployment** is an important phenomenon. It is not only the very wealthy who can afford not to work: those who receive an income from other sources (from a spouse or from the state, for example) may also find that the net wage they can earn does not compensate for lost leisure or non-market activities, including working at home or raising children. Voluntary unemployment is likely to be more widespread among low-skilled people who cannot hope to earn much, or in countries where taxes are so high that working yields little net gain. The most obvious costs are faced by families with children. The high cost of child care—or simply the unavailability of such services—explains why two-earner families are not as common in some countries as in others. Table 4.2 displays the labour force participation rate

| Table 4.2 | Female Labour Force Participation Rates, Unemployment Rates, and Employment Ratios, 1998 |

	Participation rates	Unemployment rates	Employment ratios
Belgium	53.8	11.7	47.9
Canada	69.0	8.2	63.7
France	60.8	13.9	51.8
Germany	62.6	10.3	56.6
Ireland	52.1	7.5	48.8
Luxembourg	47.6	4.2	62.4
Netherlands	62.9	5.5	59.2
Portugal	59.5	6.6	61.6
Spain	48.7	26.7	35.2
Sweden	75.5	8.0	68.3
UK	67.8	5.3	63.5
USA	70.7	4.7	67.8
Japan	59.8	4.2	61.3
Denmark	75.0	6.4	70.1
Finland	69.7	12.1	61.5
Norway	75.9	3.2	73.8

Source: OECD.

(the proportion of women of working age in the labour force, whether employed or not), the female unemployment rate, and the proportion of women of working age actually employed. The variation of these indicators across countries is significant, and points to differences in both cultures and institutions. Female participation in the labour force is very high in countries like Denmark and Sweden, which have a highly developed and subsidized child care system.

4.3   A Static Interpretation of Unemployment

Our first attempt at defining unemployment in the last section was somewhat unsatisfactory. Unemployment is more than simply labour withheld voluntarily from the market. The International Labour Organization (ILO) and the Organization for Economic Cooperation and Development (OECD) define an individual as unemployed if he or she does not have a job during the reference period *and* is actively looking for one *and* is ready to work. Let us begin anew by defining the **labour force** as the part of the population that is either working (L) or unemployed (U). The labour force mainly excludes young people in school, the retired, and those who are not looking for work. It corresponds closely to the amount of labour supplied to the market, given current conditions, including the level of real wages. Denoting the labour force as L^s, we can write:

(4.2) L^s = L + U.

labour force   employment   unemployment

The unemployment rate u is then given by the fraction of the labour force which is out of work, or $u = U/L^s$. Perhaps it is now clear why the picture of unemployment in Figure 4.7 is incomplete: according to the ILO definition, it is zero! In the rest of this chapter, we examine alternative reasons for unemployment as well as its implications for the well-being of society.

4.3.1 Involuntary Unemployment and Real Wage Adjustment

One interpretation of unemployment is the failure of markets to clear. Figure 4.9 considers the important case where the real wage is fixed at $\bar{w}$, which is higher than the level which equates supply and demand, w. At $\bar{w}$, firms are willing to hire $\bar{L}$ labour, while workers supply L^s. Since firms cannot be forced to hire more than they wish, actual employment is $\bar{L}$, and $L^s - \bar{L}$ is labour supplied but not demanded by the market. This is **involuntary unemployment**. Involuntary unemployment occurs when an individual is willing and able to work at the wage $\bar{w}$ but cannot find a job, no matter how hard he or she tries. At point B, the marginal product of labour (MPL) exceeds the valuation of leisure time by households which are out of work.

In Figure 4.9, it is the failure of the wage to decline that perpetuates unemployment. If the real wage were to fall to w at point A, demand would increase, supply would decrease, and unemployment would be eliminated at L. This is a key result: the existence

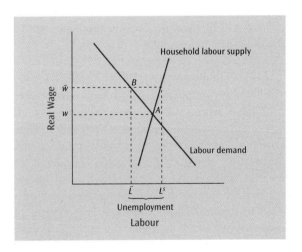

Fig. 4.9   **Involuntary Unemployment**

At the real wage rate $\bar{w}$ workers supply L^s of labour but firms demand, and hire, only $\bar{L}$. The quantity $L^s - \bar{L}$, which is supplied by households but not demanded by firms, represents involuntary unemployment. If the real wage were to adjust to the level w, the market would clear at point A.

of involuntary unemployment must be explained by **real wage rigidity**, which we examine next.

4.3.2 Collective Bargaining and Real Wage Rigidity

For sustained real wage rigidity to occur, involuntarily unemployed workers must be unable to supply their labour services at wages below $\bar{w}$, or firms must be unwilling to take up such offers, or be unable to make their own. What important institutional features of labour markets have been overlooked so far? **Labour (or trade) unions** are one of the most fundamental and universal institutions that operate in modern economies. Unions are employees' organizations which advocate interests of labour in a number of dimensions, most importantly, wages. They are matched by often equally powerful **employers' associations**, such as the CBI in the UK, the MEDEF in France, the BDA in Germany, or the SAF in Sweden. Bargaining between employers and unions contrasts sharply with the perfect-competition description of labour markets described in Section 4.2. We need to study the motives of negotiators, and how they impact on wage determination. In doing so, we discover how unemployment can be voluntary from the perspective of trade unions, and nevertheless be involuntary from the viewpoint of the individual household.[9]

The rationale for labour unions

The employer–employee relationship has inherently conflictual aspects. One is the distribution of income; while economic principles assert that income should be split according to marginal productivity, in practice marginal productivity is difficult to measure and economic principles are not always adhered to. Another more subtle reason is that firms need to monitor effort at work, a key element of productivity, which is under the control of each individual employee. Individual workers facing a large employer are in a poor bargaining position.

They have little influence over their own wage rate and may not even feel safe discussing working conditions, fearing reprisals in the form of a salary cut or dismissal. They may even feel pressure to accept conditions that would not be acceptable under competitive conditions.

Workers organized themselves into unions to help resist such pressures, but especially to achieve higher pay levels and a voice in the day-to-day operation of the workplace. How big and influential are they? As Table 4.3 shows, union organizations vary considerably from country to country. Scandinavian countries have a tradition of centralized unionization; workers in Britain are organized according to craft; France, Italy, and Spain have unions with ties to political parties. These differences reflect social history as well as the costs and benefits associated with union membership. The costs are dues that members must pay. The benefits vary, ranging from higher wages and protection from arbitrary employer decisions to more specific advantages, including priority for certain jobs and income supplements when unions are on strike. In some countries, many advantages accrue to all workers, so there is little point in paying union dues. This is the case in France, for example.[10] In other countries, such as Belgium and Scandinavia, unions help manage funds that hand out some social benefits, including unemployment insurance. In the USA, some unions even issue credit cards and provide other financial services to their members. In the end, the influence of unions is usually much stronger than simple membership statistics would suggest, and is partly related to labour laws which institutionalize their role. This is evident from the last column in Table 4.3, which shows the fraction of all workers working under contracts negotiated by unions, whether or not they are union members.

The economics of labour unions

Simplifying somewhat, we can think of two primary economic objectives which motivate unions: higher

---

[9] It should be stressed that we limit ourselves strictly to the economic significance of trade unions. As the history of the labour movement amply demonstrates, unions have had an enormous influence on modern society, which goes beyond economics.

[10] This is an example of the so-called free-rider problem. If no workers pay dues, the union disappears and no one is protected. So some workers must pay the dues for all to have a union.

| Table 4.3 | European Trade Unions: Membership and Coverage, 1950–1997 |

Country	Structure	Union membership (%)				Union coverage (%)
		1950	1970	1990	1997	1994
Sweden	Umbrella (ILO, TCO, SACO/SR)	67	67	82	86	89
Finland	Umbrella (SAK)	30	51	73	78	95
Denmark	Umbrella (LO)	56	63	75	76	69
Norway	Umbrella (LO, AF, YS)	45	50	56	55	74
Belgium	Party, religious (FGTB, CSC, CGSLB, CNC)	43	42	50	53[b]	90
Ireland	Mostly crafts in ICTU, fragmented	42	59	59	52[b]	—
Austria	Umbrella/industrial (ÖGB)	62	57	47	39	98
Italy	Party, religious (CGIL, CISL, UIL)	45	37	39	37	82
United Kingdom	Mostly crafts (96 in TUC, fragmented)	45	50	43	36[b]	47
Germany[a]	Umbrella/industrial (DGB, DAG)	38	32	36	27	92
Portugal	Local and plant-level bargaining; 'social pacts' at national level	—	—	40	30[b]	71
Netherlands	Party, religious (FNV, CNV, RMHP, AVC)	43	37	24	24	81
Switzerland	Mostly plant-level (SGB)	40	30	27	23	50
Greece		—	—	34	—	—
Spain		—	—	12	17	78
France	Party, religious (CGT, CFDT, CFTC, GGC, FO)	30	20	14	10	95
US	Mostly local plant-level (AFL–CIO)	x	x	x	16	18

[a] West Germany until 1990.   [b] 1995.
Source: Density rates from Ebbinghaus and Visser (2000); coverage from OECD *Employment Outlook* 1997.

real wages, and more jobs.[11] It is helpful to think of union preferences in terms of indifference curves shown in Figure 4.10. The slope of the indifference curve represents the willingness of the union leadership to trade off employment for wages. It is flat for 'hard-line' unions which are unwilling to trade wages against employment, steeper for unions which care relatively more about jobs than wages.

In contrast to Section 4.2, we now describe a labour market in which union indifference curves replace those of the representative individual as the relevant preferences, capturing the fact that the active agent in the labour market is not the indi-

vidual, but his or her trade union or, more generally, the collective bargaining process. The 'budget line' faced by the union is the demand for labour. From Section 4.2.2 we know that labour demand is given by the MPL (either a firm's MPL, or that of an industry or the entire economy: if firms are all alike, their individual demand does not differ from the collective one defended by an employers' association).

Given the demand for labour that it faces, the optimal choice for the union is the tangency point of the highest indifference curve with the current demand for labour. When the demand for labour shifts, the union's menu of options shifts as well. Capital accumulation or technological progress which shifts out the labour demand curve, for example, will increase the wage that can be paid at a given employment level, or increase the sustainable

[11] Unions care about many other aspects of labour markets, such as safety at work, working time, employees' rights and influence over working conditions and organization. To simplify the analysis, these aspects are not considered here.

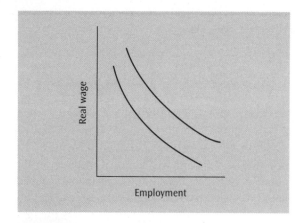

Fig. 4.10 **Trade Unions' Indifference Curves**

When a trade union values both higher wages and more employment, its preferences are described by indifference curves. A 'hard-line' union is not willing to give up much in lower wages to raise employment. A union mainly preoccupied with employment is represented by steep indifference curves.

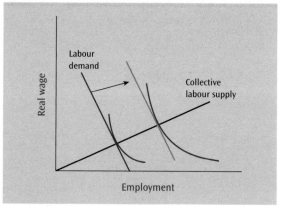

Fig. 4.11 **The Collective Labour Supply Curve**

The collective labour supply curve is obtained by connecting the points of tangency between the indifference curves and a shifting labour demand schedule.

employment that can be engaged at given wages. Inward shifts of labour demand are also possible, attributable to destruction or obsolescence of the capital stock—e.g. due to wars earthquakes, the lack of new investment, or new inventions—and have the opposite effect, shrinking available options to the union. As the labour demand schedules shifts, successive tangency points map out the **collective labour supply curve** depicted in Figure 4.11. The curve describes the most desired joint evolution of real wages and employment from the union's viewpoint.

The slope of the collective labour supply curve thus reflects the preferences of the union for employment and wages as well as its economic environment.[12] Union members who are currently employed or who enjoy seniority or job protection tend to fight for a hard-line union: if their influence

is high, the slope of the collective labour supply curve will be steep. In contrast, a 'jobs-first' union accepts to moderate real wage increases and supply more labour: it will tend to exhibit a flat collective labour supply curve. More details on different possible shapes of the collective labour supply curve are discussed in the Appendix.

Employment effects of collective bargaining

The collective labour supply curve resembles the individual supply curve of Figure 4.3, but has different origins. Collectively, through their unions, workers increase their bargaining power and accordingly aim at better outcomes. In particular, for a given amount of labour supplied, they ask for higher real wages: the union-driven collective labour supply curve can only lie above the individual labour supply curves. Without the union's influence on wage setting, equilibrium would occur in Figure 4.12 at point A: individuals would be willing to work up to L at wage w. They cannot, however, because the wage $\bar{w}$ is set through negotiations between the firms and the trade union, and individuals cannot simply underbid their employed colleagues. Unemployment ($L^s - \bar{L}$) is involuntary for affected individuals, but voluntary from the union's point of view.

---

[12] Note that the collective labour supply curve depends on the successive shifts in the demand for labour that we imagine. Different shifts can change both the position *and* the slope of the labour demand curve. A number of outcomes are possible; they are described in more detail graphically in the WebAppendix to Chapter 4.

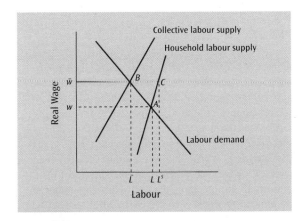

Fig. 4.12 **Labour Market Equilibrium with a Trade Union**

When a labour union represents workers at wage negotiations, labour market equilibrium occurs at point *B*. If the union collective labour supply curve is above the individual labour supply curve, the real wage $\bar{w}$ is higher and employment $\bar{L}$ (hours or number of workers) lower than at point *A*, which would be the outcome if individuals were negotiating individually. The result is the existence of **union-voluntary, individual-involuntary unemployment** $(L^s - \bar{L})$: it is the difference between actual employment $\bar{L}$ and the amount of work L^s that workers are willing to supply individually at the real wage rate $\bar{w}$ (point *C*).

Why do unions enforce wage rigidity, apparently against the will of unemployed workers? One reason is that the leadership is typically elected by the employed, sometimes called the **insiders**. Unemployed workers are almost always a small minority of the membership, even at record high unemployment rates of 10% or even 20%. Furthermore, unemployed workers often give up their membership or lose interest in union affairs. They are called the **outsiders**. Unions end up representing the insiders, who have jobs, not the outsiders, who are unemployed. Employed workers look for high real wages (for themselves) at the cost of some unemployment (for others). Box 4.2 illustrates how the relentless rise of unemployment in Europe after the two oil shocks can be explained by this effect.

The split between unions and unemployed workers cannot go too far, though. After unemployment increased to high levels in Europe in the 1970s and 1980s, unions have become more employment-conscious and real wage growth has moderated. One

reason is that members become worried that they too might become unemployed. A second reason is criticism from the non-unionized component of society. Yet another is that the loss in membership revealed in Table 4.3 has meant lower income for the union from dues as well as less overall influence.

It would be unfair to assert that unions are solely responsible for real wage rigidity. The employers' associations represent the collective interests of firms. They represent an additional mechanism for policing collective bargaining agreements reached with unions. In the end, employers' associations do not control the demand for labour: this is the prerogative of the individual companies. While it is in firms' interest to keep wages low—trade unions were often created to prevent employers from exercising rather ruthlessly their power and imposing very low wages—it is also in their interest to keep the wages of their competitors high, or at least to prevent them from hiring cheap labour. In this way, employers' associations can also contribute to real wage rigidity.

4.3.3 Social Minima and Real Wage Rigidity

Beyond trade unions and employers' associations, several other institutional and economic factors can contribute to wage rigidity, and therefore involuntary unemployment. Frequently mentioned in the European context are social minima, or minimum standards for income and earnings mandated by the government for reasons of social equity or protection.

Minimum wages set a lower bound below which wages may not fall. Many countries legislated minimum wages long ago for a variety of reasons. One was to prevent employers with too much market power from depressing wages artificially. Another reason was to protect young people from exploitation. With schooling rudimentary and poverty endemic, for many youngsters on-the-job training was the only way to get started; unscrupulous employers would offer very low wages, sometimes below minimal survival needs. Social protection was and often still is justified. Even in countries without statutory or legal minimum wages, it is frequently the case that collective agreements are

---

The European Unemployment Problem

Two major negative shifts to the demand for labour occurred during the past thirty years. Both were associated with the sudden oil price increases of the mid-1970s and early 1980s and are called the oil shocks. By all accounts, they corresponded to a significant inward shift of the aggregate labour demand curve. If trade unions respond to a narrower membership by calling for steady or even higher wages, the collective labour supply curve shifts upward. Owing to the behaviour of the 'insiders' who have jobs, employment prospects for 'outsiders' are

reduced. After the oil shocks are absorbed, the employment level is permanently reduced. That such an effect—dubbed the 'hysteresis effect'—has been observed in several European countries is suggested by the step-wise increase in the unemployment rate following each oil shock (Table 4.4). In contrast, unemployment rates in the USA increased at the time of each oil shock but then reverted towards earlier levels. As unemployment rises, pressure to do something does as well; in a number of countries, measures have been taken as will be seen below.

Table 4.4 **Average Unemployment Rates by Decade**

	1960–9	1970–9	1980–9	1990–9
France	2.0	3.8	9.0	11.2
Germany	0.8	2.4	6.8	8.0
Italy	3.8	4.7	8.4	10.7
Spain	2.5	4.4	17.5	19.6
Sweden	1.7	2.1	2.5	6.2
United Kingdom	1.8	3.6	9.5	8.0
USA	4.8	6.2	7.3	5.8

Source: OECD Economic Outlook.

---

extended to uncovered workers, and contract wages assume the characteristics of a legal minimum wage. With occasional exceptions, this is currently the case in Austria, Belgium, Denmark, Finland, Germany, Greece, Italy, Norway, and Sweden.

The primary economic[13] effect of minimum wages is to discourage firms from hiring workers with low MPL. Figure 4.13 illustrates the effect of minimum wages. To serve any purpose at all, the minimum wage w_{min} must be higher than the wage $\bar{w}$ that would obtain otherwise ($\bar{w}$), and which is itself higher than what individuals would accept with market clearing (w). The result is unemployment

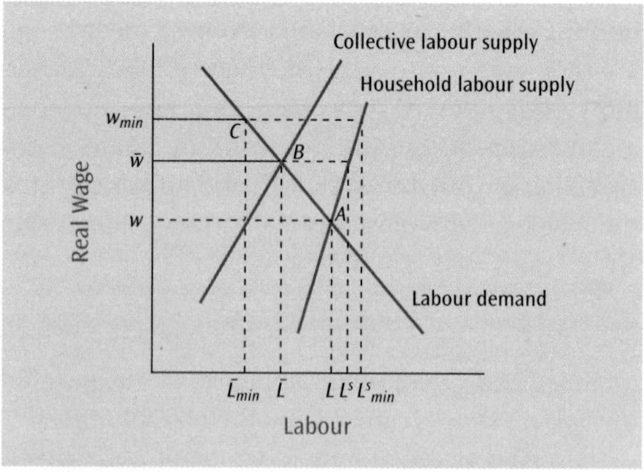

Fig. 4.13 **Minimum Wages**

Minimum wages reduce the demand for labour below the level that would result with either union-negotiated wages or individual-supplied labour.

---

[13] Emphasis is put here on the economic effects of minimum wages. Other important considerations include equity and social norms which reject the existence of 'working poor'.

$(L^S_{min} - \bar{L}_{min})$ even higher than the level implied by the wage set in collective bargaining $(L^S - L)$. Some evidence on the effect of minimum wages is discussed in Box 4.3.

Those most likely to be hurt by the existence of minimum wage legislation are poorly educated young people with no job experience and older workers with obsolete skills. The effect is quite widespread,

---

Box 4.3 **Minimum Wages and Youth Unemployment**

It is striking that teenagers in the USA often work during the summer when their European counterparts go on vacation. One reason might be that wages that must be paid for young, unskilled labour are too high in Europe. The US minimum wage amounts to about a third of the average manufacturing wage, while in many European countries it exceeds 50%. This is one reason why filling station attendants and grocery shop assistants have all but disappeared in most European countries. Table 4.5 shows non-employment and unemployment rates for young people in a number of countries as well as the average minimum wage as a fraction of the average overall wage. In interpreting the table, it is important to note that youth in Denmark younger than 18 receive a deep discount from collectively bargained minimum wage as they do in the USA. The UK did not have a statutory minimum wage, and teen-

agers are generally not unionized. It is especially noteworthy that in France, Belgium, and the Netherlands, the minimum wage as a fraction of the median wage is high, meaning that a great many jobs are paid the minimum wage.

In France the minimum wage, called the SMIC (Salaire Minimum Interpersonel de Croissance), is an important element of the collective bargaining system. It is set by a council on which both the government and unions are represented. Many government employees receive the SMIC. In 1997, roughly 11% of workers in industry, commerce, and services earned the SMIC or near it, a much higher proportion than in the USA (about 4%).

While the minimum wage in general has a negative effect on youth employment, it may lead to a substitution of adults for youths, at the same time increasing the employment of the former.

Table 4.5 **Minimum Wages and Youth Unemployment, 1997**

	Minimum wage as % of average wage[a]	% affected (at or near minimum)[c]	Youth (age) minimum as % of adult minimum[c]	Non-employment ratio for youth age 15–24:[b]	Unemployment rate for youth aged 15 to 24:[b]
Belgium	63.3	4	slight	74.8	21.3
Denmark	Collective agreements	6	40 (<18)	31.8	8.1
France	71.7	11	80 (16); 90 (17); 30–75 for trainees	79.9	28.1
Germany	Collective agreements	—	Industry agreements	55.6	10.7
Italy	Collective agreements	—	Industry agreements	74.8	33.6
Netherlands	76.1	3.2	34.5 (16); rising to 84 (22)	38.9	9.5
Spain	40	6.5	66 (<18)	71.1	37.1
UK	None	—	None	39	13.5
USA	39.0[d]	4	None	42	11.3

Sources: [a] OECD *Employment Outlook* 1998.   [b] OECD *Employment Outlook* 1999.
[c] Dolado et al. (1996).   [d] US Council of Economic Advisers (2001).

because, once a floor is set, it pushes up the lower echelons of the wage pyramid, possibly affecting better qualified workers as well. The range of qualifications for which the MPL is below the real wage is wider than just the very lowest echelons.

4.3.4 Efficiency Wages and Real Wage Rigidity

Another reason why real wages may not decline in the presence of involuntary unemployment is that firms do not wish to lower them. The phenomenon is often called **efficiency wages**, and it is related to another special aspect of labour. In contrast with other factors of production, work effort is not easily observed by firms, and yet it matters a lot. By paying a worker a wage in excess of his marginal productiv-

ity, firms may attempt to elicit more work of better quality. A worker who is dismissed for lack of effort is unlikely to obtain such a good deal elsewhere, especially if dismissals are interpreted as a sign of poor work effort. Firms may also pay efficiency wages to obtain a better selection of applicants and to keep workers from quitting too often.

In capital-intensive industries, where shirking could seriously disrupt the production process and where a high-quality workforce is of primary importance, firms have a strong incentive to pay efficiency wages. In this case, the function of real wages goes beyond simply equilibrating demand and supply in labour markets. Generally, wages will not be able to satisfy both functions, and will tend to be rigid and lie above the market-clearing level, as in Figure 4.12.

4.4   A Dynamic Interpretation of Unemployment

4.4.1 Labour Market States and Transitions

Any person in the working age population is either employed, unemployed, or out of the labour force. Figure 4.14 displays these three states and how flows occur between them. A striking aspect of labour markets in developed economies is the sheer

size of these flows. Table 4.6 shows that the flow of individuals moving into and out of unemployment per year is a multiple of the stock of unemployment at any given time. In contrast to the static picture painted in Section 4.3, labour markets are remarkably dynamic, even when unemployment is stuck at high levels.

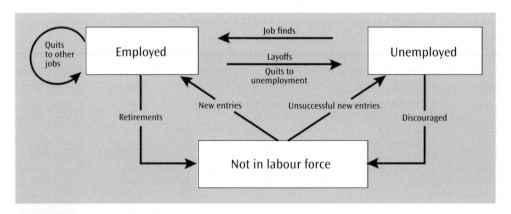

Fig. 4.14   **A Map of Labour Markets**

Every individual is in one of three states: employed, unemployed, or out of the labour force. Over any period of time, large numbers of workers are flowing from one state to another.

| Table 4.6 | Unemployment: Average Stocks and Annual Flows in 1999 (millions) |

	Unemployment Flows		Average unemployment stocks
	Into unempl.	Out of unempl.	
Germany	7.22	7.37	4.09
UK[a]	3.14	3.30	1.26
France	4.08	4.43	2.77
USA	30.80	31.23	5.87

[a] Claimant count.

Sources: Bundesanstalt für Arbeit (Germany), Dept of Labor (USA), Dept of Employment (UK), INSEE (France).

There are three ways of becoming unemployed. First, new entrants to the labour market may join the labour force before they have found work, but are unsuccessful, at least initially. Second, **separations** of workers from jobs may lead to unemployment. Voluntary separations from the employee's viewpoint (called quits) account for roughly 50% to 66% of all separations from employment in the UK, and up to 70% in the USA. Yet quits rarely lead to unemployment: most workers who quit take up another job immediately (transition from employment to employment). Most of those who quit but do not start a new job leave the labour force, usually for family reasons (maternity leave for example), return to school, retirement, etc. Finally, job losers—those who are *in*voluntarily separated—tend to flow into unemployment. Job loss may occur when short-term contracts expire (common in France and Spain), factories close or relocate, or because of unanticipated redundancies or layoffs (more common in Denmark, the UK, and the USA).

4.4.2 **Stocks, Flows, and Frictional Unemployment**

No two positions and no two persons are the same. Pairing a worker and an unfilled job opening or vacancy is not always easy and may take time. The matching of skills, occupation, industry, and geographical location requires a large amount of information. The more efficient the labour markets are, the faster the match is achieved. In the meantime, **frictional unemployment** occurs. This is an unavoidable result of the dynamics of labour force movements, and the normal process of job creation and destruction.

In addition to the efficiency of the job matching process, frictional unemployment depends on the number of job separations and the number of vacancies. If we ignore the flows from and to 'Not in the labour force' in Figure 4.14, the number of workers who become unemployed (per month or per year) represents a fraction s, called the **separation rate**, of existing jobs (L). While sL workers flow into unemployment each period, a number of unemployed workers find jobs. If we use f to denote the job **finding rate**, i.e. the fraction of the unemployed (U) who find employment during the period, the change in unemployment in a given period is given by

(4.3) $$\Delta U = sL - fU.$$

Frictional unemployment can be understood as the stock U^f of unemployment that is expected to occur, on average, when unemployment remains steady. Equality of flows into and out of unemployment occurs when $\Delta U = 0$ in (4.3), or when

(4.4) $$U^f = \frac{s}{f}L.$$

Table 4.7	Inflows into Unemployment and Unemployment Rates in the UK	
	Inflow rate into unemployment (% per month)	Unemployment rate (% of relevant labour force)
By region: Britain		
South-East	1.0	1.9
East	1.2	2.4
South-West	2.1	2.4
West Midlands	1.0	4.1
East Midlands	1.6	3.4
Yorkshire and the Humber	2.1	4.4
North West	1.8	4.3
North East	2.9	6.6
Wales	2.1	4.5
Scotland	2.4	4.8
Total	1.7	3.7
By demographic group: UK		
Aged 16–17	1.8	20.7
Aged 18–24	4.8	11.0
Aged 25–49	1.4	4.4
Aged 50 and over	1.0	4.0
Male	2.3	5.2
Female	1.1	1.9

Source: UK Labour Market Trends (1/99–8/00).

It is convenient to express unemployment as a proportion of the labour force $L^S = L + U$. Then (4.4) shows that the frictional *rate* of unemployment is[14]

(4.5) $$u^f = U^f/N = \frac{s}{s+f}.$$

We can think of the proportion s of workers separated from their jobs as the probability of losing a job when currently employed and, similarly, the proportion f of unemployed workers represents the probability of finding a job when unemployed.[15] (4.5) says that frictional unemployment is larger, the less frequent are job finds and the more frequent are job separations.

The separation rate s has two components: structural and cyclical. The structural aspect is linked to the ease with which firms dismiss workers. It is lower in countries where legal and social restrictions exist (as in most European countries) than in countries where redundancies are more acceptable (e.g. the UK and the USA).[16] The cyclical aspect simply refers to the fact that during recessions the probability of losing a job rises and so, therefore, does frictional unemployment.

Table 4.7 shows that in one particular country (the UK), job separation rates can vary considerably

[14] Since $L^S = L + U$ (see (4.2)), $1 = (L/L^S) + (U/L^S)$. Dividing (4.5) by L^S, and substituting $(L/L^S) = 1 - u$ gives (4.6).

[15] These figures naturally obscure a large degree of heterogeneity in the labour market: some individuals find a job readily after becoming unemployed, whereas others may have very low probabilities of exiting unemployment.

[16] It is, however usually the case that outflow rates in countries with employment protection are also lower, because firms are more reluctant to hire new workers.

across various characteristics of labour market participants. Those specific labour force groups that exhibit higher separation rates of inflow into unemployment indeed tend to have higher unemployment rates.

4.4.3 Job Finding and the Duration of Unemployment

The job finding rate f depends on the effectiveness of the matching process. It depends on how hard the unemployed look for jobs, how many job openings are available, and how easy it is to spot an opportunity. It may also depend on incentives to remain unemployed, and unemployment insur-

ance may therefore slow down the exit rate out of unemployment.

Table 4.8 shows that unemployment benefit systems vary considerably from country to country, with respect to eligibility criteria, income replacement, and the period over which they are paid. At the same time, unemployment benefits have adverse side-effects. While **unemployment benefits** or assistance reflect a widely perceived need for solidarity and social conscience, they may encourage unemployed workers in declining industries to wait for an unlikely recovery rather than to retrain and change sectors. They also act as a disincentive for looking for a job, or as an incentive for being

Table 4.8 Unemployment: Conditions for Eligibility and Benefits, 1999

	Eligibility conditions		Maximum duration: Benefit	Replacement rate of net earnings/Benefit level[c]	
	Employment	Period			
Austria	26 weeks.	12 months	30(50) weeks	50%	according to wage class
Belgium	312 days	18 months	∞	60%	of max earnings
Denmark	52 weeks	3 years	5 years	90%	of average earnings
Finland	43 weeks	24 months	50 weeks	121 marks	per day
France	registered employment		27 months	57.4%	
Germany	360 days	3 years	360 days	60%	of net earnings
Greece	200 days	2 years	max. 12 months	40%	
Ireland	39 weeks	last 1 year	max. 15 months	£70.50	per week
Italy	52 weeks	2 years	max. 180 days	30%	
Japan	6 months	12 months	max. 300 days	80%	of daily wages
Netherlands	26 weeks	39 weeks	7 years	70%	of minimum wage
New Zealand	resident for 24 months		∞	NZ$147.89	per week
Norway	registered employment		78 weeks	0.2%	of annual income per day
Spain	12 months	last 6 years	180 days	70%	of average earnings
Sweden	450 hours	6 months	max. 450 days	240 kr	per day
Switzerland	6 months[a]	2 years	max. 520 days	70%	of last earnings
UK			6 months	£51.40	per week
USA	15–20 weeks[b]	1 year	max. 39 weeks	50%	of last earnings, taxable

[a] 25 times the weekly lower earnings level in 1 of last 2 complete tax years (April to March).
[b] Different in various states.   [c] Single household without children.
Source: 'Social Security Programs throughout the World'; Social Security Administration, Office of Policy, Office of Research, *Evaluation and Statistics*, SSA Publication No. 13-11805; August 1999.

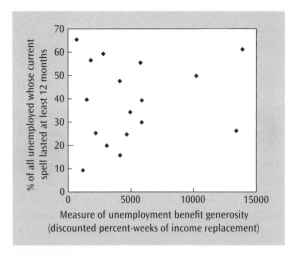

'choosier'.[17] If the benefits are generous, and particularly if they are long-lasting, unemployed workers may take more time to find an acceptable job, a time in which their skills and re-employability may deteriorate. This phenomenon is called the unemployment trap. This is especially true for unemployed low wage-earners who face loss of benefit upon taking on a new job. As can be seen in Figure 4.15, there is a tendency for people to remain unemployed longer in countries where un-employment benefits are more generous, paying more income over longer periods. As the finding rate declines, frictional unemployment rises. This confirms an uncomfortable trade-off between social concern and economic efficiency.

Fig. 4.15 **Long-Term Unemployment Rates and the Generosity of Unemployment Insurance, 1996**

The generosity of unemployment insurance systems is calculated as the maximum amount that someone who becomes unemployed can expect to receive. Generosity depends on the eligibility, the fraction of net wage replaced by benefit as well as the period of time over which they are available. The diagram indicates that, on average, where the system is more generous the proportion of long-term unemployed in the total population of unemployed tends to be higher, although this represents only one of many potential causes. Countries are: Austria, Belgium, Denmark, Finland, France, Germany, Greece, Ireland, Italy, Japan, the Netherlands, Norway, Spain, Sweden, Switzerland, United Kingdom, and the USA.
Source: OECD *Economic Outlook* 1996, 2000, and authors' calculations.

4.5 **The Equilibrium Rate of Unemployment**

4.5.1 **The Concept**

If all unemployment were voluntary, it would hardly attract any attention. The existence of high and evidently involuntary unemployment means that labour markets do not function like other markets. A large number of market imperfections, arising from both economic and institutional factors, requires that we qualify the pure-competition paradigm of Section 4.2 and consider an alternative definition of equilibrium to the equality of demand for labour by firms and the supply of labour by households.

Labour market equilibrium attempts to capture the unemployment rate that would occur in the absence of cyclical disturbances. Because of imper-fections, labour markets may be in equilibrium and yet unemployment may not be limited to voluntary unemployment. **Equilibrium unemployment** can be viewed as the sum of frictional and structural unemployment:

(**4.7**)   Equilibrium unemployment
= frictional unemployment
+ structural unemployment.

Frictional unemployment occurs because it takes time for a match to occur between a worker seeking a job and a vacancy needing to be filled. It depends on the efficiency of the labour market, including the eagerness of both parties to find a match quickly. The frictional unemployment rate may well vary over time, not just because the market's efficiency

---

[17] Strictly speaking, this applies only to those who already qualify for benefits. Prior work experience is often required before one can draw unemployment insurance benefits. In this case, indi-viduals will be more willing to accept the first job. This is often called the 'entitlement effect'.

	1970–9	1980–9	1990–9
Germany	2.4	6.8	9.2
Italy	4.7	8.4	10.9
Japan	1.7	2.5	3.1
Spain	4.4	17.5	19.7
UK	3.6	9.6	8.0
USA	6.2	7.3	5.6

Table 4.9 Estimates of Equilibrium Rates of Unemployment

Source: OECD.

rate, so exit from unemployment has become increasingly harder. Is the development of the social safety net to be blamed for having provided workers with the incentive to wait out their unemployment? Circumstantial evidence—for example Figure 4.5—points in that direction when based on a comparison between Europe, where the safety net has become extensive, and the USA. Yet there is some disturbing counter-evidence. The social safety net is even more developed in Denmark, Sweden, and Norway, where long-term unemployment has remained lower. This implies that what really matters is not the safety net itself, but the disincentives that it may generate. Unemployment benefits, for example, provide an alternative to finding a job, and help transform temporary unemployment into permanent—structural—unemployment. Long-term unemployment has become increasingly widespread, and as workers gradually lose their human capital and contact with the active labour force, they become unsuitable for any vacancy.

The strikingly different evolution of the equilibrium unemployment rate across countries also points to the importance of institutions in influencing wage levels. This concerns the process of wage bargaining. The comparison between Europe and the USA in Box 4.4 shows that high unemployment in the EC is related to steep real wage increases, amounting to what has been dubbed the European 'wage shock'. Labour costs consist not only of wages: labour taxes (social security and retirement contributions) have also been allowed to rise steeply. Of importance too is the regulation of the use of labour (length of the work-week, dismissal procedures, part-time work, etc.). We return to these aspects in detail in Chapter 17.

4.5.3 Actual and Equilibrium Unemployment

It can take a long time, often years, before real wages actually adjust to their long-run values shown in Figures 4.7 and 4.12. In the meantime, actual unemployment can deviate from equilibrium unemployment. Actual employment is below, and actual unemployment above, equilibrium when the real wage is above the equilibrium level, as at point A_1 in

changes but because economic conditions make it more or less likely for people to find jobs or to become unemployed.

Structural unemployment has many causes. The common thread is that the supply of labour is influenced by a number of institutions and regulations. Collective labour supply, which is brought into balance with labour demand in equilibrium, does not quite match individual supply behaviour. Some workers are involuntarily unemployed even when real wages equate the collective supply of labour with the demand of firms.

Estimates of equilibrium rates of unemployment are provided in Table 4.9. The contrast between Europe and North America is striking. The equilibrium unemployment rate was generally very low in Europe in the 1960s. Since then it has risen considerably while remaining stable in the USA. A comparison of Table 4.9 with Table 4.4 shows that actual unemployment has followed the same pattern. To begin to understand this dramatic evolution, we return to the two components of the equilibrium rate of unemployment.

4.5.2 The European Experience

The evidence suggests that European unemployment rose when large numbers of workers lost their jobs at the time of the oil shocks. The expected subsequent return to pre-oil-shock levels has been thwarted in many European countries by a fall in the finding

Box 4.4   'Eurosclerosis' and 'Eu-phoria'

With a few exceptions, the economies of Europe have experienced high rates of unemployment since the mid-1970s. Most of us grew up with high rates of unemployment in Europe. Yet it may be surprising that in the 1960s and early 1970s, Europe had lower unemployment rates than in the United States. A number of things happened in the 1970s which were not particularly favourable for countries with an important role for collective wage setting. First the two oil price shocks, which acted like large negative productivity shocks, shifted labour demand to the left. Second, a yet-unexplained slowdown in the rate of total factor productivity growth occurred in the 1970s, shrinking the pie over which unions could bargain. Third the late 1960s and early 1970s were notable as a particularly militant period for European trade unions, with a number of general strikes and labour unrest across the continent and the UK. 'Hard-line' European unions succeeded in pushing real wages higher and increasing their downward rigidity. The term 'Eurosclerosis' was coined by German economist Herbert Giersch of the Kiel Institute of World Economics to characterize this period of gloom and doom. Facing an apparently unstoppable rising tide of unemployment, many leaders simply accepted unemployment as beyond any influence of policy. Yet unions cannot overlook completely the plight of the unemployed.

The experience of the 1980s and 1990s in some European countries has taught us that it was possible to restore low rates of unemployment. Two outstanding examples exist for the way out of Europe's labour market misery. In the United Kingdom, the Tory government of Lady Thatcher used legislation to weaken significantly the power of trade unions, while reducing the level of social welfare and unemployment benefits. In contrast, the Netherlands chose a more cooperative path: unions and employers reached a historic agreement on wage moderation (the Wassenaar Accord) in 1982, which government rewarded with tax cuts and more favourable fiscal treatment of part-time work. It is significant that the union leader at the time, Wim Kok, later became prime minister and guarantor of the agreement, which

has held to the present and is regarded as an unparalleled success. It turns out that persistent wage moderation was one essential ingredient of both the UK and Dutch success stories. The lesson: unemployment can be brought down, but it takes time, and political will.

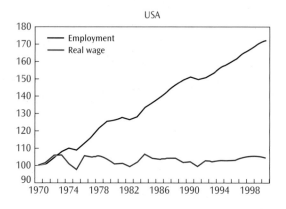

Fig. 4.16   Employment and Real Wages: Europe and USA

Over the period 1970–2000, real wages more than doubled in the Euro area, while employment stagnated. At the same time, as real wages stagnated in the USA, employment rose more than 70%. (Real wages = total compensation per employee deflated by the GDP deflator.)
Source: OECD.

Figure 4.17. When the real wage is low, firms may be able temporarily to move away from the union-set collective labour supply curve towards the individual labour supply curve (point A_2), for example by using agencies specializing in temporary jobs

or overtime work. Workers may have overestimated the real wage by underestimating the rise in the price level. Firms may be willing to hire more workers at the going wage. In such situations employment is above, and unemployment below, the

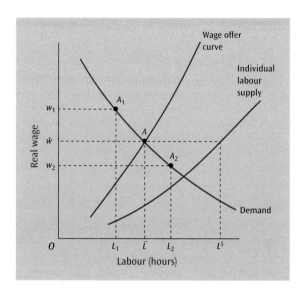

equilibrium level. These deviations, while short-term in nature, tend to be associated with fluctuations of the economy associated with the business cycle. We revisit this important topic in Chapter 12.

Fig. 4.17 **Actual and Equilibrium Employment**

When unions negotiate on behalf of workers, market equilibrium occurs at point A, and equilibrium unemployment is $L^s - \bar{L}$. Actual employment and unemployment may differ if the real wage is slow to move to its equilibrium level $\bar{w}$. If it is above the market equilibrium level ($w_1 > \bar{w}$), firms reduce employment to L_1 and actual unemployment exceeds equilibrium unemployment. Conversely, below-equilibrium real wages ($w_2 < \bar{w}$) enable firms to connect with structurally unemployed workers willing to work at lower wages than the union-set level. The resulting unemployment rate is lower than the equilibrium level.

Summary

1. Households trade off leisure against consumption (more generally, labour income). An increase in wages can induce more labour supply if the substitution effect dominates (elastic labour supply), less labour supply if the income effect dominates (backward-bending), or no change at all if the two effects offset each other (inelastic supply).

2. Individual labour supply seems to be inelastic in the short run, but in the long run is more likely to be backward bending as the higher incomes afforded by higher real wages allow households to enjoy both more leisure as well as more consumption. Aggregate labour supply is more responsive to real wage changes than that of households in the short run, as real wage increases draw new individuals into the labour force.

3. The demand for labour by firms depends on its (marginal) productivity which is determined by the available technology and the capital stock. Firms hire labour to the point where the marginal productivity of labour is equal to the real wage. The labour demand schedule is shifted outwards by an improvement in technology or an increase in the capital stock.

4. Equilibrium employment and the wage level are given by the intersection of labour demand and labour supply. Improvements in technology or increases in capital will be reflected in higher wages if labour supply is inelastic, and in higher employment if labour supply is elastic.

5. Involuntary unemployment arises when real wages do not decline to clear the market so that not all labour supplied by households is hired.

6. Labour unions care about real wages and employment. In determining their target wage, given the demand for labour firms, they ask for higher real wages than if the labour market were perfectly competitive. While the resulting unemployment rate is (optimal and) voluntary for unions, it may be involuntary for individuals.

7. Very centralized or decentralized wage negotiations deliver lower real wages and less unemployment than negotiations taking place at intermediate levels of centralization (industry by industry, or by craft).

8. Because firms cannot easily monitor work effort or wish to elicit lower turnover or improve worker quality, they may offer efficiency wages. This is yet another reason why real wages may be set above market-clearing levels.

9. Labour markets are also characterized by widespread government interventions. Minimum wages, designed to protect workers, can actually cause unemployment. Despite this, governments may see minimum wages as an effective means of guaranteeing a socially acceptable minimum income for those who want to work.

10. The labour market is characterized by a considerable amount of flow between its different states (employment, unemployment, not in the labour force). Search is an important aspect and results in frictional unemployment. Alongside structural unemployment, it is a source of equilibrium unemployment.

11. The efficiency of job search can vary across individuals and countries, and is affected by government labour market policies. Unemployment benefits, designed to make unemployment more bearable, provide disincentives to quickly finding a new job, thereby increasing frictional unemployment. Other programmes, such as training and relocation subsidies, reduce frictional unemployment.

12. Because of distortions and regulations, equilibrium unemployment is never zero or entirely voluntary. Individuals may be willing to work at lower wages than those prevailing in equilibrium, but may not be able to underbid in the market. This is the sense in which real wages are downwardly rigid.

13. Real wages are slow to adjust to disequilibria, if only because they fulfil many other roles. This speed of adjustment will depend on labour market institutions, among other things. As a result, actual and equilibrium unemployment may differ for some time.

Key Concepts

- leisure
- consumption–leisure trade-off
- real (consumption) wage
- income effect, substitution effect
- labour supply: individual and aggregate
- labour force
- participation rate
- man-hours
- marginal productivity of labour (MPL)
- labour demand
- wage and profit shares
- voluntary and involuntary unemployment
- real wage rigidity
- trade unions, labour unions

- employers' associations
- insiders and outsiders
- collectively voluntary/individually involuntary unemployment
- collective labour supply curve
- minimum wages
- efficiency wages
- unemployment benefits
- unemployment stocks and flows
- separation and separation rate
- finding rate
- frictional unemployment
- equilibrium unemployment
- structural unemployment

Exercises

1. Suppose that the household in Figure 4.3 receives an inheritance. What is the effect on its decision to work and to consume? According to this result, do rich people work more or less than poor people?

2. Suppose Robinson Crusoe is paid a higher wage ('overtime') if he works more than 8 hours a day, but only has 16 hours at his disposal.
   (*a*) Draw his budget line in this case.
   (*b*) Does the existence of overtime necessarily make him better off?
   (*c*) Show Crusoe's optimal behaviour for 'normal' indifference curves. Under which conditions will he choose to work overtime? Under which conditions will he refuse?

3. What is the effect on the labour market of a minimum wage that is actually lower than the equilibrium wage? Show in your graphical answer the new equilibrium wage and the level of employment.

4. A new labour tax is imposed which is proportional to wages. Individuals care about after-tax wages.
   (*a*) Draw the old and new individual supply curves.
   (*b*) What is the effect on the equilibrium wage and employment levels?
   (*c*) What is changed if wages are set through negotiations with a trade union which also cares about after-tax wages?

5. Derive the collective labour supply curve graphically. Show how different union preferences can interact with the same shift of labour demand and lead to (*a*) rigid wages around some 'target level' with flexible employment; (*b*) flexible wages around some target level of employment; (*c*) flexible wages when employment is rising, but rigid when employment is declining.

6. One of the immediate consequences of opening the borders between East and West Germany was the potential for migration between the two regions. Because of a more productive capital stock and more know-how, wages in the West were about three times as much as those in the East. Consequently many East Germans moved to the West. What are the consequences for this migration for real wages (*a*) in West Germany? (*b*) in East Germany? (*c*) for employment in the two regions? Can you explain why West German trade unions were eager to organize their comrades in the East?

7. It is often the case that unemployment benefits are paid out of a fund financed by taxes levied on the firms proportionately to their wage bill. How might this affect equilibrium unemployment?

8. In Japan the bonus system is widespread. Workers often receive 30% of their pay in the form of a profit-contingent payment, which can go up or down depending on the fortunes of the enterprise in which they work. What are the implications of such a system for real wage rigidity and equilibrium employment?

9. It is sometimes said that the massive influx of women into the labour force is a cause of unemployment.

(a) Draw the effect on the labour market as described by Figure 4.10. What does it mean for real wages and employment?

(b) Using Chapter 3, note that more available labour raises the MPK. Assuming that, as a result of more investment, the capital stock increases: how does your answer to (a) change?

10. Severance regulations are universally thought to influence labour markets, but it is hotly disputed whether they increase or decrease unemployment. Explain.

Suggested Further Reading

The following textbooks provide further analyses of labour economics at a basic level:

Ehrenberg, Ronald, and Smith, Robert (1988), *Modern Labour Economics*, 3rd edn., Scott Foresman.

Filer, Randall, Hamermesh, Dan, and Rees, Albert (1996), *The Economics of Work and Pay*, HarperCollins.

Layard, Richard, Nickell, Stephen, and Jackman, Richard (1991), *Unemployment*, Oxford University Press.

High European unemployment has been studied in detail. A survey is:

Bean, Charles (1994), 'European Unemployment: A Survey', *Journal of Economic Literature*, 32: 573–619.

The OECD's *Job Study* (1994).

See also the special issue of the *Swedish Economic Policy Review*, 1 (1–2), Autumn 1994 (articles by Lars Calmfors, Jorgen Elmeskov, Charles Wyplosz, Patrick Minford, Rudiger Dornbusch, Jacques Drèze and Henri Sneessens, and Richard Jackman).

Some interesting contributions are

Bentolila, Samuel, and Dolado, Juan (1994), 'Labour Flexibility and Wages: Lessons from Spain', *Economic Policy*, 18: 53–100.

Blanchflower, David, and Oswald, Andrew (1994), *The Wage Curve*, MIT Press.

Burda, Michael (1988), 'Wait Unemployment in Europe', *Economic Policy*, 7: 391–426.

Calmfors, Lars, and Driffill, John (1988), 'Bargaining Structure Corporatism and Macroeconomic Performance', *Economic Policy*, 6: 13–62.

Saint-Paul, Gilles (1993), 'On the Political Economy of Labour Market Flexibility', *NBER Macroeconomic Annual*, 8: 151–86.

Two surveys of European unionism can be found in:

Booth, Alison, Burda, Michael, Calmfors, Lars, Naylor, Robin, Cecci, Daniel, and Visser, Jelle (2000), 'Trade Unions in Europe: Problems and Prospects in the 21st Century', in Boeri (ed.), *What do Unions do in Europe*, MIT Press.

Ebbinghaus, B., and Visser, J. (2000), *Trade Unions in Western Europe Since 1945*, Macmillan.

For a review of the debate over the effects of minimum wages see:

Dolado, Juan, Kramarz, Francis, Machin, Steven, Manning, Alan, Margolis, David, and Teulings, Coen (1996), 'The Economic Impact of Minimum Wages in Europe', *Economic Policy*, 23: 317–72.

Kennan, John (1995), 'The Elusive Effects of Minimum Wages', *Journal of Economic Literature*, 33: 1949–65.

Appendix: Labour Supply and Demand, and the Collective Labour Supply Curve

Household Labour Supply

Robinson Crusoe maximizes his utility function defined over consumption C and leisure ℓ:

(A4.1)
$$U = U(C, \ell),$$

subject to the budget constraint

(A4.2)
$$w\bar{\ell} = w\ell + C,$$

Where w is the real (consumption) wage and $\bar{\ell}$ is Crusoe's time endowment. The first-order condition is found by substituting C from (A4.2) into (A4.1) and maximizing with respect to ℓ:

(A4.3)
$$U_\ell/U_c = w.$$

The ratio of the marginal utilities vis-à-vis leisure (U_ℓ) and consumption (U_c) is the marginal rate of substitution and the (absolute value of the) slope of the indifference curve. This measures the ratio of the changes in leisure and consumption that keep the utility level unchanged. At the optimum, the amounts substituted are such that this ratio is equal to the real wage rate.

The individual labour supply curve is the (implicit) function household labour supply L as to real wage w defined by (A4.3):

(A4.4)
$$L^{s,\text{individual}} = L^s(w).$$

Aggregation over many households results in

(A4.5)
$$L^s = L^s(w, \bar{L}),$$

where $\bar{L}$ is the number of individuals of working age.

The Demand for Labour by Firms

Since capital is fixed, we can write the production function simply as $Y = F(\bar{K}, L) = F(L)$. Express the firm's profit in terms of units of output, or as

(A4.6)
$$\Pi = F(L) - wL.$$

Choosing employment to maximize (A4.6) gives

(A4.7)
$$\text{MPL} = F'(L) = w.$$

The inverse of relationship (A4.7) determines the demand for labour;

(A4.8)
$$L = L(w) = F'^{-1}(w), \text{ with } L'(w) < 0.$$

Wages and the Labour Share

The wage share is $s = wL(w)/F(L)$. What is the effect of an increase in the real wage on s? Differentiating this expression yields

(A4.9)
$$\frac{\partial s}{\partial w} = \frac{L}{Y}\left[1 + \frac{wL'}{L} - \frac{wF'L'}{Y}\right].$$

Define two elasticities as

η_{Lw} = elasticity of labour demand to the real wage

$$= -\frac{dL}{dw}\frac{w}{L} = -\frac{wL'}{L}$$

θ_{YL} = elasticity of output with respect to labour

$$= \frac{dY}{dL}\frac{L}{Y} = \frac{F'L}{Y}.$$

(A4.9) can be rewritten as

(A4.10)
$$\frac{\partial s}{\partial w} = \frac{L}{Y}[1 - \eta_{LW}(1 - \theta_{YL})].$$

Since $F' = w$, θ_{YL} is also labour's share in value added and $(1 - \theta_{YL})$ is the profit share. Thus, the condition for the wage share to be increasing when the real wage rises is that $\eta_{Lw} < 1/(1 - \theta_{YL})$, or that the elasticity of labour demand be less than the inverse of the profit share. This is the more likely to happen the smaller is the profit share and the less elastic is the demand for labour, i.e. if the demand for labour does not decline 'too much' in response to an increase in real wages.

Collective Labour Supply

Consider a labour union that has utility given by $U(w - \bar{w}, L - \bar{L})$. In this formulation (sometimes known as a Stone–Geary specification), utility is dependent on the excess of wages and employment above exogenous reference levels, here $\bar{w}$ and $\bar{L}$. We assume that $U_w > 0$, $U_L > 0$ while $U_{ww} < 0$, $U_{LL} < 0$, and $U_{wL} > 0$. We consider only the case of a monopoly labour union, which sets the wage unilaterally.[18]

The union maximizes utility subject to the labour demand curve (A4.8), by choosing the real wage w that

---

[18] For more sophisticated treatments of the collective bargaining process, which allow for bargaining between unions and employer associations, see an advanced textbook, e.g. Booth (1995).

maximizes $U(w - \bar{w}, L(w) - \bar{L})$. The first-order condition is

(A4.11) $$\frac{U_w}{U_L} = -L'(w),$$

where the derivatives are evaluated at the optimum value. Equation (A4.11) has an interpretation similar to that of (A4.3): the union picks a wage such that the marginal rate of substitution of employment for wages is equal to the slope of the labour demand curve. This corresponds to points of tangency in the various panels traced out in Figure 4.11.

We can solve this condition by considering a specific form of the utility function.[19]

(A4.12) $U(w - \bar{w}, L - \bar{L}) = [\alpha(w - \bar{w})^{1/\rho}$
$$+ (1 - \alpha)(L - \bar{L})^{\delta\rho}]^{1/\rho},$$

---

[19] This form exhibits constant elasticity of substitution between isoelastic functions of 'normalized' employment and wages.

with $1 > \rho > -\infty$. First consider the case $\gamma = \delta = 1$. It can be shown that the elasticity of substitution between adjusted employment and wages is given by $(1 - \rho)^{-1}$. As ρ approaches 0, the function assumes the form

(A4.13) $U(w - \bar{w}, L - \bar{L}) = (w - \bar{w})^\alpha (L - \bar{L})^{(1-\alpha)},$

whereas the case $\rho \to -\infty$ gives

(A4.13') $U(w - \bar{w}, L - \bar{L}) = \min [(w - \bar{w}), (L - \bar{L})],$

and $\rho = 1$ yields the linear form

(A4.13'') $U(w - \bar{w}, L - \bar{L}) = \alpha(w - \bar{w}) + (1 - \alpha)(L - \bar{L}).$

An alternative class of union preferences arises when $\rho = 1$ with γ or δ less than unity:

(A4.14) $U(w - \bar{w}, L - \bar{L}) = \alpha(w - \bar{w})^\gamma + (1 - \alpha)(L - \bar{L})^\delta.$

Curves which intersect the origin in Figure 4.11 could be derived from cases in which $\bar{w} = \bar{L} = 0$. The case of a vertical collective labour supply at some positive $\bar{L}$ would correspond to a case of $\gamma = 1$, $\delta < 1$, and $\bar{w} = 0$, while a horizontal collective labour supply corresponds to the case of $\gamma < 1$, $\delta = 1$, and $\bar{L} = 0$.

Intertemporal Budget Constraints

The future influences the present as much as the past.

– Nietzsche

5.1   Overview

Each of the three sectors identified in the circular flow diagram of Chapter 2—the private sector, the government, and the rest of the world—can borrow and lend. In doing so, they shift income and spending between the present and the future. Borrowing brings future income forward to be spent today rather than in the future. Lending, or more generally, saving defers the use of current income to some later date. This link between the present and the future takes the form of **intertemporal budget constraints**: the liabilities of each sector must eventually be repaid, while accumulated assets will eventually be spent.

Lending and borrowing decisions are inevitably driven by expectations about future economic conditions. The importance of expectations for current behaviour cannot be overemphasized. Those who expect their incomes to grow rapidly will want to borrow now and raise their current standards of living instead of waiting. In contrast, the lucky winner of a lottery will likely save a large fraction of the prize, because it is unlikely to occur again. Firms'

investment decisions, too, are a gamble on future demand. Not the present, not the past, but expectations of the future exert the greatest influence on firms' capital budgeting decisions.

This chapter looks at what is called intertemporal trade: the shifting of spending over time. It is a trade because time has a price. This price is determined by interest rates. The intertemporal constraint provides the rules of the game. It may be a surprising way of thinking about things that we do everyday, but it will provide a powerful framework for understanding some fundamental features of economics. Because the future is unbounded, it can be rather overwhelming to think about it in simple terms. So we adopt two simplifying devices. First, we will reduce the flow of time to just two periods, called today and tomorrow, the present and the indefinite future. Second, we will maintain the parable of Robinson Crusoe, introduced in the last chapter, who is all at once consumer, producer, and his own government. These steps should make pretty abstract considerations a bit more familiar.

5.2   Thinking about the Future

5.2.1   The Future Has a Price

It is a basic economic principle that anything of value must have a price. This includes money and goods delivered at future dates. In fact, markets exist for the sole purpose of pricing future deliveries of primary commodities: London's Commodity Futures, New York's Mercantile Exchange, or Rotterdam's Oil Futures deal in such futures contracts. Markets for financial resources are conspicuous: in most countries, markets for loans determine the interest rate—

the price for borrowing and the return from lending. More advanced countries have stock markets which assess the value of firms, primarily on the basis of expected future earnings (profits).

Microeconomic principles can be readily used to understand how the future is priced. There is a direct parallel between *intertemporal* consumption choices (between present and future goods) and *intratemporal* consumption choices (among goods at a particular point in time). When we choose between consuming now or in the future, we effectively decide whether to save or to borrow. As rational households plan spending over time, they take into account their future incomes and needs, and balance these against the interest rate at which they can borrow or save. Similarly, rational firms forecast the profitability of plant and equipment in which they invest; they compare the return from investments with the interest rate, which represents either the cost of funds or, if funds are available, the best alternative use for them.

5.2.2 The Rational Expectations Hypothesis

Expectations about the future are crucial to all this. But how exactly do people form expectations? This book takes the view that agents' forecasts are correct *on average*. This is the **rational expectations hypothesis**. It does not imply that individual agents forecast the future perfectly; it does imply that they do not make systematic errors. Alternative assumptions about expectations are presented formally in

Box 5.1. These alternatives are logically weak, either because they rule out forward-looking behaviour, or assume that agents do not use all the available information about the future in a rational manner. The rational expectations hypothesis takes the opposite position, assuming that agents do use all available information in a way that reflects its costs, and use it in a skilled enough way to be right, on average. Some claim that this is unrealistic, because it assumes too much rationality.

We adopt the rational expectations hypothesis for two reasons. First, economics itself is based on the hypothesis that agents behave rationally. If we accept this as a description of consumption and production, why not about expectations formation? Second, even if most people are not fully rational all the time, alternatives are no closer to realism because they assert that people are repeatedly and systematically wrong. If they are, they must suffer losses. Isn't it natural to expect them to take steps to avoid such errors in the future?

> ### Box 5.1   A Formal Presentation of Expectations
>
> When thinking about expectations formally, it is necessary to incorporate uncertainty or randomness explicitly. We consider an agent's view about a random variable x_{t+1} from the perspective of period t and denote the expectation of its value in time $t + 1$ as $_tx_{t+1}$.
>
> *Rational expectations* asserts the difference between a variable's expectation and the value that actually occurs, called its realization, is unpredictable:
>
> $$_tx_{t+1} - x_{t+1} = \varepsilon_{t+1},$$
>
> where ε_{t+1} stands for a purely random forecast error, sometimes called white noise.[1] If ε is equal to zero in each period, we have the case of *perfect foresight*.
>
> *Adaptive expectations* assumes that agents act to gradually correct their mistakes over time. According to this view, if they underestimated an economic variable last time, they raise their expectation; if they overestimated it, they reduce their forecast:
>
> $$_tx_{t+1} - _{t-1}x_t = \alpha(x_t - _{t-1}x_t)$$
>
> where α measures the extent to which agents adjust their expectations for past mistakes ($0 < \alpha < 1$). While making sense, this trial-and-error process implies that agents accumulate knowledge only from their past experience. *Static* expectations, in which agents expect no change at all, can be seen as the special case $\alpha = 0$, whereas *myopic* expectations ($\alpha = 1$) implies that agents' forecasts are equal to last period's realized value.
>
> An alternative assumption related to adaptive expectations is that agents form *extrapolative expectations* of the future as a continuation of past trends:
>
> $$_tx_{t+1} = x_t + \beta(x_t - x_{t-1}),$$
>
> where β is the extent to which agents expect past trends to continue in the future. It can be thought of as a variant of adaptive expectations when expectations are myopic ($_tx_{t+1} = x_t$) but with $\alpha \neq 1$.

---

[1] A more formal description is that $_{t-1}x_t$ is the mathematical expectation of x_{t+1} based on all information available at time t, denoted as I_{t+1}: this is written $_tx_{t+1} = E(x_{t+1} \mid I_t)$.

There is an even better justification for rational expectations. We are ultimately interested in how prices, interest rates, incomes and spending interact on the market place. It is enough that a few well-informed agents behave rationally to drive the markets. If unions act on behalf of their members, it suffices that *their* expectations be correct on average. In financial markets, all that is required is that a number of professional traders be well informed with sufficient resources at their disposal. If they perceive that prices are too low compared with their valuation, they will buy, forcing prices upwards; if prices are too high to be consistent with their expectations, they will sell. Less well-informed customers end up accepting the market prices because they are on average right, even if never quite right.

5.2.3 The Parable of Robinson Crusoe

The analysis of private sector behaviour proceeds in two steps. This chapter sets up the intertemporal budget constraint facing households, firms, the government, and the nation as a whole. Chapter 6 will

use these constraints to study behaviour. Because there are millions of agents, a difficulty arises: how can we account for so many actions? One simplifying assumption is that, as a first approximation, all consumers and firms are alike. This step is by no means absurd; at the macroeconomic level, agents do face common price levels, interest rates, and macroeconomic conditions. The simplification allows us to study the behaviour of just one consumer and one firm as the average behaviour of the economy. The representative consumer and a representative firm should be understood as a parable, a way of capturing key aspects of economic life.

Following a long tradition in intertemporal economics and the shorter tradition of the previous chapter, we will work with Robinson Crusoe as our representative agent, stranded on an island and forced to fend for himself. It is convenient to collapse time into two periods, 'today' and 'tomorrow',[2] where tomorrow is a metaphor for the future. Effectively, the day after tomorrow, Crusoe will be rescued and will no longer need to concern himself with the economics of his island.

5.3   The Household's Intertemporal Budget Constraint

5.3.1 Consumption and Intertemporal Trade

Robinson Crusoe was forced to survive using a single available resource, coconuts. In fact, we initially imagine that the island does not even have coconut trees: rather, the coconuts simply wash up on the beach. The number of coconuts that he (rationally) expects to have today and tomorrow is called his **endowment**.[3] It is exogenous because, until Robinson

learns how to plant coconuts, he has no choice but to consume what nature gives him. His endowment of coconuts today (Y_1) and coconuts tomorrow (Y_2) is represented as point A in Figure 5.1. Since the coconuts are perishable, Crusoe's consumption of coconuts is also represented by point A. This is the **autarky** point. A household or a country operates in autarky when it does not trade with the rest of the world.

If, however, there is a not-too-distant island which is inhabited by economic agents, trade is possible. Because Crusoe's coconuts are just as good as his neighbours', one might conclude that there is no reason to trade. That is not correct. Crusoe may well be interested in **intertemporal trade**, or trade across time. He might lend his neighbours some coconuts today, if he expects to find only a few tomorrow. On the contrary, if today's 'harvest' is abnormally low, he may borrow coconuts now and repay later when times are better.

---

[2] The two-period version is the workhorse of intertemporal economic analysis and is attributable to the American economist Irving Fisher (1867–1947).

[3] Two caveats apply. First, we assume that there is no uncertainty and that Crusoe has a perfect foresight with respect to the future. Perfect foresight is the equivalent of rational expectations when there is no uncertainty. Second, we consider that Crusoe has little else to do with his time so that coconuts can be gathered at no personal cost. Ch. 4 has already considered the important case when Crusoe enjoys leisure and puts a price on working (picking up coconuts) albeit in an intratemporal setting.

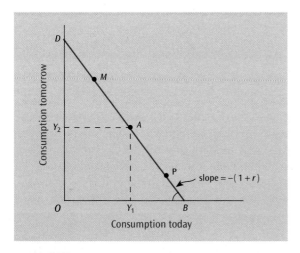

Fig. 5.1 Endowment, Wealth, and Consumption

Endowment available today and tomorrow determines wealth and available consumption choices along the budget line *BD*. The same level of wealth (*OB*) can be achieved by professional athletes (point *P*) and university students (point *M*).

5.3.2 The Real Interest Rate

Crusoe and his neighbours must agree on the terms of repayment: how much should he pay (or receive) tomorrow for one coconut borrowed (lent) today? These terms are the **real interest rate**. If the neighbours are already conducting intertemporal trade among themselves, and are willing to offer him the same rate of interest, then from Crusoe's point of view the interest rate, denoted by r, is exogenous. If he lends 100 coconuts today, he will receive $100(1 + r)$ coconuts tomorrow. Equivalently, to receive 100 coconuts tomorrow he must save $100/(1 + r)$ coconuts today. Simply put, a coconut tomorrow is worth $1/(1 + r)$ coconuts today.

The price of tomorrow's consumption in terms of today's consumption is called an **intertemporal price**, t. As the real interest rate r is positive, it says that goods tomorrow are less valuable than goods today. The real interest rate measures the cost of waiting. Valuing future goods in terms of goods today (here, dividing by the interest factor, 1 plus the real interest rate) is called **discounting**. Box 5.2

Box 5.2 **Discounting and Bond Prices**

Discounting is used in economics and finance to evaluate the value of future incomes or expenditures in terms of resources today. It is frequently used to value financial assets. Discounting asks: what is the amount required today, given an interest rate, to generate some payment or payments in the future?

Consider the simplest case of a bond which pays €100 in one year's time. (This type of bond is called a *pure discount* bond.) If the interest rate is 5%, what is the value of this bond today? It is the amount invested now that yields 100 next year. If that amount is *B*, then it must be true that

$$B(1 + 0.05) = 100,$$

so $B = 95.24$. We can ask how much this bond would be worth if it were a two-year discount bond instead:

$$B(1 + 0.05)^2 = 100,$$

so that now $B = 90.70$. The further into the future the payback is, the more heavily any amount is discounted.

Consider now any payment a_t in a future year t. Generalizing, the present value of a payment in period $t = n$ is $a_n/(1 + r)^n$; and the present value of a stream of future incomes $t = 1, \ldots, n$, discounting at rate r, is

$$\frac{a_1}{1 + r} + \frac{a_2}{(1 + r)^2} + \frac{a_3}{(1 + r)^3} + \ldots + \frac{a_n}{(1 + r)^n}.$$

A simple example is the case of a consol, a bond that promises to pay a fixed amount for ever. The price of a consol p is simply the present discounted value of its payments:

$$p = \frac{a}{1 + r} + \frac{a}{(1 + r)^2} + \frac{a}{(1 + r)^3} + \ldots + \frac{a}{(1 + r)^n} + \ldots = \frac{a}{r}.$$

The price of a consol is clearly inversely related to the interest rate. Other bonds have a finite maturity so the formula is more complicated, but the general principle remains that higher real interest rates imply lower bond prices.[4]

---

[4] More details on bond valuation and interest rates can be found in Ch. 19.

presents this important concept more generally. It can be used for example to explain the inverse relationship between bond prices and interest rates, among other things.

Intertemporal trade allows Crusoe to choose consumption combinations represented by the line BD in Figure 5.1. This line must go through his endowment point A, since he can always choose not to trade at all. At point B Crusoe forgoes consumption tomorrow completely: he borrows against his future endowment Y_2, receives $Y_2/(1+r)$ coconuts, and consumes $Y_1 + Y_2/(1+r)$ coconuts today. At point D he fasts today, and lends all his current endowment Y_1 in order to consume $Y_1(1+r) + Y_2$ coconuts tomorrow. The line BD represents all the possibilities open to Crusoe, in between the extremes just described. It is called the **budget line**, its slope is $-(1+r)$.[5] If the rate of interest increases, the budget line becomes steeper: for a given amount of saving today, more will be available tomorrow.

5.3.3 **Wealth and Present Discounted Values**

If Crusoe consumes C_1 in the first period and his income 'from nature' is Y_1, his saving is $Y_1 - C_1$. If $Y_1 - C_1$ is positive, he is lending; if $Y_1 - C_1$ is negative, he is borrowing. In the second period, his consumption C_2 will equal the sum of income Y_2 plus $(1+r)(Y_1 - C_1)$, the interest and principal on his savings from period 1. (If saving was negative in the first period, this means paying back principal plus interest.) Formally, we have

(5.1) $$C_2 = Y_2 + (Y_1 - C_1)(1+r).$$

This fully describes Crusoe's **intertemporal budget constraint**. Dividing both sides by $(1+r)$ and rearranging,

(5.2) $$C_1 + \frac{C_2}{1+r} = Y_1 + \frac{Y_2}{1+r}.$$

The left-hand side is the **present discounted value** of consumption: it is the sum of today's and tomorrow's consumption valued in terms of goods today.

[5] The slope is the ratio OD/OB. From the text we know that $OD/OB = [Y_1(1+r) + Y_2]/[Y_1 + Y_2/(1+r)] = 1 + r$. The slope is negative because the budget constraint is downward-sloping.

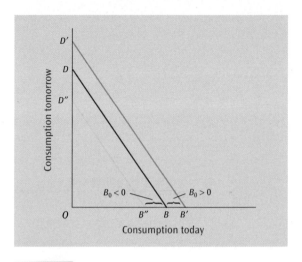

Fig. 5.2 **Inheriting Wealth or Indebtedness**

When some wealth $B_0 > 0$ is inherited, the budget line shifts from BD to $B'D'$. If it is a debt $B_0 < 0$ that is inherited instead, the budget line is $B''D''$. The lines are parallel because the real interest rate is unchanged.

The right-hand side is equal to the present discounted value of income (his endowment). It is the maximum consumption that Crusoe could enjoy today given his resources today and tomorrow, and is represented by point B in Figure 5.1. Put differently, OB is the present discounted value of Crusoe's total endowment, in fact it represents his wealth, denoted by the symbol Ω:

(5.3) $$\Omega = Y_1 + \frac{Y_2}{1+r}.$$

If lending and borrowing is available without restriction, the same menu of possible consumption over both periods can be financed by individuals with very different income profiles. It doesn't matter whether Crusoe is a university student with low current and high future income, as represented by point M in Figure 5.1, or a professional athlete with high current and low future income (point P). As long as these points are on the same intertemporal budget constraint, the present discounted value of income is the same and intertemporal trade allows income to be shifted across time by borrowing and lending.

If Crusoe has initial tradable wealth B_0 (an initial cache of coconuts), his wealth will increase by this amount and the budget constraint will be modified as follows:[6]

(5.4) $$C_1 + \frac{C_2}{1+r} = Y_1 + \frac{Y_2}{1+r} + B_0.$$

Naturally, this means that he can consume more in both periods. If he started with a debt, then B_0 is negative and he will have to consume less in order to repay the debt with interest. In general, total wealth is the sum of inherited wealth or indebtedness B_0 and of the present value of income. This is shown in Figure 5.2, where the inherited wealth or indebtedness is added to the present value of income. At a given real interest rate, it implies shifting the budget line BD to $B'D'$ or $B''D''$.

5.4 The Firm and the Private Sector's Intertemporal Budget Constraint

5.4.1 Firms and the Investment Decision

So far the endowment has been considered exogenous. In fact, income mostly comes from carefully chosen productive activities. Production normally requires that some current endowment be diverted from consumption and used to acquire productive capital. Crusoe could plant coconuts today which would grow into trees bearing coconuts tomorrow. Naturally, once planted, a coconut cannot be consumed: it is useful only for its future production. The use of valuable resources to produce more goods later is called **investment** or **fixed capital formation**. Indeed, a large quantity of goods—plant and equipment—have no consumption value whatsoever; they are designed solely to make future production possible.

Like consumption, the investment decision has a fundamental intertemporal aspect. Firms decide to accumulate capital when it is profitable to do so, and profitability depends on expected future outcomes. In order to finance their investments, firms obtain resources from the capital market (stock exchanges, bond markets, or banks) or use their own funds (retained earnings).

5.4.2 The Production Function

The investment decision depends upon the amount of output that can be produced with the available equipment (the number of coconuts to be obtained from planting a tree). The **production function** $F(K)$ captures this relationship between capital input and output and is depicted in Figure 5.3. It can be thought of as a special case of the production function of Chapter 3, in which labour input is exogenous. The shape of the curve implies that, as more capital is accumulated, the additional or marginal yield declines. That marginal output decreases when more input is put in place is the

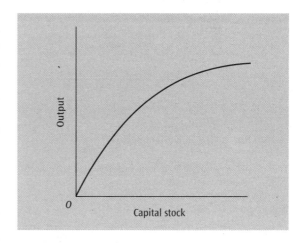

[6] This is obtained by noting that today's available resources are $Y_1 + B_0$ so that (5.2) is changed to $C_2 = Y_2 + (Y_1 + B_0 - C_1)(1 + r)$. Note also a convention of notation: implicitly there is a period 0, before Crusoe's landing on the island. At the end of period 0, there were Y_0 coconuts. When period 1 starts, upon Crusoe's arrival, the value of these coconuts is $B_0 = Y_0(1 + r)$, i.e., we call B_0 the beginning-of-period 1 value of resources available at the end of period 0.

Fig. 5.3 **The Production Function**

As more input is added, output increases, but at a decreasing rate. This is the principle of declining marginal productivity.

principle of **diminishing marginal productivity** already encountered in Chapter 3.[7]

5.4.3 **The Cost of Investment**

Starting with no capital stock (we assume that there were no coconut trees on the island), today's investment represents the total stock of capital available for production tomorrow. (Box 5.3 considers the more realistic case when previously accumulated capital already exists.) Crusoe understands that he can either invest K in productive equipment, or lend K to his neighbours. In the first case, he will have an output $F(K)$ tomorrow. In the second case, he will receive an income $K(1 + r)$. The real interest rate represents the **opportunity cost** of the resources used in investment. Because of the option of lending at rate r, the investment must yield at least $1 + r$ to be worth undertaking.[8]

Figure 5.4 shows the opportunity cost $K(1 + r)$ as the ray OR. As long as the amount of output exceeds

the cost, the technology is sufficiently productive and investment is worthwhile. At point A, investment just covers its cost, there is no economic profit. To the right of A, investment uses up more resources than it produces. Positive economic profits occur only to the left of A.

Changes in the interest rate can change the set of investment levels that are productive. If the rate of interest were to increase, the OR line would rotate upward, pushing point A to the left, reducing the return from any investment level, and thus narrowing the range of productive investments. Another angle on the problem is to compute the net return V from investing K. It is the difference between the present value of output tomorrow and investment today:[9]

$$(5.5) \qquad V = \frac{F(K)}{1 + r} - K.$$

An investment project is economically justifiable only if it has a positive present value. In terms of (5.5), that means $V > 0$ or if $F(K) > K(1 + r)$. Figure 5.5

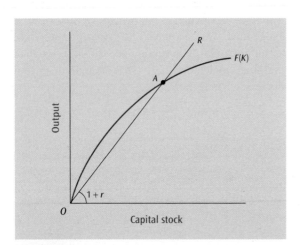

Fig. 5.4   **Productive Technology**

The cost of borrowing to finance investment is given by OR. As long as output exceeds the cost of borrowing, the technology is productive and the producer makes profit. Beyond A, she makes losses.

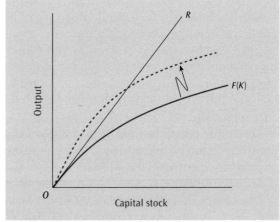

Fig. 5.5   **Unproductive Technology**

Given the interest rate, no firm will operate with a production function $F(K)$. Technological innovation may occur and open up profit opportunities.

[7] The reason behind this principle is that, given the existing amount of labour used to man the equipment (here, Crusoe's time), adding new equipment is less and less effective in raising output.
[8] Alternatively, Crusoe could borrow coconuts for investment purposes. The interest rate then is the cost of investment. This is discussed in Box 5.4 and in the Appendix.

[9] The trees are assumed not to have resale value; they die after the second period. If they didn't, one would need to add back the resale value of the depreciated trees in the second period, which would increase the value of the investment activity. This modification is described in detail in the next chapter.

illustrates a case when the technology is not productive enough given the real interest rate. In that case it does not pay to invest: it is more profitable to lend at the rate r. It would require either an improvement in technology (the production function schedule shifts upward) or a lowering of the interest rate (the ray OR rotates downward) for investment to be worthwhile.

5.4.4 The Intertemporal Budget Constraint of the Consolidated Private Sector

The budget constraint of Section 5.3 takes endowments as given. Once investment and production are taken into account, income tomorrow is no longer simply given by nature. The budget constraint now depends on the amount that is invested and on its profitability. As long as it is profitable, investment increases wealth. Figure 5.6 shows how this happens. Starting from point A, Crusoe can save either by lending to his neighbours or by investing an amount I_1 up to a maximum of his endowment Y_1. If all his savings are invested, the capital stock available for tomorrow's output production is the difference between today's endowment Y_1 and consumption C_1:

(5.6) $$K = I_1 = Y_1 - C_1.$$

The more he invests—the more we move to the left—the larger will be tomorrow's production. This is why the production function is now the mirror image of the one shown in Figure 5.4: as we move

leftward from the endowment point A, investment increases and tomorrow's output becomes larger. Tomorrow's income is the sum of the endowment Y_2 (the coconuts lying on the beach) plus output $F(K)$:

(5.7) $$C_2 = Y_2 + F(K).$$

The intertemporal budget constraint determines the present value of consumption $C_1 + C_2/(1 + r)$. With $C_1 = Y_1 - I_1$ given by (5.6) and C_2 given by (5.7), the present value of consumption is equal to wealth Ω:

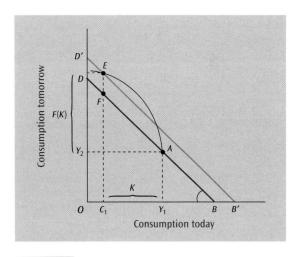

Fig. 5.6   **Investment Increases Wealth**

Investing K in the productive technology allows a household to improve its wealth over and above that corresponding to the initial endowment A. Here wealth increases by BB' as FE additional goods become available in the second period.

Box 5.4	**The Modigliani–Miller Theorem**

One of the implications of the consolidation of household and firm accounts is that households ultimately own the firms and that the activity of firms affects the value of household wealth. In practice, firms may be owned directly by households (we speak of stocks or shares in the firm, or equity ownership), or firms may borrow resources with a promise to repay in the future (they issue debt). Shareholders are therefore called **residual claimants**, since they have a claim to whatever remains after firms have incurred their costs, serviced their debt (outstanding bonds and borrowing from banks), and paid taxes. Similarly, if a firm is declared bankrupt, those who have lent to the firm (bondholders, banks, and other creditors) have priority over equity holders. Under ideal conditions, it does not matter whether a firm uses debt or equity to finance an investment project. This result is known as the Modigliani–Miller Theorem.[10]

In the same vein, there is no difference between firms' savings and household savings lent to firms, at least to first approximation. Firms' savings amount to retaining earnings instead of distributing them to shareholders. In that case, shareholders are entitled to the future earnings generated by non-distributed profits. The number of shares does not change, but each share is worth more. In the second case, the shareholders provide the firm with additional resources in return for future earnings associated with the new investment: they now hold more shares but the value of each share remains approximately unchanged. In both cases, for a given investment project, the shareholders' wealth is the same. In the first case, they implicitly lend to the firm the equivalent of undistributed earnings.

Thus, the firm is a 'veil' which acts on behalf of its shareholders. It is irrelevant whether the firm or the shareholders do the saving. In practice, the relative shares of saving by firms and households vary considerably from one country to another (Figure 5.7). But when household and corporate savings are added up, national patterns appear more similar. For example, the bulk of saving is done by households in firms in Italy and the UK. In the Netherlands, corporations account for a larger share of total savings. One reason for this variation is the difference in the tax treatment of dividends, retained earnings, and capital gains. When the capital gains associated with retained earnings are taxed less heavily than dividend income, for example, shareholders are better off when firms save on their behalf.

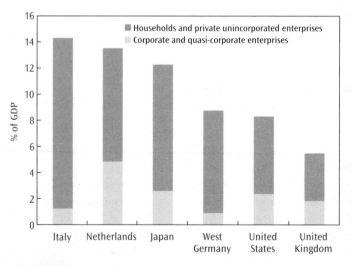

Fig. 5.7	**Corporate and Household Saving, 1981–1987**

Total saving rates differ across countries, but not as much as the share of saving of the corporate and household sectors. Tax treatment of income from saving largely explains the latter difference.
Source: OECD.

---

[10] It is named after the two Nobel Prize laureates, Franco Modigliani of MIT and Merton Miller of the University of Chicago.

(5.8)
$$C_1 + \frac{C_2}{1+r} = \Omega,$$

where wealth is now expressed as

(5.9)
$$\Omega = Y_1 - I_1 + \frac{Y_2}{1+r} + \frac{F(K)}{1+r}$$
$$= \left[Y_1 + \frac{Y_2}{1+r}\right] + \left[\frac{F(K)}{1+r} - I_1\right]$$
$$= \left[Y_1 + \frac{Y_2}{1+r}\right] + V$$

Total wealth = endowment + value of the firm

Wealth now consists of two parts. The first part is the present value of the endowment as before in (5.3). The second part is the increase in wealth by V, the net value of the investment activity, as in (5.5). In Figure 5.6 the outcome of investment I_1 is shown as point E. Note that E lies above the initial budget line; this is because the production technology is productive at the rate of interest r. The distance OB still represents the present value of the endowment. But now, for a choice of investment I_1 which brings Crusoe to point E, new total wealth is the distance OB'. Since the value of future output is discounted at the same rate r, the new budget line is parallel to BD. The distance BB' is the net return on investment.[11]

In the parable, Crusoe represents the private sector as a whole, which consists of individuals and firms. Firms ultimately belong to their shareholders, and the net return from investment raises their wealth. In effect, the firm is simply a veil. It should be valued as the present value of net income from all its activities. If shareholders anticipate that a firm will become more profitable in the future—because of a technological advance, as represented by the shift in Figure 5.6—then net expected returns rise and they are richer. This wealth gain takes the form of an increase in the value of the firm. In the real world, this would be reflected in the value of a firm on the stock market.

Does it matter how this increase in wealth occurs —whether firms borrow to finance the investment or use their own savings? In Crusoe's world the answer is simple: it doesn't. This is easy to see from Figure 5.6: if borrowed coconuts can be planted, Crusoe could bring forward the present value of his endowment to point B. Yet as long as he invests as in Figure 5.6, the value of his wealth is the same! It does not matter whether a firm uses debt (borrowing) or equity (own saved funds) to finance the investment plans. This result, known as the **Modigliani–Miller Theorem**, is discussed in more detail in Box 5.4.

5.5 Public and Private Budget Constraints

5.5.1 The Public Budget Constraint

There was no government on Robinson Crusoe's island. In the real world, there is a public sector which taxes, purchases, and transfers incomes. A government is little different from other economic agents. It can borrow and lend, and then repay its debt with interest or be repaid by its debtors. The government spends G_1 and G_2 today and tomorrow, and raises net taxes, T_1 and T_2. Because they are a central component of the intertemporal budget

constraint, we shall henceforth separate out interest payments from other transfers for the rest of this book.[12]

Suppose there is no initial debt. If Crusoe's government spends more than its income today, then $G_1 - T_1 > 0$ and it borrows. Tomorrow's taxes must cover both tomorrow's spending and the debt service on today's borrowing:

(5.10)
$$T_2 = G_2 + (G_1 - T_1)(1 + r_G),$$

where r_G is the rate of interest at which the government can borrow or lend.

[11] Note that the production schedule cuts the new budget line $B'D'$, suggesting that this result might be improved by investing a little bit less than I_1. Ch. 4 shows that, when Crusoe behaves optimally, he will invest to push out his new budget line as far as possible.

[12] It should be stressed that G represents government purchases of goods and services and should be distinguished from total government outlays, which include transfer payments. In our notation, transfer payments are deducted from taxes to give net taxes, T.

If the government runs a surplus today, $G_1 - T_1$ is negative and tomorrow's taxes T_2 can be less than tomorrow's spending. This is the government's intertemporal budget constraint, similar to the household budget constraint (5.2). It may also be rewritten in present-value terms:

$$(5.11) \qquad G_1 + \frac{G_2}{1 + r_G} = T_1 + \frac{T_2}{1 + r_G}.$$

Defining D_0 as the debt inherited from the previous period, today's budget deficit can be separated into two parts: the **primary deficit**, which is the amount by which non-interest expenditures exceed revenues, and net interest payments:

$$\text{Total deficit} = \underbrace{(G_1 - T_1)}_{\substack{\text{primary} \\ \text{deficit}}} + \underbrace{r_G D_0}_{\substack{\text{debt} \\ \text{service}}}.$$

Then the government budget constraint can be rewritten in terms of primary budget deficits:

$$(5.12) \qquad D_0 + (G_1 - T_1) + \frac{G_2 - T_2}{1 + r_G} = 0.$$

The sum of the initial debt and of the present value of primary budget deficits must be zero. The constraint is illustrated in Figure 5.8 for the case where $D_0 = 0$. In that case, the budget line passes through the origin because the government has no initial debt or assets, and the slope of the line is $-(1 + r_G)$.

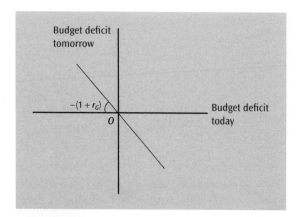

Fig. 5.8   **The Government Budget Line**

A deficit today must be matched by a budget surplus tomorrow, or vice versa, if the government is to obey its intertemporal budget constraint.

Then a budget deficit (surplus) today must be matched by a budget surplus (deficit) tomorrow:

$$(5.13) \qquad (G_1 - T_1) + \frac{G_2 - T_2}{1 + r_G} = 0.$$

Do governments actually respect their budget constraints? To be sure, there are spectacular examples of government defaults, or repudiation of past debts. Most were associated with sharp political upheavals: the turbulent years of the French Revolution, the October 1917 revolution in Russia, the end of the Weimar Republic in 1933, Castro's revolution in Cuba.[13] In most cases, however, it is politically difficult for a government to default. Latin American defaults in the 1980s, or Russia's in 1998 were traumatic events.

In order to avoid defaults, today's primary deficits require primary surpluses later, and conversely. Given spending plans, lower taxes today are followed by higher taxes tomorrow. Alternatively, for a given path of taxes, more spending today requires spending cuts tomorrow. How long does 'today' last before a government is hit 'tomorrow' by the budget constraint? Governments that start with little debt can run deficits for many years. Figure 5.9 presents examples of primary budget balances relative to the size of the economy (GDP). Some countries (the UK) show a succession of primary deficits and surpluses. In other cases (Ireland, Italy, the USA) deficits have been sustained over many years, yet eventually the budget constraint has prevailed and the primary budgets have been corrected, sometimes moving into spectacular surpluses.

5.5.2 The Consolidated Public and Private Budget Constraint

Just as the corporate veil was pierced when we consolidated the household and firm budget constraints, might it not be the case that the private sector also sees through the public sector veil? Could the private sector understand that it ultimately pays

---

[13] The public debt must be carefully distinguished from the external debt, although in some instances the public debt is held by foreigners and represents the bulk of the external debt. This chapter assumes that the public debt is held by domestic residents.

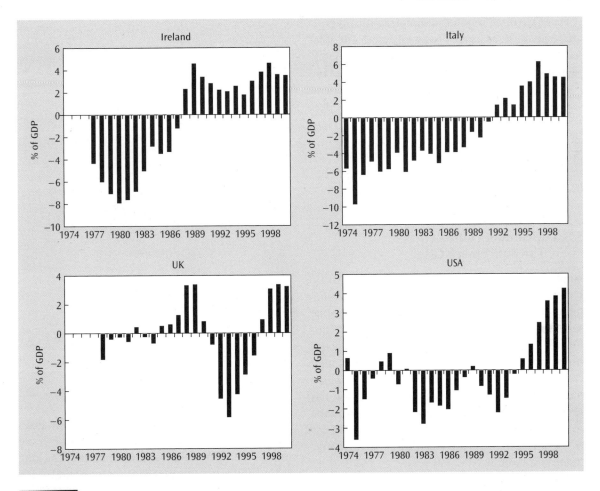

Primary Budget Surpluses, Four Countries, 1974–2000

Over time, primary budget balances must add up, in present-value terms, to initial public debt. Some governments, like the UK, have maintained primary budget balances on average over many years. Those that have allowed deficits to cumulate into large indebtedness eventually have to run surpluses, as has been the case in Ireland, Italy, and the USA.
Source: OECD.

the taxes anyway? Ignoring the existence of firms, the budget constraints of the private and public sectors are recalled:

(5.14) $$C_1 + \frac{C_2}{1 + r} = Y_1 - T_1 + \frac{Y_2 - T_2}{1 + r}.$$

(5.15) $$G_1 + \frac{G_2}{1 + r_G} = T_1 + \frac{T_2}{1 + r_G}.$$

Note that the government and the private sector do not necessarily face the same interest rates when they engage in borrowing or lending activities: the

government sector borrows and lends at rate r_G, the private sector at rate r. Starting with the case where the interest rates are the same ($r = r_G$), adding up the private and public budget constraints gives the following expression:

(5.16) $$C_1 + \frac{C_2}{1 + r} = (Y_1 - G_1) + \frac{Y_2 - G_2}{1 + r}.$$

This looks very much like the private sector budget constraint (5.14), except that taxes have been replaced by public spending.

There are three ways of interpreting this important result. First, as seen by reorganizing (5.16), total national spending—the sum of private and public spending on goods and services—cannot exceed the country's wealth. The country can borrow or lend abroad, but it must respect the nation's budget constraint:

(5.17) $\underbrace{(C_1 + G_1) + \frac{C_2 + G_2}{1 + r}}_{\substack{\text{present value of} \\ \text{total domestic spending}}} = \underbrace{Y_1 + \frac{Y_2}{1 + r}}_{\substack{\text{present value of} \\ \text{domestic incomes}}}.$

5.5.3 Ricardian Equivalence: The Benchmark Case

Equation (5.16) has a second interpretation. Private sector wealth is the difference, in present-value terms, between private endowments and public spending. It is as if the government simply confiscates the resources corresponding to its expenditures, and the private sector takes the remainder. Given public spending decisions, taxes can be levied today or tomorrow: the time profile of taxation has no effect on private wealth, what matters is public spending which pre-empts private spending and has to be financed through taxation at some point, today or tomorrow.

The result, that the private sector fully internalizes the public sector's budget constraint, is known as the **Ricardian equivalence proposition**.[14] In Figure 5.10, point A represents Crusoe's endowment measured before taxes. Once public spending is taken into account as in (5.16), the private endowment is represented by point A'. The government reduces Crusoe's private wealth by an amount represented by the distance BB', which is either the present value of taxes or the present value of public spending. (The two are equal because of the government budget constraint (5.15).) Public spending can be financed either by current taxes or by borrowing. If the government reduces taxes today without changing its

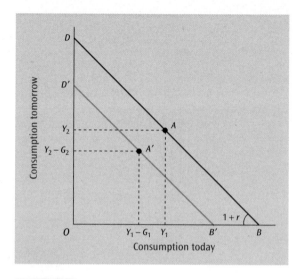

Fig. 5.10 **Ricardian Equivalence**

The government's spending and taxing activities reduce private wealth. Given government purchases, the precise scheduling of taxes does not matter.

expenditures, it borrows today and will raise taxes tomorrow. For the private sector, this means more net-of-tax income today and less tomorrow. As long as the public and private sectors borrow and lend at the same rate ($r = r_G$), these intertemporal shifts are equivalent and the public borrowing can be matched one for one by private saving along the same private budget line.

The third interpretation of (5.16) concerns private wealth. When a government borrows to cover its deficit, it issues bonds which are a promise to repay interest and principal. Do households that own the debt consider it as part of their wealth? In this interpretation, they do not: government's indebtedness does not appear as part of private wealth in the right-hand side of (5.16). The reason is that the private sector pierces the veil of government: it recognizes that the government's promises to pay—the principal and interest on public debt—is matched by taxes levied to service the debt, today or tomorrow. Public bonds are an asset to households which is exactly offset by the value of their tax liabilities. Ricardian equivalence asserts that government debt

---

[14] Named after English economist David Ricardo (1772–1823), who first formulated this idea, only to dismiss it as unlikely. The idea has been revived and championed by Harvard economist Robert Barro.

| Table 5.1 | Public and Private Borrowing Rates, March 2000: Long-Term Bonds (% per annum) |

Country	Treasury bonds	Corporate bonds
Australia	6.36	7.17
Britain	5.26	5.99
Canada	5.90	7.03
Denmark	5.48	7.18
Japan	1.87	0.84
Sweden	5.29	5.75
United States	6.12	7.56
Euro-area	5.18	5.72

Source: *The Economist*, 25 March 2000.

does not represent net wealth to the aggregate private sector.

5.5.4 **Where Ricardian Equivalence Can Fail**

The Ricardian equivalence result is highly controversial. It means that the path of taxes is irrelevant for the behaviour of the private sector. It implies that the stock of government debt does not, on net, contribute to the wealth position of households. Holding purchases of goods and services (G) constant, budget deficits do not matter. It drives home the point that governments are net drains on an economy's resources without leaving open the possibility of effects of tax and spending policies. This section considers the many assumptions, implicit or explicit, required to reach the Ricardian equivalence result. In the end, the result of this discussion is that budget deficits probably do matter, and that at least some fraction of public debt is regarded by the private sector as wealth.[15]

Mortal or new citizens

The citizens are not all alike when they face the

taxman, some pay a lot more taxes than others. So the burden of public debt service is not equally borne by all citizens. Similarly some hold government debt, and some don't. Yet, this does not imply that the aggregate household sector can escape the implications of equations (5.14)–(5.15). In the *aggregate* future tax burdens are the same.

On the other hand, citizens are certainly mortal. If they are not alive in period 2, they will not fully incorporate the intertemporal budget constraint of the government into their own budget constraints. If the current private sector fails to factor in *all* future tax liabilities, it is possible that government debt represents private wealth to some agents, and bond-financed deficits increase their wealth.

Different interest rates

It has been explicitly assumed that the government and the private sector face the same interest rate as they engage in intertemporal trade ($r = r_G$). How realistic is this assumption? In Table 5.1 two categories of borrowing rate are displayed. Interest rates on Treasury bonds represent the cost of borrowing faced by the public sector. The corporate bond rate is the interest rate charged by the bond market for firms with the best credit rating; most private borrowers face significantly higher rates (by some 1–2% more for businesses, and much more for

---

[15] Other potential failures of the Ricardian equivalence proposition are related to the behaviour of agents under uncertainty, and go beyond the scope of this book.

households). In most cases, private borrowing rates exceed the comparable public borrowing rate. This is probably because the government is considered a less risky borrower.

The table shows that these rates can differ. When $r > r_G$, combining the private and public budget constraints (5.14) and (5.15) yields, instead of (5.16),[16]

(5.18) $$C_1 + \frac{C_2}{1+r} = (Y_1 - G_1) + \frac{Y_2 - G_2}{1+r}$$
$$+ \left[\frac{r - r_G}{1+r}\right](G_1 - T_1).$$

The left-hand side is the private sector's present value of consumption, discounted at the rate of interest r at which private citizens can engage in intertemporal trade. The right-hand side must therefore represent private wealth. It includes as before the present discounted value of net private income, GDP less pre-emptive public spending, plus an additional term. This term shows that when $r > r_G$, a fraction of the deficit $G_1 - T_1$, public borrowing in period 1, increases private sector wealth. Why could a tax cut holding spending constant under these conditions increase private wealth? Because the government access to lower borrowing costs is equivalent to a subsidy to the private sector, as if the government were 'lending' the tax reduction today and demanding repayment tomorrow—through taxes—at the lower interest rate r_G. The government indirectly allows the private sector to borrow at the lower interest rate.[17]

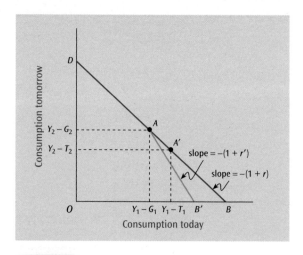

Fig. 5.11   **Borrowing Constraints**

When the household cannot borrow at all, its budget line is restricted to the segment AD, because it cannot consume today more than what is left of the endowment after public spending ($Y_1 - G_1$). If the government reduces taxes and borrows instead (abroad), the household's borrowing line extends to the segment $A'D$. When borrowing constraints take the form of a higher private borrowing rate r', the budget line is the kinked line $B'AD$. A budget deficit at A' relaxes the private household's budget constraint.

Restrictions on borrowing

Many households cannot borrow as much as future expected income would justify. They may be unable to convince lenders—typically banks—of their creditworthiness. Lenders do not have the means of fully investigating customers' statements on a credit application form. In addition, future incomes are never really certain; so lending to households is risky. Borrowing rates exceed lending rates to compensate for this risk. In the worst case, no lending is extended and individuals are said to be credit rationed. The case of credit rationing is represented in Figure 5.11. With a net private endowment represented by point A, the agent can only move along her budget line on the segment AD. The segment AB is not attainable through private borrowing. If the government runs a deficit today, the agent may reach point A' as she consumes $Y_1 - T_1$, which is larger than $Y_1 - G_1$ since $T_1 < G_1$.

---

[16] To see this, multiply both sides of (5.15) by $(1 + r_G)/(1 + r)$, and rewrite as

$$G_1 + \frac{G_2}{1+r} + \frac{r_G - r}{1+r}G_1 = T_1 + \frac{T_2}{1+r} + \frac{r_G - r}{1+r}T_1$$

so that

$$T_1 + \frac{T_2}{1+r} = G_1 + \frac{G_2}{1+r} + \frac{r_G - r}{1+r}(G_1 - T_1).$$

Substitution in (5.14) yields (5.18).

[17] Contrary to appearances, there is no 'free lunch' here: the government is simply borrowing on better terms than the private sector can. In doing so, it effects a transfer from lenders to the beneficiaries of the tax cut, who experience an increase in the present value of their resources. In reality, lenders could be foreigners, but are more likely to be wealthier residents.

Most often individuals face higher and rising costs of borrowing as the lending bank or agent (a pawn shop, the Mafia, or notaries in France) demands higher interest to compensate for additional risk. The situation is similar to the case studied in the previous section and is also illustrated in Figure 5.11. When lending, the constrained agent can move along *AD*, but for borrowing she moves along *AB'*. The budget line is now kinked at the endowment point. In this case, public debt contributes to citizens' wealth, and the time profile of taxes affects the private sector budget constraint. At point *A'* the constrained citizen is better off than anywhere along *AB'*. As in the previous section, the government borrows on behalf of its citizens, increasing the wealth of those who cannot borrow on those terms.

Distortionary taxation and unemployed resources

Ricardian equivalence also fails to hold because people change their behaviour in response to taxes. Most taxes are said to be distortionary. For example, taxation on labour income or wages may lead some to work less, and this will reduce output. In the parable of Crusoe, the endowments of coconuts are exogenous, so increasing taxes on them does not affect their supply. In the real world, taxes can reduce wealth because they reduce output. This is especially important in the presence of underutilized resources, like unemployment. If a tax cut increases the level of economic activity and generates additional income, then the associated fiscal deficit will be associated with higher wealth.

Evidence[18]

Given the list of assumptions presented in the previous sections, it would seem quite unlikely that Ricardian equivalence could hold in practice.[19] Yet,

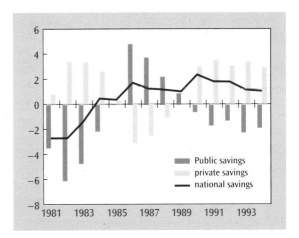

Fig. 5.12 **Ricardian Equivalence in Denmark, 1981–1994**

In the mid-1980s the Danish government put an end to a long period of budget deficits. The private sector's net saving decreased nearly one for one (not quite, since the country's current account improved). The opposite happened in the early 1990s. Both episodes conform partially with the predictions of the Ricardian equivalence hypothesis. In contrast, when the USA increased its government budget deficit dramatically in the early 1980s, the current account worsened in parallel.
Source: OECD.

it receives some empirical backing, especially when the public budget moves by large amounts that are clearly perceptible to the private sector. Figure 5.12 shows one such case. In Denmark, over the period 1981–94, the budget went from deficit to surplus and back to deficit. The private sector went exactly in the opposite direction. The country's overall balance (an issue taken up in Section 5.6 below) followed the public sector's changes, but in a muted way as the private sector partially offset the budget. A key aspect of this 'test' is the assumption that expectations of government purchases (*G*) remained roughly constant (as a fraction of GDP). This seems, *ex post*, to have been a defensible assumption: government consumption in Denmark at the beginning and the end of the 1990s represented about 26% of GDP.

---

18 An overview of the debate and existing evidence can be found in the symposium published in the Spring 1989 issue of the *Journal of Economic Perspectives*.

19 Its main advocate, Robert Barro, concludes his overview of the evidence as follows: 'I have argued that empirical findings . . . tend mainly to support the Ricardian viewpoint. However, the empirical analysis involves substantial problems about data . . . and the results are sometimes inconclusive' (Barro 1989).

5.6   The Current Account and the Budget Constraint of the Nation

5.6.1 The Primary Current Account

The budget constraint of the nation shown in (5.17) results from the consolidation of the budget constraints of the private and public sectors. The country's net saving vis-à-vis the rest of world occurs through the balance on the current account. Much like the public sector budget surplus, it can be decomposed into a **primary current account** (PCA) and net external investment income, rF:

(5.19) $CA = PCA + rF,$

where F represents the country's net asset position vis-à-vis the rest of the world, and r, as before, is the average real interest rate paid on F. Net investment income is positive when the country holds more assets than liabilities ($F > 0$), or negative, in the case of an indebted country ($F < 0$).

In the two-period framework, ignoring any initial asset position, the budget constraint of the nation requires that the present value of country's primary current accounts equal zero:

(5.20) $PCA_1 + \dfrac{PCA_2}{1 + r} = 0.$

Primary current account deficits in the first period must be repaid by primary current surpluses (in present value) in the second. Symmetrically, surpluses in the first period enable a nation to spend more than it produces in the future. It would seem wasteful for a country eventually not to take advantage of this fact; otherwise it is literally giving away resources for claims on the rest of the world which it will never use.

Condition (5.20) can be suitably modified if there is an initial net asset position F_0:[20]

(5.21) $PCA_1 + \dfrac{PCA_2}{1 + r} = -F_0.$

---

[20] For convenience, as earlier for the private sector, F_0 represents here both principal and interest inherited from the past. Later in Chapter 17 we will deal with the two explicitly and separately.

If a country has net wealth at the beginning of period 1 (F_0 is positive), it can draw on it to run future current account deficits in present-value terms. If there is external debt (F_0 is negative) the present value of current accounts must be positive, by an amount sufficient to repay the external debt.

The implication for the country as a whole is the same as for the private and public sector: primary current account deficits today must be eventually matched by surpluses, and conversely. If a country fails to satisfy its budget constraint, eventually it will face a tough situation. Many of the crises of the 1990s can be traced back to growing fears that some countries were not going to meet their constraints.

5.6.2 Enforcement of Credit Contracts and Sovereign Borrowing

We have seen in this chapter that private households, firms, and governments face an intertemporal budget constraint which limits their ability to borrow at any point in time to the present value of lifetime resources. 'Lifetime' has a clear definition for individuals; for firms and governments it is less clear, since the existence of firms and governments is never guaranteed. Nevertheless, within a legal jurisdiction, private borrowers and lenders will generally be able to rely on special institutions to enforce the budget constraint. Firms or individuals which simply walk away from debts face bankruptcy and possibly jail. Of course there are always exceptions, but they generally involve fraudulent activities such as pyramid schemes described in Box 5.5, and these tricks are usually declared illegal as soon as they are detected. In principle, these rules should also apply to governments, regardless of whether they borrow at home or abroad. As soon as they try to violate their budget constraint, the source of credit should dry up rapidly.

It is important, however, to distinguish between international borrowing by private entities and **sovereign borrowing**, or international borrowing by national governments. A country cannot be bankrupted or jailed, of course. Unlike private

---

Box 5.5 Pyramids: Running away from the Budget Constraint

Failure to understand the budget constraint can be costly to ordinary citizens and governments alike. The view that debts must be repaid tends to be lost on gullible gamblers who invest in 'pyramids'. These arrangements function as follows. A dubious financier offers depositors huge returns. When the time comes to repay, he uses freshly deposited money to pay back, principal and interest. For this to work, he must attract ever more depositors. And it works. Word of mouth spreads news of the wonderful opportunity and when the first depositors get their money back the sceptics are silenced by the 'evidence'. More and more people want their share of the pie. So the scheme grows and grows, and grow it must to simply pay back maturing deposits. But it cannot grow indefinitely, simply because there is not an infinity of people in a country, or even in the world. Pyramids must eventually collapse and the people who set up such schemes know it. So they wait until they think that they have enough deposits at hand, and they suddenly disappear with the money, and thousands of investors discover that they have just lost their life savings.

Pyramids are also called Ponzi-schemes, named after Charles Ponzi, an Italian immigrant to the USA who operated in the early 20th century. Poor Ponzi did not run away fast enough, he went to jail, and died there. Most countries ban pyramids but they flourished in the early years of transition in several former communist countries (with huge ones in Bulgaria, Romania, Russia). Apparently, ordinary citizens had not had the time to learn about the arithmetics of intertemporal trade and budget constraints. The collapse of the Albanian variety in late 1996 impoverished tens of thousands of already poor people—some of whom, lured by promises of 300% return, had sold their cattle and houses—triggered huge street demonstrations and brought down the government —which had failed to close down the pyramids—after they had collected an estimated €1 billion in a country with a GDP of €2.3 billion.

---

lending within a country, enforcement of sovereign loan contracts is legally difficult. What happens when a country's government is unable to serve its debt? The first reaction is that foreign lending immediately stops, and this often affects would-be private borrowers. The country must at least balance its current account, since it cannot borrow, which forces painful adjustments in private and public budgets. Thereafter negotiations start with the creditors to try to arrange a rescheduling of debt service. Two institutions have been set up to deal with troubled sovereign borrowers: the Paris Club which brings together official lenders (countries which lend to countries) and the London Club which brings together private lenders (banks, large financial institutions). As long as an agreement is not reached, a delinquent country is frozen out of international lending, and this may last many, many years.

 ## Summary

1. Because households may borrow or lend, their budget constraint is fundamentally intertemporal. It incorporates all current and future spending on the one hand, and all current and future income on the other. Future spending and incomes are discounted using the interest rate at which households can borrow or lend.

2. Wealth is the sum of the present value of current and future income and inherited assets less debts. The intertemporal budget constraint requires that the present value of spending be less than, or equal to, wealth. It applies to all economic agents, households, firms, the public sector, and the nation as a whole.

3. When firms invest, they forgo—on behalf of their shareholders—current consumption for future output. The profitability of investment depends both on the technology and on the rate of interest. The rate of interest is the opportunity cost of capital that investors apply to investment projects because it is available on other assets.

4. Budget constraints can be added together, or consolidated. Consolidating the households' and the firms' budget constraints gives the budget constraint of the private sector. As a first approximation, corporations are a veil: they provide their owners or shareholders with a means of increasing their wealth.

5. The public sector intertemporal budget constraint implies that, for a given time profile of government purchases, tax reductions today imply tax increases later on, and conversely. Alternatively, given a tax profile, more government spending today implies less spending later on, and conversely.

6. The Ricardian equivalence proposition asserts that the private sector internalizes the public sector budget constraint. Public debt is not considered as private wealth, and the time profile of taxes does not affect the private sector budget constraint. If the private sector can freely borrow at the same rate as the government, public dissaving (saving) is matched one for one by private saving (dissaving): the private sector pierces the veil of the government budget to keep total national saving unchanged.

7. Ricardian equivalence is unlikely to hold for several reasons. For example, individuals may expect that some current public debt will be repaid after they die; also, private interest rates typically exceed the rate at which the government borrows. Many households face borrowing constraints. Yet there is some evidence that the private sector internalize part of government debt.

8. The national budget constraint is the consolidation of the private and public sector budget constraints. It states that the present value of primary current account deficits cannot exceed the nation's net external wealth. It also implies that, all things being equal, higher primary current account deficits today will require primary current account surpluses in the future.

9. Although it must also obey an intertemporal budget constraint, sovereign borrowing by a nation may differ from private international borrowing by its residents. One difference is that governments and countries cannot be bankrupted, and the assets of defaulting governments are hard to seize.

Key Concepts

- intertemporal budget constraint
- rational expectations hypothesis
- endowment
- autarky
- intertemporal trade
- real interest rate
- discounting, discount factor, and present discounted value

- budget line
- fixed capital formation (investment)
- production function
- wealth
- diminishing marginal productivity
- opportunity cost
- gross/net investment
- primary government budget surplus or deficit

- borrowing constraints
- Ricardian equivalence proposition
- primary current account

- sovereign borrowing
- capital flight

Exercises

1. Suppose that Crusoe cannot trade with neighbours, but also that coconuts no longer spoil completely, so he can store them for consumption tomorrow. Suppose that 10% of the stored coconuts are lost because of spoilage. Represent this situation graphically.

2. If a firm decides not to distribute dividends to its shareholders, its share price often increases. Why? Are the shareholders necessarily wealthier?

3. Draw the government budget line in Figure 5.9. when there is an initial public debt D_0.

4. In the text, Robinson Crusoe does not want to leave any wealth beyond tomorrow, presumably because he knows he will be rescued. The situation would be different if he wanted to leave his friend Friday a gift of fixed amount B_2 in the second period. (B_2 might also be thought of as a bequest.) Write down Crusoe's budget constraint and represent it graphically.

5. The real interest rate is 10%. What is the value of a new firm which invests €100,000 and expects to have returns net of costs of €40,000 next year, €52,000 the year after, €56,000 the third year, and then to close down with equipment valued at zero? How does your answer change if the equipment is instead sold for €20,000?

6. What is the present value for Crusoe of 100 coconuts tomorrow if the real rate of interest is (*a*) 5%? (*b*) 10%?

Suggested Further Reading

The two-period framework is used to interpret actual economic conditions in:
Sachs, Jeffrey (1981), 'The Current Account and Macroeconomic Adjustment in the 1970s', *Brookings Papers on Economic Activity*, 1: 201–68.

The Ricardian proposition is examined by several authors in the *Journal of Economic Perspectives*, 3 (1989): 37–54, and in
Seater, John (1993), 'Ricardian Equivalence', *Journal of Economic Literature*, 31: 142–90.

Appendix: Budget Constraints over Many Periods

This appendix provides a formal treatment and a generalization of the two-period analysis of intertemporal budget contraints in the main text.

Households (without investment)

At the end of period t, the household receives income Y_t and consumes C_t. If $B_{t-1} \neq 0$ is inherited net financial wealth and r is the (constant) real interest rate, the change in wealth is given by

(A5.1) $$B_t - B_{t-1} = Y_t - C_t + rB_{t-1}$$

or

$$B_{t-1} = \frac{B_t - Y_t + C_t}{1 + r}$$

But this must also hold for $t + 1$:

(A5.2) $$B_t = \frac{B_{t+1} - Y_{t+1} + C_{t+1}}{1 + r},$$

so, by substitution,

$$B_{t-1} = \frac{C_t - Y_t}{1 + r} + \frac{C_{t+1} - Y_{t+1}}{(1 + r)^2} + \frac{B_{t+1}}{(1 + r)^2}.$$

Successive iteration yields

(A5.3) $$B_{t-1} = \frac{C_t - Y_t}{1 + r} + \frac{C_{t+1} - Y_{t+1}}{(1 + r)^2} + \ldots + \frac{B_{t+n}}{(1 + r)^{n+1}}.$$

Attention is drawn to the last term, which is the present value of agent's net assets in period $t + n$. As n goes to infinity, one would expect that the household would have to repay its debt—to transfer resources equal in present value to its initial debt. (Households cannot repay their debt by borrowing for ever.) In terms of the model of the main text, this is like the condition that no net or positive asset position remains after period 2. With an infinite horizon, this requirement can be written as

(A5.4) $$\lim_{n \to \infty} \frac{B_{t+n}}{(1 + r)^{n+1}} \geq 0.$$

At the same time, it makes little sense to go to 'the end' with unspent wealth; this would imply forgone consumption possibilities. As long as this can be ruled out, the inequality of (A5.4) can be replaced by an equality. Now we find the infinite-horizon equivalent of (5.4) in the main text, for period $t = 1$:

(A5.5) $$\sum_{i=1}^{\infty} \frac{C_i}{(1 + r)^{i-1}} = (1 + r)B_0 + \sum_{i=1}^{\infty} \frac{Y_i}{(1 + r)^{i-1}},$$

which says that the present value of consumption is equal to household's wealth, the sum of inherited financial wealth B_0, plus interest on that wealth rB_0, plus the present discounted value of income.

Firms (with investment)

In period t the firm makes a net cash flow Π_t of

(A5.6) $$\Pi_t = F(K_{t-1}) - I_t,$$

which is paid at the end of the period. Thus, today's value of the firm can be decomposed as this period's profit plus the present value of the firm next period:

(A5.7) $$V_t = \frac{\Pi_t}{1 + r} + \frac{V_{t+1}}{(1 + r)^2}.$$

Iterating on this expression gives

(A5.8) $$V_t = \frac{\Pi_t}{1 + r} + \frac{\Pi_{t+1}}{(1 + r)^2} + \frac{\Pi_{t+2}}{(1 + r)^3} + \ldots + \frac{V_{t+n}}{(1 + r)^{n+1}}.$$

As n goes to infinity, the firm cannot have a negative present value—it would be bankrupt. Nor does it make sense for the owners to reach 'the end' with unspent residual wealth. So we have the following transversality condition:

(A5.9) $$\lim_{n \to \infty} \frac{V_{t+n}}{(1 + r)^{n+1}} = 0.$$

Therefore, the value of the firm at the end of period $t = 1$ is the present discounted value of its profits:

$$V_1 = \sum_{i=1}^{\infty} \frac{\Pi_i}{(1 + r)^{i-1}}.$$

The Private Sector (with investment)

In each period, households that own the firm split total income between consumption C and investment I:

(A5.10) $$Y_t + F(K_{t-1}) = C_t + I_t.$$

Assume that capital depreciates completely each period. The present value of consumption is at most the present discounted value of available resources—the sum of endowment Y_t and net output of the firm $F(K_{t-1})$ less investment I_t. In present value terms, this can be written as

(A5.11) $$\sum_{i=1}^{\infty} \frac{C_i}{(1 + r)^{i-1}} = (1 + r)B_0 + \sum_{i=1}^{\infty} \frac{Y_i + F(K_{i-1}) - I_i}{(1 + r)^{i-1}}$$

$$= (1 + r)B_0 + \sum_{i=1}^{\infty} \frac{Y_i}{(1 + r)^{i-1}} + V_1.$$

The present value of consumption is bounded by wealth, the sum of inherited assets, the present value of endowment, and the value of the firm. This left-hand side of (A5.11) corresponds to Ω defined in the text for the two-period model.

Government

The same reasoning applies to the government as to households. The result is a condition that prohibits net public debt in 'the end' and requires that the present value of taxes must equal the initial debt and the present value of spending:

$$(A5.12) \qquad \lim_{n \to \infty} \frac{D_{t+n}}{(1 + r_G)^{n+1}} = 0.$$

It is possible to derive the infinite period equivalent of (5.11):

$$(A5.13) \qquad \sum_{i=1}^{\infty} \frac{T_i}{(1 + r_G)^{i-1}} = (1 + r)D_0 + \sum_{i=1}^{\infty} \frac{G_i}{(1 + r_G)^{i-1}},$$

where G and T occur at the end of the period.

The Public and Private Sectors

With taxes T_i in each period, the private sector's budget constraint (A5.11) becomes

$$(A5.14) \qquad \sum_{i=1}^{\infty} \frac{C_i}{(1 + r)^{i-1}} = (1 + r)B_0 + \sum_{i=1}^{\infty} \frac{(Y_i - T_i)}{(1 + r)^{i-1}} + V_1.$$

When all the taxes remain lump-sum and government and private sector borrow and lend at the same rate $(r = r_G)$, (A5.11) and (A5.13) can be combined to yield

$$(A5.15) \qquad \Omega = \sum_{i=1}^{\infty} \frac{C_i}{(1 + r)^{i-1}}$$

$$= (1 + r)(B_0 - D_0) + \sum_{i=1}^{\infty} \frac{(Y_i - G_i)}{(1 + r)^{i-1}} + V_1.$$

Since there is only one 'representative agent' in the economy, $B_0 - D_0$ can be thought of as the nation's inherited external investment position (net foreign assets/liabilities), which is the sum of private assets (B_0) and government assets $(-D_0)$.

Private Sector Demand: Consumption and Investment

6

All production is for the purpose of ultimately satisfying a consumer.

– J. M. Keynes

6.1 Overview

When defined as final goods expenditures, the GDP consists of consumption, investment, government purchases, and the net exports of goods and services. These components represent demands for goods and services by various sectors—households, firms, the government, and foreigners.

This chapter focuses on the private elements of aggregate spending: consumption and investment. Figure 6.1 shows that the variability of these components (as a share of GDP) is quite different, suggesting that they are driven by different motives; private consumption seems more stable than investment, while public spending is more volatile in the USA than in the EU. In order to explain consumption and investment, our point of departure is a parable of a representative consumer and a representative firm. Both are taken to be rational, they strive to do the best they can given their available resources and opportunities. Although rationality is sometimes understood as implying extraordinary intelligence or the ability to perform elaborate calculations, optimizing behaviour simply means that agents, possibly through trial and error, behave in consistent fashion.[1] The end product of the chapter is a **consumption function** and an **investment function**, two key building blocks of macroeconomic analysis.

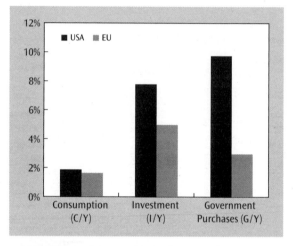

Fig. 6.1 Coefficient of Variation of GDP Components, 1970–1999

The coefficient of variation measures how much some variable fluctuates relative to its value on average. Technically, it is defined as the ratio of the standard deviation to the mean. The chart shows that the fraction of GDP represented by consumption is much more stable than investment or government spending.

6.2 Consumption

Households receive an income from their work or their asset holdings and have to decide what to do with it. The decision to consume is a decision not to save, and saving is a decision to postpone consumption. It is fundamentally intertemporal: now or later, which is better? *Micro*economics focuses on how households decide *what* to consume, e.g. apples or oranges. For *macro*economics, the emphasis is on

---

[1] Introspection often makes us sceptical about such assumptions. Who hasn't given in to the temptation of buying a pastry when not really hungry or a stereo system when short of cash? Such departures from rationality are in fact infrequent enough to be outweighed by a majority of well-thought-out decisions. This is why rationality in economics is the right way to approximate reality.

when to consume. For this reason, we make the simplifying assumption that there is only one good to consume (Robinson Crusoe's coconuts) and the focus is the choice between now and later.

6.2.1 **Optimal Consumption**

As Robinson Crusoe considers consuming the coconuts that he finds on the beach, he realizes that he can borrow or lend some of them through intertemporal trade with his neighbours. In fact, he may choose any combination of consumption today and consumption tomorrow as long as he remains on, or inside, his budget constraint. His choice depends on his preferences, which are described in Figure 6.2 by **indifference curves**. Each curve corresponds to a given level of **utility**, or well-being. A particular indifference curve represents combinations of consumption today and consumption tomorrow that leave Crusoe indifferent. Higher indifference curves correspond to higher levels of utility.

Two central aspects of indifference curves are their slope and their curvature. For a particular consumption combination, the slope of an indifference curve depicts Crusoe's willingness to swap consumption tomorrow for consumption today, holding utility constant. Where the curve is steep, for example, he is willing to give up a lot of future consumption to increase today's consumption. A flat curve indicates reluctance to give up consumption tomorrow for consumption today. The second aspect, the curvature, shows how the willingness to substitute consumption intertemporally depends on the relative abundance of consumption in the two periods. Moving along an indifference curve upwards and to the left, Crusoe is less and less willing to give up coconuts today as the expected consumption of coconuts tomorrow grows larger and larger. Box 6.1 provides more details on the phenomenon of intertemporal substitution.

Naturally, Crusoe wants to consume as much as possible in both periods, but he is restricted by his intertemporal budget, which is the straight line in

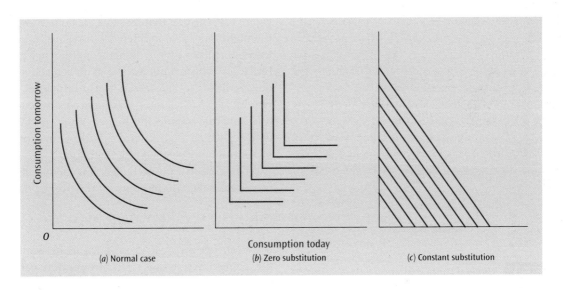

Fig. 6.2   **Indifference Curves**

Along any indifference curve, utility is constant. In panel (*a*), consumption tomorrow can be substituted smoothly for consumption today, but, as consumption today increases, at a decreasing rate. In (*b*), the consumer can be made better off only by increasing consumption today and tomorrow in fixed proportions. In (*c*), consumption today and consumption tomorrow are always substituted at the same rate. In all cases, indifference curves further up in the north-east direction correspond to higher utility levels.

Box 6.1 Indifference Curves and Intertemporal Substitution

The slope of the indifference curve shows how many units of goods tomorrow we are willing to give up for an additional unit of goods today. Along a given indifference curve, moving to the right, today's consumption increases while tomorrow's declines. The curve becomes flatter because we are willing to give up increasingly less consumption tomorrow for consumption today. The opposite occurs as we move up and to the left. The **marginal rate of intertemporal substitution** is represented by the slope of the curve.

The curvature of the indifference curve captures how readily the consumer substitutes consumption across time. In Figure 6.2, panel (a) describes the normal situation, but it is worth thinking about two opposite extremes. At one end of the spectrum, there can be no substitutability at all: the consumer is better off only if consumption is increased in fixed proportion in both periods. The indifference curves would look like the letter L in panel (b) of Figure 6.2. At the other end, the

marginal rate of substitution can be constant: the consumer is always willing to substitute the same amount of consumption today for consumption tomorrow. The indifference would be a straight downward-sloping line, as in panel (c).

Consider Figure 6.3, which characterizes optimal consumption. A key feature of point R in Figure 6.3 is that the marginal rate of substitution is just equal to the slope of the budget line, or $1 + r$. To see why, suppose that Crusoe is on his budget constraint but has a marginal rate of substitution of 1; he is willing to exchange one coconut today for one tomorrow. By lending 1 today, he gets $(1 + r)$ tomorrow, and can make himself better off, i.e. moving towards point R. If he goes too far, the marginal rate of substitution will exceed $(1 + r)$; he will then prefer to shift consumption back to the present and can increase his utility by doing so. Only when the marginal rate of substitution is equal to the intertemporal price of consumption has Crusoe exhausted the gains from intertemporal trade.

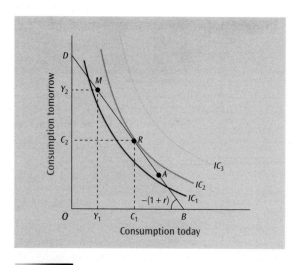

Fig. 6.3 Optimal Consumption

The budget line shows how much can be consumed today and tomorrow for given endowment (represented by point M) and real interest rate (the slope). Optimal consumption is achieved at point R. In this case the consumer borrows today $C_1 - Y_1$ and repays $Y_2 - C_2$ tomorrow. Consumption at R is also possible for an individual with endowment A, who lends today and dissaves tomorrow.

Figure 6.3. The best that he can do is point R, where the highest possible indifference curve just touches the budget line. A more desirable indifference curve like IC_3 is beyond his means, as it lies above his budget line. He can afford the utility level corresponding to IC_1 because this curve cuts the budget line, but can acquire the higher utility associated with IC_2, which is tangent to his budget line. Box 6.1 provides a more detailed interpretation.

When Crusoe is on his budget line, he spends his total wealth (OB) in the course of the two periods:

$$(6.1) \qquad C_1 + \frac{C_2}{1+r} = Y_1 + \frac{Y_2}{1+r} = \Omega.$$

If he can borrow or lend as much as he wants at the going interest rate, his consumption pattern over time depends only on the present *value* of his income—his budget constraint—and not on the particular *timing* of his income. In Figure 6.3, a 'student Crusoe' (with endowment M) borrows because his current income Y_1 is low relatively to his future income Y_2, while a 'professional athlete Crusoe' (endowment point A) with high current and low

Box 6.2   **Permanent Income and Life-Cycle Consumption**[2]

Most individuals or households do not expect a constant flow of income over their lifetimes. Typically, young people earn less than older people. The principle of optimal consumption implies that they should borrow when young and repay debts or even save when older in order to *smooth* the time profile of consumption.

Figure 6.4 displays a typical pattern of rising expected income and shows how **life-cycle consumption** would be chosen. To maintain a constant flow of consumption, the individual spends an amount corresponding to his or her **permanent income** each year. Permanent income is that income which, if constant, would deliver the same present value of income as the actual expected income path. It is a good measure of sustainable consumption over the time horizon of an individual.

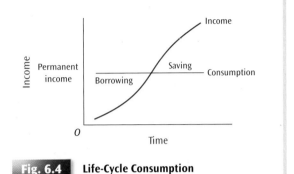

Fig. 6.4   **Life-Cycle Consumption**

When income is expected to increase over a lifetime, consumption smoothing implies borrowing when young and paying back when older.

future income will save. Since both individuals lie on the same budget line, they have the same wealth *OB*. If both have identical tastes as described by their indifference curves, saving and borrowing allows them to have identical consumption patterns. The associated principles of life-cycle and permanent income consumption are presented in Box 6.2.

6.2.2 **Implications**

Permanent versus temporary changes in income
How does Robinson Crusoe respond to a temporary increase in income? Imagine that today's harvest is unusually plentiful, rising to Y_1' in Figure 6.5, while next period's harvest Y_2 is expected to remain unchanged. For simplicity, the figure represents the case where, initially, consumption was exactly matching income in both periods so that there was no need to borrow or lend (points *A* and *R* overlap). The endowment point now shifts from *A* to *A'*, on

the new budget line *B'D'*, which is parallel to the initial line *BD* since the real interest rate remains unchanged. It is natural to expect that Crusoe will consume more. However, the key insight is that his consumption (point *R'*) will rise in *both* periods. Consumption today increases less than the windfall, as he saves some of it to spread over time. A temporary increase in income is accompanied by a permanent, but smaller, increase in consumption.

What if, instead, the increase in income is permanent, in the sense that both Y_1 and Y_2 rise by equal amounts? (Think of a lasting improvement in the harvest outlook, or an enduring improvement in Crusoe's coconut technology!) The new endowment point is *A''* and the corresponding budget line is *B''D''*. Optimal consumption moves to point *R''*. As a first approximation, points *A''* and *R''* coincide and consumption rises in both periods.[3] Being equally better off in both periods, Crusoe sees no reason to save or borrow. A permanent increase in income is absorbed in a permanent increase in consumption of similar size.

---

[2] The permanent income hypothesis was developed in the late 1950s by Chicago economist Milton Friedman and was cited as his main contribution when he was awarded the Nobel Prize. The life-cycle theory of consumption was also recognized by the Nobel Prize committee as an important contribution of MIT economist Franco Modigliani.

[3] This is only an approximation. Impatient consumers may bring forward some of tomorrow's windfall, whereas more patient agents would save some of today's windfall for tomorrow's consumption.

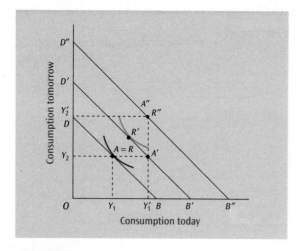

Fig. 6.5 Temporary and Permanent Income Changes

The shift from A to A' describes a temporary increase in income. Consumption rises both today and tomorrow. (The household moves from R to R'.) Part of today's income windfall is saved to sustain higher spending tomorrow. The shift to point A" represents a permanent increase in income. It does not require consumption smoothing through saving or borrowing. The best course of action is permanently to increase consumption (to point R").

Finally, consider the case when income is unchanged today, but is correctly expected to increase tomorrow. If Robinson knows that his future crop will be more plentiful, he will borrow today against his future income to afford a better standard of living immediately. This type of behaviour, far from being thriftless or incautious, actually makes him better off.

An implication of this reasoning is that only new information should alter consumption behaviour. If future incomes are correctly anticipated, they will be incorporated into current wealth and current consumption will fully reflect this information. The only reason why consumption will change is if unexpected disturbances affect income, either current or future, so that wealth is changed. Since all that is known of the future is already taken into account in the evaluation of wealth, only true surprises can alter wealth and therefore consumption. Put differently, changes in consumption must be unpredictable. This is known as the **random walk**

theory of consumption, because changes in consumption should be random.[4]

Consumption smoothing and the current account

The common theme behind the three cases examined above is that people generally dislike highly variable consumption patterns. When faced with a temporary change in income, rational consumers save or borrow to spread the effects on consumption over time. In bad times, this may take the form of dissaving (spending from accumulated savings) or borrowing (from the bank, from relatives, or using a credit card). In good times, consumers accumulate assets or repay their debts. This phenomenon is known as **consumption smoothing**. It explains why consumption is less variable than GDP in Figure 6.1, and is in general the most stable component of aggregate demand.

This does not mean that consumption is *always* more stable than GDP. Since the evolution of actual GDP is a mixture of permanent and temporary disturbances, consumption will on average reflect the nature of this mixture, responding more to permanent than to temporary changes. Indeed, there are times when consumption is more unstable than GDP. A good example is the case when income is expected to fall in the future: consumption spending declines immediately while income is still stable. The subsequent fall in GDP is then frequently seen as being caused by the consumption shortfall, while in fact it is simply the correctly anticipated consequence. Box 6.3 presents an example where consumption seems to have preceded GDP when the Czech Republic was entering into a recession.

Consumption smoothing is possible because Crusoe borrows when facing a temporary loss of income today or a windfall tomorrow, and saves when benefiting from a temporary gain or expected future bad times. Saving and borrowing play the role of a buffer in the presence of transitory income disturbances. Moving from a particular individual to the country as a whole, the logic remains the same

---

[4] The random walk theory of consumption was formulated by Robert Hall of Stanford University. It is surprisingly difficult to reject empirically.

Box 6.3   **Boom and Bust in the Czech Republic, 1997–2000**

After a few successful years of transition, the Czech economy started to slow down in late 1996. Then in the Spring its currency, the koruna, faced attacks and the Czech central bank was forced to devalue. Confidence in the Czech miracle faded. Figure 6.6 shows that the real GDP growth turned negative in early 1997 and did not go back to positive until 1999. There is very little evidence that consumption was being smoothed during this period. In fact the sharp decline from mid-1996 dragged the GDP downward much as its sudden recovery in early 1999 preceded the resumption of GDP growth. Were Czech consumers busy disproving economic principles? Two more likely interpretations run as follows. In 1996, the government started to implement policies designed to reduce the growing budget deficit, including raising taxes, which undoubtedly hurt consumer confidence. More importantly, the Czech Republic—seen as one of the most successful transition countries—had enjoyed a large inflow of foreign capital which led to a consumption boom in 1994–5. This inflow quickly reversed itself when the economy started to slow down, drying the financial market. Anticipating bad times, consumers cut down on spending. An interesting question indeed is how much the Czech slump in consumption anticipated the bust, and how much it actually *caused* it. To answer it, we will need to know much more about the way income is determined—and that is the material of later chapters.

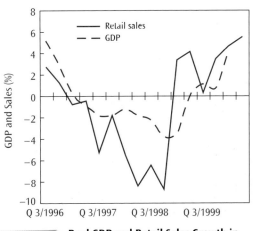

Fig. 6.6   **Real GDP and Retail Sales Growth in the Czech Republic, 1996–2000**

In the mid-1990s, growth of consumption—here represented by retail sales—in this relatively successful transforming economy slowed sharply. This slowdown was followed by a downturn in GDP. Similarly late in 1998, an upturn in retails sales seems to anticipate the general improvement in economic conditions observed from 1999 onward. Deciding whether the swings in consumption 'caused' the output fluctuations or simply 'anticipated' them is an important and recurrent question posed in macroeconomics.

but the mechanics are slightly trickier. When Mr Crusoe lends to fellow resident Mr Friday, there is no change in aggregate saving. At the country level, net borrowing or lending can only be vis-à-vis the rest of the world: saving or borrowing takes place through the primary current account.

The consequence of aggregate consumption smoothing, therefore, is temporary imbalances in the primary current account. Recall from (3.22) that the primary current account is GDP less domestic spending:

(6.2) $PCA = Y - (C + I + G).$

If GDP declines while investment and public spending remain unchanged, consumption smoothing implies a worsening PCA. Similarly, a temporary increase in GDP would lead to a temporary surplus. For most countries, primary current accounts are typically small and oscillate around zero. To some extent these may be regarded as an optimal response to temporary shifts in incomes. A specific example reviewed in Box 6.4 is the reaction to the oil price increases that occurred in the 1970s.

Consumption and the real interest rate

When the real interest rate rises, so do the rewards to saving. Put differently, the price of consumption tomorrow in terms of consumption today declines. Will saving always increase and consumption always decline? The question is harder to answer than it

---

Box 6.4 **Oil Shocks and European Current Accounts**

Oil prices have increased abruptly three times in the past quarter-century. At the end of 1973 they quadrupled. They doubled in several instalments over 1979–80, and increased by 50% in 1990, after a marked decline in 1986 (Figure 6.7). For most European countries which are heavily dependent on oil for their energy needs, an oil shock can be thought of as a reduction in income.[5] Even if the price increase is permanent, the short-run impact is larger than in the long run because conservation can attenuate this effect over time. Oil-importing countries should respond by running current account deficits, while oil and energy exporting countries would be expected to show large surpluses. Figure 6.8 shows that Europe, comprising mostly oil-importing countries, underwent a current account deficit after each shock, and a surplus after the counter-shock of 1986. Yet some European countries are energy-exporters and benefit from oil shocks. This is the case of the Netherlands, which exports natural gas, the price of which moves along with that of oil. The Dutch current account stands in sharp contrast with that of most countries in Europe, which are heavy importers of oil. After each shock, these current accounts appear to be the mirror image of each other.

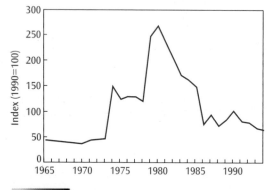

Fig. 6.7 **Real Price of Crude Oil, 1965–1994**

The real price of oil is computed as the ratio of the US dollar price of crude oil to the consumer price index of all industrialized countries.
Source: IMF.

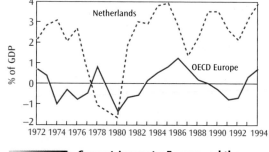

Fig. 6.8 **Current Accounts: Europe and the Netherlands, 1972–1994**

As an importer of oil, Europe suffered an income loss at the time of the oil shocks. Consumption smoothing calls for temporary borrowing now (current account deficit) and repayment later (current account surplus). The Netherlands, a gas exporter, experienced a temporary windfall which was saved abroad through current account surpluses.
Sources: OECD *Economic Outlook*; IMF.

---

first appears. Figure 6.9 shows that the effect on consumption today depends on whether Crusoe is a net borrower (e.g. a student) or a net lender (e.g. a professional athlete). Since endowments today and tomorrow are unchanged in both panels of

the figure, the budget line rotates around point *A*. Optimal consumption shifts from point *R* to point *R'*. Net lenders gain from higher interest rates, moving to a higher indifference curve and consuming more in both periods. The borrower who faces higher interest costs is in the opposite situation, as he must devote more resources to debt service, and his current consumption declines. Increases in interest rates have important redistributive effects between borrowers and lenders: an increase hurts the former and benefits the latter.

The effect of the interest rate on consumption is ambiguous because it works through two channels.

[5] At the time it was not obvious whether these shocks were temporary or permanent. Fig. 6.6 strongly suggests that they were temporary, but back in the mid-1970s or early 1980s Fig. 6.6 was not available, and the oil price increase was often regarded as permanent. Milton Friedman was a lone voice in the wilderness when he wrote in 1975: 'Almost regardless of our energy policy, the OPEC cartel will break down. That is assured by a world-wide reduction in crude-oil consumption and expansion in alternative supplies in response to high prices. The only question is how long it will take' (*Newsweek*, 17 Feb. 1975).

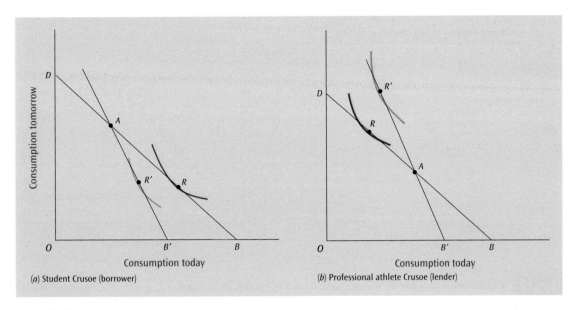

(a) Student Crusoe (borrower)

(b) Professional athlete Crusoe (lender)

Fig. 6.9   **The Effect of an Increase in the Interest Rate**

As the interest rate increases, the budget line becomes steeper and rotates about the endowment point A. The response of the consumer depends on whether she is a borrower or a lender. The borrower (a) will tend to consume less today because the interest rate at which resources are brought forward has increased. The lender (b) consumes more today, since the same amount of lending can increase the amount of consumption possible tomorrow without reducing today's.

First, it increases the cost of goods today compared with those tomorrow. An increase in the interest rate makes the budget constraint steeper, since it determines the slope of the intertemporal budget constraint. Second, it reduces the value of wealth Ω, which is the present discounted value of all income.

6.2.3 Wealth or Income?

An old tradition in macroeconomics which can be traced back to Keynes relates aggregate consumption to disposable income Y^d, roughly GDP less net taxes. The argument is simple: people set aside a fraction of disposable income for saving, and consume the rest.[6] Yet, a key implication of the theory developed in the previous sections is that consumption is driven by wealth, not current income. This is what consumption smoothing is all about. Figure 6.10 shows the evidence for France. The available measure of wealth includes liquid financial assets of families as well as the value of their fixed assets and real estate. The link between consumption and

[6] This is the assumption used in Ch. 3 by the Solow growth model.

disposable income is strong, in fact stronger than between consumption and wealth.

One possible explanation is that income and wealth grow in tandem, so that the observed consumption–income relationship may reflect a common dependence on wealth. Yet wealth appears more volatile than disposable income, partly because of fluctuations in share prices on stock markets. It could then be that households look on stock market gains and losses as temporary and only pay limited attention to short-term volatility. Another possible explanation is that private wealth is not well known, in part because people are very reluctant to provide truthful information about their assets, in part because expected future income—an important component of wealth—is not measurable and therefore left out.

A more fundamental explanation is related to a household's ability to borrow and lend. The Crusoe parable assumes that the representative household can borrow freely at a given interest rate. This might be the case if present and future incomes of individual households—against which borrowing

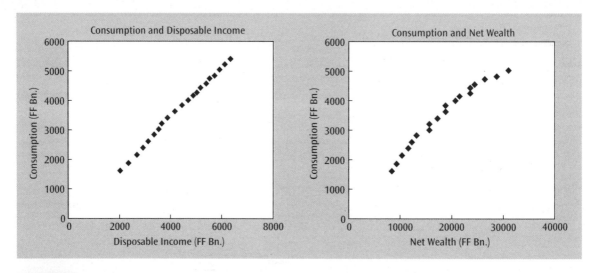

Fig. 6.10   **Consumption, Disposable Income, and Wealth in France, 1980–2000**

The link between consumption and wealth is quite strong, but less tight than the link between consumption and disposable income. *Source*: OECD.

is pledged—were known with certainty to lenders. In real life, banks and other lending intermediaries cannot know the repayment prospects of all individual borrowers with certainty. A common banking practice is to demand collateral—the borrower pledges tangible wealth such as a house in case of non-payment. This option is not available to all households. Banks charge higher interest rates to customers who appear riskier and sometimes refuse to lend at any rate, or place ceilings on the amount that can be borrowed. Consumers who cannot obtain credit in spite of future earnings potential are said to be **credit rationed**.

In the presence of credit rationing, spending is governed by current disposable income, not wealth.[7] This is shown in Figure 6.11, which uses Figure 5.11 as its point of departure. Here Robinson Crusoe is completely prevented from borrowing. His consumption possibilities are limited to the kinked line *CAB*. In particular, he cannot reach the segment *AD* of his intertemporal budget constraint and thus his preferred consumption pattern *R* is not possible. In that case, the best option for him is to be at point

A, where he consumes exactly his income in both periods. If a significant proportion of households is rationed in credit markets, disposable income also will influence consumption, along with wealth, which only matters for non-rationed households. Box 6.5 illustrates the importance of national

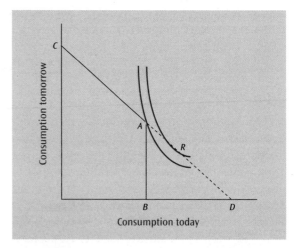

Fig. 6.11   **Credit Constraints**

If Crusoe cannot borrow, his budget constraint shrinks from *CD* to *CA*. He would like to be at point *R*, however, borrowing today and paying back tomorrow. The best outcome for him under the circumstances is to consume at point *A*, with consumption equal to income both today and tomorrow.

---

[7] Ch. 5 provides a detailed treatment of interest rates and credit rationing. It also shows that with credit rationing, Ricardian equivalence will not hold for those who would like to borrow, so that current taxes affect current consumption as well, hence the relevance of disposable income as opposed to GDP.

Box 6.5   **Current Income and Spending in East Germany and Poland**

The swift conversion of East Germany (the former German Democratic Republic) and Poland to market-based economies in 1990 provides a unique example of an anticipated increase in permanent income. In both countries, the adoption of market-based institutions implied that income levels would eventually reach Western Europe's. The transition to a market economy however is painful, possibly leading to an initial fall in income as inefficient production capacity is shut down and workers change occupations and industries. While current observable income falls, wealth is rising because future incomes are so much larger than before. Faced with an expected windfall, optimal consumption rises, both now and in the future. Actual current consumption can increase only if people are able to borrow. As part of German unification, the citizens of the Eastern Länder had access to a well-developed domestic financial market. For the former East Germany, borrowing 'abroad' meant becoming customers of West German banks, or recipients of credits or grants from the government. On the other hand, Poland started with a large external debt preventing its government from further borrowing, and its citizens and firms certainly did not have access to foreign bank credit despite high growth. Figure 6.12 shows the dramatic difference. While GDP fell in East Germany after 1990, private consumption there rose to equal total East German GDP. Public spending and private investment also rose, bringing the current account deficit to nearly 100% of GDP. In credit-constrained Poland, on the other side, spending tracked income. Because of its large external debt, Poland actually had to run a primary surplus. In contrast, East Germany's large external debt was assumed by West Germany.

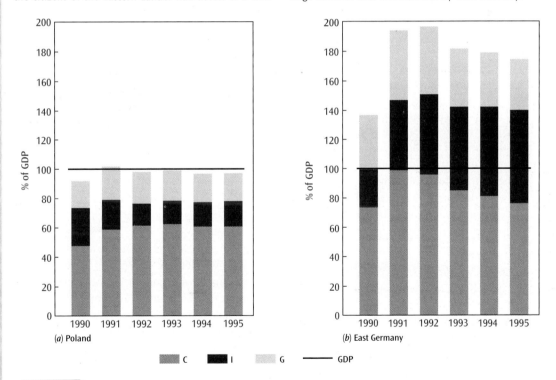

(a) Poland   (b) East Germany

C   I   G   ——— GDP

Fig. 6.12   **GDP, Domestic Demand, and the Current Account: Poland and East Germany**

Spending in East Germany rose after unification as firms, citizens, and authorities were able to borrow against higher expected future income. There is no link between consumption and spending as 'foreign' borrowing is almost as large as income. In Poland, which has similar long-run growth prospects, spending follows income because of the impossibility of borrowing large amounts abroad.

Sources: DIW Wochenbericht; World Bank; CSO; DGII.

borrowing constraints in the early phase of the process of economic transformation in Eastern Europe. But even in advanced countries, credit rationing affects a substantial proportion of households. It is therefore not surprising to observe the tight link between consumption and disposable income in Figure 6.10.

6.2.4 **The Consumption Function**

Let us now summarize the results set out thus far. Consumption is driven primarily by wealth, and wealth is based on current and discounted future incomes of households. In practice, many people are unable to borrow even though their expected future income is higher. For them, disposable income is the effective determinant of consumption. This, along with the fact that income and wealth tend to grow together, means that consumption seems to be

better explained by disposable income. In fact, both matter, as can be seen from the example in Box 6.5 and as is apparent in Figure 6.10. Section 6.2.2 also notes that the real interest rate affects consumption, but its direct role is ambiguous. In all likelihood, a negative effect of interest rates on consumption is most likely to occur indirectly through wealth: a rise in interest rates reduces wealth and consumption. In the end, we capture these various effects by writing down the consumption function, a compact notation linking consumption to its two main determinants

$$\textbf{(6.3)} \qquad C = C(\Omega, Y^d).$$
$$\qquad\qquad\qquad\quad + \quad +$$

The *plus* signs underneath reminds us that consumption increases with both wealth Ω and disposable income Y^d. This is the fundamental formulation that will be used in the rest of this textbook.

6.3 Investment

The second category of private spending decisions to be explained is investment, or gross domestic capital formation. Investment goods are not intended for consumption. They include machine tools, computers, office furniture, land-moving equipment, buses, and construction of new factory buildings, as well as increases in inventories to be sold at a future date. All these goods have the common trait that they enable the production of goods and services in the future. The decision to invest is therefore an intertemporal decision.

6.3.1 **The Optimal Capital Stock**

The amount of output that can be produced by a representative firm is described by the production function $Y = F(K)$, which gives output of coconuts Y available tomorrow when Crusoe plants K coconuts today on his bare desert island. The production function is depicted in panel (*a*) of Figure 6.13.[8] A

related concept is the **marginal productivity of capital (MPK)**. This is the amount of extra output that can be obtained when an additional unit of capital is installed ($\Delta Y/\Delta K$), and can be measured as the slope of the production function.[9] Because of the principle of declining marginal productivity, the MPK declines as more capital is put in place, as is shown in panel (*b*).

We looked at the return from capital, what about the costs? When he decides to save a coconut, Crusoe can always choose between planting it or lending it to inhabitants of neighbouring islands. In the latter case, he can expect to receive 'tomorrow' the coconut plus interest. Or else, if he does not have enough savings, he can borrow a coconut, and pay

---

[8] This paragraph summarizes the exposition of the firm's budget constraint in S. 5.4 of Ch. 5.

[9] To see why, imagine a point on the curve. An increase ΔK in the stock of capital is represented as a horizontal move from the initial point. How much output ΔY is available? It is measured as the vertical distance which brings us back to the production function. The ratio $\Delta Y/\Delta K$ is the slope of the line connecting the point of departure and the point of arrival back on the production function. As the initial step ΔK is made shorter, this slope becomes the slope of the curve itself. (Formally, the line becomes tangent to the curve.)

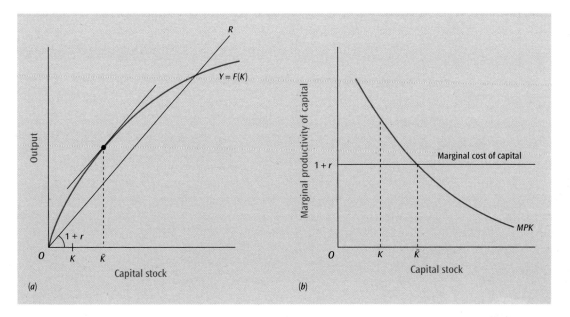

Fig. 6.13   **The Optimal Capital Stock**

The optimal stock of capital $\bar{K}$ is achieved when the firm's production function is farthest from the line OR, which represents the cost of capital. There the marginal productivity of capital is equal to its marginal cost (MPK = $1 + r$). Investment is the difference between the desired capital stock $\bar{K}$ and the previously accumulated capital stock K.

back principal and interest. The same is true for any firm. If the investment is financed by resources that could instead be invested in financial assets, the **opportunity cost** of the investment is $(1 + r)$. If the investment is financed by borrowing, the **marginal cost** of investment is $(1 + r)$.[10] In both cases, the cost is the same, it is shown in panel (a) of Figure 6.13 as the ray OR. The ray represents the total cost, $(1 + r)K$, of capital installed today and productive tomorrow, the sum of the principal and the interest charged. (The cost of equipment here is unity because it takes one coconut to start a tree.) The marginal cost of capital, or the cost of one incremental unit of productive capacity, is simply $(1 + r)$. It is represented in panel (b) by a horizontal line.

The firm's profit in the second period is the difference between what it produces and the cost of production:

(6.4) $$\text{Profit} = F(K) - K(1 + r).$$

In panel (a), this is measured as the vertical distance between the curve depicting the production function and the ray OR. To maximize profit, the manager chooses the **optimal capital stock** $\bar{K}$ such that the distance between the two schedules is as large as possible. This occurs where the slope of the production schedule (given by its tangent) is equal to the slope of the cost-of-capital schedule OR. Then the marginal productivity of capital (MPK) is equal to the marginal, or opportunity, cost $1 + r$. (Box 6.6 provides an extension of this result.)

(6.5) $$MPK \quad = \quad 1 + r.$$
$$\underset{\text{marginal productivity}}{} \quad \underset{\text{marginal cost}}{}$$
marginal productivity   marginal cost
of capital   of capital

In Figure 6.13(b), the optimal capital stock $\bar{K}$ corresponds to the intersection of the MPK and marginal cost curves.

If each and every firm behaves optimally, the same principles can be applied to the economy as a whole. Two conclusions follow. First, the optimal

[10] Some precision is required for the careful reader. Presumably, capital can be resold. Here we assume that Crusoe abandons his coconut grove upon rescue. If he could sell it, the expected resale value comes as a deduction of the cost of investment. Box 6.6 elaborates on this point.

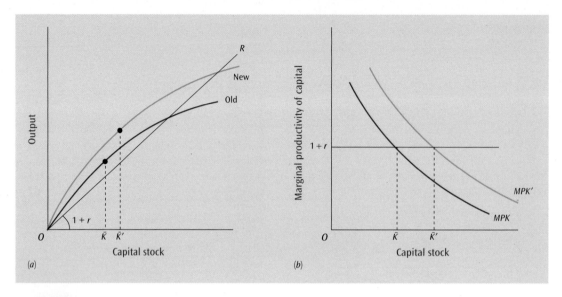

Fig. 6.14   **Technological Progress**

Technological progress makes more output possible with the same stock of capital. In panel (*a*) the production schedule shifts upward. In panel (*b*) the MPK schedule moves up to the right. The optimal stock of capital is now $\bar{K}'$, larger than initial $\bar{K}$.

capital stock depends positively on the expected effectiveness of the available technology, captured by the marginal productivity of capital. An improvement in technology or technological progress means that more output can be produced with the same capital stock. In Figure 6.14, the production function in panel (*a*) and the MPK schedule in panel (*b*) both shift upward. The optimal stock of capital increases from $\bar{K}$ to $\bar{K}'$. Second, the optimal capital stock depends negatively on the real interest rate. If the real interest rate increases, the cost schedule *OR* rotates counter-clockwise in Figure 6.14(*a*) and the marginal cost schedule shifts upward in panel (*b*). The intuition behind this important result is that, for a given state of technology, higher opportunity costs of capital reduce the amount of capital that can be employed and still be more profitable than simply 'lending' the resources in the financial markets.

6.3.2 **Investment and the Real Interest Rate**

Investment is carried out for two purposes: to bring the capital stock to its desired level, and to make

up for capital lost through physical or economic depreciation.[11] In Figure 6.13, we can find the optimal stock of capital $\bar{K}$ and the stock of capital inherited from past investment K—perhaps there were already some coconut trees around when Crusoe came to his island. Ignoring depreciation, optimal investment is simply the difference $\bar{K} - K$. Thus, given the accumulated stock of capital so far and the rate of depreciation, the determinants of optimal investment are the same as those of the optimal stock of capital. An increase in the real interest rate which lowers the optimal stock of capital also lowers optimal investment, since the pre-existing capital stock and the rate of depreciation remain unchanged. Accordingly, the investment function could be expressed as

(6.6) $$I = I(r).$$

---

[11] From Box 5.3 we know that $\Delta K = I - \delta K$, where ΔK is the increase in the stock of capital, δ is the rate of depreciation, and therefore δK is the amount of capital that was used up. This decomposition can be rewritten as $I = \Delta K + \delta K$, which shows that I—gross investment—must cover ΔK—net investment—as well as replacing depreciated capital.

Box 6.6   **Looking Beyond the Next Period and Taking Account of Capital Depreciation**

The two-period approach implicitly assumes that when Crusoe is rescued at the end of the second period he abandons his capital stock. But what if he sells it to Friday, who chooses to stay on the island? If there is a 'resale market', the results will change in an important way. When stating, as in (6.5), that the marginal cost of capital equals its marginal product, we need to include the resale value of capital as part of the firm's income. For simplicity, suppose the price of trees is equal to one (coconut). Then the optimal condition is

(6.7) MPK + 1 = $1 + r$.

marginal product   resale value   marginal cost

The cost of capital is 1, the same as the value of output since these are all coconuts. This condition can be rewritten more simply as:

(6.8) $MPK = r$.

The marginal product of capital need only be equal to the real interest rate, rather than $1 + r$ when Crusoe needed to recoup the principal of his investment. In practice, firms can usually resell their equipment at some

price, so they will require a lower productivity because they take into account the value of their equipment. So equation (6.8) rather than (6.5) is more likely to be relevant in practice. It is important to note that this does not invalidate the investment function (6.6).

But the story continues: an additional element of realism recognizes that installed capital is being worn out over time, or becomes economically obsolete. The decaying of equipment can be captured by a **rate of depreciation** δ. Tomorrow's value of today's capital is not 1 but $1 - \delta$. Taking this into account, (6.8) becomes

(6.9) MPK + $1 - \delta$ = $1 + r$.

marginal product   resale value   marginal cost

which can be simplified as

(6.10) $MPK = r + \delta$.

Here the marginal or **user cost of capital** is equal to the sum of the interest rate r and the rate of depreciation δ. Depreciation can be thought of as an additional cost of capital. From (6.11) the original case can be regarded a special case in which depreciation is complete ($\delta = 1$).

6.3.3 The Accelerator Principle

In contrast to Crusoe's treeless island, in the real world some capital stock already exists. It could be expected that, in order for the capital stock to reach its optimal level derived in Section 6.3.1, investment would have to move in roughly the same proportion. This idea gives rise to a simple way of thinking about investment. Suppose the optimal capital stock is proportional to the expected output level:

(6.11) $\bar{K}_2 = vY_2,$

which can be justified both theoretically and empirically.[12] Then, when firms invest to keep the capital

stock at its optimal level, an increase of GDP from Y_1 to Y_2 requires a change from $\bar{K}_1 = vY_1$ to $\bar{K}_2 = vY_2$. Ignoring depreciation, this means an investment of:

(6.12) $I_1 = \bar{K}_2 - \bar{K}_1 = v(Y_2 - Y_1) = v\Delta Y_2.$

This relationship captures the **accelerator principle**. Any expected increase in real GDP requires a matching increase in the capital stock. In practice, the capital–output ratio v is between 2 and 3. (Annual GDP represents between one-third and one-half of the installed capital stock.) GDP movements therefore are associated with much larger changes (an 'acceleration') in investment.[13] This provides one reason why investment is more volatile than GDP: it is based on expectations of the future. In the following sections we will develop this idea in greater detail.

---

[12] The long-run stability of the capital–output ratio is stressed in Ch. 5. Consider the case of the Cobb–Douglas production function $Y = AK^\alpha$. Here marginal productivity is $MPK = \partial Y/\partial K = \alpha AK^{\alpha-1} = \alpha Y/K$. The optimal capital stock is K^* such that $MPK = 1 + r$, so $\alpha Y/K^* = 1 + r$, and $K^* = \alpha Y/(1 + r)$. Setting $v = \alpha/(1 + r)$ gives (6.12).

[13] To account for depreciation, (6.12) is simply changed to $I_1 = v\Delta Y + \delta K_1$. The same conclusions apply.

6.3.4 **Investment and Tobin's *q***

Why do observers of the economic scene continuously monitor the evolution of stock markets? Prices of shares often move in erratic ways which may not seem particularly related to economic activity. In fact, stock prices are intimately related to macroeconomics. Aggregate economic activity affects stock prices, and stock prices are important determinants of aggregate economic activity. One important link is via wealth: when stock prices rise, shareholders become richer and spend more. Another link, which is our focus here, is investment.

Shares in publicly traded companies are titles of ownership. They represent claims on firms' present and future profits. Profits are the difference between firms' sales and their costs, which are mostly wages when the economy as a whole is considered. Share prices can be thought of as the market's best estimate of the value of those present and future profits. This value may differ from the price of the capital goods that constitute the firm itself, which is sometimes called the replacement cost of a firm's capital stock.

For a number of reasons, it is likely that the market value of a firm will differ from the replacement cost of its physical capital. One such reason is the existence of intangible assets which include by such factors as the firm's know-how, its network of distributors and retailers, its reputation among customers, etc. A more important reason, from the point of view of macroeconomics, is the fact that 'Rome wasn't built in a day'. Establishing a new firm from scratch requires time and resources. These costs are greater, the more rapidly an investment project is undertaken. To summarize this, we define a ratio, called **Tobin's *q***, which is defined as follows:[14]

(6.13) Tobin's q

$$= \frac{\text{market value of installed capital}}{\text{replacement cost of installed capital}}.$$

[14] It is named after US economist and Nobel laureate James Tobin, who in 1969 pointed out the relevance of the ratio of market valuation of the firm's stock market to the replacement value of the firm's capital stock. In the meantime, more sophisticated analyses have shown the conditions under which this average q concept is equal to the marginal concept presented in the text. For our purposes, we will simply assume that these conditions are met.

The numerator of Tobin's q is the firm's value as priced on the stock market, the total value of all existing shares. The denominator is the amount that would have to be spent to replace the capital goods incorporated in existing firms.

The **q-theory of investment** relates the behaviour of aggregate investment to Tobin's q. When Tobin's q is greater than unity, installed capital is more valuable than what it cost to purchase it, and investment is positive. For example, a Tobin's q of 1.2 would imply that a firm that spends 100 on investment increases its market value by 120. Installation adds a value of 20 to uninstalled equipment. Given the principle of declining marginal productivity, investment reduces the return on the capital over time and therefore reduces Tobin's q. Firms will continue to invest until Tobin's q has returned to unity. Alternatively, when q is lower than 1, selling off equipment at replacement cost would be profitable for the firm's shareholders, so investment should be negative. If installed equipment cannot be resold, at least investment should stop and the capital stock be allowed to decline through depreciation. The dependence of investment on Tobin's q is displayed in Figure 6.15.

How is the q-theory related to the previous section, which showed that the interest rate is a key determinant of investment? The market values firms by discounting future earnings using the real interest rate. Any increase in the rate leads to heavier

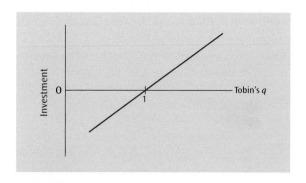

Fig. 6.15 **The q-theory of Investment**

When Tobin's q is larger than 1, it pays for firms to invest. When Tobin's q is less than 1, there is no incentive to invest, but rather an incentive to disinvest, or to dismantle or abandon productive capacity.

discounting and therefore to a decline in stock prices. Thus, the negative effect of the real interest rate on investment is actually incorporated into Tobin's q. But Tobin's q does more than just take the interest rate into account; it also incorporates two other factors in the investment decision. First, gains in productivity of capital raise future income, and thereby increase share prices and q. Second, q incorporates the role of expectations. Inevitably, investment is a bet on the future: firms buy equipment now to produce output for several years under uncertain conditions. How they will be able to take advantage of the equipment is not known when the investment occurs. Uncertainty ranges from the general economic situation, to competition in domestic and foreign markets, to the evolution of technology and even political developments. All these aspects are continuously evaluated by the stock markets. Forward-looking share prices are volatile because these factors are volatile, and in the end this explains why investment is the most volatile component of GDP. This dependence on fleeting expectations led Keynes to assert that volatile patterns of investment reflect the **animal spirits** of entrepreneurs, that is, their expectations of the future profitability of investment. It is exactly this volatility that is evident in Figure 6.1.

Figure 6.16 shows that Tobin's q typically leads investment.[15] The link is quite strong, with a variable but relatively short lag. Yet not all companies are publicly traded; in fact, most firms are too small to issue shares, and many larger ones are reluctant to 'go public'. It is often cheaper for firms to draw on their own savings (retained earnings) because profits are usually taxed less when reinvested than when distributed. Some firms prefer to finance investment by borrowing rather than by issuing shares; especially in continental Europe, bank lending plays an important if not dominant role. For these firms, Tobin's q still adequately measures the incentive to invest: it reflects both expected profitability—the numerator—and the real cost of borrowing through the discount factor and the cost of capital—the denominator.

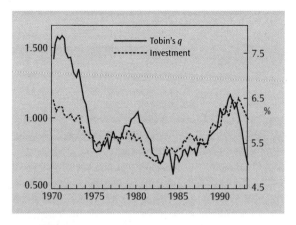

Fig. 6.16 **The Rate of Investment and Tobin's *q*, Germany 1970:1–1993:2**

Investment generally follows movements of Tobin's *q*.
Note: Tobin's *q* is computed by the authors (as marginal *q*).
Source: Bloch and Coeuré (1994).

Tobin's q explains why there is a link between national stock markets and the state of the national economy. The economic function of stock exchanges is to evaluate the future profitability of firms and to place a value today for the whole stream of future earnings from capital ownership. For the macroeconomy as a whole, average stock prices represent the value of the capital stock in place. Financial markets also assess the degree of riskiness related to unavoidable uncertainty, and this is factored into share prices. Present and especially future economic conditions affect stock prices. Conversely, we should expect stock markets to affect economic conditions since stock prices influence investment through Tobin's q.

6.3.5 **The Microeconomic Foundations of Tobin's *q*[16]**

Installation costs

We have now seen two reasons for a firm to invest. The first one is to reach the optimal stock of capital.

---

[15] As in the text, the rate of investment is the ratio of investment to the capital stock (I/K).

[16] This section is a more advanced presentation of the q-theory of investment based on the notion of installation costs. It shows the similarity with the reasoning used to establish the optimal stock of capital. It can be skipped without any loss of continuity. The Appendix presents a formal analysis.

The second one is to take advantage of the difference between the value of installed capital and its replacement cost. We would expect firms to seize such opportunities quickly. In practice, however, firms do not adjust the capital stock instantaneously to its optimal level. For this reason q can differ systematically from unity for a long time. One reason for this is that firms face **installation costs** in addition to the direct costs considered so far.

The idea behind installation costs is simple. With adequate resources, it could have been possible to dig the Eurotunnel in just six months. Doing so, however, would have been enormously 'costly' in many ways, so it was completed over several years instead. Intuitively, the bigger the investment per unit of time, the more costly it is to install it. Examples of installation costs include the fact that each addition of new equipment in a factory disrupts existing production and that workers must be trained to operate new equipment.

Installation costs explain why Tobin's q is not always equal to unity. In their absence, firms would promptly bring capital to its optimal stock level, equating marginal productivity and marginal cost as in equation (6.6), which can be rewritten as

$$(6.14) \qquad \frac{MPK}{1 + r} = 1.$$

$MPK/(1 + r)$ is the present value of the return on investment: it is next period's return on the latest addition of capital discounted back to today.[17] It must be equal to the marginal cost of equipment which is unity. When installation is costly, however, the cost of investing is not just the price of equipment: it now includes an additional cost, the marginal cost of installing new equipment, φ. This installation cost can be thought of as equipment which is 'eaten up' in the installation process. Furthermore, φ is an increasing function of the investment undertaken.[18] The optimal investment decision is to invest until the present value of the

MPK of new equipment is equal to the augmented marginal cost of equipment:

$$(6.15) \qquad \frac{MPK}{1 + r} = 1 + \varphi.$$

Comparing (6.14) and (6.15), we see that installation costs raise the MPK required to justify the investment. This can be achieved by aiming at a capital stock lower than $\bar{K}$, since marginal productivity is higher the lower is the stock of capital. If installation costs increase with the size of investment, once this level is reached, the next round of installation is cheaper, φ is lower, so firms will engage into more investment, and so on until φ is driven down to zero and (6.14) holds. That way firms break the path towards $\bar{K}$ into small steps which entail smaller costs.

Installation costs and Tobin's q

The stock market should value the return on an additional unit of investment by the present value of its marginal return, $MPK/(1 + r)$. In the case of Robinson Crusoe, the replacement cost of capital is simply the cost of coconuts (uninstalled equipment) which is 1. Tobin's q is therefore[19]

$$(6.16) \qquad q = \left(\frac{MPK}{1 + r} \right) \Big/ 1.$$

Equation (6.4) establishes the link between the two investment principles. The optimal capital stock of capital is reached when (6.5) is satisfied, that is when Tobin's q is equal to 1. When q is above 1, the MPK is larger than $1 + r$ and investment is warranted. When q is lower than 1, the MPK is low given the replacement cost of physical capital. As new capital is put in place, the MPK declines, as does q. Investment becomes smaller and installation costs φ decline until they become negligible. At that stage $q = 1$, $MPK = 1 + r$, and the stock of capital is at its optimal level. Installation costs cause firms to move towards the optimal capital stock incrementally; along the

---

[17] Remember, there are just two periods, so 'tomorrow' is a shorthand for the indefinite future. Otherwise we would have to discount all future MPKs.

[18] For example, the investment costs associated with a 10% increase in the capital stock could be four times the costs implied by a 5% increase.

[19] We cheat a bit here. The definition of Tobin's q is based on the market value of firms, while what matters in theory is the *marginal* return on investment. The market value of firms depends on the *average* return on all capital, not just the latest addition. We overlook the difference between these two definitions of average and marginal q.

Box 6.7   **The User Cost of Capital and the Price of Investment Goods**

In Robinson Crusoe's world, coconuts were used for both consumption and investment. In the real world, investment and consumption goods are different and have different prices. This complicates slightly, but does not invalidate, the main line of reasoning. Let p^k be the relative price of investment goods, defined as P^K/P, where P is the euro price of consumption goods and P^K the euro price of capital goods. If p^k is constant, profit for the firm expressed in units of the consumption good is:

$$(6.17) \qquad \text{Profit} = \frac{F(K)}{1 + r} - p^k K.$$

Comparing this expression to (6.5), the optimal stock of capital fulfils a slightly modified version of (6.6):

$$(6.18) \qquad MPK = p^k(1 + r),$$

and the definition of Tobin's q becomes

$$(6.19) \qquad q = \frac{MPK/(1 + r)}{p^k}.$$

The only difference is that Tobin's q now compares the marginal product of capital with its replacement cost, the price of investment goods. With installation costs, optimal investment must obey

$$(6.20) \qquad \underset{\text{present value of MPK}}{MPK/(1 + r)} = \underset{\text{marginal cost of capital}}{(1 + \varphi)p^k}$$

or, in terms of Tobin's q,

$$(6.21) \qquad q = \frac{MPK/(1 + r)}{p^k} = (1 + \varphi).$$

The analysis can be extended in a straightforward way to several periods and to allow the price of investment goods to vary over time. If Crusoe buys investment goods at p_1^k and sells back $(1 - \delta)$ at price p_2^k, he would maximize

$$(6.17') \qquad \text{Profit} = \frac{F(K)}{1 + r} - p_1^k K + \frac{(1 - \delta)p_2^k K}{1 + r}$$

and optimal capital stock would satisfy

$$(6.18') \qquad \begin{aligned} MPK &= (1 + r)p_1^k - (1 - \delta)p_2^k \\ &= [(1 + r) - (1 - \delta)(1 + \pi K)]p_1^k, \end{aligned}$$

where π^K is the rate of change in the price of capital goods $(p_2^k/p_1^{k} - 1)$. For small r, δ, and π^k, this can be approximated by

$$MPK \approx (r + \delta + \pi^K)p_1^k.$$

The right-hand side is a measure of the **user cost of capital** which incorporates the possibility that the relative price of investment goods may change over time.

---

way the return on investment in present-value terms exceeds the replacement, or user, cost of capital.[20] Box 6.7 provides more details.

The geometry of installation costs

Installation costs have two particular properties. First, they increase with the size of the investment. Big steps are more than proportionally more expensive than small ones. Second, they are transitory. Once the equipment is in place, the only relevant cost is the interest rate and depreciation—the opportunity cost of resources employed in production.

Figure 6.17 modifies panel (*b*) of Figure 6.14 in two ways. First, investment is measured on the horizontal axis as the investment rate I/K, which gives a better indication of the intensity of disruptions giving rise to installation costs.[21] Second, on the vertical axis, marginal costs and returns are expressed in today's present discounted values. The marginal cost of capital in present value is always 1, because one unit of capital implies giving up one unit of consumption good today. The horizontal schedule represents the cost of investment in the absence of installation costs. With installation costs, the cost of

---

[20] Another approach, pioneered by Professors Finn Kydland of Texas and Edward Prescott of Minnesota, stresses that it takes time to design, acquire, and put in place new equipment. The implications are similar to those of installation costs.

[21] In the absence of depreciation, $I/K = \Delta K/K$. Focusing on the investment rate is justified by the idea that a given amount of investment is more disruptive in a small firm (or economy) than in a large one.

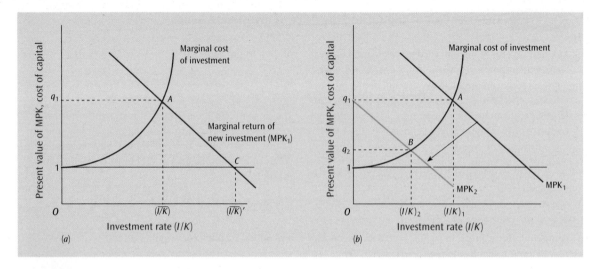

Fig. 6.17   **Tobin's *q***

In panel (*a*) profits are maximized at point *A*, where the marginal return of investment in present-value terms is equal to its marginal cost. The marginal cost of capital is 1 (unit of forgone consumption). The optimum rate of investment is $(\overline{I/K})'$. Tobin's *q* corresponds to point *A*: it is the ratio of the marginal return on new investment to the cost of new capital. In the absence of installation costs (point *B*), the optimum rate of investment $(\overline{I/K})$ brings the capital stock immediately to its optimum level. In panel (*b*) investment starts at point *A* as before. With a higher stock of capital, the MPK then declines as represented by the shift from MPK_1 to MPK_2. With Tobin's *q* still above unity, investment continues but at the lower rate $(I/K)_2$. The process continues until *q* is equal to 1, and no further investment is warranted.

investment exceeds the cost of capital. The more equipment is put in place, the higher is the marginal cost; hence the upward-sloping marginal cost of investment curve. The marginal return on investment is $MPK/(1 + r)$; it is downward sloping because of the principle of declining marginal productivity.

Firms invest until the marginal cost equals the marginal return at point *A* in panel (*a*) of Figure 6.17, where the two curves intersect. The value of an additional unit of capital installed,—Tobin's *q*— exceeds the replacement cost of capital. Without installation costs, the firm would choose point *C* instead and invest more. It may be surprising that the marginal return is higher with than without installation costs. Rather than reducing the long-term profitability of investment, installation costs simply induce firms to invest at a slower rate. In the long run, firms achieve the same desired capital stock as in the absence of adjustment costs.

Panel (*b*) shows how the investment rate moves over time. With *q* above 1, investment first occurs

at rate $(I/K)_1$ corresponding to point *A*. Each MPK schedule is drawn for a given stock of already installed capital. Moving along the schedule, we find the profitability of further additions to the existing capital stock.

Once the capital stock has increased as a result of investment, however, these additions become less productive—because of the principle of declining marginal productivity. So, as further investment accumulates, the MPK schedule shifts downwards, in the figure from MPK_1 to MPK_2.[22] As long as Tobin's *q* is greater than unity investment continues, but at declining rates, here at rate $(I/K)_2$ corresponding to point *B*. The process will continue until *q* is driven down to 1 and the capital stock has reached its long-run, optimal level.

---

[22] The observant student will note that for linear curves, and in the absence of depreciation, the intercept of each successive MPK curve with the vertical axis is determined by the value of *q* in the preceding period.

6.3.6 **The Investment Function**

The **investment function** is the relationship summarizing compactly all the ideas that have been developed until now. First, investment is inversely related to the interest rate because it measures the opportunity cost of those resources. Higher interest rates imply lower investment spending. Second, the accelerator mechanism captures the stable long-run relationship between the capital stock and output. Since the rate of proportionality is greater than 1, increases in output lead to magnified increases in investment expenditures. Finally, Tobin's q reflects the fact that some firms finance their expenditures by issuing shares on the stock market. High stock prices mean that the market places a high value on installed capital, so firms can raise more resources per share issued, and this encourages investment. Tobin's q also incorporates some, but not all, of the effect of real interest rates on investment, because a higher interest rate discounts more heavily future profits and reduces q. (For firms that raise money not on the stock market, but by issuing bonds or borrowing from banks, it is the interest rate alone that represents the cost of investment.) These results can be summarized by the following **investment function**, which will be used repeatedly throughout the book:

$$(6.22) \qquad I = I(r, \Delta Y, q).$$
$$ {-} \ \ {+} \ \ {+}$$

It says that investment depends negatively on the real interest rate r, positively on the change in GDP, and positively on Tobin's q.[23]

 ## Summary

1. Rational consumers attempt to smooth consumption over time, borrowing in bad years, saving in good ones. Consumption is driven primarily by wealth, the present discounted value of current and future incomes, and initial net asset holdings. Over a life cycle, income typically increases. To smooth out consumption, agents typically borrow when young and pay back later.

2. Individual consumption smoothing means that, in the aggregate, temporary disturbances are met by current account imbalances (national saving or dissaving) to reduce the need to adjust consumption abruptly. In contrast, permanent disturbances lead to immediate consumption adjustment rather than to borrowing or lending.

3. Financial market imperfections, arising from uncertainty about future incomes and the inability of banks to assess individual future prospects, prevent households from borrowing against future expected income. As a result, current disposable income also affects aggregate consumption.

4. The effect of changes in the real interest rate on current consumption is ambiguous. Lenders tend to increase, while borrowers decrease, consumption in response to increases in the interest rate. In the aggregate, however, higher interest rates are likely to reduce consumption by reducing wealth.

5. The consumption function relates aggregate consumption to wealth (positively) and disposable income (positively).

---

[23] In theory, Tobin's q should contain all information necessary to infer the profitability of investment, subsuming the other two arguments r and ΔY. Since many firms finance investment through borrowing and retained earnings, the interest rate also matters directly. In addition, as with households, many firms are rationed on the credit market, so they have to rely upon current income to finance spending on productive equipment, justifying the accelerator term.

6. The optimal capital stock equates the marginal productivity of capital to the marginal cost of capital. The optimal capital stock increases when the real interest rate declines and when technological gains raise the marginal productivity of capital.

7. Investment over and above capital depreciation increases the capital stock. As the optimal capital stock, investment is driven by the real interest rate.

8. The accelerator mechanism links investment to changes in output. This is both a mechanical relationship (in the long run the capital output ratio is constant) and a symptom of credit rationing.

9. The ratio of the market value of installed capital to the replacement cost of installed capital is called Tobin's q. It is an approximation of the ratio of the present discounted value of the marginal return of investment to the marginal cost of capital. This ratio is equal to unity when the capital stock has reached its optimal level. When Tobin's q is larger than unity, the capital stock is below its optimal level and firms benefit from further investment.

10. The market value of installed capital, the numerator in Tobin's q, is priced in the stock market. In setting this price, stock markets look ahead. The forward-looking nature of Tobin's q mirrors how firms take into account expected future earnings when they make investment decisions.

11. Because of various installation costs, firms do not acquire their optimal capital stock immediately. Rather, they spread investment over time, gradually bringing capital up to the optimal level.

12. The present discounted return to investment exceeds the marginal cost of capital to compensate for installation costs. Investment proceeds until the present value of its return, at the margin, equals the marginal cost of investment, the sum of borrowing and installation costs.

13. The investment function states that aggregate investment depends upon: (i) the real interest rate (negatively); (ii) Tobin's q (positively); (iii) GDP growth (positively).

Key Concepts

- preferences
- indifference curves
- utility
- marginal rate of intertemporal substitution
- life-cycle consumption
- permanent income
- permanent and transitory disturbances
- consumption smoothing
- random walk
- consumption function
- credit rationing
- marginal productivity of capital (MPK)
- marginal cost of capital
- optimal capital stock
- opportunity cost of investment
- capital depreciation
- user cost of capital
- accelerator principle
- Tobin's q
- q-theory of investment
- animal spirits
- installation costs
- investment function

Exercises

1. What are the effects on current and future consumption of an income windfall expected in the future? Show your reasoning graphically.

2. Should a temporary increase in taxes to finance a temporary increase in public spending reduce the current account deficit? What about a permanent increase in both taxes and public spending? What is the effect on the current account?

3. It is often the case that poor countries save less than richer ones. They also often have a younger population. Can you link these two features?

4. Consider a household whose income is £1000 today and £1500 tomorrow.
   (a) If the real interest rate is 5%, what is its wealth (i) in terms of today's consumption, (ii) in terms of tomorrow's consumption? Compute the household's permanent income (see Box 6.2).
   (b) If today's income unexpectedly increases by £200, what is the change in the permanent income?
   (c) If income goes up by £200 permanently, what is the effect on permanent income?
   (d) Answer the same questions with a 10% real interest rate.

5. Latin American countries in the 1980s and Russia in the late 1990s were cut off from world financial markets. What could be the effect on consumption and investment spending in these countries on an increase of world interest rates?

6. There is evidence that spending on durable goods increases faster than spending on non-durables during a temporary boom expansion. Can you give some economic reasons why? (*Hint*: think of durable goods expenditure as a form of saving.)

7. In Figure 6.5 it is assumed that initially there is no borrowing or lending.
   (a) If the consumer was initially a net borrower, what is the effect of (i) a temporary increase in income, (ii) a permanent increase? Contrast your results with the case treated in the text.
   (b) Apply the same question for the case where the consumer was initially a net lender.

8. A great deal of debate has arisen in Germany on the financing of the expenditure necessary to improve the much neglected infrastructure in its new eastern states. One side favours increased taxes, which would fall largely on households. The other side favours an increased budget deficit. Which side is right? How important to your answer is your assumption of whether the spending increase is permanent or temporary?

Suggested Further Reading

Some of the classic readings on consumption and investment are:

Ando, Albert, and Modigliani, Franco (1963), 'The "Life-Cycle" Hypothesis of Saving: Aggregate Implications and Tests', *American Economic Review*, 53: 55–84.

Friedman, Milton (1957), *A Theory of the Consumption Function*, Princeton University Press.

Hall, Robert (1978), 'Stochastic Implications of the Life-Cycle–Permanent Income Hypothesis: Theory and Evidence', *Journal of Political Economy*, 86: 971–88.

For a more advanced treatment, see:

Blanchard, Olivier, and Fischer, Stanley (1989), *Lectures on Macroeconomics*. Cambridge, Mass.: MIT Press.

Romer, David (1996), *Macroeconomics*. New York: McGraw-Hill.

Tobin, James (1969), 'A General Equilibrium Approach to Monetary Theory', *Journal of Money, Credit and Banking*, 1: 15–29.

Some applications to policy issues:

Börsch-Supan, Axel (1991), 'Aging Population: Problems and Policy Options in the US and Germany', *Economic Policy*, 12: 103–40.

Hayashi, Fumio (1986), 'Why is Japan's Saving Rate so Apparently High?', *NBER Macroeconomics Annual*, 147–210.

Summers, Lawrence H. (1981), 'Taxation and Corporate Investment: A q-Theory Approach', *Brookings Papers on Economic Activity*, 1: 67–140.

Ueda, Kazuo (1988), 'Perspectives on the Japanese Current Account Surplus', *NBER Macroeconomics Annual*, 217–55.

Appendix: Consumption, Investment, and Tobin's q

Consumption: Two Periods

We describe the preferences with a utility function over consumption in both periods: $U(C_1, C_2)$. To make things simpler, we assume that the utility function is time-separable, i.e. that the utility in each period is independent of consumption in the other:

(A6.1) $$U(C_1, C_2) = u(C_1) + \frac{u(C_2)}{1 + \rho},$$

where $u(C_i)$ is the one-period utility of consumption in period $i = 1, 2$ ($u' > 0$, $u'' < 0$) and ρ is called the subjective rate of time preference, with ρ strictly positive. Denoting wealth by $\Omega = Y_1 + Y_2/(1 + r)$, the budget constraint is

(A6.2) $$C_1 + \frac{C_2}{1 + r} = \Omega.$$

Substituting C_1 from (A6.2) into (A6.1), we maximize $U(C_1, C_2)$ and obtain the first-order condition

(A6.3) $$(1 + \rho)\frac{u'(C_1)}{u'(C_2)} = 1 + r.$$

Equation (A6.3) implies that the marginal rate of substitution of goods in period 2 for goods in period 1 is equal to the corresponding economic rate of transformation (the gross interest rate $1 + r$).

Several implications follow from (A6.3). Since $u'' < 0$, u' is a decreasing function of C. If r rises, $u'(C_1)$ must increase relatively to $u'(C_2)$, so C_1 must fall relatively to C_2. Intuitively, the price of period 2 consumption relative to that of period 1 consumption ($1/(1 + r)$) falls, making C_1 more expensive. Second, an increase in impatience (ρ increases) produces the opposite effect. Third, if $r = \rho$, consumption is perfectly smoothed out—that is, $C_1 = C_2$. This is so because the return on waiting (measured by the real interest rate, i.e. the cost of consuming now) is exactly compensated by impatience.

In order to derive the level of consumption today, more information is required (i.e. the functional form taken by the utility function). Yet it is possible, by total differentiation of (A6.3), to obtain a number of comparative-statics results as follows. The total differential of (A6.3) yields

(A6.4) $$[(1 + \rho)u''(C_1) + (1 + r)^2 u''(C_2)]\,dC_1$$
$$= (1 + r)^2 u''(C_2)\,d\Omega + [u'(C_2)$$
$$+ (1 + r)(\Omega - C_1)u''(C_2)]\,dr,$$

which, setting $dr = 0$, gives the effect of wealth on consumption as

(A6.5) $$\left.\frac{dC_1}{d\Omega}\right|_{dr=0} = \frac{(1 + r)^2 u''(C_2)}{(1 + \rho)u''(C_1) + (1 + r)^2 u''(C_2)},$$

which is unambiguously positive. A corresponding expression can be derived for C_2.

The effect of an increase in the interest rate on C_1 can likewise be derived from (A6.4), setting instead $d\Omega = 0$:

(A6.6) $$\left.\frac{dC_1}{dr}\right|_{d\Omega=0} = \frac{u''(C_2) + (1 + r)(\Omega - C_1)u''(C_2)}{(1 + \rho)u''(C_1) + (1 + r)^2 u''(C_2)}.$$

This expression, in contrast to (A6.5), cannot be signed unambiguously. One can however rewrite the right-hand side of (A6.6) as

(A6.7) $$\frac{u'(C_2)}{(1 + \rho)u''(C_1) + (1 + r)^2 u''(C_2)} +$$
$$\frac{(1 + r)(\Omega - C_1)u''(C_2)}{(1 + \rho)u''(C_1) + (1 + r)^2 u''(C_2)}.$$

Multiply numerator and denominator of the first term by $(1 + r)^2 u''(C_2)$ and substitute (A6.5) to obtain

(A6.8) $$\frac{u'(C_2)}{(1 + r)^2 u''(C_2)}\frac{dC_1}{d\Omega} + \frac{(\Omega - C_1)}{(1 + r)}\frac{dC_1}{d\Omega}.$$

Finally, define the elasticity of intertemporal substitution as[24]

(A6.9) $$\sigma = \frac{-u'(C_2)}{u''(C_2)C_2}.$$

Using this definition, rewrite (A6.8) as

(A6.10) $$\left.\frac{dC_1}{dr}\right|_{d\Omega=0} = \left[\frac{\Omega - C_1}{1 + r} - \frac{\sigma C_2}{(1 + r)^2}\right]\frac{dC_1}{d\Omega}$$
$$= \frac{(1 - \sigma)(\Omega - C_1)}{1 + r}\frac{dC_1}{d\Omega},$$

so that $dC_1/dr|_{d\Omega=0} < 0$ for $\sigma > 1$, and $dC_1/dr|_{d\Omega=0} > 0$ for $\sigma < 1$. Holding total wealth Ω constant, the effect of an interest rate increase depends on the elasticity of substitution; it is negative for a high elasticity of substitution ($\sigma > 1$) and positive for a low value ($\sigma < 1$).[25] This corresponds to the discussion in Section 6.2.4 in the main text. On the other hand, the total effect on consumption consists of (A6.10) plus the wealth effect of an

---

[24] The parameter σ can be thought of as the inverse of the elasticity of marginal utility of consumption $-[u''(C_2)C_2]/u'(C_2)$.
[25] In the case of unit elasticity—the case of log utility, or $U(C) = \log(C)$—the net effect is zero.

interest rate increase, which is always negative since $d\Omega/dr < 0$; so

(A6.11)
$$\frac{dC_1}{dr} = \underbrace{\frac{dC_1}{dr}\bigg|_{d\Omega=0}}_{(?)} + \underbrace{\frac{dC_1}{d\Omega}\frac{d\Omega}{dr}}_{(-)}.$$

Investment: Two Periods

Robinson Crusoe decides how many coconuts (I_1) to plant, given that when he does so installation costs him $I_1\Phi(I_1/K_1)$ coconuts in addition to the K_1 trees that already exist. We assume that $\Phi' > 0$, $\Phi'' > 0$ (installation costs are convex, i.e. they increase more than proportionately), and that $\Phi(0) = \Phi'(0) = 0$ (no costs are incurred when no investment is undertaken). Capital stock in the second period will be, in the absence of depreciation, $K_2 = K_1 + I_1$. If Y_i represents his period i endowment, the budget constraint is

(A6.12)
$$C_1 + \frac{C_2}{1+r} = Y_1 + \frac{Y_2}{1+r} + \frac{F(K_1 + I_1)}{1+r}$$
$$- I_1 - I_1\Phi\left(\frac{I_1}{K_1}\right).$$

Crusoe must decide how many coconuts to plant. He chooses I_1 in order to maximize his wealth, i.e. the right-hand side of (A6.12). This means that the consumption decision, which was covered above, is separated from the investment decision. The first-order condition[26] for investment is:

(A6.13)
$$\frac{F'(K_2)}{1+r} = 1 + \Phi\left(\frac{I_1}{K_1}\right) + \left(\frac{I_1}{K_1}\right)\Phi'\left(\frac{I_1}{K_1}\right).$$

Now define q as follows:

(A6.14)
$$q_1 = 1 + \left(\frac{I_1}{K_1}\right)\Phi'\left(\frac{I_1}{K_1}\right) + \Phi\left(\frac{I_1}{K_1}\right).$$

It is the marginal cost of investment. By (A6.13), q_1 is also equal to $F'(K_2)/(1 + r)$, the present value of next period's MPK, net of installation costs. This is Tobin's q. Define the function $\Psi(I_1/K_1)$ as

(A6.15)
$$\Psi\left(\frac{I_1}{K_1}\right) = \left(\frac{I_1}{K_1}\right)\Phi'\left(\frac{I_1}{K_1}\right) + \Phi\left(\frac{I_1}{K_1}\right).$$

The function $\Psi(I_1/K_1)$ is increasing when $\Phi'(I_1/K_1) > 0$ and $\Phi''(I_1/K_1) > 0$. In addition, $\Psi(0) = 0$. Then (A6.14) becomes $\Psi(I_1/K_1) = q_1 - 1$, which can be inverted to give

(A6.16)
$$I_1 = K_1\Psi^{-1}(q_1 - 1),$$

[26] The second-order condition $F''(K_2)/(1 + r) - \phi''(I_1/K_1)K_1 < 0$ is assumed to be satisfied.

where Ψ^{-1} is the inverse function of Ψ. As $\Psi^{-1}(0) = 0$, no investment occurs when $q_1 = 1$. Since Ψ is increasing in I_1/K_1, Ψ^{-1} is increasing in q_1 and the firm invests when $q_1 > 1$.

Investment: the Infinite-Horizon Case

The two-period case can be extended to the more general case of an infinite horizon by reasoning recursively. Π_t is the firm's profit in period t:

(A6.17)
$$\Pi_t = F(K_t) - I_t - I_t\Phi(I_t/K_t),$$

where $\Phi(I/K)$ is the installation of investment. Capital accumulates as follows:

(A6.18)
$$K_{t+1} = (1 - \delta)K_t + I_t,$$

where δ is the rate of capital depreciation. From period t onwards, the firm chooses its planned investment to maximize the present value V_t of its profits

$$V_t = \sum_{i=0}^{\infty} \frac{\Pi_{t+i}}{(1+r)^i}$$

under the constraint (A6.17). The Lagrangean of this problem in period t can be written as

(A6.19)
$$\mathcal{L}_t = \sum_{i=0}^{\infty} \frac{\Pi_{t+i}}{(1+r)^i}$$
$$- \sum_{i=0}^{\infty} \frac{q_{t+i}}{(1+r)^i}[K_{t+i+1} - (1-\delta)K_{t+i} - I_{t+i}],$$

where q_{t+i} is the Lagrange multiplier in period $t + i$. It has the interpretation of the shadow price of an additional unit of capital when the firm is behaving optimally. The necessary first-order conditions for an optimum are $\forall i = 0, 1, \ldots$

(A6.20)
$$\frac{\partial\mathcal{L}_t}{\partial I_{t+i}} = \frac{-1 - \Phi(I_{t+i}/K_{t+i}) - (I_{t+i}/K_{t+i})\Phi'(I_{t+i}/K_{t+i}) + q_{t+i}}{(1+r)^i}$$
$$= 0,$$

and

(A6.21)
$$\frac{\partial\mathcal{L}_t}{\partial K_{t+i}} = \frac{\partial\Pi_{t+i}/\partial K_{t+i}}{(1+r)^i} + \frac{(1-\delta)q_{t+i}}{(1+r)^i} - \frac{q_{t+i-1}}{(1+r)^{i-1}}$$
$$= 0.$$

From (A6.20), the optimal investment can be derived, conditional on the inherited capital stock, as

(A6.22)
$$q_{t+i} - 1 = \Phi(I_{t+i}/K_{t+i}) + \frac{I_{t+i}}{K_{t+i}}\Phi'(I_{t+i}/K_{t+i}).$$

Define $\Psi(I_{t+i}/K_{t+i}) = \Phi(I_{t+i}/K_{t+i}) + (I_{t+i}/K_{t+i})\Phi'(I_{t+i}/K_{t+i})$, and invert (A6.22) to get

(A6.23) $$I_{t+i}/K_{t+i} = \Psi^{-1}(q_{t+i} - 1),$$

which is a positive function of q in each period. Recursive substitution of (A6.21) yields, for any T,

(A6.24) $$q_t = \left[\frac{1-\delta}{1+r}\right]^T q_{t+T} + (1+r)^{-1} \sum_{i=0}^{\infty} \Pi'_{t+i} \left[\frac{1-\delta}{1+r}\right]^i,$$

where $\Pi'_{t+i} = [F'(K_{t+i}) - \Phi(\cdot) - \Phi'(\cdot)]$ is shorthand for the marginal net productivity of investment. If we impose the side condition that q_t not grow too fast, or

(A6.25) $$\lim_{t \to \infty} \left[\frac{1-\delta}{1+r}\right]^T q_{t+T} = 0,$$

then we obtain

(A6.26) $$q_t = (1+r)^{-1} \sum_{i=0}^{\infty} \left[\frac{1-\delta}{1+r}\right]^i \Pi'_{t+i}.$$

Equation (A6.24) gives the value of q for an infinite horizon. As in the main text, it is the present discounted value of future net marginal products of investment. With capital depreciation at rate δ, however, positive replacement investment occurs only if $q > 1$ in the long run with K constant. More precisely, combining (A6.17) and (A6.21) plus $K_t = K_{t+1} = K = I/\delta$ requires $\delta = \Phi'^{-1}(q_{t+i} - 1)$, so it must be that $q > 1$.

The Real Exchange Rate

7

Suppose a man climbs five feet up a sea wall, then climbs down 12 feet. Whether he drowns or not depends upon how high above sea-level he was when he started. The same problem arises in deciding whether currencies are under- or over-valued.

– *The Economist*, 26 August 1995

7.1 Overview

This chapter completes the analysis of the real side of the economy. As in Chapter 3, it examines the long run, when all markets are in equilibrium. The innovation is that, so far, we implicitly looked at one good, called 'output'; in this chapter the analysis is expanded to consider two goods. This important modification allows us to study **relative prices**, or prices of goods in terms of others (e.g. how many cakes can be exchanged for a car). This is not our first encounter with relative prices: the real wage (the ratio of nominal wages to a price index) or the real interest rate (the price of tomorrow's consumption in terms of today's consumption) fall in that category. Relative prices are the essence of a market economy.[1] They act as signals and provide incentives to producers and consumers to adapt their behaviour to changing market conditions.

The **real exchange rate** performs this important function. The real exchange rate is the relative price of foreign goods and services in terms of domestic goods and services. It is related to the **nominal exchange rate** (the price of domestic money in terms of foreign money) adjusted for the domestic and foreign goods prices.

The central message of this chapter is twofold: the real exchange rate affects the primary current account by shifting both production and consumption choices between the home and foreign goods. And the **equilibrium real exchange** rate is such that the intertemporal budget constraint (presented in Chapter 5) is satisfied in the long run.

Because there are many possible definitions of home and foreign goods, the real exchange rate can be defined in a number of ways. This chapter looks at two important ones. The first is simply the ratio of prices at home to those at abroad, expressed in a common currency. The second definition distinguishes between those goods and services that are traded internationally and those that are produced at home and are not subject to international competition.

7.2 The Real Exchange Rate and the Primary Current Account Function

7.2.1 The Real Exchange Rate Defined

To compare prices of goods produced at home with those of goods produced abroad, we need to express them in a common currency. For that purpose, we use the nominal exchange rate. Exchange rates are set on the foreign exchange market.[2] Exchange rates can be quoted in either of two ways: either as the number of foreign monetary units per domestic unit (this is called **British terms**, e.g. \$1.5 per £1 for Britain, or \$1.1 per €1 for the European Monetary Union) or as the number of domestic monetary units per foreign unit (which used to be called **European terms**, e.g. CHF 1.6 per \$1 for Switzerland). *This text adopts the convention of British terms* since it is commonly used for quoting the euro and the pound. With this convention, a currency **appreciation** corresponds to an increase in its value in terms of foreign currencies, so the exchange rate rises (e.g.

---

[1] Indeed, a crucial first step in the transformation of Eastern European countries to market economies was the freeing of prices so that they could play this fundamental role.

[2] Exchange markets and the nominal exchange rates are studied in detail in Ch. 19. A quick look at that chapter may be useful.

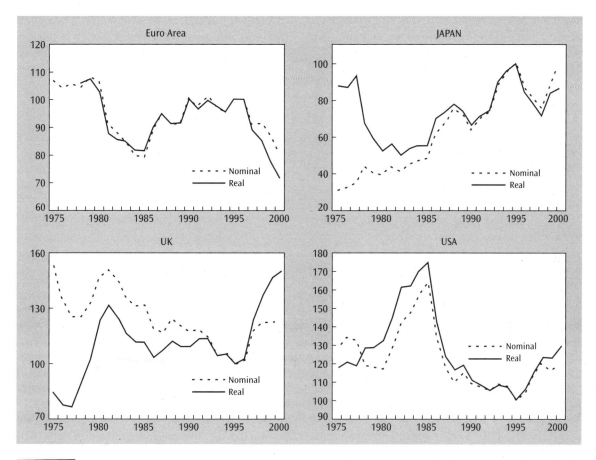

Fig. 7.1   **Nominal and Real Exchange Rates, Four Countries, 1975–2000**

Nominal exchange rates move quickly and prices move slowly. This is why sudden movements in the nominal exchange rate are reflected in the real exchange rate. Over the longer run, different evolutions of domestic and foreign prices may break the co-movements between the two exchange rates.
Sources: IMF.

from \$0.9 to \$1.1 for €1). Conversely, a loss of value, or a **depreciation**, would imply a decline in the exchange rate.

If *S* denotes the exchange rate (say, dollars per €1) and P^* is the price of foreign goods expressed in foreign currency (say, \$), then the domestic price of foreign goods is P^*/S. Conversely, if *P* is the price of domestic goods in domestic currency, their price in foreign currency is SP.[3] The real exchange rate, the relative price of foreign goods in terms of domestic goods, is

$$(7.1) \qquad \sigma = \frac{P}{P^*/S} = \frac{SP}{P^*}$$

both prices   both prices
in domestic currency in foreign currency

As long as we compare goods prices in the same currency we arrive at the same definition. The real exchange rate can be thought of as the nominal exchange rate 'doubly deflated' by foreign and domestic goods prices. Like their nominal counterparts, real exchange rates are said to appreciate (σ increases) or depreciate (σ declines).

As long as goods prices P^* and P remain unchanged or move closely together, the nominal and real exchange rates move together. As Figure 7.1

---

[3] To see this: *P* is measured in euros, P^* is measured in dollars, and *S* is expressed in terms of dollars per euro. Then P^*/S is measured in euros (since (\$)(\$/euro) = euro). Similarly, SP is measured in dollars.

illustrates, over short horizons, the nominal and real exchange rates tend to fluctuate in tandem. This is so because typically nominal exchange rates are quite volatile, while prices tend to be sticky. Over the longer run, however, nominal and real exchange rates seem to have lives of their own, which justifies studying separately the real exchange rate in the long run (this chapter) and the nominal exchange rate (Chapter 19).

In order to better grasp the distinction between the nominal and real exchange rates, it is useful to ask: when do the two move together? Clearly, when domestic and foreign price levels move together, so that their ratio is constant. For that to be the case, inflation must be the same at home and abroad. If, on the contrary, inflation pushes foreign prices (P^*) faster than domestic prices (P), the real exchange rate depreciates (σ decreases) as long as the nominal exchange rate S does not appreciate enough to fully offset the decline in P/P^*; a special case is when the nominal exchange rate is fixed. Conversely, the nominal exchange rate may appreciate and the real exchange rate change little; this occurs for instance when inflation is lower at home (P/P^* declines) by about as much as S rises, as in Germany, on average, over 1975–90. A general feature, visible in Figure 7.1, is that real exchange rates are more stable in the long run than in the short run, and also more stable than nominal exchange rates. This relative long-run stability makes it easier to first study the real exchange rate in the long run, and then to study the nominal exchange rate in the long and short run.[4]

7.2.2 Measuring the Real Exchange Rate in Practice

Measuring real exchange rates in practice poses two problems. The first concerns the definition of 'foreign'. Quite obviously, the rest of the world comprises a large number of countries which need to be aggregated in some way. The solution consists in computing P^* as a weighted average of prices in a large number of trading partner countries (ideally,

all of them) and S as a corresponding weighted average of our nominal exchange rate vis-à-vis each of them. The weights assigned to each country are chosen to represent its importance to us. Box 7.1 explains how this is accomplished. The corresponding values of S and σ are called respectively the nominal and real **effective exchange rates**. These are indices—we can no longer express the nominal exchange rate in value terms, e.g. dollars per euro—computed to take a simple value, e.g. 1 or 100, in some base year. In Figure 7.1 the indices are such that they take on the value 100 in 1985.

A second problem arises when deciding which prices to compare. A real exchange rate is the price ratio of two baskets of goods and services. Because so many baskets are possible, there is no one real exchange rate that answers all the questions one may wish to consider, so several definitions are possible. One of them is the ratio of domestically produced exports to foreign-produced import prices, sometimes called the **external terms of trade**. Another definition is the ratio of non-traded to traded goods prices, sometimes called the **internal terms of trade**. The merit of the first definition is to be more precise about where the traded goods are produced. The advantage of the second definition is that it separates out the sectors open to foreign competition (which produce traded goods) from those that are sheltered (and produce non-traded goods). Broader-based real exchange rates compare consumer price indices or GDP deflators. Other indices are designed to measure a country's competitiveness by focusing on production costs, chiefly labour costs.

7.2.3 How the Real Exchange Rate Affects the Primary Current Account

What is the link between the real exchange rate and the primary current account (PCA)? Consider, for instance, a real depreciation: domestic goods become cheaper relatively to foreign goods. Two substitution effects follow. First, on the consumption side, an increase in foreign prices will tend to reduce domestic spending on foreign goods and make domestic goods more attractive. This improves the primary current account. Second,

---

[4] This is why Ch. 7 comes before Ch. 19!

Box 7.1   **Computing and Comparing Effective Exchange Rates**[5]

Effective exchange rates are computed using a number of partner-countries. Each partner-country receives a weight typically representing its importance in trade, for example its share of our exports or our imports, or the average of both. Geometric averaging is applied to price indices in these countries and to our bilateral exchange rates vis-à-vis their currencies. If n countries are selected and S_i is the bilateral nominal exchange rate vis-à-vis country i with trade weight w_i, our effective nominal exchange rate is:

$$S = (S_1)_1^w (S_2)_2^w (S_3)_3^w \ldots (S_n)_n^w$$

where the weights sum up to 100% ($\Sigma w_i = 1$). The effective foreign price level P^* is computed by applying the same weights to each partner-country's price index Pi:

$$P^* = (P_1)^{w_1}(P_2)^{w_2}(P_3)^{w_3} \ldots (P_n)^{w_n}.$$

Then the effective real exchange rate is simply the average of our real exchange rates vis-à-vis each partner-country:

$$\sigma = \left(\frac{S_1 P}{P_1}\right)^{w_1} \left(\frac{S_2 P}{P_2}\right)^{w_2} \left(\frac{S_3 P}{P_3}\right)^{w_3} \ldots \left(\frac{S_n P}{P_n}\right)^{w_n} = \frac{SP}{P^*}$$

This approach can be applied to other classes of goods. A frequently used measure of the real exchange rate is the ratio of export to import prices. It differs from the ratio of non-traded to traded good prices in two ways: it ignores the existence of non-traded goods, and it distinguishes among the traded goods those which are produced domestically and exported from the imported goods produced abroad. In this view the 'home' goods are exports instead of non-traded, and the 'foreign' goods are imports instead of all traded goods lumped together. The choice between this or that measure really depends on the characteristics of the country at hand and on the question of interest.

---

on the production side, more resources will be diverted from producing now-cheaper domestic goods towards producing substitutes for now-higher priced foreign goods, possibly even towards goods for export. This too improves the primary current account. The **primary current account function** formally summarizes these observations:

(7.2) $$PCA = PCA(\sigma, \ldots).$$
    $$(-)$$

As usual, the minus sign indicates that an increase in the real exchange rate σ has a negative effect on the primary current account. All other things equal —which is represented by the dots in (7.2)[6]—a real depreciation leads to an improvement in the primary account, a reduction in the deficit or an increase

in the surplus. This function is represented by the downward-sloping schedule in Figure 7.2. The rest of this chapter analyses this dependence, a key macroeconomic relationship.

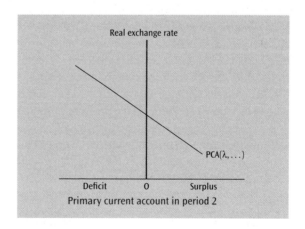

Fig. 7.2   **The Primary Current Account Function**

The primary current account function shows the relation between the real exchange rate and the primary account balance. It is downward-sloping because a more depreciated real exchange rate, everything else unchanged, leads to an improvement in the primary current account.

---

[5] Nominal and real effective exchange rates are computed and published by various sources. Among them, *International Financial Statistics*, a monthly publication of the International Monetary Fund, presents a variety of real exchange rates (using GDP deflators, export prices, CPIs, labour costs) computed using a sample of 18 advanced economies.

[6] The other variables that affect the PCA are specified further in Ch. 11.

| **7.3** | **The Real Exchange Rate as the Relative Price of Traded Goods** |

7.3.1 **Traded versus Non-traded Goods**

Among the many possible definitions of the real exchange rate, we work here with the second one presented in Section 7.2: the ratio of **non-traded** to **traded goods** prices. Losing the distinction between exports and imports is not too damning for the developed countries which trade among each other mostly very similar goods: after all a car is a car, even if brand names differ. For those developing countries which export natural resources and import industrial products, the distinction between exports and imports would be much more important.

How do we tell the difference between traded and non-traded goods? There is no clear border, but common sense takes us a long way. Examples of goods or services that cannot be physically traded are housing, construction, and transportation. The most important obstacle to trade is transportation costs: haircuts, medical services, car repair, or cement are good examples. Other goods and services could be traded but are not because country-specific regulations limit their usefulness elsewhere or prevent their exchange (e.g. standards: why are US washing machines so different from European ones?). Many goods may be non-traded but are nevertheless tradable: if protection were removed or transportation costs were to fall, they might become traded.[7] In the end, the distinction is useful and important for one good economic reason: non-traded goods do not face the same competitive pressure as traded goods. When trade is relatively free, traded goods cannot differ much in price and quality. Non-traded goods, on the other side, are purely local.

Denoting by P^T and P^N the home currency prices of traded and non-traded goods, measured in euros, the relative price of non-traded goods in terms of traded goods is

(7.3)
$$\sigma = \frac{P^N}{P^T}$$

Under pressure from world trade competition, the domestic price of traded goods P^T will align itself with foreign prices P^{T*} when expressed in the same currency, so $P^T = P^{T*}/S.$, where P^{T*} is the price of foreign-produced traded goods expressed in foreign currency. This is an extreme way of recognizing the constraint that international competition imposes on the domestic pricing of traded goods. It is roughly correct for 'small' countries which do not much influence world prices and must take P^{T*} as given. The real exchange rate can therefore be expressed as

(7.4)
$$\sigma = \frac{SP^N}{P^{T*}},$$

i.e. the relative price of non-traded goods in terms of traded goods. As given by (7.4), the real exchange rate represents an **internal terms of trade** because it is the price ratio of the two categories of domestically produced goods. It measures how much of locally produced non-traded goods must be given up in exchange for one unit of traded goods. When non-traded goods are dear in terms of traded goods, the real exchange rate is said to be appreciated relative to a situation in which they are cheaper.

7.3.2 **The Production Possibilities Frontier**

When resources are not wasted (full employment, no idle capital), producing more of one good in an economy implies producing less of the other. This trade-off is represented in Figure 7.3 by the **production possibilities frontier (PPF)**. The curve describes the whole range of combinations of traded (Y^T) and non-traded goods (Y^N) that can be simultaneously produced, given existing resources and technology. Moving along the PPF reveals how production can be shifted from one sector to the other by transferring resources. Box 7.2 explains why the PPF is concave or bowed out from the origin.

The PPF shifts outwards over time, primarily for two reasons. First, more inputs (capital, labour) may become available. Second, technical progress in either or both of the two sectors allows more

---

[7] Financial services were long considered a non-traded good, until the information technology revolution sharply reduced the costs of providing and transporting such services.

The Shape of the Production Possibilities Frontier

The shape of the PPF describes how an economy's available resources can be used to produce various combination of two goods. As we move down the curve to the south-east, the production of traded goods declines while that of non-traded goods increases. The negative slope simply says that we cannot produce more of one good without producing less of the other one since this requires reallocating capital and labour. The rate at which one good is 'transformed' into the other (called the marginal rate of transformation) is measured by the slope of the PPF at any particular point. The steeper the slope, the more non-traded goods must be given up to produce one more traded good. The PPF is bowed-out to reflect the fact that as we keep substituting, say, giving up traded for non-traded goods, we must increasingly sacrifice more and more traded goods to obtain the same additional quantity of non-traded goods. One reason is that some factors of production are fixed—the stock of capital at any time, management skills, land, natural resources. For example, given the stock of capital, as labour is shifted towards the non-traded goods sector, the MPL declines in the non-traded goods sector and rises in the traded goods sector: moving workers is increasingly costly in terms of lost traded output, and is less and less effective in producing more non-traded goods. Other reasons for decreasing returns are: labour is specialized, as some workers enjoy a comparative advantage in producing particular goods; there are costs of moving from one pattern of production to another; and technologies differ across sectors. Only if both sectors were to use the same technology, with constant returns to scale, if no particular skills were required, and if the movement of inputs across sectors were costless would the PPF be a straight line and the marginal rate of transformation be constant.

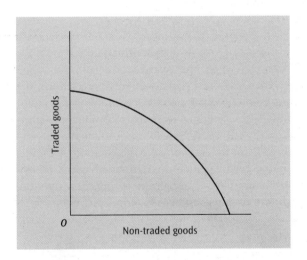

The Production Possibilities Frontier (PPF)

The production possibilities frontier (PPF) summarizes maximal combinations of different goods that an economy can produce, given its available resource and, perhaps, its markets institutions and regulations. Its slope is the marginal rate of transformation or, here, how many units of tradable goods must be given up to obtain a unit of the non-tradable good.

production with the same inputs. The PPF fully takes into account existing imperfections and distortions in goods, labour, and capital markets. For example, if a reduction in the generosity of unemployment benefits leads workers to supply more labour, such a policy would shift the PPF outwards.

For any chosen combination of production of tradable and non-tradable goods, nominal GDP in euros is given by

(7.5) $\text{nominal GDP} = P^T Y^T + P^N Y^N.$

The nominal GDP is the sum of the nominal value added in both sectors. The real GDP is obtained by deflating the nominal GDP. This can be done by using an aggregate price index (the GDP deflator, the average of P^T and P^N) or else by choosing one good as **numeraire**. A numeraire is simply a good in which other goods prices are quoted. Choosing the traded good as numeraire, the real GDP, expressed in units of traded goods, is obtained by dividing the nominal GDP by P^T, the price of *traded goods*:

(7.6) $Y = Y^T + \sigma Y^N \text{ with } \sigma = P^N / P^T.$

A particular value of real GDP could correspond to any number of different combinations of the two

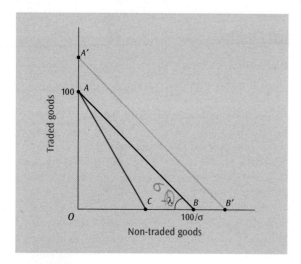

Fig. 7.4   Price Lines

A price line corresponds to a particular value of real GDP evaluated in terms of traded goods. Given the relative price σ of non-traded goods, a real GDP of 100 can be attained by producing 100 traded goods (point A) or 100/σ non-traded goods (point B), or any combination of both goods along the line AB. A′B′ represents a higher real GDP with the same relative price. If non-traded goods become more expensive (σ rises) the price line becomes steeper, with the intercept moving from point B to point C. The intersection of the price line with the y-axis (point A) is the real value of total GDP in terms of the traded good.

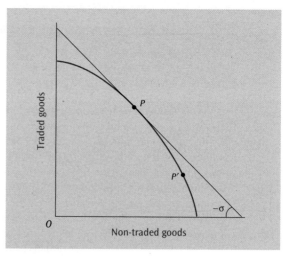

Fig. 7.5   Optimal Production

Given technology and resources, the highest real GDP is achieved at point P, where the price line (which is as high as possible) is tangent to the production possibilities frontier. If the relative price of non-traded goods rises, maximum GDP is reached at a point like P′, where more of the more highly valued non-traded good is produced.

goods. These combinations are shown in Figure 7.4 as the **price line** AB. The slope of the price line (−σ) is given by the real exchange rate. The intersection with the y-axis represents the value of GDP in terms of the numeraire (traded goods). If the real exchange rate appreciates (non-traded good prices rise relatively to traded goods prices), a given real GDP (measured by OA in terms of traded goods) corresponds to less of the more valuable non-traded good (from OB to OC); the new price line AC is steeper. A higher real GDP with the same σ corresponds to a higher price line, like A′B′.

Figure 7.5 shows that, for a given value of the real exchange rate, the most-preferred outcome is attained at point P where a price line is tangent to the PPF. At this point there is no incentive to shift production in favour of either of the two goods: given the relative price σ, this output mix maximizes real GDP given existing resources. When relative prices change, so does the optimal output mix. For example, when the relative price of non-traded goods rises (a real exchange rate appreciation), the price line becomes steeper and the tangency point moves to P′. Quite reasonably, production shifts towards the more valuable non-traded good and away from the less valuable traded good. A decline in the relative price of non-traded goods (a real exchange rate depreciation) triggers the opposite shift of resources and production.

7.3.3 The Case of a Balanced Primary Current Account

The real exchange rate determines the optimal production mix, but what determines the real exchange rate? The answer is that the market does. Technology, resources, and consumer tastes meet each other in the market place. Technology and resources are summarized by the PPF. Once we know about tastes and the budget constraint of consumers, we can find the real exchange rate that delivers equilibrium between demand and supply for

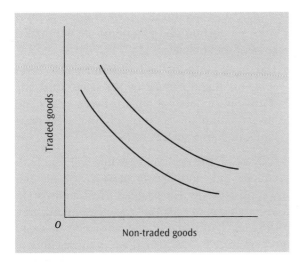

Fig. 7.6   **Indifference Curves**

Consumers' intratemporal preferences are described by indifference curves. Each curve becomes flatter towards the right because as more non-traded goods are consumed the willingness to give up more traded goods for one more non-traded good declines. Curves to the north-east correspond to increasing levels of satisfaction.

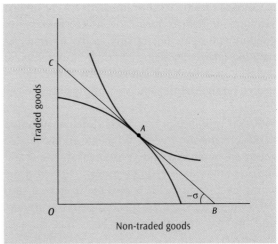

Fig. 7.7   **Optimal Production and Consumption**

Available technology and resources constrain efficient production to points on the PPF. The highest satisfaction is attained at point A, where one indifference curve is tangent to the PPF. The common slope of the PPF and the indifference curve at this point represents the relative price that will lead markets to achieve optimality: the production mix reflects what consumers want.

both traded and non-traded goods simultaneously. This **equilibrium real exchange rate** is relevant for the long run, when resources are not idle and all markets have reached equilibrium.

Figure 7.6 depicts tastes of households in the usual way. Much like the preferences between consumption today and consumption tomorrow (intertemporal choice), preferences between traded and non-traded goods (*intra*temporal choice) can be summarized by indifference curves, with the same shape for the same reasons. And as usual, moving outward gives higher utility levels.

Free choice in the market place permits consumers to achieve the highest possible utility given the available technology and endowment of productive resources.[8] In Figure 7.7 this occurs at point A, where the PPF and the indifference curves are tangent to each other. Their common slope at the tangency

point is the relative price that makes both producers and consumers aim at precisely that point. At this market-clearing relative price, producers maximize value added and consumers are happy to buy both goods exactly in the proportion produced. The PPF plays a role similar to a budget line: it describes the country's existing resources, except that a relative price is needed to value these resources. The interaction between technology (the PPF) and tastes (the indifference curves) in the market place determine the equilibrium relative price.

7.3.4 The Case of a Non-zero Primary Current Account: The Role of the Real Exchange Rate

An important feature of Figure 7.7 is that at point A the primary current account is balanced. Aggregate income and total spending are equal, as are production and spending in each of the two sectors. But in reality the current account is not always balanced; in fact, it is rarely balanced! How should we think

---

[8] Technically, the relative prices reflect the marginal rate of substitution for consumers and the marginal rate of transformation of non-traded for traded goods.

of primary current account imbalances? Put briefly, surpluses or deficits break the link between production and spending at any point in time, as nations take advantage of their intertemporal budget constraint.[9] The full geometry of this case is treated on the website, and we outline only the key ideas here.

Market equilibrium has a very different meaning in markets for non-traded and traded goods. Traded goods are produced and consumed at home and abroad so that market equilibrium is achieved at the world level. At home, it is possible to have a situation where, for example, spending exceeds production. In that case, the difference is met through imports. (These are paid for by an increase in foreign debt or a decrease in domestic holdings of foreign assets.) Similarly, exports absorb the excess of local production over local consumption. Nontraded goods, on the other side, are produced and consumed locally. The market is local and equilibrium requires that production be equal to consumption at home. Graphically, the production point P shown in Figure 7.5 and the absorption point A shown in Figure 7.7 need not coincide. Trade offers freedom, but it is not the case that 'anything goes':

- The budget constraint imposes that the primary current account deficit today be matched by surpluses later on, and conversely.

- Point A must be vertically above or below point P, since production and absorption of non-traded goods must be equal.

- The slopes of the PPF and the indifference curves at points P and A must be the same, since the relative price does not differ between sellers and buyers within the country (of course, ignoring tariffs and taxes, such as VAT).

Changes in the real exchange rate will lead both producers and consumers to revise their behaviour in a consistent way. For example, a real appreciation leads producers to reallocate resources towards producing less traded goods, and consumers to spend more on traded goods. The result is a worsening of the primary current account. Two conclusions follow:

First, the PCA function is downward-sloping, as depicted in Figure 7.2. The exchange rate affects the primary current account by shifting production and spending between traded and non-traded goods in opposite directions.

Second, if the primary current account needs to change to reach a particular value—to meet the intertemporal budget constraint—the real exchange rate will have to change accordingly. For example, it will have to depreciate sufficiently to induce producers and consumers to change their behaviour in a way consistent with a required improvement in the current account.

7.4 The National Intertemporal Budget Constraint and the Equilibrium Real Exchange Rate

7.4.1 The Long Run and the Primary Current Account: A Review

The nation's intertemporal budget constraint introduced in Chapter 5 states that a nation cannot borrow beyond its means and that accumulated assets can and should be eventually spent.[10] In

present-value terms, the country meets its external constraint when the current and future primary current account deficits match the initial net asset position of the country (or the surpluses must at least match the initial debt). In the simplified two-period framework, this statement was written formally as:

$$(7.7) \qquad PCA_1 + \frac{PCA_2}{1+r} = -F_0(1+r)$$

where F_0 is the net external position of the country inherited from the past (before interest is paid). F_0 is positive when the country was a net lender, allowing

---

[9] Remember that Chapter 2 establishes that the primary account is the *difference* between income (from production) and spending. This is the same point again.

[10] This section presents a review of the two-period framework developed in Ch. 5. When an infinite horizon is considered, the problem becomes somewhat more complicated; see Ch. 15 for details.

the country to run external deficits, and negative when the country is a net debtor and must must run surpluses.

As long as it meets its intertemporal budget constraint, the country is free to choose the pattern of its primary accounts over time. This degree of freedom evaporates in the second and 'last' period. Tomorrow's primary account must match the accumulated net external position. As in Chapters 5 and 6, 'tomorrow' is a metaphor for the long-run steady state: on average, short-run fluctuations simply cancel out. Then the primary current account must be such that, by the end of period 2 (the proverbial end of time) the country repays its accumulated debt, or spends its assets, principal and interest, inherited from period 1:

$$(7.8) \qquad PCA_2 = -(1 + r)F_1.$$

where F_1 is the net external position of the country at the end of the first period. A positive asset position allows a deficit, while a position of external indebtedness requires a surplus. The external position F_1 inherited from period 1 is the initial net position F_0, plus interest rF_0, plus PCA_1, the primary surplus incurred in period 1 (today).[11]

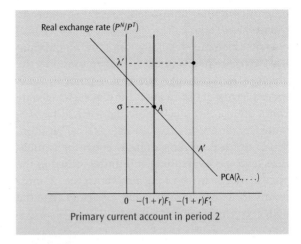

Fig. 7.8   The Equilibrium Real Exchange Rate

Long-run equilibrium requires that the primary current account match the net asset position, inclusive of interest payments $-(1 + r) F_1$. To point A corresponds the equilibrium real exchange rate σ. A less favourable net asset position $F_1' < F_1$ means that a lower primary current account deficit (or a larger current account surplus) is necessary. The vertical schedule is shifted to the right. This requires a lower real exchange rate to generate a larger primary current account surplus to serve the external debt if $F_1 < 0$, or a smaller deficit as net foreign repayments are reduced if $F_1 > 0$.

7.4.2 The Equilibrium Real Exchange Rate and the Primary Current Account in the Long Run

The requirement that the long-run primary current account be consistent with the country's external budget constraint defines the **equilibrium, or long-run, real exchange rate**. The primary current account function depicted in Figure 7.2 shows what real exchange rate is needed to achieve a given primary current account. The second period's budget constraint given by (7.8) requires that the primary

current account be equal to the negative of the country's net foreign asset position, plus interest: it means paying off the debt (when F_1 is negative) through a surplus, or running down accumulated assets (when F_1 is positive) through a deficit. The constraint is shown as the vertical schedule $-(1 + r)F_1$ in Figure 7.8. If a country is indebted, then $F_1 < 0$, and the schedule $-(1 + r)F_1$ will lie to the right in the figure. If on the other hand a country is a net creditor with $F_1 > 0$, the vertical schedule will lie to the left in the figure. For the budget constraint to be satisfied in period 2, the economy must be at the intersection of the primary current account schedule and this vertical line. At point A, the equilibrium exchange rate can be read off the vertical axis. Quite simply, the downward-sloping primary current account schedule shows how the real exchange rate affects the primary current account, the long-run budget constraint shows how the required

---

[11] Formally, at the *end* of the first period, the net external investment position carried forward is $F_1 = (1 + r)F_0 + PCA_1$, representing capital and interest on the previous investment position, *plus* any new net saving (PCA_1). If nothing is to be left for the 'afterlife', then $F_2 = 0$, that is, net assets at the end of the second period are zero. But $F_2 = (1 + r)F_1 + PCA_2$. This means that $PCA_2 = -(1 + r)F_1$: it is a surplus used either to repay the debt plus interest if $F_1 < 0$, or a deficit to allow more absorption than production if $F_1 > 0$. It follows that $PCA_2 = -(1 + r)F_1 = -(1 + r)^2F_0 - (1 + r)PCA_1$.

primary current account determines the equilibrium real exchange rate.[12]

As it represents the long run, the equilibrium real exchange rate is unlikely to correspond to the observed real exchange rate at any point in time. Indeed, Figure 7.1 shows that the real exchange rate varies quite a bit, much more than would be warranted by the evolution of the net external position. When the real exchange rate is above its equilibrium level it is **overvalued**; it is **undervalued** in the opposite case. In the long run, however, it must return to its equilibrium value to ensure that the budget constraint is not violated.

7.4.3 The Fundamental Determinants of Real Exchange Rates

The result that the net external investment position drives the equilibrium real exchange rate is a very powerful one. It means that, eventually, market forces will take the real exchange rate to where it should be. The time required to get there can be considerable, however, taking several years or longer. A **misaligned exchange rate** implies either that the country is living beyond its means, which it can do only as long as it can continue to borrow, or that it is consuming and investing below its potential, and can keep doing so only as long as its households, firms, and government are willing to save. The concept of an equilibrium real exchange rate looks beyond such transitory phases to focus on the steady state. It is the beacon that shows where the real exchange rate is headed.

Graphically, this conclusion looks deceptively simple: the equilibrium exchange rate is determined by the PCA schedule and the initial net foreign asset position. It is possible, however, to go beyond the curves and ask which variables, known as the **fundamental determinants**, or **fundamentals** for short, are responsible for the evolution of the real exchange rate. While the analysis is motivated by Figure 7.7, which shows the special case of a balanced current account, it is consistent with the more general case treated on the website: the real exchange rate must be such that production and consumption decisions are consistent with the primary current account required by the budget constraint and, conversely, that any change in the real exchange rate is associated with changes in the relative production and consumption of traded and non-traded goods. What follows is a list of the most important fundamentals.

Net external position

Most evidently, the net external investment position is a fundamental determinant. The more positive the external investment position, the more appreciated is the equilibrium exchange rate. Similarly, indebted countries will require depreciated real equilibrium exchange rates in order to generate the resources for debt service. Figure 7.8 depicts the latter case: if foreign indebtedness grows from F_1 to F_1', the net asset position schedule shifts to the right, and the equilibrium real exchange rate must depreciate. In order to satisfy its budget constraint, a country that has been borrowing abroad must generate primary current account surpluses to service its debt. Productive resources have to be shifted towards the traded goods sector, and local demand must be curtailed. The real exchange rate depreciation provides the incentives needed for these changes to occur.

The net external position of a country is determined by history and is difficult if not impossible to change at any point in time. Examples abound of countries such as Indonesia and Nigeria which were made fabulously wealthy by oil discoveries, but then squandered their wealth and even became highly indebted as a result. Sometimes a sudden change in asset prices can bring about a change in the external position: a good example here is Sweden, shown in Figure 7.9. Note that an increase of the real interest rate paid on the external debt has the same effect as an increase in the debt itself.

Production: resources and structure

The PPF summarizes a country's resource endowments, productive capacities, and sectoral structure. These characteristics differ across countries and vary over time within a country. One general tendency is that the more the country production structure

---

[12] The same result can be reached with the help of Figure 7.7. It is presented on the website.

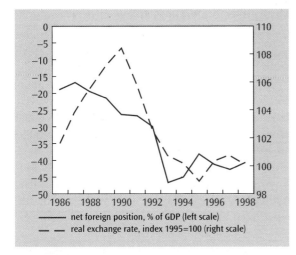

Fig. 7.9 Net External Position and the Real Exchange Rate: The Case of Sweden, 1986–1998

In the early 1980s, Sweden enjoyed a moderate current account surplus, hence a nearly stable net external position, with an indebtedness of about 20% of GDP. Then the real exchange appreciated and became overvalued as witnessed by a severe deterioration of the current account and the associated external debt build-up. In the early 1990s the real exchange rate started to depreciate. By the mid-1990s it had reached an equilibrium level as the debt stabilized.

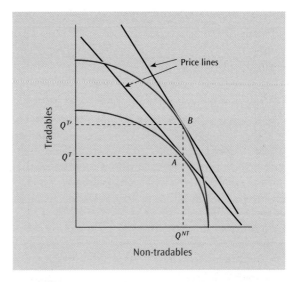

Fig. 7.10 The Equilibrium Real Exchange Rate and Productivity in the Traded Goods Sector

An increase in the productivity of the traded goods sector, which may also represent an exogenous tradable resource discovery, shifts the PPF upwards in a biased fashion. A real exchange rate which maintains constant non-tradable production (point B) must be appreciated relative to the original position (point A), as can be seen in the steeper price line.

is geared towards the production of traded goods, the higher is its equilibrium exchange rate. The reasoning is as follows: the more the country produces traded goods at the expense of non-traded goods, the less of the latter are available for domestic consumption. But domestic consumption is met by domestic production. To induce the economy to produce and consume in this way, *ceteris paribus*, the relative price of non-traded relative to traded goods, the real exchange rate σ, must rise to shift spending away from non-traded goods.

The best way to demonstrate this point is to ask the following question: what would happen if the traded goods sector suddenly became more productive? Figure 7.10 shows how the PPF would react, shifting upwards so that more tradable good output is feasible at any given output of non-tradable goods. Keeping production of non-tradables constant and continuing to assume external balance, the equilib-

rium exchange rate must appreciate (σ must rise) and the slope of the price line must become steeper.

Why could such a shift occur? A good example is the discovery of natural resources, which are highly tradable. When oil was discovered in the UK's North Sea in the mid-1970s, sterling's real exchange rate soon appreciated by more than 30%. Ironically, the result was a shift away from 'traditional' industry (other traded goods besides oil) towards services, with massive plant closures and unemployment as industrial workers could not be immediately absorbed by the oil industry or the non-traded goods sector. This striking process of de-industrialization is called the **Dutch disease**, ever since it was first diagnosed in the 1960s when gas was discovered in the Netherlands' side of the North Sea.[13] The Dutch disease explains why resource-rich countries typically

[13] The website presents the phenomenon in detail.

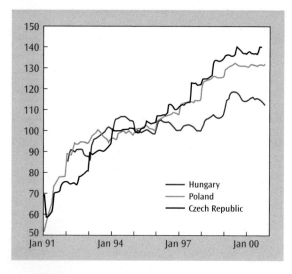

Fig. 7.11 **Real Exchange Rates in Transition Countries, 1991–2000 (Index: Jan. 1995=100)**

The figure depicts the evolution of the ratio of the price of services to the producer price index, a measure of the real exchange rate. All three successful transition countries show a strong upward trend, with accumulated real appreciation of 100% over a decade in the case of Poland.

find it more difficult to develop and maintain an industrial sector, as can be seen in contemporary Russia. This should not be a source of long-term concern though: why produce industrial goods when mother Nature provides easy exports? In the short run, however, the adjustment can be rather painful.

Another example is the kind of restructuring which has followed the end of central planning in Eastern and Central Europe. Under the previous regime, much emphasis had been put on producing heavy industry products which are normally considered tradable but were rarely sold outside of the Soviet block, while services were deliberately undersized. The transformation process has led to the quick emergence of the service sector and the gradual restructuring of the industrial sector toward producing goods which are effectively tradable. The result has been a strong trend towards appreciation as seen from Figure 7.11.

Absorption: preferences and wealth

Changes in consumption patterns also affect the equilibrium real exchange rate. For example, as we grow richer we spend more on non-traded goods. Nontraded services such as leisure (movies, restaurants, etc.), education, and medical services may even take an increasing importance in our budgets. Since non-traded goods must be produced domestically, an increased demand must be accompanied by a higher relative price to elicit more production. Anything which increases the wealth of resident households—a real estate or stock market boom, the repatriated earnings of foreign relatives, or foreign aid—can have similar effects.

The size of government, a big consumer, may also affect the real exchange rate. Governments spend a large part of their budgets on non-traded goods and services (public services, roads and other utilities). Since such spending is financed by taxes levied on people who tend to spend more on traded goods, an increase in the size of government tends to shift domestic absorption towards non-traded goods, and thus to raise their relative price, i.e. the real exchange rate.

In the end . . .

Any change that reflects 'deep' or structural changes is likely to affect the current account and therefore the equilibrium real exchange rate. In practice, however, disturbances large enough to produce significant changes in the equilibrium real exchange rate are rather rare events. This is why it is often a good rule of thumb to consider that the equilibrium real exchange rate remains roughly unchanged. But then one must be always on the watch for the possibility that a major change is under way. A point in the case is the catch-up process whereby poorer countries successfully enter a take-off growth phase. As they accumulate capital, import advanced technology, and become more productive their economies undergo a systematic transformation. The result is a continuing appreciation of the real exchange rate. This is known as the **Balassa–Samuelson effect**, which is described in Box 7.3.

Box 7.3	**The Balassa–Samuelson Effect**[14]

Travellers frequently note that wealthier countries are systematically more expensive than poorer ones. This is documented in Table 7.1, which shows the GDP deflators in various countries converted into a common currency. The GDP deflator is a weighted average of traded and non-traded goods prices. If the prices of internationally traded goods are roughly equalized in a common currency,[15] then differences in average price levels reflect differences in non-traded goods prices—such as haircuts, hotel rooms, transport, bread, and so on. The table then suggests that non-traded goods are cheaper in poorer countries. Why is that so? We have seen already that services, which constitute a large share of traded goods,

are 'luxury' goods. In poor countries, demand for services is limited and their prices are accordingly low.

A second reason is supply. Poorer countries are characterized by lower stocks of physical and/or human capital (Chapter 3), which implies low productivity in the traded goods sector. When productivity is low, for this sector to be competitive in world markets, wages must be commensurably low. Wages will also be low in the non-traded sector since worker mobility, customs (desire of fairness), and trade union activity typically prevent wages from differing much from one sector to another. With lower wages, prices in the non-traded goods sector will therefore be lower in poorer countries.

Table 7.1	**Price Level Comparison, 1992 (USA = 100)**

	Price Level GDP			Price Level GDP
Europe			**Asia**	
Austria	138.3		Bangladesh	10.9
Belgium	120.5		India	16.8
Denmark	147.1		Israel	106.6
France	126.2		Japan	148.6
Germany, West	136.0		Pakistan	22.2
Iceland	155.9		Singapore	97.6
Ireland	111.6			
Italy	126.5		**Africa**	
Netherlands	121.5		Chad	43.6
Norway	154.1		Egypt	28.6
Spain	113.3		Mozambique	7.1
Sweden	155.0		Nigeria	26.5
Switzerland	161.6			
UK	110.6		**Central and South America**	
			Brazil	52.2
North America and Oceania			Chile	47.9
			Mexico	49.2
Canada	97.9		Peru	77.1
USA	100.0		Venezuela	35.7
Australia	91.1			
New Zealand	77.6			

Source: Heston and Summers 1991 and update http://www.nber.org/data_index.html

[14] Named after the late Bela Balassa, Hungarian-born and for long at Johns Hopkins University in Baltimore, also known as gourmet and author of a confidential restaurant guide, and after Paul Samuelson, a Nobel Prize winner from MIT. A formal derivation of the Balassa–Samuelson effect is available on the web.

[15] The assumption that prices of internationally traded goods are equalized is sometimes called the Law of One Price. Reasons for and exceptions to this rule are developed in Ch. 8.

Summary

1. Real exchange rates measure the price of domestic goods in terms of foreign goods. A variety of prices can be used (export price index, CPI, WPI, GDP deflator, labour costs) to 'double-deflate' the nominal exchange rate and address different questions. A convenient definition is the ratio of non-traded to traded good prices.

2. Effective nominal and real exchange rates are weighted averages of a country's exchange rates vis-à-vis the rest of the world, in practice its main trading partners.

3. Regardless of the definition, the real exchange rate affects the primary current account. An decrease in the real exchange rate (a depreciation) will tend to improve the primary current account. Indeed, relatively lower non-traded good prices encourage producers to shift to the traded good sector away from the non-traded good sector, and encourage consumers to substitute non-traded for traded goods.

4. While the production and consumption of non-traded goods must be equal, the primary current account is the difference between the production of and spending on traded goods.

5. The primary current account is driven in the long run by the nation's budget constraint. So the equilibrium long-run real exchange rate depends on the country's inherited net external position. Countries that accumulate large external indebtedness will tend to have depreciating real exchange rates, and countries with large external asset positions will tend to have appreciating real exchange rates.

6. The equilibrium real exchange rate changes in response to disturbances that affect a country's structure: productivity, tastes, other relative prices. These are generally rare events.

7. Increases in wealth and productivity, especially in the traded goods sector, are associated with more appreciated real exchange rates. This explains why price levels measured in a common currency are lower in poorer countries.

Key Concepts

- relative prices
- real exchange rate
- nominal exchange rate
- European/British terms
- appreciation/depreciation
- effective exchange rates (nominal and real)
- primary current account function
- traded and non-traded goods
- production possibilities frontier (PPF)

- numeraire
- price line
- terms of trade: internal and external
- real equilibrium exchange rate
- over- and undervaluation
- misalignment
- Balassa–Samuelson effect
- fundamental determinants/fundamentals
- Dutch disease

Exercises

1. Are the following goods traded or non-traded? On what does your answer depend?
   (a) Restaurant meals
   (b) Banking services
   (c) Architectural services
   (d) Newspapers
   (e) Meat
   (f) Car rentals

2. What happens to the real exchange rate between two countries if the price level at home doubles, all other things given? If the price of foreign goods doubles? If the nominal exchange rate doubles?

3. Explain why it is optimal to produce along the PPF and not inside it. Picking a point on the PPF in Figure 7.7 that is not at the tangency with the price line, explain why it is desirable to move towards the tangency point.

4. After wars, victor-countries often exact reparations from the losers in the form of valuable resources, financial assets, or other forms of tradable wealth. What would you expect to be the effect of such action in each of the two countries? Thinking in terms of traded and non-traded goods, explain the effect on the relative price of traded goods, production, consumption, and the primary current account.

5. Redraw Figure 7.7 to represent the case of a primary current account surplus; of a primary current account deficit.

6. In the European Monetary Union, there is single monetary policy which aims at the area-wide inflation. Are there good reasons to expect inflation to differ systematically across countries?

7. What would you expect the effect of debt relief (i.e. the reduction of the debt in present-value terms) to have on the real exchange rate of a highly indebted country?

8. Estonia has tied its nominal exchange rate to the DM (and to the euro). Yet, inflation is significantly higher than in Germany. Why? Does it mean that its exchange rate is becoming overvalued?

9. Developing countries typically borrow abroad in foreign currency and therefore face interest costs determined by the foreign interest rate. Why do they fear increases in world interest rates?

Money

Until now our attention has been restricted to the real side of the economy. We have not yet recognized the existence of money and the fact that goods we buy and wages we earn are measured in units of money, or in *nominal terms*. This part corrects this important oversight. It also shows that it is possible to separate out the real from the nominal side in the long run. In the shorter run, however, the real and monetary sectors are intertwined. This interaction—among other things—gives rise to the phenomenon of business cycles, the succession of periods of rapid economic growth and recession.

The main objective of Part III is to establish what money is, how it is created, and what role it plays in a modern, open economy. We also study how central banks operate, torn between objectives that may be at times conflicting: setting the interest rate, the exchange rate, the rate of money growth, and ultimately the rate of inflation.

Money and the Demand for Money

8

Money is not, properly speaking, one of the subjects of commerce; but only the instrument which men have agreed upon to facilitate the exchange of one commodity for another. It is none of the wheels of trade: it is the oil which renders the motion of the wheels more smooth and easy.

– David Hume

The invention of a circulating medium, which supersedes the narrow, cumbrous process of barter, by facilitating transactions of every variety of importance among all sorts of people, is a grand type of advance in civilization.

– *Chambers's Encyclopedia, 1870*

8.1 Overview

All societies since time immemorial have used one form of money or another. Money is a very special form of wealth. Its return is typically very low— banknotes yield no interest at all—and yet it is perceived as desirable, even the ultimate form into which all other assets can be transformed. The reason is that money facilitates transactions between economic agents. It is indispensable to the proper functioning of a modern economy. To be convinced of this, we need only imagine the costs a barter economy would impose on our daily lives. Yet, the definition of money is far from clear. Banknotes and coins are money. What about chequebook

balances? Travellers' cheques? Savings accounts? Other financial instruments? There are indeed various forms of money, some of them even produced by different institutions. This chapter therefore starts with several definitions of money. The question of the supply of money, however, is left for the next chapter.

The present chapter focuses on the demand for money. Since money is not an ideal form for holding wealth, we need to understand why it is held at all. This is the first step towards understanding money's role in the macroeconomy: its effect on prices, interest rates, and, eventually, real economic activity.

8.2 What is Money?

The definition of money has been an issue of dispute for a long time, and the difficulties have been compounded recently by the computer and internet revolution. Once upon a time, gold, silver, and other commodities served as money. Slowly but surely, paper money (banknotes) edged out these **commodity monies**. Next came the widespread use of sight deposits. Nowadays, the speed, ease, and low cost of converting one type of asset into another have blurred conventional distinctions between money and other related forms of wealth. Plastic cards are a familiar sight and e-money is on the rise. A proper definition must capture the enduring qualities that

characterize money, while abstracting from those that are transient, arbitrary, or country-specific.

8.2.1 A Narrow Definition

Currency (banknotes and coins) is undoubtedly a form of money, even though a century ago there were doubts that these forms were as trustworthy as coins made from precious metals. Yet, the use of currency to settle transactions is relatively limited, economic agents often use bank deposits instead. This is the rationale for a first definition of money: currency in the hands of the public (households, firms, and governments) plus sight deposits (bank accounts that are payable on demand, often called demand deposits or checking accounts). This **monetary aggregate** is denominated as M1. One key characteristic of M1 is that it is generally accepted as a means of payment.

M1 = currency in circulation + sight deposits.

This measure is open to different interpretations which highlight the danger of rigid definitions. For example, should travellers' cheques be counted as money? They do not fit the bureaucrat's definition, but they seem to function much like the other stuff. Some countries do include travellers' cheques in M1. What about credit cards or even prepaid telephone cards, or foreign currency, which in some countries, such as post-communist Eastern Europe, is used alongside domestic currency? Practices differ, and changing circumstances and technology can call any definition into question.

8.2.2 Broader Aggregates

Sight deposits at banks have two main characteristics: (1) cheques can be written or transfers can be made against them, and (2) the interest paid is either nil or lower than what other assets offer. This is why banks often offer more attractive accounts that bear interest, but cannot be drawn on with cheques. Yet such funds can often be transferred into regular sight deposits—often a phone call, a series of key-strokes on a telephone handset or an internet connection, is enough. The ease of transfer renders these assets very similar to sight deposits. This is why they are included in our second definition of money, M2:

M2 = M1 + time (or savings) deposits at banks with unrestricted access.

An even broader measure includes instruments such as large certificates of deposit, or time deposits with a longer term and possibly restricted access, foreign currency deposits, and deposits with non-bank institutions. The precise meaning of 'larger' and 'longer maturity' depends on local rules and regulations. The distinction is one of degree: these instruments are less liquid, meaning that they are more costly or difficult to convert into cash or checking accounts. This is called M3:

M3 = M2 + larger, fixed-term deposits + accounts at non-bank institutions.

8.2.3 Liquidity versus Yield

Beyond currency and M1, all definitions are inevitably arbitrary and vary from country to country. This is why **monetary aggregates** like those presented in Table 8.1 are not directly comparable across countries. Still, all the aggregates measure the 'liquid wealth' of the non-banking sector. M1 is considered perfectly liquid, whereas M2 and M3 are not suitable for transactions and must generally be converted into M1 for that purpose.

Table 8.1   Money in Five Countries, December 2000

		Currency	M1	M2	M3
UK	(£bn)	27.1	459.8	804.5	926.1
	% GDP	3.0	47.9	85.0	96.7
Euro-zone	(€ bn)	347.5	2074.3	4287.2	5080.0
	% GDP	1.2	15.8	25.5	35.3
USA	($ bn)	530.5	1091.3	4945.7	7098.8
	% GDP	2.9	11.0	50.0	71.7

Sources: IMF; various central banks' bulletins.

Box 8.1 **The Vision of Wicksell: A Moneyless Society**

Once upon a time, money was gold or silver, or seashells, or large stones on South Pacific islands. Such **commodity money** has an *intrinsic* value, since it is made of goods that can be used for other purposes. These goods are 'wasted' when used as money, and this is one reason why paper and cheap metal have replaced silver or gold. A century ago, the Swedish economist Knut Wicksell went further. He asked: Why have money at all? He envisioned a central record keeper who would keep a tally of all credits and debits. Whenever an individual worked, his balance would be credited; whenever he spent, the balance would be debited. In principle, it would be possible to run a negative balance, i.e. to borrow from the system. In the end, instead of producing currency, the central bank would operate and guarantee the system and determine the value of the unit of account. At the time, Wicksell's moneyless society was dismissed as impractical science fiction.

A century later, the technical problems of establishing such a 'moneyless society' have been largely solved.

Large powerful computers can keep accurate, up-to-date records and investigate the creditworthiness of households and businesses. In Swindon, a community near London, a large-scale experiment with electronic cash cards was conducted by Mondex and NatWest Bank from 1995 to 1998, and pointed up a number of hurdles which still remain. Would there be a demand for money, as we have defined it, in a 'moneyless society'? If the system were perfect and all transactions could be recorded at point of sale, probably not. Yet the amount of trade that occurs in informal settings is still large, and often convenient. It may be a long time before the local newspaper kiosk installs such a system. More importantly, a significant portion of society may have something to hide from a system like Wicksell's. Anyone trying to evade taxes, work in the underground economy, or engage in other illicit activity will always desire a means of payment that is not necessarily traceable to the transacting party. Right or wrong, the very intrusiveness of Wicksell's system might be its most objectionable trait.

Beyond the definitions, differences across countries reflect the stage of development of banking services as well as national regulations. Banks and financial institutions (savings banks, unit trusts, investment management firms, and life insurance companies) compete for customers' wealth. In some countries banks are able to offer interest on checking accounts; in others they have to compete through different means (free bank accounts, proximity of branches, computerized services). Competition and technical change force banks and financial institutions to invent new types of accounts that are not part of M1 but are better remunerated and yet easily transformed into a form suitable for transactions. The computer revolution has made complex transfer agreements virtually costless and has thereby rendered money definitions increasingly arbitrary. Many believe we are not so far from reinventing the moneyless society that the Swedish economist Knut Wicksell once imagined and is described in Box 8.1. As a simplification, we will generally think of money in terms of its narrower definition, M1.

8.3 Why Is This Money?

Technology makes the search for a definition of money very difficult indeed. Perhaps it would make more sense to look for defining characteristics of money. Why is M1 money? Why do businesses and individuals use it? On the surface, both questions seem trivial. Good business sense would say that money is whatever is generally accepted in payment, and it is used because others will accept it. The reasoning is circular: money is money because it is accepted, and it is accepted because it is money! In a perplexing way, this circularity is one of money's most intrinsic and durable aspects, despite its other rapidly changing attributes over the centuries. In the end, the best definition of money is: an asset that is generally accepted as a means of payment.[1]

8.3.1 Economic Functions of Money

An alternative, and widely used, approach is to define money by its attributes, that is by what money does for us and why we use it. This section presents several key ideas from this rich tradition.[2]

A medium of exchange

Money is a **medium of exchange**. People use it to settle accounts, regardless of what is being bought or sold. In a remarkably convenient way, money solves the **double coincidence of wants**. Thomas is selling apples. François is interested in purchasing some, but he is selling tomatoes which Thomas does not want to buy (he is looking for potatoes). Direct trade may not take place between the two of them. They would need to find Vittorio, who happens to be selling potatoes and is interested in buying tomatoes. Money admirably solves that problem.

A unit of account

In a moneyless or barter economy, all goods would be traded according to their relative prices (tomatoes versus apples versus potatoes versus tomatoes). As the number of goods grows, the number of relative prices rises rapidly. With two goods there is a single relative price; with three goods, there are three relative prices; with five goods, ten. If there are 50 goods, the number of relative prices rises to 1225; and so on.[3] The need for a 'common denominator' or **unit of account** is obvious. Money serves as a numeraire or a benchmark in which all other goods are priced.

A store of value and standard of deferred payment

Money is indeed an asset, and is therefore one way of holding wealth. Wealth transfers resources from the present to the future, for later consumption or further wealth accumulation. The value of money may change over time, but that is true of any other **store of value**. Similarly, money can be used as the numeraire in which debt contracts are written: it serves as a **standard of deferred payment**.

8.3.2 A Dominated Asset

Money is a **dominated asset**. It bears a lower rate of return than assets of comparable riskiness, such as Treasury bills (short-term government bonds), which are also backed by the state. This yield disadvantage can be seen as the cost of 'staying liquid' and is the reason for the systematic inverse relationship between liquidity and returns: the larger the yield on a monetary instrument, the more restrictions are attached to it. Examples are the need to maintain a minimum (and often substantial) balance, limitations on the minimum amount that can be settled per cheque, charges on cheque writing or transfers to other accounts, and so on. As a rule, the more liquid an asset is, the lower is its yield; the price of liquidity is forgone interest.

8.3.3 A Public Good

Money compensates for its inferiority in terms of interest by serving as the means of payment. In other words, it is so generally accepted that it can be used as payment without asking. But *why* is it so generally accepted? The following example can illustrate this very special feature of money.

Suppose a shopkeeper accepts a written promise from a trustworthy customer to pay his grocery bill at some future date. This promise, or IOU,[4] represents the shopkeeper's claims on his customer's future resources, and is simply a loan. This loan has value; if the customer in question is particularly trustworthy, the shopkeeper might be able to use this IOU to pay for his own purchases. The IOU could end up held by parties completely unrelated to the shopkeeper or his customer; it might be used as *money*. For that to happen, the public will require significant information about the initial customer's

---

[1] In a way, we know about as much as a US Supreme Court Justice knew when asked to define pornography: I can't tell you what it is, but I know it when I see it.

[2] This tradition starts with the work of British economist William Jevons (1875).

[3] The mathematical formula for the number of relative or bilateral prices is $n(n-1)/2$, where n is the number of goods.

[4] IOU = I owe you.

Box 8.2   Parallel Currencies

There have been a number of episodes in history when private money has circulated alongside, or even in lieu of, fiat money created by the state. Some examples of such 'free issue' environments are Scotland in the eighteenth century, the USA in the nineteenth century, and Hong Kong today. In these episodes banknotes privately issued by local banks circulated along with gold, silver, or national banknotes. Even assuming its authenticity, however, it was often difficult for those presented with such banknotes to know their true value, since this involved information about the solvency of the bank in question, as well as what others thought of the notes. Generally, banknotes were sold at a discount from face value. (In nineteenth-century USA, it was related to the distance from the issuing bank.) Banknotes were treated as the senior debt of the issuing bank: their holders were the very first to be paid off in the event of bankruptcy. All the same, bank failures often meant that the money became worthless. It was common for 'banknote reporters' to publish regular listings of counterfeit banknotes as well as discounts or premiums in terms of gold, so that transacting parties might agree on an exchange value.

Nowadays parallel currencies are observed in countries with extreme economic instability and mistrust of the government, but they usually circulate in the form of foreign exchange rather than private issue. US dollars and Deutschmarks circulated freely in many Eastern European and Latin American countries, as well as in Israel during the hyperinflation of the early 1980s. This phenomenon of *dollarization* became very widespread in the former communist countries early on in their process of economic transformation; Table 8.2 shows the extent of currency substitution that occurred. Dollarization usually comes to an end as soon as conditions stabilize and public trust is restored.

Table 8.2   Currency Substitution in Central and Eastern Europe, 1993[a]

Albania	18	Poland	28
Bulgaria	30	Romania	35
Estonia	5	Russia	35
Latvia	25	Slovenia	42
Lithuania	25	Ukraine	28

[a] Currency substitution is defined as the ratio of foreign currency deposits to broad money.
Source: Sahay and Végh (1995).

---

creditworthiness. And yet, if they simply *assume* that the customer is creditworthy, the money could circulate as a means of payment without any difficulty. In the end, the reputation of the initial issues of the IOUs determines the acceptability of this type of money. Yet it is very unlikely that the shopkeeper himself, much less third parties, will ever know, or care to know, enough about individuals to accept their IOUs as money. Private IOUs are a victim of **information asymmetry**: the fact that others know less about the customer than he himself does. As a result, if his IOUs were widely accepted, he could very well one day succumb to the temptation of issuing more IOUs than he is able to repay. Since this potential misbehaviour is easily suspected, no one will accept these IOUs.

Money is accepted either because it has intrinsic value (gold, for example), or because it is an IOU from an institution with a solid reputation. The creditworthiness of the state is essential for **fiat money**[5]—non-commodity money—to circulate. Confidence emerges as the key characteristic of money. Other institutions may attempt to acquire sufficient reputation to issue their own parallel currencies, and Box 8.2 reports on some historical experiments with them.

For IOUs to circulate in the above example, several costs are incurred. The value of the IOUs must be ascertained at each transaction, and in case of default the shopkeeper may be required to guarantee the bad debt. The safety of money is a **public good**, meaning that it is enjoyed simultaneously by different people. The social benefit (the gains to all members of the community) from this activity exceeds its

---

[5] Fiat comes from the Latin 'let there be', or 'let it be'.

private cost (to the shopkeeper). Unfortunately, the shopkeeper cannot charge others for providing this service and so he has little incentive to supply private money, even if it is desirable from a social point of view. It is a general result that, if left to the market, public goods are undersupplied, no matter how useful they are. This is where governments have a special responsibility. Because they are easily

recognized and enjoy more credibility than the average citizen, governments usually establish the monetary standard and supply the medium of exchange, declaring it to be legal tender and requiring that it be accepted in exchange for goods. In the end, this is probably the most efficient way of satisfying the definition given at the beginning of this section.

8.4 Money: A Balance Sheet Approach

8.4.1 Consolidated Balance Sheets

Money is an asset for those who hold it. With the exception of commodity money, however, it is also someone else's liability. This can be seen by examining the **balance sheets** of the banking system displayed in Figure 8.1. A balance sheet is a snapshot of an entity's financial status. **Net worth** is the difference between the value of its assets—listed on the left side of the balance sheet—and its liabilities—listed on the right side. We consider three big players: the central bank, the commercial banking sector, and the non-banking sector, which includes households, corporations, and the government.

The balance sheets depicted in Figure 8.1 are *consolidated*: the assets and liabilities belonging to the same sector cancel. For example, within the non-bank sector, borrowing by the government or corporations from private citizens cancel out and do not appear. The money stock M1 is represented by the tinted area, the sum of currency held by the public and sight deposits. It is on the asset side of the non-financial sector.[6] It appears simultaneously as a liability of the consolidated banking sector.

8.4.2 Currency as a Liability of the Central Bank

Cash held by the public is a liability of the central bank. When central banks first began issuing paper money, or currency, in the nineteenth century, they committed themselves to exchanging these banknotes against gold on demand. This is how the public eventually came to trust paper money and regard it as good as gold or silver. Today, the gold backing is gone, gold holdings represent a very small fraction of a central bank's assets, and silver has all but disappeared from their vaults. As Table 8.3 shows, precious metals have since been supplanted by the debt of the Treasury, the commercial banking system, or foreign central banks. These assets now constitute the 'backing' for currency.

8.4.3 Sight Deposits as a Liability of Commercial Banks

Sight deposits, the larger part of M1, are liabilities of the commercial banking sector. Figure 8.1 shows that sight deposits are backed by three types of asset. First, banks hold some currency and deposits with the central bank; both of these are the central bank's liability. (We ignore here their holdings of foreign currency.) Second, banks may own government debt. Third, banks hold debt of households and firms. If we consolidate the liabilities of the central bank and commercial banks, we arrive at M1 and the government's own deposits. Money is thus as good as the consolidated assets of the central bank and the commercial banks, and that is the

[6] Following common practice, we have excluded government deposits at the central bank from M1. Government accounts tend to be quite volatile and are not really under the control of the private sector. Volatility is a problem because the aggregates often move too much to be used as a gauge of monetary conditions. In some countries (for example the USA), as a result of a sharp distinction between the Treasury and the central bank, the Treasury actually refrains from using the central bank for the bulk of its transactions, preferring accounts at commercial banks.

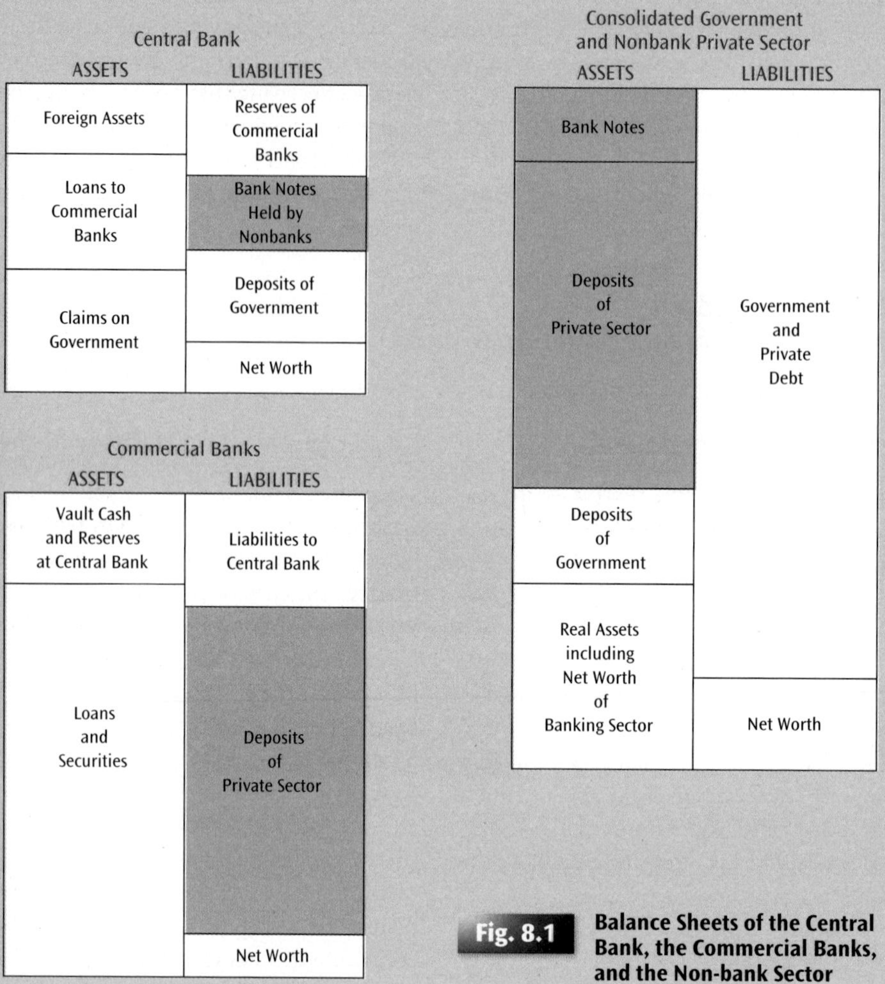

Fig. 8.1 Balance Sheets of the Central Bank, the Commercial Banks, and the Non-bank Sector

Table 8.3 Assets of Central Banks in Selected Countries, Mid-year 2000 (bn euros)

	Gold	Foreign assets	Loans to commercial banks	Claims on gov't
Euroland	117.3	341.8	477.3	112.8
USA	11.8	61.0	—	561.3
UK	4.8	30.3	—	22.7
Japan	1.2	268.9	39.9	487.9
Sweden	0.3	17.5	4.8	2.5
Poland	1.0	27.0	1.7	4.7

Source: IMF.

indebtedness of the government and of the private sector.

This is why, in the end, modern money—in contrast to gold or silver money—ultimately rests on the trust of agents in their own economies. To bolster this trust, regulations are designed to enhance the creditworthiness of the banking sector. Yet, banking panics may occur in troubled times, when the value of such regulation may be called into question. Out of concern for their wealth, people withdraw their deposits to acquire foreign currencies or other non-financial assets such as gold or durable goods. When the chain of confidence breaks in one place, the whole fragile edifice can come tumbling down.

8.5   The Demand for Money

It is the exceptional individual indeed who derives pleasure from owning and holding money per se. For most households and firms, money is useful because it facilitates transactions. Since money is a dominated asset, however, most people will not hold a significant fraction of their wealth in that form. Figure 8.2 shows the evolution of M1 and M2, scaled by nominal output (M/PY). Because the money stocks are nominal, it is natural to measure them relative to nominal rather than real output. Recent

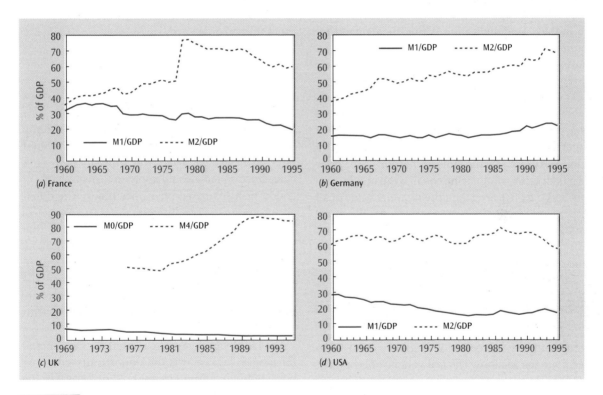

Fig. 8.2   **Narrow and Wide Monetary Aggregates, Four Countries, 1960–1995**

Changing definitions over time and across countries makes it difficult to track down the evolution of monetary aggregates. For Britain, we show the monetary base M0, a very narrow aggregate, and M4, a very wide aggregate. In France, M2 was redefined in 1978, hence the break in the series. Possible economies of scale may encourage a downward trend in the narrow aggregates. In Germany and the UK the narrower aggregate has declined in part because depositors have shifted part of the wider aggregates into better remunerated bank accounts.

Sources: IMF; CSO (UK).

innovations in payment technologies have provided a convenient means of shifting resources from non-interest-bearing, or low-interest, sight deposits (M1) to better remunerated accounts (M2). This may explain the upward trend in M2 although the expected downward trend in M1 is at best modest. In fact, the figure suggests that where a downward trend occurred it was reversed after 1985. Both ratios also fluctuate quite sizeably. This section is devoted to explaining these evolutions in money demand.

8.5.1 The Price Level as a Determinant of Money Demand

Money demand is largely motivated by the need to carry out transactions, that is, by its command over goods and services. Money is valued for its purchasing power, and this purchasing power is measured by the price level—effectively the cost of goods in terms of money. The implication is that the demand for money is a demand for *real* rather than nominal balances. The real value of money can be represented as:

$$\text{Real money stock} = M/P,$$

where M is the nominal stock of money and P is the consumer price index (CPI). The real money stock remains unchanged when the nominal stock increases exactly by the same proportion as the price level. All other things being equal, if the money supply and the price level (and the nominal value of all other assets in the economy) were to double, there would be no effect on the real economy. This property is called the **neutrality of money**. Its importance for macroeconomics cannot be exaggerated.

8.5.2 Real Income as a Determinant of Money Demand

The main reason for holding money (M1) is to facilitate transactions. The real volume of economic activity must therefore be an important factor in determining the demand for money, and we should expect a positive relationship between real GDP and the real money stock. Is this relationship proportional? The Appendix shows that **transaction costs** (bank commissions, or time and effort spent converting money from and into other assets) lead

people to use money more efficiently. If we ignore this effect, however, the demand for money should be positively related to the level of economic activity, approximated by the GDP.[7]

The elasticity of money demand with respect to GDP is defined as the percentage increase in money demand resulting from a 1% increase in the GDP.[8] If it is equal to unity, money demand is proportional to GDP. The presence of scale economies would correspond to elasticities less than unity. Table 8.4 presents elasticities of money demand for a number of countries, separating the short run (within one quarter) from the long run. For the long run, when adjustment of money balances is complete, the elasticities are as often above as they are below unity, the average being 1.2. Bearing in mind the lack of precision inherent in obtaining such estimates, it is acceptable, as a rule of thumb, to consider that money demand is about proportional to income, all other things equal.

8.5.3 Nominal Interest Rates as a Determinant of Money Demand

The **nominal interest rate** is the rate actually paid by borrowers for loans or bonds that are denominated in money terms. By contrast, real interest rates—which have been the only interest rates considered so far—would apply to loans in terms of goods, or loans based on a price index. The difference between the two interest rates is that the prices of goods typically rise because of inflation, so that repayment of loans in money rather than 'in kind' at the same interest rate would penalize the lender. If he expects to receive money worth less in the future, he will require a higher nominal interest rate as compensation: the nominal rate increases with inflation (see Section 8.7.2).

The nominal interest rate matters for the demand for money because it is the **opportunity cost** that households and firms face for holding wealth in the fallow form of money. Money bears a zero nominal interest rate—and a negative real interest rate, as

---

[7] GDP is not an ideal measure of transactions; total sales, as opposed to final sales, might be preferable.

[8] The formal definition is $\dfrac{\Delta(M/P)/(M/P)}{\Delta Y/Y}$.

Table 8.4	**Elasticities of Money Demand (effect of a 1% increase in income (GNP) or of a 1 percentage point increase in the nominal interest rate)**			

	Real income		**Nominal interest rate**	
	Short run	**Long run**	**Short run**	**Long run**
Belgium	0.06	0.41	−0.50	−3.57
Denmark	0.27	1.67	−0.30	−1.88
Finland	0.64	1.13	−0.77	−1.57
France	0.10	0.36	−0.19	−0.70
Germany	0.35	1.19	−0.53	−1.83
Greece	0.16	1.25	−0.13	−1.00
Ireland	0.07	1.48	−0.45	−9.00
Italy	0.11	1.88	−0.31	−5.17
Netherlands	0.41	0.71	−0.86	−1.51
Norway	0.09	1.74	−0.23	−4.60
Portugal	0.18	0.95	−0.51	−2.68
Sweden	0.49	1.40	N.A.	N.A.
Switzerland	0.04	0.36	−0.79	−7.18
UK	0.12	1.70	−0.43	−6.14
Japan	0.05	1.76	−0.44	−6.29
USA	0.06	1.18	−0.12	−2.40
Unweighted av.		1.20		−3.70

Note: The short-run effect is measured within a quarter. The long-run effect corresponds to a complete adjustment of indefinite duration. The demand concerns the real stock of money.
Source: Fair (1987).

explained below—which must be compared with the nominal rate available for other assets. Holding money implies forgoing that nominal interest rate. For firms which work with large cash balances, these costs can be significant, so cash management, the art of keeping these balances low, is very serious business. Table 8.4 shows estimates of the elasticity of money demand vis-à-vis the interest rate. The negative signs confirm that money demand declines when interest rates rise. The average long-run effect means that, when the nominal interest rate rises by one percentage point, real money demand falls by 3.7%.[9]

[9] There is a subtle difference between the income elasticity of money demand (the percentage effect of a 1% increase in income) and the semi-elasticity of a one-percentage-point increase in the interest rate. Formally, the elasticity of y with respect to x is $(\Delta y/y)/(\Delta x/x)$ and the semi-elasticity is $(\Delta y/y)/\Delta x$.

8.5.4 The Money Demand Function

Summarizing, we have found that the demand for nominal money is proportional to the price level, or, equivalently, the demand for money is a demand for real money. Real money, in turn, is demanded to facilitate real transactions and therefore increases with the real GDP. Holding money, though, has a cost that is measured by the nominal interest rate. Higher interest rates discourage the holding of wealth in the form of money. On the other hand, if it is costly to turn other assets into liquidity, real money holdings are larger. The **money demand function** is a compact way of describing these various effects:

$$(8.1) \qquad M/P = \mathscr{L}(Y, i, c),$$
$$\qquad\qquad\qquad + \; - \; +$$

Box 8.3 **The Many Reasons for Holding Money**

The demand for money is explained in the text by its role in facilitating transactions. This is often called the *inventory theory of money* because it comes from the trade-off between the cost of holding that inventory—interest costs—and the transaction cost of converting interest-bearing assets into money. The inventory explanation may also be expanded to account for uncertainty and the perceived risk of being caught without liquidity in emergencies. This behaviour is dubbed the *precautionary motive* and generally predicts that the demand for money rises when economic conditions become more uncertain.

A very different approach emphasizes that money is one asset among several. The *portfolio balance view* argues that agents spread their wealth so as to diversify their assets, considering not only the returns (zero for currency, the nominal yield on bonds) but also the risk

characteristics of each asset. The corresponding demand-for-money function includes the interest rate and transaction costs as before, but instead of transactions and the real GDP it is related to wealth. One particular aspect of the portfolio approach is the *speculative motive*. In fast-moving financial markets, traders must be ready to buy or sell quickly very large amounts of assets. When interest rates are low and expected to rise, bond prices are expected to fall. (Box 3.2 explains the inverse relationship between bond prices and the interest rate.) It is then considered better to 'stay liquid', to hold more money and fewer bonds on which capital losses are possible. Conversely, when interest rates are high and expected to fall, traders want to acquire bonds and take advantage of capital gains when their prices rise: the speculative demand for money declines.

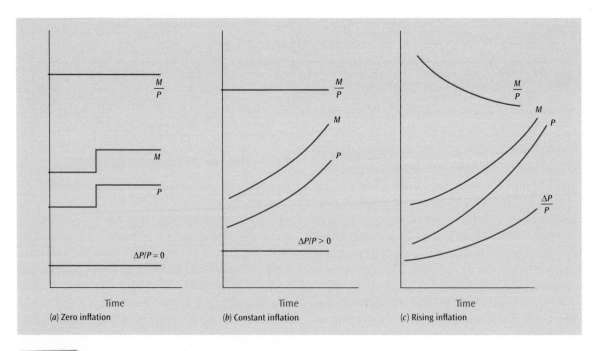

(a) Zero inflation   (b) Constant inflation   (c) Rising inflation

Fig. 8.3 **Money Demand and Prices (assuming no real GDP growth)**

When expected inflation is constant, real money demand is constant and nominal money demand just moves with the price level. This is true for both panels (a) and (b). In panel (a) there is a one-shot unexpected price increase. In panel (c) prices rise at an increasing rate. As inflation increases, real money demand declines, which means that the nominal money demand grows less quickly than prices.

where M is the nominal stock of money, P is the price level, Y is real GDP, i is the nominal interest rate, and c is the average cost of converting other forms of wealth into money. The signs underneath remind us of the effect of each variable on the demand for money. The Appendix shows how (8.1) can be formally justified by inventory management principles. Other justifications are summarized in Box 8.3.

The effect of the price level on money demand is shown in Figure 8.3, where it is assumed, for simplicity, that real GDP is constant. Then, as long as the inflation rate ($\Delta P/P$) is constant, the real demand for money remains unchanged. Panel (a) shows the case of zero inflation ($\Delta P/P = 0$). The price level is constant, except for a single jump which is perceived by agents as one-off (for example, an increase in sales tax or VAT). Panel (b) shows the case of a non-zero but constant inflation rate ($\Delta P/P > 0$). Real money demand is constant, but lower than with zero inflation, and the nominal money demand rises in proportion to the price level. Panel (c) shows the case where inflation is rising. Real money demand

declines while nominal money grows increasingly faster, yet more slowly than the price level.

The **velocity of money** measures how many times on average a unit of money is spent during the measurement period (usually a year). It is defined as $V = PY/M$, and is the inverse of the ratio shown in Figure 8.2. For example, if $V = 3$, the money stock M is spent on average three times on the GDP, or the money stock 'turns round three times' over the year. Given the money demand function, velocity is:

$$(8.2) \qquad V = Y/\mathcal{L}(Y, i, c)$$

In the particular case where real money demand is proportional to real GDP, velocity is independent of GDP.[10] In the short run, transaction costs do not change much so that velocity simply moves as the interest rate changes. When the interest rate rises, holding money becomes more expensive and people save on cash balances; the money turns round faster, and velocity increases. Over the longer run, if transaction costs decline, people will hold less money and velocity will show a rising trend.

8.6   Equilibrium in the Money Market: The Short Run

The real money demand function is depicted in Figure 8.4. Its negative slope reflects the opportunity cost of holding money. Its position corresponds to a particular GDP level. If the GDP increases, so does the demand for money at any nominal interest rate. The schedule shifts to the right.

Chapter 9 is devoted entirely to the way central banks control the supply of money. Here we simply assume that the central bank fixes the nominal money supply which, for a given price level, renders the real money supply exogenous, hence the vertical line in Figure 8.4. Money market equilibrium is described by the intersection of both schedules. This simple apparatus can be used to explain the short-run relationship between money and interest rates. It is only a short-run view because it takes as exogenous the real GDP, the price level, and the inflation

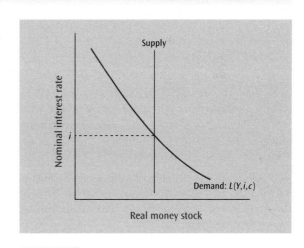

Fig. 8.4   **Equilibrium in the Money Market**

Given the level of economic activity and the cost of converting funds, the negative slope of the money demand curve reflects the effect of the opportunity cost of holding money. When the central bank sets the money supply (the vertical supply schedule), the interest rate adjusts to clear the money market.

---

[10] When money demand is proportional to real GDP, it can be rewritten as $L(Y, i, c) = Y\, l(i, c)$ and $V = Y/Y\, l(i, c) = 1/l(i, c)$.

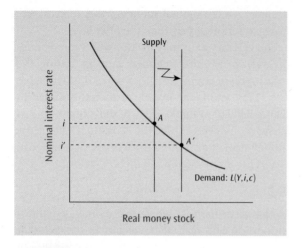

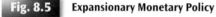

Fig. 8.5   **Expansionary Monetary Policy**

An increase in the real money supply lowers the nominal interest rate. A decline in interest rates induces a higher demand so as to match the higher supply.

rate: over the short run (say, a quarter) these variables normally change very little. With a constant inflation rate, the results that follow apply to both the nominal and real interest rates.

8.6.1 Money Supply Effects

Figure 8.5 shows the effect on interest rates of an increase in the real money supply, represented by a rightward shift in the vertical schedule. The demand curve does not shift, since its other determinants (real GDP and transactions costs) are assumed to remain unaffected.[11] As the equilibrium moves from A to A', the interest rate declines. This illustrates the power of the central bank to influence interest rates. A restrictive or 'tight' monetary policy occurs when the central bank contracts the real money supply, which would be represented by a leftward shift of the vertical supply schedule. In that case nominal and real interest rates rise.

8.6.2 Cyclical Fluctuations

An increase in real GDP increases money demand, and the demand schedule shifts to the right as

[11] Ch. 10 directly addresses the effects of money supply on GNP.

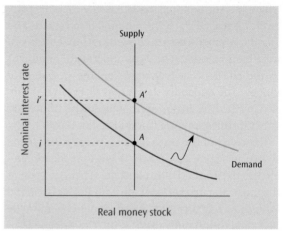

Fig. 8.6   **An Increase in Real Economic Activity**

An increase in real economic activity increases the demand for money and the schedule shifts to the right. Starting at point A, the new equilibrium occurs at point A' and the nominal interest rate increases from i to i'. With supply unchanged, demand cannot increase in equilibrium. The interest rate must rise until its negative effect on demand exactly offsets the positive effect of the increase in GDP.

shown in Figure 8.6. If the real money supply remains unchanged, the interest rate must rise until the increased demand induced by the higher GDP is entirely offset by the higher opportunity cost of holding money. This is one reason why interest rates are procyclical, rising in booms and declining in recessions.

8.6.3 Transaction Costs

If the nominal cost of converting wealth between interest-bearing assets and money decreases, more wealth is held in the form of interest-bearing assets and less in the form of money. The money demand curve shifts to the left, as in Figure 8.7, and interest rates fall to the point where the opportunity cost is low enough to persuade agents to hold the existing money supply. An example of a decrease in transaction costs is the development and introduction of automatic teller machines. On the other hand, transaction costs might increase if banks decided to charge more for transfers, or if an increase in wages made individuals' leisure time more valuable.

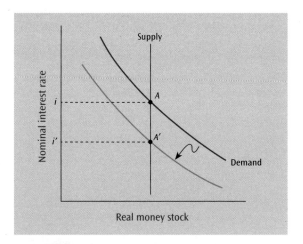

Fig. 8.7   A Decline in Transaction Costs

A decline in the cost of converting assets from money to interest-bearing forms reduces the demand for money and shifts the demand schedule to the left. Since the supply does not change, the interest rate must fall to reduce the opportunity cost of holding money until demand is restored to its initial level.

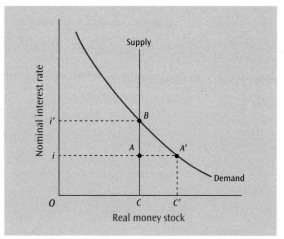

Fig. 8.8   Money Market Disequilibrium

Point A to the left of the demand curve describes a situation of excess demand for money. At the relatively low interest rate i, agents want to hold more real money balances (at point A' on the demand curve). They attempt to sell other assets or borrow money, but with unchanged supply the interest rate rises until equilibrium is restored at point B at interest i'.

8.6.4 The Equilibrating Role of the Interest Rate and Asset Prices

How is equilibrium achieved in the short run? Point A in Figure 8.8 is to the left of the demand curve: it depicts the case of an excess demand for money. At interest rate i, agents would like to hold real balances (point A') in excess of the available supply (point A). To obtain additional liquidity, they attempt to sell other assets such as bonds or to borrow funds from each other. With a fixed money supply OC, however, these efforts cannot be successful in the aggregate. The interest rate increases as the result of competi-tion for more money, and bond prices fall as more bonds are offered for sale.[12] Equilibrium is restored at point B at interest rate i'.

Financial markets react extremely quickly to dis-equilibria. This is because large losses can be incurred by holding bonds when their prices are falling. Similarly, very large capital gains are available to those who buy bonds before their prices increase. Any disequilibrium in the money market is elimin-ated by swift interest rate and bond price changes, and the economy promptly returns to its money demand schedule.

8.7   Equilibrium in the Money Market: The Long Run

The money market equilibrium condition also settles the long-run link between money, prices and inflation, and the exchange rate. Two very simple and powerful results emerge. First, in the long run, inflation is determined by the rate of money growth. Second, in the long run, the rate of exchange rate depreciation is determined by the rate of inflation. Figure 8.9(a) presents long-run averages of money growth and inflation rates for all the OECD countries.

---

[12] The link between interest rates and bond prices is presented in Box 5.2.

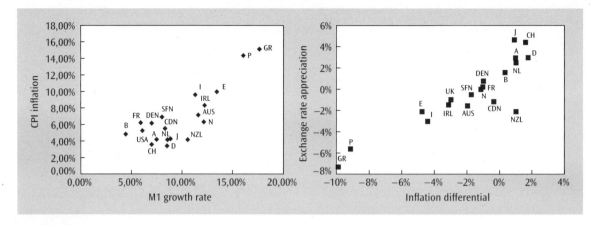

Fig. 8.9 Money, Inflation, and Exchange Rate Appreciation in the Long Run: OECD Countries, 1970–1998

Averaging over many years eliminates short-run effects. Panel (*a*) shows that countries that have experienced high inflation rates are those where nominal money has grown faster. Panel (*b*) shows that the rate of exchange rate depreciation vis-à-vis the USA is about equal to the inflation differential exchange vis-à-vis the USA, as suggested by purchasing power parity.
Source: IMF.

Panel (*b*) does the same for exchange rates and inflation (relatively to the dollar and US inflation). While not perfect, the positive relationship between all three variables is unmistakable.

8.7.1 Long-Run Inflation

As the economy grows, more money is needed to facilitate more transactions. In Figure 8.10, this means that the demand schedule continuously shifts to the right. If the real money stock were held constant, the interest rate would grow from point *A* to point *A'* and then continuously further up as the demand schedule moves rightward. But we know that nominal interest rates do not grow without bounds over the long run. The two examples in Figure 8.11 show that the British and Dutch nominal interest rate rose at times of sustained inflation (after the Second World War and then in the 1970s). But they seem to have returned to lower levels, rather than continuing to rise. What must happen in Figure 8.10 is that the supply schedule eventually moves rightward until it passes through a point like *B* where the real money supply matches the long-run growth in its demand. How can that be?

In the long run, the central bank controls only the *nominal* money stock. It can affect neither prices,

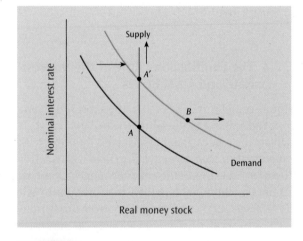

Fig. 8.10 Money and Long-Run Growth

As real GDP increases, so does the demand for real money. The demand schedule shifts to the right. If the real money supply did not respond, the interest rate would rise, as shown by the move from point *A* to point *A'*. Continuous growth would result in an ever shifting demand schedule and an ever rising interest rate. The absence of long-run trend in the nominal interest rate means that, somehow, the supply curve must shift over time to move from *A* to *B*, and further to the right.

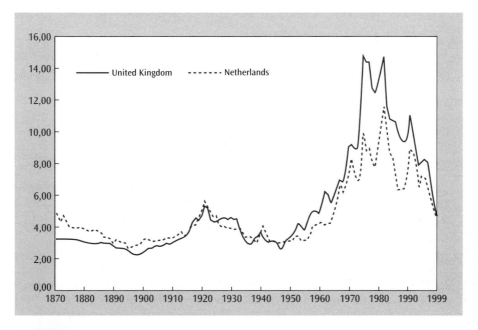

Fig. 8.11 **Nominal Interest Rates, UK and the Netherlands, 1870–1999**

Over very long periods the nominal interest rate is trendless, despite shorter-run fluctuations and possible 'staircase behaviour' reflecting the higher inflation rate of the 1970s and 1980s.
Sources: Homer (1963); IMF.

Table 8.5 **Inflation and Money Growth in the Long Run: A Rule of Thumb (assuming that real money demand grows at 3% p.a.)**

Nominal money supply (%)	Inflation rate (%)
0	−3
3	0
8	5
50	47
103	100

nor inflation, nor the real money supply. The only possibility of reconciling any discrepancy between real money demand (*M/P*) and nominal supply (*M*) growth is for prices and inflation to play the balancing act as endogenous variables. Inflation is

the channel through which, in the long run, money market equilibrium is ultimately achieved. (See Box 8.4 for details.)

Consider the case shown in Table 8.5, where economic growth implies a 3% average annual increase

---

Box 8.4   The Algebra of Long-Run Inflation

The money demand function $\mathcal{L}(Y, i, c)$ identifies three determinants of the real money stock. As long as the transaction cost c is constant in real terms, it can safely be ignored. Similarly, when the interest rate does not exhibit any long-term trend, despite considerable variability, it does not affect real money in the long run. This just leaves the real GDP. If η is the elasticity of the demand for money with respect to GDP, an annual GDP growth rate of g translates into an annual growth rate ηg in money demand. Noting that the growth rate of the real money stock is the difference between the growth rates of the nominal money stock and the price level, we have the equilibrium condition:

$$(8.3) \qquad \Delta(M/P)/(M/P) = \mu - \pi = \eta g$$

where $\mu = \Delta M/M$ and $\pi = \Delta P/P$. Given the real growth rate g, this expression shows that the long-run inflation rate is the difference between the nominal money growth rate and the rate of growth of real GNP, up to the elasticity factor η:

$$(8.4) \qquad \pi = \mu - \eta g.$$

Looking ahead, the relationship (8.4) can be combined with relative purchasing power parity (PPP) in equation (8.9) to yield the long-run rate of exchange rate depreciation:

$$(8.5) \qquad \Delta S/S = (\mu^* - \mu) - (\eta^* g^* - \eta g).$$

Faster money growth abroad than at home ($\mu^* > \mu$) leads in the long run to an appreciation. Faster output growth at home than abroad ($g > g^*$) also leads to an appreciation, if the faster demand for money is not accommodated by a faster growth in the money supply.

---

in real money demand. If the central bank allows the nominal money stock to grow at the same 3% per year, demand and supply will coincide when the average inflation rate is 0%. Were the nominal money stock to grow at an average annual rate of 8%, inflation would have to be 5%: only then would the real money stock grow at the same 3% rate (8% nominal less 5% of inflation) as real money demand. This is why in the long run inflation is a monetary phenomenon. It is due to money growth in excess of what is strictly demanded by the public. Figure 8.9 confirms the strength of this conclusion.

8.7.2 Inflation and the Fisher Principle

Section 8.5.1 looked at the role of the price level in the demand for money. The rate of inflation, i.e. the rate of increase in the price level, has an independent effect on money demand. The distinction is subtle and is illustrated in Figure 8.3 above. A once-and-for-all and unexpected increase in the price *level* raises nominal money demand proportionately. In contrast, continuous price increases—

inflation—erode the purchasing power of money. For example, with a 10% annual inflation rate, a given stock of money in real terms is worth 10% less a year later.

The effect can be understood by the distinction between nominal and real interest rates. By definition, the real interest rate (r) is the difference between the nominal interest rate (i) and the expected rate of inflation (π^e):

$$(8.6) \qquad r = i - \pi^e.$$

$$\begin{array}{ccc} \text{real interest} & \text{nominal} & \text{less} \quad \text{expected} \\ \text{rate} & \text{interest rate} & \text{inflation} \end{array}$$

For decisions such as consumption and investment, we have seen that the real interest rate is the one that matters. In principle, no one would lend money at a nominal interest rate lower than expected inflation because the interest payment does not compensate for the loss of purchasing power. Implicitly, at least, borrowers and lenders agree that a positive real interest rate should remunerate the lender. Over long periods, real interest rate shows no trend. The nominal rate can therefore be seen as the sum of the reward to the lender, or the cost of borrowing

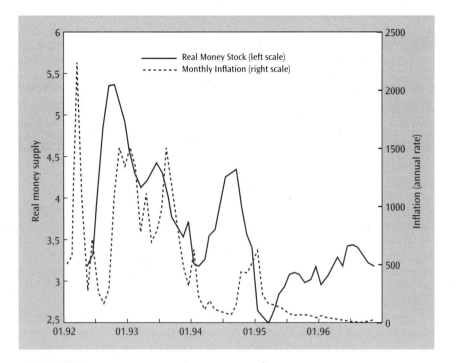

Fig. 8.12   **Money Demand and Hyperinflation in Russia, 1992–1996**

The ratio of money to GDP or GNP declines when the expected rate of inflation rises. When hyperinflation is credibly eliminated, the ratio should go back up to normal levels. The recent example of Russia following the collapse of the Soviet Union and the end of central planning well illustrates how it works, including setbacks. After a burst of inflation in the wake of price liberalization in early 1992, a temporary decline in inflation was achieved in 1993–4, due to artifical administrative price controls. This move failed to persuade the public and confidence in the ruble was not restored; the public continued to shun domestic money and use dollars instead. Following the successful onslaught on inflation in 1995, it took time for the Russian public to gradually and cautiously return to the ruble.
Source: IMF.

(the real interest rate), and expected inflation. This is just (8.6) rewritten as

(8.7) $i = r + \pi^e.$

This relationship, known as the **Fisher principle**,[13] shows that the negative effect of expected inflation on real money demand works itself through the nominal interest rate. The nominal rate includes both the forgone real opportunity cost (r) and the expected capital loss on the nominal value of the loan (π^e). The long-run stability of the real interest rate implies therefore that the nominal interest rate fully reflects expected inflation. The store-of-value and standard-of-deferred-payment properties of money are eroded when its value in terms of the goods it can buy is deteriorating because prices keep increasing. Figure 8.12 shows the spectacular example of **hyperinflation**—when inflation reaches rates in excess of 50% per month—in Russia. As expected, domestic money holdings fall dramatically and shattered confidence is not easily restored once inflation returns to low levels. More details on some fascinating episodes of hyperinflation are provided in Box 8.5.

---

[13] After Irving Fisher, the Yale economist referred to in Ch. 3.

Box 8.5   Money in Hyperinflations

There is no clear border between high inflation and hyperinflation but, conventionally, hyperinflation corresponds to price increases in excess of 50% per month. Under such circumstances, inflation seems to assume a life of its own and to continue rising inexorably. In Central Europe a wave of hyperinflations occurred in the early 1920s, and again early in the transition period. Rates of 10% per *hour* were actually observed for brief periods.

In countries with chronically high inflation, nominal interest rates are often indexed: loan contracts include a clause that stipulates that the interest rate be adjusted for inflation over the lifetime of the loan. Alternatively, lending is restricted to short maturity, sometimes not longer than a week. Because these loans are then renewed at the prevailing interest rate, it is roughly equivalent to indexation. Consequently, as inflation rises borrowers and lenders attempt to keep the real interest rate unchanged, and the nominal interest rate rises along with inflation. This explains why, in Figure 8.12, the real money stock (M/P) dramatically declines when inflation picks up speed. Fearing ever-increasing losses on the real

value of money and with nominal interest rates rising, people hold increasingly smaller amounts of cash, sometimes just enough for the day's shopping. The velocity of money increases. People convert their wealth into assets immune to inflation. They hold durable goods of all sorts, including precious metals as well as less standard assets such as TVs, refrigerators, or even cigarettes. Foreign currency begins to circulate openly, with goods prices quoted and traded in both local and foreign (mostly dollar) currencies, a phenomenon called *currency substitution* (see also Box 8.2).

When inflation is finally beaten, nominal interest rates decline, and the demand for money rises again in real terms. This effect is called *reliquification*. It is a signal that people believe the inflationary episode to be over. Yet, Figure 8.12 show that successes against inflation are not always convincing. Temporary successes can be followed by relapses—as was the case in Russia in 1998—and even long after hyperinflation is vanquished, real cash balances remain low, suggesting that once-burned agents continue to be sceptical.

8.7.3 The Exchange Rate in the Long Run: Purchasing Power Parity

The real exchange rate (σ) is defined in Chapter 7 as the ratio of domestic to foreign prices, expressed in same currency ($\sigma = SP/P^\star$). Its rate of change is the sum of the rate of nominal appreciation plus the domestic inflation rate less the foreign inflation rate:

$$(8.8) \qquad \frac{\Delta\sigma}{\sigma} = \frac{\Delta S}{S} + \frac{\Delta P}{P} - \frac{\Delta P^\star}{P^\star}$$

In the long run, the real exchange rate is driven by real factors—tastes, relative productivity, accumulated external net asset position—and the need to meet the nation's budget constraint. When these real factors remain unchanged, the equilibrium real exchange rate is constant. The real exchange rate is constant when the nominal exchange rate appreciates at a rate ($\Delta S/S$) equal to the difference between the foreign ($\pi^\star = \Delta P^\star/P^\star$) and domestic ($\pi = \Delta P/P$) inflation rates, the **inflation differential**:

$$(8.9) \qquad \Delta S/S = \pi^\star - \pi.$$

To keep the real exchange rate unchanged—that is to maintain external competitiveness—a country with a higher rate of inflation than the rest of the world (when $\pi^\star < \pi$) must have a depreciating currency ($\Delta S/S < 0$), whereas a low-inflation-rate country will have an appreciating currency. This principle is called **relative purchasing power parity** (PPP). Figure 8.9 provides strong evidence for PPP. As predicted by (8.9), for each country the link between the depreciation of its currency vis-à-vis the dollar and the inflation differential vis-à-vis the USA is quite tight.

Bringing together PPP and the explanation of long-run inflation, we see that the long-run rate of exchange rate depreciation depends on the difference between the rate of money growth at home and abroad. This reasoning is formalized in Box 8.4. Countries with fast money growth have more inflation than those with slow money growth. If the real exchange rate is constant, their nominal exchange rate must depreciate. On the other hand, the demand for real money rises rapidly in fast-growing economies. Given the rate of growth of the nominal money supply, the nominal exchange rate tends to appreciate.

A much stronger version of this idea is **absolute purchasing power parity**. This asserts that price levels are equalized across countries once they are converted in the same currency: not only is σ assumed to be constant, but it is assumed to be equal to unity, and therefore $P^* = SP$. Box 8.6 provides some details on the failure of absolute PPP to hold.

Box 8.6   **The Law of One Price and Absolute Purchasing Power Parity**

A key ingredient in the logic behind absolute PPP is the law of one price. This 'law' asserts that the same good should trade everywhere at the same price, when prices are expressed in the same currency. If prices were to differ significantly, it is asserted, enterprising traders would buy the goods where they are cheapest and sell them where they fetch a higher price. This process would push prices towards each other until all profit opportunities have disappeared. In practice, the law of one price is known to be grossly violated. Table 8.6 provides an

example, using prices of a standardized good (mirrors) sold by the same firm in different (international) markets. More examples and some of the reasons behind the results were presented in Chapter 7. Yet in the long run, if countries have access to similar technologies and converge to similar wealth levels, absolute purchasing parity becomes a much more reasonable proposition—not good by good, but across broad baskets of goods. This might well characterize price-level convergence in Europe.

Table 8.6   **Prices of IKEA Mirrors across Europe, 1998 US$**

	Mirrors		
	Alg (square mirror tiles)	Guldros (round mirror)	Krabb (wavy mirror)
Austria	24	113	48
Belgium	22	111	28
Denmark	13	119	34
Finland	15	107	21
France	21	100	33
Germany	22	97	51
Italy	23	79	44
Netherlands	20	101	20
Norway	12	82	27
Spain	32	112	34
Sweden	15	94	24
Switzerland	19	67	27
United Kingdom	25	115	30

Source: Jonathan Haskel and Holger Wolf, 'Why does the "Law of one Price" Fail?', CEPR Discussion Papers, July 1999 No. 2187.

Summary

1. Money is an asset that is generally accepted as a means of payment. This definition leaves some room for interpretation, especially as payment technologies change over time.

2. Money has four attributes: it is a medium of exchange, a unit of account, a store of value, and a standard for deferred payment. Bearing no or low interest, it is dominated by other assets. Its desirability stems from its unique ability to resolve the problems of the double coincidence of wants and of information asymmetry.

3. Money is a public good. The fact that it is easily recognized and generally accepted generates benefits for the community. This is why there is a role for the government in issuing and guaranteeing money.

4. Money is simultaneously an asset of the private non-banking sector and a liability of the banking system. Currency is a liability of the monetary authority (central bank), while sight deposits are a liability of commercial banks.

5. The demand for money is a demand for real money. Agents are interested in the purchasing power of money, not in its nominal or face value.

6. The demand for real money increases with the volume of transactions, approximated by the real GDP. It decreases, with the nominal interest rate, the opportunity cost of holding money. The demand for money increases with transaction costs because agents have an incentive to limit the number of transactions between money and other assets.

7. An unexpected and once-for-all increase in the price level does not affect the real demand for money. It affects the nominal demand for money, which increases in proportion with the price level.

8. Inflation reduces the purchasing power of money. An expected increase in inflation leads agents to reduce their real demand for money. This effect is captured by the nominal interest rate, the sum of the real interest rate, and the expected rate of inflation.

9. In the short run, money market equilibrium occurs rapidly through changes in the interest rate and bond prices. In the long run, money market equilibrium is achieved through changes in the price level and/or the rate of inflation.

10. In the long run, relative purchasing power parity holds in the absence of real disturbances. Then the rate of nominal exchange rate depreciation is equal to the inflation differential.

 ## Key Concepts

- commodity monies
- monetary aggregates (M1, M2, etc.)
- medium of exchange
- double coincidence of wants
- unit of account
- store of value

- standard of deferred payment
- dominated asset
- information asymmetry
- parallel currency
- fiat money
- public good

- balance sheet
- net worth
- neutrality of money
- transactions costs
- nominal interest rate
- opportunity cost
- money demand function

- velocity of money
- Fisher principle
- inflation, hyperinflation
- inflation differential
- purchasing power parity (PPP), absolute and relative

Exercises

1. Each central bank publishes the definition of its own monetary aggregates. Find the definitions for money aggregates in your own country.

2. If inflation is positive, simply maintaining the nominal money supply at some constant level amounts to a contractionary monetary policy. True or false?

3. Banks routinely exchange domestic currency against foreign currencies for their customers. Imagine that a customer brings in a large amount of foreign currency and asks that her checking account be credited by the corresponding amount in domestic currency. In the balance sheet of the commercial banking (Figure 8.1), show what happens:
   (a) when the commercial bank keeps the foreign currency in its vaults.
   (b) when the bank turns over the foreign currency to the central bank and receives domestic currency in return.

4. The real interest rate rises from 2% to 4% while the nominal interest rate remains unchanged at 9%. All other determinants of money demand are assumed to be constant.
   (a) How can you explain this?
   (b) What is the effect on the demand for real money?

5. In the consolidated balance sheet of the government and non-bank private sector, suppose we know the following:
   (a) Deposits of the government and the private sector amount to 2000.
   (b) Total net worth is 400.
   (c) The net public debt of the government is 800 and its gross debt 1000, the difference being in bank deposits. (The government has no real assets.)
   (d) The gross private debt is 1600.
   (e) Private real assets total 600.

   What is the value of bank notes and currency in circulation? What is M1?

6. The percentage effect on real money demand of an increase of one percentage point of the interest rate (say, from 5% to 6%) is sometimes called the interest rate semi-elasticity of the demand for money. Suppose it takes the value −0.1. The income elasticity of money demand (the percentage effect of an increase of 1% of real GDP on real money demand) is 0.8. Find the increase in the interest rate required to maintain money market equilibrium, at unchanged real money supply, when output increases by 1%, 2%, and 5%.

7. Credit cards offer their holders the ability to obtain immediate credit up to a given ceiling. What are arguments for
   (a) including the total amount of ceilings in the definition M1?
   (b) using only the amounts actually used up?
   (c) not including it at all?

8. Give a reason why the ratio of money to nominal GDP might increase when standards of living are rising. (*Hint*: think about leisure.)

9. What is the effect on the velocity of money of an unexpected increase in the rate of inflation that is:
   (a) temporary?
   (b) permanent?

 ## Suggested Further Reading

The classic formal articles on the inventory theory of money demand are:

Baumol, William (1952), 'The Transactions Demand for Cash: An Inventory Theoretic Approach', *Quarterly Journal of Economics*, 56: 545–56.

Tobin, James (1956), 'The Interest Rate Elasticity of the Transactions Demand for Cash', *Review of Economics and Statistics*, 38: 241–7.

A survey of the large number of empirical studies of the demand for money is:

Goldfeld, S., and Sichel, M. (1989), in B. M. Friedman and F. Hahn (eds.), *Handbook of Monetary Economics*, North-Holland.

Appendix: An Inventory Model of the Demand for Money

This appendix presents a simple inventory model of money demand by individual households. It is due to Baumol (1952) and Nobel Prize laureate James Tobin (1956).

We imagine an agent who receives a nominal income of PY in each period and consumes at a constant rate over the period. There are no savings carried over from one period to the next. She receives her income in the form of a cheque at the beginning of the period, say, the month. At a minimum, she must visit the bank once, in order to deposit all her salary in her bank account, so that it is available for spending. In general, she will probably choose to keep some wealth in the form of an interest-bearing savings account as well as in her current account. Each visit to the bank or transaction has a nominal cost c. (c should be thought of as the opportunity cost of time spent queueing, 'shoe leather' used up while running to the bank, and or bank fees for such transactions.) If n is the number of visits to the bank during the month, the monthly cost will be nc. To reduce such costs, she might want to hold more sight deposits, but then she faces an opportunity cost. If i is the monthly interest rate served on the savings account, holding an average nominal balance M over the month implies an opportunity cost iM.

Figure A8.1 shows the amount of money that the agent has in her checking account for various numbers of monthly trips to the bank. The height of each triangle represents the amount withdrawn from the savings account and deposited in the checking account. It is PY/n. As trips to the bank, which are evenly spaced, occur every $(1/n)$th day of the month, the area of each triangle represents her average money held between two trips:

Average money held between two trips

$$= \frac{1}{2} \times \frac{PY}{n} \times \frac{1}{n} = \frac{PY}{2n^2}.$$

Her opportunity cost is the interest forgone on this average money holding:

Opportunity cost = $\underset{\text{interest rate}}{i} \times \underset{\text{no. of trips}}{n} \times \underset{\substack{\text{av. holding in} \\ \text{between two trips}}}{(PY/2n)^2}.$

Total costs TC (trips plus opportunity costs of holding M1) are therefore

(A8.1) $$TC = i\frac{PY}{2n} + cn.$$

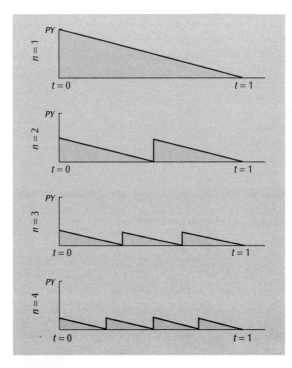

Fig. A8.1 Trips to the Bank and Average Money Holdings

For one trip per month to the bank ($n = 1$), the average balance is simply $PY/2$. For two trips ($n = 2$), there are two triangles, each with area $(PY/2) \times (1/2) \times (1/2)$, so the average monthly balance is $PY/4$. For n trips per month, the average holding between trips is $PY/2n^2$ and the average monthly balance is $PY/2n$.

Table A8.1 presents the breakdown of total costs when $PY =$ ECU 2000 per month, with a cost of transferring money of $c =$ ECU 1 and a nominal interest rate of 12% (about 1% per month). Total costs are minimized for three trips to the bank over the month.

The more general mathematical formulation of the problem is:

(A8.2) $$\min_n TC = i\frac{PY}{2n} + cn.$$

Ignoring the fact that n must be a whole number, the optimum is obtained by setting the marginal cost equal to zero:[14]

---

[14] This is a local minimum because the second-order condition is satisfied.

No. of trips	Interest cost $(PY/2n)i$	Trip's cost (cn)	Total cost
1	10.00	1.00	11.00
2	5.00	2.00	7.00
3	3.33	3.00	6.33
4	2.50	4.00	6.50
5	2.00	5.00	7.00
6	1.67	6.00	7.67

Table A8.1 Costs of Cash Inventory (in ECUs)

(A8.3)
$$\frac{\partial TC}{\partial n} = -\frac{iPY}{2n^2} + c = 0.$$

The optimal n is:

(A8.4)
$$n^{\star} = \sqrt{\frac{iPY}{2c}},$$

which leads to the 'square root' formula describing the optimal holding money stock:

(A8.5)
$$M^{\star} = \frac{PY}{2n^{\star}} = \sqrt{\frac{PYc}{2i}}.$$

As the demand-for-money function (8.1), this expression states that the optimal average money holding is:

- a positive function of real economic activity Y
- a positive function of the price level P
- a positive function of transactions costs c
- a negative function of the nominal interest rate i

If we further define the *real* cost of transactions c^R as $c^R \equiv c/P$, the square root formula can be expressed in terms of real money demand:

(A8.6)
$$\frac{M^{\star}}{P} = \sqrt{\frac{Yc^R}{2i}}.$$

We can further rewrite (A8.6) as

(A8.7)
$$\left(\frac{M}{P}\right)^{\star} = Y\sqrt{\frac{c^R/Y}{2i}}.$$

If the transaction cost is a fixed proportion of income, c^R/Y is constant and the demand for money is proportional to the real GDP. The income elasticity of money demand is unity, and the elasticities with respect to (c^R/Y) and i are both 0.5:

$$\frac{\partial(M/P)^{\star}/\partial(c^R/Y)}{(c^R/Y)/(M/P)} = \frac{1}{2}$$

and

$$\frac{\partial(M/P)^{\star}/\partial(i/Y)}{(i/Y)/(M/P)} = -\frac{1}{2}.$$

The Supply of Money and Monetary Policy

9

By playing upon the reserves of the bank, the note-issuing authority can induce an expansion or a contraction of credit at will. But in order to do so, it must have at its disposal some machinery for issuing and withdrawing notes easily and promptly. A Government which can only withdraw notes by raising the necessary funds from the public by taxes or loans does not fulfil this condition. The best instrument for the regulation of the supply of paper money is a State Bank or else a Central Bank which, while not itself a part of the Executive Government, is willing regularly to co-operate with it.

– R. G. Hawtrey

9.1 Overview

In Chapter 8 we studied the demand for money. It is now time to study the other side of the market, the supply of money, in more detail. Money, that is bank notes and demand deposits, is supplied jointly by the commercial banks and the central bank, but control of the process rests solely with the central bank. The following four broad questions are addressed in this chapter: (1) What are the central bank's objectives, and how does it meet them? (2) How does the central bank exert control over the money supply process, given that money is generated primarily by commercial banks? (3) What are the links between domestic and foreign monetary conditions? (4) How can the central bank help safeguard the integrity of the financial system, given its inherent fragility?

Central banks are typically required to deliver low and stable inflation. We already know from Chapter 8 that this requires a low rate of money growth, but that the link between money growth and inflation is usually slow to emerge. In the meantime, the central bank needs additional guideposts. It typically focuses on intermediate targets that it can control using its instruments. A particular difficulty is that the central bank can control M1, M2, or wider aggregates only indirectly, mostly through the cost of money, the interest rate.

The choice of a target has been changing, partly in response to prevailing conditions, partly as new techniques are developed. In recent years, a number of central banks have begun to target inflation directly, instead of targeting money growth, the standard strategy used in the 1980s to bring inflation down. Exchange rate targeting, which proved useful too in reigning in inflation, is also receding because of conflicts that arise between the central bank's domestic and foreign monetary policy objectives of which can occasionally result in serious crises.

While the guiding principles of monetary control are fundamentally the same across countries, institutions and procedures differ across countries. These differences may appear important in the day-to-day operation of a national central bank, but they tend to cloud and confuse discussion of the unifying aspects of monetary policy. For that reason we downplay them, highlighting instead similarities and describing a monetary system that should be thought of as a common denominator of various arrangements observed in developed economies.

9.2	**Objectives, Targets and Instruments**

Most central banks are responsible for establishing and maintaining price stability. For instance, the Maastricht Treaty provides an explicit mandate for the ESCB (European System of Central Banks, or **Eurosystem**):

The primary objective of the ESCB shall be to maintain price stability. Without prejudice to the objective of price stability, the ESCB shall support the general economic policies in the Community with a view to contributing to the achievement of the objectives of the Community.

Article 105

The ESCB defines price stability as 'an annual increase in the price level below 2% over the medium run', i.e. an inflation rate between 0% and 2%. In 2001, the Bank of England had an inflation objective of 2.5%. The US Federal Reserve does not have an explicit quantitative objective and seems to adapt to current conditions, but leaves no doubt that it wants inflation to remain low.[1]

Inflation may be the **objective**, but central banks cannot control it directly. In Chapter 8, we saw that inflation is determined in the long run by the growth rate of money, more precisely by the confrontation of the real demand for money with a nominal money supply. Real demand is driven by the (non-bank) public, the nominal supply is the responsibility of the central bank. The 'art of central banking' is to match the supply of money today with its ultimate, long-run impact on inflation. Thus achievement of the inflation objective is indirect. To that effect, central banks rely on targets and instruments.

Targets are indirect objectives which, while closely related to the ultimate inflation objective, are better controlled by the central bank. Three main targets are often mentioned. The first is the rate of growth of monetary aggregates (M1, M2, M3, M4, etc.) which determine the subsequent rate of inflation once demand is taken into account. The ESCB, for instance, has identified M3 growth as the first 'pillar' of its monetary policy strategy. Another frequently mentioned target is the exchange rate. Like the nominal money supply, the nominal exchange rate is closely associated with the rate of inflation, as was shown in Chapter 8. The ESCB lists the exchange rate as a component of the second 'pillar'. Some central banks may fix the exchange rate or attempt to influence its course. This was the case within the European Monetary System which existed from 1979 to 1998. Many Eastern and Central European countries have also relied on the exchange rate target to stabilize prices. More recently, inflation has become a popular target. The question of a choice of a target is addressed in Section 9.4.5.

Unfortunately, targets are not under the *direct* control of the central bank, either. Central banks use **instruments**, which they control with precision and which influence the targets. Nowadays, interest rates set directly by the central bank have become the instrument of choice. In the past, central banks sometimes worked primarily with narrow monetary aggregates, like M0 or domestic credit. The link between these instruments is illustrated in Figure 9.1 which depicts the public's nominal demand for money as a function of the interest rate i (the figure relates to the narrow aggregate M0 for reasons that will become clear later). Chapter 8 showed that the public demands money on the basis of what it can buy. Its demand for nominal money depends on both the price level P and the real money demand $L(Y, i, c)$:

(9.1) Nominal demand for money $= M^d$

$$= P\mathcal{L}(Y, i, c)$$

Given the price level, the central bank faces the demand schedule shown in Figure 9.1. The schedule is downward-sloping because the real demand for money declines when the interest rate rises.

---

[1] Inflation has become the objective of central banks only since the 1980s. In the 1960s, many central banks were more preoccupied with economic growth and unemployment. The general increase in inflation rates in the late 1970s and early 1980s has prompted a re-examination of what central banks do and led to the change of objective. Some central banks have not fully repudiated the growth objective, e.g. the US Federal Reserve.

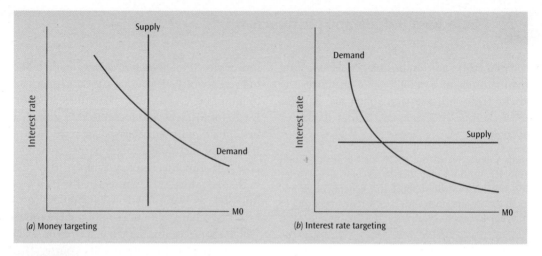

Fig. 9.1   **Monetary Policy Procedures**

The central bank may use the money supply as its policy instrument, leaving the market to determine the interest rate (Panel (*a*)). Conversely it can set the interest rate; in that case it must provide the market with whatever volume of base money is demanded at the chosen rate (Panel (*b*)).

The central bank cannot do anything about the public's preferences; it can only decide where to be on the demand schedule. If it chooses to set the quantity of money, as shown in Figure 9.1, Panel (*a*), it must accept whatever interest rate is compatible with the public's behaviour. When it operates with an interest rate instrument, as shown on the right-most graph, it gives up the possibility of controlling the monetary supply. In short, the central bank can aim at the price or the quantity of money, not both. Today, most central banks focus on the price of money, i.e. the interest rate.[2]

9.3   Money Creation

This section makes two main points. First, most of what we have defined as money is actually created by commercial banks in the process of lending to private customers. Money creation by the monetary authorities only concerns cash (banknotes and coins) and reserves held at the central bank by commercial banks. Second, the central bank exerts indirect control on private money creation by commercial banks by restraining the volume of their reserves. The instruments that a central bank ultimately uses are those that influence the bank's lending behaviour and demand for reserves.

9.3.1   **The Roles of Central and Commercial Banks**

The central bank and the monetary base

The **central bank** is a public or quasi-public agency with an explicit, exclusive legal mandate to control

---

[2] Note that the interest rate i is the price of one period loans repaid in money, and therefore represents the opportunity cost of holding money; the price level P refers to the price of goods and services in terms of money.

Table 9.1	The Balance Sheet of the European Central Bank, September 2000 (€ billions)		

Assets		Liabilities	
Gold and foreign reserves	459.0	Currency in circulation	373.5
Claims on governments	112.8	Reserves held by commercial banks	113.1
Claims on banks and financial institutions	481.7	Other deposits by banks and financial institutions	233.0
Other assets	76.3	Government deposits	58.1
		Other liabilities	130.0
		Net worth	222.1
Total	1129.8	Total	1129.8

Source: Monthly Bulletin, ECB, November 2000.

money and credit conditions.[3] It is the 'bankers' bank', through which banks can settle claims against each other, and it may also serve as a clearing house of cheques written by depositors. It generally does not take deposits from the private sector but may serve as the government's bank. It may also gather, process, and analyse information about the financial and real economy. Most importantly, the central bank guarantees the value of the currency by aiming at price stability. It does so by issuing currency, one of the components of M1. It also creates **bank reserves**, which are claims on the central bank held by commercial banks. The sum of currency in circulation and commercial bank reserves is known as the **monetary base**, sometimes called M0.[4] The monetary base is represented by the shaded area in Figure 9.2 and is the sum of the first two liability

entries in the balance sheet of the European Central Bank shown in Table 9.1.

The role of commercial banks in money creation

As **financial intermediaries**, commercial banks collect funds from depositors and lend them to customers, channelling resources from savers to borrowers. They also perform a payment-clearing role in settling accounts among their customers and with those of other banks. Much more important, however, is their role in the money supply process. Were it not for banks, the only circulating medium of exchange would be currency. In fact, the bulk of the money supply used in modern economies is bank deposits, and these deposits are actually created by the commercial banking system. The money-creating function of banks is what distinguishes them from other financial intermediaries such as savings banks, brokers, and stock markets. All of those institutions collect, lend, and invest funds, but none of them has the right to create money, because none of them may legally lend more than they have received in deposits.

By lending money that they do not directly possess, commercial banks are in effect issuing money. How do they do it? We will learn below that, by issuing a loan to a customer, a bank increases the volume of its assets, as shown in Figure 9.2. The

[3] The Bank of England was a private institution from its founding in 1694 until its nationalization in 1946, much like the Banque de France, founded in 1800 and nationalized in 1945. The Bundesbank was established in 1949 as a successor to the Deutsche Reichsbank founded in 1876. The oldest central bank is the Swedish Riksbank, founded in 1668, while other dates of foundation are: Bank of Japan, 1882; Banca d'Italia, 1893; Austrian National Bank, 1816; Swiss National Bank, 1905. The Federal Reserve of the USA was founded in 1913 and is owned by the member banks, although profits above a statutory maximum are remitted, as in most countries, to the government (Goodhart 1988).

[4] Other expressions used are 'high-powered', 'base money', or 'central bank money'.

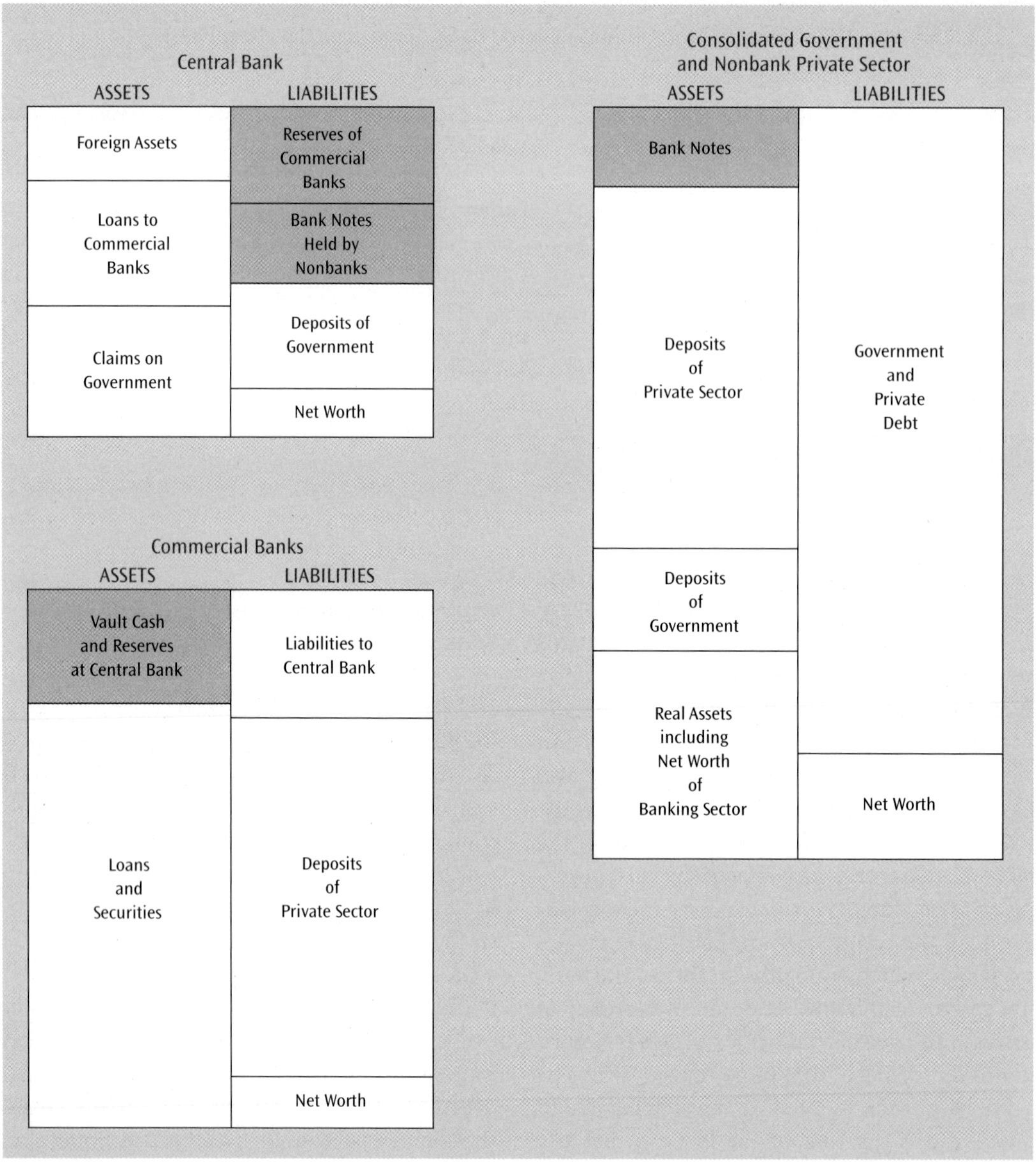

Fig. 9.2   The Balance Sheets, Again

increase is matched on the liability side by the amount of the loan credited to the customer's bank account. That is, in a nutshell, how new money is created by a bank.

Prudential and legal reserves requirements

Bank reserves can be thought of as the 'money' that commercial banks use to conduct transactions among themselves and with the central bank. The reserves pay little or no interest, so commercial banks would rather keep them at a minimum. What determines this minimum, then? First, banks must have enough currency at hand to meet everyday withdrawals by customers. For that purpose, they use vault cash or draw on their deposits at the central bank which are immediately convertible into cash. Further, banks require a means of settling payments among themselves and on behalf of their customers. Settlements between banks are usually made by transfers from the central bank account of one bank to another.

Suppose, for example, that a customer of Bank A receives some payment in the form of a cheque drawn on Bank B.[5] He deposits the cheque in his checking account at Bank A. Bank A simultaneously credits its customer's account and deposits the cheque with the central bank. The central bank then debits Bank B's reserves account and credits Bank A's reserve account. For such transactions, a positive reserve balance is obviously necessary at the central bank. During a given period, any commercial bank may receive large amounts in deposits and face large withdrawals. If the two about balance, which is normally the case, they actually need very limited amounts of reserves; but sometimes withdrawals may exceed deposits by a large amount. This is why commercial banks always find it *prudent* to hold some fraction of their assets in the form of either vault cash or deposits at the central bank.

A second reason for banks to hold reserves can be legal. In many countries, deposit-taking banks are *required* by law to hold a fraction of outstanding deposits in the form of bank reserves at the central bank. These so-called **reserves requirements** are one of many regulations that are imposed on banks, and are normally set as a proportion of deposits. This proportion is called the **reserve ratio**. In the euro area, the reserve ratio is set at 2% of banks' deposits. It is 3% in the USA (rising to 10% for large deposit holdings). There are no reserve requirements in a number of countries (e.g. Canada, the UK, and Switzerland), which rely solely on prudential

behaviour. Reserve requirements are not always binding, and banks sometimes hold reserves in excess of the legal amount. Except under extraordinary conditions, however, excess reserves holdings by commercial banks are usually kept to a minimum because of the associated opportunity costs—forgone lending business.

9.3.2 The Money Multiplier

Whether compulsory or prudential, there is a linkage between checking deposits at banks, which are liabilities of commercial banks to their customers, and bank reserves, which are assets of the commercial bank and liabilities of the central bank. This linkage is the central bank's source of control over the money supply. Whenever a bank makes a loan to a customer, it creates a new deposit, and it will need to hold more reserves at the central bank. This link implies a relationship, known as the **money multiplier**, between the monetary base and each monetary aggregate. The multiplier process is both simple and striking. It is presented in two different ways. The first stresses the end result, while the second, developed in the WebAppendix, tracks the relatively involved process by which money is actually created.

Reserve ratios and reserve multipliers

Two of the main items in a bank's balance sheet (Figure 9.2) correspond to costly activities:

- Reserves, when borrowed from the central bank, carry an interest charge. Unborrowed reserves held at the central bank yield little or no interest income, hence an opportunity cost.

- Customers' demand deposits require setting up and maintaining a network of branches with personnel, equipment, and office rental. In addition, depositors may even earn some interest.

So how do banks make a profit? The answer is: make sure that the asset side of the balance sheet is earning a good rate of return. Holding interest-yielding assets is one way, lending to their customers is another, more profitable one. Good banking practice therefore calls for lending as much as is prudently possible. This can be done easily enough: it is sufficient to credit the customer's account. As long as the

---

[5] A cheque is a piece of paper, issued by a payer, which entitles its bearer (payee) to payment drawn on the payer's checking account at a commercial bank. In many European countries, cheques are no longer the payment mechanism of choice, going the way of the phonograph player and the tape recorder. Electronic debit cards now allow payers to transfer their balances directly, bypassing the need for writing cheques and worrying about their acceptance. Despite this technological advance, the need for a central bank remains: at the end of any given day, some bank may come up short and will need extra liquidity to cover its obligations. Only the central bank is available for this task.

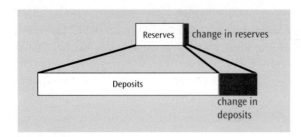

Fig. 9.3   **The Reserves–Money Stock Link**

When reserves are a constant proportion (*rr*) of deposits
(*R = rrD*), deposits cannot grow without an increase in
reserves. Conversely, a change in reserves Δ*R* allows banks
to increase their deposits—by granting loans—in much
larger amounts. The money multiplier is the inverse of the
reserve ratio.

interest on the loan exceeds the cost of managing
the deposit, it is profitable to do so.

If this is the case, why don't banks simply increase
customer credit, and the corresponding deposits,
without bounds? Naturally, prudential banking
means identifying good credit risks and excluding
borrowers who will not repay their loans; for the
moment, let us assume that there are enough good
credit opportunities around. Even in this case, the
reserve ratio will restrict lending by commercial
banks. As illustrated in Figure 9.3, banks' reserves
may not be less than the (required or prudent)
reserves ratio (*rr*) *times* the volume of deposits:

$$\text{(9.2)} \qquad \text{Reserves} \geq rr \times \text{deposits.}$$

The figure may also be read in reverse: the volume
of deposits cannot exceed a multiple of existing
reserves. The dark purple area in Figure 9.3 shows that
an increase in reserves can be multiplied up into a
larger volume of deposits. If reserves are a fraction of
deposits, then deposits are a multiple of reserves.
Formally, rearranging (9.2) gives:

$$\text{(9.3)} \qquad \text{Deposits} \leq (1/rr) \times \text{reserves.}$$

The factor (1/*rr*) is often called the *reserve multiplier*.
Equation (9.3) means that together, commercial
banks cannot expand their money creation beyond
a multiple of reserves. Here is the catch: in the aggregate, reserves can only be obtained from the central
bank.

The monetary base multiplier

We now understand how the central bank can put a
cap on the volume of bank deposits by controlling
the volume of bank reserves. But two difficulties
arise. The first is that the central bank can only control M0, the sum of bank reserves and currency.
Second, the central bank is not just interested
in controlling bank deposits, but rather the wider
aggregates (M1, M2, M3, M4) which ultimately
determine the rate of inflation. Both of these facts
mean that monetary control may be less precise
than implied by the simple reserve multiplier.

Consider first that, although the central bank is
the sole (legal!) producer of M0, the sum of currency
and bank reserves, it cannot control its components.
It is the public that decides how much of M0 it
wishes to hold in the form of currency. Effectively,
the remainder is deposited at banks and can serve as
bank reserves. Since the central bank is interested in
controlling the aggregate money stock (M1, M2, or
broader aggregates), rather than reserves *per se*, more
attention is paid to the *monetary base multiplier*, or
money multiplier, which relates the monetary base
to a monetary aggregate, for example M1:

$$\text{(9.4)} \qquad \text{Monetary base multiplier} = \text{M1/M0.}$$

Next, we ask what happens if some of the newly
created monetary base, M0, does not entirely end
up as bank reserves. Figure 9.3 does not distinguish
between currency and bank deposits at the central
bank, in Figure 9.4 this omission is corrected.

Table 9.2 presents actual ratios of the money
supply (M1) to the monetary base (M0). They are
much smaller than the inverse of the reserves ratio
as predicted by formula (9.2), because of currency
holdings by non-banks. To see this, imagine first
a world without currency, so that all transactions
are carried out using bank deposits (cheques, plastic
cards, transfers). All of M1 takes the form of bank
deposits and the monetary base is entirely held by
commercial banks (see Figure 9.2). Now, if the public chooses to hold part of their money in the form
of currency, any loan by the banking system results
in some cash withdrawal. The banks lose some of
their reserves, which limits their loan-making activity. The larger is the share of currency in M0, the
less reserves remain in the banking system, and the

Table 9.2	M0, M2, Money Market Multipliers, and Currency, 2000			
	M0 (% of GDP)	**M2** (% of GDP)	**Multiplier** M2/M0	**Currency** (% of M2)
Japan	14.9	128.4	8.6	9.9
USA	6.0	11.0	1.8	54.4
Euro-zone	5.8	31.0	3.1	18.7
UK	3.7	61.9	16.9	5.9

Source: Central bank websites.

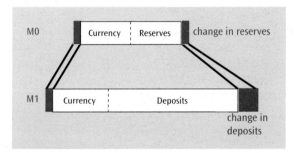

Fig. 9.4 **The Reserves–Money Stock Link with Currency**

The public holds currency as well as bank accounts. As reserves are a constant proportion of deposits, any increase in reserves allows an increase in deposits, with a multiplier equal to the inverse of the reserve ratio. The central bank, however, controls the monetary base M0, not the breakdown between its components, currency and reserves. If the money multiplier is defined as the effect of an increase in the monetary base on the money supply M1, it is smaller because part of the money created by the commercial banks will be converted in currency, leaking out of the banking system.

smaller is the multiplier. Box 9.1 shows formally that the monetary multiplier is indeed lower, the more currency the public holds. Table 9.2 confirms that countries with a predilection for currency tend to have low money multipliers.

Leakages

The money multiplier is lower when conversion of bank deposits into currency acts as a drain on commercial banks' reserves. Other leakages produce the same effect and help explain the relatively low money multipliers reported in Table 9.2. Leakages occur when money is deposited in non-bank financial institutions (e.g. savings banks or the post office) which operate with a 100% reserve requirement. Money can also leak abroad, and this reduces the amount of reserves available for the banking system. Box 9.2 shows that this leakage can be sizeable.

A variable multiplier

We assumed that commercial banks use any reserve in excess of the minimum level to make loans, and that they have no difficulty finding customers. Neither of these assumptions need *always* be correct. Banks manage their assets and liabilities very carefully, with an eye to the future. They may consider that some loan applications are too risky, or that it may be a good idea to keep some extra reserves for future business. As a result, banks routinely hold excess reserves. The volume of excess reserves is variable, and depends on economic conditions (which affect the risk that loans will go unpaid) and on the likely evolution of interest rates (expected *future* increases increase the attractiveness of holding reserves now).

The private sector's behaviour too can be variable. For example, fears of worsening economic conditions, or the expectation of declining interest rates, may limit the amount of new credit that the public wants to borrow. As a result, the response of banks to reserve availability is less automatic than implied by the money multiplier formulae. As conditions change, or are expected to change, the actual multiplier can fluctuate.

Box 9.1   **The Money Multiplier with Currency**

Assuming that the public wishes to hold a proportion cc of M1 in the form of currency (CU), and that the banks keep a fraction rr of deposits (D) in bank reserves (R) (for simplicity, ignore vault cash), the two aggregates M0 and M1 can be written as

$$(9.5) \qquad M0 = CU + R = ccM1 + rrD$$

$$(9.6) \qquad M1 = CU + D = ccM1 + D.$$

Then (9.5) implies $D = (1 - cc)$M1. Inserting this value of D in (9.4) gives

$$(9.7) \qquad M0 = [cc + rr(1 - cc)]M1,$$

so

$$(9.8) \qquad \text{Money multiplier} = M1/M0$$

$$= \frac{1}{cc + rr(1 - cc)}.$$

The money market multiplier is $1/rr$ if the public holds no currency (if $cc = 0$). It is equal to 1 if all M1 is cash ($cc = 1$). Table 9.3 shows how the multiplier varies with different values of the currency-to-M1 ratio cc and the reserves ratio rr.

Table 9.3   **Theoretical Values of the Money Multiplier (M1/M0)**

Currency/M1	Reserve ratio		
	5%	10%	20%
0%	20.0	10.0	5.0
5%	10.3	6.9	4.0
10%	6.9	5.3	3.6
20%	4.2	3.6	2.8
30%	3.0	2.7	2.3

Box 9.2   **Where is the Money?**

In 1996, US dollars in circulation amounted to $390 billion, or roughly $1481 for every man, woman, and child in the USA, almost $6000 per four-person family. Surveys indicate that the average US four-person household held about $300 in cash in 1995, some $20 billion in total. Business holdings are estimated to amount to another $20 billion. So where is the rest? It seems likely that much of it is abroad, something like $200 billion. Currency shipments over the period 1988–96 are estimated to amount to well over $100 billion, half of it to Europe (largely the former Soviet Union), 30% to the Middle East and the rest to Latin America. Why? Obviously, shady characters use dollars to avoid traceable transactions. 'Greenbacks' are also known to circulate as the sole currency (Ecuador, Liberia, Panama) or as a **parallel currency** in many countries where high inflation makes local currencies unappealing as a store of value. It is believed that 60 billion dollars worth is in circulation in the former Soviet Union alone. Similarly, it is estimated that about 25% of all Japanese currency and 40% of all German currency is held abroad.
Source: Rogoff (1998).

Required or self-imposed reserves ratios?

Some countries, Switzerland and the UK for example, have zero or symbolic reserve requirements, and yet they are considered perfectly safe places to hold banking accounts. Reserve requirements serve several purposes. Initially, they were imposed to reduce the riskiness of banking systems. Next, they guaranteed a role for the central bank in the business of money creation. Finally, they became the means for central banks to control the money supply. Whether reserves are required or self-imposed reserves, as long as $rr > 0$ deposits are linked to reserves, and the central bank retains control over money supply .

Why impose reserve requirements, then? One reason is that they represent a form of taxation on the banking system since they are poorly remunerated. Indirectly, they allow governments to tax households and firms who get below-market interest on bank deposits as part of a deal between commercial banks, who argue that their own deposits at the central bank are poorly remunerated, and their regulators. At a time of globalization, reserve requirements subject the domestic banking sector to a competitive disadvantage relative to other countries with lower or non-existent minimum ratios. And indeed, as financial integration deepened in the 1990s, reserve requirements declined. The ESCB now imposes the same low ratio throughout the Euro area, but competition with outside financial centres in Europe—London and Zurich in particular —remains.

9.4 Controlling the Money Supply

9.4.1 Derived Demand for Base Money

Summarizing so far, we have reached three important conclusions:

- The public (households and firms) have a reasonably clear and stable view of the amount of nominal money (M1, M2, M3, etc.) they wish to hold. This is represented by equation (9.1).

- The banking system creates the money in the process of granting loans to customers. In doing so, they need—for regulatory or prudential reasons— to hold reserves, as represented by equation (9.2).

- In spite of the various leakages that affect money created by banks, there is a reasonably stable link between the monetary base and the money stock, this is the money multiplier m (described in equations (9.4) or (9.8), depending on what is assumed about the leakages).

Bringing this all together we find that the public's demand for money M^6 translates into a **derived demand** by commercial banks for the monetary base M0, which we shall call M0^d:

(9.9) $M0^d = M/m = P\mathcal{L}(Y, i, c)/m$

This is the behaviour captured in Figure 9.1 and reproduced in Figure 9.5: the downward-sloping schedule describes the derived demand for the monetary base for given price level P, real GDP Y and transaction costs c.

[6] From now on we overlook the distinction between the different definitions of money (M1, M2, etc.) and refer to broad money as M.

Now imagine that, starting at point A, the economy is growing. Where will households and firms find the extra money that they need to carry out an ever increasing volume of transactions? They will want to borrow from their banks. As the banks respond by granting loans, their need for reserves increases. Although individual banks may be able to obtain reserves from each other, viewed as a

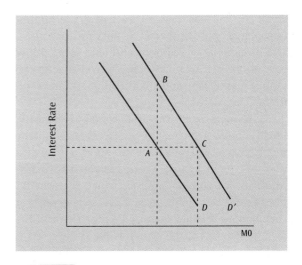

Fig. 9.5   **The Money Market**

The public's demand for money translates into a demand for the monetary base by commercial banks. If the public wants to hold more money, the derived demand schedule shifts to the right. The central bank may decide not to respond, in which case the interest rate rises (point B), or to keep the interest unchanged (point C), or any combination of M0 and the interest rate as long as it lies on the demand schedule.

whole, the increase in the total demand for money translates into an increase in the demand for the monetary base, captured by the rightward shift of the demand schedule from D to D'. How the central bank responds is examined in the following section. At this stage we just note that any change in the demand for the overall money stock M is transmitted to a change in the demand for monetary base.[7]

9.4.2 Open Market Operations

Figure 9.5 represents the market for the monetary base, called the **money market**, or the **open market**, the linchpin of all financial markets. The 'commodities' traded on this market are deposits at the central bank. The market does not have a physical location, rather it operates a network complete with brokers. The players are commercial banks and financial—sometimes non-financial—institutions (e.g. insurance companies, large corporations) and the central bank. As the sole producer of base money, the central bank exercises the dominant influence on the market. Because commercial banks know that they ultimately need reserves to grant credit to their customers, they regard the interest rate charged on this market as their primary indicator of monetary conditions and tend to promptly pass on to their own customers any change in the money market rate, and all other interest rates soon follow.

Institutional details vary from country to country, but the broad features are similar. Dealers on the money market typically trade very short-term maturities, overnight to two weeks. Market participants primarily deal with one another, which allows banks to obtain better yields on any excess reserves that they happen to hold than by keeping them in the form of deposits at the central bank. If the reserves available on the market exceed participant needs, the interest rate declines, while it rises when there is excess demand. The central bank closely monitors

the situation and can intervene on the market as it wishes, conducting **open market operations**. Box 9.3 describes the various open market operation procedures adopted by the ECB. The main features are the following:

- Open market operations typically take the form of a short-term loan from the central bank to commercial banks.

- These loans are guaranteed by a collateral presented to the central bank by the borrower. Each central bank has a list of assets admitted as collateral, typically Treasury bills or bills issued by large corporations which are considered very safe. Indeed, it is not in the mission of a central bank to take risks in lending.

- By lending reserves, the central bank allows M0 to increase. Thereafter commercial banks step up lending to their customers, which increases M1 and the wider monetary aggregates.

- Because these loans are short-term, commercial banks continuously need to pay back and borrow again, a procedure called rolling over. This dependence allows the central bank to influence money market conditions with great precision: it can step up lending to increase liquidity, or it can absorb liquidity and reduce the monetary base by not renewing maturing loans.

9.4.3 The Practice of Monetary Policy

On any normal business day, some commercial banks hold reserves in excess of what is required or desired, while others fall short. The money market allows participants to trade these reserves, borrowing and lending among themselves at very short maturities. As it reflects the cost of money to banks, the money market interest rate is the best gauge of monetary conditions, it determines how much banks charge their own customers. This rate is called the money market rate, with special names in some countries, the Federal Funds Rate in the USA and EONIA in the Euro area (see Box 9.3). As the ultimate net supplier of bank reserves—the 'commodity' being traded—the central bank orients the market on a minute-by-minute basis.

---

[7] The transmission is not necessarily one for one because the multiplier is not perfectly constant. Here, if the commercial banks were holding excess reserves at point A, they will be able to partly satisfy their customers without needing more reserves, but if growth continues, sooner or later they will have exhausted this margin. From there on, we assume that the money multiplier is constant.

Box 9.3   **How the ECB does it**

The ECB conducts four types of open-market operations:

- Main refinancing operations, which are weekly auctions for loans of two-week maturities. Commercial banks submit bids and the ECB chooses how much to allocate at which interest rate. This is the main source of liquidity provision to the market.

- Longer-term refinancing operations, which are monthly auctions for loans of one-month maturity. This is a limited source of financing.

- Fine-tuning and structural operations, which are occasionally conducted to deal with special circumstances.

- Standing facilities, which set a ceiling and a floor for the short-term (overnight) interest rate. These operations are undertaken by individual banks to either deposit funds at the marginal deposit rate (the floor) or borrow from the ECB at the marginal lending rate (ceiling). These facilities are used daily at the commercial banks' initiative.

These operations take the form of a **reverse transaction** or **repurchase agreement** ('repo' for short), loans of limited duration. To signal its intentions, the ECB publicly announces the rate at which it will conduct its next main refinancing operations as well as the floor and ceiling rates. Figure 9.6 shows that the key short-term market rate EONIA (euro overnight index average) moves within the tunnel set by the lending and deposit rates, closely following (sometimes even anticipating) the ECB's main rate, the refinancing rate. The ECB's control of the very short-term interest rate is perfect.
Source: Annual Report, ECB, 1999.

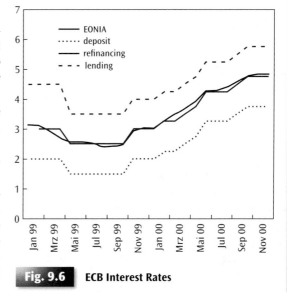

Fig. 9.6   **ECB Interest Rates**

The ECB conducts weekly auctions at the pre-announced main refinancing interest rate. Its lending and deposit rates determine, respectively, a ceiling and a floor for the interbank rate EONIA (Euro OverNight Index Average) which tends to closely follow the refinancing rate.
Source: Monthly Bulletin, ECB, November 2000.

At normal times, when the economy is growing, the public's demand for money expands and the derived demand for the money base increases with it. This is represented in Figure 9.5 by the shift from D to D'. How does the central bank react? It may wish to keep the money supply unchanged, but then it must be aiming at point B, where the interest rate has increased. Instead, it may wish to keep the interest rate unchanged, aiming at point C. In that case, it must provide more monetary base by intervening on the open market. The multiplier then takes over and, eventually, the wider monetary aggregates will follow suit. What the central bank definitely *cannot* do is determine both the money supply and the interest rate. This is why it must choose an instrument.

9.4.4 Reserve Requirements as a Tool of Monetary Policy

When the central bank has imposed a reserve requirement which is binding, changing the reserve ratio can serve as an additional instrument of monetary policy. For example if the required reserve ratio is raised from 5% to 6%, with unchanged supply of reserves, deposits must contract by roughly 20%.[8] This is a drastic move, which not only stops commercial banks from lending, but might even cause them to *call in* (demand immediate repayment of) some existing loans. Because this move can be very costly to banks, reserve ratios are normally changed only in small increments, and then only in emergency situations.

9.4.5 **Monetary Policy Targets**

A short history of monetary targetry

During much of the 1950s and 1960s, conventional wisdom was that central banks ought to maintain low and stable interest rates. This was deemed to be good for investment and growth. As a result, money was allowed to grow endogenously, often quite fast. The reasons can be inferred from Figure 9.5. Ultimately this policy led to high inflation rates in the 1970s.

Reminded of their duty to deliver price stability, most central banks in the OECD area opted then to target the rate of money growth explicitly. In Chapter 8, it was shown that as long as the public's demand for monetary aggregates is stable, money growth ultimately determines inflation. A low and stable rate of money growth is therefore a clear signal that inflation too will be low and stable. During the 1980s, nearly all central banks in the OECD countries operated with a money growth target, with the result that interest rates were quite volatile (to see why, look again at Figure 9.5).

Monetary targeting can be credited for the successful disinflation of the 1980s, but then disenchantment with money targets has set in. The link between money growth and inflation has become less predictable over the policy planning horizon (two to three years), much as the link between money base and wider monetary aggregates has become clouded. Widespread financial deregulation in the mid-1980s first, the information technology

on banking and financial markets in the 1990s next, have resulted in instability in the public's demand for money. With unexpected and poorly understood shifts in the derived demand for reserves, the link between the money supply and inflation has become unreliable and, with a variable money multiplier, control of the money base M0 does not deliver a precise handle on the wider aggregates.

Inflation targeting

One answer has been to target inflation directly. Initially implemented by the Bank of New Zealand in the late 1980s, inflation targeting has been adopted e.g. in Canada, Chile, Israel, Mexico, Poland, Sweden, and the UK. The appeal of this target is that it is closest to the central bank's mandate, which makes it easiest to communicate monetary policy actions and to reassure the public that these actions are driven by a clear and transparent commitment to a verifiable definition of price stability.

The two crucial elements of inflation targeting consist of an inflation target—which may be set by the constitution of the central bank or by the government—and the central bank's own forecasts of inflation over the medium run—two to three years ahead of time. Comparing the target with forecasts provides a straightforward guide to policy action: if the forecast exceeds the target, for instance, monetary policy is tightened by raising the interest rates and slowing down money growth.

A key concern is that inflation forecasts are inherently uncertain, especially two or three years ahead. What if the central bank makes a mistake? For example, if it overestimates future inflation, it will unnecessarily raise interest rates. Naturally mistakes are possible: the great oil price increases of the 1970s would have knocked any inflation forecast off target. There is no perfect solution to this difficulty. One answer, proposed by the Bank of England, is presented in Box 9.4.

Other popular targets

Not all central banks have adopted inflation as their only target. Instead of targets, the ECB has adopted two indicators called 'pillars': one of them is the traditional money growth rate—not a target but a 'reference value' in the language of the ECB—and the

---

[8] When banks hold no excess reserves and currency holdings are nil, equation (9.3) implies that, if reserves are constant deposits change in the same proportion but in the opposite direction, like the reserve ratio. In the example, $\Delta rr/rr = +0.2$ implies that $\Delta D/D = -0.2$.

Box 9.4   The Bank of England's Fan

Since 1993 the Bank of England has employed inflation targeting in guiding monetary policy. In 1998, the Bank was made formally independent. On both dimensions of inflation targeting and monetary independence, it has strongly influenced central banking practice. The Bank does not decide its inflation target which is set, instead, by the Chancellor of the Exchequer, e.g. 2.5% for 2001. Thus the Bank's task is technical—achieve the set target—rather than political—decide on the appropriate rate of inflation. It is fully independent, however, in the way it goes about achieving its target and has no other duty to fulfil. The bank is said to be goal-dependent and instrument-independent. If it misses its target by more than 1% on either side of the 2.5% target, the Bank's Governor must write an open letter to the Chancellor. The Bank publishes every quarter its inflation forecast in the *Inflation Report*. This forecast is produced on the assumption that interest rates remain unchanged. Thus, any discrepancy between the forecast and the target can be dealt with by a change in the interest rate. Interestingly, the forecast is published as a fan, shown in Figure 9.7.

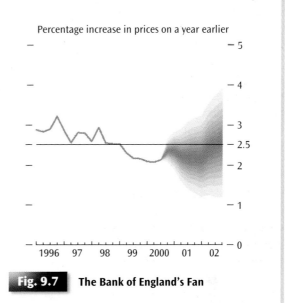

Percentage increase in prices on a year earlier

Fig. 9.7   The Bank of England's Fan

The figure shows the inflation forecast as of November 2000. It covers the next two years. Rather than publishing just one number for each period ahead, sensibly the Bank of England recognizes the uncertainty inherent in the exercise and presents a 'fan', which is darker where the estimate is considered more probable, and increasingly lighter where the odds seem low. The fan thus reveals the Bank's thinking, its best guess and the size of its doubts.
Source: *Inflation Report*, Bank of England, November 2000.

other one includes numerous indicators (inflation, the output gap, the exchange rate, etc.). Still, committed to an inflation rate between 0% and 2%, the ECB is an implicit inflation-targeter. The US Federal Reserve System, the US central bank, does not have any explicit target, it operates with a high degree of pragmatism.

A number of countries aim at the external value of their currency, making the exchange rate the target of monetary policy. As will become clear in the next section, exchange rate targeting seriously constrains monetary policy. Some countries allow some flexibility in the exchange rate target, either in the form of a band of fluctuation (for example within the European Monetary System), or by letting the exchange rate depreciate along a pre-specified trend (this has been the policy followed by Hungary since 1995). Others have completely linked their currency to another one, operating what is called a currency board: this is the case of Argentina, Bosnia, Bulgaria, Estonia.[9] The most extreme form of exchange rate targeting is the complete adoption of a foreign currency, which completely eliminates domestic monetary policy. It is called dollarization when the adopted currency is the dollar (e.g. Ecuador, Panama) or euroization when the euro becomes the national currency (e.g. in Bosnia-Herzegovina).

[9] For more details on the European Monetary System or currency boards, see Chapter 20.

9.5   Monetary Policy in an Open Economy

9.5.1 Foreign Exchange Market Interventions

Monetary policy is influenced by foreign exchange markets. The link is the foreign assets that the central bank holds (Figure 9.2), which mostly consist of deposits with foreign central banks denominated in foreign currencies, foreign Treasury bills, and some gold. Central banks use their foreign assets to *intervene* on the foreign exchange market to influence the exchange rate. For instance, if the central bank wishes to prevent a depreciation, i.e. a loss in the external value, it buys back its own currency on the foreign exchange markets, and pays for it by drawing on its stock of foreign assets. On the asset side of its balance sheet, foreign reserves decline; on the liability side, the monetary base is reduced since the domestic currency bought back on the foreign exchange market is effectively withdrawn from circulation. At this point, the money multiplier comes into play and the wider aggregates decline as well. Similarly, to prevent an appreciation, the central bank sells its own currency and acquires foreign assets; the monetary base increases, and so do the wider aggregates. Unless something else is done, the link is direct and automatic.

There is a similarity between exchange and open market interventions. Both affect the liabilities of the central bank (monetary base) as well as its assets and in both cases the money multiplier then amplifies the initial effect of the intervention. The difference lies in which asset holding changes. In the case of an open market operation, it is the holdings of domestic assets that are affected (repurchase agreements, bills or other private paper, Treasury bills). In an exchange market intervention, it is the holdings of foreign exchange that are affected. This similarity highlights the possibility of a conflict between monetary control and exchange rate control. Indeed, since foreign exchange market interventions directly affect the size of the monetary base, monetary policy autonomy is lost when the central bank is compelled to intervene on foreign exchange markets to fix the exchange rate. Later chapters explore this

issue in detail. The next section outlines a procedure often used in an attempt to break the automaticity.

9.5.2 Sterilization

The similarity between money and foreign exchange market intervention suggests a 'quick fix' for the tension between monetary policy and exchange rate control. A central bank can offset, or sterilize, the impact of its foreign exchange intervention on the money supply by intervening on the open market with a transaction of the same volume, but with the opposite effect on money market liquidity.

Take a particular example of the defence of the exchange rate depicted in Figure 9.8(*a*). To support its currency, the Danish Krone (DKK), the Danish central bank—Danmarks Nationalbank—sells €10 million of its foreign exchange reserves and buys the equivalent amount of its own currency, say DDK 80 million. As a result, the asset side of the central bank declines by DKK 80 million, and the monetary base shrinks by the same amount. If the central bank simultaneously purchases DKK 80 million worth of securities on the open market, it injects the same amount of monetary base that was destroyed during the foreign exchange market intervention. Panel (*b*) of Figure 9.8 shows that the end effect of **sterilization** is a reshuffling of the asset side of the central bank's balance sheet—an increase in domestic asset holdings matched by a reduction of foreign exchange—leaving the liability side, in particular the monetary base, unchanged.

Later, we shall see that this 'quick fix' is just that—and not at all free of problems of its own. In particular, the cause of currency's weakness, which called for intervention in the first place, is not addressed. Attempting to divorce the exchange rate from domestic monetary conditions may result in speculative attacks—crises in South East Asia, Russia, Brazil in the late 1990s are a reminder of the limits of this strategy. At this stage, we just note that there is an automatic link between foreign exchange market interventions and the money supply, but that this automaticity can be broken through sterilization.

Danmarks Nationalbank		Danmarks Nationalbank	
Assets	Liabilities	Assets	Liabilities
Foreign exchange − 80,000,000	Monetary base − 80,000,000	Foreign exchange − 80,000,000	Monetary base + 0
		Government bonds + 80,000,000	
(a)		(b)	

Fig. 9.8   **Foreign Exchange Market Intervention and Sterilization**

In panel (a) the central bank intervenes in the exchange market to support its currency. It sells some of its foreign exchange reserves and buys back its own currency. With some currency withdrawn from circulation, the monetary base is reduced, and the money supply will decline further through the multiplier effect. In panel (b) the central bank counters the money-reducing effect by sterilizing its exchange market intervention. It buys an equivalent amount of securities from commercial banks. This replaces the monetary base previously destroyed.

9.6   Monetary Financing of the Government: A Slippery Objective

We now look more closely at the relationship between a central bank and its government. The central bank is a public institution and therefore part of the 'government', broadly speaking. While many central banks were created by private commercial bankers, they typically ended up being nationalized and brought under government control. The proximity between an inherently cash-hungry institution (the government) and the exclusive producer of cash (the central bank) creates temptations beyond imagination. Indeed, few are the countries that in their past have refrained from including 'provider of cash' in the central bank's list of objectives. The result has most often been uncontrolled inflation, prompting institutional reforms that establish thick walls between the central bank and its government. Future chapters will look into that issue. Here we describe the various ways in which a central bank can provide resources to the government.

9.6.1 Direct Credit to the Government

A central bank can lend directly to the government by simply crediting its account (see Figure 9.2). This is monetary base (M0) creation, equivalent to printing banknotes and turning them over to the government, very much like a commercial bank creates money (M1) by lending to one of its customers. The difference is the multiplier. Indeed, as soon as the government uses its loan to purchase goods or services, the monetary base enters the commercial banking system as recipients of government payments deposit these funds in their bank accounts. At that stage, the multiplier process takes over. Exactly the same occurs when the government borrows from commercial banks by issuing Treasury bills which are then acquired by the central bank on the open market, another modern version of the printing press called **monetization** of the public debt.

It is often the case that governments in dire financial conditions are unable to borrow from the public or from banks. In that case, their natural tendency is to ask the central bank to do the lending. If the central bank obliges, and it may be forced to if it is under direct government control, easy financing of that sort is not conducive to public budgetary rectitude. Most of the episodes of high inflation are associated with direct financing of budget deficits and/or monetization of the debt.

Table 9.4	Seigniorage around the World (% of GDP)			
	Seigniorage		Inflation	
	1980–91	1992–95	1980–91	1992–95
Advanced Economies	0.8	0.3	7.2	3.3
USA	0.4	0.4	5.4	2.8
Germany	0.5	0.3	2.9	3.5
Japan	0.6	0.3	2.6	0.9
Hungary	0.4	4.1	12.7	23.1
Poland	7.0	2.2	99.5	34.6
Israel	1.9	0.5	111.1	11.3
Africa	1.4	1.3	19.6	22.2
Asia	1.5	2.0	7.6	7.1
Latin America	3.2	2.4	251.4	110.1

Source: Paul Masson, Miguel Savastano, and Sunil Sahrma (1998), 'Can Inflation Targeting Be a Framework for Monetary Policy in Developing Countries?', Finance and Development, 35(1): 34–7.

9.6.2 Indirect Credit: Seigniorage and the Inflation Tax

Producing the monetary base is virtually costless: a stroke of a pen—more precisely keying in a few zeros in the computer—or activating the printing press. Yet, the central bank does not give out its production for free, it sells it at face value, thus making comfortable profits. The revenue from this lucrative activity is called **seigniorage**, a reminder of the Middle Ages when local lords had the monopoly of coinage on their lands and charged a fee for every coin they minted. Seigniorage is the main source of profit for central banks. As public institutions, central banks are usually required to pass most of their profits to their governments. Table 9.4 shows, however, that seigniorage is rarely a substantial source of revenue in advanced economies.[10]

Seigniorage should not be confused with the related **inflation tax**. Seigniorage income accrues as the government uses newly created money to pay its bills. The inflation tax, in contrast, erodes the value of all nominal government liabilities that are not protected against inflation, not just the monetary base.[11] If the public debt is not indexed to inflation, and it rarely is, an unanticipated increase in inflation benefits the government by reducing the debt's real value (in general, unanticipated inflation hurts all creditors and benefits all borrowers, but within the private sector it is a redistribution of wealth and not a tax). In contrast, real assets such as property, artwork, rugs, jewels, and explicitly indexed financial instruments are immunized from inflation's effects. Only if inflation is correctly anticipated is the private sector protected from the inflation tax, since the nominal interest rate increases one-for-one

---

[10] The higher the rate of inflation, the more people must keep acquiring money to make up for its declining purchasing power, hence a seemingly endless source of revenue. In fact, when inflation rises and the value of money keeps declining, people reduce their cash balances, often drastically, thus limiting the central bank's ability to extract yet more resources.

[11] Formally, seigniorage is the real value of the monetary base created: $\Delta M0/P = (\Delta M0/M0)M0/P$. In contrast, the inflation tax on the monetary base is the inflation rate π times the real stock of the base, or $\pi(M0/P)$. It turns out that $\Delta M0/P = \pi(M0/P) + \Delta(M0/P)$: seigniorage is the sum of the inflation tax on the monetary base and the increase in the real stock of monetary base.

with expected inflation (the Fisher principle): the capital loss on the principal is exactly compensated by the higher nominal yield (Chapter 8). In that case, the inflation tax boils down to seigniorage.

9.6.3 Independence of the Central Bank

The temptation for governments to engage in inflationary finance is strong: borrowing from the central bank provides resources and, as it is inflationary, it further delivers seigniorage and the inflation tax. The benefits accrues immediately, the costs (inflation) later. Since central banks are responsible for price stability, their instinct is to refuse to finance government budget deficits. It is no surprise that governments have a perpetual desire to control the central bank, mostly for bad reasons. For this reason, an increasing number of central banks have been made formally independent of their governments. Typically they are often forbidden by law to lend directly to public authorities and are explicitly requested to deliver low and stable inflation rates. This is the case in the Euro area, where central bank independence, the primacy of the price stability objective and the interdiction of government lending are explicitly stated in the Maastricht Treaty.

9.7 Bank Regulation and Monetary Control

9.7.1 Central Bank Oversight

The privilege of creating money conferred to commercial banks does not come without risks and restrictions. Banks are officially registered by the central bank or related agencies. They must satisfy strict operating requirements designed to deal with the risks involved in creating money. These risks reflect the **information asymmetry** problem: commercial banks have less information about their customers' creditworthiness than the customers themselves. A customer who seeks a loan from a bank has an incentive to misrepresent her situation if it is likely to lead to a refusal of credit. For this reason, bank lending may be riskier than intended. Since most of the money supply is created by commercial banks, confidence and acceptability of money is at stake.

Much as confidence in the currency (i.e. money issued by the central bank) rests on the quality of the central bank, confidence in money created by the commercial banks requires that it be freely and immediately convertible into currency at any time. The history of commercial banking is strewn with bank failures, which often turned into bank panics as worried depositors attempted to withdraw as much cash as possible, not only from the failing bank but from all financial institutions.

The reason for such chain reactions is **systemic risk**. Systemic risk arises first because banks (and, more generally, financial institutions) hold each other's assets, often in large amounts. Should one bank go bankrupt, its liabilities, held as assets by other banks, become worthless. These losses may lead in turn to more bankruptcies. In addition, if the public becomes suspicious that one bank is in trouble and could contaminate others, it will attempt to withdraw what it perceives to be endangered funds. Generalized collapses of the banking system have been observed in the 1990s e.g. in Hong Kong, Russia, Korea, Indonesia, and Ecuador.

To reduce these risks, all countries have instituted bank regulations, and international agreements are being worked out. Regulations include the supervision of bank accounts and operations, limits on competition perceived dangerous to the stability of banks, and restrictions on asset ownership and banking activities. The purpose is to limit risk-taking by banks, to give monetary authorities advance warning in case of failure, and to guarantee the supply of good banking services. An example of protection is compulsory bank insurance. If a bank fails, its customer can be insured against loss. Table 9.5 provides a few examples of insurance systems.

9.7.2 Lender of the Last Resort

Another example of public protection of bank customers is the function of **lender of last resort**. In principle at least, the central bank is expected to provide failing banks with sufficient monetary base to

Table 9.5	Bank Insurance in the Euro Area

Country	Coverage of deposits (€)
Austria	20000
Belgium	20000
Denmark	40000
Finland	25000
France	60000
Germany	90% up to ceiling 20000
Greece	20000
Ireland	90% up to ceiling 20000
Iceland	20000
Italy	103000
Netherlands	20000
Norway	250000
Portugal	25000
Sweden	25000
Spain	20000
UK	90% up to ceiling 22000

avoid immediate bankruptcy and reassure depositors that they can always exchange bank deposits for currency. Bank crises occurred on a large scale in the USA during the Great Depression of the 1930s. The failure of the Federal Reserve Board (the US central bank) to act as lender of last resort at the time is widely blamed for having deepened the recession. In the wake of the first oil shock in 1974, many central banks conducted a 'lifeboat' operation to keep a number of financial institutions afloat. In view of the consequences of contagion, several central banks created the Basle Committee, described in the next section.

The lender of the last resort function of a central bank represents a delicate balancing act. On the one hand, it is known and recognized that the banking system can be unstable in the face of large, sudden withdrawals, which may be based as much on irrational fears or misinformation as the truth. Supplying liquidity in crises can spare financial systems considerable pain and suffering. On the other hand, commercial banks which know that the central bank will bail them out in emergencies will behave differently, possibly in ways which are bad for the financial system as a whole. Box 9.5 summarizes the policy dilemma faced by central banks in this regard.

Box 9.5	Bank Runs and Lender of Last Resort: A Double-Edged Sword

When the value of commercial bank deposits becomes suspicious, bank account-holders attempt to withdraw their funds and convert them into cash. During such *bank runs* it is impossible for all deposits to be paid out, because banks hold only part of their assets in cash, this is a consequence of the money multiplier. Suspicion is contagious, and can be fatal to healthy banks, indeed to the whole banking system. This is why the monetary authorities may intervene as lender of last resort. As they stand ready to create whatever money is required to honour withdrawals, it is in their power to placate depositors' anxieties and put an end to bank runs.

On the other side, lender-of-last-resort protection may encourage banks to take excessive risks, a phenomenon known as *moral hazard*. For that reason, central banks maintain a large degree of uncertainty as to what they would do in case of bank failure, or even deny in public that they are ready to carry out lender-of-last-resort operations. The lender-of-last-resort function is not extended automatically, encouraging depositors to keep an eye on their banks in good times as well. The accepted procedure is to follow the Bagehot principles (named after Walter Bagehot, a British economist of the late 19th century):

(1) lend only against marketable collateral;

(2) lend in large amounts at a higher rate than the market interest rate;

(3) then sell or liquidate insolvent banks, with the losses being borne by their owners and uninsured depositors.

Initially injecting cash into a bank and then letting it go bankrupt allows partly at least to protect hapless depositors while 'punishing' shareholders for their improper control over management.

9.7.3 **Capital Adequacy Ratios**

In the 1970s, and at an increasing rate in the 1980s, financial integration among the advanced economies brought their financial and banking systems into close contact with each other. Increasing integration had two consequences. First, systemic risk is not limited to any one country but can spread across national borders at great speed. Even with relatively slow communication, the 1929 collapse of Wall Street quickly affected financial centres throughout the world. Modern bank regulators see an increase in global financial instability which must be met with new rules and strengthened sanctions. The crises of the late 1990s are evidence that their fears are well founded.

Second, banks compete directly with each other across borders. This calls for a level playing field to ensure fair competition. In 1989, an international agreement among most advanced economies was reached to establish minimum levels of **capital adequacy**. Banks are required to have minimum net worth as a fraction of total risky assets (see Figure 9.6). Net worth is sometimes called owners' capital or equity; it represents the owners' stake in the bank, i.e. what is left of total assets after the value of liabilities have been subtracted. Capital adequacy regulations ensure that sufficient capital (the property of the banks' owners) can act as a 'shock absorber' for the bank's balance sheet and protect depositors against bad contingencies. Details are provided in Box 9.6.

> ### Box 9.6   **Capital Adequacy Ratios**
>
> Capital adequacy regulations are designed to protect the integrity of the banking system from individual bank risk, by requiring that capital (on the right-hand side) be a constant fraction of total risky assets (on the left-hand side) in their balance sheets. While a good case can be made for bank capital regulations, they sometimes put banks at a competitive disadvantage in international markets. Countries with little or no regulations may operate with lower levels of capital for a given stock of earning assets, and may earn better rates of return. In response to this problem, the Committee on Banking Regulation and Supervision (also know as the Basle Committee) has agreed on standard measures of bank capital adequacy.[12] The G-10 (the ten largest industrial countries) and the EC agreed to enforce these capital adequacy standards by end 1992 (by March 1993 in the case of Japan).
>
>   The principle is to link the amount of risky assets that banks hold with owners' equity, i.e. resources committed by the shareholders of the bank. Figure 9.9 shows the symmetry with the reserves ratios. The capital adequacy ratios cover the weak part of a bank's assets with the captive part of its liabilities, while reserves ratios cover the weak part of the liabilities with safe assets. One capital adequacy rule requires that primary or 'core' capital, consisting of paid-in equity and retained earnings, not fall below 4% of total risk assets. Secondary capital should equal at least an additional 4% of risk assets. Secondary capital is defined as hidden reserves, general loan-loss provisions, asset revaluation, and certain 'near equity' such as convertible bonds, subordinated debt, and perpetual
>
> floating rate notes. The volume of risk assets is defined by a weighting scheme that increases with the riskiness of the asset involved. With the growing complexity of financial instruments and the rising importance of 'emerging markets', risk classification is becoming both more arduous and less relevant. In 2001, a new agreement has been reached. It aims at encouraging individual institutions to develop their own risk assessment mechanisms, but under the control of supervisory agencies.
>
>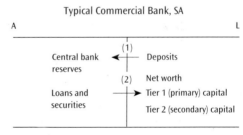
>
> > ### Fig. 9.9   **Reserve and Capital Adequacy Ratios**
>
> Primary or 'core' capital consists of the stakes of the owners in the bank. Secondary capital includes resources close to equity, such as hidden reserves, general loan-loss provisions, asset revaluation, convertible bonds, subordinated debt. Reserve ratios (1) link safe assets to potentially volatile deposits. Capital adequacy ratios (2) link safe liabilities to risky assets.

---

[12] The Basle Committee (established 1975) is a permanent forum for the discussion of international aspects of bank regulation. It consists of representatives of the G-10 central banks and bank supervisory bodies. Its name comes from the fact that it is housed by the Bank for International Settlements (BIS) situated in Basle. The BIS was founded after the First World War to provide settlement, research, and other services to the world's central banks.

9.7.4 Technological Innovation in Banking and Monetary Control

Banks are constantly devising new ways of satisfying the financial needs of their customers. Many of these developments are also prompted by the banks' attempts to escape monetary policy and regulation. The central banks' objective of reining in money growth generally runs counter to individual banks' attempts to increase their profitability. Similarly, banking regulation aims at protecting customers by limiting the range of banking activities, including risk-taking. Pressed by competition and aided by continuous technological innovations—in financial instruments, computer power and communications systems—banks often innovate by exploiting loopholes in existing legislation. As a result, monetary control is weakened and banks may become more fragile. This fragility is confirmed by continuing bank failures as well as the collapse of prestigious institutions like Barings of Britain (one of the oldest banks) or LTCM (Long-Term Capital Management, a firm created and run by several Nobel Prize winners) in the USA.

 ## Summary

1. The main objective of central banks is to achieve price stability, i.e. low and stable inflation. Some central banks may also try to stabilize output and employment. In pursuing their objective(s), central banks define one or more targets, which are related to the overall objective. To meet these targets they may have one or more instruments of monetary policy at their disposal.

2. Since most of the money stock is created by commercial banks, control of the money supply by the central bank is only indirect. The key instrument is the reserve ratio, which is either imposed by regulation or self-imposed by commercial banks themselves. This ratio establishes a link between bank reserves of the monetary base—a liability of the central bank—and bank deposits, a component of the money stock.

3. Bank reserves represent a fraction of deposits. An increase in the monetary base and in bank reserves translates into a much larger increase in deposits. This multiplicative factor is called the money multiplier.

4. The multiplier establishes a fairly stable link between the money base and the wide monetary aggregates (M1, M2, M3, M4, etc.). Thus the public's demand for money translates into a derived demand for the monetary base. This demand is expressed on the money market.

5. Facing the derived demand for the monetary base, central banks carry out open market interventions, providing commercial banks with base money. In doing so, they decide on a quantity to supply, or to supply whatever quantity is demanded to deliver the desired interest rate on the money market. An additional instrument available to the central bank is the required reserve ratio, when it exists.

6. The most popular targets in formulating monetary policy are (expected) inflation, money growth and the exchange rate. When the exchange rate is fixed, the central bank is committed to intervene on the exchange markets. There exists an automatic link between foreign exchange market interventions and the money supply. Sterilization is one way of breaking the automaticity.

7. As a public institution, a central bank can assist the government in the financing of its expenditures in three ways: (1) it can lend directly to the government; (2) it usually transfers some of its seigniorage revenues; (3) by allowing inflation to rise, it creates an inflation tax which lowers the burden of the public debt when the latter is not indexed.

8. Because the monetary financing of public spending is a permanent temptation, an increasing number of central banks have been made independent of their governments. Independence is designed to allow central banks to refuse to jeopardize their price stability objective. It sometimes specifies that the central bank may not lend directly to the government, or sets a limit on such loans.

9. In addition to establishing the standard of payment, the central bank ultimately guarantees the value of money. This is done by a variety of regulations and the lender-of-last-resort function. Bank deposits are guaranteed—sometimes up to a certain level—through a combination of insurance schemes and implicit understanding that the central bank will create sufficient monetary base in case of bank failure. In return, the central banks may impose on banks constraints designed to reduce their vulnerability.

Key Concepts

- central bank
- monetary base
- bank reserves
- objectives, targets and instruments
- financial intermediaries
- reserves requirements, reserve ratio
- money multiplier
- open market operations
- interbank market

- monetization
- seigniorage
- inflation tax
- foreign exchange market interventions
- sterilization
- information asymmetry
- systemic risk
- lender of last resort
- capital adequacy

Exercises

1. Box 9.3 presents the open market procedures of the ECB. Why are lending and deposit rates the ceiling and floor for the market's interest rates?

2. Consider the case when the government runs a budget deficit. Explain why monetization of the debt (when the central bank buys Treasury bills on the open market) is equivalent to direct lending to the government.

3. Draw a parallel between the central bank's profit from seigniorage and a commercial bank's profit from lending to its customers.

4. The central bank can control the sum of its liabilities, the monetary base, but not its breakdown between currency and banks' reserves. Explain why, and who does decide.

5. Explain why and how an unstable demand for money creates problems for the central bank's objective of price stability. What does it imply for the choice of a target?

6. Consider the case of a country where banks are not forced to hold reserves but do so voluntarily. How might the behaviour of commercial banks frustrate the efforts of the central bank to control the money supply?

7. We have seen two sorts of reserves: bank reserves and foreign exchange reserves. Carefully distinguish between them.

8. In Box 9.1, the money market multiplier is computed as $1/[cc + rr(1 - cc)]$ when the public maintains a constant fraction, cc, of the total money stock in currency form. If instead the private sector holds a constant fraction α of its deposits in the form of currency, show that the money multiplier is $(1 + \alpha)/(\alpha + rr)$, where rr is the reserves ratio.

9. Compute the multiplier when the required reserves ratio is 1% and the public chooses to hold 25% of its money (M1) in cash. What should the central bank do to increase M1 by €10 million?

10. What are the costs of money creation for a commercial bank?

11. The central bank buys €50 million worth of Treasury bills from commercial banks. It pays for it partly in foreign currency—the equivalent of €10 million—and partly in local currency.
    (*a*) Show the effects in the balance sheets of the central bank and of the commercial banking system.
    (*b*) Show what commercial banks will do if the required reserves ratio is 25%.

Suggested Further Reading

Historical references:
Goodhart, Charles A. E. (1988), *The Evolution of Central Banks*, MIT Press.
Deutsche Bundesbank (ed.) (1999), *Fifty Years of the Deutsche Mark*, Oxford University Press.

On the debate on how central banks should behave (objectives, targets, accountability):
Bernanke, Ben S., and Frederic S. Mishkin (1997), 'Inflation Targeting: A New Framework for Monetary Policy?', *Journal of Economic Perspectives*, 11(2): 97–116.
Blinder, Alan (1998), *Central Banking in Theory and Practice*, MIT Press.
Blinder, Alan, Goodhart, Charles, Hildebrand, Philipp, Lipton, David, and Wyplosz, Charles (2001), 'How Do Central Banks Talk', *Geneva Report on the World Economy* 3, CEPR.
Fischer, Stanley (1995), 'The Unending Search for Monetary Salvation', *NBER Macroeconomic Annual*, 1995: 275–86.
Issing, Otmar (1994), 'Experience Gained with Monetary Policy Instruments in Germany', *Bankhistorisches Archiv*, Beiheft 27, Fritz Knapp Verlag.
Leiderman, Leonardo, and Svensson, Lars E. O. (eds.) (1995), *Inflation Targets*, CEPR.
Walsh, Carl (1995), 'Recent Central Bank Reforms and the Role of Price Stability as the Sole Objective of Monetary Policy', *NBER Macroeconomic Annual*, 1995: 237–52.

The European debate:
Buiter, Willem (1999), 'Alice in Euroland', *CEPR Policy Paper* 1.
Issing, Otmar (1999), 'The Eurosystem: Transparent and Accountable or Willem in Euroland', *CEPR Policy Paper* 2.
See also the *Monitoring the ECB* series at http://www.cepr.org

On where the money is, see:
Rogoff, Kenneth (1998), 'Blessing or Curse? Foreign and Underground Demand for Euro Notes', *Economic Policy*, 26: 261–304.

All central banks maintain interesting and up-to-date websites which present their data and views. A good starting point is the Central Banking homepage: http://www.centralbanking.co.uk/

Macroeconomic Equilibrium

Money is absent from Part II. There workers, households, and firms take decisions based on real or relative prices, with no role for the monetary sector studied in Part III as if money does not affect macroeconomic outcomes. While the nominal–real dichotomy is a crucial assumption to think about the long run, it is questionable for the short run. The next two chapters bring the goods, money, and labour markets into a single, consistent framework. This **macroeconomic model** is then used to analyse the simultaneous determination of output, employment, the price level, and the interest rate. The outcome is called **macroeconomic equilibrium**.

Chapter 10 clarifies the roles of output and prices in achieving equilibrium. Two competing hypotheses are presented and characterized. In the classical view, price adjustments bring demand and supply relatively quickly into line with each other; in contrast, the Keynesian view regards prices as changing only slowly, leaving the burden of adjustment to output and employment. Chapter 11 then takes the Keynesian view as the relevant starting point for analysis of short-run fluctuations in real economic activity and interest rates. The exchange rate plays a crucial role in shaping these fluctuations as well as potential policy responses.

Output, Employment, and Prices

10

At the core of the Keynesian polemics . . . is the relationship between price flexibility and full employment. The fundamental argument of Keynes is directed against the belief that price flexibility can be depended upon to generate full employment automatically. The defenders of the classical tradition, on the other hand, still insist upon this automaticity as a basic tenet.

– Don Patinkin

10.1 Overview

This chapter integrates the real macroeconomy of Part II, where money played no role, with the monetary sector of Part III. It proposes a coherent framework which looks at the macroeconomy across its three key markets: the goods market, the labour market, and the money market. This framework is then used to analyse the conditions under which equilibrium is achieved simultaneously in all three markets. Yet, there are two different ways of thinking about market equilibrium. The first—sometimes called the **classical (or neoclassical) approach** to macroeconomics—assumes that prices perform the task of bringing the economy to equilibrium. By 'prices' we mean here not only the price level of goods in terms of money, but also the interest rate and real wages. An important result is that when all prices can adjust freely, the real and monetary sectors do not affect each other.

A second approach takes a different tack. It assumes that some prices are sticky, at least for a while. Equilibrium in this case is achieved through the adjustment of quantities traded: the volume of goods and services (i.e. GDP) and the quantity of labour employed. This second viewpoint is called **Keynesian**, in reference to J. M. Keynes, who criticized the classical approach.

Despite the fact that both approaches arrive at radically different conclusions, both are derived from the same underlying framework. This framework consists of two powerful graphical tools: the *IS–LM* model, which highlights interactions between the goods market and the money market; and the aggregate supply–aggregate demand (*AS–AD*) model, which brings in the labour market and the behaviour of firms that produce and sell goods and services. Both tools are used extensively in the rest of this textbook; they are the bread and butter of macroeconomics.

Chapter 10 stresses the concept of equilibrium in both approaches. A market is said to be in equilibrium when it is at rest and there are no forces moving it away from that resting point. Chapter 10 can be thus seen as an intermediate step towards the analysis of Chapter 11, which examines the effect of changes in exogenous variables on the equilibrium of the economy. Chapter 10 first considers the case of the **closed economy**, which does not trade with, borrow from, or lend to other countries. A closed economy can be regarded as a metaphor for the world economy; this chapter will therefore be most suitable for dealing with global issues of macroeconomic equilibrium. Chapter 11 analyses the case of a small open economy, which trades goods, services, and assets with the rest of the world.

10.2   The Goods Market and the *IS* Curve

10.2.1 Equilibrium in the Goods Market

The first market to consider is that for goods and services produced domestically, the goods market for short. The point of departure is the behaviour of households, firms, and the government, all of which demand consumption and investment goods in pursuit of their activities. The general focus is on the short run, we take the long run as given; the analysis can be thought of as period 1 of the two period framework of Chapters 5 and 6.

In a closed economy, the GDP consists of private consumption, investment, and government purchases. In the 'first period', this can be written as

(10.1) $$Y_1 = C_1 + I_1 + G_1.$$

The components of private demand were analysed in Chapter 6. Today—in period 1—the consumption and investment functions are:

(10.2) $$C_1 = C(\bar{\Omega}, Y_1^d) \qquad \text{(consumption function)}$$
$$+\quad +$$

(10.3) $$I_1 = I(r_1) \qquad \text{(investment function)}$$
$$-$$

The signs underneath functions remind us that consumption spending (C) depends positively on private wealth $\bar{\Omega}$ and disposable income $Y^d = Y - \bar{T}$, and that investment spending (I) depends negatively on the real interest rate (r). Private wealth is considered to be exogenous, hence the bar symbol. For simplicity, investment is a function of the interest rate only: an increase in the real interest rate reduces the attractiveness of investment by increasing the opportunity cost of capital.[1] In addition to private spending by households and firms, government spending and taxing is set exogenously by the government:

(10.4) $$G_1 = \bar{G}_1 \qquad \text{(government purchases)}$$
$$T_1 = \bar{T}_1. \qquad \text{(net taxes)}$$

In Chapter 2, equation (10.1) is presented as true by definition. The crucial step taken in this chapter is to go beyond a mere accounting identity and think of it as the condition for equilibrium in the goods market. The right-hand side represents the *demand* for the nation's output, the left-hand side depicts the *supply* of it, and equilibrium is achieved when the two are equal. Demand is driven by disposable income, the interest rate, government spending, taxes, and wealth. The supply of output is determined by an economy's productive capacity: its capital stock, its labourers and their skill endowments, and the state of technology.[2]

How is equilibrium, the equality between demand and supply of goods and services, achieved? In one view, prices are assumed to perform this task, adjusting to whatever extent necessary. Most economists consider this to be an accurate representation of the long run, or the second period in our two-period framework. In Section 10.5, this also characterizes the first period accurately, but an alternative view is that prices are sticky and that supply adjusts passively to demand. The implications of this alternative assumption are studied in Section 10.6.

To start with, we ask not how equilibrium is achieved, but what it looks like when it is achieved. More precisely, we seek values of the interest rate and output for which (10.1) holds, that is, when the goods market is in equilibrium. For the moment, the price level in the first period is taken as given, and equal to the price level in the second period. Inflation is zero, so the nominal interest rate i_1 is equal to the real interest rate r_1. Later, this assumption will also be relaxed.

10.2.2 Desired Demand and Equilibrium Output

The demand for goods is described by the right hand side of (10.1). It is summarized by the planned or **desired demand function**, which combines the behavioural relationships (10.2), (10.3) and (10.4):

---

[1] Put in terms of Ch. 6, a rise in interest rates reduces Tobin's q and thereby makes investment less attractive.

[2] The determinants of long-run output were discussed in detail in Ch. 3.

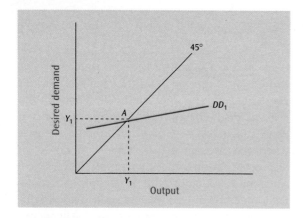

Fig. 10.1 **The 45° Diagram**

Total desired demand responds positively but less than proportionately to a temporary increase in real GDP; hence the slope of the upward-sloping demand schedule is less than 45°. Equilibrium output is the GDP level Y_1 at which demand equals actual output along the 45° line.

(10.5) $DD_1 \quad = \quad C(\bar{\Omega}, Y_1 - \bar{T}_1) + I(i_1) + \bar{G}_1$

  desired demand = sum of demands for goods given i and Y

Current income (GDP) Y_1 affects planned consumption, and therefore desired demand, via two channels. First, it exerts a positive influence on household wealth Ω, the present value of income today Y_1 and tomorrow Y_2. This effect is suppressed here as we take wealth as exogenous ($\Omega = \bar{\Omega}$). Second, it affects disposable income, which is current income minus taxes ($Y_1 - \bar{T}_1$). This is the link we focus upon and represent in Figure 10.1 with the upward-sloping desired demand schedule. The schedule is flatter than the 45° line because, when income or GDP rises, demand increases by less.[3]

In equilibrium, demand equals output—which is supplied by firms. But output supplied equals income Y_1, since both represent another definition of GDP. Equilibrium thus occurs when desired demand is equal to income. In Figure 10.1, this is the intersection of the DD_1 schedule and the 45° line at

point A. Desired aggregate demand (measured along the vertical axis) is equal to output voluntarily produced (measured along the horizontal axis). This state is called **goods market equilibrium**.

10.2.3 The *IS* Curve

We have described goods market equilibrium, holding the interest rate constant. In Figure 10.1, the DD_1 schedule depicts the positive dependence of demand on output, holding the interest rate constant. What happens if the interest rate changes? The answer is given by the first panel of Figure 10.2. The starting point A is on the desired demand schedule drawn for an interest rate i_1. A decline in the interest rate, from i_1 to i'_1, means that the cost of capital declines and future profits are discounted at a lower rate. Consequently, investment increases.[4] As a result of the decline in interest rates, investment spending increases—as implied by the investment function (10.3). At each level of income, desired demand is higher. The DD curve shifts upwards. The move from point A to point B means that equilibrium output increases from Y_1 to Y'_1.

The second panel of Figure 10.2 summarizes this discussion. Points A and B correspond respectively to the initial (interest rate i_1 and GDP Y_1) and final (i'_1 and Y'_1) outcomes. The same reasoning can be repeated for any a number of interest rates, producing more points like A and B. They will trace out a negative relationship between the interest rate and equilibrium output depicted by the downward-sloping schedule known as the ***IS* curve**.[5] *For given values of exogenous variables, the IS curve represents the combinations of nominal interest rate i and real GDP that are consistent with goods market equilibrium.* Formally, the *IS* curve is the set of Y_1 and i_1 such that output Y_1 is equal to desired demand DD_1:

(10.6) $\qquad Y_1 = C(\bar{\Omega}, Y_1 - \bar{T}_1) + I(i_1) + \bar{G}_1.$

---

[3] If the increase in income or GDP is temporary, consumption smoothing implies a smaller increase in consumption (in all rigour, wealth is endogenous, then). If the increase in GDP is permanent, consumption should rise by the same amount. Since tomorrow's situation is assumed to be exogenous, changes in today's income are always considered temporary, so demand increases less than proportionately to GDP.

[4] The discussion could be formulated in terms of Ch. 6: a decline in interest rates leads to in increase Tobin's q.
[5] The name of this curve comes from the identity (2.6): $I - S = T - G + PCA$, and was first derived by Nobel Prize laureate Sir John Hicks. For simplicity, he assumed the government budget to be in equilibrium and no foreign trade, so the identity reduced to $I = S$. We draw the *IS* curve as a line because we do not really know, nor do we need to know, its exact shape. For a derivation of the *IS* curve using calculus, see the WebAppendix.

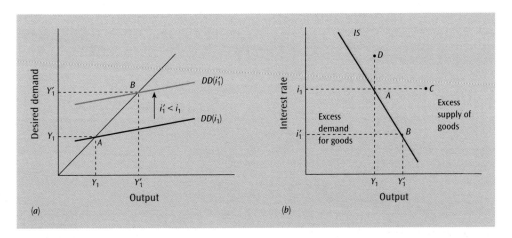

Fig. 10.2 Deriving the *IS* Curve

The *IS* curve traces out combinations of the nominal interest rate (i) and output (Y) for which the goods market is in equilibrium, for given values of the exogenous variables. A reduction in interest rates from i_1 to i_1' leads to an increase in real investment at any level of income. In panel (*a*) the *DD* demand curve shifts up, leading to a new equilibrium output Y_1', corresponding to moving along the curve from point *A* to point *B*. The results are shown in panel (*b*).

The *IS* curve is downward-sloping because a higher interest rate reduces private spending. For equilibrium to be maintained, output Y_1 must be lower.

The *IS* curve represents points of goods market equilibrium, and all points *off* the *IS* curve correspond to market **disequilibrium**. Disequilibrium occurs when, at given output or interest rate levels, desired demand is not equal to output. What happens if, starting from point *A* in Figure 10.2(*b*), today's output increases holding the interest rate constant so that we move to point *C*? A higher income implies a higher level of demand, but, because of consumption smoothing of temporary fluctuations, demand will rise by less than output/income. At point *C*, therefore, there is not enough demand to absorb all of the new output: this is a situation of **excess**

supply on the goods market. Similarly, moving vertically up from point *A* to, say, *D* corresponds to an increase in the interest rate with unchanged output. This leads to excess supply in the goods market as aggregate demand declines. The region above and to the right of the *IS* curve therefore represents a situation of excess supply in the goods market. Similarly, the region below and to the left of the *IS* curve corresponds to a situation of **excess demand** for goods and services. The *IS* curve divides panel (*b*) into those pairs of interest rates and output levels that imply excess supply, and those that imply excess demand. The *IS* curve, the boundary of the two regions, represents those combinations of GDP and the interest rates which are consistent with goods market equilibrium.

10.3 The Money Market and the *LM* Curve

The next step applies the same logic to the money market. In Chapters 8 and 9, the money market was characterized in terms of an equilibrium between the demand for money by households, firms and the

government, and a supply of money determined by the central bank, with the help of the banking system. As in Section 10.2, we ask which real GDP and interest rate levels are compatible with equilibrium

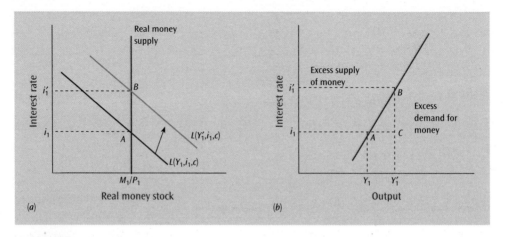

Fig. 10.3 **Deriving the *LM* Curve**

The *LM* curve traces out the combinations of interest rates and output consistent with money market equilibrium. Panel (*a*) depicts the money market equilibrium. The demand curve going through point *A* corresponds to output Y_1. For a higher output level Y_1', demand for money is higher; a higher interest rate i_1' is required to restore equilibrium. Points *A* and *B* in panel (*b*) correspond to the same points in panel (*a*).

in the money market, given the price level. Panel (*a*) of Figure 10.3 reproduces the equilibrium condition established in Chapter 8. The nominal money supply, which is controlled by the central bank, is assumed exogenous and equal to $\bar{M}_1$. Because the price level is taken as given, the real money supply is equal to $\bar{M}_1/P_1$, hence the vertical supply schedule. Money demand corresponds to a particular GDP level Y_1 and to an exogenous level of transaction costs. **Money market equilibrium** occurs where supply and demand are equal:

(10.7) $$\bar{M}_1/P_1 = L(Y_1, i_1),$$

which occurs at point *A*.

Now consider the effect of an increase in GDP from Y_1 to Y_1' in Figure 10.3, holding all else constant. The immediate consequence for panel (*a*) is to raise the demand for money. At each interest rate, the transactions demand of households and firms increases, and the money demand schedule shifts out at any given interest rate. A new equilibrium occurs at point *B*, and the interest rate rises from i_1 to i_1'. This result is summarized in panel (*b*) of Figure 10.3, with corresponding equilibrium points *A* (Y_1 and i_1) and *B* (Y_1' and i_1'). Money market equilibrium implies a

positive relationship between GDP and the interest rate. This is the **LM curve**.[6] *The LM curve is the combination of income and interest rates for which the money market is in equilibrium, given the price level and the exogenous variables.*[7]

Since the *LM* curve traces out equilibrium in the money market, all points *off* the *LM* curve signal conditions of disequilibrium. To see this, suppose that the economy is in equilibrium at point *A* in Figure 10.3. What is the consequence of an increase in real GDP from Y_1 to Y_1' at unchanged interest rate, say to point *C*, holding all else constant? In the money market, a higher GDP raises the demand for real money balances. By assumption, the real supply of money is unchanged and an excess demand for money results. To restore equilibrium under these conditions, a higher interest rate is necessary to re-establish equilibrium, say, point *B*. A higher interest rate increases the opportunity cost of holding money and therefore brings demand back into line with given real money supply.

[6] '*LM*' originates from the fact that along the curve, the demand for liquidity (*L*) equals the money supply (*M*) in eq. (10.7).
[7] For an explicit derivation of the slope of the *LM* curve using calculus, see the Appendix to this chapter.

The region below and to the right of the LM curve thus represents disequilibrium situations of excess demand on the money market. Restoration of equilibrium requires either a rise in the interest rate, or a reduction in income and output levels. Similarly, the region above and to the left of the LM curve corresponds to an excess supply of money: equilibrium can be restored with a decrease in the interest rate or an increase in income and output. The border between these two regions, the LM curve, is where the money market is in equilibrium, i.e. in a state of neither excess supply nor excess demand.[8]

10.4 General Equilibrium

10.4.1 Goods and Money Markets

The two previous sections established equilibrium conditions for the interest rate and GDP in goods and money markets, given the price level and exogenous variables. A natural next step is to look at when both markets are simultaneously in equilibrium. This is shown in Figure 10.4 as the intersection of the IS and LM curves. Given the price level, there is one interest rate and one level of GDP compatible with equilibrium in both markets. This GDP level can be thought of as representing **aggregate demand**, for it is the amount of income which, given the interest rate, wealth, public spending, taxes, and the price level, gives rise to an equal amount of *desired* spending. The IS–LM diagram is an example of a more general approach followed to find the **general equilibrium**. First, each market is examined separately and independently, and equilibrium conditions are established. Then these conditions are brought together, and the intersection of these conditions gives the general equilibrium.

For two reasons, the IS–LM diagram does not alone suffice to establish a general equilibrium in the economy. First, the price level must be determined, or at least accounted for; until now it was simply taken as given while other variables were studied. Second, until now we have not mentioned the labour market, an important element intimately connected with the production or aggregate supply of GDP. In the following sections these omissions are redressed.

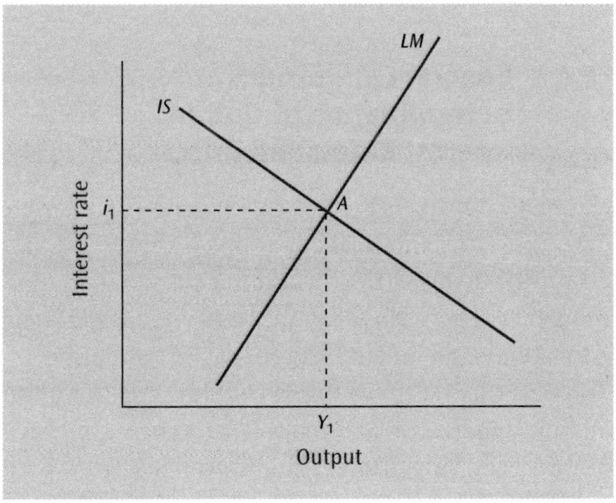

10.4.2 Output and the Labour Market with Flexible Real Wages

Figure 10.5 recalls and summarizes a number of results of Chapters 3 and 4. Since variables always refer to the first period, subscripts will be suppressed henceforth for convenience. The leftmost panel represents the labour market. The capital stock is given by accumulated past net investment and is exogenous. As a result, the marginal productivity of

Fig. 10.4 Goods and Money Market Equilibrium

The IS curve describes the output and interest rate levels compatible with equilibrium in the goods market. Similarly, along the LM curve, the money market is in equilibrium. At point A both markets are simultaneously in equilibrium: there is just one such point, and just one combination of output and the interest rate.

[8] The result is more powerful than it appears. The LM curve also describes equilibrium in the market for interest-bearing assets. The reason is that the demand for money represents the choice of keeping wealth in non-interest-yielding form. Implicit is a decision of how much wealth is held in the form of interest-yielding assets such as bonds or stocks.

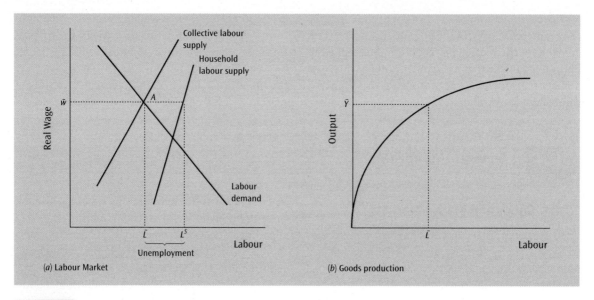

Fig. 10.5   **Output and Employment**

Wages adjust to establish equilibrium in the labour market at point A (panel (a)). This determines the amount of labour used by firms. Given the stock of capital, output is fully determined by employment by the production function (panel (b)).

labour is declining, hence the downward-sloping labour demand schedule. The labour supply curve represents collective wage-setting. It is upward-sloping as workers or their representatives trade off employment and higher real wages. If real wages adjust to equilibrate demand and supply, the market settles at point A. If there is involuntary unemployment (U), it is only from the perspective of households.[9]

The rightmost panel of Figure 10.5 displays the production function of the economy. Given the stock of capital, the production function shows how much output can be produced using given labour input. At the real wage determined in the labour market, the firms hire a level $\bar{L}$ of employment (man-hours) and produce $\bar{Y}$. Thus, equilibrium in the labour market

determines the equilibrium level of output supplied by firms.

10.4.3 General Equilibrium Determination of Output, Interest Rates, and Prices

Figure 10.6 brings these results together in a single diagram. This graphical apparatus is important and powerful. It shows how to find the general equilibrium, i.e. when all three markets—goods, money, and labour—are in equilibrium at the same time.

Panels (a) and (b) in the left part of the figure can be found in Figure 10.5. They depict the supply side of the economy: how equilibrium in the labour market determines today's output Y. This is the level of output that firms are willing to supply at current nominal wages and prices. The top centre panel (c) shows the IS and LM schedules of Figure 10.4. The intersection of these two curves determines the aggregate demand of the economy: how much households, firms, and the government want to spend on today's output Y given prevailing

[9] The difference between collective and household labour supply was discussed extensively in Ch. 4. The real wage/employment outcome is associated with involuntary unemployment from the household perspective. None of the main conclusions of the present chapter hinges on real wage flexibility, however. An exercise asks you to check this.

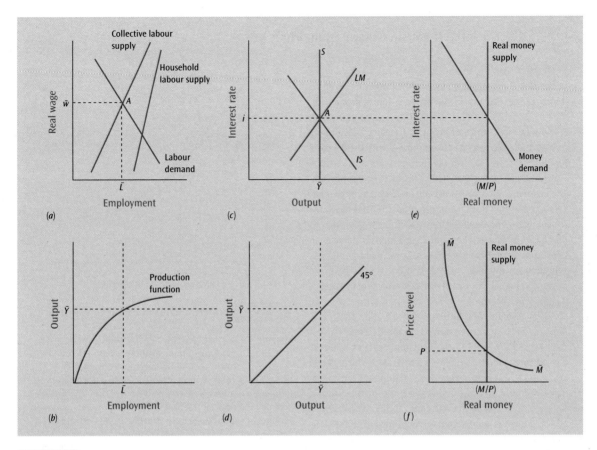

Fig. 10.6 **General Equilibrium**

When real wages are fully flexible, they adjust to clear the labour market at point A (panel (a)). This determines the amount of labour used by firms. Given the stock of capital, the level of output is fully determined by employment as shown in panel (b). Using the 45° degree line in panel (d), the level of output that firms intend to supply is shown as the economy's vertical supply schedule S in panel (c). Panels (e) and (f) show the money market and the corresponding price level. At point A in panel (c), all three markets (labour, goods, money) are simultaneously in equilibrium. This is called the general equilibrium of the economy.

interest rates.[10] Box 10.1 links the interest rate thus determined with consumers' desires to allocate their consumption over time, as was derived in Chapter 6. The supply of goods $\bar{Y}$ is represented in panel (c) by a vertical line S. It is found by 'reflecting' the output level found in the lower left panel (b) using the 45° line in panel (d).

The top right panel (e) reproduces the money market equilibrium condition shown in Figure 10.3(a),

and links the interest rate to the observed real supply of money. Finally, for a constant nominal money stock, the price level and the real money stock move inversely to one another, and this relationship is captured in the lower right panel (f).[11] With the nominal money supply given at $\bar{M}$, the $\bar{M}\bar{M}$ curve in panel (f) associates a higher price level with a lower

---

[10] In Ch. 11, we include the net demand for goods and services from the rest of the world in an open economy.

[11] It is given by the simple formula $P = \bar{M}/(M/P)$. In words, it tells us what price level P is necessary to make an exogenous nominal money supply consistent with a given level of real balances M/P.

Box 10.1 The Interest Rate in General Equilibrium

In Chapters 5 and 6, the interest rate was taken as given by the rest of the world. In fact, in the long run it is *determined* by the world's preferences, resources, and production possibilities. The interest rate will be that which equilibrates the supply of savings—excess of output over private and government consumption—with the demand for goods used for investment purposes.

Figure 10.7 shows the properties of this equilibrium. The economy starts with a private endowment at point A, which represents the consumption possibilities available if no investment is undertaken, and given government purchases G_1 (investment and government purchases in the second period have been set to zero). By forgoing consumption in amount I_1, the economy can increase the present value of its wealth as described in Chapter 3 (Figure 3.7). The amount of consumption households are ready to give up for additional consumption tomorrow depends on tastes, summarized by indifference curves. By moving from A to A', the economy reaches a higher indifference curve. The real interest rate which clears the world's supply of savings and its demand for investment will be equal to the marginal rate of substitution between goods tomorrow for goods today. It will generally be positively related to the impatience of households (preference for today over tomorrow) and to the marginal productivity of investment (its effectiveness in transforming goods today into goods tomorrow).

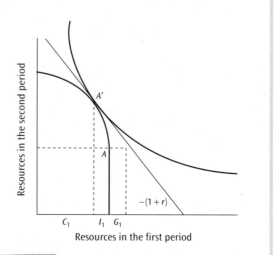

Fig. 10.7 Interest Rate in General Equilibrium

The interest rate is determined endogenously as the price that allocates output Y_1 among various types of demand $(C_1 + I_1 + G_1)$. It will depend on tastes for consumption today versus consumption tomorrow, which are given by indifference curves, and productive possibilities, which are given by the slope of the production function (the marginal product of capital tomorrow). Starting from a private endowment at A, savings and investment allow the economy to reach point A'.

level of real money balances, and a lower price level with a higher level of real balances. Along with private behaviour described by the demand-for-money schedule, the real money supply determines the *LM* curve in panel (*c*).

The central question is whether output produced and supplied in panel (*b*) is compatible with equilibrium in the goods and money markets depicted in panel (*c*). As drawn, the *IS* and *LM* curves intersect at point A on the supply line S, so that demand, income and supply are equal. This is an instance of simultaneous equilibrium in all three markets.

It may seem like a lot of luck for all three markets to be in equilibrium at the same time. What would happen if aggregate demand—given by the

intersection of *IS* and *LM* schedules—should differ from supply $\bar{Y}$, the outcome delivered by the labour market plus the production function? This situation is represented by point B in Figure 10.8, panel (*c*); equilibrium reached in goods and money markets lies to the left of the S curve. Equilibrium in goods and labour markets occurs at point A off the *LM* curve (with excess demand in the money market). Equilibrium in the money and labour markets occurs at point C off the *IS* curve (income exceeds demand for goods). The beauty of market economies is that a number of powerful forces are at work to eliminate such disequilibria. The rest of this chapter studies these mechanisms and how they operate.

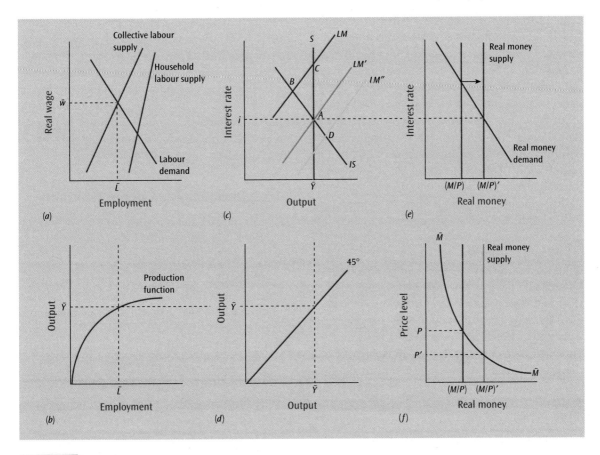

The Role of the Price Level

When the three schedules do not go through the same point as shown in panel (c), the price level adjusts and affects the real value ($\bar{M}/P$) of a given stock of nominal money supply. The result is a shift in the LM curve until it passes through the point where the supply and IS schedules intersect. At point B demand falls short of supply, so a reduction of the price level is needed to shift the LM curve to the right. Conversely, at point D supply falls short of demand, which is curtailed when the real money supply decreases following an increase in the price level. At point A equilibrium obtains in goods, money, and labour markets.

10.5   General Equilibrium with Flexible Prices

10.5.1 Supply-Determined Output

In the classical view, prices—more accurately, the general level of goods prices in terms of money—play the equilibrating role. This section shows that, with full price flexibility, all three markets are always jointly in equilibrium. At point B in Figure 10.8, the level of demand and income compatible with

goods and money equilibrium Y is less than the output $\bar{Y}$ produced and supplied by firms, given labour market equilibrium. A decrease in the price level prompted by the excess supply of goods can restore equilibrium. The process is as follows.

First, note that in panel (e) the demand-for-money schedule is defined for the supply level $\bar{Y}$ and will not shift. The money supply schedule plus the demand for money schedule yield the *LM* curve, which passes through point *C* where output is $\bar{Y}$. A reduction in the price level will increase the real money supply (panel (*f*)). This translates into a rightward shift of the real money supply line in panel (*e*) and a corresponding move from *LM* to *LM'* in panel (*c*). Thus there exists a price level low enough for *LM'* to go through point *A*, where general equilibrium is achieved. In the figure, the equilibrating price level is *P'*, which in panel (*e*) corresponds to the real money supply schedule (*M/P*)'.

This example shows that there is a price level that establishes general equilibrium when the interest rate and the real wage adjust to clear the money and labour markets. Put differently, full flexibility of all relevant prices (the price of goods, the interest rate, i.e. the price of money, and the real wage, i.e. the price of labour) results in general equilibrium.[12] The adjustment does not affect the supply side, which is shown in panels (*a*) and (*b*). These panels correspond to the labour market and the firms' decision to hire labour and to supply a given output level. Two important conclusions can be drawn.

First, when the price level adjusts freely, the economy's general equilibrium is always found at the intersection of the *IS* and the goods supply schedule *S* in the top centre panel. The *IS* schedule can be interpreted as the economy's demand schedule. The output level is said to be **supply determined**.

Second, price adjustments restore equilibrium through the real value of money. By changing the volume of real balances, changes in the price level shift the *LM* curve until it goes through the intersection of the supply and *IS* schedules. In the case of point *B*, i.e. a situation where demand is weak relative to what firms are prepared to supply, a fall in the price level is needed to raise the real value of money.

This in turn leads to a lower interest rate, and a higher level of aggregate demand. A similar story can be told for the case in which aggregate demand exceeds aggregate supply. If the *IS* and *LM* curves were to intersect at point *D*, an increase in the price level would be required to restore equilibrium, by reducing real money balances, raising the interest rate and slowing consumption and investment spending.

10.5.2 Dichotomy and Money Neutrality

The economy we have studied thus far exhibits an important property: nominal and real variables do not affect each other. More precisely:

1. Real variables (real GDP, equilibrium unemployment, relative prices, including the real exchange rate) are unaffected by the level of the money supply;

2. Changes in the money supply affect *all* nominal variables (i.e. those denominated in terms of the domestic currency) by the same proportion.[13]

Why this is so can be seen by returning to Figure 10.8. The general equilibrium is found at the intersection of the *S* and *IS* schedules, which describe the real side of the economy (goods and labour markets). The *LM* curve, which describes the nominal side of the economy (money and other financial markets), plays no role in determining the equilibrium. It simply shifts to pass through the intersection of the two 'real curves'. When the price level adjusts immediately and the economy is always in general equilibrium, the principle of **classical dichotomy** holds: nominal variables do not affect real variables. Only technology and tastes affect the real side of economic activity (growth, unemployment, real consumption, etc.). In particular, output is determined entirely by aggregate supply conditions. Monetary factors, such as the money supply and nominal interest rates, play no role.

---

[12] We have only established the existence of general equilibrium. More technical issues such as the uniqueness of equilibrium and that the relevant prices always move in the right direction to achieve general equilibrium (the issue of stability) are beyond the scope of this book. The question of price adjustment is developed more fully in Chs. 12–14.

[13] This is linked to the proposition in Ch. 8 that the rate of inflation is proportional to the rate of money growth.

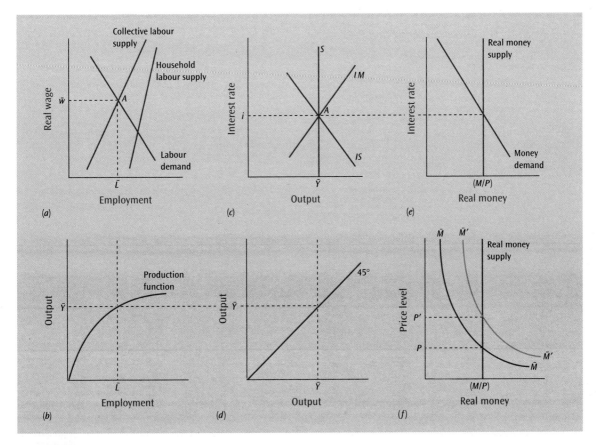

Monetary Neutrality

An increase in the nominal money supply causes a shift from $\bar{M}\bar{M}$ to $\bar{M}'\bar{M}'$, which leads to a proportional increase in the price level. All real variables are unchanged.

To see why, imagine that the supply of nominal money increases. In Figure 10.9 the $\bar{M}\bar{M}$ curve shifts out to $\bar{M}'\bar{M}'$ in panel (f). At a given price level, the supply of real balances rises and shifts down the LM schedule. This is not consistent with general equilibrium, however, since aggregate demand exceeds aggregate supply in panel (c). To restore equilibrium, a price-level adjustment is necessary to return the LM curve to its original position. For that to occur, nominal money changes must be offset by proportional changes in the price level, leaving the real money supply unchanged, as is shown in panel (f).[14]

The property that money does not affect the real side of the economy is known as **monetary neutrality**. In Figure 10.9, monetary neutrality means that neither the labour market conditions (panels (a) and (b)), which determine the supply of goods (the S line in panel (c)), nor spending decisions (the IS curve) are influenced by changes in the money supply (the LM curve).

At one level, the idea of monetary neutrality seems almost obvious: money delivers the unit of account, and the unit of account should be irrelevant for the real terms of trade on which agents engage in market transactions. An excellent recent example of this is the adoption of the euro (see Box 10.2), which is merely a relabelling of prices, in

---

[14] When M and P change in the same proportion, M/P remains constant.

Box 10.2 **The Euro and Monetary Neutrality**

On 1 January 1999, the euro officially became the currency for the 'Euro-11', members of the European Union: Austria, Belgium, Luxembourg, Finland, France, Germany, Ireland, Italy, the Netherlands, Portugal, and Spain; Greece joined in 2001. (The list reflects the result of the Danish referendum in September 2000 not to adopt the euro immediately.) On 1 January 2002, euro banknotes became legal tender for transactions for the first time, although the adoption of irrevocable exchange rates three years earlier had already rendered these national currencies 'non-decimal units' of the euro.

At first glance, the introduction of the euro is nothing but a mere rescaling of prices, and it would be tempting to assert that the introduction of the euro is an excellent example of a purely monetary event, with no consequences for the real economy. What remains to be seen, however is how the conversion will affect the behaviour of firms, households, and governments. For example, central banks can be coerced by national governments into financing budget deficits; this option is no longer available to individual national governments which adopt the euro. A common currency will make it easier for agents to trade across the borders of Euroland member countries; prices will become more transparent and competition should increase. This could change the structure of demand and supply of goods

and services across national boundaries. Implicitly, workers will find themselves in competition with those of other nations.

In addition, one should not underestimate the one-off costs associated with a currency conversion of the magnitude of the euro. Some 50 billion coins and 10 billion banknotes must be brought into circulation. Were the banknotes stacked, they would make a pile 1000 kilometres high. The logistics of the monetary conversion are staggering, although not insurmountable. Who pays for the insurance, transport, and management of the currency conversion is clear, the consumer and the taxpayer. In practice there are always difficulties with the introduction of new currencies, especially since actual conversions involve transactions costs for households, firms, and especially banks. Furthermore, it is inevitable that some people will be left out of the picture, or be fooled by unscrupulous swindlers. This kind of fraud can occur in the absence of monetary unions, however. There is also the 'rounding-up' problem; it is well known that retailers like to choose prices that are round numbers (or end in '49' or '99'). The introduction of the euro will make the new prices 'non-rounded' and will lead to price changes, which will necessarily represent real price changes. What will be the net impact of all these effects? It will take years to sort out these effects; we'll have to wait and see.

---

principle. In Chapter 8 it was shown that over the long run inflation and exchange rate depreciation are driven entirely by growth of the nominal money supply. The more extreme view that prices adjust even in the short run, so that the economy is always dichotomized, is the **(neo)classical assumption**.[15] Its validity for the real world remains controversial.

Evidence presented in Figure 8.9 does suggest that to a first approximation, the principles of dichotomy and money neutrality provide a good benchmark for the long-run behaviour of the macroeconomy. At the same time, Figure 10.10 suggests that strict monetary neutrality does not obtain from year to year. Changes in nominal money do not lead to instantaneous price changes, and appear to be related to changing rates of economic activity. This opens up an interesting question: how does the economy behave when prices *don't* adjust perfectly to every change in the environment? The next section examines more closely the implications of price rigidity.

---

[15] This is the rival to the Keynesian view that prices are sticky. The term 'classical' comes from Keynes's initial critique. 'Neoclassical synthesis' refers to the revival of pre-Keynesian ideas and their incorporation into Keynesian models in the late 1960s and early 1970s.

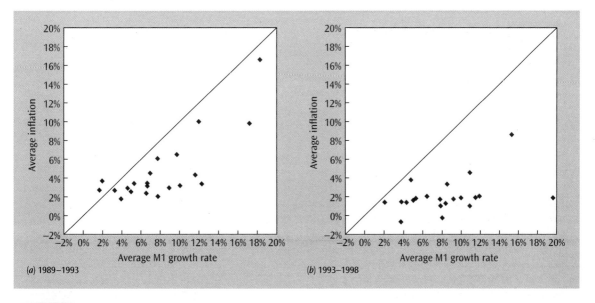

(a) 1989–1993

(b) 1993–1998

Fig. 10.10   **Money and Prices in the Short Run, 21 Countries, 1985–1993**

Over short five-year intervals, the linkage between monetary growth and inflation is less obvious than in Figure 8.9.
The 21 countries are: USA, Japan, Germany, France, Italy, UK, Canada, Australia, Austria, Belgium, Denmark, Finland, Greece,
Iceland, Ireland, Netherlands, New Zealand, Portugal, Spain, Sweden, Switzerland.
Sources: IMF, OECD.

10.6   General Equilibrium with Sticky Prices

10.6.1 Demand-Determined Output

A radically different approach to thinking about the macroeconomy assumes that the price level is no longer perfectly flexible, but instead is *constant* over the short run. The equilibrating role played by prices, which is so central to the classical approach, is shut down. Instead, adjustment takes place in quantities of goods demanded and produced, and thereby in output and employment as well. This backdrop for studying macroeconomics is often called the **Keynesian assumption**. We will see that it changes our perspective in a fundamental way.

Is this assumption realistic? Chapter 1 (Table 1.4) offered evidence that prices are considerably less variable than output. Common day-to-day experience suggests that firms, which generally set prices

for most goods that are purchased, do not change them every day. Why this is so is not entirely well understood. Discussion of these issues will be postponed until Chapter 12, but Box 10.3 presents a few good reasons why firms change prices only infrequently.

Under the Keynesian assumption, output is **demand determined**. This means that suppliers produce whatever is demanded at the given price level. In this sense, the Keynesian case can be thought of as the polar opposite of the classical case, in which output is set by supply conditions alone. Figure 10.11 reproduces Figure 10.8 to illustrate the key differences between the flexible and sticky price equilibria. The starting point is the same: the three schedules in panel (*c*) do not go through the same point. The demand-for-money schedule in panel (*e*) corresponds to output level *Y* since the

---

Box 10.3   The Keynesian Assumption

The assumption that the price level is insensitive to aggregate demand in the short run follows a tradition in macroeconomic analysis that began with John Maynard Keynes (1883–1946) and his *General Theory of Employment, Income and Money*, published in 1936. His purpose was to explain how the level of economic activity could fall dramatically and become stuck at such low levels as observed in the Great Depression. (Industrial production declined by 10–20% between 1929 and 1931.) Today the Keynesian assumption is a practical step towards constructing a macroeconomic framework; but Keynesians would go beyond that, claiming its validity as a good 'working assumption'. For example, Dennis Carleton of the University of Chicago found that firms in the United States change prices infrequently, often no more than once every 18 months, even during periods of moderate inflation.

Critics of the Keynesian assumption argue that it lacks microeconomic foundations. They often ask: Why don't price-setters adjust to changing economic conditions? What kind of behaviour could rationalize price rigidity? The Keynesians have three responses. First, **menu costs** might be significant. These are administrative costs associated with changing prices, relabelling packages, and advertising these changes. Surely these costs must be more than the mere relabelling of prices, since catalogue prices, which are easy to change, are not changed very often either. Similarly, modern supermarkets which use bar codes to price their goods should not find it costly to change entries in the central computer. This suggests that there must be other important reasons for nominal price rigidity.

A second explanation emphasizes *customer relationships*. To invest in consumer relations and maintain a good reputation vis-à-vis its customers, a firm may keep its price lists unchanged in the face of considerable fluctuations in demand. For example, in August 1995 VAT tax was raised by 2% in France. Many stores announced that they would not change their prices *inclusive of the tax*. Thus, to keep prices constant, they seemed willing to absorb—for a time at least—the 2% tax hike and to pay for advertisements to make this known to their customers. A third explanation of price stickiness relates to the role of *contracts*. Firms may be locked into implicit or even explicit contracts to deliver goods at a specified price for some period of time.

---

corresponding *LM* curve in panel (*c*) goes through point *B*. Now the price level *P* does not change. With a fixed money supply $\bar{M}$ and a fixed price level, the real money supply in panel (*e*) is exogenous, which fixes the position of the *LM* curve in panel (*c*). The *IS* curve, which gives conditions for equilibrium in the goods markets, has no reason to move. As a result, the only resting point for the economy is at point *B*, where the *IS* and *LM* curves intersect. Point *B* must be the equilibrium.

The equilibrium cannot be completely described without looking at the labour market. In general equilibrium, if one market does not clear, others will not clear either; in particular, the labour market will not clear. If all nominal prices are rigid, then this includes nominal *wages* as well, so the real wage (the

ratio of rigid nominal wage to the rigid price level) is also fixed at some level $\bar{w}$. When prices are rigid and demand- and supply-determined outputs differ, the 'short side' of the market determines the outcome. In this case, aggregate demand is exceeded by the supply-determined level $\bar{Y}$ corresponding to point *A* in panels (*a*) and (*c*). If firms produce less, they need less labour; panel (*b*) shows that employment is *L*, below the level $\bar{L}$ corresponding to the previous equilibrium in the labour market. Employment is thus determined as the volume of labour needed to produce the level of output demanded, *Y*. In panel (*a*), the real wage $\bar{w}$ has been drawn as the marginal productivity of labour at the previous equilibrium. Unemployment is the outcome, as labour supply exceeds demand by the distance *AB*. This is,

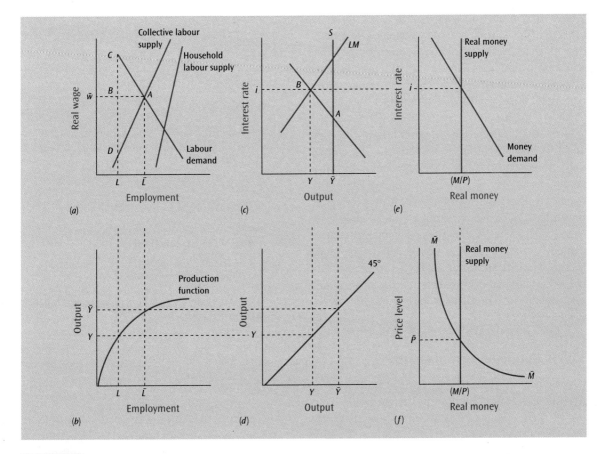

Fig. 10.11 **Sticky Price Equilibrium**

Starting from a situation where all three schedules do not go through the same point in panel (*b*), with sticky prices and a given nominal money supply, the real money stock ($\bar{M}/P$), and therefore the *LM* curve, cannot change. It is the aggregate structure of demand, and therefore the *IS* schedule, that determines the sticky price equilibrium at point *A*. Reflecting the demand-determined output level via panel (*d*), we find in panel (*b*) the level of employment *L* needed to produce *Y*. The labour market need not be in equilibrium however, and in general will be characterized by unemployment. In panel (*a*) it is assumed that firms pay real wage $\bar{w}$ compatible with employment $\bar{L}$, so that there is involuntary unemployment corresponding to *AB*.

however, one of many possibilities, all depending on the value of real wages at the outset.[16]

The main difference between the flexible and sticky price cases can now be summarized in a

---

[16] It is important to note that, because aggregate demand determines output, firms generally will not be on their labour demand curves. In fact, any wage between *B* and *C* is possible: not being on the labour demand curve means that firms make extra profits as they pay less for labour than its marginal productivity.

convenient way. With flexible prices, the direction of causality in Figure 10.6 is counter-clockwise, moving from panel (*a*) to panels (*b*), (*d*), and (*c*): labour market equilibrium determines output. Panels (*e*) and (*f*) then show what price level is consistent with general equilibrium. With sticky prices, the right-hand panels (*e*) and (*f*) are no longer useful, since the *LM* curve already incorporates this information. The logic now is to 'move clockwise', from panel (*c*) to panels (*d*), (*b*) and (*a*): the labour market no longer determines the goods market, *but rather is determined by it*. The difference between the labour demanded and labour supplied at some non-clearing real wage $\bar{w}$ represents involuntary unemployment. The case considered here, where demand falls short of supply, is the archetypal sticky-price Keynesian case.[17]

With sticky prices, general equilibrium does not occur as in Figure 10.6, except by chance. Goods and money markets are in equilibrium, but the labour market is not. At an intuitive level this appears realistic. We do not observe firms producing unwanted goods for very long when demand is weak, nor do we see persistent shortages when demand exceeds supply. As was noted in Chapter 8, money markets are notoriously fast to adjust. On the other side, labour markets require more time, and unemployment seems to be a feature of everyday life.[18]

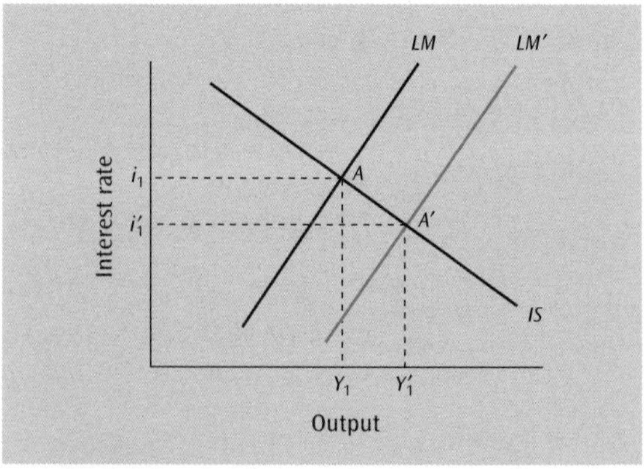

Fig. 10.12 **Monetary Neutrality Fails when the Price Level is Fixed**

An increase in the money supply leads to excess supply of money on points along the old *LM* curve. The new *LM* curve lies below and to the right of the old one. Equilibrium in goods and money markets implies a lower interest rate and higher real GDP than at *A*.

10.6.2 **Non-neutrality of Money**

An important implication of a sticky price level is that the classical dichotomy no longer holds. This can be seen in Figure 10.12 using a single diagram, panel (*c*) of Figure 10.11. Output determines employment, so all the variables involving the real side of the economy (GDP, employment, consumption, investment, real interest rates, etc.) are subject to influences originating in the money market. Since

the price level does not move, changes in nominal money have real effects.

A corollary of the failure of the classical dichotomy is the non-neutrality of money. In Figure 10.12, changes in the nominal money supply shift the *LM* curve, and thereby affect output, employment, and other real variables. In the classical case, monetary neutrality held because the price level moved to equate real money supply $\bar{M}/P$ with real money demand $L(Y, i, c)$ consistent with equilibrium levels of output and interest rates. In effect, the price level moved enough to bring the *LM* curve through the intersection of the goods supply and *IS* schedules. When the price level is fixed, it is money demand that adjusts to money supply. This, in turn, requires changes in the interest rate and output. These changes remain compatible with goods market equilibrium: graphically, the economy moves along the *IS* curve from *A* to *A'*.

---

[17] It is possible to consider the opposite case, where demand exceeds supply. This case, sometimes called 'repressed inflation', is rare, but was frequently observed in centrally planned economies, when prices were set low relative to market clearing values, probably for political reasons. As a result, scarcities were common.

[18] Such 'sticky price general equilibria' are sometimes called non-Walrasian, referring to Léon Walras (1834–1910), a French mathematical economist who first conceptualized the idea of general equilibrium. Walras emigrated to Lausanne in Switzerland when his theories were rejected by his French peers, who ultimately drove him to exile.

Summary

1. The *IS* curve is the set of real GDP levels and interest rates compatible with goods market equilibrium, given the price level. This schedule is downward-sloping because an increase in the interest rate depresses consumption and investment spending, and thereby the aggregate demand for goods and services; goods market equilibrium requires that output be lower.

2. The money market equilibrium condition is represented by the *LM* curve, a positive relationship between real GDP and the interest rate, given the real money supply. The slope of the *LM* curve is positive because an increase in the interest rate, which reduces the demand for money, must be offset by an increase in GDP, which increases demand.

3. In the labour market, there exists a real wage and a level of employment which deliver equilibrium with no involuntary unemployment, at least from the perspective of the collective bargaining parties.

4. When all three markets (goods, money, labour) clear simultaneously, the economy's general equilibrium is achieved. Whether, and how, it is reached depends very much on how the price level adjusts.

5. Price-level adjustments affect the real money supply and drive the *LM* curve to pass through the intersection of the supply-determined output schedule and the *IS* curve, which represents demand conditions.

6. When the price level is flexible, the economy is dichotomized: real and nominal variables do not affect each other. Monetary neutrality is the absence of real effects of nominal money changes. Money affects only prices and other nominal variables.

7. The assumption that prices are flexible is a useful way of thinking about the long run of the economy. While borne out in the long run, full price flexibility is less likely to characterize the short run.

8. When prices are sticky, output is determined by demand conditions. The equilibrium occurs at the intersection of the *IS* and *LM* curves. In general, the corresponding output differs from intended supply. This discrepancy leads to disequilibrium on the labour market, often resulting in involuntary unemployment.

9. With sticky prices, the classical dichotomy and monetary neutrality principles do not apply. Money matters for the real side of the economy.

10. The Keynesian assumption, which maintains that the price level is constant and that output adjusts to achieve goods market equilibrium, is a convenient short cut for analysing the short-run determination of GDP and interest rates.

11. The flexible and sticky price cases can be analysed with the same graphical apparatus. With flexible prices, GDP is supply determined and prices adjust; with sticky prices, GDP is demand determined and the output of firms adjusts.

Key Concepts

- classical (neoclassical) approach
- closed economy
- desired demand function
- goods market equilibrium
- *IS* curve
- disequilibrium
- money market equilibrium
- *LM* curve

- aggregate demand
- general equilibrium
- supply- and demand-determined output
- classical dichotomy
- monetary neutrality
- classical (neoclassical) assumption
- Keynesian assumption
- menu costs

Exercises

1. The *IS* and *LM* curves define four quadrants in Figure 10.4. Any position off a curve corresponds to market disequilibrium, which can be characterized as excess demand or supply in either goods or money markets, or both. Define each quadrant accordingly, e.g. excess demand in the goods market and excess supply in the money market; etc.

2. Suppose that real desired demand is represented by the following simplified function: $2000 + 0.5(Y - T) + G - 200i$. Output Y, taxes T and government purchases G are in real (constant euro prices) terms. The nominal interest rate in per cent per annum is given by i. Government purchases G are constant and equal to 3000.

   (a) What value of GDP compatible with equilibrium when $T = 3000$ and $i = 5\%$? Trace out the *IS* curve by answering the same question for $i = 2\%$ and $i = 8\%$. Give the equation for the *IS* curve.

   (b) Answer all parts of question (a) when instead $T = 4000$. Where is the curve in relation to (a), and why?

   (c) Answer all parts of (a), now assuming that desired demand is now given by $2000 + 0.5(Y - T) + G - 400i$. Explain the differences in your answers to (a).

3. Using the diagram in Figure 10.6, show the effect of a one-time productivity gain (an outward shift of the production function) on employment, output, prices, real wages, and interest rates when prices are flexible. How does your answer change when prices are sticky?

4. Suppose the money demand curve is represented by the following linear function: $L(Y, i) = 0.5Y - 300i$. Suppose $M/P = 2000$.

   (a) Plot the *LM* curve in the i, Y space.

   Use the IS curve from Exercise 2 with $\bar{G} = \bar{T} = 3000$ to solve for equilibrium output Y and interest rate i.

5. Consider the case where real wages are sticky and such that, in Figure 10.6(a), there is some involuntary unemployment. Show that, if prices are flexible, equilibrium is still possible in other markets and that output remains supply determined. Show that the economy is dichotomized and that money is neutral. (This exercise establishes that the flexible price results apply in the presence of real wage rigidity.)

6. The desired demand function is $DD = 4000 + 0.5(Y - \bar{T}) + \bar{G} - 200i$ with $\bar{G} = \bar{T} = 3000$, and assume that output is produced using the production function $Y = \sqrt{(KL)}$. Further, assume that $K = 20{,}000$. Assume that labour is supplied exogenously by households with $L = 5000$.
   (a) What is the equilibrium level for output, real wages, and interest rates?
   (b) Using the money demand function $L(Y, i) = 2Y - 800i$, solve for the price level in this economy for $\bar{M} = 18{,}000$.

7. Using the graphical apparatus, show the effects on GDP, employment, the price level, and the interest rate of an increase in the transaction costs c which affect money demand. You should consider the cases of both fixed and flexible prices.

8. Now assume the Keynesian case for problem 6 with $\bar{P} = 1$ for simplicity. Solve for the effect of an increase in $\bar{M}$ from 16,000 to 17,000 on Y and i. What happens to employment L? What key assumptions have you made in solving this problem?

9. Formerly planned economies emerged with an antiquated capital stock. This means that new investment will quickly raise productivity. Assuming that they start from general equilibrium as in Figure 10.6,
   (a) Show the effect of investment in panels (a) and (b).
   (b) Interpret the resulting situation in panel (c).
   (c) In the case of flexible prices, what is expected to happen to GDP, the interest rate, and prices?
   (d) Now answer the same question as (c) in the case of sticky prices.
   (e) Can the outcome of question (c) be reached with sticky prices if the central bank changes the nominal money supply in a judicious manner?

10. Suppose that a blight wiped out half of an agricultural economy's current harvest (period 1 endowment), which can be either planted today and harvested tomorrow, or consumed today. Use Figure 10.7 apparatus to predict the consequences for the interest rate. Now employ these implications in the six-panel diagram of Figure 10.6 to predict implications for the general equilibrium of the economy. Assume that the nominal money supply is constant, that agents perceive the shortfall as temporary—so that wealth is unchanged—and that the productivity of investment is unchanged, meaning that the production function shifts downwards by an equal amount. *Harder*: what happens to nominal GDP in the first period, if the demand for money has unit elasticity?

Suggested Further Reading

The classic is:

Keynes, John Maynard (1936), *The General Theory of Employment, Interest, and Money*, Macmillan/ Harcourt Brace.

The paper that founded macroeconomics and 'summarized' the *IS–LM* framework is:

Hicks, John (1937), 'Mr Keynes and the Classics', *Econometrica*, 5: 147–59.

The seminal characterization of flexible and sticky price equilibria is:

Patinkin, Don (1948), 'Price Flexibility and Full Employment', *American Economic Review*, 38: 543–64.

Advanced treatments can be found in:

Romer, David (1996), *Advanced Macroeconomic Theory*, McGraw-Hill.
Sargent, Thomas, J. (1987), *Macroeconomic Theory*, Academic Press.

Appendix: A Mathematical Treatment of the Macroeconomic Equilibrium with Flexible and Fixed Prices

This appendix derives formally some of the results presented in the text.

Macroeconomic Equilibrium under Flexible Prices (the Classical Model)

The Labour Market

Aggregate labour supply is assumed to be given by

(A10.1) $$L^S = L^S(w, \bar{N}),$$

where w is the real wage and $\bar{N}$ is the exogenous number of individuals of working age. Assumptions are $L_W^S > 0$, $L_{\bar{N}}^S > 0$. The supply of labour could be viewed more generally as the role of collective bargaining or union behaviour instead of households.

Aggregate labour demand was derived in (A6.8) as

(A10.2) $$L^D = L^D(w, \bar{K}),$$

with $L_W^D < 0$, $L_K^D > 0$. Equilibrium is given by

(A10.3) $$L^D(w, \bar{K}) = L^S(w, \bar{N}) = L,$$

which determines two unknowns, employment L and the real wage w.

The Goods Market

Goods supply is given by the output of firms that produce goods using labour which they have hired according to (A10.2). Capital is fixed in the first period, so we can write the production function simply as $Y = F(\bar{K}, L)$. Since employment is determined in the labour market as the solution to (A10.3), we can define $\bar{L}$ and $\bar{w}$ as the corresponding equilibrium employment and wage, so

(A10.4) $$Y^S = F(\bar{K}, \bar{L}).$$

To derive goods demand, set inflation expectations $\pi = 0$, so the real interest rate r is the same as the nominal interest rate i. Following Chapter 4, final expenditure of households, firms, and government can be written for this closed economy as

(A10.5) $$Y = C(\Omega, Y^d) + I(i) + \bar{G},$$

where Y is GDP, C is consumption, I is investment expenditures, and $\bar{G}$ is government purchases, denominated in real terms. Government purchases $\bar{G}$ are exogenous, as is the lump-sum (net) tax $\bar{T}$. Disposable income Y^d is given therefore by $Y - \bar{T}$. In principle, $\bar{T}$ need not be positive; if negative it could be an exogenous transfer or a tax exemption. Wealth Ω is taken as exogenous.

Equation (A10.5) is the *IS* curve drawn in Figure 10.2, which is an equation in Y, i, and (trivially) the price level P. Total differentiation of (A10.5) results in

(A10.6) $$dY = C_\Omega d\Omega + C_{Y^d} dY - C_{Y^d} d\bar{T} + I_i di + d\bar{G}.$$

The slope of the *IS* curve in (i, Y) space is given when all exogenous variables are constant in (A10.6), when we set $d\Omega = d\bar{G} = d\bar{T} = 0$:[19]

$$dY = C_{Y^d} dY + I_i di$$

or

(A10.7) $$\frac{dY}{di} = \frac{I_r}{1 - C_{Y^d}} < 0$$

for any value of the price level P. Goods market equilibrium obtains when supply and demand of goods are equal, or

(A10.8) $$F(\bar{K}, \bar{L}) = Y = C(\Omega, Y^d) + I(i) + \bar{G}.$$

Money Market

The supply of nominal money is determined by the central bank at $\bar{M}$. Demand for real balances was derived in Chapter 8 as

(A10.9) $$\mathscr{L}(Y, i)$$

with $\mathscr{L}_Y > 0$, $\mathscr{L}_i < 0$. Equilibrium in the money market is given by

(A10.10) $$\bar{M}/P = \mathscr{L}(Y, i),$$

which is the *LM* curve. Total differentiation of (A10.10) results in

(A10.11) $$\frac{d\bar{M}}{P} - \frac{\bar{M}}{P^2} dP = \mathscr{L}_{Y^d} Y + \mathscr{L}_i di.$$

For P, given $dP = 0$, the slope of the *LM* curve can be found when $dM = 0$ in (A10.11), or

(A10.12) $$\frac{di}{dY} = -\frac{\mathscr{L}_Y}{\mathscr{L}_i} > 0.$$

Note that the 'last market', the market for interest-bearing assets, can be assumed to clear if the money market clears. This is said to be an application of Walras's Law, discussed in any good microeconomics textbook.

---

[19] The assumption that wealth is constant could be modified, as will be done in the next chapter's appendix. It reflects the view that transitory (current) movements in interest rates and output should not affect household wealth, which is based on a longer-term horizon.

General Equilibrium with Flexible Prices

Thus, we have:

S curve: $Y = F(\bar{K}, \bar{L})$

IS curve: $Y = C(\Omega, Y - T) + I(i) + \bar{G}$

LM curve: $\bar{M}/P = \mathcal{L}(Y, i)$,

a system of three equations for Y, i, and p. They are represented by the three curves in panel (c) of Figure 10.6. Since output supply is given, the equilibrium interest rates solves

$$\bar{Y} = C(\Omega, Y^d) + I(i) + \bar{G},$$

and the price level adjusts to obey (the MM curve)

$$P = \frac{\bar{M}}{\mathcal{L}(\bar{Y}, i)}.$$

Macroeconomic Equilibrium under Fixed Prices

We now assume that, for whatever reason, P is exogenously given at level $\bar{P}$. Generally, not all markets will clear; in particular, it is assumed that the labour market remains out of equilibrium, and that $L = L^D < L^S \neq \bar{L}$. For simplicity, we also assume that the nominal wage is fixed at $W = \bar{W}$ so that the real wage is also fixed at $\bar{W}$.[20] Labour demand is demand-determined; that is, employment is simply labour demanded to produce output Y. Under these conditions, we can consider equilibrium only in the goods and money markets. Equilibrium in the bond market will obtain if the money market clears, as before.

[20] This assumption is not necessary. For example, Keynes (1936) assumed that only nominal wages were rigid, while prices could adjust fully. Alternatively, one could assume rigid prices plus flexible nominal *wages*, assuming that individuals are on their labour supply curve, or rigid prices plus flexible nominal wages but with the latter determined along a *collective* rather than the household labour supply schedule.

Goods Market

Demand for goods is given by (A10.5). The supply of goods is perfectly elastic at price $\bar{P}$; firms are willing to supply more output at that price. The goods market equilibrium is given by

$$Y = C(\Omega, Y^d) + I(i) + \bar{G}.$$

Because changes in Y are considered short-run, Y is assumed not to affect wealth, or $\Omega_Y = 0$. The slope of the IS curve remains as given in (A10.7).

Money Market

The money market equilibrium condition is unchanged except for the exogeneity of prices:

(A10.10)′ $\bar{M}/\bar{P} = \mathcal{L}(Y, i)$.

The LM curve has slope given by (A10.12). The MM curve is given by

$$P = \frac{\bar{M}}{M/P} = \frac{\bar{M}}{\mathcal{L}(Y, i)}.$$

General Equilibrium with Fixed Price Level

IS curve: $Y = C(\Omega, Y - T) + I(i) + \bar{G}$.

LM curve: $\bar{M}/\bar{P} = \mathcal{L}(Y, i)$.

These two relationships are shown in panel (c) in Figure 10.9. The S curve depicts the output that would have obtained under flexible wages and prices, but is shown only for reference purposes. Note that equilibrium output and interest rates will not generally coincide with those under flexible prices.

Unemployment

Unemployment is given by $L^S(\bar{w}, \bar{N}) - L$, where L satisfies $\bar{Y} = F(\bar{K}, L)$.

Aggregate Demand and Output

11

The nature of the exchange rate regime has an important bearing not only on the relative effectiveness in influencing income and output of the two types of financial policy—monetary policy and budgetary policy—but also on their relative practicability or sustainability.

– J. Marcus Fleming

11.1   Overview

The main message of Chapter 10 was that when the price level is free to adjust, money is neutral. Monetary neutrality means that changes in the money supply do not affect aggregate economic activity. When prices are sticky and do not adjust, however, the economy loses the neutrality property. More generally, demand changes can cause output and employment to deviate from the flexible price equilibrium. This chapter takes the Keynesian assumption that prices are constant as a point of departure for the short run. Later chapters study how output and prices move together. Under the Keynesian assumption, output is determined by demand. Equilibrium in the goods market is achieved through changes in production, which adjusts passively to aggregate demand with little or no change in prices and wages. The resulting **Keynesian model** provides a first interpretation of cyclical fluctuations, successive phases when an economy grows faster (a boom or an expansion) or slower (a recession) than its trend growth rate. Figure 11.1 presents a stylized illustration of these departures of real GDP from its long-run trend. Because demand lies behind cyclical fluctuations in the Keynesian view, governments can use monetary and fiscal policies to reduce the amplitude of macroeconomic swings, or even to eliminate them entirely.

For many decades the Keynesian model was considered the alpha and omega of macroeconomics. Many policy-makers adopted this framework in the 1960s, paying detailed attention to the demand side of the economy and more or less neglecting how the supply side sets prices. The result was inflation in the 1970s and unemployment in the 1980s. Even

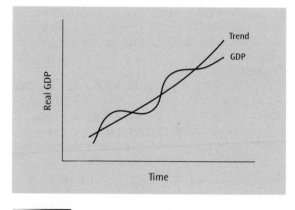

Fig. 11.1   **Cyclical Fluctuations**

The Keynesian assumption helps explain short-run fluctuations of real GDP around its long-run growth trend.

though the shortcomings of the sticky price view are now well recognized, the analysis presented here remains a most useful 'rule of thumb' for thinking about the short run. Most macroeconomists and policy-makers have this framework in mind when they assess current macroeconomic conditions or make policy decisions.

Outcomes in goods, money, and foreign exchange markets are highly interdependent in the Keynesian model. The money market described in Chapters 8 and 9 will affect outcomes in the goods market, and thus the level of output and employment. This is because the interest rate affects investment spending and, at least indirectly via wealth, consumption spending. At the same time, the level of real economic activity influences the demand for money and thereby the interest rate, a feedback from money to goods markets. Moreover, Chapter 7 showed how the real exchange rate can influence the demand for domestic goods in an open economy. If prices are sticky, movements in the *nominal* exchange rate, which often result from changing financial conditions at home and abroad, affect the *real* exchange rate and the demand for goods and services. Figure 11.2 summarizes this conceptual framework.

An important step taken in this chapter is to draw attention to the crucial role of external, or foreign, influences on the macroeconomy. An open economy is affected by trade in both goods and assets. In goods markets, the role of the primary current account requires an important modification of the *IS* curve. In the money markets, cross-border movements of financial assets and other forms of wealth require that we explicitly address the market for foreign exchange and the **exchange rate regime**. The exchange rate may be fixed, meaning that the central bank commits to maintain the value of its currency in terms of other currencies. Alternatively, the central bank may let the exchange rate float

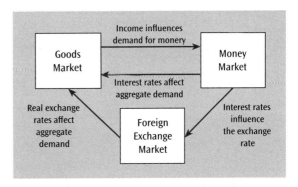

Fig. 11.2   **General Macroeconomic Equilibrium in the Open Economy**

Conditions in domestic money and goods markets affect each other: interest rates and exchange rates influence the level of aggregate demand, while income affects the demand for money and, for given money supply, interest rates. General equilibrium occurs when equilibria in the three markets are consistent with each other.

freely. The exchange rate regime turns out to be crucial to the behaviour of the economy. For this reason, the two regimes of fixed and flexible exchange rates need to be studied separately.

11.2   Short-Run Fluctuations of Output, Employment and Unemployment

11.2.1 Output, Hours, and Employment

We have seen in previous chapters that the long-run output of an economy increases as the result of additional inputs and improvements in technology. In contrast, production changes in the short run are achieved mostly by varying labour input, with capital accumulation and technical progress making at best a small contribution. In times of high demand, overtime work allows firms to utilize the same equipment more hours per day, and possibly more days per week. Similarly, if demand declines temporarily, firms can implement short-time work schedules, substitute part-time for full-time labour, freeze hirings, or in the worst case, dismiss employees. In summary, firms change production by varying either the number of hours per worker, the number of employed workers, or both. As a result of these short-run changes in labour input, employment and GDP deviate from their

respective long run paths, or trends. The temporary deviations of GDP from its trend which appear in Figure 11.3 constitute the **output gap**. The figure shows how, in Germany, cyclical variations in the output gap are accompanied by deviations of unemployment and the total number of hours worked per week or per month from their own trends: firms use both margins of adjustment in varying proportions.

11.2.2 Output and Unemployment: Okun's Law

The relationship between output growth and unemployment is known as **Okun's Law**. Okun's Law associates fluctuations of real GDP Y around its trend growth path $\bar{Y}$, with fluctuations in the opposite direction of the unemployment rate U around its equilibrium rate $\bar{U}$:

(11.1) $$U - \bar{U} = -g(Y - \bar{Y}).$$

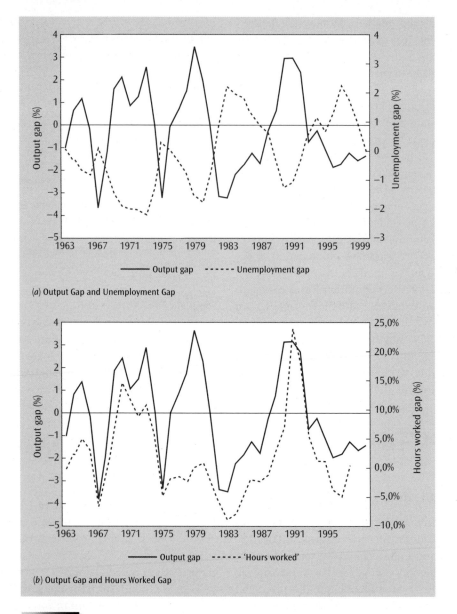

(a) Output Gap and Unemployment Gap

(b) Output Gap and Hours Worked Gap

Fig. 11.3   **Output Gap, Man-Hours, and Unemployment in Germany, 1960–2000**

The output gap (deviations of real GDP from its trend) is presented alongside deviations from the trends of the rate of unemployment and of total hours worked per month. When business conditions vary, firms adapt the supply of goods and services and their demand for labour. For example, when the economy goes into a recession, firms reduce man-hours, partly by using fewer workers, partly by reducing the number of hours worked.

Notes: Trend real GDP and unemployment are estimated as second-order polynomial functions of time.
Sources: OECD.

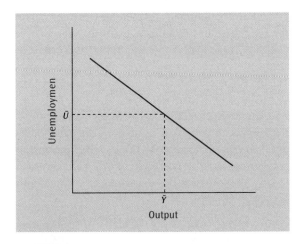

Fig. 11.4 **Okun's Law**

Okun's Law implies that, when the economy slows down, unemployment increases; when output rises relative to trend, unemployment declines.

where $g > 0$ is a reasonably stable parameter.[1] A stylized representation of Okun's Law is displayed in Figure 11.4.

Okun's Law is related to the production function which predicts that employed man-hours and output move together. If the number of workers in the labour force is fixed and hours worked per worker are unchanged, an increase in output is possible only by putting unemployed workers to work. Thus a decline in unemployment is a natural consequence of increasing output. For two reasons, the intensity of this relationship goes beyond what

the production function predicts, however. First, labour supply is procyclical, meaning that when the economy expands more rapidly, individuals tend to enter employment directly without passing through unemployment. Second, firms sometimes retain production staff that are not needed at the moment, so changes in effective employment can be greater than those measured in the statistics.

11.2.3 Aggregate Demand as a Causal Force

The distinction between cyclical fluctuations of output, employment and unemployment around trend levels on the one hand, and the evolution of structural or trend levels of these variables on the other, is an important and recurrent one in macroeconomics. The long-run evolution of the supply side—the sustainable productive potential of an economy—is determined by factors already studied in detail in Chapters 3 and 4. It is the deviations of output, employment, and unemployment around trend associated with the business cycle that we wish to explain in this and the following chapters.

This chapter takes the Keynesian assumption to its logical conclusion. When prices are given, demand becomes the proximate 'cause' of output fluctuations. This is not to say that supply factors are irrelevant, but they will be taken as given as a first approximation for the short-term analysis which is the focus of this chapter. As a result, demand-driven output will also represent the cause of employment fluctuations, and by Okun's Law, fluctuations in the unemployment rate.

11.3 The *IS–LM* Model in the Open Economy

11.3.1 Exogenous versus Endogenous Variables

An essential element of economic analysis is the separation of variables under study into those which are exogenous and taken as given, and those which

are endogenous and thus to be explained. For example, the Keynesian assumption implies that the price level $\bar{P}$ is exogenous. Fiscal policy instruments such as government purchases $\bar{G}$ and taxes $\bar{T}$ are assumed to be under direct control of the government and thus are also treated as exogenous.[2] As in

---

[1] The original observation of the US economist Arthur Okun associated a 1% drop in unemployment rate to a rise in growth of 3% above trend in the United States. This would imply a value for g of one-third.

[2] Net taxes $\bar{T}$ are exogenous; in the appendix to this chapter, net taxes are allowed to depend positively on income Y. This assumption is more realistic, since at given tax *rates*, tax revenues tend to rise with output and income.

Chapter 10, household wealth $\bar{\Omega}$ is also assumed to be exogenous, meaning that it is unaffected by changes in current income and interest rates. Foreign variables such as foreign GDP (Y^*) and the price level (P^*) are also not influenced by the economy under consideration.

Some variables are exogenous or endogenous depending on the **exchange rate regime**. For example, since both domestic and foreign prices $\bar{P}$ and P^* are assumed constant, the real exchange rate ($\sigma = S\bar{P}/P^*$) is exogenous when the nominal exchange rate is fixed ($S = \bar{S}$), but endogenous when the exchange rate is flexible. Similarly, the analysis of Chapter 9 implied that it is impossible to set exchange rates and the money supply at the same time. When the exchange rate is flexible and endogenously determined by market forces, the money supply is controlled by the central bank and thus exogenous ($M = \bar{M}$). In sharp contrast, when the exchange rate is set at an exogenous parity $\bar{S}$, the money supply is endogenous. Since prices are constant, inflation (π) is zero and nominal and real interest rates are equal ($i = r$).

11.3.2 The Primary Current Account Function

We now return to the primary current account, which was discussed at length in Chapter 7. Recall from Chapter 2 the fundamental accounting identity:

$$(11.2) \qquad Y = C + I + G + PCA.$$

Under the Keynesian assumption, this relationship is more than an accounting identity. It asserts that output, the left-hand side, is driven by demand, the right-hand side. As in Chapter 10, we use simplified versions of the consumption and investment functions established in Chapter 6. Consumption expenditures depend positively on household wealth, which is assumed exogenous, as well as disposable income Y^d, which we now write as $Y - \bar{T}$:

$$(11.3) \qquad C = C(\bar{\Omega}, Y - \bar{T}). \qquad \text{(consumption function)}$$
$$\qquad\qquad\qquad\quad + \qquad + $$

Investment spending is described as

$$(11.4) \qquad I = I(\bar{q}, r), \qquad \text{(investment function)}$$
$$\qquad\qquad\qquad + \quad - $$

The investment function resembles that of Chapter 10, but now also takes account of the positive effect of Tobin's q.[3] This modification allows us to study the effects of exogenous changes in **animal spirits** discussed in Chapter 6—the expectations of businessmen with respect to the rate of return and thus the attractiveness of capital investment. Exogenous increases in animal spirits raise q, all other things equal; an exogenous spell of pessimism concerning prospective future returns will depress q. Finally spending by the government is exogenous and given by:

$$(11.5) \qquad\qquad G = \bar{G}. \qquad \text{(government purchases)}$$

In an open economy it is necessary to track the behaviour of the primary current account (PCA). Chapter 7 linked the PCA to the real exchange rate σ, the relative price of goods produced at home in terms of those produced abroad. A real depreciation—a decrease in σ—makes foreign goods more expensive, and therefore discourages imports. At the same time, it makes domestic output more attractive to foreigners and stimulates exports. Conversely, a real appreciation—an increase in σ—boosts imports which are now cheaper, and depresses exports, which are more costly. At the same time, Chapter 2 defined the primary current account surplus as the difference between exports (X) and imports (Z) of goods and services:

$$(11.6) \qquad\qquad PCA = X - Z.$$

Let us consider first imports. A part of domestic spending, or absorption, is always spent on imports, so the greater is overall absorption, the greater will be imports.[4] Second, the analysis of Chapter 7 concluded that a higher real exchange rate (σ) implies a greater demand for imports. These observations lead to the **import function**:

$$(11.7) \qquad\qquad Z = Z(A, \sigma).$$
$$\qquad\qquad\qquad\qquad + \quad + $$

---

[3] As a simplification, q will be treated as exogenous and captures the component of Tobin's q associated with expectations of future profitability of investment and 'animal spirits'.

[4] Recall that absorption (A) is total final spending by residents and defined as $A = C + I + G$.

Since our exports are the imports of the rest of the world, exactly the same arguments apply, from the foreign perspective: our exports depend on foreign absorption A^* and its determinants, foreign wealth Ω^*, disposable income Y^{d*}, Tobin's q^*, etc. The result is the **export function**:

$$\text{(11.8)} \qquad X = X(A^*, \sigma).$$
$$\qquad\qquad\qquad\; + \quad -$$

The signs underneath are the same as for the import function with the exception of the real exchange rate. A real appreciation (σ rising) makes our goods more expensive and depresses exports, hence the '$-$' sign.

The primary current account is given by the difference between exports and imports in (11.8) and (11.7):

$$\text{(11.9)} \qquad PCA = X(A^*, \sigma) - Z(A, \sigma)$$
$$\qquad\qquad\qquad\;\; + \quad - \qquad + \quad +$$
$$\qquad\qquad = PCA(A, A^*, \sigma)$$
$$\qquad\qquad\qquad\quad - \quad + \quad -$$

Those factors which boost domestic absorption (increases in wealth, disposable income, Tobin's q, real growth, or a decline in the interest rate) increase imports and worsen the primary current account. In contrast, anything that boosts foreign spending (increases in foreign wealth, disposable income, Tobin's q, real growth, or a decline in the foreign interest rate) will increase exports and lead to an improvement of the primary current account. Finally, a real exchange rate appreciation (an increase in σ) leads to a deterioration of the primary account as imports rise and exports fall.

Finally, absorption is defined as the difference between GDP and the PCA, so in principle, the dependence of the PCA on absorption is fundamentally a dependence on GDP. This observation leads us to rewrite (11.9) as:

$$\text{(11.10)} \qquad PCA = PCA(Y, Y^*, \sigma).$$
$$\qquad\qquad\qquad\qquad - \quad + \quad -$$

The **current account function** relates PCA negatively to domestic real income, positively to foreign income, and negatively to the real exchange rate. It completes the picture of aggregate demand in an open economy.

11.3.3 The 45° Diagram Revisited

One major innovation of this chapter is to open up the economy to international trade. The qualitative characteristics of the *IS* curve remain unchanged, however. To see this, we briefly review the steps followed in Chapter 10. The desired demand function, which represents the demand for domestic goods, adding exports and subtracting imports, is now written as[5]

$$\text{(11.11)} \quad DD = C(\bar{\Omega}, Y - \bar{T}) + I(i, \bar{q}) + \bar{G} + PCA(Y, Y^*, \sigma).$$

The desired demand schedule was shown in Chapter 10 to be an increasing function of GDP (Y). But now GDP exerts a negative effect on demand via the PCA function. The presence of the PCA function reduces the net effect, but does not change the fundamental determinants of absorption, which remain household wealth, personal income, interest rates, and Tobin's q. The desired demand schedule shown in Figure 11.5 is upward-sloping as in Figure 10.1, but it is flatter to account for the fact that the primary current account worsens as income increases, as more

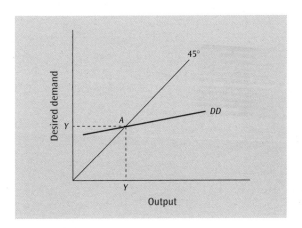

Fig. 11.5 The 45° Diagram

Total desired demand responds positively but less than proportionately to increases in real GDP, hence the slope of the upward-sloping demand schedule. Equilibrium output is the GDP level Y at which demand equals supply along the 45° line.

---

[5] Subscripts referring to the time period will be henceforth supressed.

is imported from abroad, reducing the net effect the demand for domestically produced output.

11.3.4 Demand Leakages and the Multiplier

Under the Keynesian assumption that prices are sticky, the 45° diagram shows how output adjusts to desired demand. The output level corresponding to point A at the intersection of the desired demand schedule and the 45° line is equal to demand. Fluctuations in output are driven by exogenous changes in demand. Figure 11.6 provides an illustration, the case when one component of demand, government purchases of goods and services, increases by $\Delta \bar{G}$, from $\bar{G}$ to $\bar{G}'$.

The economy starts at point A with real GDP level Y. The change in government expenditures $\Delta \bar{G}$ increases aggregate demand at any level of output. The desired demand schedule shifts upward by that amount. If output remains unchanged at Y, the new situation is described by point B, with desired demand exceeding output. What happens when desired demand and output differ? Normally, if demand exceeds output, producers make up the difference by sales from inventories of finished goods; we say that inventories are decumulated. Producers then adjust output to match demand until equilibrium output is reached. Thus, unexpected drawdowns of inventory are likely to be followed by production increases. (Conversely, when production exceeds demand, inventories are involuntarily accumulated and this will lead to a production slowdown.) As output expands to meet demand, the economy moves to point A' on the 45° line.

The process does not stop at A'. The increase in production and income leads to higher consumption, further increasing aggregate demand and, by the 45° line, output. Demand and output both rise again until equilibrium is reached at point A''. The process continues until, step by step, the economy reaches E, which is on the new desired demand schedule and the 45° line. What is important to notice is that, in the end, GDP increases by a *multiple* of the initial demand increase $\Delta \bar{G}$, an effect called the (Keynesian) **demand multiplier**. No matter where they originate, positive or negative disturbances are transmitted to the whole economy as aggregate demand responds to income changes in a process that may take several months to complete.

This is the simplest interpretation of cyclical fluctuations: the GDP responds to fluctuations in aggregate demand. The multiplier effect corresponds to the fundamental insight provided by the circular flow diagram in Chapter 2: each individual's spending is someone else's income. An exogenous increase in demand induces further increases in spending by other households. As long as output responds passively to demand, this will lead to additional income; and so on. The expansion of GDP cannot continue *ad infinitum*, however. The multiplier is finite, because at each stage of spending some fraction of income leaks from the circular flow of income, into taxes, savings and imports.[6] For example, adding the *PCA*, as we have done in this chapter, flattens the desired demand schedule; it is easily verified that the flatter the schedule, the smaller is the multiplier effect.

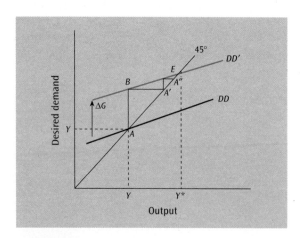

Fig. 11.6 **The Multiplier**

An exogenous increase in government spending shifts up the demand schedule vertically by $\Delta \bar{G}$. Supply equals demand, and the economy's equilibrium output increases to point Y^*. The multiplier effect—that $Y^* - Y$ exceeds the initial impulse $\Delta \bar{G}$—can be understood by following the staircase up from point A. The direct effect, an increase in demand and output, raises GDP to point A'. This point however is still not an equilibrium, because DD lies above the 45° line. Thus, desired demand and output increases again, to point A'', and so on.

[6] In theory, if at each spending decision all additional income were spent on domestic goods, the multiplier would be infinite, an implausible outcome.

Table 11.1	Demand Multipliers: Five Examples		
	Years after change		
	1	**2**	**3**
Euro area	1.43	1.31	0.41
UK	0.75	0.33	0.01
USA	1.05	0.49	−0.38
Canada	1.24	0.52	−0.17
Japan	1.85	1.58	−0.09

Note: The numbers represent the effect of a change in government expenditure of 1% of real GDP in 2000 and 2001 in all five regions on each economy's output (as percentage deviation from baseline).
Source: Deutsche Bundesbank (2000), authors' calculations.

How does the multiplier look in practice? Table 11.1 presents some values of the demand multiplier for the largest economies as estimated by the German central bank, the Bundesbank. It is obtained from relationships like (11.1)–(11.9), but with consider-

ably more detail. These estimates also reveal that the multiplier takes time to work out its effects; according to the Bundesbank, residual effects still persist three years later.

11.3.5 The *IS* Curve

Slope of the *IS* curve

The open-economy *IS* curve is derived just as in Chapter 10 by examining the effect of changes in the interest rate on desired demand and output in the 45° line diagram. Starting from *A* in Figure 11.7, what happens if the interest rate declines from *i* to *i'*? All else held constant, a lower interest rate stimulates investment spending, because the present value of future profits is higher. The desired spending schedule shifts up in Figure 11.7(*a*), and the goods market equilibrium can only be restored at point *B*, with output having risen from *Y* to *Y'*.

The move from point *A* to point *B* can be decomposed in Figure 11.7(*b*) into two steps. The drop in the interest rate, keeping GDP constant, takes the economy from point *A* to point *C*, off the *IS* curve. This corresponds to a situation of excess demand in the goods market. To restore equilibrium at the

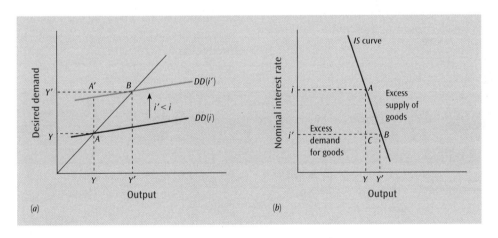

Fig. 11.7 Slope of the *IS* Curve

A reduction in the interest rate from *i* to *i'* leads to an increase in consumption and investment, which is met by an increase in output. The *IS* curve is flatter the larger is the required output increase, as measured by the distance *CB* in panel (*b*). The length of *CB* in turn depends on: (1) the responsiveness of demand to interest changes, represented by the size of the vertical shift of *DD*, or *AA'*, in panel (*a*); (2) the multiplier effect, measured by distance *A'B*. The multiplier is larger the steeper the desired demand schedule, i.e. the more sensitive is demand to changes in output.

lower interest rate, an increase in output is necessary, from point C to point B, to accommodate the rise in demand. The IS curve is flatter, the longer CB. The slope of the IS curve is flatter (1) the greater the sensitivity of consumption and investment to changes in interest rates, as measured by the vertical shift of the desired demand schedule (AA') in panel (a), and (2) the larger the multiplier that translates the initial exogenous change into higher total demand, as measured along $A'B$.

The multiplier in turn increases with the slope of the desired demand schedule, which is flatter than the 45° line. The multiplier is finite because **leakages** in demand occur in the circular flow of income. Figure 2.2 shows that taxes, savings, and imports can be seen as subtractions from GDP. These three leakages represent domestic income not *automatically* respent on domestic goods and services. The size of the leakages, and therefore of the multiplier, depends on saving behaviour, on the tax system, and on how much additional income is spent on imports, a measure called the *marginal propensity to import*. Table 11.2 presents a crude measure of openness, imports as a fraction of GDP, for a number of countries. The large economic blocs (Euroland, the USA, Japan) are fairly closed and able to lock in the effects of demand disturbances. Individual smaller countries, in contrast, are often quite open.

A key distinction: movements along or shifts of the IS curve

It is important not to confuse *shifts* of the IS curve with movements *along* it. To do this, one must keep in mind the distinction between exogenous and endogenous variables stressed in Section 11.3.1. The IS curve is the goods market equilibrium condition imposed on two endogenous variables, GDP (Y) and interest rates (i), *everything else held constant*. The position of the IS curve is determined by the exogenous variables, and as long as these remain unchanged, the economy is restricted to the same IS curve. Whenever any of the exogenous variables changes, the IS curve shifts. Figure 11.8 shows that the IS curve shifts up and to the right when the exogenous change is expansionary. In the opposite case of exogenous declines in aggregate demand, the IS curve shifts leftwards.

Which exogenous variables are relevant? Fiscal policy is a premier source of shifts in the IS curve. The government is a large player in the macro-economy, and changes in government purchases of goods $\bar{G}$ (e.g. military procurement or road construction) or services (e.g. the wages or number of civil servants) can exert a significant influence on aggregate demand. Similarly, changes in taxation $\bar{T}$ will alter disposable income available to households and consumption demand. It may also affect investment through profit taxes.

Table 11.2   **Measures of Openness: Import as Percentage of GDP, 1998 (%)**

Austria	32.1	Netherlands[a]	49.4	Euro area	12.3
Belgium	64.9	Norway	24.8	United States	11.1
Denmark	25.8	Portugal[a]	33.1	Japan[a]	8.1
France[a]	19.4	Spain	23.1		
Germany[a]	21.2	Sweden	30.2		
Greece[a]	23.2	Switzerland	27.9		
Ireland[a]	53.7	United Kingdom[a]	23.8		
Italy[a]	18.3				

[a] 1997
Source: IMF.

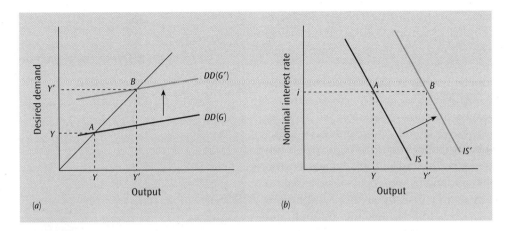

Fig. 11.8   **An Exogenous Increase in Aggregate Demand**

At unchanged interest rate i, an increase in any of the exogenous components of demand is represented in panel (a) by an upward shift of the aggregate demand schedule. Equilibrium occurs at point B and the new equilibrium output Y' is higher than the initial level Y. Panel (b) shows that the IS curve shifts to the right for the given interest rate.

A second important factor shifting the IS curve is changing expectations of businessmen, which motivate investment decisions. These expectations concern the future profitability of investment—the second period in the two-period analysis of Chapter 6. These expectations can be driven as much by gut feelings as rational calculus; for this reason Keynes called them 'animal spirits'. These factors are summarized in the variable $\bar{q}$.

Third, changes in household wealth $\bar{\Omega}$, which result from fluctuations in the value of assets such as stocks (another influence of Tobin's q), bonds, housing, etc. can affect aggregate demand and thus the position of the IS curve. Thus, the Great Depression of the 1930s is associated with the worldwide collapse of stock prices following the crash of Wall Street. Similarly, sharply falling housing prices preceded the recession of the early 1990s in the UK, Sweden, Japan, and many other countries. The recent collapse of internet- and technology-related stock prices is regarded as an important reason for the slowdown of the US economy in late 2000.

The preceding examples describe homemade sources of fluctuations. A fourth source of shifts in the IS curve is related to the openness of an economy. The current account is not only a source of leakage, but a transmission mechanism for foreign disturbances. Export-led expansions or recessions occur when demand from trading partners rises or falls, affecting exports, as summarized in equation (11.10) by the term Y^*. All other things equal, an increase in Y^* will increase the PCA and cause the IS curve to shift outwards.

11.3.6 International Capital Flows, Interest Parity, and the *LM* Curve

Capital Flows and Interest Parity

The primary current account function captures the link with the rest of the world operating through the goods market, i.e. trade in goods and services. The second link is financial: it operates through international capital movements. Under the **small country assumption**, financial conditions abroad are not affected by what is happening domestically. The 'foreign' rate of return i^* is exogenous. This return includes the possible expectation of a depreciation or appreciation of the exchange rate. For example, if the domestic currency depreciates, the value of foreign assets expressed in the domestic currency increases, and domestic owners of those foreign assets realize a capital gain. Conversely, they suffer a capital loss when the exchange rate appreciates. The overall return on foreign assets is therefore made up of two parts: the interest rate and capital gain or loss.

When capital is freely mobile, returns on similar assets will not differ systematically across countries.[7] This is because financial traders will sell assets or borrow where the rate of return is low, and buy assets or lend where the return is high. When this activity is more or less riskless, it is known as **arbitrage**. Arbitrage among asset yields is practised on a minute-by-minute basis by financial institutions which have access to large amounts of funds and face negligible transaction costs. As they restlessly scan the world, they promptly eliminate any difference in returns. No matter how successful they are individually, their activity means that worldwide returns for assets of similar characteristics are equalized across countries. The result is the following **interest rate parity** condition:[8]

$$(11.12) \qquad i = i^*.$$

This condition is depicted as the horizontal **financial integration line** in Figure 11.9.

Slope of the *LM* curve

The *LM* curve, which characterizes the money market and more generally the financial markets, is not directly affected by the interest parity condition. The *LM* curve describes equilibrium on the *domestic* money market. The financial integration line represents the equilibrium condition on the *international* financial market. In general equilibrium, both conditions must be satisfied.

The slope of the *LM* curve is understood by returning to its derivation, already seen in Chapter 10. The condition for money market equilibrium is given by

$$(11.13) \qquad \bar{M}/\bar{P} = \mathcal{L}(Y, i, \bar{c})$$

The left-hand side is the real supply of money, the right-hand side is the demand for real money

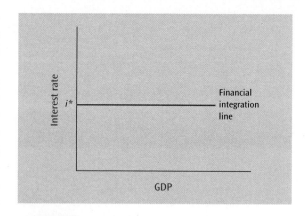

Fig. 11.9 **The Financial Integration Line**

When capital can move freely across borders, assets of similar quality (in terms of maturity and risk) should yield the same return. Otherwise, unexploited profit opportunities would exist (borrowing where interest is low and lending where it is high); this is incompatible with the assumptions of free mobility. Note that *i** denotes the return on foreign assets, which includes expected capital gains or losses resulting from changes in the exchange rate.

balances, which has now been extended to include the exogenous transactions costs of holding money, $\bar{c}$. The *LM* curve is depicted in Figure 11.10(*b*). Consider point *C* which is off the *LM* curve, and thus corresponds to disequilibrium in the money market. The move from *A* to *C* corresponds to an increase in GDP. For a given interest rate, money demand rises. To restore equilibrium, the excess demand for money must be eliminated, since the money supply is exogenous and assumed unchanged. To induce households and firms to reduce their demand for money, the interest rate must rise until point *B* is reached.

The *LM* curve is steeper, the longer the segment *BC*. First and foremost, the length of *BC* depends on the sensitivity of money demand with respect to real economic activity. If a given increase in output raises money demand by a large amount (we say that the income elasticity of money demand is large), a return to money market equilibrium requires a large compensating interest rate increase, and the *LM* curve is steep. Second, the length of *BC* depends on the sensitivity of money demand with respect to the interest rate, or the flatness of the money demand function *D* in Figure 11.10(*a*). If the money demand

---

[7] Here, 'similarity' refers to riskiness (e.g. short-term government bills and bonds are usually considered safe, as are those issued by large corporations) and the nature of the asset's payoffs, mainly its time to maturity.

[8] Ch. 19 describes the arbitraging activity of financial markets and presents the interest rate parity condition, in which the exchange rate figures explicitly.

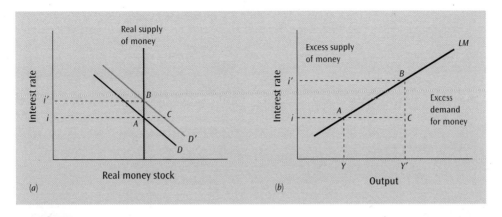

Fig. 11.10   Slope of the *LM* Curve

An exogenous increase in GDP raises the demand for money at any interest rate, hence the shift from *D* to *D'* in panel (*a*). At the initial interest rate *i*, we now have excess demand, as represented by point *C* in both panels. The size of the excess demand (measured by the length *AC*) is proportional to the responsiveness of money demand to output. The return to money equilibrium is achieved through an increase in the interest rate which reduces demand. The required increase from *i* to *i'* (measured by *AB* in panel (*a*) and by *BC* in panel (*b*)) is inversely proportional to the responsiveness of money demand to the interest rate. If money demand is very interest sensitive, a small increase in the interest rate is sufficient to eliminate the excess demand.

function is steep, the demand for money is little responsive to changes in the interest rate (we say that the interest elasticity of demand is low). Then the interest rate must move a lot to re-establish equilibrium for a given increase in GDP, hence again a steep *LM* curve; if the money demand is flat, small changes in the interest rate are sufficient to restore equilibrium and the *LM* curve will be flat.[9] To summarize, the *LM* curve is steeper, the more sensitive money demand is to output, and the less sensitive it is to the interest rate.

Moving along or shifting the *LM* curve

To avoid confusion between shifts of the *LM* curve and movements along it, the same rule applies as for the *IS* curve. A particular *LM* curve is drawn for given (fixed) values of the exogenous variables: the real money supply ($\bar{M}/\bar{P}$) and transaction costs ($\bar{c}$). As long as these exogenous variables remain unchanged, the economy remains on the same *LM* curve. Whenever any of the exogenous variables change, the *LM* curve shifts. It is intuitive, and easy to check, that the *LM* curve shifts rightward when the real money supply increases (the nominal supply increases or the price level falls) or if money market transactions become cheaper. For example, Figure 11.11 shows how changes in the nominal money supply shift the *LM* curve out. Since the price level is taken as constant, any increase in the nominal money supply is also an increase in the real supply. Then, the *LM* curve shifts to the right; when supply is held down, the *LM* shifts to the left.

In reality, inflation is never really zero but positive, and prices are constantly rising, even if very slowly, every day or month. The rule then is that the *LM* curve shifts, say, to the right when the rate of growth of the real money supply—the difference between the growth rate of the nominal supply and the rate of inflation[10]—is greater than zero.

[9] For an explicit derivation of the slope of the *LM* curve using calculus, see the appendix to this chapter.

[10] The growth rate of real balances is equal to the difference between nominal money growth and inflation: $\Delta(M/P)/(M/P) = \Delta M/M - \Delta P/P$.

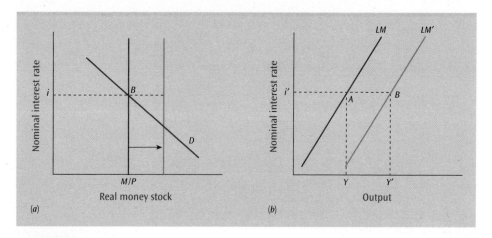

Fig. 11.11 **An Increase in the Money Supply Shifts the *LM* Curve Outward**

An increase in the money supply at a given level of interest rates creates a situation of excess money supply. This means that all points on the original *LM* curve now represent (*i*, *Y*) combinations of excess supply of money. To restore equilibrium, the demand for money must be higher. To achieve this, either the interest rate must be lower or income must be higher. Thus, the new *LM* curve lies below and to the right of the old one.

11.3.7 **Macroeconomic Equilibrium and the Exchange Rate Regime**

We now summarize the results of this section and note the most important differences with the analysis of Chapter 10. There, we studied equilibrium in three markets—the goods market (*IS*), the money market (*LM*), and the labour market. We saw that equilibrium employment in the labour market, combined with the given stock of capital and the production function, determined the supply side of the economy. In contrast, the present chapter assumed that prices and wages are sticky and that supply adjusts passively to demand. Employees supply whatever amount of labour is needed to produce the required output. This is perhaps the most radical departure, and is the decisive distinction between the classical and Keynesian analysis of the macroeconomy. It allows us to ignore the labour market which is assumed to adjust passively.

On the other hand, this chapter explicitly recognizes links with the rest of the world. First, trade in goods and services modifies, but does not fundamentally alter, the analysis of the goods market. The openness of the macroeconomy is simply incorporated in the *IS* curve. Second, trade in assets brings in the international financial markets. Under conditions of full capital mobility, equilibrium in this market is repres-

ented by the financial integration (*FI*) line. Finally, the *LM* curve remains, to a first approximation, unaffected.[11] So we now consider three markets: the goods market (*IS*), the money market (*LM*), and the international financial market, the latter replacing the labour market. When all three markets are in Keynesian, or fixed-price equilibrium, the three corresponding schedules all pass through a common point, for example point *E* in Figure 11.12.

The approach embodied in Figure 11.12 is often referred to as the **Mundell–Fleming model**.[12] The rest of this chapter uses this framework to explain how GDP and interest rates respond to various exogenous disturbances in the economy. The approach is always the same. The first step is to determine which of the three schedules shifts in response to an exogenous disturbance. The second step is to find out what must happen for the three schedules to go through a single point. The last step is to interpret the result: how and why has the economy moved from the initial to the new general equilibrium?

---

[11] It is possible that *foreigners* could demand *domestic* money for transaction purposes, and that domestic residents might demand foreign money for similar reasons. These aspects are of secondary importance and will be neglected.

[12] It is named after the Nobel Laureate Robert Mundell from Columbia University and the Briton J. Marcus Fleming, who worked at the IMF.

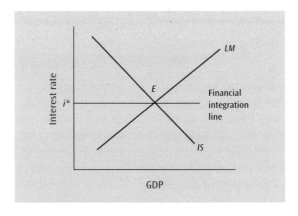

Fig. 11.12 General Equilibrium

When goods, money, and international capital markets are in equilibrium, real GDP and the interest rate are determined by the intersection of three schedules: the *IS* and *LM* curves and the arbitrage (financial integration) line.

We require that the three schedules go through the same point because none of the three markets can be out of equilibrium for very long. Inventory adjustment and output changes restore equilibrium in the goods market. Disequilibrium in the goods market would manifest itself by persistent queues in front of empty stores in the case of excess demand, or by unsold goods in the case of excess supply. It is a distinguishing feature of market economies that these situations do not occur on any significant scale. Money and international financial markets, are especially known for the rapidity at which they clear.

The implications of openness to trade and particularly to capital movements in the Mundell–Fleming model are dramatic. In particular, the exchange rate regime profoundly affects the results. Section 11.4 describes the case of a country committed to a fixed exchange rate regime. This is the case in many European countries, either because they are explicitly part of the European Monetary System, or because they peg their currency, formally or informally, to another currency of their choice. Section 11.5 considers the polar opposite case, in which the exchange rate is freely floating. This corresponds to the situation of Switzerland, the USA, and Japan, or the Euroland countries jointly vis-à-vis the rest of the world. In between these two extremes are various degrees of managed floating, where the authorities do not commit themselves to a particular rate but nevertheless attempt to prevent large fluctuations. Box 11.1 reviews the policies of European countries in early 2001.[13]

Box 11.1 Exchange Rate Regimes in Europe, 2001

At the beginning of 2001, European countries could be grouped in five categories. A first category, the members of the European Monetary Union, have fixed exchange rates irrevocably among themselves by the adoption of a common currency, the euro.[14] A second group includes countries which did not join the monetary union and have instead fixed their exchange rate vis-à-vis the euro. A third group, mostly from Eastern Europe, has pegged unilaterally to the euro or some combination of the euro and the US dollar. Some of them—Hungary for example —have an explicit programme of frequent depreciation, the so-called crawling peg. Countries in the third group do not declare any official parity but actively limit exchange rate fluctuations. Countries in the fourth group of 'free floaters' have freedom to set monetary policy, in principle. The countries that make up the fifth and final group have adopted currency boards: they peg to the euro and allow the money base to change only when their foreign exchange reserves change.

1. *European Monetary Union*: Austria, Belgium, Finland, France, Germany, Greece, Ireland, Italy, Luxembourg, Netherlands, Portugal, Spain

2. *Euro-peggers* (pegged to the euro): Denmark, Croatia, Hungary, Iceland

3. *Managed floaters*: Norway, Sweden, Czech Republic, Finland, Latvia, Macedonia, Romania, Slovak Republic, Slovenia, Ukraine

4. *Free floaters*: UK, Sweden, Albania, Moldavia, Poland, Russia, Switzerland

5. *Currency board*: Estonia, Lithuania, Bosnia-Herzegovina, Bulgaria

Source: IMF.

---

[13] More detail is provided in Ch. 20. The situation can, and will, change over time.

[14] Before 1999, these countries belonged to the Exchange Rate Mechanism of the European Monetary System. Ch. 20 presents details.

11.4   Output and Interest Rate Determination under Fixed Exchange Rates

11.4.1 Money Supply Disturbances

To study the role of monetary policy under fixed exchange rates, suppose the central bank increases the money supply from M to M'. In Figure 11.13 the LM curve shifts down and to the right from LM to LM'. Starting from initial general equilibrium at point A, there are now two candidates for the new equilibrium: point B at the intersection of LM' and IS, and point C at the intersection of LM' and the financial integration line.

Which point is relevant? At point B, the domestic interest rate is lower than the yields available on foreign assets. This prompts both foreign and domestic agents to sell domestic assets, and to purchase the more attractive foreign assets. As a result, the exchange rate comes under pressure to depreciate; this forces the monetary authorities to step in and buy the domestic currency on foreign exchange markets, using its foreign exchange reserves. This intervention reduces the money supply, and the

LM curve shifts leftwards.[15] The process must go on as long as the return on domestic assets (i) is less than the return on foreign assets (i*), that is until the LM curve has returned to its initial position. We asked whether the new equilibrium occurs at point B or point C. The answer is that neither of these points can be a general equilibrium, because neither lies on all three schedules describing the three equilibrium conditions. The economy returns to the original point A. Monetary policy has no effect. In effect, the LM curve is endogenous and moves to pass through where the two other schedules intersect.

The result that monetary policy is ineffective under fixed exchange rates should not be too surprising. Chapter 9 has already established that monetary policy independence is lost under a fixed exchange rate regime. The balance sheet of the central bank, simplified to the monetary base on the liability side and to foreign exchange (F) and domestic credit or securities (DC) on the asset side, implies that

(11.14) $$M0 = F + DC.$$

Initially, in order to expand the money supply, the central bank creates additional monetary base (M0) by extending domestic credit (DC).[16] In the course of its foreign exchange market interventions, however, the central bank spends foreign exchange rate reserves (F), and thereby withdraws monetary base from the banking system, thus offsetting its initial action.

In principle, the central bank could sterilize its sale of foreign exchange reserves in order to maintain the initial increase in the money supply, raising DC one for one as F declines. This cannot go on for

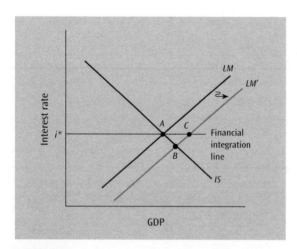

Fig. 11.13   **Money Supply Disturbance under Fixed Exchange Rates**

An increase in the money supply implies a rightward shift of the LM curve from LM to LM'. At point B, with i < i*, capital outflows force the central bank to intervene and the money supply contracts until the economy returns to point A. Monetary policy is ineffective.

---

[15] Chapter 9 explains the links between foreign exchange rate market interventions and the money supply in detail.

[16] Domestic credit is a general term describing any form of loan by the central bank to non-bank (private or government) sectors. It could take the form of direct lending to the government, purchase of government debt, or refinancing of commercial lending by private banks.

Box 11.2 **Capital Controls and Monetary Independence**

Capital controls refer to a variety of administrative measures which prevent the residents of one country from freely moving assets across borders. Some measures are designed to repel capital inflows, others to forestall outflows. When capital movements are restricted, as they were from time to time in many European countries until the late 1980s, arbitrageurs cannot equalize returns on domestic and foreign assets, and the interest rate parity condition need not hold. The domestic interest rate is decoupled from foreign returns—or at least, the link is less tight. In the case of a monetary expansion as represented in Figure 11.13, it becomes possible to aim for point *B*. In principle, the monetary authorities recover

some independence as the financial integration line is 'suspended'. In practice, however, the rewards to dodging the controls—exploiting the difference between asset returns—are so high that many agents develop great skills and invest large amount of resources in this activity. Given time—sometimes a few months, more often a few days—monetary policy independence is eroded again. A similar result holds for the case of aggregate demand disturbances studied in the next section: in Figure 11.13, point *B* becomes possible under fixed exchange rates, at least for some time. While capital controls have fallen into disrepute, they are occasionally invoked in crisis situations, for example in Malaysia after the crisis of 1997.

---

ever, though, because the stock of foreign exchange reserves is depleted along the way. The financial integration line in Figure 11.13 simply says that the central bank of a 'small' open economy must accept that the domestic interest rate cannot be altered. In order to forestall this outcome and to break the link between *i* and *i**, some countries have employed **capital controls** or restrictions on the international movement of capital. Box 11.2 explains how these capital controls operate.

11.4.2 Real Demand Disturbances

Figure 11.14 illustrates the effect of an increase in any of the exogenous components of demand for goods described in Section 11.3.5, such as improving business expectations, expansionary fiscal policy (an increase in public spending or tax reductions), or rising exports (following a foreign expansion). As in Figure 11.8, the positive demand disturbance is represented as a rightward shift of the *IS* curve, from *IS* to *IS'*. As in the previous section, two points are candidates for the new equilibrium: point *B* at the intersection of *IS'* and *LM*, and point *C* at the intersection of *IS'* and the financial integration line.

Moving from *A* to *B* along *LM*, output increases to meet higher demand, and money demand rises to

finance more transactions. Since the money supply (nominal and real) is by assumption constant, the interest rate must rise to maintain equilibrium in the money market. The higher interest rate, in turn, adversely affects investment spending.[17] This last effect is often referred to as **crowding out**, the fact that an exogenous increase in demand can reduce some investment due to higher interest rates.

Point *B* cannot represent complete equilibrium since the domestic interest rate exceeds the foreign rate of return, *i**, and the interest rate parity condition is not satisfied. The higher domestic return immediately triggers a capital inflow. As foreign currency is converted into domestic currency, the exchange rate comes under pressure and an appreciation will occur unless the monetary authorities intervene. Committed to a fixed exchange rate, the central bank sells its own currency and acquires foreign exchange reserves. The logic of equation (11.13) is that the money stock must rise and the *LM* curve will shift rightward. This process will continue

---

[17] A careful student might observe that the increased interest rates increase the discounting of future profits and should thereby reduce Tobin's *q* and further depress investment. A full consideration of this (entirely correct) point would require treating *q* as an endogenous variable; a mathematical treatment of the issue can be found in the appendix to this chapter.

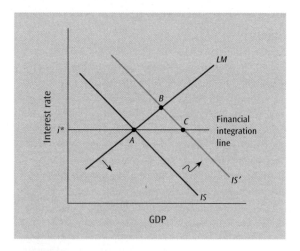

Fig. 11.14 **Demand Disturbance under Fixed Exchange Rates**

The demand expansion is shown as shifting the *IS* curve from *IS* to *IS'*. At point *B*, the goods and money markets are in equilibrium but the interest rate exceeds the world level. The combination of capital inflows and exchange market interventions raises the money supply, shifting the *LM* curve down and to the right. This proceeds until the *LM* curve passes through point *C*.

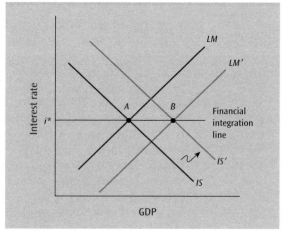

Fig. 11.15 **Policy Mix**

When both monetary and fiscal policies are combined in an expansionary fashion, the economy moves from point *A* to point *B*. While the outcome is the same as with just a fiscal policy expansion (Figure 11.14), in the present case the increase in the monetary supply is achieved through securities purchases by the central bank.

until point *C* is reached, when general equilibrium occurs at the intersection of the three equilibrium schedules.

It is essential to stress that monetary independence is lost under fixed exchange rates. The *LM* curve must pass through the point defined by the *IS* and *FI* schedules. The money supply—and the position of the *LM* curve—is endogenous and beyond the control of the monetary authorities. One way a country may attempt to reassert control is to restrict capital movements, as explained in Box 11.2.

11.4.3 The Policy Mix

The **policy mix** refers to the joint use of monetary and fiscal policies. An expansionary monetary policy under fixed exchange rates alone does not work, because its tendency to lower the interest rate generates capital outflows which offset the initial expansion. In contrast, an expansionary fiscal policy puts upward pressure on the interest rate and generates capital inflows. When well balanced, a joint

fiscal and monetary expansion leaves the interest rate unaffected, as both the *IS* and *LM* curves move rightward to point *B* in Figure 11.15. The only difference between the policy mix and a fiscal expansion can be seen on the asset side of the central bank. In both cases the money supply rises by the same amount. With a policy mix, however, it rises because the central bank provides additional monetary base by lending to or buying securities from banks; with pure fiscal expansion, the central bank provides the additional monetary base by increasing its foreign exchange reserves.

11.4.4 International Financial Disturbances

When returns on foreign assets rise from *i** to *i*'*, the horizontal financial integration line shifts upwards in Figure 11.16. The *IS* and *LM* schedules intersect at point *A*, so goods and money markets are in equilibrium, but the interest rate which results is too low. Capital outflows prompt foreign exchange

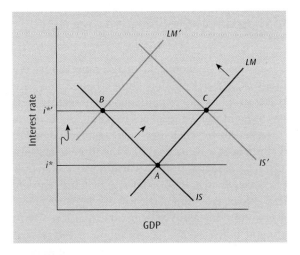

Fig. 11.16 **A Financial Disturbance**

The increase in the rate of return on foreign assets induces a capital outflow. Under a fixed exchange rate, the central bank intervenes to prevent a depreciation. The money supply contracts and the *LM* curve shifts to *LM'*. The new general equilibrium is at point *B*. Under flexible exchange rates, the exchange rate depreciates. The gain in competitiveness increases the demand for domestic goods. The *IS* curve shifts to *IS'* and equilibrium occurs at point *C*.

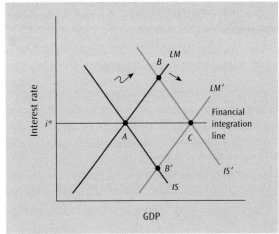

Fig. 11.17 **A Devaluation**

A devaluation shifts the *IS* curve out to *IS'*. At the same time, the money supply rises as central banks purchase foreign exchange, and the *LM* curve shifts downwards.

intervention by the central bank, the money supply contracts, and the *LM* curve shifts leftwards until it goes through point *B*. The domestic economy cannot be shielded from international financial disturbances. If interest rates rise worldwide, they must rise at home, which provokes a recession (*Y* declines). This example illustrates the phenomenon of *monetary interdependence*. Under fixed exchange rates, changes in foreign interest rates are transmitted directly to domestic interest rates.

11.4.5 **How to Think about a Parity Change**

The fact that monetary policy is ineffective under fixed exchange rates does not mean that monetary policy cannot be used. If exchange rate changes are possible, as is the case with most fixed exchange rate regimes, a weaker form of monetary policy independence can be restored. (Naturally, the ultimate

form of fixed exchange rate system, the monetary union, excludes parity changes.) In **revaluation** or **devaluation**, the monetary authority unilaterally changes the parity rate at which it buys and sells foreign exchange. For given price levels at home and abroad, a nominal devaluation, for example, implies a depreciation of the real exchange rate, and shifts the *IS* curve outwards in Figure 11.17. In order to enforce the new parity, the central bank must sell its own currency and purchase foreign exchange. The supply of high-powered money and thus of the money supply itself expands and the *LM* curve shifts out to the right in Figure 11.17.[18] A devaluation thus is tantamount to a monetary expansion, whereas a revaluation corresponds to a monetary contraction. In brief, monetary and exchange rate policies are just two sides of the same coin.

---

[18] Another possibility is that the devaluation has already been anticipated by the market. In this case, the *FI* curve shifts upwards because financial markets require a higher return in the home currency. Capital outflow ensues, and the rest can be understood in the context of the preceding section. This explains why interest rates often rise sharply before a devaluation actually occurs.

11.5.1 **Demand Disturbances**

An exogenous increase in aggregate demand under flexible exchange rates is shown as the rightward shift of the *IS* curve from *IS* to *IS'* in Figure 11.18. Again, the question is whether the economy will settle at point *B* or point *C*, or indeed anywhere else. The key rule is that, when the exchange rate is freely floating, the central bank does not intervene in the money market and therefore controls the money supply. The position of the *LM* curve is exogenous. At point *B* the domestic interest rate exceeds the return available on foreign assets. Capital flows in, but now, in the absence of central bank intervention, the exchange rate appreciates (*S* rises). With domestic prices assumed constant, the real exchange rate also appreciates (σ rises), which hurts competitiveness and leads to a deterioration of the primary current account. Total demand for domestic output declines, and the *IS* curve shifts leftward. This process goes

on as long as the domestic interest rate is above the financial integration line: the exchange rate continues to appreciate until the loss in competitiveness has brought the *IS* curve back to point *A*.

Under flexible exchange rates, aggregate demand disturbances leave output and the interest rate unaffected, in sharp contrast with the fixed exchange rate case. Increases in domestic demand entirely leak abroad as a result of the loss of competitiveness. Every additional euro of demand expansion originating at home leads to a worsening of the current account by one euro. The return to point *A* is, however, not instantaneous. In contrast to the exchange rate, which responds immediately to capital inflows, the effect on trade and the current account will take time to complete.

The result applies to any of the exogenous components of demand in equation (11.11). In particular, an expansionary fiscal policy—raising public spending or reducing taxes—merely leads to an exchange rate appreciation and to a worsening of the current account. Similarly, a surge in business optimism and the resulting investment boom has no demand effect: it simply crowds out net demand in the foreign sector. Under flexible exchange rates an economy cannot lift itself up via demand, nor can it be lifted up by world demand. As foreign customers attempt to purchase more of our exports, they end up bidding up the exchange rate, which discourages their initial move. In the end, under floating exchange rates, *domestic demand impulses are neutralized by exchange rate changes and the economy is insulated from foreign demand disturbances.*

11.5.2 **Money Supply Disturbances**

A monetary expansion is represented by the shift of the *LM* curve from *LM* to *LM'* in Figure 11.19. At point *B*, the low interest rate prompts capital outflows and therefore an exchange rate depreciation. The attendant gain in external competitiveness increases foreign demand for domestic goods, and the current account improves. Graphically, the additional net foreign demand—more exports and

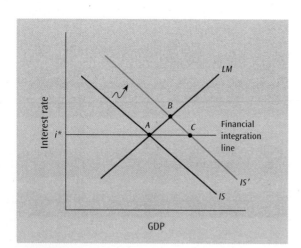

Demand Disturbance under Flexible Exchange Rates

As real demand increases, the *IS* curve shifts rightwards. At point *B*, capital flows in and the exchange rate appreciates (*S* rises). This loss of external competitiveness leads to a fall in net foreign demand for domestic goods until the *IS* curve returns to its initial position *A*. The demand disturbance is 'crowded out'.

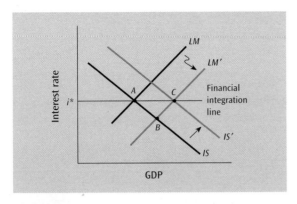

Fig. 11.19 Money Supply Disturbance under Flexible Exchange Rates

An increase in the money supply shifts the *LM* curve to *LM'* from *LM*. At point *B*, with low domestic interest rates, the exchange rate depreciates which leads to a current account surplus. This shifts the *IS* curve rightwards until local interest rates are equal to the foreign rate of return *i** at point *C*.

fewer imports—shifts the *IS* curve to the right until it passes through point *C*.

In contrast to the fixed exchange rate case, monetary policy is effective under flexible rates. As described, monetary policy works entirely through its effect on the exchange rate and the current account, rather than through the interest rate, which remains governed by foreign returns. Monetary policy is sometimes considered a **beggar-thy-neighbour** policy: it diverts world demand away from foreign goods and towards domestic goods. Beggar-thy-neighbour policies raise opposition from trade partners if the exchange rate depreciation is perceived as being unjustified, merely an attempt to achieve an 'artificial' trade advantage. Box 11.3 describes tensions in Europe resulting from sharp devaluations in the 1990s. The legacy of bruising trade fights in the 1930s is often cited as an important

---

Box 11.3 **Beggar-Thy-Neighbour Policies in Europe?**

The first half of the 1990s witnessed a number of spectacular devaluations. The dissolution of the Soviet Union in 1991 and the resulting economic chaos had severe repercussions for Finland, which suffered a drop of exports of roughly 25%. At the time, the Finnish currency, the markka, was pegged to a basket of currencies which included the Deutsche Mark and the US dollar. Just as the *IS–LM* model predicts, in the course of the year the central bank spent enormous foreign exchange reserves defending the exchange rate, while the domestic economy went into a tailspin and unemployment rose to nearly 20%. On 15 November 1991 the Finnish markka was devalued by 12.3%. While this move allowed the Finns to relax monetary policy, reduce interest rates, and stimulate demand, it was not especially helpful for neighbouring Sweden, an important trading partner with Finland which also pegged its rate to a basket of currencies. On Thursday, 5 December, the Swedish central bank raised the interest rate from 11.5% to 17.5%. The increase was said to be necessary after a sudden capital outflow of SKR 26 billion in the course of two-and-a-half weeks, which many observers blamed on the Finns' devaluation. The initial monetary tightness was regarded as a cause of the recession which ensued. Shortly thereafter, Sweden devalued its currency as well.

Similarly, in the summer of 1992 two large member-countries in the fixed exchange rate mechanism of the European Monetary System, Italy and the UK, gave up their fixed exchange rates in the face of violent speculative crises.[19] In both cases, the exchange rate immediately depreciated by nearly 20%. In addition, interest rates declined, a sign of monetary relaxation. The British Chancellor of the Exchequer, Norman Lamont, celebrated the recovery of policy independence by stating that from then on 'British monetary policy [would] work for Britain'. Within a few months, the Spanish peseta, the Portuguese escudo, and the Irish punt, while remaining pegged within the EMS, were also devalued by sizeable amounts (between 10% and 20%). Given price stickiness, the real exchange rates depreciated in similar proportions. Those countries which did not devalue their currencies suffered serious competitiveness losses. Figure 11.20 shows that Lamont was right: countries with devalued currencies such as Finland, Italy and the UK enjoyed a pick-up in growth following the depreciation of their currencies. In the aftermath, a number of firms in 'strong' currency countries complained loudly about 'unfair trade practices'.

---

[19] The events that led to this outcome, and their analysis, are discussed in Ch. 20.

Box 11.3 **Continued**

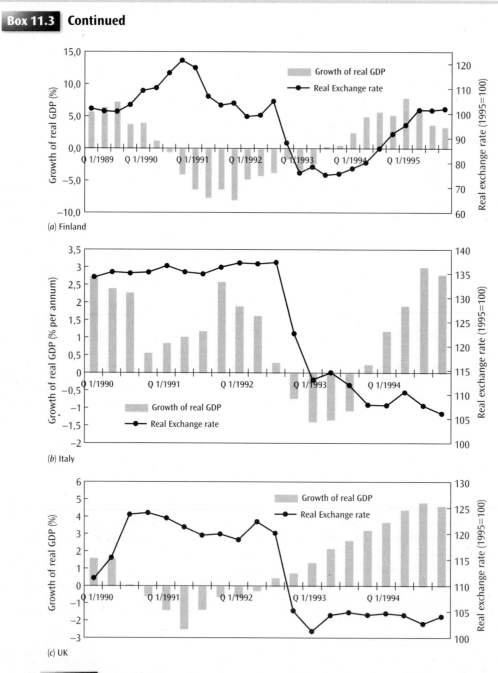

(a) Finland

(b) Italy

(c) UK

Fig. 11.20 **Growth after Devaluation**

Italy and the UK were in a recession when the 1992 exchange crisis erupted. Forced out of the exchange rate mechanism of the EMS, the lira and the pound depreciated by about 20%, boosting growth. Some of their trading partners felt that they had been made victims of a competitive depreciation. In Finland, a similar recovery can be observed after the depreciations of the markka in 1991, as well as in late 1995.

Sources: IMF; OECD.

reason for Europe's marked preference for a fixed exchange rate regime.

The impotence of monetary policy under fixed exchange rates is directly related to the fact that monetary policy is effective under flexible rates precisely because it works through exchange rate changes. In the end, monetary policy is the same as exchange rate policy. When the authorities wish to use the monetary instrument, they must decide what exchange rate they will be aiming at if they want to have any effect on the real economy. If capital controls are in place, or if financial integration is less complete than hitherto assumed, the domestic interest rate can depart somewhat from the foreign rate of return. (Box 11.2 elaborated on this case.) In particular, part of the effect of monetary policy may come through a decline in interest rates.

11.5.3 **The Policy Mix**

Fiscal policy is ineffective under flexible exchange rates because it exerts an upward pressure on interest rates and the resulting capital inflows lead to a currency appreciation. The authorities may prevent this exchange rate movement by changing the money supply. A monetary expansion appropriately coupled with a fiscal expansion prevents the exchange rate from appreciating. This case is shown in Figure 11.15 as the move from point A to point B. With no reduction in foreign demand, the additional spending generated by the fiscal expansion materializes at home instead of leaking abroad. What is the difference between a combined fiscal and monetary policy mix and just monetary policy? When an expansionary monetary policy is used alone, the exchange rate depreciates: world demand is shifted towards domestic goods, and it is the primary account improvement that boosts demand for domestic goods. With a policy mix, the exchange rate remains unchanged. In this case, the expansionary effect originates in domestic demand while the current account deteriorates.

11.5.4 **International Financial Disturbances**

The effect of an increase in returns on foreign assets (i^*) was described in Figure 11.16 for the case of fixed exchange rates. The same diagram can be used to describe the effects of an international financial disturbance under flexible exchange rates. Capital flows out to take advantage of better returns abroad and the exchange rate depreciates. The country's external competitiveness and current account improve. The IS curve shifts to the right until it goes through point C.

This disturbance could correspond to a situation where the 'rest of the world' adopts a stricter monetary policy. (This can be thought of as a shift in the LM curve of the rest of the world, upwards and to the left, resulting in higher foreign interest rates and lower foreign GDP.) While GDP declines abroad, it rises at home. This is just another instance of the beggar-thy-neighbour effect, except that it now works in reverse: the monetary contraction abroad has an anti-contractionary effect at home as 'their' exchange rate appreciation is 'our' depreciation. In contrast, under fixed exchange rates, domestic GDP also falls following a monetary contraction abroad (point B in Figure 11.17).[20] 'Foreign' monetary policy has the same qualitative effect on foreign and domestic GDPs under fixed exchange rates—the transmission is said to be positive—and the opposite effect under flexible rates—a negative transmission.

11.5.5 **Fixed versus Flexible Rates: Which is Better?**

This chapter has presented a number of new results for understanding short-run macroeconomic fluctuations. In addition to the role of the Keynesian assumption, which establishes the role of aggregate demand, it was shown that the exchange rate regime is a decisive determinant of the behaviour of the open macroeconomy. Table 11.3 summarizes the impact of various disturbances under fixed and flexible exchange rates. When the exchange rate is fixed, demand disturbances—including both fiscal policy actions as well as those originating in the

---

[20] That monetary policy abroad reduces foreign GDP under fixed exchange rates might appear to contradict the result that monetary policy is ineffective under fixed exchange rates. Remember that we have made the 'small country assumption' and consider 'abroad' as the rest of the world. The rest of the world cannot be a 'small country'. One way to think about it is that 'abroad' represents a larger foreign economic power.

Table 11.3	The Mundell–Fleming Model: A Summary	

Exogenous change	Effect on real GDP	
	Fixed exchange rates	Flexible exchange rates
Expansionary demand disturbance	Increase	No effect
Expansionary monetary policy	No effect	Increase
Increase in foreign interest rates	Decrease	Increase

Source: Schneider and Enste (2000).

private sector—affect domestic GDP. Monetary disturbances have no effect on real GDP. Monetary policy is ineffective because the central bank's commitment to uphold the declared parity of its currency renders the money supply endogenous. In contrast, when the exchange rate is freely floating, the economy is shielded from real demand disturbances. Discrepancies between the domestic and foreign interest rates trigger capital flows, which lead to offsetting movements in the exchange rate and the current account. Thus, fiscal policy is ineffective because the primary current account entirely offsets the policy effect on domestic demand. In contrast, monetary policy is effective precisely because it works through the exchange rate and the current account.

For policy-makers it is not always evident which regime is preferable. Each has advantages and disadvantages, depending on which types of shock predominate. While an economy with a floating exchange rate maintains the option of an independent monetary policy, it will be vulnerable to shifts in the domestic financial system, e.g. exogenous shifts to the demand for money or innovations in financial transactions technology. Monetary policy in this case will generally be crafted with an eye on the exchange rate; one often speaks of a 'dirty' or 'managed' float. A fixed exchange rate regime—of which the limiting case is a monetary union—tends to magnify shifts in real demand from home and abroad, while providing a shield against disturbances to the domestic money and financial markets. This shield does not work for shocks to international financial conditions, however. Foreign financial disturbances affect domestic interest rates and GDP in both regimes, either forcing a painful contraction or a devaluation-driven expansion. Box 11.4 and Table 11.4 illustrate how different the outcome can be by examining how two city-states, Hong Kong and Singapore, reacted to the international financial crisis of 1997–8 which hit East Asia.

Box 11.4   Reacting to the Crisis of 1997: Hong Kong versus Singapore

In 1997 the world financial system was rocked by severe crisis. After more than a decade of extraordinary economic growth, a number of Eastern Asian economies—starting with Thailand, then Indonesia, Malaysia, Phillipines, South Korea—were subject first to severe stock market crashes, followed by speculative attacks on the national currencies and spectacular outflows of short-term capital and finally, devaluation and deep recessions.

These events—with the exception of the timing and severity of the initial crash of national bourses—can be readily understood using the *IS–LM* open economy model. The stock market declines can be seen either as a rational expectation of what was to come, or more realistically, the exogenous collapse of a speculative bubble associated with East Asian 'emerging economies'. This stark decline in Tobin's *q* led to a sharp drop in

Box 11.4   **Continued**

investment and overall spending, an exogenous shift leftwards of the *IS* curve. At the time, these countries had pegged their currencies to the US dollar, and the outflow of short-term funds which ensued corresponds to the shift from *A* to *B* in Figure 11.16. (An upward shift in the *FI* curve may also have been at work here, as international investors demanded higher returns to compensate for an expected devaluation or risk thereof; see Chapters 19 and 20 for more details.) These capital flows were so strong in the end that national foreign exchange reserves were rapidly depleted and devaluations were unavoidable.

One exception was Hong Kong, which pegged its currency to the US dollar in the special form of currency board. Because of its close economic links with the People's Republic of China and its role as a financial centre, a devaluation of the Hong Kong dollar would have had grave consequences, triggering a devaluation of the Chinese currency. The monetary authorities of Hong Kong refused to devalue, and lost more than $8 billions in reserves in August 1998 alone. Although the defence of the Hong Kong dollar was successful, it came at considerable economic cost. It is interesting to compare the economic performance of Hong Kong and Singapore—two economies, with striking similarities in their robust health before the crash and their city-state economic structure. Unlike Hong Kong, Singapore devalued early on in the crisis and was able to recover fairly rapidly.

Table 11.4   **Dealing with the Crisis: Singapore versus Hong Kong**

Singapore

	Nominal exchange rate S-$ per US-$	Growth in real GDP (%)	Growth rate of real exports (%)	Growth rate of real imports (%)	Deposit rate (%)	Total reserves minus gold (billions US$)
1995	1.42	7.9	10.7	9.7	3.5	68.7
1996	1.41	7.5	3.9	3.7	3.4	76.8
1997	1.48	−0.4	−3.9	−3.1	3.5	71.3
1998	1.67	9.3	9.7	−1.4	4.6	74.9
1999	1.69	5.4	7.2	9.0	1.7	76.8

Hong Kong

	Nominal exchange rate HK-$ per US-$	Growth in real GDP (%)	Growth rate of real exports (%)	Growth rate of real imports (%)	Deposit rate (%)	Total reserves minus gold (billions US$)
1995	7.73	3.8	11.2	16.0	5.6	55.4
1996	7.74	4.5	−0.7	−2.7	4.6	63.8
1997	7.75	4.9	−2.2	−0.6	6.0	92.8
1998	7.75	−5.3	−7.8	−12.1	6.6	89.7
1999	7.77	3.2	6.6	3.1	4.5	96.2

Source: IMF.

Summary

1. Short-run fluctuations in output over the business cycle are associated primarily with movements in hours worked and employment. The Keynesian assumption relates those output fluctuations to shifting aggregate demand.

2. The empirical relationship between output growth around trend and changing unemployment is known as Okun's Law. It shows how the observed unemployment rate can fluctuate around its equilibrium rate.

3. The primary current account improves when income and output in the rest of the world expands and the real exchange depreciates, and worsens when GDP and absorption rise at home.

4. An autonomous increase in demand for domestic goods triggers a multiplier mechanism: more demand means more output, and more output means a higher income and hence a new round of demand increases.

5. The multiplier process is dampened by leakages in the income–demand chain: savings, taxes, and imports.

6. The *IS* curve is flatter, the more sensitive demand is to the interest rate, and the larger is the multiplier.

7. When a country's financial markets are well integrated in world markets, the domestic interest rate is tied to worldwide financial conditions. Under conditions of complete capital mobility, a third equilibrium condition is the equality of the domestic interest rate is equal to the (home currency) rate of return on foreign assets.

8. The *LM* curve is steeper the more sensitive money demand is to output and the less sensitive it is to the interest rate.

9. When the exchange rate is fixed, demand disturbances affect domestic GDP while monetary disturbances have no effect on real GDP.

10. When the exchange rate is freely floating, the economy is shielded from demand disturbances, while monetary policy is effective.

Key Concepts

- Keynesian model
- exchange rate regime
- output gap
- Okun's Law
- cyclical versus equilibrium unemployment
- import, export, and PCA functions
- (Keynesian) demand multiplier
- leakages
- small-country assumption

- arbitrage
- interest rate parity
- financial integration line
- Mundell–Fleming model
- crowding out
- capital controls
- policy mix
- monetary interdependence
- revaluation/devaluation
- beggar-thy-neighbour policies

Exercises

1. The *IS*, *LM*, and financial integration curves define six regions in Figure 11.12. Any position off a curve corresponds to market disequilibrium which can be characterized as excess demand or supply in either goods or money markets or short-term capital inflow or outflow. Define each region accordingly, e.g. excess demand in the goods market and excess supply in the money market.

2. Desired demand (*DD*) is represented by the following simplified function:

$$DD = 3000 + 0.8(Y - \bar{T}) + \bar{G} - 100i - 500S.$$

   Domestic and foreign price levels have been assumed constant and equal to one. Let $i = 5\%$ throughout. Initially $\bar{G} = \bar{T} = 3000$. *S* is the nominal exchange rate and is assumed fixed at one.
   (*a*) Compute the effect on GDP of an increase in $\bar{T}$ from 3000 to 3500. Show your result graphically. What is the value of the lump-sum tax multiplier?
   (*b*) Compute the effect on GDP of an increase in $\bar{G}$ from 3000 to 3500. Show your result graphically. What is the value of the government spending multiplier?
   (*c*) Compute the net effect on GDP when both $\bar{G}$ and $\bar{T}$ increase by the same amount, from 3000 to 3500. Show your result graphically. What is the value of the balanced budget multiplier? Compare your answers and discuss.

3. *France, 1981–3.* In 1981 a Socialist government took power in France and attempted to reflate the economy while the rest of the world was falling deeper into recession. The expansionary policy consisted of increased government spending with no tax increases and an accommodative to expansionary monetary policy. (One-third of the deficit was money financed.) Despite this, growth was only 1.8% in 1982 and 0.7% in 1983.
   (*a*) Using the *IS–LM* diagram, map out the Mitterrand policy in 1981–2. France fixed its exchange rate in the European Monetary System. What must have happened to the current account?
   (*b*) Within a few months of the programme's outset, capital outflows were significant. What does this indicate? (*Hint*: think about the current account.) What was the gain (at least, the perceived gain) of instituting capital controls in France?
   (*c*) Why was the demand policy of Mitterrand doomed to failure before it even began?

4. Suppose the demand for real money balances has the form $\mathcal{L}(Y, i, c) = 0.5Y - 300i + 50c$. Let $\bar{P} = 1$, $\bar{M} = 2500$ and $\bar{c} = 10$. Plot the *LM* curve in the *i*, *Y* diagram. What is the effect of an increase in $\bar{c}$ from 10 to 20 on the *LM* curve? What is the effect of an increase in the price level from $\bar{P} = 1$ to $\bar{P} = 2$, holding $\bar{c} = 10$? Of $\bar{M} = 2500$ to $\bar{M} = 3000$?

5. *Norway, 1986.* Norway faced a precipitous drop in the real value of oil exports in 1986. This occurred both because the dollar price of oil declined and because the dollar depreciated. Describe the impact using the *IS–LM* diagram. What options were available to Norway? Norway fixed its exchange rate to a basket of currencies.

6. Using the initial *IS* and *LM* curves from problems 2 and 4, consider a fixed exchange rate regime with $\bar{S} = 1$ and $i^* = 10$.
   (*a*) Find the equilibrium interest rate and real GDP. What is the equilibrium value of the nominal money supply? Explain.

(*b*) What is the effect of an increase in government expenditure from 3000 to 3500? What happens to the money supply as a result? Explain in words how the central bank allows this to occur.

7. Suppose the exchange rate in Problems 4 and 6 is fixed at 0.5, and the economy is at equilibrium ($i = i^* = 10$). Assess the effect of an increase in the foreign interest rate i^* to 15 on equilibrium output and interest rates. If the exchange rate is allowed to float and M/P is exogenous, how will your answer change?

8. Using the same initial *IS* and *LM* curves from problems 2 and 4, consider now a flexible exchange rate regime with $\bar{i}^* = 10$.
   (*a*) Solve for the equilibrium interest rate and real GDP. Explain the differences with your answer to 4(*a*).
   (*b*) What is the effect now of an increase in government expenditure from 3000 to 3500? How does your answer change if the money supply is increased at the same time from 3500 to 4000?
   (*c*) What is the effect of an increase in taxes from 3000 to 3500, all other things held equal? Give your answer for both flexible and fixed exchange rate regimes, and in the latter assume $S = 1$.

9. *German reunification and the EMS, 1990.* One result of German economic and monetary union in 1990 was the huge requirements of the former German Democratic Republic for needed infrastructure and transfers. These were assumed by West Germany.
   (*a*) What is the effect of increased public spending on the *IS* curve in Germany? Recall that Germany fixes its exchange rate in the European Monetary System.
   (*b*) Suppose the German central bank decides instead not to increase the money supply. Is such a decision consistent with a fixed exchange rate regime?
   Other countries have perceived higher German interest rates as an upward movement of the financial integration line. How might this help explain the prolonged recession observed in Germany's EC neighbours in 1991?

10. *Poland* has experienced high real growth since the mid-1990s, driven primarily by exceptionally strong investment spending and export growth. Explain how Poland's fixed exchange rate policy has contributed to this boom. What do you expect the consequences to be for the current account? For foreign exchange reserves? For the Polish money supply?

Suggested Further Reading

The Mundell–Fleming model refers to:

Fleming, J. M. (1962), 'Domestic Financial Policies under Fixed and Floating Exchange Rates', *IMF Staff Papers*, 9: 369–79.

Mundell, R. A. (1962), 'Capital Mobility and Stabilization Policy under Fixed and Flexible Exchange Rates', *Canadian Journal of Economic and Political Science*, 29: 475–85.

More advanced treatments can be found in:

Gärtner, M. (1993), *Macroeconomics under Flexible Exchange Rates*, Harvester Wheatsheaf.

Obstfeld M., and Rogoff, K. (1998), *The Foundations of International Macroeconomics*, MIT Press.

Romer, D. (1996), *Advanced Macroeconomics*, McGraw-Hill.

Appendix: A Mathematical Treatment of Policy Multiplier in the *IS–LM* System

This appendix derives formally some of the results presented in the text for the *IS–LM* model of an open economy, under fixed and flexible exchange rates. Both foreign and domestic price levels are exogenous throughout, so changes in the nominal exchange rate are equivalent to changes in the real rate; if S is the nominal and σ is the real exchange rate, then $dS = d\sigma$.

The Model

The *IS* curve is given by

(A11.1) $Y = C(\Omega, Y^d) + I(q, i) + \bar{G} + PCA(Y, Y^*, \sigma)$,

where Y is GDP, C consumption, I investment expenditures, $\bar{G}$ government purchases, and PCA the current account, all denominated in real terms (at constant prices). The functions are largely as in the main text. Government purchases are exogenous, as is the tax rate and the lump-sum (net) tax. Disposable income Y^d is given therefore by $Y(1 - \tau) - \bar{T}$. In principle, $\bar{T}$ need not be positive; if negative, it might be regarded as an exogenous transfer or a tax exemption. Investment is a positive function of q and the interest rate. q is assumed to be a positive function of expected future marginal products of capital (exogenous) and a negative function of the interest rate (endogenous). Note also that the primary current account is only a function of domestic GDP, foreign GDP, and the real exchange rate.

Total differentiation of (A11.1) yields the following local characterization of the *IS* curve:

(A11.2) $dY = C_Y(1 - \tau)dY - C_Y Y d\tau - C_Y d\bar{T}$
$\qquad + C_\Omega(\Omega_i di + \Omega_S dS) + I_q q_i di + I_i di$
$\qquad + d\bar{G} + PCA_\sigma d\sigma + PCA_Y dY$,

where subscripts here refer to partial derivatives of the underlying functions; i.e., $C_Y \equiv \partial C / \partial Y^d$. By assumption, $1 > C_Y > 0$, $C_\Omega > 0$, $\Omega_i < 0$, $\Omega_E \lessgtr 0$ (depending on whether the net foreign asset position is positive or negative), $I_q > 0$, $q_i < 0$, $I_i < 0$, $PCA_\sigma > 0$, and $PCA_Y < 0$. The slope of the *IS* curve is given when $d\tau = d\bar{T} = dS = d\bar{G} = d\sigma$:

$$\frac{di}{dY} = \frac{1 - C_Y(1 - \tau) - I_Y - PCA_Y}{C_\Omega \Omega_i + I_q q_i + I_i} < 0.$$

The *LM* curve is given by equilibrium in the money market, i.e. by

(A11.3) $M/\bar{P} = \mathcal{L}(Y, i)$,

so total differentiation results in (setting $d\bar{P} = 0$)

(A11.4) $dM/\bar{P} = \mathcal{L}_Y dY + \mathcal{L}_i di$,

with $\mathcal{L}_Y > 0$ and $\mathcal{L}_i < 0$, for reasons given in Chapter 8. The slope of the *LM* curve is $di/dY = -\mathcal{L}_Y/\mathcal{L}_i > 0$.

Fixed Exchange Rates

The nominal exchange rate (units of domestic currency per unit of foreign currency) is pegged at $\bar{S}$, and the domestic interest rate i is continuously equal to the exogenous foreign required rate of return i^*. Thus, $d\bar{S} = di = 0$. The money supply is endogenous. The *IS* curve reduces to

(A11.5) $dY = C_Y(1 - \tau)dY - C_Y Y d\tau + C_Y d\bar{T} + d\bar{G} + PCA_Y dY$,

and the *LM* curve is

(A11.6) $dM/P = \mathcal{L}_Y dY$.

The money supply is endogenous, and we will ignore the *LM* curve for the rest of the fixed exchange rate analysis. It is sufficient to manipulate (A11.5). To derive the fiscal multipliers, we seek the change in the endogenous variable Y for changes in the policy instruments: $\bar{G}$, τ, and $\bar{T}$. Thus, the government spending multiplier obtains from (A11.5) when $d\bar{G} \neq 0$ but $d\tau = d\bar{T} = 0$:

$$\frac{dY}{d\bar{G}} = \frac{1}{1 - C_Y(1 - \tau) - PCA_Y} > 0.$$

Similarly, the lump-sum tax multiplier obtains when $d\bar{T} \neq 0$ and $d\tau = d\bar{G} = 0$:

$$\frac{dY}{d\bar{T}} = \frac{-C_Y}{1 - C_Y(1 - \tau) - PCA_Y} < 0.$$

Note that $dY/d\bar{G} > -dY/d\bar{T}$, so one might think of a balanced budget multiplier which applies when changes in government purchases are matched by tax increases or transfer reductions ($d\bar{G} = d\bar{T} \neq 0$, $d\tau = 0$):

$$\frac{dY}{d\bar{G}}\bigg|_{d\bar{G}=d\bar{T}} = \frac{1 - C_Y}{1 - C_Y(1 - \tau) - PCA_Y} > 0.$$

The tax rate multiplier ($d\bar{G} = d\bar{T} = 0$, $d\tau \neq 0$) is given by

$$\frac{dY}{d\tau} = \frac{-YC_Y}{1 - C_Y(1 - \tau) - PCA_Y} < 0.$$

Floating Exchange Rates

Under a floating exchange rate regime, the money supply is exogenous, so $M = \bar{M}$. As before, i^* is given as well.

Consequently, the domestic interest rate clears the domestic money market, and the exchange rate moves to clear the demand and supply of foreign exchange, assumed to be determined by relative rates of return. The financial integration condition is simply[21]

(A11.7) $\qquad dS = \theta(i - i^*) \quad \text{with } \theta > 0.$

Equation (A11.7) simply states that, when nominal interest rates exceed the required rate of return abroad, the exchange rate tends to appreciate. The IS curve is given by (A11.2), the LM by (A11.4). It is possible to solve (A11.2), (A11.4), and (A11.7) to obtain the analogous multipliers under floating exchange rates:[22]

It is revealing to compare these multipliers with those of the previous section. For two reasons, the fiscal multipliers are smaller than they are under fixed exchange rate regimes. First, there is a crowding out of interest-sensitive expenditure as interest rates rise. Second, higher domestic interest rates are associated with an appreciated exchange rate (S higher), which crowds out exports and encourages imports. The extent of this crowding out depends on the slope of the LM curve—$(\mathcal{L}_Y/\mathcal{L}_i)$; as the LM curve becomes flatter, we move closer to the fixed exchange rate regime case. Note also that, as capital becomes perfectly mobile $(\theta \to \infty)$, the fiscal multipliers tend to zero, and the monetary policy multiplier tends to $1/(\bar{P}\mathcal{L}_Y)$.

$$\frac{dY}{d\bar{G}} = \frac{1}{1 - C_Y(1 - \tau) - PCA_Y + (\mathcal{L}_Y/\mathcal{L}_i)[C_\Omega\Omega_i + I_q q_i + I_i + \theta(PCA_\sigma + C_\Omega\Omega_S)]} > 0,$$

$$\frac{dY}{d\bar{T}} = \frac{-C_Y}{1 - C_Y(1 - \tau) - PCA_Y + (\mathcal{L}_Y/\mathcal{L}_i)[C_\Omega\Omega_i + I_q q_i + I_i + \theta(PCA_\sigma + C_\Omega\Omega_S)]} < 0,$$

$$\frac{dY}{d\tau} = \frac{-YC_Y}{1 - C_Y(1 - \tau) - PCA_Y + (\mathcal{L}_Y/\mathcal{L}_i)[C_\Omega\Omega_i + I_q q_i + I_i + \theta(PCA_\sigma + C_\Omega\Omega_S)]} < 0.$$

It is also possible to derive the monetary policy multiplier as

$$\frac{dY}{d\bar{M}} = \frac{[C_\Omega\Omega_i + I_q q_i + \theta(PCA_\sigma + C_\Omega\Omega_S)]/\bar{P}\mathcal{L}_i}{1 - C_Y(1 - \tau) - PCA_Y + (\mathcal{L}_Y/\mathcal{L}_i)[C_\Omega\Omega_i + I_q q_i + I_i + \theta(PCA_\sigma + C_\Omega\Omega_S)]} < 0.$$

[21] In Ch. 9 we explored this relationship in detail.

[22] These three equations are a system in three unknowns dY, di, and dS. These unknowns can be solved for in terms of the exogenous variables in a variety of ways. One is brute force.

Another is to write the system in matrix form $Ax = b$, where x is the vector of endogenous variables, A is a conformable matrix of the coefficients, and b is the set of exogenous terms; if A is invertible, the solution is $x = A^{-1}b$.

Inflation and Business Cycles

The next three chapters bring together the material of the first half of the book in a way that can be used in the analysis of historical episodes as well as contemporary policy dilemmas. It is the core of modern macroeconomics, and follows a tradition which distinguishes between forces of demand and supply affecting the evolution of output. Chapter 12 focuses on inflation and aggregate supply, relaxing the Keynesian fixed-price assumption and stressing the role of labour markets. Chapter 13 introduces inflation in the *IS–LM* analysis and derives the aggregate demand schedule. Bringing together the aggregate demand (*AD*) and aggregate supply (*AS*) schedules provides a powerful tool for explaining the behaviour of inflation and output. Chapter 14 then focuses on business cycles. It presents a number of stylized facts and examines how well they are explained by the *AD–AS* framework. It also introduces an alternative and competing view, the Real Business Cycle theory, which is based on an equilibrium interpretation of macroeconomic fluctuations.

Aggregate Supply and Inflation

12

When the demand for a commodity or service is high relative to the supply of it we expect the price to rise, the rate of rise being greater, the greater the excess demand. Conversely when the demand is low relatively to the supply we expect the price to fall, the rate of fall being greater, the greater the deficiency of demand. It seems plausible that this principle should operate as one of the factors determining the rate of change of money wage rates, which are the price of labour services.

– A. W. Phillips

12.1 Overview

Up to now, the price level in the economy was taken as fixed. Of course, prices do in fact change. A cup of tea in London that cost 5p in 1965 goes for £1.10 in 2001. The baguette in Paris which cost 40 centimes in 1965 fetched more than 4 francs 35 years later. Inflation is not about changes in the price of tea in Britain and bread in Paris, however, but rather about changes in the general price level; inflation involves *all* prices in an economy. And wages also seem to change: gross of deductions, an hour's labour by an average UK factory worker was compensated at 0.48 £/hour in 1965, compared with more than £14 in 1999; the representative French manufacturing worker earned 8.64FF per hour in 1965 in contrast to more than 158 FF in 1999.[1] Part of these wage increases represents rising productivity, but the bulk reflects inflation, the decline in the purchasing power of money. Chapter 8 established that inflation in the long run depends on how rapid the money supply is increasing relative to an economy's output of goods and services, but how is the long run actually reached? This is the topic of the present chapter.

As we track down the inflation phenomenon we find ourselves once again studying the **supply side** of an economy. In earlier chapters, we already looked at the supply side as the potential output of the economy: Chapter 3 derived the economy's trend growth in productive capacity as a function of capital, labour, and technology; Chapter 4 examined how the labour market settles on an equilibrium unemployment rate. In this chapter we explore explicitly what puts inflation in motion and how persistent it is. In fact, the present chapter can be seen as a counterpoint to the previous one. There the familiar GDP decomposition was reinterpreted as a causal relationship running from demand to output, but how output really responds to the **demand side** was left open. What are the incentives for producers to react to demand? Or for workers to change the numbers of hours they work? This and the next chapter develop the idea that demand increases are actually met by a combination of output expansion *and* price increases. The mix varies over time, however. In the short run, prices are sticky and most of the response is in output, as in Chapter 11. In the long run, prices rise and the economy returns to its trend growth path, as in Chapters 8 and 10. The short run is Keynesian; the long run is characterized by the neutrality principle.

In recent years, inflation has declined considerably, stabilizing at 2–4% in United Kingdom, Euroland, and the USA. In Japan, the price level is stable or even falling. Yet inflation remains at high and unstable levels in Turkey, many Latin American countries, and the new market economies of Central and Eastern Europe. It remains a primier topic of macroeconomics precisely because it has a tendency to come back when most have come around to believe that is has been vanquished.

---

[1] Source: US Bureau of Labor Statistics, Office of Productivity and Technology, October 2000.

12.2 The Phillips Curve: Chimera or a Stylized Fact?

12.2.1 A. W. Phillips's Discovery

The traditional starting point is the **Phillips curve**, a negative *trade-off* observed between inflation and unemployment, the twin 'bads' of macroeconomics. It is named after the late New Zealander A. W. Phillips of the London School of Economics. In the late 1950s Phillips plotted the annual rate of growth of nominal wages, or **wage inflation**, in Britain during the period 1861–1957 against the rate of unemployment and found a remarkably robust negative correlation, that was confirmed for a number of other countries.[2] Figure 12.1 plots Phillips curves—using the rate of price inflation instead of wage inflation—for Britain and the average of sixteen advanced economies for the period 1921–73 (excluding war years). While far from perfect (a number of outliers correspond to exceptional events), the Phillips curve is suggestive of an important systematic relationship: a stylized fact.

12.2.2 A Supply Curve Interpretation

Figure 12.2 presents the stylized version of a Phillips curve. A country could suffer from high inflation but have low unemployment (point *A*), or from high unemployment but with low inflation (point *B*). The message of the Phillips curve to policy-makers was simple and appealing: pick a point on the Phillips curve, i.e. choose a politically acceptable combination of unemployment and inflation, and then steer the economy to that point.[3] In theory, this could be achieved by moving the *IS* curve using fiscal policy (public spending and taxes) or the *LM* curve using monetary policy, or a mix of both. A country that favoured low unemployment would choose a point

like *A* in Figure 12.2; a country interested in low inflation would aim at a point like *B*, accepting some unemployment. The Phillips curve was seen as a trade-off.

The discovery of the Phillips curve played a central role in the early development of macroeconomics and its everyday use by policy-makers. Economists had been frustrated by the 'missing link' between output and inflation: they knew well that the fixed price assumption used to derive the *IS* and *LM* curves could not literally be true. The *IS–LM* system explained output fluctuations given prices; Okun's Law explained how unemployment varies with output. Explaining how prices respond to unemployment was all that was needed for a complete macroeconomic theory. By filling this gap, the Phillips curve provided the foundation of the **aggregate supply curve** presented in the second panel of Figure 12.2: when output increases relative to trend, unemployment declines (Okun's Law) and inflation rises (the Phillips curve). The aggregate supply curve answers the question raised earlier: under what conditions is an economy willing to supply the output that households and firms demand? The answer was: inflation must increase, because under those conditions wages and profits are increasing.

12.2.3 The Phillips Curve in Demise

Weak foundations

Not long after its discovery, the interpretation of the Phillips curve—that higher prices elicit more output —was perceived as standing on weak theoretical legs. In the late 1960s, Milton Friedman, the Nobel Laureate of 1976 and Edmund Phelps of Columbia University[4] independently attacked the Phillips curve idea. Their challenge was to ask: how could the rate of change of nominal variables, such as nominal wages and prices, be related to real variables such as employment, unemployment and output in the long run? If the theory of monetary neutrality as

---

[2] It turns out that Phillips was not the first to discover the Phillips curve: the American economist Irving Fischer (of Robinson Crusoe fame) published a paper in the *International Labor Review* of 1926 in which he confirms a similar relationship in the United States.

[3] This view of a trade-off was echoed by Helmut Schmidt, the ex-chancellor of West Germany, who stated in a newspaper interview in 1978 that he would prefer 5% inflation to 5% unemployment. How times have changed!

[4] This is the same Phelps who formulated the golden rule of economic growth, in Chapter 3.

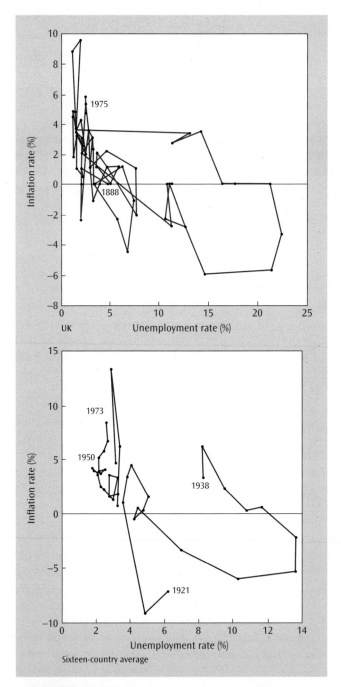

Fig. 12.1 **Phillips Curves: The UK (1888–1975) and a Sixteen-Country Average (1921–1973, excluding 1939–1949)**

Sources: Maddison (1991); Mitchell (1998). Unweighted average of observations for Australia, Austria, Belgium, Canada, Denmark, Finland, France, Germany, Italy, Japan, Netherlands, Norway, Sweden, Switzerland, the UK, and the USA. For some years, some countries are missing.

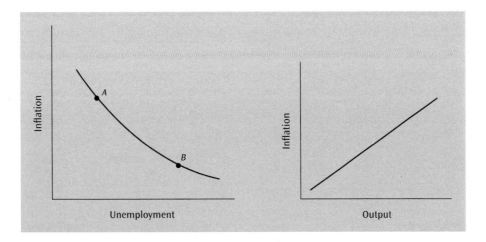

Fig. 12.2   **The Phillips Curve and Aggregate Supply**

The Phillips curve was once seen as a negative trade-off between unemployment and inflation, representing a set of possible options from which governments could choose. For example, it could keep unemployment down (point *A*) at the cost of some inflation, or could limit inflation (point *B*) but only by accepting unemployment. Combining the Phillips curve and Okun's Law delivers a supply curve. The supply curve states that inflation must rise to induce suppliers to produce more output.

outlined in Chapter 8 is valid, then rates of change in the price level and other nominal variables should be unrelated to the real economy.[5] In particular, a simultaneous rise in prices and wages should leave relative prices—real interest rates, real wages, and real exchange rates—unchanged. Only if workers and firms suffer from **money illusion**—that is, if they act on increases in their own prices or wages without taking contemporaneous increases in all other prices into account—will they raise output.

To understand the critique of Friedman and Phelps, it is helpful to think about the long-run behaviour of labour markets and output. The principle of monetary neutrality asserts that the economy is dichotomized in the long run: real and nominal sectors of an economy cease to influence each other. If we define the long run as the situation when the output level is on its trend growth path $\bar{Y}$ and unemployment is at its equilibrium rate $\bar{U}$, *no matter what the rate of inflation is*, then the rate of inflation is determined by the rate of money growth. Graphically, if in the long run unemployment returns to its equilibrium level, the **long-run aggregate supply curve** as well as the Phillips curve must be vertical lines, as displayed in Figure 12.3.

Wobbly evidence

The critique of Friedman and Phelps, while largely ignored in the late 1960s, proved to be right on target in the 1970s. As Figure 12.4 shows, the Phillips curve seems to have disappeared at times. The link, still present in the late 1960s, breaks down in the following decade. The vanishing Phillips curve had as profound an influence on policy-making as the Phillips curve itself.[6] To start with, it was a puzzle: over nearly a century, the inverse relationship between inflation and unemployment seemed relatively robust and yet, it broke down in all countries at about the same time. That could not just be bad luck! The challenge is to explain both the existence of a Phillips curve and its disappearance, as well as the striking similarity between different countries' experiences.

[5] In his address to the American Economic Association in 1967 Friedman argued that '. . . there is always a temporary trade-off between inflation and unemployment, there is no permanent trade-off. The temporary trade-off comes not from inflation *per se*, but from a rising rate of inflation.' Friedman (1968: 10).

[6] For more details see the appendix to this Chapter.

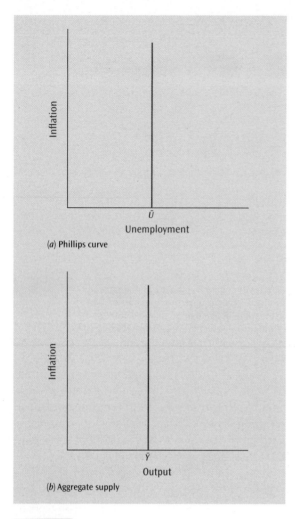

(a) Phillips curve

(b) Aggregate supply

Fig. 12.3 The Long Run

In the long run, unemployment is at its equilibrium rate and output is on its trend growth path. Both the Phillips curve and the aggregate supply curve are vertical. Inflation is determined by money growth, independently of output or unemployment.

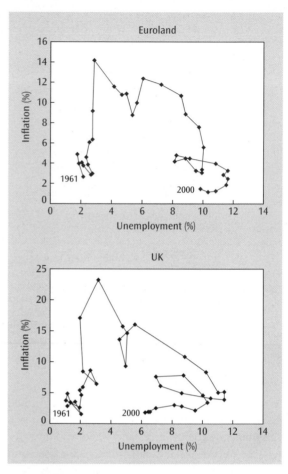

Fig. 12.4 Phillips Curves: The Recent Experience, Euroland and the UK, 1961–2000

The Phillips curve broke down at the end of the 1960s. In both Euroland and the United Kingdom, the sharpest departures occur during the years 1973–5 and 1979–81. In the most recent period the Phillips curve seems to have returned.
Sources: Eurostat.

Solving the Phillips curve mystery requires us to make use of some important clues. First, the timing of the sharpest increases in inflation—first around 1973–4, and then around 1979–80—can be related directly to two **oil shocks**, when oil prices increased fourfold in 1973–4 and then doubled over again in 1979–80.[7] Second, in between the oil shocks, and

after the second oil shock, it is possible to observe the re-emergence of Phillips curves. Third, each of these curves seems to lie to the right of the previous one. This last fact suggests that the equilibrium unemployment rate, about which the actual rate fluctuates, had increased over time. In the following section we dissect the rate of inflation to show exactly where it comes from. The end result is a rehabilitated Phillips curve.

---

[7] The evolution of oil prices is displayed in Fig. 12.7.

12.3 Accounting for Inflation: The Battle of the Mark-ups

If we view prices as sticky in the short run but perfectly flexible in the long run, then their medium-run behaviour holds the key to understanding the disappearance of the Phillips curve. To study the medium run, we break down inflation into its most important components—an accounting exercise of sorts. We start with the observation that firms set prices. They do so with one eye on the market and the other on production costs. Focusing next on production costs, emphasis is shifted to nominal wages, labour productivity, and the cyclical state of the labour market. Consolidating price-setting and wage-setting shows not only why the Phillips curve exists, but also under which conditions it can disappear.

12.3.1 The Battle of the Mark-ups: A Simple Story

Prices as a mark-up on costs

When perfect competition reigns in product markets, firms are unable to set prices. A good example is the fruit grower who sells his apples in the town market. With many other sellers around, the farmer finds it difficult to set his price very far from the average price for apples of the same variety: if he raises his price a few cents, he has no customers; if he lowers his price by a few cents, he will sell everything, but regret the forgone profits. We conclude that producers of standard products such as milk or copper have little or no **market power**.

Yet in reality, most firms *do* set prices. For this, they must have some market power. Either there is little competition among firms—generally hard to believe—or they must do something to acquire market power. In fact, they go to extreme lengths to establish it. They strive to **differentiate** their products, making them different from those of the competitors. They do so through design (similar cars always differ in many subtle ways) and through advertising to win consumer loyalty (some people like Volkswagen, others Renault), or both. This is what marketing is all about. The payoff is some monopoly power, firms can raise prices without

losing all customers, market power allows for higher profits. The difference between perfect competition and monopolistic pricing is explained in detail in the WebAppendix.

When firms set prices, the result is **mark-up pricing**: a firm with market power sets the price (P) of its product above the nominal marginal production cost (MC), by 10% or 30%, say.[8] Mark-up pricing is summarized as follows:

$$(12.1) \qquad P = (1 + \theta)MC \qquad \text{where } \theta > 0.$$

To keep things simple at the moment, we assume that the mark-up θ is constant; later we relax this assumption and look at the consequences.

Labour costs and wages

To discover how and why prices are changed, then, we need to study nominal marginal costs. Yet marginal costs—the costs of producing another unit of output, all other things held constant—are difficult to measure. As is customary, we approximate them by **average** or **unit costs**—total costs divided by the number of units produced.[9] It is convenient to break down total costs into two main categories: labour and non-labour costs. For the economy as a whole, labour costs are the single largest component of production costs. Table 12.1 shows that their share of value added ranges from 50% to 70% in developed countries, and are usually higher in labour-intensive services than in capital-intensive industries.[10]

(12.2) Average costs in euros
= total costs in euros/number of
  units produced
= unit labour costs + unit non-labour costs

---

[8] Microeconomic principles state that, in the presence of perfect competition, firms are driven to set prices equal to marginal costs; the mark-up is then zero.

[9] The WebAppendix to this chapter provides a justification of this assumption.

[10] In interpreting these numbers, it is important to remember the distinction between value added and turnover or total sales, which was stressed in Chapter 2. As a percentage of total sales, wage shares are much lower because total turnover in an economy includes the costs of intermediate goods. The figures reported in Table 12.1 have netted out payments for intermediate inputs produced by other firms.

Table 12.1 Wage Share of Value Added by Country and Selected Industries, 1997 (%)

	Total economy	Manufacturing	Chemicals	Basic metal industries	Wholesale/ retail trade
Belgium	51.2	61.6	54.7	73.0	49.3
Germany	52.7	69.6	n.a.	n.a.	63.1
Denmark[a]	55.4	62.6	54.6	59.4	61.6
Italy	41.3	53.1	55.2	38.7	27.1
Japan	56.4	58.6	30.5	38.9	67.5
Netherlands[a]	51.2	54.8	34.6	51.6	59.9
United States	59.9	63.0	48.8	72.1	57.8

[a] 1995
Source: OECD.

Because labour costs are the largest component of total costs, they are our first focus of attention, ignoring other costs for the moment. Unit labour costs, labour cost in euro per unit of output, can be further broken down into two components: cost per hour, and what can be produced in one hour. The first component is the gross nominal wage per hour worked (W), which includes not only direct wage and salary but also costs like paid vacations, direct labour taxes, social security contributions, and other benefits paid by employers on behalf of their workers. In many European countries this component can be nearly equal to the net pay received by the worker. The second component, the amount of output that is produced by labour in an hour, is labour productivity. Following the notation of previous chapters, this is Y/L, total output Y divided by total hours worked L (measured in man-hours). To summarize, nominal *total* labour costs are measured as the product WL of the hourly wage W and hours worked L, so nominal *unit* labour costs are measured as the ratio of total costs to output: WL/Y. Nominal unit labour costs can also seen as the ratio of the hourly wage to average labour productivity:

(12.3)   Nominal unit abour costs

$$= \frac{\text{gross hourly wage}}{\text{average labour productivity}}$$

or $$\frac{WL}{Y} = \frac{W}{(Y/L)}$$

To simplify things, we first suppose that productivity is constant and equal to one: one hour of labour produces one unit of output. In this case, as we ignore non-labour costs, unit labour costs are simply the nominal wage, W, and the mark-up equation (12.1) becomes

(12.4) $$P = (1 + \theta)W.$$

Prices are a mark-up on nominal wages.

Wages as a mark-up on prices

Let us take the process one step further: what determines hourly wages? A good starting point for answering this question is Chapter 4. There we saw that both employees and employers care about *real* labour costs and *real* wages. Yet wage bargaining can only be about *nominal* wages for a number of reasons. First, everyone consumes a different bundle of goods, and it would be difficult to decide whose bundle to use for measuring real wages. Second, the price level, even when measured by the CPI, is measured only with a lag. Third, and most importantly, the future is unknown. Naturally, employees want to protect their nominal wages from inflation. Employers normally agree to incorporate inflation in wage settlements but worry about overestimating it and paying their workers 'too much'. Both sides can agree on what real wage W/P to aim at, but uncertain what nominal wage W will hit the target. Inevitably, they must form a view on the inflation rate which will prevail in the future. Indeed, the expected rate of inflation, to be incorporated into wage settlements, is a central part of wage negotiations. We will denote the expected price level by P^e.

The upshot is that wage negotiations will set a nominal wage W compatible with an expected real wage target W/P^e, which emerges from factors studied in Chapter 4. The real wage normally tracks labour productivity, but we know that collective wage bargaining can do better or worse at times, trading off income against employment. So unions will aim for a target real wage which is a mark-up over productivity. Since we assume, for the time being, that labour productivity itself is constant and set to unity, the outcome is:

$$(12.5) \qquad W/P^e = (1 + \gamma) \quad \text{or} \quad W = (1 + \gamma)P^e, \quad \text{with } \gamma > 0$$

Thus nominal wages are a simple mark-up on the expected price level.

Isn't this a clear case of circular reasoning? We saw earlier that prices themselves were a mark-up on nominal wages (equation (12.4)), and the last equation holds that nominal wages are a function of prices! In some sense, the wage-price determination process is circular, and has thus earned the title **'battle of the mark-ups'**.[11] Prices depend on wages which depend on expected prices, so *actual* prices depend on *expected* prices. This circularity can be summarized by combining the price equation (12.4) with the wage equation (12.5) to obtain

$$(12.6) \qquad P = (1 + \theta)(1 + \gamma)P^e.$$

Note that the circular process has an anchor: P^e, the level of prices expected by wage negotiators to prevail over the course of the contract. We will later see that this expectation is the central determinant of inflation in the medium run.

12.3.2 The Role of Productivity

We have assumed that labour productivity is constant but we know from Chapter 3 that labour productivity is growing all the time. This directly

reduces labour costs. As equation (12.3) makes clear, if labour productivity Y/L increases by 5%, holding nominal wages W constant, unit labour costs decline by 5%. Average labour costs grow as the difference between hourly wage growth and productivity growth.[12]

How does labour productivity growth affect the process of wage and price determination? We need to review both mark-ups. The price mark-up (12.1) is set above unit labour costs $WL/Y = W/(Y/L)$ (we still ignore non-labour costs), so (12.4) is modified as follows:

$$(12.4') \qquad P = (1 + \theta)\frac{W}{(Y/L)}.$$

Growth in labour productivity reduces labour costs, and should reduce the price level, all other things given. But the story does not end here. As already noted, workers expect and usually receive some share of the fruits of their rising productivity. Their real wage can be thought of as a mark-up over productivity Y/L, so the new wage mark-up equation is:

$$(12.5') \quad W/P^e = (1 + \gamma)(Y/L) \quad \text{or} \quad W = (1 + \gamma)(Y/L)P^e.$$

And now, if we combine (12.4') and (12.5') as before, we obtain (12.6) again! We have a striking result *given the mark-ups*, productivity does not affect the price level of the economy. The reason: productivity growth reduces labour costs for a given hourly wage, but hourly wages increase with labour productivity. Labour and other factors of production (capital, mostly) divide the cake of productivity gains just as before. The price level remains driven by the two mark-ups and the nominal price level expected to prevail over the contract period.

12.3.3 Cyclical Effects on Mark-ups

Equation (12.6) is still too simplistic. The assumption that the two mark-ups are constant violates both intuition and the facts. They tend to move over business cycles. To see which side would 'win' the battle of the mark-ups, we need to separate out the two, distinctly different mark-up decisions.

---

[11] The battle of the mark-ups approach to understanding inflation has found empirical support in OECD countries in pathbreaking work by researchers at the London School of Economics Richard Layard, Steven Nickell and Richard Jackman, among others.

[12] Nominal labour costs are defined as $W/(Y/L)$, and therefore change at the rate $\Delta W/W - \Delta(Y/L)/(Y/L)$.

Box 12.1   **Short-Run Keynesian Assumption and Long-Run Neutrality**

The Keynesian assumption that prices are sticky needs to be justified. In principle, it is not in the interest of anyone to keep prices 'wrong'. A firm with market power will set the price higher than under perfect competition, but will adjust the price whenever the situation changes: different demand, different costs of production. This does not explain stickiness per se.

One explanation relates to the existence of long-term contracts, or agreements to trade at a given price. If conditions change, the agreed-upon price remains binding until a new contract is set, unless the contract is contingent on such changes. Contracts can be formal, but they may also be implicit: buyers and sellers are engaged in a long-term relationship, and often do not need to write down exact terms of agreement. But why do such contracts exist if they are not always optimal? The story here is that it may be costly to change prices frequently or to write extremely detailed contracts. Explicit or implicit contracts make life easier for all those concerned, as long as conditions do not change too much. The so-called menu costs explanation is based on this idea. Just as it is too expensive for a restaurant to change its price list every day as the prices of its inputs (fruits, vegetables, meat) fluctuate, so it is impractical to renegotiate contracts, or to write down contracts that account for all possible contingencies. Firms may find it easier to set prices today for some period of time and sell whatever demand is forthcoming at the price.

The effects of menu costs are intuitive. If, for example, demand declines, the firm will have an incentive to reduce its price. If it does not, its profits will not be as high as they could be. However, in the presence of menu costs, the firm will compare the potential for better profits when the price is changed, with the menu costs of changing prices. Small changes in demand are likely to be better dealt with by unchanged prices. Menu costs may be explicit (like printing a new menu or price-list) or implicit (like having to explain to customers how and why the price has been changed). They explain why prices do not move in response to small disturbances but do react to large ones.

Start with the price mark-up. If competition heats up in good times, as new goods and producers enter the market, the mark-up θ should decline in booms. But market demand may be so strong that all competitors instead raise their price mark-ups and θ could increase in booms. Turning now to the wage mark-up γ, it rises in booms if workers need higher real pay for motivation to work harder. Furthermore, since wages are collectively negotiated, rising employment generally improves the bargaining position of unions, which is reflected in a higher wage mark-up.[13] The evidence is that, together, the combined mark-ups rise during booms and decline in recessions. This result is represented in the following fashion:

(12.7) $\theta + \gamma = a(Y - \bar{Y}) = -b(U - \bar{U})$

By Okun's Law (Chapter 11) we know that output and unemployment move inversely around their equilibrium values; the positive parameters a and b summarize the relationship of the mark-ups to these cyclical indicators.

Equation (12.7) is consistent with evidence presented in Section 11.2 that labour market outcomes deviate over the cycle from equilibrium levels derived in Chapter 4. There we saw that **real wage rigidities** prevent equilibrium unemployment from achieving full employment in the long run, thus explaining involuntary unemployment. In this chapter, we study **nominal wage rigidities** which can explain cyclical deviations of output and unemployment from trend.[14] (Already Figure 4.17 gave the first hint that the actual unemployment rate can deviate from equilibrium.) Box 12.1 gives some reasons for nominal rigidities. In the next section we show how this disequilibrium pressure on price and wage mark-ups are translated into changes in the inflation *rate*.

---

[13] This is the short-run equivalent of the collective labour supply curve of Ch. 4, where unions trade off higher real wages against more employment.

[14] That deviations of output and unemployment from trend can be associated with changes in the mark-up is the disequilibrium view of the business cycle developed in Chapter 14.

12.3.4 **Moving from Price Level to Inflation**

Until now we have reasoned using the price level, actual P or expected P^e. Most people monitor the rate of inflation, which is the rate of increase of prices. Denoting the inflation rate by π, we can define it as:

$$(12.8) \qquad \pi = \frac{P - P_{-1}}{P_{-1}} = \frac{P}{P_{-1}} - 1$$

or, in percentage terms: $\quad \pi = 100 \left(\frac{P}{P_{-1}} - 1 \right)$

Similarly, the price level P^e expected by wage negotiators defines an expected rate of inflation which we call **core inflation**:

$$(12.9) \qquad \bar{\pi} = \frac{P^e}{P_{-1}} - 1$$

where P_{-1} stands for the past price level observed at the time of the previous wage negotiation.

The circular process equation (12.6) can be turned into an equally circular relationship between actual and core inflation. Taking into account the cyclical behaviour of the combined mark-ups (12.7), the relationship can be written as:[15]

$$(12.10) \quad \pi = \bar{\pi} - a(Y - \bar{Y}) \quad \text{or} \quad \pi = \bar{\pi} - b(U - \bar{U}).$$

The dissection of the rate of inflation shows that it depends on the core rate of inflation and the state of the business cycle. The core rate of inflation is a central part of the analysis. It is forward-looking in the sense that wage negotiators attempt to guess as correctly as possible price changes which will occur in the future over the course of the contract under discussion. It is also backward-looking to correct from past mistakes: if, during the previous round of negotiations, future inflation was underestimated, the employees were penalized, if it was over-estimated, wages went up too fast and profits were squeezed. This backward-looking part of wage nego-tiations sometimes takes the form of explicit or implicit **indexation** clauses which commit nominal wages to make up for past price increases. During periods of high inflation, wages are set for short periods because forward-looking guesses are too difficult and errors lead to very significant dis-tortions; indexation then can become automatic. In low-inflation periods, there is little difference between the backward and forward-looking com-ponents, and between core and actual inflation.

12.3.5 **Completing the Picture: The Effect of Supply Shocks**

It is now time to look at the non-labour costs of production which have been studiously ignored so far. These costs correspond to the other factors of production—capital and land, for example—as well as to intermediate inputs such as unfinished goods, materials, and energy. The costs of intermediate inputs to a firm are the sales prices charged by another firm so, at the country level they are auto-matically reflected in the overall inflation rate and do not add anything to the analysis. Of course, this does not apply to imported intermediate goods and raw materials, which are set abroad and trans-lated into domestic costs via the exchange rate. As long as PPP remains approximately true, the costs of imported intermediate goods simply follow domestic inflation. Similarly, the cost of capital includes dividend payments to shareholders and interest payments on bonds or bank loans. These costs also broadly track the inflation rate and do not change our previous results.

It is useful to think of non-labour costs as follow-ing core inflation $\bar{\pi}$ plus an additional component —denoted s—which is meant to capture **supply shocks** such as sharp oil price rises, deep devalu-ations, or other exogenous increases in non-labour production costs such as tax hikes or additional regulation. The supply shock term can be positive or negative. It is a catch-all for exogenous disturbances affecting production costs. As long as non-labour costs simply follow the core rate of inflation, the supply shock term is zero. The way to think about it is that it is close to zero most of the time, or on average, with occasional significant positive or negative deviations.

Supply shocks may also be created by the gov-ernment, especially when it changes taxes. The variety of taxes borne by the firms relate directly to

---

[15] Dividing by P_{-1} and subtracting 1 from both sides of (12.6) gives: $\pi = (1 + \theta)(1 + \gamma)(1 + \bar{\pi}) - 1 = 1 + \theta + \gamma + \gamma\theta + \bar{\pi} + \theta\bar{\pi} + \gamma\bar{\pi} + \gamma\theta\bar{\pi} - 1 \approx \theta + \gamma + \bar{\pi}$, where the last step is an acceptable approximation as long as $\bar{\pi}, \theta$, and γ are small.

production and affect the final selling price—value added or excise taxes, profit taxes, establishment and property taxes, and so on. Other costs imposed by governments are implicit, but may have a significant impact (environmental or consumer protection legislation, for example). All of these government-induced costs affect only the *price level*; to have an effect on the rate of inflation, they would have to increase continuously, which is unlikely. Under these conditions, it is possible to modify equation (12.10) to

$$
(12.11) \quad \pi = \bar{\pi} \begin{cases} + a(Y - \bar{Y}) \\ -\text{or}- \\ - b(U - \bar{U}) \end{cases} + s.
$$

$$
\begin{array}{cccc}
\text{actual} & \text{core} & \text{cyclical} & \text{supply} \\
\text{inflation} & \text{inflation} & \text{demand pressure} & \text{shock}
\end{array}
$$

with s taking the value of zero when non-labour costs rise at the core rate of inflation. Note that the cyclical effects are captured alternatively by fluctuations of output about trend or of unemployment about its equilibrium rate.

12.4 Inflation, Unemployment, and Output

12.4.1 The Phillips Curve Rehabilitated

Can the accounting framework summarized by eq. (12.11) solve the Phillips curve puzzle—both its existence over decades and its apparent instability over particular periods of time? The original Phillips curve claims that inflation depends only on the level of unemployment. The inflation account (12.11) shows that cyclical labour market conditions do indeed matter, but so do core inflation, equilibrium

unemployment, and occasional supply shocks. For a Phillips curve to be visible, these latter factors must be stable. Indeed, when supply shocks are zero and when actual unemployment equals its equilibrium rate, actual inflation equals its core rate:

$$
(12.12) \quad \text{With } s = 0, \quad \pi = \bar{\pi} - b(U - \bar{U});
$$

$$
\text{thus:} \quad \pi = \bar{\pi} \text{ when } U = \bar{U}.
$$

This situation corresponds to point A in the left panel of Figure 12.5. At point B unemployment is

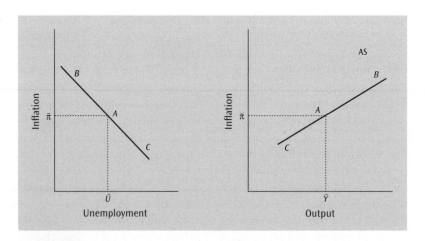

Fig. 12.5 **The Augmented Phillips Curve and the Aggregate Supply Curve**

By definition, point A represents the case where actually observed inflation π is at its core rate $\bar{\pi}$ and where unemployment is at its equilibrium rate, and output is at its trend value. When unemployment is low and output high, actual inflation is above core inflation rate (point B). When unemployment is high and output low, actual inflation is below core inflation (point C).

Table 12.2	**Variability of Inflation, Unemployment, and Imported Commodity Prices in Britain, 1888–1990**[a]		
	1982–90	**1969–82**	**1888–1965**
Inflation	0.36	0.44	2.29
Unemployment	0.20	0.49	0.92
Real commodity prices	0.09	0.20	0.17

[a] Variability is measured as the coefficient of variation, the ratio of the standard deviation to the mean. Commodity prices are deflated by the consumer price index.
Sources: Mitchell (1978; 1988); Maddison (1991).

below equilibrium so the demand pressure pushes inflation above its current core rate $\bar{\pi}$. Conversely, point C corresponds to the case where inflation is below its core rate because the unemployment rate is above equilibrium. While this resembles the Phillips curve, there is a crucial difference: its position is determined by point A, that is, by the core inflation rate $\bar{\pi}$ and the equilibrium rate of unemployment $\bar{U}$.[16]

Table 12.2 presents the year-to-year average variability in the rate of inflation, the rate of unemployment, and commodity prices over selected historical subperiods in Britain. It turns out that, over the period surveyed by Phillips, commodity prices were quite stable. Furthermore, the general level of prices was largely trendless; inflation therefore was negligible, and core inflation was probably near zero, at least rather stable. During this period, focusing only on unemployment fluctuations in (12.11), as the Phillips curve does, makes sense.

During the 1970s, however, price and commodity shocks were a major source of instability. As inflation rose, core inflation rose as well, and became more variable, reflecting rapidly changing expectations. The Phillips curve's demise reflects the emergence of core inflation and supply shocks, the two other explanatory factors of inflation. The modern Phillips curve is therefore **augmented**, meaning that

it incorporates core inflation and allows for supply shocks.

There is no presumption whatsoever that either core inflation or the equilibrium rate of unemployment is constant over time. If either changes, point A moves, and so does the Phillips curve. Potentially, there exists an infinity of Phillips curves, corresponding to the infinity of values that the core inflation rate or the equilibrium rate of unemployment can take. It just so happened that, over the hundred years surveyed by Phillips, the core rate of inflation and the equilibrium rate of unemployment did not change much, so there seems to have been just one Phillips curve.[17] The recent revival of the Phillips curve described in Box 12.2 can be explained by recent stability of inflation and the equilibrium rate of unemployment.

12.4.2 Core Inflation and the Long Run

Core inflation, we saw, captures the rate of inflation agreed upon during wage negotiations. It has both a backward-looking (catching up with past inflation due to previous contracts) and a forward-looking component (what inflation is expected to be in the future). Somehow, it must be related to the actual rate of inflation. How this is so in the short run is considered in the next chapter. In this section we deal with the long run.

---

[16] This is why the equilibrium rate of unemployment is sometimes called the NAIRU: the non-accelerating inflation rate of unemployment. At point B inflation accelerates above its core rate; at point C it decelerates. Only at A does it stabilize.

[17] There are good reasons for this: the period corresponds to the time of the gold standard and the Bretton Woods system, both of which constrained inflation from rising too much and kept core inflation in check.

Box 12.2 **The Re-emergence of the Phillips Curve in the 1990s**

Just as the Phillips curve was threatened twenty years ago with an ignominious demise, it is now making a comeback, as the last ten years of the inflation-unemployment data in Figure 12.4 seem to suggest. What explains this revival? The analysis of this chapter offers several alternatives. First, oil prices and other sources of dramatic supply disturbances characteristic of the 1970s and 1980s have disappeared. (Oil prices did spike by nearly 30% in 1990 in the aftermath of Iraq's invasion of Kuwait, and again in 1999–2000, but not enough, or not for long enough to have a powerful effect). Second, the low inflation experience of the 1990s has undoubtedly stabilized inflationary expectations, providing one reason for a low value of core inflation. Third, and more subtly, Chapter 9 tells us that monetary policy is now governed by a new set of rules which has as its primary objective a low inflation rate, and this policy has been judged credible by participants in goods, labour, and financial markets. The lesson may well be that a Phillips curve exists as long as the monetary authorities can refrain from exploiting it unduly to manage the business cycle.

As negotiators consider the amount of inflation to be factored in wage settlements, they strive to guess it accurately. Of course, employees have an incentive to overstate the core rate of inflation, but employers have the opposite incentive. If there were no uncertainty and both sides always knew *ex ante* what inflation would be over the lifetime of the wage contract, core and actual inflation would just be equal. Uncertainty means that core inflation must be guessed. More often than not, the guesses are wrong. Yet, the principle of rational expectations implies that wage negotiators do not make systematic forecast errors. Although forecasts are almost always incorrect, the errors are largely unsystematic and average to zero. At the same time, not all workers are present at the bargaining table every year. Their wage developments reflect agreements struck in the past, and based on dated, less well-informed expectations of inflation.

These observations have two important implications. One is that there must be a link between actual inflation π and core inflation $\bar{\pi}$. Core inflation must track, albeit imperfectly, actual inflation. The backward-looking component implies that core inflation *lags* behind actual inflation, but the forward-looking component implies that core inflation *leads* actual inflation. It is the presence of both components that makes the link rather murky in the data.

The second implication relates to the long run. If actual and core inflation rates are equal on average, eq. (12.11) establishes that, in the absence of supply shocks, on average unemployment is at its equilibrium level. This is why the long-run Phillips curve is vertical as in Figure 12.3. The long run corresponds to the time it takes for core and actual inflation to catch up with each other. Views vary about how quickly this happens, and herein lie some of the most fundamental controversies in macroeconomics. These are studied in Chapter 16.

The vertical Phillips carries a crucial implication: there cannot be a long-lasting trade-off between unemployment and inflation. Demand policies cannot move the actual unemployment rate permanently away from its equilibrium level. This is why one of the lessons to be learned from Figure 12.4 is that actual unemployment rates move about equilibrium levels that are shifting over time. These successive changes in equilibrium unemployment, which were documented in Table 4.9, imply rightwards shifts of short-run Phillips curves.

12.4.3 **Aggregate Supply**

Focusing on the cyclical effect on the mark-ups captured by fluctuations in unemployment about its equilibrium rate, we have interpreted (12.11) as an augmented Phillips curve. If the cycle is captured by fluctuations in output Y about its trend $\bar{Y}$, we

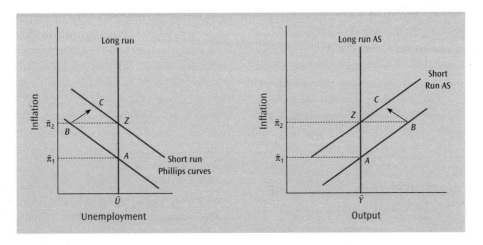

From the Short to the Long Run

For a given core rate of inflation, the economy can sustain lower unemployment at the cost of higher inflation. This trade-off is not permanent, however. When core inflation rises to be consistent with higher actual inflation, the short-run Phillips curve shifts up. In the long run (point Z) there is no trade-off.

obtain an aggregate supply schedule. The right panel of Figure 12.5 follows exactly the same logic as the left panel. In the absence of any supply shock ($s = 0$), when the core and actual inflation rates are equal ($\pi = \bar{\pi}$), output must be on trend ($Y = \bar{Y}$), hence point A. Point B describes a cyclical boom: output is above trend ($Y > \bar{Y}$)—and unemployment is below its equilibrium rate—and inflation, fuelled by the mark-ups, rises above its current core rate $\bar{\pi}$. Similarly, a recession is described by point C, and inflation falls. The result is a short-run upward-sloping aggregate supply curve.

The aggregate supply curve conveys two messages. In the short run, it is possible for GDP to fluctuate about its trend growth path, and such fluctuations are accompanied by movements of inflation about the core rate. In the absence of supply shocks, output and inflation move in the same direction. In the long run, GDP must return to its growth path, regardless of what the inflation rate is: real forces determine the growth of real activity and the growth of money supply determines inflation. The long-run aggregate supply schedule is vertical. It will, however, shift continuously to the right as a consequence of long-run economic growth.

12.4.4 **From the Short to the Long Run**

Figure 12.6 displays a short-run and a long-run Phillips curve, and the corresponding short-run and long-run aggregate supply curves. Point A, which is on both short and long-run curves, represents the long-run equilibrium, when actual and core inflation are equal ($\bar{\pi}_1$) and actual unemployment is at its equilibrium level while output is on trend. By construction, the particular short-run curve that goes through point A corresponds to core inflation rate $\bar{\pi}_1$. Now imagine a demand expansion designed to reduce unemployment and shift the economy to a point like B: the short-run trade-off means less unemployment and more output, but more inflation. However, at point B the actual rate of inflation is now π_2, higher than the core rate $\bar{\pi}_1$. Sooner or later, wage negotiators will recognize that inflation has now increased to the higher level π_2. When they do so, the short-run curves shift upward, passing through point A', which corresponds to the new core inflation rate $\bar{\pi}_2 = \pi_2$. (The equilibrium rate of unemployment and trend output are assumed constant.) The unemployment-inflation trade-off worsens: any level of unemployment now requires a higher rate of inflation. If the authorities react by picking point C, both unemployment and inflation will rise, while output will decline. Yet point C is not permanently sustainable either, since inflation remains above core inflation $\bar{\pi}_2$. Through a succession of shifts in the short-run Phillips and AS curves and associated—increasingly desperate—policy reactions, eventually unemployment and output must return to their equilibrium positions.

12.4.5 Factors that Shift the Phillips and Aggregate Supply Curves

The original position of the Phillips and aggregate supply curves in Figure 12.6 is determined by point A, that is by core inflation and by the equilibrium unemployment rate and trend GDP, respectively. This gives two reasons for the curves to shift. The first is a change in the core or underlying inflation rate: an increase in core inflation shifts the curves up. The second reason is that equilibrum unemployment and trend GDP may change. Shifts in the

equilibrium unemployment rate occur occasionally. Trend output continuously rises as the outcome of long-run growth. To avoid dealing with a curve that constantly moves to the right, later chapters will draw the AS curves with the output gap $(Y - \bar{Y})$ on the horizontal axis.

A third reason why the supply curve may shift is the occurrence of supply shocks. Let α be the share of non-labour costs in total production costs. A 1 % increase in real non-labour production costs—owing to an exchange rate depreciation or to a rise in commodity prices—raises inflation and the curve by α %. If the increase is temporary, the curve will return to its initial position, but may continue to influence inflation via core inflation. The next chapter discusses cases when this can happen.

Are commodity prices an important source of disturbances affecting the aggregate supply curve? Figure 12.7 recalls the oil shock and also illustrates the role of exchange rates. A currency appreciation makes foreign goods cheaper when expressed in domestic prices, including imported materials and

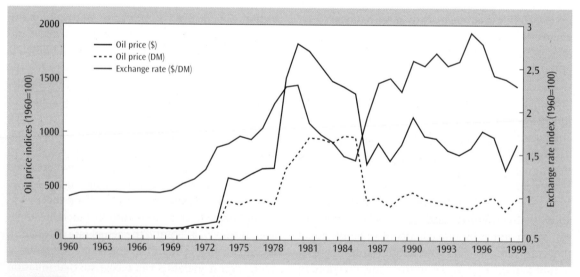

Fig. 12.7   **The Oil Shocks and the DM, 1965–1999**

The Deutschmark (DM) propitiously appreciated in the early 1970s when oil prices, set in US dollars, quadrupled. Valued in DM, oil prices rose much more modestly. At the time of the second oil shock in 1979–80, in contrast, the DM depreciated vis-à-vis the dollar, which worsened the supply-side effect in Germany. In 1986 the counter-oil shock was accompanied by another appreciation of the DM, and therefore an even stronger positive supply shock for Germany. In recent years oil prices have jumped up again, posing an inflation threat for Germany and the Euro area.
Source: IMF.

primary commodities. Exchange rate changes and commodity price changes may reinforce or offset each other. For example, the well-timed appreciation of the German currency in the 1970s had the effect of cushioning the blow of the first oil shock on Germany, since it made the price of oil increase by less in Deutschmarks than in dollars. The more recent oil price surge in the year 2000, in contrast, was aggravated by the depreciation of the euro.[18]

Summary

1. The Phillips curve was once considered a sufficient description of the supply side. Its message was that a permanent trade-off existed between unemployment and inflation. Output could rise to meet an increase in demand but would, in the process, generate a higher rate of inflation that might or might not be acceptable.

2. From the late 1960s to the late 1980s, Phillips curves vanished. Contrary to the notion of an inflation–unemployment trade-off, both inflation and unemployment rose in the mid-1970s and early 1980s, a phenomenon called stagflation.

3. Accounting for inflation starts with the study of how firms set their prices. The result is mark-up pricing, setting prices as a mark-up over production costs.

4. Production costs are separated into two broad categories: labour and non-labour costs. Labour costs rise when wages—and related costs—increase faster than labour productivity. They often represent the most important source of cost changes.

5. Nominal wages are also set as a mark-up on the nominal price level.

6. Wages are set through negotiations that acknowledge three main factors: core inflation, productivity gains, and the state of the business cycle which largely reflects the relative bargaining strength of employees and employers.

7. Wage contracts attempt both to catch up on past inflation and to protect wages from future inflation. Core inflation captures both these backward- and forward-looking aspects.

8. The consolidation of inflation accounts describes the actual rate of inflation as responding to: core inflation, demand pressure transmitted from the labour markets to goods markets, and occasional supply shocks.

9. The inflation accounts explain both why a Phillips curve may have existed for a century, and why it disappeared as the result of mounting inflation in the 1960s and early 1970s, and the two oil shocks of 1973–4 and 1979–80.

10. In the long run, unemployment returns to its equilibrium rate. Equivalently, real GDP cannot permanently stray away from the productive potential of an economy. In the long run the Phillips curve and aggregate supply schedules are vertical. The economy is dichotomized, growth and real rigidities determine the GDP and unemployment, money growth determines inflation, and there is no trade-off between inflation and unemployment.

---

[18] Formally, let P^* be the price of oil in US dollars, P the oil price quoted in euros, and S the exchange rate ($ per euro). Then $SP = P^*$, or $P = P^*/S$. Thus when S increases (the euro appreciates) P increases by less than P^*. Formally: $\Delta P/P = \Delta P^*/P^* - \Delta S/S$.

11. The Phillips curve describes the supply side and can be transformed into an aggregate supply curve using Okun's Law. The supply curve says that, for increased output to be supplied, inflation increases because production—mainly labour—costs rise faster than anticipated, or than is reflected in core inflation.

12. The core rate of inflation and the equilibrium unemployment rate determine the position of the short-run Phillips curve. The position of the aggregate supply curve is determined by the core rate of inflation and trend GDP. Any change in one of these variables leads to shifts in the short-run schedules.

Key Concepts

- supply side, demand side
- Phillips curve
- wage inflation
- aggregate supply curve
- long-run aggregate supply
- market power
- product differentiation
- oil shock
- mark-up pricing

- average or unit costs
- core inflation
- battle of the mark-ups
- real wage rigidity
- nominal wage rigidity
- menu costs
- indexation
- supply shocks
- augmented Phillips curve

Exercises

1. Suppose a government underestimates the equilibrium rate of unemployment and attempts to reduce the unemployment rate below the equilibrium rate by stimulating aggregate demand. Show the likely outcome of such a policy using the short- and long-run Phillips curves.

2. Show the effect on the short- and long-run Phillips curves of an oil shock, i.e. a once-and-for-all increase in the price of imported energy, assuming that core inflation remains unchanged. Does it matter whether the country is self-sufficient, or an oil importer?

3. A Phillips curve is represented by the following relationship: $\pi - \bar{\pi} = -10(U - \bar{U}) + s$, where s is a supply shock term. Draw the curve when $\bar{\pi} = 4\%$ and $\bar{U} = 7\%$; when core inflation rises to 6%.

4. It is sometimes claimed in the popular press that the 'new economy' will have permanently lower inflation and lower unemployment. Can you make sense of this claim using the augmented Phillips curve? What is your assessment of its validity?

5. Why might an expansionary monetary policy under flexible exchange rates increase inflation? (*Hint*: How could a depreciation be a supply shock?) How might an expansionary fiscal policy be a source of reduced inflation in an open economy with flexible exchange rates?

6. What could be the effect on inflation of an increase in value added taxes (VAT)? Of an increase in corporate profit taxes? Of an increase in personal income taxes? State your assumptions carefully.

7. The rational expectations hypothesis (Chapter 5) asserts in its weak form that agents use all available information efficiently and do not make systematic mistakes. Applied to the labour market and core inflation, what does the rational expectations hypothesis imply about core inflation and the behaviour of the short-run Phillips curve? Can you think of reasons why core inflation might require time to equal actual inflation even under rational expectations?

8. Three types of consumer price index are being used in the UK: the retail price index (RPI), RPIX, which excludes the interest charge on mortgage loans, and RPIY, which also excludes indirect taxes (VAT, duties, local taxes, etc.). These distinctions have been introduced because, using the CPI, a restrictive monetary or fiscal policy might be *inflationary* in the short run. Explain why.

9. It is often asserted that some central banks (e.g. the old German Bundesbank or the Swiss National Bank) have anti-inflation 'credibility': they have a reputation for keeping inflation low. How might this affect the core inflation rate? In particular, how might it influence the reaction of core inflation to commodity price shocks?

10. A reform of labour market institutions reduces equilibrium unemployment to 5%. Explain the effect on inflation and unemployment in the short term and in the long term.

Suggested Further Reading

The three classics on the Phillips curve are:

Friedman, Milton (1968), 'The Role of Monetary Policy', *American Economic Review*, 58: 1–17.

Phelps, Edmund S. (1968), 'Money-Wage Dynamics and Labor Market Equilibrium', *Journal of Political Economy*, 76: 687–712.

Phillips, A. W. (1958), 'The Relationship between Unemployment and the Rate of Change of Money Wage Rates in the United Kingdom, 1861–1957', *Economica*, 100: 283–99.

For critical views, see:

Gordon, Robert J. (1990), 'What is New Keynesian Economics?', *Journal of Economic Literature*, 28: 1115–71.

Tobin, James (1972), 'Inflation and Unemployment', *American Economic Review*, 62: 1–18.

More recent explorations of the inflation–output trade-off can be found in:

Ball, Lawrence, Mankiw, N. Greg, and Romer, David (1988), 'The New Keynesian Economics and the Output–Inflation Trade-off', *Brookings Papers on Economic Activity*, 1: 1–65.

Leiderman, Leonard, and Svensson, Lars O. (eds.) (1995), *Inflation Targets*, CEPR.

Symposium: The Natural Rate of Unemployment, *Journal of Economic Perspectives*, 11(1): 3–108.

The Return of the Phillips Curve, a special issue of the *Journal of Monetary Economics* Volume 44 (October 1999).

For an article that gives a precise statistical quantification of the concept of core inflation, see:

Quah, Danny, and Vahey, S. P. (1995), 'Measuring Core Inflation', *Economic Journal*, 432: 1130–44.

Many central banks (in Canada, the UK, Spain, Sweden) regularly publish an *Inflation Report* which contains detailed analyses and data about current inflationary developments.

Appendix: Mark-up Pricing

The Geometry of a Price Setter

The situation of a typical firm with market power is described in Figure A12.1. It faces a downward-sloping demand schedule; if competition were perfect, the demand curve would be perfectly horizontal and the firm would have to take prices or leave them. The demand schedule also represents average revenue, i.e. the price of one unit sold. The marginal revenue from selling one more unit, in contrast, is the sales price *less* the loss from lowering the price charged to all other consumers. This is why the marginal revenue schedule (MR) lies below the demand schedule.[19] The figure also shows the marginal cost curve (MC): it measures how much it costs to produce one more unit, all things given. The marginal cost curve is rising: since the stock of productive capital is fixed in the short run, the marginal productivity of other factors decreases when production is expanded. Microeconomic principles formally establish that the firm maximizes its profit

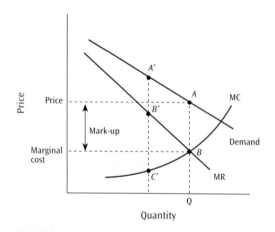

Fig. A12.1 Mark-up Pricing

Given the demand curve for its product, the firm chooses point A because that is where it maximizes its profits. The optimum occurs when the marginal revenue from an additional unit of output and the marginal cost of producing it are equal. The corresponding point B determines how much to produce, and point A shows how to price the product accordingly.

[19] Formally, the demand curve is the function $P(Q)$ linking the price P and the quantity sold Q. Total revenue is $TR = P(Q)Q$. Average revenue is $TR/Q = P(Q)$, the demand curve. Marginal revenue is $MR = \partial TR/\partial Q = P(Q) + Q(\partial P/\partial Q)$. Since $\partial P/\partial Q$ is negative (it is the slope of the demand curve), we have $MR < AR$.

when its marginal cost equals its marginal revenue, i.e. at point B where the two schedules intersect. Point B corresponds to production level Q.

The reasoning is intuitive. To sell quantity Q, the firm must choose point A on the market demand schedule by setting the price at P. To see why this is the best that it can do, consider point A'. Starting from the price and quantity corresponding to A', the firm weighs the costs and benefits of selling one more unit. Its profit increases because its marginal revenue (point B') exceeds its marginal cost (point C'). The firm will produce more until marginal revenue equals marginal cost, that is at point A. The same reasoning can be applied to any point to the right of A on the demand schedule: profits rise by selling and producing less.

For our purposes, the key result is that the selling price will be set equal to (marginal) cost—corresponding to distance BQ—plus a profit margin or mark-up—corresponding to the distance AB. The mark-up depends on the sensitivity of the market to price changes, measured by the price elasticity of demand. When demand is highly elastic—the demand curve is flat—the mark-up is small because the firm has little market power; even a small price increase would reduce demand dramatically. This is the case of perfect competition. Conversely, with a less elastic demand, the firm has an incentive to take advantage of the market's insensitivity to price increases and to charge a high mark-up. If the elasticity is constant—a reasonable approximation—the mark-up will also be constant.

Mathematical Exposition

The demand for output Q declines with the price of the good. It is represented by the demand function $Q(P)$, where $Q'(P) < 0$. The elasticity of demand η is (minus, to be positive) the logarithmic derivative:

$$(A12.1) \qquad \eta = -\frac{\partial \ln(Q)}{\partial \ln(P)} = -\frac{\partial Q/\partial P}{Q/P}.$$

Let total costs $C(Q)$ be the sum of fixed costs f and variable costs $c(Q)$, with $c'(Q) > 0$, and $c(0) = 0$. The firm's total profit is:

$$(A12.2) \qquad \text{Profit} = \underset{\substack{\text{total} \\ \text{revenue}}}{R(Q)} - \underset{\text{total costs}}{C(Q)}$$

$$= \underset{\substack{\text{total} \\ \text{revenue}}}{QP(Q)} - \underset{\substack{\text{fixed} \\ \text{costs}}}{f} - \underset{\substack{\text{variable} \\ \text{costs}}}{c(Q)}.$$

To maximize profit, the firm sets its derivative of (A12.2) with respect to output equal to zero. This implies that marginal revenue equals marginal cost:

(A12.3) $\qquad R'(Q) = C'(Q)$ or $MR = MC.$

The firm can choose either the quantity produced and sold or the price level, given demand $Q(P)$. If it chooses quantity, then the first-order condition for maximization of profit (A12.2) is:[20]

(A12.4) $\qquad P + Q\dfrac{\partial P}{\partial Q} - C'Q = 0,$

where $C'(Q)$ is the marginal cost MC. Note that

(A12.5) $\qquad Q\dfrac{\partial P}{\partial Q} = \dfrac{P(\partial P/\partial Q)}{P/Q} = -\dfrac{P}{\eta}.$

Then we find that the profit is highest when

(A12.6) $\qquad P = \dfrac{C'(Q)}{1 - 1/\eta}.$

---

[20] We assume that the second-order condition is satisfied.

This says that the price level is set as a mark-up θ over marginal cost:

(A12.7) $\qquad P = \theta MC$ where $\theta = \dfrac{1}{1 - 1/\eta} > 1.$

The mark-up is larger than unity. If the elasticity of demand is constant, so is the mark-up. (In the limiting case where competition is perfect, the elasticity of demand is infinite, the mark-up is equal to one, and firms set marginal costs equal to the (exogenously) given price level.) Note also that, when average costs are constant, average and marginal costs are equal. Average costs $AC(Q) = C(Q)/Q$ are constant when $\partial AC/\partial Q = (QC' - C)/Q^2 = 0$. This implies that $QC' = C$, or that C' (marginal costs) $= C/Q$ (average costs). If average costs are constant, then it should be clear that if (A12.7) holds then $\pi = \Delta P/P = \Delta MC/MC.$[21]

---

[21] Here we apply the rule (called rule of logarithmic differentiation) that, if $z = xy$, then $z/z = x/x + y/y$. Since we assume that the mark-up is constant, $\Delta\theta/\theta = 0$.

Aggregate Demand and Aggregate Supply

13

Money influences only monetary variables and not real variables in the long run. The problem is 'how long is long?' The 'Keynesian' answer embodied in the concept of the Phillips curve was 'too long to matter!': the 'monetarist' rejoinder was 'shorter than the Keynesians think!'; extreme rationalism provides the answer 'too short for anything else to matter!'— answers that no one concerned with either the history or the practice of stabilization policy is likely to accept.

– Harry G. Johnson

13.1 Overview

This chapter presents a unified framework for thinking about output and inflation. This framework integrates and unifies many results of previous chapters, and, together with the *IS–LM* diagram, represents the 'workhorse' of macroeconomists. Its main analytical strength lies in the distinction between aggregate demand and aggregate supply. Aggregate demand has been analysed within the *IS–LM* framework under the assumption that prices are constant. The first task is to amend this framework to account for variable prices (inflation). The result is the downward-sloping curve labelled *AD* in Figure 13.1: a higher inflation rate, all other things equal, reduces aggregate demand. The upward-sloping aggregate supply curve is already familiar from the previous chapter. In a market economy demand equals supply, so the position of the economy is described by the intersection of the *AD* and *AS* curves. Separating the two blades of the scissors is often the best way to approach any economic issue, and macroeconomics is no exception.

The *IS–LM* analysis of Chapter 11 showed that the exchange rate regime (fixed or freely floating) is of crucial importance in understanding an economy's reaction to real and financial disturbances. This observation remains valid in the presence of inflation, and this chapter maintains the sharp distinction between the two regimes.

The aggregate supply curve stresses the difference between the short run, when a trade-off is possible between unemployment and inflation, and the long run, when the supply curve is vertical. This distinc-

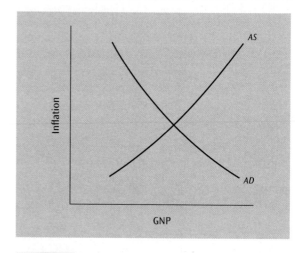

Aggregate Demand and Aggregate Supply

The macroeconomy can be fully described by the intersection of the aggregate demand and supply curves. Movements of these curves help to interpret fluctuations in output and inflation.

tion is fundamental. In the long run, demand and monetary factors have no effect on real economic variables—for example real GDP, unemployment, or the real exchange rate—while nominal variables such as inflation and the nominal exchange rate depend only on the money supply. In the short run, however, monetary and real factors interact with each other. Linking the economy's short run to the long run is a key function of the aggregate demand and supply framework. The chapter concludes with examples of the framework's usefulness.

Aggregate Demand and Supply under Fixed Exchange Rates

13.2.1 **Aggregate Demand**

A long-run restriction

Under fixed exchange rates, changes in the price level affect aggregate demand primarily via the real exchange rate. When the nominal exchange rate (S) is fixed, the real exchange rate (σ) depends on the evolution of prices at home (P) and abroad (P^*). The real exchange rate is:[1]

(13.1) $$\sigma = \frac{SP}{P^*}.$$

If domestic inflation (π) exceeds the foreign inflation rate (π^*), the real exchange rate appreciates (σ rises), external competitiveness worsens, the primary current account deteriorates, and demand for domestic goods decreases. Conversely, if inflation is lower at home than abroad, the real exchange rate depreciates (σ falls) competitiveness is enhanced, the primary current account improves, and demand for domestic goods rises. The link between the real exchange rate and the inflation differential under a fixed exchange rate is

(13.2) $$\frac{\Delta\sigma}{\sigma} = \pi - \pi^*.$$

As a first approximation for the study of an open economy, we will adopt the principle of **purchasing power parity (PPP)**. To recall, PPP is based on the idea that prices at home, prices abroad, and the nominal exchange rate move to keep the real exchange rate constant.[2] When the nominal exchange rate is fixed, PPP rules out *permanent* differences between domestic and foreign inflation. If domestic and foreign inflation rates were to diverge, the real exchange rate would appreciate or depreciate without end. As long as the exchange rate is truly fixed, deviations between domestic and foreign inflation can only be temporary. Formally,

(13.3) $$\pi = \pi^* \text{ in the long run.}$$

[1] Various definitions of the real exchange rate were presented in Ch. 7.
[2] PPP is studied in detail in Ch. 8.

This restriction is represented in Figure 13.2(*b*) as the horizontal long-run PPP line.

It was shown in Chapter 8 that money growth is the determinant of inflation in the long run. Therefore, the PPP line represents a restriction on monetary policy. Recall that in a fixed exchange rate regime with fixed prices—the *IS–LM* (Mundell–Fleming) framework—monetary policy independence is lost. This turns out also to be true in the

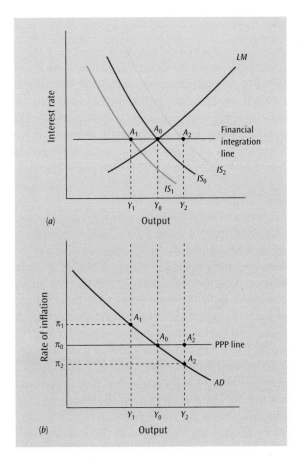

(*a*)

(*b*)

Fig. 13.2 *IS–LM* **and Aggregate Demand under Fixed Exchange Rates**

Starting from inflation π_0 at point A_0, an increase in the rate of inflation to π_1 reduces the country's external competitiveness. The *IS* curve shifts leftward in panel (*a*). The resulting decrease in demand is reported in panel (*b*). Conversely, a reduction in inflation to π_2 improves competitiveness, shifts the *IS* curve rightward, and increases aggregate demand.

| **Box 13.1** | **Money Growth under Fixed Exchange Rates** |

The real money supply must match the needs of a growing economy. If the economy grows at a rate g, and the elasticity of demand is η, then money demand, in real terms, grows at rate ηg. The nominal money growth rate is the sum of the real money growth rate and inflation. In the long run, GDP growth is given by real factors, while the inflation rate is determined by the rest of the world; the rate of nominal money growth consistent with a fixed exchange rate is[3]

(13.4) $\qquad \Delta M / M = \mu = \pi^* + \eta g.$

The same relation applies to the rest of the world, linking inflation abroad to the rate of money growth (μ^*) abroad and to the real growth rate of the rest of the world (g^*):

(13.5) $\qquad \mu^* = \pi^* + \eta g^*.$

Combining (13.4) and (13.5) we find that, for the exchange rate to be held fixed, domestic money grows at the same rate as abroad, after due adjustment has been made for relative GDP growth:

(13.6) $\qquad \mu = \mu^* - \eta(g - g^*).$

---

presence of inflation. When the central bank intervenes in foreign exchange markets to defend the parity, domestic money supply becomes endogenous and money growth must be consistent with the requirement imposed by PPP on the domestic inflation rate. Box 13.1 formally derives the endogenous rate of growth of money under fixed exchange rates.

The effect of inflation on demand

In the shorter run, what happens to aggregate demand when the inflation rate increases—or decreases—while nothing else changes? The question can be answered using the IS–LM system, keeping all other factors affecting the position of the IS and LM curves constant. The first panel of Figure 13.2 illustrates the economy in equilibrium as the intersection of the IS curve with the financial integration line at point A_0. Under fixed exchange rates with full financial integration, the nominal money supply is endogenous and the LM curve will shift to meet the IS curve and the financial integration line at the same point. In this equilibrium, the rate of inflation (π_0) is the same as abroad ($\pi_0 = \pi^*$).[4] Since $\pi_0 = \pi^*$, the real exchange

rate σ is constant. The curve IS_0 corresponds to this real exchange rate.

What happens when the rate of inflation rises from π_0 to π_1? At the given foreign rate of inflation π^*, the real exchange rate appreciates and competitiveness is eroded. The primary current account worsens and demand for domestic output declines. In the IS–LM diagram, the IS curve has shifted to IS_1. Along the LM curve, the interest rate declines, triggering capital outflows and sales of the domestic currency on the exchange markets. To maintain the same parity, the central bank intervenes and buys back its own currency. The money supply declines, and the LM curve moves to the left until it passes through point A_1 at the intersection of the new IS curve and the financial integration line. Over the span of about one year's time, the effect of a higher inflation rate is to reduce aggregate demand.

The effect on aggregate demand of a decline in inflation can be studied in the same way. If inflation falls below the foreign rate, competitiveness improves and the real exchange rate depreciates (σ falls). Consequently, the IS curve shifts to the right, and the higher demand—after the period of a year or so—is described by a point like A_2 in panel (a).

In panel (b) the inflation rates correspond to output levels given by points A_0, A_1, and A_2, and trace out the **aggregate demand curve**. The curve is

---

[3] The link between money growth, inflation, and real GDP growth is established in Ch. 8, Box 8.5.

[4] Box 13.1 shows that if the real money supply is constant, the nominal money supply grows at the same rate as the foreign price level ($\mu = \pi^*$); if the economy is growing over time, nominal money will grow faster, namely at rate $\pi^* + \eta g$, where g is the real growth rate of the economy and η is the elasticity of money demand with respect to real income.

downward-sloping because a rising inflation rate weakens the country's external competitiveness, which reduces demand for domestic goods by both domestic and foreign residents. Along the aggregate demand curve, both goods and money markets are in equilibrium. This is because the AD schedule is derived by tracking intersections of IS and LM schedules: being on the IS schedule captures goods market equilibrium, while being on LM corresponds to the money market equilibrium. It is a short-run curve because, as long as domestic inflation differs from foreign inflation, demand continues to change (so that a year later, say, output would have moved further away from Y_0 in Figure 13.2, flattening the demand curve).

Factors shifting the aggregate demand schedule

Under fixed exchange rates, any exogenous variable that shifts the IS curve also shifts the aggregate demand curve. For example, starting from an initial inflation rate π_0, an increase in government spending $\bar{G}$ is represented in Figure 13.2(a) by a shift from IS_0 to IS_2. In panel (b) the corresponding point is A'_2. The new demand schedule which passes through A'_2 must lie to the right of the initial schedule as shown in Figure 13.3. To review, other exogenous variables studied in Chapter 11 which affect the position of the IS curve include taxes $\bar{T}$, household wealth $\bar{\Omega}$, Tobin's q ('animal spirits') $\bar{q}$, and foreign income Y^*. Note that the real exchange rate is *not* included in this list, since it is now *endogenous*, depending on the evolution of domestic prices relative to foreign prices. It should be straightforward to see that an exogenous decline in these exogenous variables reduces aggregate demand at any inflation rate and therefore shifts the AD curve leftwards.

13.2.2 The Complete System

Figure 13.4 brings together aggregate demand and supply. The demand side comes in two parts: the downward-sloping short-run aggregate demand schedule AD, and the horizontal long-run PPP line results from the endogeneity of money in fixed exchange rate regimes. The supply side was derived

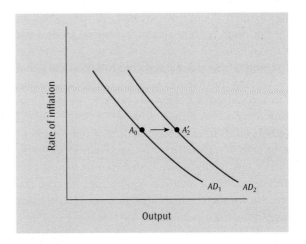

Fig. 13.3 **Shifts in the Aggregate Demand Curve**

Exogenous changes in demand which shift the IS curve also shift the short-run aggregate demand curve in the same direction. Point A'_2 corresponds to the same point in Figure 13.2, showing a demand increase at the initial inflation rate π_0.

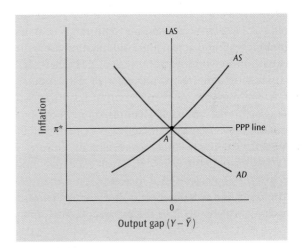

Fig. 13.4 **Aggregate Demand and Supply under Fixed Exchange Rates**

In the long run output is at its trend growth level, the output gap is zero, and inflation is equal to the foreign inflation rate. The short run is determined by the AD and AS curves. The figure depicts a situation of long-run equilibrium where all four curves intersect.

in Chapter 12 and also comes in two parts: an upward-sloping short-run supply curve *AS*, and the vertical long-run schedule *LAS*. In the long run, on the supply side, actual and core inflation are equal ($\bar{\pi} = \pi$). On the demand side, the domestic inflation rate is equal to the foreign rate ($\pi = \pi^*$). The two long-run schedules intersect at point *A*, where actual GDP is on its trend growth path. The output gap of zero ($Y - \bar{Y} = 0$) reflects the principle of long-run dichotomy.[5] The situation depicted in Figure 13.4 corresponds to a long-run equilibrium because the two short-run schedules also go through the long-run equilibrium point *A*. In the following sections, we examine several cases of short-run equilibria distinct from the long-run position and explain how the economy moves from the short to the long run.

13.2.3 Fiscal Policy and Demand Disturbances

Short run

An example of fiscal expansion—an increase in government purchases ($\Delta \bar{G} > 0$) or a tax reduction ($\Delta \bar{T} < 0$)—is shown as the rightward shift of the *AD* curve in Figure 13.5. Initially, at point *A*, the economy is long-term equilibrium. (Output *Y* is at its trend level $\bar{Y}$ and actual and core inflation are both equal to the world inflation rate π^*.) The new *AD'* curve shows the short-run effect of fiscal policy, say after one year. At point *B* output has increased —as with the Mundell–Fleming framework—but inflation has risen as well, and is now higher than abroad.[6] The rise in inflation worsens the country's external competitiveness: the real exchange rate $\sigma = SP/P^*$ appreciates as *P* increases faster than *P**. The result is a deterioration of the primary current account which cuts into the expansion. Had infla-

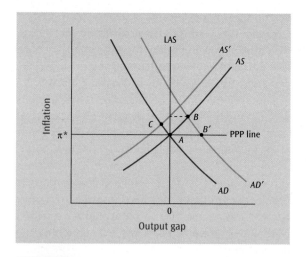

Fig. 13.5 **Fiscal Policy under Fixed Exchange Rates**

Starting at point *A*, a fiscal policy expansion shifts the *AD* curve rightwards to *AD'*. In the short run, the economy moves to point *B*. Thereafter, the expansion is reversed to meet the budget constraint, so the *AD* curve shifts back. In the long run the economy will return to its initial position, because inflation must equal foreign inflation: it cannot change if the exchange rate is to remain fixed. In the short run, as trend inflation trails actual inflation, the *AS* curve shifts upward and the economy moves to point *C*. As trend inflation returns to its long-run level, the economy ultimately returns to point *A*.

tion remained constant, and competitiveness been preserved, the outcome would have been at point *B'* with a larger increase in output. The horizontal distance between *B* and *B'* is a measure of the deterioration of the primary current account.

Long run

The long run is characterized by three observations. First, the government budget constraint rules out permanent fiscal expansions: expansionary policies must eventually be reversed and the aggregate demand curve must return approximately to its initial position *AD*.[7] Second, output must return to

---

[5] For convenience, the horizontal axis has been redrawn to measure deviations around trend output, or the output gap. This rescaling allows us to focus on the business cycle and to ignore trend output $\bar{Y}$, which is growing continuously over time.

[6] This shows that the Mundell–Fleming framework can be seen as a special case when the *AS* curve is flat. Indeed, with prices constant and supply meeting all demand fluctuations, the *AS* curve is horizontal at the $\pi = 0$ level.

[7] In the meantime, the public debt has risen and must be paid for by a permanent primary budget surplus, which requires that the *AD* curve shifts back beyond *AD*. Overlooking this effect is acceptable if the initial expansion does not last long enough to seriously increase the debt–GDP ratio. Ch. 15 returns to this issue at length.

the long-run aggregate supply line, so there can be no permanent real effect of a fiscal expansion. Third, and most importantly, inflation cannot deviate for very long from the foreign inflation rate if the exchange rate is to remain fixed. Thus, the inflation rate must return to its long-run PPP line. The conclusion is that in the long run the economy must return to point A.

Transition

The actual path taken by the economy from the immediate short run at point B to the long run at point A can be reconstructed using a couple of observations. First, the budget constraint of the government implies that an expansion today must be matched by a contraction later on to pay for debt. That means that the AD curve must eventually shift back, and even remain for some time *below* its initial position. Figure 13.5 is drawn on the assumption that the policy reversal occurs soon after point B has been reached. Another reason for the demand curve to shift back towards its initial position is that, under fixed exchange rates, *only the foreign rate of inflation π^* can ultimately sustain a permanently higher demand curve, i.e. a permanently higher inflation rate at zero output gap.* This is merely a restatement of the logic of the PPP line.

Second, the supply side will affect the adjustment path to the new equilibrium. The backward-looking component of core inflation reacts to actual inflation conditions, 'catching up' with (and the forward-looking perhaps even anticipating) current inflation. As a result, the short-run AS curve will shift upward. This leads to a position like point C or even further down along AS'; since AD is temporarily below its initial and long-run position, GDP falls below trend level and the inflation rate declines. GDP is below trend because fiscal policy is no longer expansionary and is possibly contractionary, while higher inflation worsens the primary current account. From now on, with output below trend, core inflation exceeds actual inflation.[8] With core inflation declining, the AS curve continues to shift

down. The economy moves down along the AD curve which eventually settles back at its long-run position as a period of low inflation re-establishes external competitiveness. The trajectory is roughly from point C to point A.[9]

To summarize, a fiscal expansion, or more generally a real demand disturbance, is necessarily temporary. Initially it leads to an expansion of output, although at the cost of an increase in the inflation rate and a deterioration in the external position. Over time the GDP returns to its trend path while inflation winds down, tracing out a broad spiral from A to B, to C, and then towards A from below. The recent experience of Ireland in the 1990s, described in Box 13.2, is an excellent illustration of how an economy reacts to an exogenous expansion of demand and illustrates the role of a fixed exchange rate regime in shaping economic policy responses.

13.2.4 Monetary Policy and Realignments

In fixed exchange rate regimes, monetary policy is beyond the control of the central bank. The bank's task is to keep its interest rate close to the rate prevailing in the country to which it pegs its exchange rate, and therefore to supply money as demanded by the public at that interest rate. This loss of monetary independence was often seen in Europe, where smaller countries in the European Monetary System fixed their exchange rates and effectively handed over control of monetary policy to larger, more influential countries, most often Germany. A consequence of this means accepting monetary policy decisions 'from abroad', even when they are unrelated to national conditions. Growing frustration in this area is said to have been a prime motivation for European Monetary Union, although a monetary union per se does not change that fact that member countries relinquish national autonomy over monetary policy.

The only possibility of retaining some degree of monetary independence under fixed exchange

---

[8] This is a key result of the analysis of the supply curve in Ch. 12: whenever we are to the left of the long-run AS curve, by construction, actual inflation is below core inflation.

[9] Actually, the economy will need to move below point A, because a period of lower inflation than abroad is required to bring the real exchange rate back to its initial level.

Box 13.2 Ireland

Ireland will go down in economic history as the economic miracle of the last decade of the twentieth century. In the 1980s, this country was counted among the 'sick men of Europe', with unemployment in excess of 15%. Disappointing growth, high inflation, and alarming state finances—the public debt exceeded 140% of GDP in 1988—prompted MIT Professor Rudi Dornbusch in 1989 to describe Ireland as 'locked in a high unemployment and high debt trap'. Ten years later, virtually everyone was taken by surprise. Table 13.1 gives details. From 1991 to 2000 annual real growth averaged 8%, compared with the EU average of 2%; by 1996, inflation had declined to under 2%. By the end of the decade, the government ran such large budget surpluses (2–3% of GDP in the last half of the decade) that by 2000 the national debt had fallen to 40% of GDP. The most striking indicator of Ireland's success was the reversal of more than a century of persistent outmigration of its citizens, mostly young men, and mostly to the USA and the UK. By the mid-1990s Ireland was a significant net receiver of migrants.

What triggered the initial boom can be readily understood using the AS–AD framework. In the early 1990s, Ireland worked hard to encourage foreign direct investment using EU subsidies and its own tax breaks, and was successful in attracting major foreign corporations with its low labour costs and 'hard punt' strategy of fixing the exchange rate. Especially US firms saw Ireland as an export gateway to all EU markets. Investment and exports grew rapidly during the period, often at double-digit rates. On the supply side, fiscal austerity built up credibility in low inflation, while a national consensus on nominal wages (so-called 'Partnership Agreements') tended to make nominal wages and prices more rigid in the short run. Finally, the effects of a decade of high real capital investment and return migration certainly shifted the *LAS* curve to the right at a faster pace than in previous decades.

By 2000 however, Ireland began to show tell-tale signs of an inflationary economy in a fixed exchange rate regime. While inflation was initially low enough to admit Ireland to Euroland in 1998, by the end of 2000 it had reached 6–7%. House prices roughly doubled in the period 1995–2000. As a member of the European Monetary Union, Ireland could no longer raise the nominal exchange rate to cool off the economy; furthermore, at 1–2% of Euroland GDP, it has negligible influence on ECB monetary policy. Ironically, the budget surplus was so large that the government actually *cut* taxes and granted high pay increases to public sector employees, adding fuel to the fire! In the end, the Irish boom will probably be choked off by a real exchange rate appreciation, inducing a recession similar to the move from *B* to *C* in Figure 13.5. It is likely that a slowdown of investment and consumer spending will occur, the latter driven by a deflation of real estate and other asset prices. At the advent of the introduction of the Euro, Ireland has become a symbol for benefits, as well as potential problems that arise when regions in a currency union experience uneven, or asymmetric shocks.

Table 13.1 Irish Economic Performance, 1980–2000

Period	GDP growth (% p.a.)	Inflation (% p.a.)	Debt/GDP ratio (%)	Gov't budget surplus/GDP ratio (%)	Unemployment rate (%)
1981–1985	2.6	11.3	93.3	−11.4	14.3
1986–1990	3.7	3.2	109.0	−5.4	15.6
1991–1995	5.4	2.5	92.8	−2.1	14.5
1996–2000	10.4	1.9	61.9*	1.7	8.7*

* 1996–1999.
Source: OECD, Eurostat, EU.

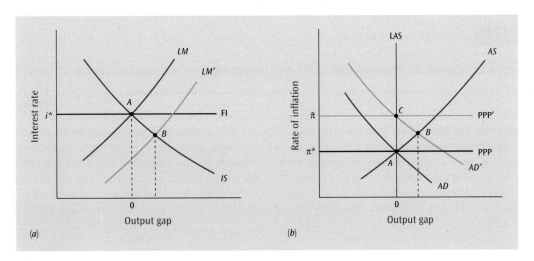

(a)   (b)

> **Fig. 13.6**   **Monetary Policy under Fixed Exchange Rates with Capital Controls**
>
> Capital controls, if effective, suppress the interest rate constraint in panel (a). A monetary expansion can then shift the *LM* curve to *LM'* and the *AD* curve to *AD'*. At the new equilibrium (point *B* in both panels) domestic inflation exceeds the foreign rate. Periodic devaluations of this sort shift up the PPP line and make point *C* possible.

rates is to introduce capital controls and change the parity from time to time. Figure 13.6 illustrates the case of a country that undertakes a monetary expansion. When capital controls work, they prevent arbitrageurs from linking domestic interest rates with the foreign rate of return. Consequently, the financial integration line ceases to be binding in panel (a) and the monetary authorities can shift the *LM* curve to *LM'*, raising the rate of growth of money and reducing the interest rate. In panel (b), the monetary expansion is represented by a rightward shift in the aggregate demand schedule to *AD'*. Point *B* in both panels shows that the desired expansionary effect is achieved at the cost of some inflation.

The expansion is temporary, however, for two reasons. First, at point *B* actual inflation exceeds core inflation. Over time, core inflation catches up and the *AS* curve shifts upward until it passes through point *C*. There, the rate of inflation has increased by the same amount as the rate of money growth ($\Delta\pi = \Delta\mu$); the real money supply is constant—more precisely, it is growing along with the economy's real growth—and monetary policy has run its course and ceases to have any expansionary impact. Yet

—and this is the second reason—point *C* is not sustainable in the long run either, because it is above the PPP line. Inflation is higher at home than abroad, the real exchange rate keeps appreciating, and competitiveness deteriorates. As demand weakens, the *IS* curve shifts to the left and the *AD* curve moves back from *AD'* to *AD*.

There are two ways of restoring external competitiveness eroded by inflation. The first is to reduce inflation below the foreign rate for some period of time. This is rarely done because it implies a long period of low output and high unemployment. One celebrated case—that of Britain after the First World War—is recounted in Box 13.3. Most countries choose the second option, changing the exchange rate parity. A **devaluation** resets an overvalued real exchange rate to a level that restores external competitiveness.[10]

---

[10] When the exchange rate is allowed to float, its movements occur in response to market conditions, on a continuous basis. These movements are called an **appreciation** when the currency's value increases, or a **depreciation** in the opposite case. When the exchange rate is fixed, it is the monetary authorities that decide its value. They can change the parity: they can make the currency more valuable in terms of foreign currencies (a **revaluation**), or they can lower its value (a **devaluation**).

> ### Box 13.3   Churchill versus Keynes
>
> During the First World War the price level doubled in Britain, and the fixed exchange rate of sterling against gold was suspended. It was always understood that, once the war was over, sterling would return to the pre-war parity of 85s. per ounce of fine gold. Winston Churchill, the young Chancellor of the Exchequer, was determined to carry out this task and indeed restored the gold parity in 1925. By ruling out a devaluation, Britain's competitiveness could be restored only through falling domestic prices. Table 13.2 shows that the deflation was massive and, true to the Phillips curve, was accompanied by a significant rise in unemployment. In fact, although Britain maintained the gold parity until 1931, prices never quite fell to pre-war levels, and unemployment remained high, even before the onset of the Great Depression. John Maynard Keynes, who was critical of this policy, wrote later that 'the loss of national wealth entailed . . . was enormous. If we assume that only half the unemployment was abnormal, the loss of national output may be estimated at more than £100 million per annum—a loss that persisted over several years.'[11]
>
> ### Table 13.2   Britain after the First World War: The Consumer Price Index, Inflation, and Unemployment, 1913–1931
>
> | | CPI (1913 = 100) | Inflation (%) | Unemployment (%) |
> |------|-----|------|------|
> | 1913 | 100 | 2.0 | 2.1 |
> | 1919 | 219 | 9.5 | 2.4 |
> | 1920 | 248 | 13.2 | 2.4 |
> | 1921 | 224 | −9.7 | 14.8 |
> | 1922 | 181 | −19.2| 15.2 |
> | 1923 | 176 | −2.8 | 11.3 |
> | 1924 | 176 | 0.0 | 10.9 |
> | 1925 | 176 | 0.0 | 11.2 |
> | 1926 | 171 | −2.8 | 13.7 |
> | 1927 | 167 | −2.3 | 10.6 |
> | 1928 | 167 | 0.0 | 11.2 |
> | 1929 | 167 | 0.0 | 11.0 |
> | 1930 | 157 | −6.0 | 14.6 |
> | 1931 | 148 | −5.7 | 21.5 |
>
> Sources: Maddison (1991); Mitchell (1978).

Figure 13.7 shows how a devaluation restores the real exchange rate to its competitive value. By the use of occasional devaluations—supported by capital controls—a country may maintain inflation at a level permanently higher than abroad.

Similarly, a country with lower inflation than abroad sees its competitiveness rise. To get back to the initial situation with unchanged nominal exchange rate, it needs to endure a period of higher inflation. It may instead choose periodically to **revalue** its currency. Provided capital controls are effective, a country can regain limited monetary policy independence under fixed exchange rates; temporary effects (point B in Figure 13.6) may be sustained for a while. With recurrent revaluations, inflation may remain permanently lower than abroad.

[11] J. Keynes (1930: 165).

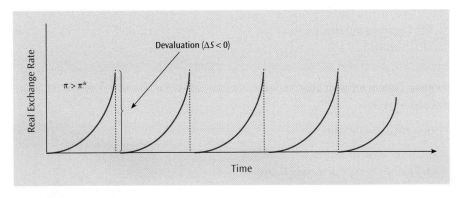

Fig. 13.7   **Realignments Restore the Real Exchange Rate**

With a higher rate of inflation at home, the real exchange rate appreciates (σ rises). A devaluation resets the real exchange rate and restores competitiveness. For a time at least, periodic devaluations permit the economy to sustain a higher rate of inflation than abroad while fixing the exchange rate.

13.3   Aggregate Demand and Supply under Flexible Exchange Rates

Under flexible exchange rates, aggregate demand reacts differently to inflation, because the roles of nominal money and nominal exchange rates trade places. The nominal money supply, endogenous under fixed exchange rates, is now exogenous and under the control of the central bank. The nominal exchange rate in contrast, is no longer exogenously fixed, but is determined by market forces and is endogenous. Before discussing the flexible exchange rate regime in detail, we must first understand how a flexible exchange rate changes the required rate of return demanded by investors (the interest rate parity condition) and how a permanent change in inflation will affect the position of the financial integration line in the Mundell–Fleming model. When this has been established, we can see how inflation affects aggregate demand when the exchange rate is flexible.

13.3.1   Interest Rate Parity Revisited

The financial integration condition of the Mundell–Fleming framework states that the domestic interest rate is equal to the foreign rate of return. Exactly

what this foreign rate of return was, was intentionally left open. In this section we make this condition more precise. The foreign rate of return is not simply the rate of interest abroad, because it pays its return in a different currency. An appreciation of the domestic currency in terms of dollars, for example, reduces the domestic value of dollar assets and therefore the return from holding them. When international investors compare interest rates in various countries, they take that aspect into account by equating returns *given expected exchange rate changes*. Denoting by $\Delta S/S$ the expected rate of nominal appreciation of the domestic currency, the modified **interest rate parity** condition is[12]

(13.7) $$i = i^* - \Delta S/S.$$

In this expression, i^* represents the nominal foreign interest rate. If the domestic currency is expected to appreciate by, say, 5% over the next year, the foreign interest rate must be 5% higher to compensate for the

---

[12] The exact derivation of this condition as well as its modification for risk is presented in Ch. 19.

expected capital loss.[13] If instead a depreciation is anticipated, $\Delta S/S$ is negative and the domestic interest rate is higher than abroad.

13.3.2 Aggregate Demand and the Complete System

The effect of inflation on demand

To see why inflation affects aggregate demand differently under flexible exchange rates, consider Figure 13.8. As before, we assume that all other exogenous factors that affect demand (the *IS* and *LM* curves) remain unchanged. This applies not only to the money supply, but also to fiscal policy instruments and the exogenous determinants of consumption and investment. An 'unchanged monetary policy' means a constant rate of nominal money growth (μ), which, under flexible exchange rates, determines the rate of inflation in the long run.[14] Holding money growth constant, an increase in the rate of inflation from π to π' reduces the rate of growth of the real money supply (M/P)—measured as ($\mu - \pi$). This change in real balances implies a leftward shift in the *LM* curve, which after some time reaches the position *LM'* in panel (*a*).

At the same time, the higher inflation rate prompts the expectation of an exchange rate depreciation, by purchasing power parity. The previous section argued that financial markets will incorporate this expectation into the required return for internationally mobile capital. The expected return on foreign assets increases and the financial integration line shifts upwards.[15] Under flexible exchange rates, the position of the *IS* curve is endogenous (see Chapter 11): the exchange rate will appreciate until, through its effect on the primary

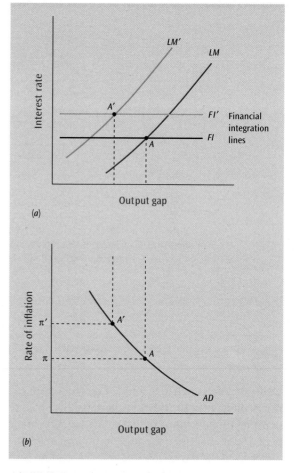

Fig. 13.8 *IS–LM* and Aggregate Demand under Flexible Exchange Rates

The figure shows the effect of an increase in the rate of inflation on aggregate demand when the rate of nominal money growth remains constant (μ). Starting at point *A* with an inflation rate π, inflation rises to π'. This reduces the rate of real money growth and moves the *LM* curve to the left in panel (*a*). Demand is reduced (point *A*), hence the downward-sloping curve in panel (*b*).

---

[13] In Ch. 11 we implicitly assume that $\Delta S/S = 0$. Given that prices are taken to be constant at home and abroad, PPP would indeed predict a constant exchange rate.

[14] According to (8.4), the long-run inflation rate is $\pi = \mu - \eta g$.

[15] Strictly speaking, this will only hold if money growth increases permanently. If the money growth is only temporary, the financial integration line may remain unchanged. In this case, the intensity of the effect will be greater, but the qualitative conclusions are not affected.

current account, the *IS* curve passes through point *A'*. The *LM* curve and financial integration line fully characterize the outcome.

The overall effect of a higher rate of inflation is a decline in output. Reporting this result in panel (*b*) establishes that the short-run aggregate demand curve is downward-sloping. It is a short-run curve because, as long as the inflation rate stays high, the real money stock growth rate is declining and the *LM* curve keeps shifting to the left.

To summarize, the short-run aggregate demand curve is downward-sloping under both fixed and flexible exchange rates, but for different reasons. When exchange rates are fixed, inflation affects demand through external competitiveness. Inflation does not affect the real money supply because money is endogenously supplied by the central bank through exchange market interventions. Under flexible rates, the situation is reversed. Competitiveness is under the dominating influence of the nominal exchange rate, not of prices. Inflation affects the evolution of the real money supply for any nominal growth rate μ set by the central bank.

What moves the demand curve

The strong result from Chapter 11—that movements in the *IS* curve are 'crowded out' by exchange rate changes over time—remains valid. In the end, neither fiscal policy, nor animal spirits, nor any other exogenous change in demand can shift the aggregate demand curve for very long because these impulses are offset by a change in the real exchange rate. The aggregate demand curve shifts when the *LM* curve does, primarily when the real money supply is changing. *Under flexible exchange rates, the nominal growth rate of the money supply is the sole determinant of the position of the AD curve.*

The complete system

Figure 13.9 presents the complete system under flexible exchange rates. It includes the short- and long-run aggregate supply curves as well as the short-run aggregate demand curve. The horizontal **money growth line** is the equivalent of the PPP line under fixed rates, except that now the monetary authorities control its position. Being free to choose the rate of growth of nominal money, they can determine the long-run inflation rate. The PPP principle ensures that, in the long run, the exchange rate makes up the difference between the domestic and foreign inflation rates. The figure depicts a long-run equilibrium: actual output is equal to

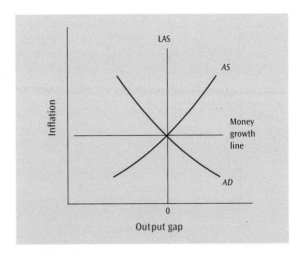

Fig. 13.9 **Aggregate Demand and Supply under Flexible Exchange Rates**

In the long run output is at its trend growth level (a zero output gap) and the money growth rate determines the rate of inflation. The figure depicts long-run equilibrium when the short-run aggregate demand and supply curves pass through the same point as the long-run schedules.

trend output—a zero output gap—as required by the supply side, and inflation is set by money growth as required by the demand side. If the foreign rate of inflation is below the domestic rate, the exchange rate is depreciating; in the opposite case, it is appreciating.

13.3.3 **Monetary Policy**

Long run

The long-run effects of an expansionary monetary policy, i.e. of an increase in the rate of growth of the nominal money supply, are straightforward. Monetary neutrality implies that inflation will increase permanently by the same increase in monetary growth, as will the rate of exchange rate depreciation ($-\Delta S/S$). The real side of the economy is left unaffected. In Figure 13.10, the economy moves from point A to point C and the vertical distance AC represents the increase in the money growth rate.

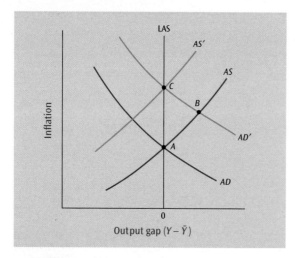

Fig. 13.10 **Monetary Policy under Flexible Exchange Rates**

Starting at point *A*, a monetary policy expansion shifts the *AD* curve rightwards to *AD'*. In the long run the economy will settle at point *C*, with GDP equal to trend output and the increase in inflation equal to the increase in the money growth rate. Short-run equilibrium occurs at point *B*. Thereafter core inflation tends to its long-run level and the economy moves from point *B* towards point *C*.

Short run

The expansionary effect of an increase in money growth is described in Figure 13.10 by the shift of the aggregate demand curve from *AD* to *AD'*. The economy moves to point *B* in the short run: output is raised (and unemployment declines); inflation increases, but by less than the money growth rate; and therefore the real money supply expands. If inflation were to rise immediately in the same proportion as money, the long run would be achieved instantaneously. For a temporary expansionary effect to occur, the wage- and price-setting process must have some inertia arising from rigidities somewhere in the economy. This is given by the slope of the AS curve.

Transition

The transition will take the economy in steps from point *B* to point *C*. At point *B*, where output is above its growth trend level, the actual rate of

inflation exceeds the core rate. What happens during the transition—and therefore the details of the trajectory—depends on the behaviour of the core rate of inflation. To the extent that it is backward-looking, core inflation is sluggish. Initially the *AS* curve does not move and the economy reaches point *B*. As core inflation begins to track actual inflation, the short-run *AS* curve shifts upward and the economy moves from *B* towards *C*, along curve *AD'*. Along the path from *B* to *C*, actual inflation exceeds the core rate of inflation, while output declines as the real money growth rate is eroded by the rise in inflation.

Yet, core inflation has a forward-looking component which could anticipate that the long run is achieved at point *C*. If core inflation were purely forward-looking, it would immediately adjust to the long-term inflation rate. If the short-run *AS* curve shifts at once to position *AS'*, the transition bypasses point *B* and the economy jumps directly from point *A* to point *C*. In that case neutrality occurs instantaneously and monetary policy loses its effectiveness. Two conditions are required for that to happen. First, core inflation must be entirely forward-looking. Second, price- and wage-setters must be willing and ready to raise prices and wages to the full extent of the change in core inflation. The existence of either price or wage stickiness or of a backward component in core inflation is what makes the short run different from the long run.

In summary, an expansionary monetary policy increases output and inflation in the short run. In the long run, the effect falls entirely on higher inflation and not at all on output—this is the neutrality result under flexible exchange rates. In the short run, the backward-looking component of core inflation and price or wage stickiness create the non-neutrality needed for an output effect, while the forward-looking component tends to bring neutrality forward to the shorter run. The role of core inflation obviously requires closer scrutiny. This is the task of Chapter 16.

13.3.4 Fiscal Policy

For reasons which were treated in detail in Chapter 11, fiscal policy fails to move the *IS* curve, and therefore aggregate demand, because its effects are ultimately frustrated by the exchange rate reaction. A fiscal expansion leaks abroad because a real appreciation leads to a worsening of the primary current account. A fiscal contraction provokes a real depreciation which generates an increase in demand. For all practical purposes, the aggregate demand curve does not move.

13.4   How to Use the *AS–AD* Framework

This section illustrates how the complete system may be used to analyse important questions. It serves three main purposes: to develop familiarity with the framework; to bring up the role of a number of principles developed earlier; and to consider some recent economic developments of general interest.

13.4.1 **Supply Shocks**

Supply shocks occur when the production conditions change. Adverse supply shocks include the exogenous loss of factors of production or natural disasters (crop failures, earthquakes). It also characterizes the shift from central planning to markets in Eastern and Central Europe. Examples of favourable supply shocks are technological advances and the discovery of natural resources. They create difficult problems for policy-makers who are typically ill-equipped to face the consequences—Box 13.4 recalls how oil shocks shattered the world economy after 1973.

Box 13.4   **The Oil Shocks of the 1970s and 1980s**

The two oil shocks of 1973–4 and 1979–80 represent a turning point in post-war economic history. We can see from Figure 13.11 how the oil shocks marked the end of the rapid growth performance of most European countries and Japan, and were followed by markedly higher inflation and unemployment rates. By the end of the 1980s inflation had been rolled back, but employment and output growth remained significantly below the golden levels of the 1960s. The challenge posed by oil shocks in fact led to the development of many of the ideas presented in this chapter, just as the *IS–LM* framework was a response to the Great Depression.

    Major commodity prices started to rise in the early and late 1970s. While most of these increases were quickly reversed, nominal oil prices increased sixfold in two steps, with a partial reversal in 1986. The role of policy is highlighted by the choice of the exchange rate regime. At the time of the first shock, the industrial countries were trying to preserve a system of fixed exchange rates, including several European countries regrouped in the 'Snake' arrangement.[16] Countries that were determined not to let inflation rise did not wish to maintain a fixed exchange rate with a more complacent rest of the world. Some countries, including Austria, Germany, Switzerland, and the Netherlands, opted for the low-inflation strategy; Japan, Italy, Spain, and the UK implicitly opted for the high-inflation approach; most other European countries adopted an intermediate stance with little or no policy reaction. Along the way, the international monetary system based on fixed exchange rates could not accommodate such policy divergences and collapsed.

---

[16] Ch. 19 describes the international monetary arrangements; Ch. 20 discusses the European experience.

Box 13.4   **Continued**

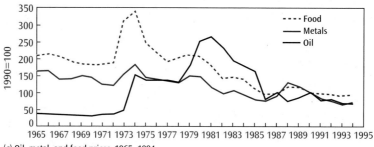

(a) Oil, metal, and food prices, 1965–1994

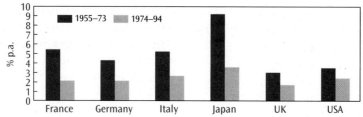

(b) GDP growth, 1965–1994

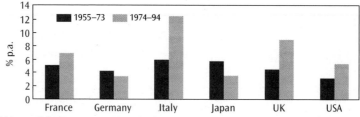

(c) Average inflation

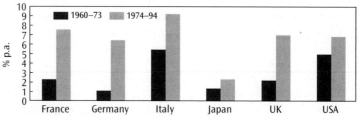

(d) Average unemployment

Fig. 13.11   **The Oil Shocks: A Turning Point for Six Countries, pre- and post-1973**

Panel *(a)* shows the prices of key commodities relative to the average consumer price index in the advanced economies. Real oil prices increased from 1973 until 1981, then declined significantly at the time of the counter-oil shock in 1986. Other commodity prices increased earlier, in 1971–2, but were quickly reversed, and in fact declined over the following decade. Panels *(b)*–*(d)* confirm that, with few exceptions, since the first oil shock of 1973–4 all key macroeconomic variables (growth, inflation, unemployment) have changed for the worse in OECD countries. *Sources*: IMF; OECD *Main Economic Indicators*.

A short-term policy dilemma

Until now, the short-run aggregate supply curve was considered assuming away supply shocks. Supply shocks occur when the supply curve shifts, when imported commodity prices increase faster than inflation. Under these circumstances, producers face increased production costs. Yet Chapter 12 showed that producers pass on higher intermediate goods prices on to their own prices. As a result, inflation will be higher for any level of output and of the core rate of inflation:

$$(13.8) \qquad \pi = \bar{\pi} + a(Y - \bar{Y}) + s.$$

In Figure 13.12 the short-run aggregate supply curve shifts upward from AS to AS'. The move from point A to point B represents **stagflation**, a combination of declining real growth and rising inflation. If the relative price increase is just a one-off event, it might seem that the AS curve will shift back to its initial position. This interpretation is optimistic, however. Facing higher prices, workers may demand

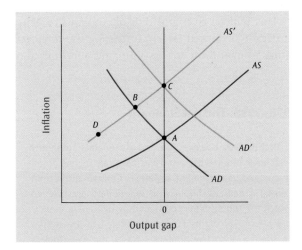

An Adverse Supply Shock

An adverse supply shock shifts the AS curve up to AS'. The economy undergoes stagflation as it moves from point A to point B. If the authorities decide to avoid a fall in output and a rise in unemployment, they can adopt expansionary demand-side policies and drive the economy back to long-run equilibrium at point C. If instead they decide to prevent inflation from rising, they can adopt contractionary demand-side policies and aim at point D.

higher nominal wages. Formally, the backward-looking component of core inflation $\bar{\pi}$ rises, which means that, even after the commodity price increase has been absorbed (s goes back to zero in equation (13.8)), the AS curve is unlikely to shift back quickly.

This poses a serious policy dilemma for governments. One approach is to soften the blow on output and unemployment by adopting an expansionary policy (monetary or fiscal, depending on the exchange rate regime). Aiming at point C, and shifting the AD curve to AD' in Figure 13.12, hastens the return to trend growth but at the cost of higher inflation. Another approach is to prevent inflation from ever rising so that core inflation never changes. This calls for a prompt *contractionary* policy reaction, moving down the short-run aggregate demand schedule until it goes through point D. Once the shock has worked itself through (and $s = 0$), the aggregate supply curve moves back to AS and the restrictive demand policy may be lifted to return to point A.

The exchange rate regime

The previous discussion makes it clear that core inflation is the driving force behind the short-run aggregate supply curve after the initial shock. It tends to increase because of its backward-looking component. The forward-looking component depends on which long-run equilibrium is expected to be reached eventually. If the authorities are known or are expected to aim at point D in Figure 13.12 with a restrictive monetary policy, the forward-looking component is likely to act towards bringing core inflation down and the trajectory will shift roughly from A to B and back to A. If instead policy is lax, aiming at point C, core inflation will rise for a while, pushing the AS curve above AS'. The trajectory will be from A to B and beyond, higher and to the left of B along the new AD' curve. However, since we have a negative output gap, core is above actual inflation, so the AS curve will eventually start shifting back towards AS', even though the one-off supply shock is over. The economy winds up at point C.

Under flexible exchange rates, each country can choose its long-run inflation rate and therefore can determine whether point *A* or point *C* will be reached. This is not the case with a fixed exchange rate regime where the long-run position is determined by the PPP line, i.e. the 'foreign' rest of inflation. What this means is that, in presence of a serious supply shock, a fixed exchange rate regime can be maintained only among like-minded countries which have compatible views of how they will react. Box 13.4 explains the role this issue played in the aftermath of the oil shocks.

Lessons from supply shocks

Three general lessons can be drawn. First, an adverse supply shock is bad news. It adversely affects growth, unemployment, and inflation at the same time, in contrast with the Phillips curve trade-off. Second, demand management instruments are not appropriate for a supply shock. When the aggregate supply curve moves up and to the left, demand management cannot deal with both inflation and output. Demand-side policies must make the difficult choice between taking the shock as an increase in inflation or as a drop in output with higher unemployment. Third, the exchange regime becomes crucial. A fixed exchange rate can be maintained only among countries that adopt the same strategy.

13.4.2 Demand Shocks

Exogenous shifts in demand are another source of movements in output. It is sometimes difficult, however to identify these shifts. German reunification is a striking example of a source of an unexpected demand surge in Europe during the first half of the 1990s. Even more interesting is the fact that the shift in demand hit European countries asymmetrically. Box 13.5 describes the situation faced by the Netherlands, which from the early 1980s until the advent of the euro had committed to a fixed exchange rate regime with Germany.

In Figure 13.14 an adverse demand shock is represented by a leftward exogenous shift of the short-run aggregate demand curve. The economy moves from point *A* to point *B*. In principle, the government has instruments at its disposal—monetary or fiscal policy, depending on the exchange rate regime—that could restore the *AD* curve to its original position. This was the standard policy response of the 1960s. During the 1990s, however, the reaction has been remarkably subdued in European countries.

This reluctance is not difficult to explain. After a decade dedicated largely to erasing the inflation scars from the oil shocks (bringing core inflation

---

Box 13.5 **Monetary Policy in the Netherlands 1978–1998: The DM Standard**

From the European Monetary System's creation in 1979 until its twilight in 1998, the Bank of Netherlands maintained a fixed parity of the guilder vis-à-vis the Deutschmark. Only in two instances, in 1979 and 1982, was the Dutch currency depreciated, each time by a mere 2%. Figure 13.13 shows how a truly fixed exchange rate regime must function. The increasing closeness of Dutch and German interest rates seen in panel (*a*) vividly captures the meaning of the financial integration line in the Mundell–Fleming framework. Panel (*b*) shows that the obligation of the Bank of Netherlands to accommodate domestic money demand at the German interest rate leads to an erratic money growth pattern from year to year. The contrast with the smooth pattern of money growth in Germany until 1989 is striking.

In the 1990s, however, the loss of monetary autonomy which was implied by a fixed exchange rate regime posed a demand management problem. German unification caused a demand boom with inflationary pressure, to which the Bundesbank responded by tightening monetary policy. The Netherlands, of course, had less reason to adopt a restrictive monetary policy, but nevertheless followed the German lead and let interest rates rise. Later, the tables turned: in the latter half of the 1990s, the Dutch economy experienced a surge in growth which exceeded Germany's. Just as the theory predicts, money supply growth in the Netherlands was also higher, adding fuel to an already hot economy. Contractionary fiscal policy remained the only available instrument of demand management.

Box 13.5   **Continued**

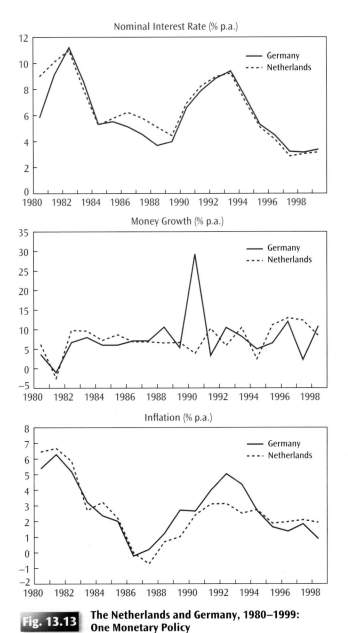

Fig. 13.13   **The Netherlands and Germany, 1980–1999: One Monetary Policy**

During the last two decades before monetary union, Germany and the Netherlands experienced a deepening of financial integration under conditions of a credible fixed exchange rate regime. In the 1990s, the Netherlands had to face both a period of slower and faster growth than Germany without the ability to use monetary policy to moderate these swings.

Sources: OECD, IMF.

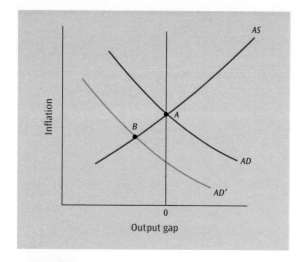

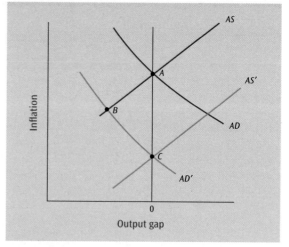

Fig. 13.14 **An Adverse Demand Shock**

An adverse demand shock is represented by a leftward exogenous shift of the short-run aggregate demand curve. The economy moves from point A to point B. In principle, the government has instruments at its disposal—monetary or fiscal policy, or both—which could restore the AD curve to its original position. This was the standard policy response of the 1960s. During the 1990s, however, the reaction has been remarkably subdued in European countries.

Fig. 13.15 **Disinflation**

Disinflation aims at bringing the economy from point A to point C. Using demand-side policies implies adopting contractionary monetary or fiscal policies, pushing the aggregate demand curve from AD to AD'. The short-run equilibrium at point B explains why disinflation is usually painful: it requires a period of low output and high unemployment. Long-run equilibrium is achieved at point C when the short-run aggregate supply curve has shifted to AS'. The speed of this shift depends on the time taken by core inflation to catch up with lower actual inflation.

down), most countries felt that the results had to be consolidated. This meant that monetary growth could not be allowed to rise again. Another policy achievement of the 1980s was the generally successful control over public indebtedness. Most governments felt that their intertemporal budget constraint precluded any decisive use of fiscal policy to counteract a weakening of aggregate demand.[17]

13.4.3 **Disinflation**

Once an economy has settled on a high rate of inflation, how can policy bring it down again? Under flexible exchange rates, the answer is simple:

reduce the growth rate of the nominal money supply. Under a fixed exchange rate arrangement, real appreciation is necessary. In both cases, it means shifting down the short-run aggregate demand curve from AD to AD' in Figure 13.15, in an attempt to move from point A to point C on the long-run aggregate supply curve. The short-run effect of disinflationary policy corresponds to point B: inflation declines but so does output, while unemployment rises. At point B actual inflation is below core inflation. Eventually, the short-run aggregate supply curve returns to AS' and the disinflation is complete.

The interesting question is: how long does it take to move from point B to point C, and how much output is lost along the way? One measure of the **output cost of disinflation** is the **sacrifice**

[17] Ch. 16 provides more details on governments' reluctance to use their demand management instruments. Ch. 15 studies the public debt situation.

ratio. It compares the cumulated increase in the rate of unemployment with the reduction in inflation achieved during that period. For example, the Phillips curves of Figure 12.4 show disinflation in Euroland and the UK over the period 1980–4. In both countries the unemployment rate rose significantly; the corresponding sacrifice ratios over this period were roughly 2.5 percentage points of inflation for 1 point of unemployment for Euroland, compared with a ratio of 7 : 1 for the UK. Clearly, this ratio is only a descriptive device, as it does not control for the credibility of disinflation policies —an important determinant of how quickly core inflation declines.

The output cost of disinflation is lower the faster the *AS* curve comes down. That, in turn, depends on the speed at which core inflation adapts to a declining inflation rate. The backward component of core inflation causes sluggishness in shifts of the *AS* curve, while the forward-looking component accelerates the adjustment. The importance of the backward-looking component is that it depends on wage- and price-setting institutions. The next section looks at the role of wage indexation, and Box 13.5 evaluates the role of the timing of wage negotiations. The forward-looking component is often referred to as the 'psychological' nature of price- and wage-setting. Wage negotiators may have opposing incentives in stating their expectations. It may be good bargaining tactics for workers to argue that inflation is high, while employers prefer to predict declines in the rate of inflation. Jointly, however, employers and employees have an incentive to be as close as possible to target, for errors may be costly in terms of competitiveness and profitability. This often leads to a conservative approach in assessing the future path of inflation: core inflation tends to move slowly over time. Negotiators may be influenced by outside indicators. In particular, the government may play a role by signalling its intentions and calling for moderation.[18] In some countries the government may actually even sit at the negotiating table.

13.4.4 Nominal Rigidities and Wage Indexation

Departures from trend growth and equilibrium unemployment occur because of **nominal wage and price rigidities**. Why do those who set prices and wages fail to bring them to a level that would keep the economy on its long-run trend with unemployment at its equilibrium level? Even if wages could be reset every day or every month, it takes time to know with some degree of accuracy the evolution of the price level. Errors, even if short-lived, are unavoidable.

One solution is to index wages to the price level, matching price increases with wage increases, one for one. Partial indexation compensates for only some fraction of inflation. **Wage indexation** has been adopted, formally or informally, in many countries in an attempt to reduce the risks involved in setting wages when there is much inflation uncertainty. However, indexation institutionalizes the backward-looking component of core inflation. This is a drawback at times of disinflation: Section 13.4.3 has shown that disinflation is faster and less painful the weaker is the backward-looking component of core inflation. As explained in Box 13.6, this is one reason why the practice was abandoned in the 1980s.

---

[18] One such signal is the rate of wage increase in the public sector, which is part of government spending (*G*) but also acts to set a lower bound on expected $\Delta W/W$. More on this can be found in Chs. 15 and 16.

Box 13.6 **Wage Negotiations: The Time Dimension**

In most European countries and in the USA, wage negotiations are *staggered* over a year or more. One wage negotiation takes into account the previous one, and may even anticipate the next one. Employees do not want to be bettered by other employees. Employers do not want to be underpriced and must hold their labour costs in line. In contrast, in Japan wage negotiations are *synchronized*. They take place every year at roughly the same time, the so-called 'spring offensive' (*shunto*). Each industry opens up bargaining, but closely monitors the state of play elsewhere. When one bargain is struck, it sets the trend and all the others follow quickly. For a time, wage negotiations in Northern Europe were centralized and therefore highly synchronized. Elsewhere they are staggered, but some negotiations are *trend-setting*: they result in similar agreements later on and sometimes even trigger readjustments to previously reached ones, thus injecting a dose of synchronization. With wage staggering, aggregate nominal wages (the average of all nominal wages) move slowly, which retards the return to equilibrium unemployment. The *AS* curve will appear flatter. With full synchronization, average nominal wages are stable between negotiations, and then jump. This implies a steeper *AS* curve. The implications for the economy are profound: either a quick return to the equilibrium unemployment rate if the real wages are set right, or a prolonged departure if they are set incorrectly.

The situation is different in economies where inflation is high and has been so for a long time. There it is common to have mandatory or mutually agreed indexation schemes for wages. Brazil was particularly advanced in this regard, indexing virtually *all* nominal prices, including house rents, corporate balance sheets, taxes, and public utilities rates. Such indexation schemes can often reduce the staggering considerably, with the same effect as an increase in synchronization of wage-setting.

Although wage indexation removes some of the costs of high inflation to households and firms, it has serious adverse side-effects. First, indexation generally perpetuates any real wage gain achieved. This gives an incentive to any group of wage-earners to be the first to bid for higher wages. The result is that all groups rush to be first, as much to protect themselves as to achieve a head-start. Second, indexation reduces both public and government support for anti-inflation policies. This is why Germany, ever since its famous hyperinflation in the 1920s, has made indexation illegal. The third drawback is that indexation makes disinflation costlier in terms of unemployment. When inflation is on the way up, nominal wages trail behind prices: real wages are reduced and labour demand is robust. When inflation is on the way down, wages indexed on past inflation trail actual inflation: real wages rise, firms' profits are squeezed, and unemployment rises. This is why most European countries with legal or simply widespread indexation clauses eliminated them in the 1980s (Belgium, France, the UK, and possibly Italy), much against the will of trade unions. Fourth, indexation eliminates downward real wage flexibility as real wages are at least constant unless there is a sharp burst in inflation. The lack of flexibility is a source of unemployment when an adverse supply shock occurs.

Summary

1. The macroeconomy is analysed as the interplay of aggregate demand and aggregate supply. This framework emphasizes the distinction between the short run and the long run, when output returns to its trend growth path.

2. The short-run aggregate demand curve is downward-sloping. Under fixed exchange rates, an increase in inflation above the foreign rate erodes external competitiveness and reduces total demand for domestic goods. Under flexible exchange rates, for a given growth rate of the nominal money supply, an increase in the inflation rate lowers the rate of growth of the real money stock, and hence has a contractionary effect on aggregate demand.

3. In the long run, inflation is restricted to be equal to foreign inflation under fixed exchange rates. Under flexible rates, the inflation rate is determined by the rate of growth of the nominal money supply.

4. Only under flexible rates can the monetary authorities set the money growth rate. Some independence can be achieved under fixed exchange rates by the use of capital controls. The possibility of devaluing or revaluing the currency further allows a country under otherwise fixed exchange rates to choose its long-run rate of inflation.

5. Under fixed exchange rates, fiscal policy can affect aggregate demand and output. The effects of a fiscal policy action are temporary. First, in the long run output must be back on trend and inflation is determined by the foreign rate of inflation. Second, the fiscal policy action itself is temporary because of the government's budget constraint.

6. A fiscal expansion initially raises the output level at the cost of a higher rate of inflation. Over time, as core inflation rises and the unavoidable retrenchment of fiscal policy occurs, demand returns to trend output.

7. Under fixed exchange rates monetary policy is ineffective. This is also the case for fiscal policy under flexible exchange rates.

8. Under flexible exchange rates, a monetary expansion initially raises output and inflation. Over time, inflation continues to increase, eroding the real money supply and bringing output back to its trend growth path.

9. An adverse supply shock simultaneously lowers output and raises inflation. Demand management policies are ill-equipped to deal with a supply shock. They may cushion the fall in income at the cost of more inflation, or reduce the inflationary impact at the cost of a deeper fall in output and more employment.

10. Disinflation requires reducing the rate of monetary growth. It can be costly in terms of lost output and above-equilibrium unemployment.

11. The faster core inflation adjusts, the lower the costs of disinflation. Wage indexation and the staggering of wage negotiations are among the institutional factors that reinforce the backward-looking component of core inflation.

Key Concepts

- PPP line
- aggregate demand curve
- appreciation, depreciation
- revaluation, devaluation
- interest rate parity
- money growth line
- stagflation
- output costs of disinflation
- sacrifice ratio
- nominal wage and price rigidity
- indexation

Exercises

1. Consider the following *AD* curve given by $Y = Y_{-1} + \alpha - \beta\pi + \gamma\mu + \phi\Delta G$. How do the values of γ and ϕ depend on whether the economy has fixed or flexible exchange rates? Interpret what 'β' means under the two regimes.

2. Explain, using the *AS–AD* and *IS–LM* framework under flexible exchange rates, why a monetary expansion which is permanent is more likely to have an expansionary effect than a temporary expansion.

3. Use the two *AD* curves given in Exercise 1 combined with the following aggregate supply curve:

$$\pi = \bar{\pi} + a(Y - \bar{Y}) + s.$$

Trace out the *short-run* effect under both fixed and flexible rate regimes of: (i) a one-off increase in government spending; (ii) a permanent increase in money growth.

4. Disinflation is associated with output loss for two reasons. Explain.

5. A government wants to use monetary policy under a flexible exchange rate to keep actual GDP above its trend growth rate for ever. In the *AS–AD* diagram, show graphically the consequences of such a policy.

6. Assume that core inflation is entirely forward-looking and that expectations are rational. What are the effects of fiscal policy (under fixed exchange rates) and monetary policy (under flexible exchange rates) on output and inflation? Consider both cases of expansionary or restrictive policies, at your discretion.

7. The adoption of a *currency board* has become one method of choice for stabilizing the transforming economies of Central and Eastern Europe. Simply put, a currency board fixes the exchange rate to a foreign currency and removes all discretion of the central bank in choosing monetary policy instruments; its sole function is to trade foreign exchange for domestic currency at the declared parity. Why might this be a particularly effective way of stabilizing in a country with a bad history of inflation?

8. Suppose in the future a large region of Euroland is hit by a negative shock to investment. Trace out the initial effects and the adjustment to the long run. How might expectations of inflation in a monetary union versus a floating exchange rate regime affect the adjustment?

9. In the 1990s, when both countries used different monies, the Netherlands fixed its exchange rate with that of Germany. What is the effect on output and inflation of (*a*) a temporary and (*b*) a permanent increase in German inflation? (*Hint*: use the *AS–AD* diagram.) Discuss possible policy reactions.

10. In the course of their transformation to market economies, most Eastern and Central European countries underwent a burst of very high inflation (monthly rates of 20–50% or more) while output collapsed. Using the *AS–AD* framework, what is the most coherent explanation of why this occurred?

Suggested Further Reading

The aggregate demand and supply framework is fully set up and used to analyse the oil shock and its aftermath in:

Bruno, Michael, and Sachs, Jeffrey (1985), *The Economics of Worldwide Stagflation*, Harvard University Press.

Episodes of inflation and its eradication in Western Europe are described in the following articles:

Bean, Charles, and Symons, James (1989), 'Ten Years of Mrs. T', NBER *Macroeconomics Annual*, MIT Press.

Blanchard, Olivier J. (1987), 'Reaganomics', *Economic Policy*, 5.

Giavazzi, Francesco, and Spaventa, Luigi (1989), 'Italy: The Real Effects of Inflation and Disinflation', *Economic Policy*, 8: 133–72.

Sachs, Jeffrey D., and Wyplosz, Charles (1986), 'The Economic Consequences of President Mitterrand', *Economic Policy*, 2: 261–322.

Episodes of very high inflation in Eastern Europe and history can be found in:

Balcerowicz, Leszek (1994), 'Poland: The Economic Outcomes', *Economic Policy*, 19S: 71–87.

Dornbusch, Rudiger, and Fischer, Stanley (1986), 'Stopping Hyperinflations Past and Present', *Weltwirtschaftliches Archiv*, 122: 1–47.

Havrylyshyn, Oleh, Miller, Marcus, and Perraudin, William (1994), 'Deficits, Inflation and the Political Economy of Ukraine', *Economic Policy*, 19: 353–401.

Sargent, Thomas (1982), 'The End of Four Big Inflations', in R. E. Hall (ed.), *Inflation*, University of Chicago Press.

Appendix: The *AS–AD* Model

Derivation of *AS* and *AD* curves

This appendix provides a formal presentation of the model underlying the *AD–AS* framework. The aggregate supply curve is described by the following linear equation:

(A13.1) $$\pi = \bar{\pi} + h(Y - \bar{Y}) + s.$$

where $\bar{\pi}$ is core (i.e. expected inflation), $\bar{Y}$ is trend output, assumed to be constant, and h is a parameter. The supply shock term s will be assumed to remain equal to zero. Generally a bar over a variable indicates the steady state level.

The real exchange rate is

(A13.2) $$\sigma_t = \frac{S_t P_t}{P_t^\star}$$

with long-term level $\bar{\sigma}$. As we assume purchasing power parity (PPP), $\bar{\sigma}$ is constant. The PPP assumption is also taken to imply that the expected rate of nominal exchange rate depreciation is equal to the expected inflation differential $\bar{\pi} - \bar{\pi}^\star$. Then, the interest rate parity condition, which says that domestic interest rate is equal to the given and constant foreign rate $i^\star$ plus expected depreciation, can be written as:

(A13.3) $$i_t = i^\star + \bar{\pi}_t - \bar{\pi}^\star$$

An interesting result is that the previous assumption implies that the domestic and foreign real interest rates are always equal:

(A13.4) $$r_t = i_t - \bar{\pi}_t = i^\star - \bar{\pi}^\star = r^\star$$

To simplify notation, we will assume that $r^\star = 0$. If μ_t is the growth rate of the nominal money stock between period $t-1$ and t, we have:

(A13.5) $$\frac{(M/P)_t - (M/P)_{t-1}}{(M/P)_{t-1}} = \mu_t - \pi_t \quad \text{or}$$

$$(M/P)_t \cong (M/P)_{t-1}(1 + \mu_t - \pi_t).$$

Aggregate demand is derived from the *IS* and *LM* curves. The *IS* curve, linearized around the long-run equilibrium,[19] is written as:

(A13.6) $$Y_t - \bar{Y} = \beta FP_t - \gamma(\sigma_t - \bar{\sigma}) - \phi(r_t - \bar{r}),$$

where β, γ, and ϕ are fixed parameters and *FP* is a catch-all indicator of fiscal policy which includes both public

[19] The only exception is trend inflation, noted $\bar{\pi}_t$ out of equilibrium and $\bar{\pi}$ in equilibrium.

spending and tax effects, and is equal to zero in the long run. The real exchange rate captures the effect on demand via the current account. Note that (A13.4) and the assumption $r^\star = 0$ imply that the long-run real interest rate is zero; i.e. $\bar{r} = 0$.

The *LM* curve describes equilibrium in the money market. It is expressed, again in a linearized form, as:

(A13.7) $$(M/P)_t = aY_t - bi_t$$

Using (A13.5) the money market equilibrium condition *LM* can be rewritten as:

(A13.8) $$(M/P)_{t-1}(\mu_t - \pi_t) = a(Y_t - Y_{t-1}) - b(i_t - i_{t-1}).$$

Long-Run Equilibrium

It is useful first to characterize the long-run state to which the economy converges. The no-growth assumption implies that the economy is stationary and settles to its long-run equilibrium when all real variables are constant. The *IS* curve (A13.6) shows that output is on its trend ($Y = \bar{Y}$), fiscal policy is back to neutral ($\overline{FP} = 0$), and the real exchange rate returns to its level implied by the PPP assumption ($\sigma = \bar{\sigma}$). The LM curve then implies $\bar{\mu} = \bar{\pi}$, the money neutrality proposition.

Fixed Exchange Rate Regime

Aggregate demand

Under a credibly fixed exchange rate regime, the nominal money supply is endogenous, at the level needed to satisfy demand, i.e. driven by the LM curve. The interest parity condition, which ties down the domestic interest rate to the foreign rate, recognizes that the exchange is expected to be constant:

(A13.9) $$i_t = i^\star.$$

From (A13.8), the rate of money growth is:

(A13.10) $$\mu_t = \pi_t + \frac{a(Y_t - Y_{t-1})}{(M/P)_{t-1}}.$$

Aggregate demand is entirely determined by the *IS* curve:

(A13.11) $$Y_t - \bar{Y} = \beta FP_t - \gamma(\sigma_t - \bar{\sigma}) - \phi(i^\star - \bar{\pi}_t).$$

Note that, to preclude realignments, long-run inflation must be equal to the foreign inflation rate, which applies to the core rate:

(A13.12) $$\bar{\pi}_t = \pi^\star.$$

The aggregate demand curve is found by substituting (A13.3) and (A13.4) in (A13.11), with $r = r^* = 0$:

(A13.13) $\qquad Y_t - \bar{Y} = \beta FP_t - \gamma(\sigma_t - \bar{\sigma})$

Demand depends on: (1) fiscal policy, as in Chapter 11; (2) domestic inflation since an increase in the rate of inflation leads to a real appreciation as domestic goods become more expensive, via (A13.2). This is the reason why the *AD* curve is downward-sloping.

Fiscal policy

A one-period fiscal expansion is captured by a one-off increase in *FP* from $FP_0 = 0$ to FP_1.[20] We assume that at time $t = 0$ the economy was in its long-run equilibrium position. This allows us to compute the rate of change of the real exchange rate:

(A13.14) $\qquad \dfrac{\sigma_1 - \bar{\sigma}}{\bar{\sigma}} = \pi_1 - \pi_0 = \pi_1 - \pi^*$

In period $t = 1$ demand and supply are given by, respectively,

(A13.15) $\qquad Y_1 - \bar{Y} = \beta FP_1 - \gamma\bar{\sigma}(\pi_1 - \pi^*)$

(A13.16) $\qquad \pi_1 = \pi^* + h(Y_1 - \bar{Y})$.

Solving (A13.15) and (A13.16) we obtain period 1 inflation and output, and we then use (A13.14) to retrieve the real exchange rate:

(A13.17) $\qquad \pi_1 = \pi^* + \dfrac{\beta h FP_1}{1 + \gamma h \bar{\sigma}}$

(A13.18) $\qquad Y_1 = \bar{Y} + \dfrac{\beta FP_1}{1 + \gamma h \bar{\sigma}}$

(A13.19) $\qquad \dfrac{\sigma_1 - \bar{\sigma}}{\bar{\sigma}} = \dfrac{\beta h FP_1}{1 + \gamma h \bar{\sigma}}$

The first-period effect of the fiscal expansion is an increase in both inflation and output, and a real appreciation arising from higher inflation at a constant nominal exchange rate.

Moving to period $t = 2$, *FP* returns to its initial value $FP_0 = 0$. We have demand and supply given respectively by

(A13.20) $\quad Y_2 - \bar{Y} = \beta FP_0 - \gamma(\sigma_2 - \bar{\sigma}) = -\gamma\bar{\sigma}(\pi_2 - \bar{\pi})$

(A13.21) $\qquad \pi_2 = \bar{\pi} + h(Y_2 - \bar{Y})$

The solution is $Y_2 = \bar{Y}$ and $\pi_2 = \bar{\pi}$, i.e. a return to the steady state.

---

[20] The government budget constraint implies that there cannot be a permanent expansion. It also requires that an expansion be matched by an eventual contraction. We disregard the latter for simplicity. Eager students will explore this case on their own.

Flexible Exchange Rate Regime

Aggregate demand

With the exchange rate no longer expected to remain constant, the domestic interest rate is obtained from the parity condition (A13.3) and $r = r^* = 0$. The real exchange rate is now determined by the goods market equilibrium condition *IS* (A13.6):

(A13.22) $\qquad \sigma_t - \bar{\sigma} = \dfrac{\beta FP_t - (Y_t - \bar{Y})}{\gamma}$

This equation says that an increase in output requires a depreciation to increase foreign demand for domestic goods. An increase in domestic demand, via fiscal policy, requires a real appreciation to crowd out foreign demand.

Domestic demand is determined by inserting (A13.3) and the money market equilibrium condition *LM* (A13.8) in the goods market equilibrium condition *IS* (A13.6):

(A13.23) $\quad Y_t - Y_{t-1} = \dfrac{(M/P)_{t-1}(\mu_t - \pi_t) + b(\bar{\pi}_t - \bar{\pi}_{t-1})}{a}$

For given inflation expectations and a given rate of nominal money growth, an increase in actual inflation leads to a reduction in demand by reducing real cash balances. This is the reason why the *AD* curve is downward-sloping.

Fiscal policy

Fiscal policy is ineffective under flexible exchange rates by the same reasoning as in Chapter 11. Indeed (A13.25) shows that any change in fiscal policy is entirely absorbed by the real exchange rate—an expansionary fiscal policy leads to a real appreciation and (A13.23) shows that demand cannot change unless the real money supply is changed. When the fiscal policy impulse is reversed, the real exchange rate returns to its original position.

Monetary policy with backward-looking core inflation

We first consider the case when core inflation is backward-looking, as would be the case with full wage and price indexation:

(A13.24) $\qquad \bar{\pi}_t = \pi_{t-1}$.

We look at an exogenous permanent increase in its growth rate from μ_0 to μ_1, again assuming that the economy initially was in steady state equilibrium, so both actual and core inflation, the nominal interest rate, and the rate of change of the exchange rate all increase in the long run by the same proportion as the increase in money growth:

(A13.25) $\bar{\pi} - \pi_0 = i^\star - i_0 = \dfrac{S_0 - \bar{S}}{\bar{S}} = \mu_1 - \mu_0.$

This raises a small difficulty with the monetary equilibrium condition $M/P = \mathcal{L}(Y, i)$. The increase in core inflation $\bar{\pi}$ implies an equal increase in the nominal interest rate and a permanent reduction in the real money stock. This requires that, for some period of the adjustment process, inflation overshoots its long-run level $\bar{\pi}_1$. In period 1, aggregate demand and supply are given respectively as:

(A13.26) $Y_1 - Y_0 = \dfrac{(M/P)_0(\mu_1 - \pi_1) + b(\bar{\pi}_1 - \bar{\pi}_0)}{a}.$

(A13.27) $\pi_1 = \bar{\pi}_0 + h(Y_1 - \bar{Y}_0).$

Since inflation expectation in period 1 is assumed in (A13.24) to be $\pi_1 = \bar{\pi}_0$, the solution of (A13.29) and (A13.30) is:

(A13.28) $\pi_1 - \pi_0 = \dfrac{(M/P)_0 h}{a + (M/P)_0 h}(\mu_1 - \mu_0)$

(A13.29) $Y_1 - Y_0 = \dfrac{(M/P)_0}{a + (M/P)_0 h}(\mu_1 - \mu_0)$

The monetary expansion leads to an increase in inflation which is less than the increase in money growth, unless we have extreme cases ($a = 0$, $h = \infty$). Since long-run inflation will ultimately reach the rate of money growth, see (A13.25), we find that the acceleration is gradual. Output rises as well.

In subsequent periods inflation continues to rise as core inflation tracks actual inflation with a lag, which raises nominal interest rates and decreases the demand for money. Inflation will eventually overshoot its long-run level in order to reduce real money balances to the starting (equilibrium) value.

Monetary policy with forward-looking core inflation

The case when core inflation is forward-looking is more delicate and not fully treated here. If people recognize that inflation will eventually increase exactly as money growth, core inflation is set at its new long-run rate:

(A13.30) $\bar{\pi}_t = \bar{\pi} = \mu_1 \quad \forall t = 1, 2 \ldots$

In that case, and assuming that prices are fully flexible, monetary policy has no effect on the real economy. Nominal variables jump immediately to their new long-run equilibrium (which is the same as in the previous case) and all real variables (output, the real interest and exchange rates) remain unchanged. Indeed, the *IS* curve implies that, with no changes in fiscal policy, real output too remains unaffected. The price level must jump discretely and immediately after the event to bring down the real money stock as demand has been reduced by the increase in the nominal interest rate.

Business Cycles

14

Almost all of the phenomena of economic life, like many other processes, social, meteorological, and others, occur in sequences of rising and falling movements, like waves.

– Eugen E. Slutsky

14.1   Overview

Economies tend to grow over time, but in an uneven fashion. They tend to *fluctuate* around their long-term trends, as shown in Figure 11.1. Just as Chapter 3 studied trend growth and neglected shorter-run fluctuations, this chapter studies fluctuations around trend growth in more detail. The tendency for an economy to behave in a cyclical fashion has been considered a key puzzle of economic life for centuries, going as far back as the biblical observation that seven years of feast are followed by seven years of famine. It has long been observed that these patterns of expansion and contraction in activity, or **business cycles**, occur with some regularity. A recession does not necessarily mean negative growth, however. For fast growing countries like South Korea and China, a year of 4–5% growth is sometimes considered a slump!

Many questions come to mind when thinking about business cycles. Is there such a thing as a 'typical' cycle? What is its frequency? Are cycles a result of purely predictable, or *deterministic* factors, or are they random in nature? Does each period of expansion sow the seeds of an unavoidable future recession? Conversely, is it the case that **recessions** are invariably followed by **booms**, if one is willing to wait long enough? Which aspects of economic life are subject to cyclical movements and which ones seem unaffected by boom and bust? This chapter begins with some stylized facts about the business cycle. Economic forecasters and policy planners intently study the economic scene to detect signals of future macroeconomic developments. They watch a number of variables that tend to move systematically with, or even anticipate, the business cycle. Especially important are **turning points**, when the economic cycle reaches a **peak** or a **trough**. Firms which correctly anticipate the end of a recession will

hire more workers and invest in additional capacity ahead of the upturn, in order to have ample goods to sell. Firms which correctly foresee the end of a boom can slow down or cancel hiring and investment plans, and thus avoid more costly adjustments later on.

This chapter's goal is to explain business cycles. Previous chapters have given us most of the tools we need. Yet, while the *IS–LM* and *AS–AD* models are designed precisely to explain deviations of GDP from trend, more is needed. First, it is useful to track the behaviour of variables besides GDP—unemployment, prices, wages, firms' profitability, interest rates, etc. Second, we have used the *IS–LM* and *AS–AD* frameworks by assuming some exogenous changes (e.g. in the money supply, or in entrepreneurial spirits), but is there something more systematic in these changes? Can they be themselves explained as endogenous phenomena?

In fact, there are two ways of thinking about business cycles. One is that business cycles are largely predictable, self-perpetuating phenomena, much like the mythical perpetual motion machine. Section 14.3 describes what would be needed for that to happen and concludes that it is highly unlikely. A second, more fruitful, insight conceives of the economic system as a black box, which receives stimuli at one end and transforms them into business cycles at the other. This 'impulse-propagation' mechanism approach is now generally accepted among business cycle students as the most fruitful way of proceeding, and is the subject of the rest of the chapter.

It remains to identify the primary source of stimuli which drive the cycle—the impulses—and how exactly they are transmitted—the propagation mechanism. Here macroeconomists often disagree. The two premier contending views correspond to the distinction introduced in Chapter 10 between price stickiness and flexibility. Section 14.4 presents the sticky price view, which can be seen as an extension of ideas introduced in Chapters 11–13.

Section 14.5 explains the alternative case of flexible prices, which is often called the theory of **real business cycles**. The last section summarizes the current state of thinking on the two competing paradigms.

14.2 Stylized Facts about Business Cycles

As with growth in Chapter 3, a useful first step is to identify 'stylized facts', i.e. features that tend to be common to all business cycles over time and across countries. Business cycles are usually studied using quarterly data, in order to reveal enough details within the time period—usually just a few years—that a typical cycle takes to unfold.

14.2.1 The Duration and Magnitude of Cycles

Panel (a) of Figure 14.1 presents the path of GDP in the UK since 1961. It displays an estimated trend which 'smooths out' the uneven movements of real GDP. These fluctuations are even more evident in panel (b), which presents the deviations of actual from trend GDP, or **detrended** GDP, magnifying the deviations revealed in the upper panel. Cycles seem to be recurrent, with two to three years above trend, two to three years below. When the economy turns down from its peak, the recession phase starts. As it runs up from a trough, this is the time of recovery, leading to an expansion.

Stylized Fact 1:

In advanced economies, real GDP growth fluctuates in a recurrent but irregular fashion, with an average cycle length of five to eight years.

Although business cycle episodes tend to be similar, Figure 14.1 shows that they are far from identical. For example, the 1976 recovery was short-lived, leading to a 'double-dip' in 1977 following the 1975 recession. Conversely, the recovery that followed the early 1980s recession was long-lived. This irregularity makes it a delicate exercise to pinpoint peaks and troughs in the business cycle. In the USA, the task has long been performed by the National Bureau of Economic Research (NBER), which appoints a business cycle committee of independent economists. They declare as a peak the quarter that immediately precedes two consecutive quarters of decline in GDP. Similarly, a trough immediately precedes two consecutive quarters of positive growth. In Europe, business cycle dating is just as widely practised, although not on such a formal basis. For comparison, Table 14.1 identifies

Table 14.1 Descriptive Statistics of Business Cycles, 1970–1994

	No. of completed cycles	Av. cycle length (quarters)	Max. cycle length (quarters)	Min. cycle length (quarters)	Av. deviation from midpoint (%)
UK	2	31.5	42	21	2.5
France	2	35	48	22	2.1
Germany	2	36	48	24	2.9
Italy	3	24	41	11	3.4
Japan	2	36.5	44	29	2.7
USA	3	22	35	6	3.0

Source: IMF, authors' calculations.

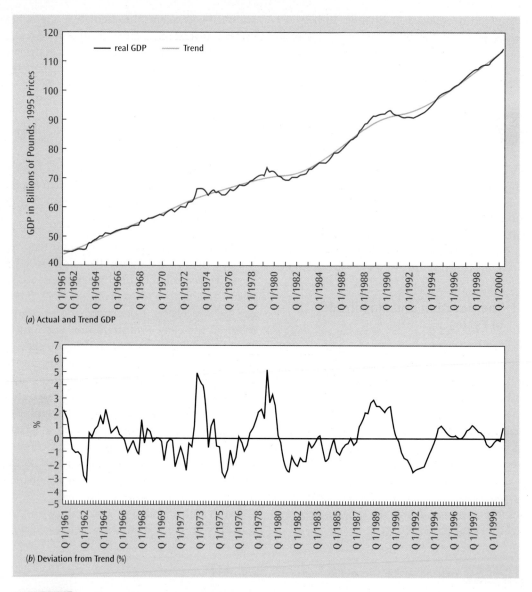

(a) Actual and Trend GDP

(b) Deviation from Trend (%)

Fig. 14.1 **Actual and Trend GDP and Detrended GDP, UK, 1961–2000**

Panel (a) shows the evolution over time of actual and trend real quarterly GDP in the UK. Panel (b) displays the series after it has been detrended, or separated from its trend.
Source: OECD, *National Accounts*.

peaks as immediately preceding declines in output below trend for a period of four or more quarters. Troughs are defined in a similar fashion. In the case of the UK between 1970 and 1994 (see Figure 14.1), this rule identifies three troughs and three peaks. From peak to peak, the first cycle lasted just over five years while the second one spans more than ten

years. Table 14.1 presents a few descriptive statistics for business cycles in several countries.[1] The average peak-to-peak cycle length is about 30 quarters or

---

[1] The table presents data on *completed* cycles, from peak to peak. Looking at Fig. 14.1, it might seem that we observe three cycles but the last one is not yet complete; i.e. the peak had not been reached in the interval observed.

Box 14.1   Famous Cycles

Business cycles, like comets, bear the names of their discoverers. Simon Kuznets was a Russian-born US economist who received a Nobel Prize for his work on growth. Russian economist Nikolai Kondratieff developed his theory of long-wave cycles in the 1920s before he was arrested and disappeared; the official *Soviet Encyclopaedia* then wrote about his work: 'this theory is wrong and reactionary'. It was also in the 1920s that Joseph Kitchin, a South African statistician and gold trader, uncovered his own more rapid cycles of 2–4 years periodicity, which are associated with inventory movements, bank clearings, and wholesale prices. Clement Juglar, a 19th-century French physician, first studied cycles in human births, deaths, and marriages before turning his skills to

interest rates and credit conditions. These *Juglar cycles*—which involve fluctuations of investment spending, GNP, inflation, and unemployment—are perhaps the closest thing to the business cycle that we will study in this chapter.

Interestingly, one of the most robust and regular cycles in economic activity is the *seasonal cycle*, which coincides with the seasons of the year. Movements of output in agriculture, manufacturing, construction, and tourism have obvious seasonal components which sometimes swamp business cycle fluctuations in magnitude, as do patterns in overall output associated with bank holidays, summer and winter weather, and harvests.

7.5 years, with large differences in minimum and maximum length. While these are the cycles most widely monitored and referred to as business cycles, a number of cyclical fluctuations in economic activity have long fascinated researchers. Box 14.1 describes some of these cycles.

Popular discussions of economic conditions emphasize short-run fluctuations associated with business cycles, to the point that cycles can have significant political repercussions, including bringing governments down. Yet the last column of Table 14.1 shows that these fluctuations represent only 2–5% of average GDP from peak to trough. Movements of GDP around its trend are clearly dwarfed by the evolution of the trend itself, as Figure 14.1 amply illustrates. Thus, the second stylized fact:

Stylized Fact 2:
Measured relative to average GDP and to the growth process, the amplitude of business cycle fluctuations is small.

To detect common aspects of business cycles, we will use **Burns–Mitchell diagrams**. These diagrams give a visual summary of the average behaviour of macroeconomic variables over a typical business cycle, measured in relation to (as a deviation from) their

respective values at the cyclical peak.[2] Figure 14.2 displays these 'reference cycles' for real GDP for several OECD countries. Note that the data are not detrended to keep them free of manipulation. Consistent with Stylized Fact 2, the figures reveal the importance of the growth trend, even at the short horizon of business cycles. Business cycles do appear to be similar across countries; for example, the average recession seems to last four to five quarters in all countries examined, and much shorter than the average expansion. This is an encouragement to search for regularities in other variables, too.

14.2.2 Correlation with Output over the Cycle

The behaviour of GDP is used to identify business cycles, but what can we say about other important

---

[2] Named after US economists Arthur Burns and Wesley Mitchell, two of the most influential empirical researchers on the 'trade cycle' in their time. They developed this technique at the NBER in the 1940s and 1950s. Their work was severely criticized in 1947 by Dutch-born Chicago economic theorist and econometrician Tjalling Koopmans as 'measurement without theory'. His attack turned several generations of economists away from the descriptive approach developed by Burns and Mitchell. A half-century later, Burns and Mitchell are making a comeback of sorts.

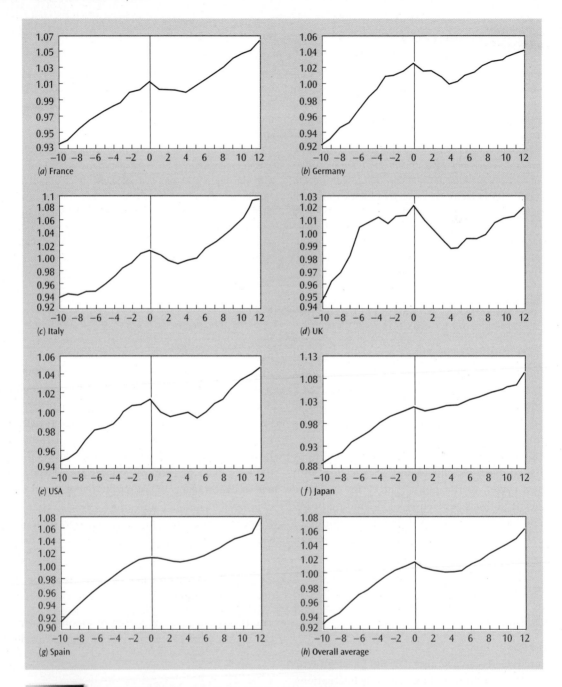

Fig. 14.2   **Burns–Mitchell Diagrams for Real GDP, 1970–1994**

The Burns–Mitchell procedure can be described as follows. First, for each country, cyclical peaks over the period are identified. Second, within a standard 'business cycle window' of 22 quarters (10 before the peak, 12 afterwards), GDP is normalized relative to its cyclical peak. Third, real GDP is averaged across all identified business cycle periods. The figure displays this average for each country and, in the last graph, for the average of all seven countries. Note that the scale differs across countries; for example, it is larger in Japan than in the UK, reflecting higher trend growth rates.
Source: OECD, *Quarterly National Accounts*.

	Consumption	Investment	Gov. spending	Exports	Imports	Prices	Inflation
EU	0.84	0.89	0.11	0.79	0.92	−0.76	0.09
Japan	0.49	0.81	−0.19	−0.10	0.16	−0.27	0.17
USA	0.85	0.90	0.09	0.18	0.56	−0.59	0.19

Table 14.2 Business Cycle Correlations of Macroeconomic Variables with Output[a]

[a] The 'European Union' is computed as the unweighted average of the UK, France, Germany, and Italy. Correlations are taken over quarterly time intervals ranging from 1957–89 to 1965–89.
Sources: Danthine and Donaldson (1993: Table 3); inflation rate correlations are taken from Chadha and Prasad (1994). Except for inflation, variables are seasonally adjusted and detrended using the Hodrick–Prescott filter.

macroeconomic variables? Are they systematically affected by the cycle? Which ones tend to be **procyclical**, moving in the same direction as GDP, and which ones are **countercyclical** instead? Or are they seemingly independent of the cycle, or **acyclical**? One way of answering these questions is to look at the degree of covariation, or co-movement, of each variable with GDP.[3] Table 14.2 presents correlation coefficients of output with other macroeconomic variables in Europe, Japan, and the USA after they have been detrended. Private domestic spending—consisting of consumption, investment, and imports—is procyclical. Public spending is quite smooth and acyclical: it would be countercyclical if the government were systematically offsetting movements in private spending, procyclical if it were stimulating it. This is robust enough to be a stylized fact:

Stylized Fact 3:
The components of private expenditures are procyclical, while on average government consumption is acyclical.

[3] The concept of correlation is introduced informally in Ch. 1. Two variables are statistically correlated when they exhibit a tendency to move together, and this tendency is summarized by the correlation coefficient. Procyclical variables would have positive values of the correlation coefficient near +1; countercyclical variables would have negative correlation coefficients with output near −1; acyclical variables would have correlation coefficients near 0.

14.2.3 Leading and Lagging Indicators

The correlations reported in Table 14.2 only tell us which variables move together simultaneously. If one variable systematically leads or lags another, contemporaneous correlation may be nil and yet an important link may still exist. The Burns–Mitchell diagrams in Figure 14.3 display the average cyclical behaviour of important macroeconomic variables for the UK, France, Germany, Italy, and the USA. The vertical line indicates the peak of the average reference cycle for GDP over all the countries. The figure shows that some variables tend systematically to peak ahead of, and others systematically to trail behind, real output. For example, the degree of capacity utilization, investment in inventory, real share prices, and real money balances are examples of **leading indicators**. They tend to predict the emergence of recessions and expansions. Other variables, such as unemployment and inflation, tend to be **lagging indicators**. Interest rates are an example of a **coincident indicator**.

Stylized Fact 4:
Some variables systematically lead GDP over the cycle (inventories, capacity utilization, stock prices, real money balances), while others (inflation, unemployment) systematically lag behind. Others (interest rates) are coincident.

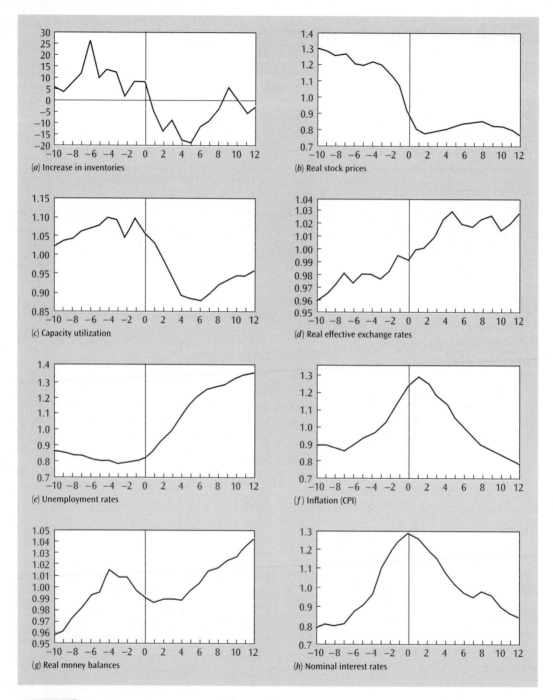

Fig. 14.3   Leading and Lagging Indicators, 1970–1994

These Burns–Mitchell diagrams show the evolution of key economic variables averaged over five countries (France, Germany, Italy, the UK, and the USA) and over each country's business cycles. The vertical line corresponds to the cyclical peak (of output).

Sources: OECD, *Quarterly National Accounts, Main Economic Indicators*; IMF, *International Financial Statistics*.

| **Table 14.3** | Variability of Key Macro Variables over the Cycle[a] |

	Output	Consumption	Investment	Gov. spending	Exports	Imports	Prices (GDP deflator)
	(%)	standard deviation relative to standard deviation of output					
EU	1.12	0.87	2.23	0.47	2.35	3.26	1.00
Japan	1.66	0.73	2.80	3.76	6.99	11.67	1.98
USA	1.73	0.71	3.01	1.18	6.82	5.17	0.90

[a] Variability is measured as the standard deviation of seasonally adjusted and detrended values using the Hodrick–Prescott filter; see Appendix for details.
Source: Danthine and Donaldson (1993: Table 3).

Our knowledge of the macroeconomy can account for many of these regularities. For example, capacity utilization (panel (*c*) in Figure 14.3) tends to decline two to three quarters before a cyclical peak, i.e. before that of GDP, which measures spending and income. How can aggregate output and spending differ from each other? When spending exceeds production, inventories of finished goods are sold to make up the difference. When output exceeds spending, inventories are accumulated.[4] Thus, moving towards a cyclical peak, firms begin to satisfy demand by selling from inventories. In contrast, near the trough, firms start restocking inventories in anticipation of a recovery. A similar logic applies to total investment spending, another leading indicator. As the cyclical peak approaches, forward-looking firms reduce spending on new productive equipment, which is not needed in a recession; conversely, anticipating rising demand, they begin expanding capacity in advance of cyclical peaks.

Financial variables are frequently useful leading indicators. The analyses of the last three chapters make it easy to understand why real money balances could help predict output. According to panel (*g*) of Figure 14.3, the real money supply starts to decline about a year in advance of the onset of a recession. Similarly, panel (*b*) suggests that real share prices start declining roughly four quarters in advance of a downturn. Since real stock prices are a measure of Tobin's *q*, it is easy to see why they are a leading indicator: financial markets also anticipate the next phase of the cycle and, for example, expect poorer profitability during the downturn phase. On the other hand, the real exchange rate in panel (*d*) contains little evidence of any systematic relationship.

14.2.4 Relative Variability

Another feature of business cycles is how much key economic variables move over the cycle relative to each other. Table 14.3 indicates several regularities across countries. At least for the EU and the USA, prices are less variable than output, which is consistent with the 'Keynesian assumption' that was introduced in Chapter 10. Consumption is smoother than output, output is smoother than investment expenditures, and trade (exports and imports) represents the most unstable component of GDP. Figure 14.4, which presents the components

[4] Inventories are goods produced but not yet sold as well as goods in process and intermediate goods used in production. In the National Income Accounts (see Chapter 2), inventory changes are counted as part of investment, so additions to inventories represent positive investment.

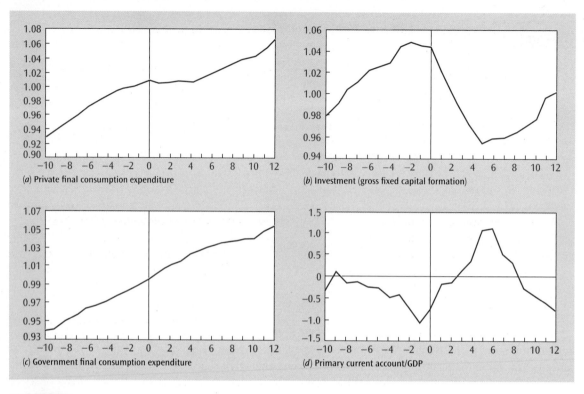

Fig. 14.4 Components of Aggregate Spending, 1970–1994

These Burns–Mitchell diagrams show the evolution of the components of aggregate spending averaged over five countries (France, Germany, Italy, the UK, and the USA) and over each country's business cycles. The vertical line corresponds to the cyclical peak.
Source: OECD, *Quarterly National Accounts*.

of GDP in Burns–Mitchell format, confirms that investment spending and the current account are the most volatile; in comparison, private consumption and government purchases of goods and services are relatively smooth. We conclude this discussion with the following stylized fact:

Stylized Fact 5:
Investment—especially inventory investment—is more volatile and consumption less volatile than GDP. Exports and imports are highly variable, while government purchases are relatively acyclical.

The fact that consumption is less volatile than GDP is consistent with the consumption smoothing principle established in Chapter 6; the volatility of investment is a consequence of its forward-looking nature, as captured by Tobin's q. Two main factors account for the acyclical nature of government purchases. First, as a policy variable, government purchases are likely to be employed countercyclically, rising to reduce a recession and declining during expansions. Second, a large component of government consumption is the wages and salaries of civil servants, which also tend to be smooth over time.

14.3.1 **Business Cycles as an Endogenous Phenomenon**

Why should economic fluctuations occur in a seemingly endless and systematic way? The long-held belief that cycles occur with perfect regularity has been disproved by closer scrutiny. Yet the list of stylized facts shows that cycles do not unfold in a completely random fashion, either. They exhibit important regularities and seem to follow an internal logic. This tension lies behind all theories of the business cycle. The question to answer is: does the cycle sow the seeds of its own reproduction, and if so, how? Might it be possible that cycles go on reproducing themselves, just like the rising and falling of the tides? This would be the case if the economic system constantly generated forces that successively speeded it up and then slowed it down. It turns out that it is quite possible to imagine how this can come about.

One necessary condition, which applies to any explanation of business cycles, is some systematic delay in economic responses to changing conditions. For example, the consumption function links current spending to current income and wealth. This may just hold for consumers' *intentions*, but they may take time in transforming that into effective *action*. This is the so-called **Robertson lag**. It is equally plausible that output does not rise immediately to meet increases in demand: the behaviour of inventories shows that firms initially supply additional demand by running down inventories, the so-called **Lundberg lag**.[5] In what follows both of these lags will be useful for studying mechanisms behind the business cycle.

14.3.2 **Deterministic Cycles: The Example of the Multiplier-Accelerator**

In the end, we expect GDP to depend on its own past—in fact, in a fairly rich and complex way. The appendix to this chapter shows how the *AS–AD* model indeed displays this pattern. To motivate this idea using a much simpler example, we study the so-called multiplier-accelerator model, which played an important role in the early development of ideas about business cycles.[6] The model ignores the price level, the monetary sector, the government sector and the role of expectations, among other things. The model is only sketched in this section; a formal framework is presented in Box 14.2 and the Appendix.

As its name suggests, the main elements of the multiplier-accelerator model are the spending multiplier introduced in Chapter 11, which translates exogenous changes in demand into changes in total final demand, and the accelerator principle presented in Chapter 6, which relates the level of investment positively to changes in GDP. Consumption in period t, C_t, responds to income with a Robertson lag:

(14.1) $$C_t = a_0 + a_1 Y_{t-1},$$

where a_0 and a_1 are positive constants, with a_1 representing the marginal propensity to spend out of income with $0 < a_1 < 1$. Investment behaves according to the accelerator principle:

(14.2) $$I_t = b_0 + b_1(Y_{t-1} - Y_{t-2}),$$

with both b_1 and b_1 positive. Again, a Robertson lag is operative here. According to (14.2), for investment spending to exceed b_0, output must increase. Since there is no government or foreign sector, the model is closed by the GDP identity $Y_t = C_t + I_t$, which after substituting (14.1) and (14.2) can be written as

(14.3) $$Y_t = (a_0 + b_0) + (a_1 + b_1)Y_{t-1} - b_1 Y_{t-2}.$$

Equation (14.3) is called a **difference equation**. It traces out an endogenous dynamic path of output Y, given its past values and the constants a_0 and b_0.

---

[5] Named respectively after the British economist D. H. Robertson and the Swedish economist Erik Lundberg.

[6] This model was developed by Paul Samuelson of MIT and the late Sir John Hicks from Oxford, both Nobel Prize laureates, as well as the late Chicago economist Lloyd Metzler.

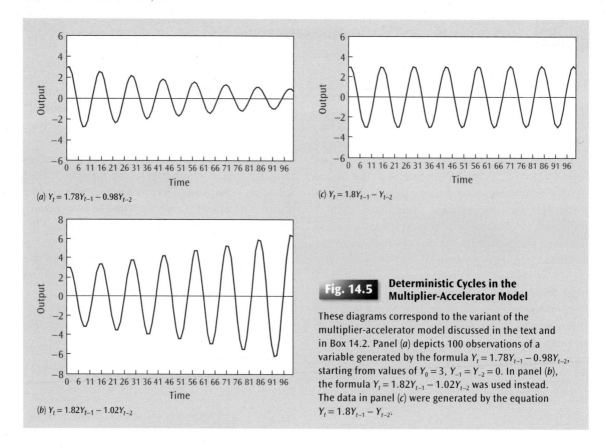

(a) $Y_t = 1.78Y_{t-1} - 0.98Y_{t-2}$

(b) $Y_t = 1.82Y_{t-1} - 1.02Y_{t-2}$

(c) $Y_t = 1.8Y_{t-1} - Y_{t-2}$

Fig. 14.5 **Deterministic Cycles in the Multiplier-Accelerator Model**

These diagrams correspond to the variant of the multiplier-accelerator model discussed in the text and in Box 14.2. Panel (a) depicts 100 observations of a variable generated by the formula $Y_t = 1.78Y_{t-1} - 0.98Y_{t-2}$, starting from values of $Y_0 = 3$, $Y_{-1} = Y_{-2} = 0$. In panel (b), the formula $Y_t = 1.82Y_{t-1} - 1.02Y_{t-2}$ was used instead. The data in panel (c) were generated by the equation $Y_t = 1.8Y_{t-1} - Y_{t-2}$.

Usually the solution to more complicated models, difference equations are an important tool for researchers. Only when the model is at rest in steady state equilibrium ($Y_t = Y_{t-1} = Y_{t-2}$) will dynamics be absent. Figure 14.5 presents the dynamic paths of output of three difference equations, all of the form of equation (14.3), but for different values of a_1 and b_1.

In panel (a), the economy exhibits cycles that die out over time, or are **damped**. The response of the model to deviations from its steady-state equilibrium is to make these deviations ever smaller. In panel (b), the cycle is **explosive**: when consumption and investment react strongly to past GDP, each step takes the economy further away from its equilibrium. The last and most interesting is panel (c) in which $b_1 = 1$. In this case, the economy oscillates forever around equilibrium, but never reaches it. This is the case of **undamped oscillations**. Under these conditions, business cycles can recur in a sys-

tematic, never-ending fashion, like self-perpetuating cycles. This example illustrates the deterministic view of the business cycle.

Box 14.2 explains in more detail how the structure of the model is translated into the model's dynamic behaviour. As might be expected, a more detailed description of the behaviour of aggregate demand and aggregate supply is associated with even richer dynamic patterns. What matters at this stage is not the details of the cycles themselves, but the general idea of explaining actual business cycles with this approach. Could it be, indeed, that what we observe is the consequence of a pendulum-like motion started some time far back in the past and self-perpetuating ever since?

The answer is no, for two reasons. First, cycles produced by deterministic models are too regular to be consistent with Stylized Fact 1. Second, the overwhelming majority of cycles generated by deterministic difference equations either die down

---

Box 14.2   The Multiplier–Accelerator Model in More Detail

The model in the text, in which both consumption and investment react with a one-period (Robertson) lag to output and output changes, respectively, led to equation (14.3), sometimes called the *reduced form* of the model. It takes the form of a difference equation of second order, since it contains variables lagged up to two periods.

It is often useful to *solve* difference equations like (14.3), that is, to express them as a function of time only. First note that the value of output in the steady state—when $Y_t = Y_{t-1} = Y_{t-2}$ is given by

$$\bar{Y} = (a_0 + b_0)/(1 - a_1),$$

which can be thought of as the autonomous spending $(a_0 + b_0)$ times the multiplier $1/(1 - a_1)$, which is greater than one. The solution of difference equations like (14.3)

take the form $Y_t = k_1\lambda_1^t + k_2\lambda_2^t$, where λ_1, λ_2, k_1, and k_2 are constants, and depend on a_0, b_0, a_1, b_1, and the initial values of Y. The crucial parameters λ_1 and λ_2 are the roots of the quadratic equation

$$\lambda^2 - (a_1 + b_1)\lambda + b_1 = 0.$$

It can be shown that the solution to (14.3) will be oscillatory if $(a_1 + b_1)^2 < 4b_1$, and will be dampened or explosive, depending on whether λ_1 and λ_2 are smaller or larger than unity in absolute value. In the oscillatory case, this condition is equivalent to whether b_1 is greater or less than one. Three cases of dynamics generated by this example are shown in Figure 14.5. In the first example, $b_1 = 0.98$, in the second, $b_1 = 1.02$, and in the third—the only case with truly perpetual cycles, $b_1 = 1$.

---

or explode, which is in clear contradiction with the endless recurrence of business cycles. Recurrent cycles such as the last panel of Figure 14.5 require a precise constellation of the economy's characteristics (in this particular example, $b_1 = 1$). Most economists believe that the probability that this combination arises is so low as to make it an unlikely candidate to explain business cycles. This opens the way for an alternative approach.[7]

4.3.3 Stochastic Cycles: The Impulse-Propagation Mechanism

A more plausible explanation starts by asking a question. In the previous section, the economy oscillated because it started away from its stationary-state equilibrium; but what displaced it out of the stationary state in the first place? Suppose an economy were constantly subject to random disturbances, or shocks. These might originate in demand

(e.g. alternatingly optimistic and pessimistic entrepreneurial animal spirits or the consumer mood, or policy actions) as well as supply (e.g. exceptionally bad or good crops and natural disasters; important inventions or discoveries like the steel furnace, railroads, electricity, or computers, as well as minor ones; social unrest). The list of potential shocks is endless. Like drops of rain generating ripples on a lake, these shocks constantly buffet the economy, moving it away from its former position.

These shocks, often referred to as **impulses**, change the demand or supply conditions in the economy. Once randomly disturbed, the economy embarks on the kind of deterministic adjustment described in the previous section, until the occurrence of the next shock. The propagation mechanism transforms, or cumulates, impulses into oscillations. It does not crucially matter any more whether the oscillations are damped or not: they are continuously replaced by new ones corresponding to new shocks. In contrast to the previous section, it is unnecessary to search for the unlikely existence of a self-perpetuating cycle. In this vision of the business cycle shown in Figure 14.6, it is sufficient to accept the view than an economy is regularly buffeted by endless series of shocks, and never really settles down to its stationary state. The rest of this chapter

---

[7] The example given in the text was a linear model. It is true that more general, *non-linear* models are capable of delivering a more exotic and less regular dynamics. Under certain parameter constellations, the results are so irregular as to be called *chaotic* by researchers. Nevertheless, the criticism continues to apply that the range of parameters for which business cycle-like behaviour is generated is limited.

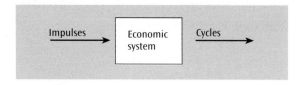

Fig. 14.6 The Impulse-Propagation Mechanism

Random shocks hit the economic system, which reacts by generating business cycles. The cycles result from the averaging or cumulation of these random disturbances over time.

follows on this lead, which is the cornerstone of modern business cycle theory.[8]

How likely is it that purely random impulses working their way through the economy actually generate the kind of behaviour corresponding to our earlier stylized facts? Can shocks which continuously move the economy away from its steady state and followed by the cyclical response shown in Figure 14.6 actually explain business cycles? Box 14.3 recalls how this question received an affirmative answer at the dawn of the computer era. Random shocks can even transform the rather boring multiplier-accelerator model into realistic cycles. In panel (*a*) of Figure 14.7, 200 purely random shocks drawn over time are plotted.[9] Such observations —the impulses—could represent a succession of unforeseeable events, big or small. Panel (*b*) shows the evolution of GDP when these shocks are 'filtered' through a propagation mechanism; in this case we use the example of the multiplier-accelerator

---

Box 14.3 Computers, Scientists, and Business Cycles

The discovery that purely random events can be responsible for cycles was made independently by Slutsky and Frisch in the 1930s. Evidence that such events can generate cycle-like behaviour typical of actual economies was not forthcoming until the late 1950s with the first computers. Frank Adelman, a nuclear physicist, and his wife Irma, an economist, studied an economic model developed by Lawrence Klein, Nobel Prize laureate from the University of Pennsylvania, and Arthur Goldberger, of the University of Wisconsin. (This model consisted of 25 equations summarizing the most important macroeconomic relationships in the US economy.) First, the Adelmans found that the Klein–Goldberger model could not generate a cycle on its own (a deterministic cycle), because the fluctuations were dying down as in Figure 14.5(*a*). Yet, when perturbed by random shocks, it produced data that had the same statistical properties as *actual* US business cycles. They concluded that:

Ever since the pathbreaking article of Frisch on the propagation of business cycles, the possibility that the cyclical movements observed in a capitalistic society are actually due to random shocks has been seriously considered by business cycle theories. The results we have found in this study tend to support this possibility . . . The agreement between the data obtained by imposing uncorrelated perturbation upon a model which is otherwise non-oscillatory in character is certainly consistent with the hypothesis that the economic fluctuations experienced in modern, highly developed societies are indeed due to random impulses. (Adelman and Adelman 1959: 620)

The Adelmans simulated, or solved, their model 100 years into the future on an IBM 650 and were proud that 'computations for one year could be made during an operating time of about one minute'. Now that simulations take seconds or less on a laptop, this approach has become routine. Much effort has gone into improving and enlarging the models and the algorithms used for simulations. More recently, Robert E. Lucas of the University of Chicago and 1995 Nobel Prize laureate in economic sciences, made this research strategy explicit:

Our task as I see it . . . is to write a FORTRAN [a programming language] program that will accept specific economic policy rules as 'input' and will generate as 'output' statistics describing the operating characteristics of time series we care about, which are predicted to result from these policies.

---

[8] The discovery that cycles can be generated from purely random factors was made in the late 1920s and early 1930s by the Russian Eugen Slutsky and the Norwegian Ragnar Frisch, who was awarded the first Nobel Prize. Slutsky was a researcher at the Conjuncture Institute in Moscow during Stalin's dictatorship and was unable to publish this discovery until eight years later when his work was finally translated into English.

[9] Such a random variable which is identically and independently distributed is often called *white noise*. White noise has the property that current and past values contain no information helpful in forecasting future values.

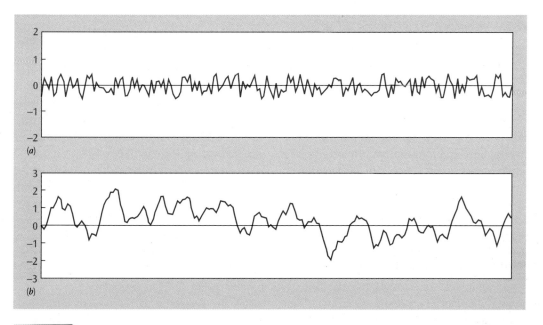

Fig. 14.7   **Impulses and Propagations: An Example**

Panel (*a*) depicts 200 observations of a random variable, ε_t. Panel (*b*) displays data from panel (*a*) after they were transformed, or 'filtered', by the formula $Y_t = 1.3Y_{t-1} - 0.4Y_{t-2} + \varepsilon_t$, starting from a given Y_0 and Y_{-1}. This 'filter' has the ability to mimic a true data series.

model described in Box 14.2. The result is a succession of artificial business cycles which resemble the UK data presented in Figure 14.1(*b*). Although the impulses themselves are not cyclical, the transformed variable exhibits irregular, periodic movements similar to business cycles.

This impulse-propagation mechanism is the dominant way of thinking about business cycles because it accords well with the stylized facts. Since they are random, the shocks will typically generate cycles of different sizes and magnitudes, as in Stylized Fact 1. If many of these impulses are related to permanent technological innovations, not only will they trigger cycles, but in the long run they will also cumulate into a process of unending growth. This is consistent with Stylized Fact 2: in the long run, the growth process (the accumulation of positive shocks) dwarfs business cycles (the reaction to individual productivity and other shocks).[10]

Some of the most important questions remain unanswered, however. First, what is the exact nature of these impulses? Second, what is the impulse-propagation mechanism? We have used a simple example to show that such a mechanism is plausible. Yet this is not good enough: the objective is to show that the 'shocks' correspond to well-known disturbances. A good business cycle theory is one that can also replicate the key stylized facts discussed at the beginning of this chapter.

Two competing approaches to thinking about the impulse-propagation mechanism have been developed. The first follows the Keynesian tradition of sticky prices and takes the *AS–AD* framework as its point of departure; it is presented in the next section. The second asks whether cycles may exist when all prices are perfectly flexible; it is studied in Section 14.5.

[10] Chapter 18 revisits the issue of innovations and low frequency growth cycles.

14.4 Sticky Price Business Cycles

14.4.1 Impulses and Propagation in the AS–AD Framework

Chapter 13 showed how to use the *AS–AD* model to understand the determinants of output and inflation in the short and long run. It can also be used to study business cycles. The point of departure is to identify the shocks as factors that shift either the *AS* or *AD* curves. **Demand shocks** shift the *AD* schedule, while **supply shocks** affect the position of the *AS* curve. Both demand and supply shocks can be positive or negative. Positive shocks, for example, move the relevant schedule rightwards.

The multiplier-accelerator model of the last section showed that lags in economic relationships are the central source of dynamics. This is also true in the *AS–AD* framework. Lags exist for various reasons: slow responses of demand to income and of supply to demand imply that the *AD* schedule reacts gradually to demand disturbances; the supply side may also be a source of **persistence**, if core inflation only gradually catches up with past inflation.

As an example, consider a permanent increase in money growth in a system of flexible exchange rates. Core inflation is simply equal to last period's inflation. The cycle triggered by this disturbance is tracked down in Figure 14.8. (A formal analysis is provided in the appendix to this chapter.) For simplicity, we start with an economy in stationary state at point *A*.[11] The monetary growth expansion takes the economy to point *B* in panel (*a*), with an increase in both output and inflation. Owing to

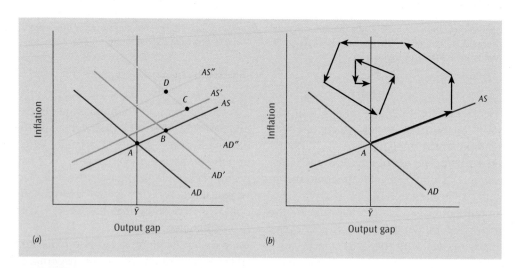

Fig. 14.8 The Propagation Framework in the *AS–AD* Model

In this example, the initial impulse is an increase in the rate of money growth. In panel (*a*), from its initial stationary equilibrium at point *A* the economy first moves to point *B*, as the *AD* curve begins to respond to the monetary impulse. Gradually, core inflation catches up with actual inflation, and the *AS* curve—whose position depends on core inflation—slides to *AS′*: when the *AD* curve reaches position *AD′* the economy is at point *B*. Further lagged responses of demand to money growth, and of core inflation to actual inflation, result in gradual shifts of the *AD* curve towards *AD″* and of the *AS* schedule towards *AS″*, bringing the economy to point *D*. Because output has begun to decline, the *AD* curve begins a descent. As inflation declines, core inflation follows and the *AS* curve also moves downwards. The economy follows a loop of the kind exhibited in panel (*b*).

[11] This is simpler because there is no cycle under way that would interfere with the one under study.

demand lags, the initial shift of the *AD* curve to *AD'* represents only an initial, partial, response. For a time, the *AD* schedule will continue to move rightwards towards *AD"*. Indeed, the lagged response of output means that the longer-run shift of the *AD* curve always exceeds that of the short run and that, as output rises, the *AD* keeps moving to the right.

At the same time, the *AS* curve shifts upward as core inflation gradually catches up with the actual inflation rate. Over time, the economy moves towards point *C*. With actual output in excess of its trend level, inflation catches up and eventually overtakes money growth.[12] This implies that the real money stock starts declining and with it output. Declining output means that the *AD* curve begins to move leftwards. Actual inflation then starts to decline, followed by core inflation and a downward shift of the *AS* schedule (not shown). Pursuing this reasoning, it appears that the adjustment will be characterized by the 'loops' shown in panel (*b*), with alternating periods of output above and below equilibrium level—i.e. business cycles.

14.4.2 Identifying Demand and Supply Shocks and their Propagation

The example of the previous section shows how the *AS–AD* framework can be used to explain business cycles. The next step is to identify the characteristics of cycles, as predicted by the *AS–AD* framework. This naturally points to a distinction between demand and supply shocks. The case studied in the previous section—an increase in money growth—is an example of a demand shock. Is the theory's prediction, that demand shocks lead to loops of the type depicted in Figure 14.8, borne out by the facts?

The case of German unification, seen from the perspective of West Germany, provides an easily identified demand shock.[13] While output in the

east was collapsing, consumption, investment, and government spending by East German residents was rising rapidly. Consumers who had been repressed for several decades and anticipated an increase in their future incomes met West German banks eager to attract new customers, especially as none of them was indebted. This also applied to local governments, which loaded up on new infrastructure and equipment. Most of this spending went to West German firms, which were poised to produce this extra demand.

Figure 14.9 shows that the outcome was indeed a counterclockwise loop. The initial demand was accommodated without significant inflationary pressure. After two years of expansion, the tell-tale signs of overheating emerged: increasing nominal wage demands by unions, high capacity utilization rates, etc. In the end, the Bundesbank refused to allow any further money growth. By allowing market interest rates to rise, and by raising the discount and Lombard rates several times, the German central bank effected a prompt return to non-inflationary conditions.

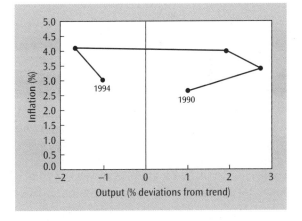

Fig. 14.9 **A Demand Shock: The Effect of German Unification on West Germany, 1990–1994**

German economic and monetary unification occurred in 1990. Spending by former East German households, firms, and governmental authorities increased dramatically, and most of this demand fell on West German producers. The figure traces out the effect on West German GDP—measured as a deviation from its trend—and rate of inflation.

Sources: OECD National Accounts; *Main Economic Indicators*.

---

[12] How do we know? We know that, as long as money growth exceeds inflation, the real money stock *M/P* rises. In the long run, the economy returns to trend GDP and the demand for money roughly returns to its initial value (since *M/P* = *L*(*Y, i*) and both *Y* and *i* approximately return to their initial levels). For *M/P* to return to its initial level, inflation *must* exceed money growth at some point.

[13] For East Germany, it was more likely a mixture of negative demand and supply shocks.

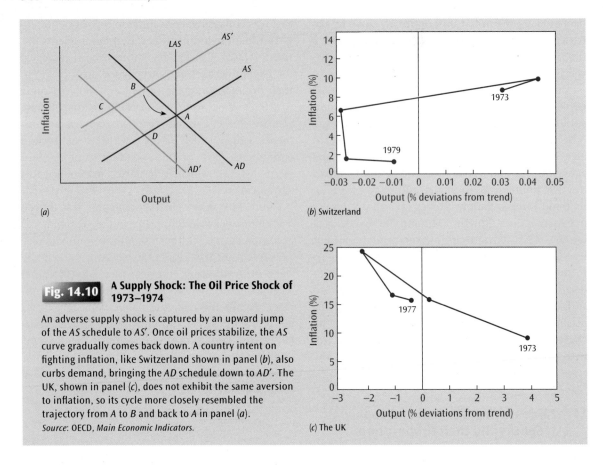

(a)

(b) Switzerland

Fig. 14.10 **A Supply Shock: The Oil Price Shock of 1973–1974**

An adverse supply shock is captured by an upward jump of the AS schedule to AS'. Once oil prices stabilize, the AS curve gradually comes back down. A country intent on fighting inflation, like Switzerland shown in panel (b), also curbs demand, bringing the AD schedule down to AD'. The UK, shown in panel (c), does not exhibit the same aversion to inflation, so its cycle more closely resembled the trajectory from A to B and back to A in panel (a).

Source: OECD, *Main Economic Indicators*.

(c) The UK

The second example traces an economy's reaction to a supply shock, the first oil price increase in 1973–4. Panel (a) of Figure 14.10 shows the theory. The AS curve shifts up to AS' because the cost of a major input, energy, abruptly rises. Without any policy reaction, the shock moves the economy from point A to point B. Thereafter, once the initial burst of cost increases is absorbed, the AS curve moves back to its initial position—but only gradually so, since core inflation is on the rise, trailing actual inflation. Similarly, with a reduced GDP, the AD curve also moves down, so that the return is shown as the curved trajectory from B to A. If instead the authorities decide to fight the inflationary implication of the oil shock and tighten up demand, the AD curve shifts leftwards to AD' and the economy moves from B to C and will return to point A via point D, for example.

Panels (b) and (c) give two examples of reactions to the oil shock. Panel (b) shows that the Swiss

National Bank adopted an explicitly anti-inflationary strategy. After the shock, in 1974 inflation increased and output continued to grow as it completed the expansion phase started a few years before. But then, restrictive policies provoked a sharp recession followed by a gradual decline in inflation—the overall cycle matching trajectory ABCD in panel (a). In contrast, authorities did not act to curb inflation in the UK, which was already high at the time: panel (b) depicts a loop similar to the ABA trajectory in panel (a).

14.4.3 The Contribution of Demand and Supply Shocks

With plausible lags on both the demand and supply side, the AS–AD framework can broadly explain patterns observed in actual business cycles. The results of this analysis are consistent with an

Table 14.4	Decomposition of the variance of GDP, 1979:1–1993:4 (%, 1 year after shock)			
Country	**Demand**	**Supply**	**Money**	**Total**
Canada	54	34	12	100
France	19	80	1	100
Germany	66	31	3	100
Italy	40	51	10	100
Japan	11	87	2	100
UK	32	64	4	100
USA	20	71	8	100

Source: Gerlach and Smets (1995).

impulse-propagation interpretation of business cycles, operating through the sticky price framework developed in Chapter 13. In the next section we consider an alternative interpretation.

An important feature of the *AS–AD* analysis is the distinction between demand and supply shocks. To think about cycles—and how to deal with them—it helps to know which types of shock are more frequent. Table 14.4 presents estimates for the importance of these shocks in five of the G7 countries.

Two kinds of demand shock were identified in this study: (1) monetary shocks, which are related to exogenous changes in monetary policy, and (2) real demand shocks, reflecting public (fiscal) policy, private spending behaviour, or foreign demand via the current account.[14] According to this study, monetary shocks are less important while demand and supply shocks are predominant. At the same time, there are significant differences from country to country.

14.5   Real Business Cycles

14.5.1 Productivity Shocks as Impulses

The *AS–AD* framework implies that business cycles are propagated because prices are sticky. Does this mean that business cycles are impossible when prices are perfectly flexible? This is the challenge undertaken by the real business cycle (RBC) theory, which argues that business cycles can be viewed as a market-clearing, equilibrium phenomenon. The challenge is demanding. As Chapter 10 shows, an economy with fully flexible prices is perfectly dichotomized, even in the short run, and departures from the long-run *AS* (*LAS*) schedule are impossible. In that case, the only shocks that affect the real economy are supply shocks, which shift the *LAS*

schedule. To the extent that monetary and fiscal policies do not affect the *LAS* line, they are irrelevant. At the same time, if the economy is always on its long-run supply schedule, the propagation mechanism of the *AS–AD* model is shut down: real GDP simply moves randomly in response to random supply shocks. So it would seem that such an economy would be free from cyclical tendencies.

---

[14] How this is done is somewhat technical. The authors identify the shocks by *defining* them in terms of their effects on real GDP: demand shocks do not have permanent effects (they do not affect the *LAS* schedule); supply shocks have both temporary and permanent effects (both the *AS* and *LAS* schedules shift); monetary shocks have neither instantaneous nor permanent effects. (It takes time for money to affect output and it leaves the *LAS* schedule unchanged.)

The hallmark of RBC theory is the emphasis of propagation mechanisms besides those related to price stickiness. It starts by focusing on supply shocks related to the production technology: the main source of impulses are new discoveries, inventions, product innovations, or process improvements. These shocks alter the productivity of factors of production, change the environment of economic agents, and cause them to change their behaviour.

Figure 14.11 shows movements in total factor productivity—as measured by the Solow residual—in the case of Germany. The Solow residual, introduced in Chapter 3, is the percentage change in output minus a weighted average of growth in labour and capital inputs, where the weights are the respective factor shares of labour and capital respectively. In the RBC framework, these are the exogenous impulses that hit the economy.[15] The propagation mechanism assumed in the RBC theory can be linked to the paradigm of Robinson Crusoe developed in Chapters 5 and 6. In fact, the RBC approach is frequently associated with more advanced versions of the growth theory presented in Chapter 3.

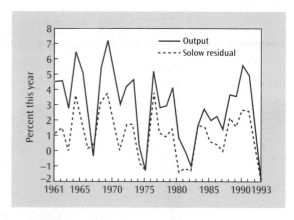

Fig. 14.11 **The Solow Residual and GDP, Germany, 1961–1993**

Growth in total factor productivity, as measured by the Solow residual, is strongly correlated with output. To some extent, the innovations themselves appear random.

Sources: OECD; *Statistisches Bundesamt*; authors' calculations.

Figure 14.12 illustrates the initial impact of a favourable temporary productivity shock. In the first instance, it raises the marginal productivity of both capital and labour. Given the stock of capital, the

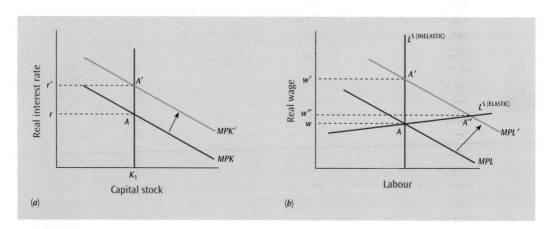

Fig. 14.12 **A Productivity Shock**

A productivity shock raises the marginal productivity of capital and labour. In the short run, the stock of capital is unchanged and the real interest rises. In the inelastic aggregate labour supply (*LS(INELASTIC)*) case, the labour supply curve is assumed to be vertical so the effect on productivity gain is to raise the real wage rate without any change in employment. When aggregate labour supply is elastic (*LS(ELASTIC)*), the response is little change in wages and a larger fluctuation in employment.

---

[15] In the sticky price interpretation, fluctuations of the Solow residual—which is highly correlated with real GDP—are endogenous and constitute one of several manifestations of a normal business cycle.

rate of return on capital rises.[16] For the time being, labour supply is assumed inelastic—the labour supply schedule is vertical—so the real wage rises. Output goes up since the same amounts of capital and labour are now more productive. On the demand side, wealth rises because both wage and profits are higher, so consumption also increases.

14.5.2 Propagation Channels in Real Business Cycles

How does the RBC approach translate the shock into a cycle? The RBC identifies two main channels. The first propagation mechanism involves physical capital. The increase in marginal productivity of capital provides an incentive to accumulate more. At a given real interest rate, we now have $MPK > r$. (Alternatively, Tobin's q increases). The build-up of capital takes time, and contributes to a higher output level along the way. Since the technology shock is temporary, its passing will mark a decline in the productivity of capital, triggering a process of decumulation and a fall in productive capacity back to the initial level. The result is a flexible-price business cycle.

The second propagation mechanism is related to the other factor of production, labour. One feature of the previous story is unappealing: if labour supply is inelastic, there is no change in employment over the cycle. This contradicts evidence that employment and unemployment fluctuate a lot, suggesting that aggregate labour supply is **elastic**. In that case, productivity shocks will be accompanied by changes in the supply of labour, and the overall response of output will be reinforced. For this channel to work, we need a good reason for the aggregate elasticity of labour supply to be so high.

The primary determinant of the slope of labour supply, as Chapter 4 showed, is the contemporary leisure–consumption choice: each period a worker decides whether to work, earn money, and consume —or to enjoy leisure. Our conclusion, backed by empirical evidence, was that the labour supply

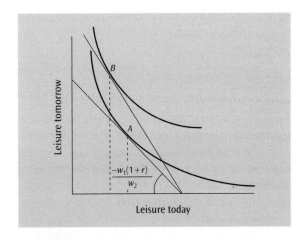

Fig. 14.13 **Intertemporal Substitution of Leisure**

Robinson Crusoe decides on his work effort by comparing, in present value terms, the wage today w_1 and tomorrow $w_2/(1 + r)$: the slope of his 'budget line' is the ratio of these wages. The combination of an increase in both today's wage w_1 and the real interest rate triggers substitution (work more today, less tomorrow) and income (work less today and less tomorrow) effects. In this particular case, Robinson reacts to a temporary wage increase by enjoying less leisure and working harder today, and taking more leisure tomorrow.

is quite inelastic at the household level. A flat aggregate labour supply curve would only result from the aggregation of different households (see Figure 4.4).[17] In addition, the RBC approach emphasizes another channel: the *intertemporal* choice between leisure today and leisure tomorrow.

This choice is represented in Figure 14.13 and resembles Robinson Crusoe's choice of consumption over time analysed in Chapter 6. Preferences are represented by indifference curves, and express the trade-off that workers perceive between leisure today, ℓ_1, and leisure tomorrow, ℓ_2. Ignoring profits and other financial wealth, Robinson's 'budget constraint' is determined by wealth Ω, which in turn is determined by wage income, i.e. today's wage plus the discounted value of tomorrow's wage:

(14.4) $\Omega = w_1(\bar{L}_1 - \ell_1) + [w_2/(1 + r)](\bar{L}_2 - \ell_2)$

The slope of this constraint is $-w_1(1 + r)/w_2$, that is, the ratio of today's wage w_1 to the present value of

---

[16] If the same shock affects the whole world, the world real interest rate is likely to rise. If it affects only one country, the real interest rate can still rise temporarily even if the nominal interest rate cannot change when the exchange rate is fixed: expected inflation absorbs the difference.

[17] In principle, a flat collective bargaining curve would achieve the same result, but the RBC approach has generally avoided considering these forms of market imperfections.

tomorrow's wage $w_2/(1 + r)$. As usual, the optimum choice is where the utility curve is tangent to the budget line.

A productivity shock that is temporary will raise today's wage w_1 and the real interest rate. This in turn will have two effects. A higher wage and a higher real interest rate mean a steeper budget line; work effort is worth more today relative to tomorrow. (Put differently, leisure today is more expensive than leisure tomorrow.) The substitution effect means that Crusoe works harder today. The income effect, in contrast, implies that Robinson Crusoe works less in both periods, since with the same work effort more leisure can be afforded in both periods. If the substitution effect dominates the income effect, the labour supply schedule in Figure 14.13 is elastic and more labour is supplied.

This is the second propagation mechanism of the RBC theory. A favourable productivity shock leads workers to supply more labour today, so GDP rises over and above the direct productivity effect of total factor. In the following period, workers 'cash in' and work less; as labour supply is reduced, GDP decreases. All of that occurs without invoking any wage or price rigidity.

14.5.3 **Optimality Properties of the Cycle**

RBC theory offers an alternative view of business cycles. Technology and other factors shift the production function out and raise the productivity of capital and labour. This causes firms to increase the stock of capital and workers to supply more labour. These reactions of the factors of production during the upswing phase of the cycle amplify the direct effect of the productivity impulse. More interesting, in a second stage, GDP declines as capital is decumulated and workers enjoy leisure or households incurring high costs of going to work stay home. These cyclical responses are optimal for all concerned. It is the best that agents can do, and there is no (involuntary) unemployment and no lost opportunities. This interpretation stands in sharp contrast to the sticky price interpretation, which stresses unemployment and inefficient utilization of resources in recessions.

Thus, one important conclusion of the RBC approach—and one that is disturbing for many economists and therefore highly controversial—is that it is impossible to use demand management policies to attempt to improve matters. Indeed, a striking implication of the RBC theory is that it is not even desirable to even out business cycles, since by definition both households and firms are doing the best they can given changing constraints, so there is nothing to lament. Deep recessions, for example, are seen as the economy's best response to severe adverse productivity shocks. In Chapter 16 we shall return to this important issue in more detail.

14.6 **Taking Stock of the Two Theories**

The previous sections introduced two self-contained, internally consistent accounts of how impulses—shocks to demand, supply, or both—are translated via a propagation mechanism into business cycles. The *AS–AD*, or sticky price, account of business cycles relies on disequilibrium in markets—prices do not adjust immediately to changing demand and supply conditions. In contrast, the RBC theory views the rising and falling tides of economic conditions as an equilibrium response to productivity shocks. It studiously avoids the terms 'demand' and 'supply', since in the RBC framework shocks to technology affect both simultaneously, and economic agents are fully aware of this. Most important, agents have exhausted any potential for improving matters, so policy has no role to play.

Where do we stand? How do the theories match up with the facts? The following sections assess some of the evidence.[18]

---

[18] To save space, we do not use our graphical apparatus (*IS–LM*, *AS–AD*, demand and supply as in Fig. 14.12) to explain every point. Careful readers will find it useful—indeed, an excellent exercise—to check their understanding by drawing their own graphs and reproducing the arguments.

14.6.1 **Productivity, Real Wages, and Employment**

Additional stylized facts about the labour market over the business cycle can be used to sharpen the debate. Figure 14.14 shows the cyclical behaviour of labour productivity, employment, the real wage, and the wage share for several OECD countries. Labour productivity—the ratio of output to employment—is procyclical and a coincident indicator. Employment is also procyclical. On the face of it, these facts are good news for the RBC view and a potential weakness of the *AS–AD* framework. With diminishing returns, given that the stock of capital cannot change much during a cycle, the marginal product of labour (and thereby the average product for all workers)

should decline when production and employment increase. The RBC theory provides a plausible interpretation. If business cycles are driven by productivity shocks, then upswings necessarily coincide with periods of high productivity. High productivity plus intertemporal substitution of leisure or a flat aggregate supply curve then explain why labour demand and supply both rise during the upswing.

However, the extreme volatility of total factor productivity seen in Figure 14.11 is suspect. Neither labour nor capital is always fully employed by firms. Because dismissal costs are positive and human capital is often firm-specific, firms avoid firing employees immediately in downturns, even though production is reduced; workers are often asked to perform tasks less related to the direct production

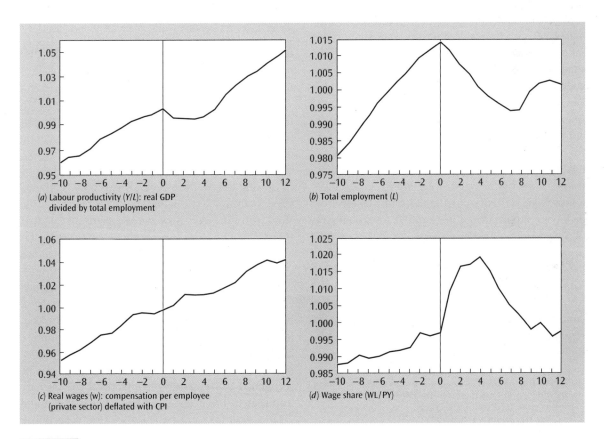

(a) Labour productivity (Y/L): real GDP divided by total employment

(b) Total employment (L)

(c) Real wages (w): compensation per employee (private sector) deflated with CPI

(d) Wage share (WL/PY)

Fig. 14.14   **Cyclical Patterns in the Labour Market, Average of G5 Countries, 1970–1994**

In France, Germany, Italy, the UK, and the USA, labour productivity and employment are procyclical and coincident. Wages are acyclical, while the wage share is countercyclical and lagging.
Source: OECD *National Accounts*; Business Sector Data Base.

process, such as maintenance, building improvements, painting, and cleaning. During the expansion phase, there is a reserve of workers' effort which can be tapped. The same argument applies to the stock of capital. Indeed, capacity utilization is not constant over the cycle (see Figure 14.3). The stylized fact of procyclical total factor productivity might therefore be due to a faulty measure of inputs: in recessions labour is employed but not in directly productive activities—we say it is *hoarded*—and it is gradually put back to more directly productive use in the upturn that follows. Similarly, capital is not discarded but used less intensively in downturns, leading to underestimation of its productivity in these periods. The extreme procyclical behaviour of the Solow residual may therefore reflect hoarded factors of production.

Another interesting feature of Figure 14.14 is that real wages are acyclical.[19] Since the wage share is the ratio of real wages to labour productivity, it follows that the wage share—the proportion of total value added paid out in labour costs—is countercyclical.[20] Panel (*d*) confirms that the wage share promptly rises once the peak of the cycle has passed. Given its emphasis on intertemporal substitution of labour, the RBC approach now fares poorly: the procyclicality of employment is predicated on *procyclical* wages. Even if real wages were mildly procyclical, a very high elasticity of intertemporal substitution or labour supply would be required to explain the observed employment response. As noted in the previous section, most available data on individual behaviour point to inelastic labour supply, at least for heads of households. To the contrary, the small responsiveness of real wages to labour market conditions favours the sticky price view, and also represents evidence for the view that real wage rigidity is the source of involuntary unemployment.[21]

---

[19] Inspection of the individual countries reveals no distinguishing patterns; in some cases there is weak evidence of procyclicality, in other cases, weak countercyclicality.

[20] The wage share is $WL/PY = (W/P)/(Y/L)$.

[21] RBC theorists counter that the reason is that job contracts do not usually provide for flexibility in the number of hours worked: they are rather of the all-or-nothing variety, i.e. work the normal work-week or don't work at all. If individual labour supply responses are 'discontinuous', with individuals shifting from zero hours to a fixed normal work-week and back, this might explain the high aggregate elasticity of employment observed.

14.6.2 Money, Credit, and the Cycle

The direct relevance of money and credit for the business cycle has been an issue for a long time in macroeconomics. It is interesting that, while the real business cycle idea has gained momentum only since the early 1980s, the difficulty of associating business cycles with money and credit was evident to another keen observer, Karl Marx, who wrote:

Among other things, the superficiality of political economy becomes apparent when it assigns a causative role to the expansion and contraction of credit, which is really only a symptom of boom and bust of the industrial cycle. Just as heavenly bodies constantly repeat their revolutions once set in motion, so it is with production as soon as it is hurled into its pattern of expansion and contraction. Effects become for their part causes, and alternating conditions of the process, which constantly reproduce themselves, take on a periodic form. (Marx 1867: I, ch. 23)

Keynes himself was less than convinced that monetary conditions were always relevant for business conditions, arguing articulately in the *General Theory* that interest rates may not fall sufficiently in recessions to offset the negative effect on investment spending of a spell of bad 'animal spirits' among businessmen.

As noted above, the RBC admits no role for money in causing the business cycle. This is because the *AS* curve is always vertical, and money is neutral in the short run. We saw however, in Figure 14.3, that the real money stock is procyclical and in particular a leading indicator. In the sticky price business cycle (*AS–AD*) model, this is consistent with money growth leading and causing booms. It is not, however, consistent with the fact that nominal and real interest rates are procyclical and coincident. Indeed, in the *IS–LM* framework, a money supply impulse is expected to work on output via *declining* interest rates. Procyclical money and interest rates can be reconciled in the sticky price world if the primary impulses to the cycle come from the real demand side (spending, fiscal policy, the current account). In that case, an increase in demand-led GDP is accompanied—or even led—by an increase in demand for money that is passively supplied by the central bank. Indeed, private spending—investment and inventory accumulation in particular—is both procyclical and leading (Stylized Fact 4). In addition, forward-looking variables are likely to react more forcefully to expectations (the stock market and other indicators of consumer sentiment). This explains why investment and spending on durable goods are so volatile. In recent years, new generations of models stressing the instability of the real demand side—some using techniques pioneered by RBC theorists—have had some successes in reconciling the *AS–AD* model with the facts.

Does such evidence seal the debate in favour of the sticky price view? Certainly not! The RBC view is that credit and money demand are passive, expanding with the economy but without any notable influence on real variables. This is also consistent with the coincident and strongly procyclical behaviour of interest rates in Figure 14.3, which the *AS–AD* framework can explain only if shifts to the underlying *IS* curve predominate, and if monetary policy works with a lag. After long focusing on technology, RBC researchers have begun to explore other disturbances to the economy, including fiscal policy, tastes, and institutions. A convergence of the two approaches may be on the horizon.

In the end, a central issue remains the flexibility of the price level. Evidence indicates that prices—measured as aggregate indices—do appear to be rigid in the short run. It is this element of realism that is lacking in the RBC theory of macroeconomic fluctuations and limits its acceptance by a wide spectrum of the economics profession, despite its intellectual rigour. While realism is not an essential element of a good macroeconomic model, this particular detail has such wide-reaching implications that it would appear essential to include it, or at least to explain why it is unimportant.

 ## Summary

1. Real output in economies tends to grow, but in a fluctuating, unsteady manner. Cyclical fluctuations of 5–10 years' duration are known as business cycles. They seldom deviate by more than 2–5% of output from average, and yet are assigned considerable significance in modern industrial societies.

2. Fluctuations in output are accompanied by fluctuations in many other macroeconomic variables. Some lead, some lag, and most are coincident.

3. Components of GDP exhibit differing degrees of volatility, which confirms that the economic forces behind them are different. Private consumption is smoother than investment, and exports and imports are perhaps the most volatile of all for small open economies.

4. Two theoretical approaches have been used to study business cycles: deterministic cycles, and stochastic cycles. The more modern and widely accepted view is that cycles represent the cumulation of random shocks over time.

5. The impulse-propagation mechanism transforms purely random shocks into more regular fluctuations. Crucial to the mechanism is the existence of lags in responses of some key variables to their determinants.

6. The *AS–AD* framework—which rests on the assumption that prices are sticky in the short run—is one example of an impulse-propagation framework. It rests on lags in the response of demand to GDP and of core to actual inflation. This view emphasizes the distinction between demand and supply shocks.

7. The real business cycle theory offers an alternative to the sticky price interpretation of business cycles. Random, exogenous productivity shocks are the underlying impulses that are propagated

through two main channels: capital accumulation, and the intertemporal substitution of leisure.

8. Both interpretations of the business cycle have strengths and weaknesses. The *AS–AD* framework has difficulties explaining procyclical productivity and procyclical interest rates. Yet it can account for the high variance of employment and the apparent short-run rigidity of nominal prices and real wages.

9. The RBC theory is ill-equipped to account for high fluctuations in employment given the acyclical behaviour of real wages. Most problematic for RBC theory is its assumption that prices are perfectly flexible and that fluctuations represent society's best response to a changing environment which cannot be improved upon.

Key Concepts

- business cycles
- boom, recession
- turning points
- peak, trough
- detrending
- Burns–Mitchell diagram
- procyclical, countercyclical, acyclical
- leading and lagging indicator
- coincident indicator
- multiplier–accelerator model

- Robertson and Lundberg lags
- difference equation
- stationary GDP
- damped, explosive, and oscillating cycles
- impulse-propagation mechanism
- sticky price business cycle theory
- demand shock
- supply shocks
- persistence
- real business cycle (RBC) theory

Exercises

1. Using the *AS–AD* diagram, trace graphically the dynamic reaction of an economy under fixed rates to a permanent decline in the foreign rate of inflation.

2. We saw that in the long-run steady state of the multiplier-accelerator model $Y_t = Y_{t-1} = Y_{t-2} = \bar{Y}$, which implies that $\bar{Y} = (a_0 + b_0)/(1 - a_1)$. In what sense can $1/(1 - a_1)$ be thought of as a multiplier?

3. Trace the effect of a positive technological shock on the *AS–AD* model with constant monetary and fiscal policy. Contrast this with the effect of the same shock in a real business cycle model as described in the text.

4. Suppose supply shocks predominated in an economy. What would the *AS–AD* model predict the sign of the correlation to be between output and inflation? What if demand shocks predominated instead?

5. Flip a coin 50 times, recording the outcomes in the order they occur (e.g. heads, tails, tails, heads, tails, etc.) by assigning the value +1 to heads, −1 to tails.

(i)   Now construct a data series according to the formula $x_t = 1.3x_{t-1} - 0.5x_{t-2} + \varepsilon_t$, for $t = 1, 2, \ldots$ 50, where ε_t is the outcome of the flip. (Assign the value 0 to the initial conditions x_0 and x_{-1}.) How many cycles do you observe?

(ii) How does your answer to question (i) change if you use instead the formula $x_t = 1.3x_{t-1} - 0.9x_{t-2} + \varepsilon_t$. Can you explain the difference?

(iii) Now compute the coin-flipping exercise using $x_t = 1.3x_{t-1} - 0.3x_{t-2} + \varepsilon_t$. What do you notice about the behaviour of x over time? Can you explain what is going on here?

6. In Figure 14.4, it is evident that, on average, PCA is a leading indicator and is countercyclical, meaning that the primary current account begins to deteriorate before the peak is reached.

(i)   Given the evidence from Figures 14.3 and 14.4, which components of aggregate demand best account for this fact? Why does the cyclical behaviour of the *PCA* depend on whether cycles are synchronized or not at home and abroad, i.e. whether we reach our peak at the same time as do our main trading partners?

(ii) In the Burns–Mitchell diagram below, (West) German net exports exhibit a clear divergence from the 'average' pattern displayed in Figure 14.4; i.e. they lead the cycle in a *procyclical* fashion. How might the sticky price view of the business cycle explain this fact? Can you think of a real business cycle interpretation of procyclical net exports?

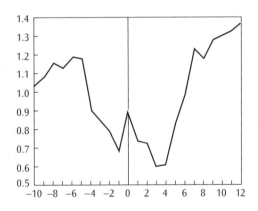

7. If you were to construct a Burns–Mitchell diagram for spending on consumer *durable* goods, what would you expect to find and why?

8. How can the *AS–AD* account for the strongly procyclical behaviour of real and nominal interest rates in the data? (*Hint*: go back to the *IS–LM* diagram.) What does this tell you about the relative importance of real versus monetary shocks in the data? (*Hint*: look at Table 14.3.)

9. In Sweden in the early 1990s, a drastic collapse in house and share prices significantly reduced net wealth of Swedish households. For the first time in many years, households' net savings turned positive. Trace through the effects of such an event on Swedish output. (You should know that Sweden was fixing its exchange rate during the period.) What would you have expected had Sweden been pursuing a floating exchange rate regime?

10. In Figure 14.14, real wages are evidently acyclical. How can the RBC theory account for this fact if labour markets are constantly clearing? How can the sticky price view of the cycle account for this fact?

Suggested Further Reading

The classics:

Burns, Arthur, and Mitchell, Wesley (1946), *Measuring Business Cycles*, NBER.

Friedman, Milton, and Schwartz, Anna (1963), *A Monetary History of the United States*, Princeton University Press.

On historical episodes:

Bruno, Michael, and Sachs, Jeffrey (1985), *Economics of Worldwide Stagflation*, Basil Blackwell.

Kindleberger, Charles (1986), *The World in Depression*, University of California Press.

Romer, Christina, and Romer, David (1989), 'Does Monetary Policy Matter? A Test in the Spirit of Friedman and Schwartz', *NBER Macroeconomic Annual*, 121–84.

Temin, Peter (1989), *The Cause of the Great Depression*, MIT Press.

On the modern debate:

Plosser, Charles I. (1989), 'Understanding Real Business Cycles', *Journal of Economic Perspectives*, 3: 51–77.

Mankiw, N. Gregory (1989), 'Real Business Cycles: A New Keynesian View', *Journal of Economic Perspectives*, 3: 79–90.

Stadler, George W. (1994), 'Real Business Cycles', *Journal of Economic Literature*, 32: 1750–83.

Summers, Lawrence (1986), 'Some Skeptical Observations on Real Business Cycles', *Federal Bank of Minneapolis Review*, 10(4): 23–7.

Appendix I: Trends in Macroeconomic Data and Detrending Procedures

Most macroeconomic data are trended: real variables like real GDP, consumption, exports, etc., have a tendency to grow secularly. Nominal variables also increase because inflation is positive on average. These trends dwarf fluctuations that are more relevant for the study of business cycles or the dynamics of inflation. To see these fluctuations around trend, we need to detrend the original variable.

Many techniques are available for removing trends. Some of them are shown in Figure A14.1, using the real GDP of Italy. Panel (a) illustrates the simplest procedure, a *linear trend*. A linear trend is simply a linear function of time: $y_t = a + bt$. Because GDP tends to grow exponentially, this is an undesirable procedure. Panel (b) displays a *linear logarithmic trend*, which looks like a linear trend once the real GDP is plotted on a logarithmic scale. The corresponding formula is $\log(y_t) = a + bt$. While this trend performs better, it fails to capture an apparent long-lasting slowdown in growth which occurred in the late 1970s. One way to cope with this difficulty is to use *split* log-linear trends, as in panel (c): we look for two different trends, one for the period 1970:1–1980:4 and one for the period 1981:1–1994:4. Yet another alternative is to model the trend as a nonlinear function of time. We often use, as in Figure 12.1, a fourth-degree polynomial (of the form $y_t = a_0 + a_1 t + a_2 t^2 + a_3 t^3 + a_4 t^4$). In panel (d) a more elaborate technique, the *Hodrick–Prescott filter* is employed, producing a smoothly variable trend. This procedure minimizes the distance between actual GDP and the estimated trend, while allowing the user to choose how smooth the trend should be.[22] The corresponding cyclical component shown in panel (e) is simply the difference between actual GDP and its estimated trend, and thereby magnifies the fluctuations.

These methods all assume that the trend is *deterministic*: the trend is estimated as a smooth continuous function of time and is not allowed to jump over time. In that case, all the randomness of the original GDP series is absorbed by the difference between the actual variable and its trend as in Figure 14.1. Another approach assumes that the trend itself evolves randomly. For example, one might think that the evolution of technology—or total factor productivity, as measured by the Solow residual in Chapter 3—is simply the cumulation of random shocks, representing important discoveries and innovations that occur by chance. One way to allow for a random trend is *first-differencing*, simply subtracting the previous value from the current one and considering that this is the cyclical component.[23] The result, shown in panel (f), is not very different from the detrended series obtained in panel (e).

---

[22] Known to engineers as the Whittaker type B, this trend $\bar{y}_t$ is formally the solution to the problem: choose the sequence $\{\bar{y}_t\}$ for $t = 1, T$

$$\min \Sigma(y_t - \bar{y}_t)^2 + \lambda \Sigma[(y_t - \bar{y}_t) - (y_{t-1} - \bar{y}_{t-1})]^2,$$

where T is the length of the sample, and λ can be chosen at will. The higher is λ, the smoother is the series.

[23] Decompose GDP y_t into a trend T_t and a cyclical component C_t. The trend includes a determinist part $(a + bt)$ and a random component ε_t. Taking the first difference gives $y_t - y_{t-1} = (T_t - T_{t-1}) + (C_t - C_{t-1}) = b + (\varepsilon_t - \varepsilon_{t-1}) + (C_t - C_{t-1})$. The fluctuations in the first difference of real GDP reflect fluctuations in the cyclical component $(C_t - C_{t-1})$ *plus* fluctuations in the random component of the trend $(\varepsilon_t - \varepsilon_{t-1})$.

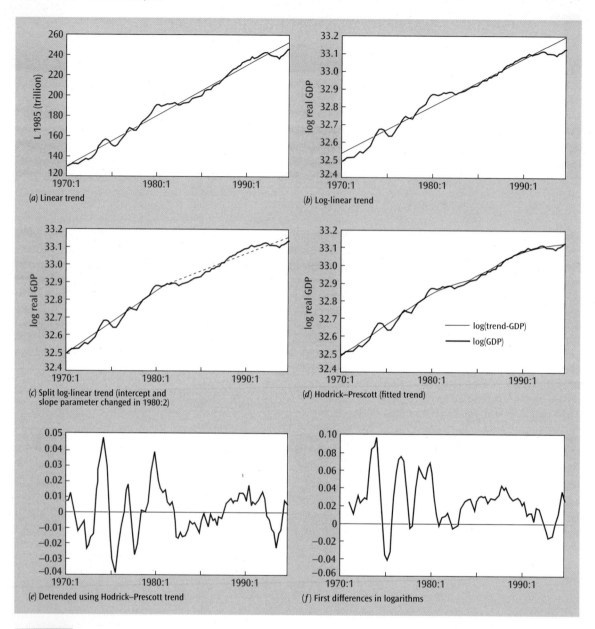

Fig. A14.1 Detrending Italy's Real GDP, 1970:1–1994:4

Source: OECD, *National Accounts*.

Appendix II: A Dynamic *AS–AD* Model of the Business Cycle[24]

This appendix presents an example of a formal dynamic *AS–AD* model and solves it. The model takes the form of a system of linear difference equations. For simplicity, most absolute constants are set to zero. Aggregate demand is given by

(A14.1) $\qquad Y_t = a_1 Y_{t-1} + a_2(\mu_t - \pi_t) + d_t,$

where

- Y_t = real output in t
- μ_t = nominal rate of money growth in t
- π_t = inflation rate in t
- d_t = one-off non-monetary demand shocks (fiscal policy)

It is assumed that $a_1 > 0$, $a_2 > 0$, and that d_t is a random variable with expected value zero; that is, it averages to 0 over time.

Aggregate supply is given by

(A14.2) $\qquad \pi_t = \bar{\pi}_t + b_1(Y_t - \bar{Y}_t) + s_t,$

where

- $\bar{\pi}_t$ = core inflation rate in t
- $\bar{Y}_t$ = trend (equilibrium) level of output
- s_t = one-off supply shocks (e.g. oil price increases, indirect tax increases)

It is assumed that $b_1 > 0$, and that s_t also has expected value 0.

Finally, core inflation is determined by

(A14.3) $\qquad \bar{\pi}_t = \lambda \pi_t + (1 - \lambda)\pi_{t-1},$

where $\bar{\pi}_t$ = core inflation rate in t. The constant λ is restricted so that $0 < \lambda < 1$.

The model can be solved in the following fashion:[25] Substitute core inflation from (A14.3) into (A14.2) and solve for π_t to obtain

(A14.4) $\qquad \pi_t = \pi_{t-1} + \dfrac{b_1}{1 - \lambda}(Y_t - \bar{Y}_t) + \dfrac{s_t}{1 - \lambda}.$

Next, subtract from equation (A14.1) the same equation holding in period $t - 1$:

(A14.5) $\quad Y_t - Y_{t-1} = a_1(Y_{t-1} - Y_{t-2}) + a_2[(\mu_t - \mu_{t-1})$
$\qquad\qquad\qquad - (\pi_t - \pi_{t-1})] + d_t - d_{t-1}.$

From (A14.4),

$$\pi_t - \pi_{t-1} = \frac{b_1}{1 - \lambda}(Y_t - \bar{Y}_t) + \frac{s_t}{1 - \lambda},$$

so (A14.5) can be rewritten as

(A14.6) $\quad Y_t = \alpha_1 Y_{t-1} + \alpha_2 Y_{t-2} + \alpha_3 \Delta\mu_t + \alpha_4 \Delta d_t + \alpha_5 \bar{Y}_t + \alpha_6 s_t,$

where

$$\alpha_1 = \frac{(1 + a_1)(1 - \lambda)}{1 - \lambda + a_2 b_1}$$

$$\alpha_2 = \frac{-a_1(1 - \lambda)}{1 - \lambda + a_2 b_1}$$

$$\alpha_3 = \frac{a_2(1 - \lambda)}{1 - \lambda + a_2 b_1}$$

$$\alpha_4 = \frac{1 - \lambda}{1 - \lambda + a_2 b_1}$$

$$\alpha_5 = \frac{a_2 b_1}{1 - \lambda + a_2 b_1}$$

$$\alpha_6 = \frac{-a_2}{1 - \lambda + a_2 b_1},$$

and where Δ signifies first difference, e.g. $\Delta\mu_t = \mu_t - \mu_{t-1}$, etc. Equation (A14.6) will be stable (non-explosive) as long as $a_1 < 1$.[26] The model will exhibit cyclical or oscillating deterministic behaviour in response to a

---

[24] We are very grateful to Francis X. Hof (Technische Universität Wien) for numerous constructive suggestions concerning this appendix.

[25] The model can also be written and solved in matrix form. The system $[Y_t \; \pi_t]'$ then can be written

$$\begin{bmatrix} Y_t \\ \pi_t \end{bmatrix} = \left(\frac{1 + a_2 b_1}{1 - \lambda} \right)^{-1} \left\{ \begin{bmatrix} a_1 & -a_2 \\ \dfrac{a_1 b_1}{1 - \lambda} & 1 \end{bmatrix} \begin{bmatrix} Y_{t-1} \\ \pi_{t-1} \end{bmatrix} \right.$$

$$\left. + \begin{bmatrix} a_2\mu_t + d_t + \dfrac{a_2}{1 - \lambda}(b_1 \bar{Y}_t - s_t) \\ \dfrac{b_1(a_2\mu_t + d_t) - (b_1 \bar{Y}_t - s_t)}{1 - \lambda} \end{bmatrix} \right\}.$$

Obtaining this form requires writing (A14.1) and (A14.3) as a vector equation with the vector $[Y_t \; \pi_t]'$ as a function of itself, $[Y_{t-1} \; \pi_{t-1}]'$ and a vector of constants. This equation is then solved to eliminate $[Y_t \; \pi_t]'$ on the right-hand side, yielding the above equation.

[26] Technically, stability for a second-order difference equation requires that the characteristic roots must lie inside the unit circle (i.e. have modulus less than unity). The roots of (A14.6) are

$$\left\{ \left[\alpha_1 - \sqrt{(\alpha_1^2 + 4\alpha_2)} \right] \Big/ 2, \left[\alpha_1 + \sqrt{(\alpha_1^2 + 4\alpha_2)} \right] \Big/ 2 \right\}.$$

Given the other assumptions on the parameters, the equation is stable as long as $a_1 < 1$.

single shock if and only if output is sufficiently sluggish (a_1 close to 1) and/or expectations are sufficiently forward-looking (λ close to 1).[27] Naturally, if the model is hit by many random shocks, oscillatory behaviour can arise all the same, just as Slutsky predicted.

It is useful to observe that, as the backward-looking element of core inflation becomes dominant ($\lambda \to 0$), equation (A14.6) becomes

(A14.6′)
$$Y_t = \frac{1+a_1}{1+a_2 b_1} Y_{t-1} - \frac{a_1}{1+a_2 b_1} Y_{t-2} + \frac{a_2}{1+a_2 b_1} \Delta \mu_t$$
$$+ \frac{1}{1+a_2 b_1} \Delta d_t + \frac{a_2 b_1}{1+a_2 b_1} \bar{Y}_t - \frac{a_2}{1+a_2 b_1} s_t,$$

whereas, as the forward-looking element of core inflation becomes dominant ($\lambda \to 1$), equation (A14.6) becomes

(A14.6″)
$$Y_t = \bar{Y}_t - (1/b_1) s_t.$$

Thus the effects of demand shocks decline as core inflation becomes forward-looking. The case $\lambda = 1$ corresponds to full price flexibility: output only responds to supply shocks as in the RBC model.

---

[27] Cyclical behaviour in the deterministic version of the model (that is, when d, s, and μ are identically zero) arises when the characteristic roots are conjugate complex. From the previous footnote, this occurs when $\alpha_1^2 + 4\alpha_2 < 0$, or when $(1 - a_1)^2 (1 - \lambda) < 4 a_1 a_2 b_1$.

Inflation can be solved as a second-order difference equation in a way similar to (A14.6):

(A14.7)
$$\pi_t = \alpha_1 \pi_{t-1} + \alpha_2 \pi_{t-2} + \frac{a_2 b_1}{1 - \lambda + a_2 b_1} \mu_t$$
$$+ \frac{b_1}{1 - \lambda + a_2 b_1} d_t - \frac{b_1}{1 - \lambda + a_2 b_1} \bar{Y}_t$$
$$+ \frac{a_1 b_1}{1 - \lambda + a_2 b_1} \bar{Y}_{t-1} + \frac{1}{1 - \lambda + a_2 b_1} s_t$$
$$- \frac{a_1}{1 - \lambda + a_2 b_1} s_{t-1}.$$

As the backward-looking element of core inflation becomes dominant ($\lambda \to 0$), equation (A14.7) becomes

(A14.7′)
$$\pi_t = \frac{1+a_1}{1+a_2 b_1} \pi_{t-1} - \frac{a_1}{1+a_2 b_1} \pi_{t-2} + \frac{a_2 b_1}{1+a_2 b_1} \mu_t$$
$$+ \frac{b_1}{1+a_2 b_1} d_t - \frac{b_1}{1+a_2 b_1} \bar{Y}_t + \frac{a_1 b_1}{1+a_2 b_1} \bar{Y}_{t-1}$$
$$+ \frac{1}{1+a_2 b_1} s_t - \frac{a_1}{1+a_2 b_1} s_{t-1}.$$

As the forward-looking element of core inflation becomes dominant ($\lambda \to 1$), equation (A14.7) becomes

(A14.7″)
$$\pi_t = \mu_t + \frac{1}{a_2} d_t - \frac{1}{a_2} \bar{Y}_t + \frac{a_1}{a_2} \bar{Y}_{t-1}$$
$$+ \frac{1}{a_2 b_1} s_t - \frac{a_1}{a_2 b_1} s_{t-1}.$$

Macroeconomic Policy

Macroeconomics originated as a field largely because of its proximity to policy-making. Part V has shown how, in theory, macroeconomic policies can prevent recessions, unnecessarily high unemployment, and inflation. Part VI explores the limits of demand management—ranging from the government's budget constraint to the interactions of private expectations with policy effectiveness—and the role of politics in policy-making. It also develops the principles of supply-side policies, the possibility of altering incentives to work, save, and produce, and how this affects the long-run capacity of the economy.

Fiscal Policy, Debt, and Seigniorage

Chancellor: In my old age I have been freed from pain.

Listen and look at this portentous bill

Which has made welfare out of all our ill:

'Be it known to all men who may so require;

This note is worth a thousand crowns entire.

Which has its guarantee and counterfoil

In untold wealth beneath imperial soil.

And this is hereby a substitute approved

Until such time as the treasure can be moved.'

Emperor: And do my people think it negotiable?

Do army and court take it for pay in full?

Strange though I think it, I must ratify it.

Steward: To collect those fluttering notes, one couldn't try it;

once issued, they are scattered in a flash.

The Exchanges stand wide open for the queue

Where every bill is honoured and changed for cash—Silver and gold—

at a discount it is true.

And then to butcher, baker, pub it goes,

Half the world only seems to think of stuffing;

While the other half in brand new clothes goes puffing.

The clothier cuts the cloth, the tailor sews.

Long live the Emperor! Makes the cellars gush

In a cooking, roasting, platter-clattering crush.

– Goethe, Faust, trans. L. MacNeice

15.1   Overview

Governments play an important role in our economic lives. Especially in Europe, they are big, and have been growing bigger for most of the post-war period. Table 15.1 shows that governments in the European Union spend and tax close to half of GDP. A large part of this spending represents redistribution of income among citizens—about a third of GDP on average. Yet, governments are also big consumers. They spend close to one-fourth of what all households do on goods and services. Nor are governments known to be particularly strict in managing their budgets. Deficits are frequent, and most governments are heavily indebted to the private sector and foreigners. While European countries have consolidated their budgets in recent years, public debt still represents about three-fourths of a year's GDP, and in some countries, such as Belgium and Italy, the stock of public debt still exceeds a full year of national output.

This chapter looks at the economic functions of governments and how they fulfil their tasks. Why do governments have an economic role to play at all? This question has been debated since time immemorial between right, left, and centre, between partisans of laissez-faire economics and interventionists. In this chapter we focus on two roles of government in the national economy: microeconomic (the provision of public goods and services, income redistribution) and macroeconomic (stabilization of aggregate activity). The stabilization function is

Table 15.1	**General Government Spending and Finances: EU, USA, and Japan, 2000**		

	EU	USA	Japan
Total spending (% of GDP)	47.5	31.3	39.6
Public consumption			
as % of GDP	17.5	13.9	9.7
as % of private consumption	29.4	20.1	16.2
Budget surplus (% of GDP)	−0.9	1.3	−8.8
Gross debt (% of GDP)	76.8	59.8	120.3

Source: OECD *Employment Outlook*; Eurostat.

performed both through active policies designed to negate the effects of business cycle fluctuations —perhaps originating in the private sector—and through the working of automatic stabilizers embedded in the public budget.

In this process, governments often find themselves running budget deficits: they pay out more than they take in. To meet their intertemporal budget constraints, they must either close the deficit or borrow and accumulate public debt. This process is inherently explosive, since existing debt must be serviced, meaning that at the very least interest must be paid. An alternative for the government is to pay its bills simply by borrowing from the central bank. Crudely put, it could print money as did Mephistopheles in Faust, effectively exploiting its monopoly right to create legal tender. **Seigniorage**, as this is called, relieves the government of the need to borrow, but it has potential implications for money supply and inflation. Still another, less frequently used, option is partial or total default, whereby the government solves its budget constraint by a confiscation of wealth from its creditors. This is the most radical of all approaches, reserved for times of national emergency.

15.2 Fiscal Policy and Economic Welfare

15.2.1 Provision of Public Goods and Services

Governments 'produce' goods and services, mostly for collective consumption. Why are they involved in that activity? The usual argument is that without the state, these goods would not be provided at all, or would be provided in insufficient quantity. First, these goods are often public goods. Second, they are produced under increasing returns.

The particularity of public goods is that they cannot be appropriated for individual consumption. This applies, for example, to law and order, defence, public gardens, or foreign affairs. Another characteristic of public goods is that their use by one person benefits another person. This is called an **externality**. A good example is education. All of society benefits from mass literacy; workers can interact more effectively, which raises their productivity. Indeed, there is considerable evidence of a direct link between the education level of a population—its **human capital**—and a country's growth performance and well-being. The generic feature of collective goods is that, without the government, they would not be produced at all privately, or would be produced in socially insufficient quantities, because individuals would not be willing to pay for the externality that benefits society as a whole.

Another reason for the undersupply of some categories of goods and services is the presence of increasing returns in production. One example is the usage of streets: the cost of paving and maintaining a road is roughly the same whether there are few or many users. Streets could be private and their use charged to users, and this would undoubtedly relieve traffic congestion in cities.[1] On the other hand, there is a risk that each of us reacts to street tolls by reducing use of streets to the point where the cost per remaining user leads to the curtailment of street provision in some areas.

While there is a strong justification for *some* government consumption—in reality, the provision of collective goods—there is no clear-cut border between goods and services that can be provided only publicly and those that could be provided privately. This relates to such differing cases as education (private schools and universities exist alongside public education), social security (health and retirement insurance are increasingly often privately provided), and utilities (highways are built and run by private companies; electricity and telephone networks are privately owned and operated). Police protection, for example, could be privately organized, but it benefits all concerned whether they pay for it or not; in practice, only better-off, homogeneous neighbourhoods could afford to set it up. Furthermore, the state has an incentive to combat lawlessness on a wider scale than do individuals interested only in protecting their own safety.

The absence of unequivocal criteria for deciding what should be publicly provided explains why there is much soul-searching on the issue. Recent privatizations throughout Europe reflect a trend towards reduced public ownership, a reversal of a long trend in the other direction. Whatever the ultimate evolution of thought on this matter, however, some government spending will always be considered desirable.

15.2.2 Redistributive Goals: Equity versus Efficiency

Productive efficiency—meaning the optimal use of available productive resources—is achieved when each factor of production is paid its marginal productivity. This may result in a very unequal distribution of income and wealth. The reality of economic life is the coexistence of much individual wealth alongside grinding poverty. While this outcome may be efficient from a productive point of view, an altogether different logic emphasizes that human beings have similar basic needs that should be met under all circumstances. **Equity** or fairness is often seen as a requirement for society to be cohesive and stable. Yet equity and efficiency often work against each other; there is a fundamental **equity–efficiency trade-off**.

Governments can reduce inequalities. Progressive income taxes reduce the differences in post-tax incomes. Taxes levied on the better-off pay for transfers to the worse-off. In fact, a significant part of public spending is dedicated to income redistribution. Table 15.2 shows the size of transfers, both as a share of GDP and as a proportion of total government outlays. In some countries, this is the single largest item in the government budget. Not surprisingly, different countries deal differently with the equity–efficiency trade-off. Sweden and the Netherlands seem to place more weight on equity than Japan or the USA, for example.

There is a trade-off however: income redistribution for the sake of equity has disincentive effects. Highly paid—and presumably highly productive—people may reduce their work effort in response to heavy taxation, or may even move abroad. On the other hand, those who receive transfers from the state may find it pointless to work hard for little net reward.[2]

---

[1] Just as public goods are undersupplied by the market, free goods tend to be overconsumed or overused.

[2] The topics of incentives and taxation are treated in Ch. 17.

Table 15.2   Government Transfers, Various Countries, 1960 and 2000

	Transfers as % of GDP		Transfers as % of government outlays	
	1960	2000	1960	2000
Austria	14.8	33.2	51.8	66.0
Belgium	12.7	31.0	44.8	62.0
Denmark	7.6	37.2	35.1	68.5
Finland	9.0	31.8	41.6	66.7
France	16.3	33.3	53.5	65.2
Germany	14.1	31.5	50.2	66.7
Greece	5.3	22.0	30.6	51.4
Ireland	9.6	19.6	38.7	55.4
Italy	11.2	28.7	45.4	66.7
Japan	4.5	17.2	34.5	44.7
Netherlands	8.6	25.5	n.a.	56.7
Portugal	3.7	27.1	24.5	56.1
Spain	2.9	22.8	23.1	56.0
Sweden	8.6	20.9	32.2	37.3
UK	9.0	24.5	30.7	62.7
USA	6.0	10.8	24.4	36.4

Source: European Economy, *OECD Fiscal Positions.

15.3   **Macroeconomic Stabilization**

Providing public services and redistributing income does not imply that total government spending differs from revenues. The government could perform its functions without running budget imbalances. As Table 15.3 shows, however, significant surpluses and deficits are the rule rather than the exception. This section looks at a second function of public budgets: stabilizing aggregate income and spending. To achieve these goals, governments shift resources intertemporally, dissaving during recessions and saving at times of expansions. Just because public imbalances can be justified, however, does not mean that they always are.

15.3.1 Long-Run Consumption and Tax Smoothing

The flow of (usually freely provided) public goods and services constitutes an integral part of each individual's consumption. In general, individual agents prefer a smooth pattern of collective as well as private consumption over time. It is the social responsibility of governments—and determinant of their electoral success—to provide a steady flow of public goods and services. At the same time, to purchase goods and services, the government must levy taxes. Taxes, however, reduce individuals' incomes

| Table 15.3 | Primary Budget Balances, Various Countries, 1972–1999 (% of GDP) |

	1972	1975	1980	1985	1990	1995	1999
Austria	3.0	−1.2	0.0	0.2	0.8	−1.4	1.4
Belgium	1.3	−1.8	−4.0	−0.1	4.0	4.5	6.0
Denmark	2.7	−2.4	−2.8	4.1	2.7	0.8	5.0
Finland	3.3	1.9	1.9	2.8	3.6	−2.8	3.9
France	1.1	−1.7	0.8	−1.0	0.3	−2.3	1.2
Germany	−0.8	−5.6	−1.6	1.1	−0.1	1.2	2.0
Greece	0.6	−2.1	−0.3	−7.1	−7.4	1.0	5.9
Ireland	−1.4	−8.5	−8.5	−4.3	3.4	1.7	3.5
Italy	−7.4	−8.1	−3.9	−5.1	−2.2	3.5	4.5
Japan	−0.4	−2.8	−3.4	1.0	3.7	−3.1	−5.7
Netherlands	1.2	−1.2	−1.5	0.3	−1.6	0.6	4.3
Norway	4.6	3.9	5.9	8.7	0.4	2.9	4.3
Spain	0.3	0.1	−1.9	−4.8	−1.1	−2.4	2.2
Sweden	2.5	0.6	−4.4	−0.8	4.2	−5.2	4.8
UK	1.2	−1.2	−0.3	0.5	0.8	−2.8	3.3
USA	0.7	−2.9	−0.1	−1.8	−0.8	0.6	3.8

Surplus (+) or deficit (−).
Source: OECD *Economic Outlook*.

and, their private consumption possibilities. For this reason, it is inefficient to lighten the tax burden for a while and then raise it sharply to satisfy the government intertemporal budget constraint.[3] A well-run government wants to finance a steady flow of spending by a steady rate of taxation. **Tax smoothing** is the normal companion to **consumption smoothing**.

This principle has a central implication for the conduct of fiscal policy. If a series of bad years reduces the country's income and its the tax base, the government's best course of action is not to cut spending and maintain the budget in balance. Nor should it raise tax rates. Rather, it should endeavour to maintain a steady flow of public goods and services, and finance the tax revenue shortfall by borrowing.[4] Conversely, a few particularly good years during which taxable income rises sharply should be used not to raise government consumption temporarily, but to increase savings. Acting on behalf of the public at large, a government should behave like any economic agent, meeting temporary income disturbances by saving or borrowing, within the limits of its budget constraint. Similarly, if the need for public spending rises or declines temporarily, the appropriate response is to borrow or save while keeping tax pressure steady. Box 15.1 applies the principle of tax smoothing to the controversial case of Germany's unification.

[3] This is especially true if households have imperfect access to credit markets, and thus cannot offset the government's actions. Consumption smoothing is studied in Ch. 6.

[4] S. 15.3.4 returns to this issue. Public sector borrowing can be done domestically or abroad. Globally, a country with a temporary fall in income must borrow. As a first approximation, it does not matter whether it is the private or the public sector that borrows abroad.

Box 15.1 **Tax Smoothing after German Reunification**

When he endorsed swift reunification early in 1990, Chancellor Helmut Kohl promised that there would be no new taxes for West Germans. Yet, the former East Germany entered the Federal Republic with precious little dowry, a hugely inefficient productive sector, a large external debt (mostly to West Germany), poor infrastructure, and considerable environmental liabilities. In the eastern states, output fell by about 50%, unemployment —official and unofficial—rose to about 30%, and state-owned enterprises needed cash to stay afloat until they could be sold. From a budgetary viewpoint, the eastern provinces required massive public spending but could not contribute much to the financing. The pressure on the federal budget is apparent in Table 15.4 and con-

tinues to amount to roughly €75 billion per year. Yet, this evolution is best regarded as temporary. Within a decade or two the eastern provinces will have very good prospects of catching up with the West. Facing a temporary shock, tax smoothing calls for accumulating public debt and limiting tax increases, as well as for current account deficits (i.e. foreign borrowing). Yet, as the full costs of reunification were tallied many have begun to question how much of the obligations of the eastern states are temporary. Kohl's successor, Schröder, and his finance minister Eichel have come under public pressure to stem the rise of the national debt and close the external deficit, even if there are good economic reasons to put up with it.

Table 15.4 **Fiscal Implications of German Reunification (% of GDP)**

	1988	1989	1990	1991	1992	1993	1994	1995	1996	1997	1998	1999	2000[a]
Goverment expenditures	46.3	44.8	45.1	46.4	47.2	48.5	48.2	48.8	49.9	48.6	47.7	47.8	47.2
Budget surplus	−2.2	0.1	−2.0	−3.3	−2.6	−3.2	−2.4	−3.3	−3.4	−2.6	−2.0	−1.9	−1.9
Gross public debt	43.4	41.0	43.2	41.3	44.4	50.1	50.2	60.5	63.0	63.6	63.1	63.3	63.0
Current account	4.5	4.9	3.4	−1.0	−0.7	−0.5	−1.1	−0.8	−0.2	−0.1	−0.2	−0.9	−0.5

[a] OECD-Projection.
Source: OECD *Economic Outlook*.

Budget deficits met by public borrowing increase the public debt. Figure 15.1 shows how public debts (as a percentage of GDP) have evolved over the past century. It is fairly clear that debts rise, sometimes spectacularly, during wars and decline afterwards. Wars are periods of unusually high public expenditure, yet they are rarely expected to last very long. The tax-smoothing principle seems to have been applied here (even if some countries eventually defaulted on part of their debts). Similarly, the oil shocks of the 1970s were met in many countries by debt accumulation.

15.3.2 **Short-Run Stabilization**

The principle of public spending and tax smoothing applies to shorter-run cyclical fluctuations as well. A cyclical downturn means that personal incomes decline temporarily. The laissez-faire view is that, facing a temporary income fluctuation, individuals should borrow and/or save to smooth their consumption pattern, with government playing no particular role. This prescription would be correct if all individuals could indeed borrow during a recession. Credit rationing, however, changes the

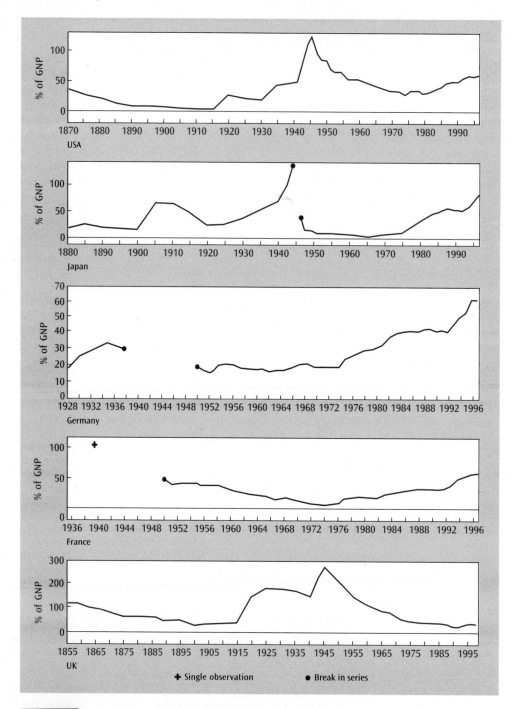

Historical Evolution of Public Debts, Five Countries

The UK had a debt to GDP ratio of over 100% in 1855, a legacy of the Napoleonic wars. During the First World War the British debt rose to about 200%, and during the Second World War to 300%. The war efforts are also visible for the USA (including the Civil War) and Japan.
Source: OECD.

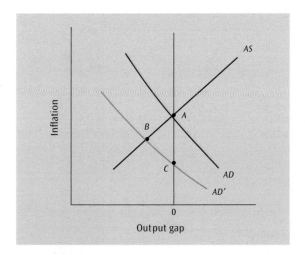

Fig. 15.2 **Stabilization Policies**

When demand exogenously falls, the economy moves from point *A* to point *B*. In the absence of stabilization policy, the economy will eventually move to point *C*. Fiscal policy can be used to speed up a return to trend output at point *A*, or even to prevent the *AD* schedule from shifting.

situation.[5] Individuals who cannot borrow, or cannot borrow as much as needed, are unable to smooth out their consumption. Not only are they hurt, but their declining demand deepens the slowdown through the demand multiplier effect. In Figure 15.2, starting from long-run equilibrium at point *A*, the aggregate demand curve shifts from *AD* to *AD'*. Under fixed exchange rates, the government can stop this process of spiralling demand decline. To keep the curve in its *AD* position and prevent the move from point *A* to point *B*, it either increases its own spending or provides tax relief. In effect, the government borrows on behalf of its credit-constrained citizens. Conversely, a demand boom provides the government with the opportunity to run a budget surplus and pay back the debt accumulated during previous downturns.[6]

When demand exogenously falls, the economy moves from point *A* to point *B*. In the absence of stabilization policy, it will eventually move to point *C*. Fiscal policy can be used to speed up a return to trend output at point *A*, or even to prevent the *AD* schedule from shifting.

The fact that unemployment rises during recessions provides another rationale for countercyclical fiscal policies. The mere increase in unemployment is not a justification for active fiscal policies. If unemployment rises because its equilibrium level has permanently increased, the economy will eventually settle along its long-run aggregate supply schedule and demand management is bound to fail. Attempts to keep unemployment below equilibrium through fiscal expansions will only lead to more public debt. However, short-run fluctuations in unemployment around its equilibrium rate occur because price and wage rigidities prevent an optimal utilization of available resources. **Countercyclical fiscal policy** may be a corrective device to keep unemployment at its equilibrium level, and output near its trend growth path. Sustaining aggregate demand with public spending when private demand weakens, or directly boosting private demand with tax relief, could eliminate business cycles altogether.

15.3.3 **Automatic Stabilizers**

Public budgets tend to go into surplus during upturns and into deficits during recessions. While government consumption is largely unaffected by cyclical fluctuations, net taxes, i.e. taxes less transfers from the government to the private sector, are strongly procyclical, as shown in Figure 15.3.[7] The reason is that nearly all taxes are set as *rates* applied to incomes or spending. When incomes and spending rise, tax collection automatically rises, and conversely. Public transfers, on the other hand, and unemployment benefits in particular, rise during recessions and decline during booms. Only if the government takes explicit steps to alter its budget can the cyclicality of public budgets be avoided.

---

[5] Ch. 6 explains the mechanism and importance of credit rationing.

[6] The principle does not apply in case of permanent disturbances, i.e. when adjustment is required.

[7] Remember that the budget deficit is the difference between government purchases and net taxes or, equivalently, is purchases plus transfers less tax revenues.

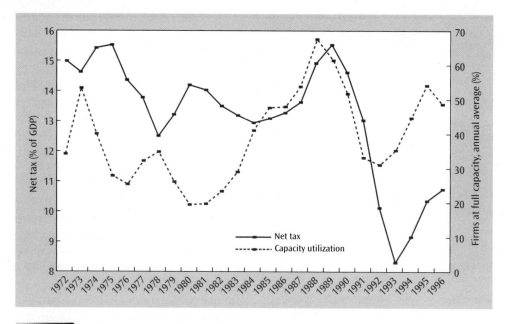

Fig. 15.3   **Cyclical Behaviour of Net Taxes in the UK, 1972–1996**

When the economy enters into a slowdown (the rate of capacity utilization declines), usually with a lag of a year or two, tax receipts fall and transfers rise. Taxes net of transfers are procyclical.
Source: OECD.

Given the nature of the budgetary process described in Box 15.2, this seems unlikely.

When an economy slows down, the budget deficit will normally increase, or its surplus will shrink or even shift into deficit. This automatic lowering of taxes amounts to an implicit fiscal expansion. Conversely, a better-than-expected economic performance reduces the budget deficit or increases the surplus because of enhanced tax income for the government, a contractionary fiscal policy of sorts. In the end, we see that exogenous shifts in private demand are automatically cushioned—if not completely offset—by shifts in public demand: these are the so-called **automatic stabilizers**. They work in the absence of any policy action: simply by enacting the budget as approved by the parliament, the government finds itself conducting a countercyclical fiscal policy, dampening both recessions and expansions.

15.3.4 **How to Interpret Budget Figures**

With automatic stabilizers in place, the budget is partly endogenous. Policy choices determine a planned surplus or deficit; economic conditions determine the outcome. This is why raw budget figures do not always fully reveal the government's intentions and are often misleading. Table 15.3 shows that most countries underwent budget deficits in 1975 and 1980. Did this reflect a collective enthusiasm for expansionary policies? To be contrary, these years coincided with the post-oil-shock recessions (the exception being Norway, an oil-exporting country).

The endogeneity of budgets means that it is not straightforward to determine whether the stance of fiscal policy is tight or easy. While the endogenous response dampens a recession, it does not pack the punch of an actively expansive tax cut or spending

Box 15.2   **The Budgetary Process**

All democracies follow roughly the same budgetary process. Once a year, the government presents a budget to its parliament, which then debates on—and sometimes amends—each item before voting on it. One part of the budget concerns spending by the various ministries or departments; the other part concerns tax revenue. The parliament approves tax rates, literally hundreds of them, from VAT to income, from petrol to corporate profits or property. While spending authorizations are set in amounts, tax receipts are uncertain, depending upon how much is to be taxed at the set rates. This is why parliament cannot decide exactly what the deficit or surplus will be. Instead, it is presented with a forecast of GDP which underlies a forecast of tax receipts and the associated deficit or surplus. It is well understood that economic conditions will settle the matter as the fiscal year goes on. Table 15.5 shows the amount of 'error' involved,

first in the case of France. Higher-than-expected GDP growth of 1988 delivered a slightly lower deficit than planned, with the opposite effect in 1992. Naturally, most governments have a tendency to forecast high growth, large tax receipts, and small deficits, since such forecasts are not binding. It takes an unusually good year to have a better budgetary outcome then announced, while a moderate slowdown easily results in massive slippages.

Table 15.5 also shows the particular situation of Russia in 1995. The budget passed by the Russian parliament was based on an unrealistically low inflation target. The higher outcome led to higher tax receipts but not to higher spending, since spending had been voted upon in nominal terms. This was the ploy used by the government to get a spending-oriented parliament to adopt a rigorous budget.

Table 15.5   **Expected and Realized Budgets, France, 1988–1992, and Russia, 1995**

	France					Russia			
	Budget deficit (FF bn)		Real GDP growth (%)				Budget deficit (% of GDP)		Inflation (%)	
	Target	Actual	Target	Actual			Target	Actual	Target	Actual
1988	115.0	114.7	2.2	4.5		1995	7.9	3.1	30	131
1992	89.9	226.3	2.1	1.3						

Sources: France: Les Notes Bleues, IMF; Russia: RECEP.

hike. In order to separate out exogenous policy decisions from endogenous responses to cyclical fluctuations, we ask what would have happened to the budget balance if real GDP had been on its trend path. In Figure 15.4 a given upward-sloping schedule represents a budget as approved by parliament. The positive slope of each schedule represents the automatic stabilizer: given tax and spending rules, an increase in the GDP improves the budget balance. The budget corresponding to schedule *FP* is tighter

—less expansionary—than the budget represented by *FP'*: for any given GDP level, the surplus is larger because of either less spending, or more taxes, or a combination of both.

The figure reveals why it is difficult to interpret budget figures. If, for example, the economy moves out of a recession at the same time as tax rates are reduced, it goes from point *A'* to point *B'*. As drawn, the budget improves, from a deficit to a surplus. The reason for the improvement is purely cyclical,

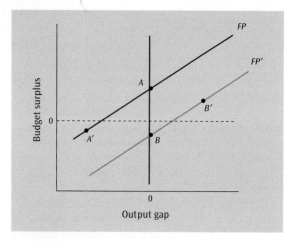

Fig. 15.4 **Endogenous and Exogenous Components of Budgets**

The line *FP* describes how the actual budget responds to cyclical fluctuations of output about its trend for a given fiscal policy stance. The move from line *FP* to line *FP'* describes a more expansionary policy stance. The cyclically adjusted budget is measured assuming a zero output gap. For fiscal policy stance *FP* it is given by point *A*, and for *FP'* by point *B*.

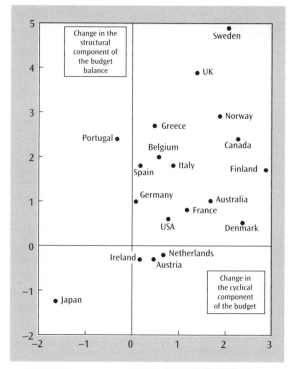

Fig. 15.5 **Decomposition of Budgets, 1993–1996: Estimates by OECD (% of GDP)**

Forecasted budget deficit changes between 1993 and 1996 are decomposed into two parts: on the vertical axis are shown changes in the cyclically adjusted budget (i.e. exogenous changes in the stance), sometimes called the structural component; the horizontal axis measures the remaining cyclical part (computed as the total change less the cyclically adjusted change). Towards the south-east, for example, are countries in which fiscal policy is expanding but where the budget is improving due to a cyclical upturn (i.e. moving from point *A* to point *B* in Figure 15.4). Between 1993 and 1996, budget balances improved as most countries emerged from the recession of the early 1990s. At the same time, they pursued restrictive fiscal polices. Japan stands out: it was in recession, hence a worsening of the cyclical component of the deficit, and is conducting expansionary fiscal policies, hence a worsening in the cyclically adjusted component.
Source: OECD, *Economic Outlook*, June 1995.

however; in fact, the authorities have relaxed the budget by cutting taxes. The actual improvement in the budget can easily be misconstrued as a sign that fiscal policy has been tightened.

In order to better interpret the fiscal stance of the authorities, we would like to have a measure free of cyclical effects. The usual procedure is to compute the **cyclically adjusted budget**. This is the budget surplus or deficit that would occur if the economy were on its trend growth path, when the output gap is nil. In the figure, cyclically adjusted budgets are represented by points *A* and *B*. For *FP*, the cyclically adjusted budget is in surplus, even though a recession could lead to an actual deficit at point *A'*. The fiscal relaxation from *FP* to *FP'* is confirmed by the move from point *A* to point *B* where the cyclically adjusted budget is in deficit. Yet, the exogenous relaxation is more than offset by the endogenous effect of the cyclical expansion, so that the actual budget is in surplus at point *B'*. Figure 15.5 applies the distinction between actual and cyclically adjusted deficits. Countries where the cyclically adjusted

budget has improved (above the horizontal axis) are countries where fiscal policy has been exogenously tightened up. The diagram makes clear that many countries have used the recent period of cyclical improvement in the budget as an opportunity to correct structural imbalances.

15.4   Deficit Financing: Public Debt and Seigniorage

Whether budget imbalances are justified by tax smoothing and consumption smoothing considerations, by active stabilization policies, or by the spontaneous operation of the automatic stabilizers, the intertemporal budget constraint prevents the permanent accumulation of public debt. Yet, in many industrialized countries public debts are very large, as seen in Table 15.6.[8] What is troublesome in the more recent period is that the largest European debts have grown in peacetime, mostly during the 1970s. This section, which extends the two-period reasoning of Chapter 3 to many periods, shows that the debt process can be explosive and requires careful management. For this reason, **debt stabilization** has emerged as a central concern of fiscal policy.

15.4.1 The Public Debt with No Growth and No Inflation

Let us first consider the case in which seigniorage is equal to zero: no central bank financing of public deficits. The government budget deficit is the sum of the primary deficit—the excess of purchases G over net tax receipts T—and of debt service—the real rate of interest r times the existing debt stock B. To finance the deficit, in the absence of monetary financing, the government must borrow and issue new debt ΔB:

$$\text{(15.1)} \qquad \underset{\substack{\text{debt} \\ \text{accumulation}}}{\Delta B} \;=\; \underset{\substack{\text{primary budget} \\ \text{deficit}}}{G - T} \;+\; \underset{\substack{\text{debt} \\ \text{service}}}{rB.}$$

$$\underbrace{\qquad\qquad\qquad\qquad}_{\substack{\text{total budget} \\ \text{deficit}}}$$

Table 15.6	Gross Public Debt, Various Countries, 1970–1999 (% of GDP)

	1970	1980	1990	1999	2000
Austria	18.9	36.6	57.9	63.3	62.9
Belgium	64.0	77.1	125.7	113.2	109.9
Denmark	n.a.	43.7	65.8	55.6	52.0
Finland	11.8	11.6	14.4	47.2	45.4
France	n.a.	30.9	40.2	67.4	67.7
Germany	18.1	31.1	43.2	63.3	63.0
Greece	17.6	22.9	90.1	105.6	103.5
Ireland	n.a.	72.7	97.2	49.2	43.0
Italy	38.4	58.6	105.4	118.5	116.8
Japan	10.6	47.9	61.4	107.2	117.6
Netherlands	51.5	46.9	78.8	66.7	66.1
Norway	41.8	43.4	32.4	35.4	35.4
Spain	n.a.	20.8	50.6	72.8	71.2
Sweden	31.5	44.3	44.3	67.5	61.8
UK	n.a.	n.a.	39.1	55.2	54.0
USA	41.3	36.8	55.3	54.2	51.7

Source: OECD *Economic Outlook*.

[8] The table presents gross debts. In contrast, net debt takes into account the state's assets. Net debt figures exist but are considered unreliable because of the difficulty in determining the value of state assets.

| Table 15.7 | Net Debts and Primary Budget Balances, 2000[a] (% of GDP) |

	Net debt in 2000	Actual primary budget surplus in 2000	Required primary surplus:[b]	
			to stabilize absolute size of debt	to stabilize debt/GDP-ratio
Belgium	106.6	4.6	5.5	2.7
Germany	48.7	1.6	3.2	1.6
Ireland	43.0	2.3	2.1	1.1
Italy	104.4	3.4	5.8	2.9
Netherlands	52.0	3.6	3.3	1.7

[a] These are forecasts produced in 1995 by the OECD.
[b] The required surplus assumes a 5% real interest rate and a 2.5% real GDP growth rate.
Source: Eurostat and OECD, *Economic Outlook*.

The overall budget deficit ΔB is sometimes called the net public borrowing requirement. If the overall budget is in surplus, the government retires some of its existing debt or accumulates assets ($\Delta B < 0$). In the rare few instances when it is a net asset holder ($B < 0$), the government can accumulate wealth.

Expression (15.1) shows that debts tend to be explosive. Even when the primary budget is balanced ($G - T = 0$), the debt continues to grow. In this case, the government is borrowing to pay interest on the existing debt, which accumulates at the rate r. This feature of indebtedness is general and applies to any debt, be it public or private, domestic (i.e. held by domestic residents) or external.[9]

To halt the accumulation of debt at some given level, the government must run a permanent primary surplus large enough to cover the existing debt service. Expression (15.1) shows that the primary surplus required to stabilize a debt that has reached the level B is

(15.2) $T - G \quad = \quad rB.$

primary   debt service
budget surplus

[9] The tendency to grow is seen by looking at (15.1) when the primary budget is balanced: then, $\Delta B = rB$ or $\Delta B/B = r$. The same logic applies to a country's external debt (net external investment position).

Enforcing (15.2) can be a formidable task. The longer the government puts off the day of reckoning, the larger the debt becomes, and the larger is the surplus ultimately required to stabilize it. Table 15.7 presents debt levels and primary budget balances. The third column gives the primary surplus needed to stabilize the debt level in 1999 according to (15.2), assuming a real interest rate of 5%. Of the countries shown, only Ireland and the Netherlands were able to reduce the absolute value of the debt in 2000. In some cases—Germany and Italy—doing so would have required a considerable tightening of public finances. Fortunately, the following sections show that this debt stabilization criterion is excessively stringent, because it ignores both growth in GDP (the tax base) and the possibility of monetary finance.

15.4.2 The Public Debt with Growth and No Inflation

No one would seriously compare the indebtedness of the USA with that of France and Sweden. The ability to service, or pay for, the debt is obviously related to the size of the country. This is precisely why all the data presented so far have been in terms of ratios to GDP, and why the appropriate objective

Box 15.3   **Debt-Deficit Arithmetic**

Growth, no Inflation. The annual budget account (15.1), when divided by real GDP, can be transformed into a relationship which shows that the debt–GDP ratio increases with the budget deficit (as a share of GDP) and debt service on the debt–GDP ratio adjusted for GDP growth rate (g):[10]

$$(15.3) \qquad \Delta \frac{B}{Y} = \frac{G - T}{Y} + (r - g)\frac{B}{Y}.$$

As long as the real interest rate exceeds the growth rate, the debt process is explosive. For a given primary deficit as a fraction of GDP, more debt means more deficit and greater borrowing requirements. The primary budget surplus ($T - G$) required to stabilize the debt–GDP ratio is

$$(15.4) \qquad \Delta\left(\frac{B}{Y}\right) = 0 \text{ when } \frac{T - G}{Y} = (r - g)\frac{B}{Y}.$$

If the rate of interest is below the growth rate, the debt–GDP ratio can be stabilized while running a budget deficit: the economy outgrows its public debt. Of course, as long as $r > g$, a surplus is still needed to stabilize the debt–GDP ratio.

Growth and Inflation. In the presence of inflation, money has to be accounted for. The Appendix shows that the budgetary accounts are simply modified to recognize that the deficit can be financed by new debt issues or by the creation of additional monetary base M0:

$$(15.5) \qquad \Delta\left(\frac{B}{Y}\right) + \frac{\Delta M0}{PY} = \frac{G - T}{Y} + (r - g)\frac{B}{Y}.$$

Stabilizing the debt–GDP ratio now requires an even smaller primary budget surplus, or can even be achieved with a primary deficit if enough monetary base is created:

$$(15.6) \qquad \Delta\left(\frac{B}{Y}\right) = 0 \text{ when } \frac{T - G}{Y} = (r - g)\frac{B}{Y} - \frac{\Delta M0}{PY}.$$

is to stabilize the ratio of debt to GDP ratio rather than the debt level.

This distinction assumes greater importance when one recognizes that GDPs grow secularly over time. Box 15.3 shows how the debt level accounts in (15.1) and (15.2) change when we look at ratios to GDP. We see that the debt to GDP *ratio* can remain constant even if the public debt *level* keeps increasing for ever. By the same reasoning, were the stock of the debt to remain stable in a growing economy, the debt-to-GDP ratio would vanish over time. Implicitly, there is a 'race' between the GDP and the public debt, or, more precisely, between the economy's trend growth rate ($g = \Delta Y/Y$) and the real interest rate (r) which determines the rate at which the debt cumulates. When the GDP growth rate exceeds the real interest rate, a balanced primary budget is sufficient for the debt–GDP ratio to shrink. When the real interest rate exceeds the economy's growth rate, the debt process is explosive; yet, the primary surplus required to stabilize the *ratio* of the debt to GDP

is significantly smaller than that required to stabilize the *level* of the debt. This is illustrated by the last column in Table 15.7. Assuming a 5% real interest rate and a 2.5% real GDP growth rate, most countries had stabilized their debt–GDP ratio in 1996. The actual data from 2000 validate this prediction.

But why have debts increased so much in peacetime? The evolution of real interest rates and growth rates after 1975 provides part of the explanation. Over the 1960s and early 1970s, real GDP growth exceeded the real interest rate in most countries. For example, real interest rates in the UK during the period 1960–80 averaged 0.9% while real growth was 2.4%. Under such conditions, budget deficits need not result in growing debt–GDP ratios. The debt accumulation process was not explosive, at least relative to GDP, a fact that probably encouraged complacency about deficits and debts. In contrast, in the period 1980–95, UK real growth had hardly changed (2.4%), while real interest rates averaged 4.7%! The debt process became explosive and required prompt and vigorous action, but some countries failed to adjust quickly enough.

---

[10] See the Appendix for a formal derivation.

15.4.3 The Public Debt with Growth and Inflation

Inflation is a way of further relaxing the budgetary stringency required for debt stabilization. Monetary financing of the deficit occurs when the central bank purchases part of the public debt, either directly from the Treasury or indirectly on the money market. To pay for it, the central bank simply issues additional monetary base M0, a process sometimes called **seigniorage**.[11] Naturally, greater use of seigniorage results in faster money growth (via the money multiplier effect) and, eventually, higher inflation. Seigniorage is just another way of financing a deficit, as is seen by modification of the budget account (15.1) to recognize that any increase in the nominal monetary base ΔM0 provides real resources to the government valued as ΔM0$/P$:

$$(15.7) \quad \Delta B \; + \; \Delta \text{M0}/P = G - T + \quad rB.$$

$$\underset{\text{new debt}}{} \quad \underset{\text{seigniorage}}{} \quad \underset{\substack{\text{primary}\\\text{deficit}}}{} \quad \underset{\substack{\text{interest}\\\text{payments}}}{}$$

Seigniorage is a cheap source of financing because little or no interest is paid on the monetary base.[12] More importantly, the absence of debt service on the monetary base severs the link that makes the debt process explosive. Can generous money growth allow the deficit to be financed without borrowing? Possibly in the short run, but the explosiveness is simply transferred elsewhere—into inflation. All high or hyperinflationary episodes can be linked to a government's attempt to break away from its budget constraint. Hyperinflations end when governments close their deficits, or when central banks stop financing them.

15.5 Three Ways to Stabilize the Public Debt

What are the options open to a government that wants first to stabilize, and then to reduce a high and exploding debt–GDP ratio? There are three, and only three, known ways of achieving that objective: (1) cutting the deficit, possibly going to a surplus, either by reducing public spending or by raising taxes; (2) financing by money creation (monetization); (3) defaulting on some or all of the existing debt. All three amount to forms of taxation: standard taxation in the first case, taxing those who happen to hold nominal assets (money, and nominal bonds) in the second case, and taxing those who own Treasury debt in the last case.

15.5.1 Cutting the Deficit

Deficit reduction is a virtuous road to debt stabilization. Politically, though, it is also the hardest of all to implement. Public spending gives rise to interest groups that resist cuts, for example government employees who will fight for their jobs. Raising taxes is notoriously unpopular. And yet, deficit reduction has been the solution chosen and achieved in several European countries. As can be seen from Figure 5.9 and Table 15.3, countries with some of the most serious debt problems—Belgium, Denmark, Ireland, and Italy—have turned their primary budgets around. The recent European consolidation can be attributed largely to preparations for monetary union, as noted in Box 15.4.

15.5.2 Seigniorage and the Inflation Tax

Inflationary finance reduces the debt burden in two ways.[13] The first is seigniorage. While not trivial,

---

[11] This expression finds its origins in the medieval practice of local lords who had the power to mint coins and used it to reduce—debase—their gold content. In a similar fashion, governments exploit the monopoly power of the central bank in creating the medium of exchange to acquire valuable resources from the private sector. Modern seigniorage too is just another form of taxation, because the authorities exchange money, which is costless to produce, against goods and services: it is as if these goods and services were just taken away.

[12] Ch. 9 described monetization of government deficits in more detail.

[13] Both are explained in S. 9.5.1 of Ch. 9.

Box 15.4 **Euroland and the Stability and Growth Pact**

A critical step towards achieving monetary union in Europe was the convergence of monetary and fiscal policies among participating countries. While more details are provided in Chapter 20, the most important reasons for convergence imposed 'from above' are relatively easy to understand. First, and most obviously, Chapter 13 establishes that under a fixed exchange rate regime, inflation rates are equal in the long run. This also applies to a monetary union. If core inflation is persistent— because there is scepticism that the monetary union will last, or more plausibly, because of backward-looking long-term contracts and price rigidity—then member countries with different inflation rates at the outset can expect to experience protracted exchange rate misalignments and economic dislocation (see Section 13.2.3). In their wisdom, the founding fathers of the euro perceived inflation as having enough inertia to warrant harmonizing monetary policies before the consummation of the marriage.

Second, when a country has its own currency and monetary independence, it must manage its financial deficits by raising taxes, cutting spending or borrowing from its own central bank (seigniorage). As a member of a wider union, this element of fiscal responsibility is modified: recourse of individual countries to seigniorage finance is banned explicitly by the ECB Treaty. Nevertheless, it is impossible to rule out future political or financial crises in a member country which—under extreme circumstances—might lead to national default on government

debt. The consequences for Europe might be so grave as to necessitate 'bailing out' the country or region deemed 'too big to fail' by the ECB. Because European solidarity has limits, it seems sensible to keep a lid on national deficit spending, without excluding the possibility of stabilizing fiscal policy.

The initial measures for harmonization of macroeconomic conditions were stipulated in the Maastricht Treaty of 1991, and included convergence criteria on inflation, nominal interest rates, public deficits, debt, and exchange rate stability. On the basis of these criteria, which were relaxed in some cases of 'exceptional progress' towards their fulfilment (Ireland, Italy, Belgium), the current list of 'in' countries was determined. To prevent Euroland countries from misbehaving in the future, the 'Resolution of the European Council on the Stability and Growth Pact' was finalized on 17 June 1997 at the Amsterdam Summit. Embodied in Article 104 of the Treaty of Europe, the Pact focuses on net borrowing by member states, and in its current form allows a total financial deficit of member governments of up 3% of GDP. Should this be exceeded, the errant country must justify its sins to the European Commission, which can demand a hefty deposit or impose a fine as long as the deficit condition is not met. In exceptional cases or clearly recessionary situations, penalties may be deferred. While frequently criticized, the Stability Pact is plainly one reason why European budgets have moved further towards fiscal stringency as documented in Table 15.3.

---

seigniorage income is too limited to be a major factor in large-debt stabilization. It has traditionally been highest in those countries, like Spain and Italy, that imposed relatively high reserve ratios on their banks, thus generating an artificially large demand for the monetary base. (Recently, in Portugal, which has moved in the opposite direction and reduced reserve requirements, seigniorage in 1995 was negative!) The second effect is the **inflation tax** on nominal assets. Most government debts take the form of nominal non-indexed assets. When prices rise, the value of that debt is eroded and debt-holders suffer a capital loss. The inflation tax is just the mirror image of this loss: the reduction of the real value of the debt.

Seigniorage and the inflation tax go hand in hand. Seigniorage leads to money growth and therefore to inflation and debt relief via the inflation tax. Naturally, the inflation tax applies only to debt issued in local currencies. In addition, the tax works only if inflation is unexpected. The reason is that, when debt-holders anticipate inflation, they demand a nominal interest rate which compensates them for the expected erosion of the principal. The nominal interest rate rises in line with expected inflation, leaving the real interest rate unchanged.[14] In that case, there is no gain from inflation for the government and no cost to bond-holders.

---

[14] This is the Fisher principle studied in Ch. 8.

Box 15.5   **Mussolini and the Public Debt**[15]

Italy emerged from the First World War with a large debt and a sizeable budget deficit. Between 1923 and 1926, having eliminated all political opposition, Mussolini re-established near budget balance and brought the debt–GDP ratio down by reducing spending and raising taxes (Table 15.8). Yet, concerned that the debt was too short in maturity, and therefore vulnerable to market conditions, the government in November 1926 imposed a mandatory conversion of debt of less than seven-year maturity into fixed-rate (5%) longer-term bonds. In 1934, these bonds were again forcibly converted into 25-year loans bearing a 3.5% interest. The first conversion is estimated to have resulted in a partial default of 20%, the second one in a loss of 30%. After these moves, the government found it very hard to undertake new borrowing. It was forced to cease issuing short-term debt in 1927 and paid a premium estimated at 2–3% on borrowing from banks.

Table 15.8   **Public Finances in Italy, 1918–1928**

	1918	1922	1924	1926	1928
Tax revenues as % of public spending	23	46	90	100	90
Debt–GNP (%)	70.3	74.8	65.1	49.7	53.8

Source: Alesina (1988a).

In the budget accounts ((15.1) for example) it is the real interest rate that appears. For the inflation tax to work, the real interest rate must fall. When inflation rises unexpectedly and quickly enough, nominal interest rates on existing assets cannot be changed; *ex post* real interest rates fall. For long-maturity assets, the nominal interest rate cannot be modified as it is contractually fixed. This explains why *ex post* real interest rates are just the mirror image of inflation. Negative interest rates mean that bondholders actually pay for the right of lending money! This is a measure of the inflation tax.

Ex ante real interest rates are always positive, so to raise tax permanently governments must repeatedly produce inflation surprises. This is exactly how hyperinflations get under way. Indeed, hyperinflations do succeed in wiping out nominal assets. However, stopping a hyperinflation is so costly that it is an option used only in extreme political situations, for example in the Eastern European countries at the time of the collapse of the communist regimes.

In the end, monetary financing of the deficit is just another form of taxation, like excise, income, or consumption taxes. It operates by reducing the value of the money base (the central bank's liability) and of the public debt (the Treasury's liability). Inflationary finance is a tax on money and bondholders.[16]

15.5.3 Default

The most brutal way of stabilizing the debt is simply to repudiate it. Except for post-war or post-revolution periods (when the blame can be put on exceptional circumstances or previous regimes), only governments under very severe stress resort to default. This can be outright default, which is perceived as breach of confidence and leaves long-lasting scars on the reputation of governments; Box 15.5 describes the Italian experience in the Fascist era. On the other

---

[15] This box draws on Alesina (1988).

[16] More generally, inflation redistributes wealth from borrowers to lenders when the assets are nominal, i.e. set in money terms and not indexed to a price level.

hand, it can be seen as a form of taxation, one that affects bondholders, much as inflation. Indeed, partial default is exactly equivalent to a tax on bond income. If, for example, a government reduces the value of its debt by half, this is the same as imposing a 50% tax on interest and repayment of the principal.

The issue of default has different implications when the debt is owned by foreigners. Thus far, it was implicitly assumed that the public debt was held by residents. In that case, debt accumulation or stabilization amounts to a redistribution of income across generations, between those who are taxed now and those who will be taxed in the future.

When debt is owned by foreigners, the situation is different. As Chapter 5 showed, honouring external debt implies transferring resources to the rest of the world. This will require running a current account surplus, i.e. spending less than is earned. In the case of domestically held debt, the government can always correct the income distribution effects through adequately counteracting taxes and transfers. This option is not available for the foreign-held public debt, and this is one reason why it is more painful. It also explains why sovereign nations are often more willing to default on external debt when the going gets rough.

 ## Summary

1. One fundamental purpose of fiscal policy is to provide public goods and services. The boundary between what has to be produced publicly and what can be produced privately is not clear-cut.

2. A second function of fiscal policy is the redistribution of income and the alleviation of inequities that may be generated by the market mechanism. Doing so, however, may lead to inefficiencies.

3. A third function is to use the budget to offset temporary or cyclical fluctuations. This is done by running deficits in bad years—financed by borrowing—and surpluses in good years—to repay the borrowing. Countercyclical fiscal policy has three main benefits. One is tax smoothing—or the avoidance of temporary changes in tax rates; others are private consumption smoothing and private income maintenance.

4. The fact that in bad years some citizens cannot borrow on their own provides a justification for fiscal policy to step in and support private consumption smoothing.

5. If prices and wages are not fully flexible, fiscal policy can be used to stabilize demand, either directly through government spending, or indirectly through taxation by reducing fluctuations in private sector incomes. This prevents or attenuates the underutilization of productive resources during recession.

6. When they vote on the budgets, parliaments set public spending levels and tax rates. During a recession (respectively, expansion) tax receipts decline (resp. increase), leading to a deficit (resp. surplus). As a result, the budget acts as an automatic stabilizer.

7. Indebtedness is an inherently explosive process. When the primary budget is balanced and the debt is positive, it is necessary to keep on borrowing merely to service existing debt. The real debt accumulates at a rate given by the real interest rate.

8. To stabilize the level of the real debt, in the absence of money financing and real growth, the government must run a primary budget surplus equal to the interest charge. The longer it waits, the larger will be the debt and the interest burden that it faces, and the larger the required primary budget surplus.

9. In a growing economy, stabilizing the ratio of debt to GDP is a less stringent condition than stabilizing the absolute debt level. The required primary surplus is proportional to the difference between the real interest rate and the real GDP growth rate. Not only is this smaller than the real interest rate, it may well be negative, thus allowing permanent primary deficits.

10. Monetary financing reduces the debt burden for two reasons. Seigniorage provides resources directly to the government, virtually free of charge. As money growth eventually leads to inflation, the real value of nominal debt declines.

11. The inflation tax can be collected, however, only if inflation is unexpected. Otherwise the nominal interest rate rises, which protects lenders.

12. In addition to lowering the deficit—through spending cuts or tax increases—or resorting to money finance, debt can be stabilized by defaulting. This drastic form of taxation considerably hurts a government's reputation.

13. As long as the public debt is held by residents, debt stabilization or reduction implies income redistribution within the country. When part of the public debt is held by non-residents, stabilization requires a net transfer by residents to the rest of the world.

Key Concepts

- seigniorage
- public goods
- externalities
- productive efficiency
- equity–efficiency trade-off
- distortionary taxation
- consumption smoothing

- tax smoothing
- stabilization policies
- countercyclical fiscal policy
- automatic stabilizers
- cyclically adjusted budgets
- debt stabilization
- inflation tax

Exercises

1. Income taxes are typically progressive, meaning that they increase more than proportionately with income. What might be the purpose of progressivity?

2. A country has a large portion of its public debt issued in foreign currency. What effect does this have on the government's incentive to engage in inflationary finance? What does a devaluation do to the debt burden?

3. 'The national debt is a great scam, because it will never be repaid.' 'The national debt is irrelevant because we owe it to ourselves.' Comment.

4. What are the differences in terms of government revenue between an anticipated and a non-anticipated increase in the rate of inflation? The Tanzi effect refers to the loss of real revenues that governments face during hyperinflations when they cannot collect revenues sufficiently quickly. Explain why such an effect makes it difficult for governments to eliminate hyperinflations. What are some possible solutions?

5. The velocity of money is $V = PY/M$, where P is the GDP deflator, Y the real GDP, and M a monetary aggregate (e.g. M1 or M2). How does an increase in velocity affect the monetary financing of the deficit?

6. A country growing at a rate of 3.5% has a debt–GDP ratio of 40%. What is the primary budget surplus that keeps this ratio constant when the real interest rate is 2%? When it is 6%?

7. Are bank notes and coins part of the public debt? Should they be? Why or why not?

8. Suppose the debt–GDP ratio is 100%, growth is 3% per annum, and the real interest rate is 5%.
   (*a*) What is the primary government budget surplus (as a percentage of GDP) that can stabilize the debt–GDP ratio?
   (*b*) How does your answer change if interest rates fall to 2%? If growth falls to 1%?

9. The demand for central bank money H is described by the function $H/P = A \exp(-\alpha\pi)$. In long-run equilibrium the inflation rate is stable ($\partial\pi/\partial t = 0$). Seigniorage is $(\partial H/\partial t)/P$. Compute seigniorage in the long run and find the inflation rate for which the revenue is maximum.

10. The demand for (real) central bank money, the source of seigniorage, declines with the rate of inflation. Suppose, as an example, that this demand (in billions of ECUs) is given by:

π	0%	1%	2%	5%	10%	20%	25%	50%
H/P	1000	905	819	607	368	135	82	7

Seigniorage is a tax applied to this demand, whose rate is just the rate of inflation. Compute seigniorage as a function of the inflation rate. (*Hint*: an inflation rate of 5% corresponds to a tax rate equal to 0.05.) Which inflation rate maximizes seigniorage?

Suggested Further Reading

For a careful analysis of public accounts, see:
Buiter, Willem (1985), 'A Guide to Public Sector Debt and Deficits', *Economic Policy*, 1: 13–80.

For a technical exposition of the link between budget deficits, the intertemporal budget constraint, seigniorage, and inflation, see:
Sargent, Thomas J., and Wallace, Neil (1981), 'Some Unpleasant Monetarist Arithmetic', *Federal Reserve Bank of Minneapolis Quarterly Review*, 5(3): 1–17.

Studies that deal with the public debt problem in Europe and elsewhere include:
Alesina, Alberto, and Perotti, Roberto (1996), 'Fiscal Adjustments: Fiscal Expansions and Adjustments in OECD Countries', *Economic Policy*, 21: 205–48.
Bartolini, Leonardo, Symansky, Steven, and Razin, Assaf (1995), 'G7 Fiscal Restructuring in the 1990s: Macreoconomic Effects', *Economic Policy*, 20: 109–46.

Appendix: The Algebra of Budget Deficits

Real GNP Growth

We start from the budget account (15.1) and divide both sides by real GDP, Y:

$$(A15.1) \qquad \frac{\Delta B}{Y} = \frac{G}{Y} - \frac{T}{Y} + \frac{rB}{Y}.$$

Note next that an approximation of $\Delta(B/Y)$ is:

$$(A15.2) \qquad \Delta\left(\frac{B}{Y}\right) = \frac{\Delta B}{Y} - \frac{\Delta Y}{Y}\frac{B}{Y}.$$

Then, if real growth $\Delta Y/Y$ is denoted by g, we find (15.3) in the text:

$$(A15.3) \qquad \Delta\left(\frac{B}{Y}\right) = \frac{G-T}{Y} + (r-g)\frac{B}{Y}.$$

Growth, Seigniorage, and Inflation

With seignorage and inflation, it is convenient to start from the annual budget account expressed in nominal terms, where P is the price level. (So PG is nominal public spending, PB nominal public debt, etc. Recall that $M0$ is the nominal stock of central bank money.)

$$(A15.4) \qquad \Delta(PB) + \Delta M0 = PG - PT + i(PB).$$

The nominal interest rate i is used for computing debt service consistently. Dividing both sides by the nominal GNP (PY), we have:

$$(A15.5) \qquad \frac{\Delta(PB)}{PY} + \frac{\Delta M0}{PY} = \frac{PG}{PY} - \frac{PT}{PY} + i\frac{PB}{PY}.$$

Using the approximation

$$\Delta\left(\frac{PB}{PY}\right) = \frac{\Delta(PB)}{PY} - \frac{PB}{PY}\frac{P\Delta Y + Y\Delta P}{PY}$$

$$= \frac{\Delta(PB)}{PY} - \frac{PB}{PY}(g + \pi),$$

and substituting into (A15.5), we obtain (15.5) in the text:

$$(A15.6) \qquad \Delta\left(\frac{B}{Y}\right) + \frac{\Delta M0}{PY} = \frac{PG}{PY} - \frac{PT}{PY} + (i - \pi - g)\frac{B}{Y}$$

$$= \frac{G-T}{Y} + (r - g)\frac{B}{Y},$$

since the real interest rate is $r = i - \pi$. Note that a surprise inflation occurs when actual inflation exceeds expected inflation $\bar{\pi}$. The *ex ante* real interest rate is $\bar{r} = i - \bar{\pi}$, while the *ex post* real interest rate is $r = i - \pi$. The difference is $r - \bar{r} = -(\pi - \bar{\pi})$. With a positive inflation surprise, $\pi > \bar{\pi}$ and $r < \bar{r}$.

The Limits of Demand Management

16

. . . the ideas of economists and political philosophers, both when they are right and when they are wrong, are more powerful than is commonly understood. Indeed the world is fuelled by little else. Practical men, who believe themselves to be quite exempt from any intellectual influences, are usually the slaves of some defunct economist.

– J. M. Keynes

As an advice-giving profession we are way over our heads.

– R. E. Lucas Jr

16.1 Overview

Since Keynes, the possibility of ironing out the business cycle by clever macroeconomic management has inspired politicians and policy-makers. Despite the theoretical possibility of demand management developed and discussed in past chapters, there are many reasons to be cautious. The sceptical tone of this chapter reflects an ongoing reappraisal of what macroeconomic policy can actually achieve in reality. The rise in inflation, unemployment, and public indebtedness in the 1970s, as well as the painful medicine applied in the early 1980s, left a bitter taste and little stomach for experimenting again with policy activism. At the same time that macroeconomic theory has raised doubts about the general efficacy of demand management, there is even less confidence that governments are capable of using monetary policy systematically to smooth out aggregate fluctuations.

The age-old controversy between monetarists and Keynesians centres on relatively narrow and technical disagreements which can have wide-ranging implications for economic policy. The first bone of contention is the speed at which goods and labour markets clear, the degree of nominal wage and price rigidity in an economy. If markets adjust rapidly, the economy is better left alone. If markets are slow to adjust, we are back in a world of trade-offs—if still only temporary—between inflation and real economic performance. In such a world, there is a place for active **demand management** policies.

The debate is also about expectations. How do expectations of inflation, which largely influence core inflation, relate to government policy or exogenous events? Shifts in policies affect expectations and, through expectations, many aspects of agents' behaviour. The implications are troubling. For example, the past may cease to be a reliable guide for the future, as 'facts' based on past experience become irrelevant.

Expectations look to the future, but the future is unbounded. When a government announces its intentions for the next year or two, or for the next legislature, we still need to ask: And what happens afterwards? What are the government's next intentions, or the next government's intentions? The absence of long-term commitments has deleterious effects; the mere freedom to carry out policy actions can have costs. The usual response has been the setting up of rules, institutions, and practices dedicated to establishing and maintaining credibility and reputation. A new trade-off emerges between rules, which anchor the future but limit freedom of action, and discretion, which permits policies to deal with unforeseen events but creates its own uncertainties.

These ideas inevitably lead us into the realm of politics, as we require an understanding of how present and future governments act and react to each other. If voters care about economic policies, politicians will need to address this concern to stay in power, or to get into power. Economic policies are no longer exogenous. Similarly, political events, in particular electoral outcomes, may become endogenous too. One implication is that political institutions are important for economic performance, if only to create the proper backdrop for economic activity.

16.2   Policy Activism and Demand Management: What are the Issues?

16.2.1 Monetarists and Keynesians: The Debate Made Simple

For almost three decades after the publication of *The General Theory*, a fierce academic debate raged between those who had embraced the Keynesian way of thinking about the macroeconomic short run, called **Keynesians**, and those who defended the classical framework of flexible prices and relying on the inherent self-corrective nature of the economic system. The latter group, known as **monetarists**, were led by stalwarts such as Milton Friedman and Harry Johnson and put much emphasis on the role of money and monetary developments while de-emphasizing the usefulness of fiscal policy. Many disagreements which persisted into the late 1960s were focused on arcane issues such as the slopes of the *IS* and *LM* curves and the endogeneity of the money supply which have since been more or less resolved. There has even been some, but by no means complete, convergence on the contentious subject of nominal price rigidity.

Monetarists and Keynesians have never stopped disagreeing, however, about the proper role of government. Heirs of the laissez-faire school of thought, monetarists focus on the dysfunctions of government interventions and attempts to stabilize the economy; they ask whether it is possible to stabilize. Keynesians worry about unemployment and slow growth. Because they believe that market outcomes can be improved upon, they contrive ways of correcting them by **activist policies**.

The debate is illustrated in Figure 16.1. Starting from point *A*, an expansionary policy (monetary policy under flexible exchange rates, fiscal policy under fixed exchange rates) takes the economy first to point *B*, and then to point *C*, where the effect is entirely absorbed by a permanently higher rate of inflation, ratified by a proportional exchange rate depreciation. The move from *B* to *C* depends on the speed at which the short-run *AS* curve shifts. This in turn depends on how core inflation reacts to actual inflation. Quick adjustment means a fast move to *C*: policy only creates inflation, at best with a fleeting

boost to GDP. A superior solution, then, is to aim at point *D*, where inflation is low, which in this view can be achieved at little or no output cost. That is the monetarist perspective.

The Keynesian case stresses a different initial position, starting from point *A* in Figure 16.2. For one reason or another, output is below its trend level, and unemployment is above its equilibrium level. Then actual inflation is below its expected level; over time, core inflation will decline and the short-run *AS* curve will shift downward until point *C* is reached. Adjustment may take a very long time, during which unemployment is high and output is forgone. This means frustration among the unemployed, and inefficiency as productive resources remain underutilized. The preferred solution for Keynesians is to pursue an expansionary policy, bringing the *AD* curve up and, by the same token, bringing the economy swiftly to point *B* where things would settle.

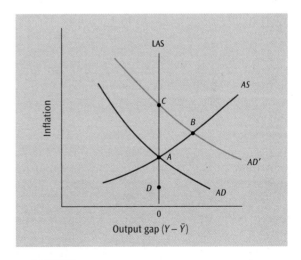

Fig. 16.1   **The Monetarist Case**

A monetary expansion moves the economy from point *A* to point *B* in the short run and to point *C* in the long run. If deviations from trend *Ȳ* are short-lived, the move is actually from point *A* to point *C*, which is not really helpful. It is more desirable to aim at point *D*, where inflation is low.

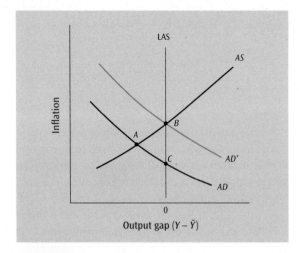

Fig. 16.2   **The Keynesian Case**

When the economy is below trend at point A, waiting for prices to adjust to reach point C may take a long time. A monetary policy boost takes the economy promptly back to full employment at point B.

The disagreement boils down to a simple question: can the economy stay away from the long-run AS schedule for a long time? Put differently, is the short-run AS curve really distinct from the vertical LAS? This, in turn, raises two issues. The first is the slope of the short-run AS curve. If it is relatively steep, there can be no lasting departure of GDP from its trend, unemployment cannot differ much from its equilibrium level, and there is no unemployment–inflation trade-off. The second issue is the time it takes for the short-run curve to give way to its long-run version. Even if it is flat but moves quickly to its long-run position, departures from trend output are short-lived.

Monetarists argue that GDP is never far from its growth trend; Keynesians disagree. It is remarkable that so sharp a divergence about the desirability of policy actions arises from an apparently narrow dispute concerning a point of detail. Indeed, it is possible to agree on the entire analysis of demand and supply, and yet disagree on every aspect of economic policy simply because there is doubt about the slope of the AS curve or about the speed at which it shifts.

16.2.2 Market-Clearing and Rational Expectations

The slope of the aggregate supply curve

What then determines the slope of the AS curve and the speed at which it shifts? The slope depends on the process of **market-clearing**. Economies in which prices and wages react strongly to conditions of excess demand in either labour or goods markets will tend to have steep AS curves. The economy tends to spend most of its time at or near trend output and equilibrium employment: all markets must clear simultaneously. This is the view that Keynes criticized in the *General Theory*. As millions of disturbances, big and small, occur all the time everywhere, the central issue is how fast prices—and wages—move in response. Monetarists believe that markets achieve equilibrium employment roughly all the time; Keynesians disagree, arguing that there is scope and need for demand management.

The speed of AS curve shifts and core inflation

The second reason the economy may stay near the vertical AS curve is because core inflation adjusts rapidly to actual inflation, i.e. the AS curve shifts. When core inflation is mostly driven by its forward-looking element and expectations are rational, the AS curve always shifts so that the economy remains on its long-run aggregate supply curve. This is often associated with the monetarist view, although some might concede that expectations take time to adjust.

Keynesians consider it misleading to think of core inflation only as expected inflation. Even if all agents perfectly anticipate the future, they may have signed nominal contracts that lock them into prices and nominal wage increases that are based on rationally expected inflation, but at some earlier period in time. Thus, when inflation deviates from these older expectations, there will be some interval of time when agents can do little or nothing about their errors. During that interval, the economy deviates from trend output.

Unemployment: Is it equilibrium or demand-driven?

The Keynesian view associates unemployment and recession with underutilization of resources. But

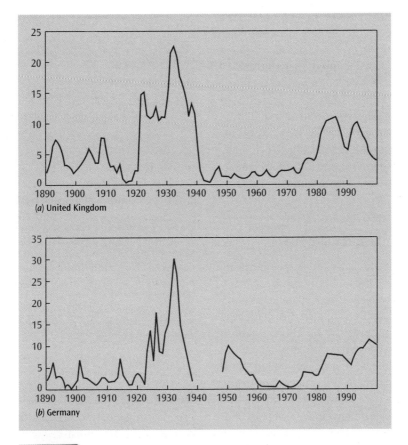

(a) United Kingdom

(b) Germany

Fig. 16.3   **British and German Unemployment Rates, 1890–1999**

Unemployment rates display considerable variability. The peaks in both countries correspond to difficult post-war conditions, the Great Depression (1929–31), and the post-oil-shock period.

Sources: Mitchell (1978); OECD *Main Economic Indicators*.

how do we know that output and employment are not at their equilibrium levels? Chapter 4 and later Chapter 11 decomposed unemployment at any point in time into a structural or equilibrium component, and that part due to cyclical fluctuation around equilibrium.[1] The first panel of Figure 16.3 shows that the British unemployment rate has fluctuated very widely over a century, ranging from under 3% at times in the early 1900s, the 1950s, and 1960s, to almost 25% of the labour force in

the early 1930s. Are these joint fluctuations in the actual and equilibrium unemployment rates, or are changes in unemployment mostly cyclical in nature, and susceptible to demand management?

While the rise in unemployment during last two decades of the twentieth century remains a subject of much debate, it is now evident that both sources of fluctuation were present. This can best be learnt by comparing different countries which have had identifiably common shocks. The second panel of Figure 16.3, which shows the German experience, shows similar experiences in the first decade of the twentieth century as well as the post-war boom. More recently, the 1980s were characterized in both

---

[1] Chs. 4 and 17 study reasons behind the increase in European equilibrium unemployment.

countries by a sharp increase in unemployment. During that decade contractionary demand policy was associated with the rise. In the 1990s, the two countries parted ways: unemployment in the UK has fallen to below 5%, while it remains stubbornly high in Germany despite a return to growth. This suggests that a different evolution of equilibrium unemployment may be at work here, associated with persistent labour market rigidities in Germany and the long-run effect of the reforms taken by Thatcher in the 1980s and maintained by successor governments.

16.2.3 Uncertainty and Policy Lags

The other battlefront between Keynesians and monetarists concerns the ability of governments to conduct policy effectively. Even if markets do not function perfectly, a case has to be made that governments can improve the situation. Establishing this case is also the subject of considerable discussion. To make the case that markets fail to adjust, Keynesians argue that many prices are set in advance because of an imperfect knowledge of future conditions, and that governments may be able to offset the effects of nominal rigidities. Yet the same uncertainty or incomplete information that prevents prices from delivering full employment of available resources may also plague government actions. Why should policy-makers have a superior ability to improve market outcomes? Incorrect pricing policies last only as long as it takes for private agents to discover the problems and take remedial action. On these grounds, monetarists assert, the best policy is to do nothing at all. If uncertainty is the main problem, governments can help simply by not making matters worse. If the government has no information advantage over the private sector, it might even do more harm than good by trying to stabilize the economy.

This critique of macroeconomic policy goes beyond the issue of government's informational advantage. Milton Friedman has argued that, in addition to the **recognition lag** (the lag in discovering that policy intervention is called for), governments need time to formulate policy, leading to

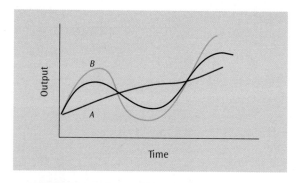

Fig. 16.4 **Lags and Demand Management Policy**

The dark line shows the business cycle arising from fluctuations in aggregate demand in the private sector. A demand management policy correctly implemented would smooth out the fluctuations (curve A). If there are significant effectiveness lags, the government may need to enact these measures well in advance of the turning points in the cycle. If instead the government reacts passively, it may simply reinforce the cycle (curve B).

decision lags. Depending on the government structure, this can be coupled with **implementation lags**, as ministries must originate and parliaments must pass legislation. Even if implemented quickly, policies take time to produce their effects. This is especially true of monetary policy. It takes several months before the easing of money market conditions and depreciating exchange rates have an impact on real activity. To make matters even worse, this **effectiveness lag** contains a large amount of uncertainty about it; economists cannot always get it right.

Figure 16.4 illustrates the debate. The dark line represents the path of output subjected to business cycle fluctuations of an economy left to itself. A perfectly thought-out and implemented policy would begin to stimulate the economy just when it is nearing a peak so that, given the various lags described above, its effects come into play just at the time it is needed. Similarly, it would turn restrictive just when the trough is passed, so as to moderate the strength of the upturn. Ideally, the outcome would be curve A. Now add uncertainty about the recognition, decision, implementation, and effectiveness lags. In the worst case, we face the risk of achieving curve *B*: the stimulus planned for the downturn affects the economy exactly when it is coming out of the recession while restraint comes into play just when the economy has peaked. Here, policy worsens matters!

In order to avoid this outcome, governments must enter the forecasting business, either generating their own 'in-house' predictions or employing outside consultants to help. In practice, national policy-makers use many of the indicators of business conditions discussed in Chapter 14 and displayed in Figure 14.3. For example, real stock prices and real money balances are relatively reliable leading indicators, and anticipate downturns by roughly four to six quarters. Another increasingly popular leading indicator is the differential, or spread, between interest rates on debt of private corporations and 'safe' government bonds; when the spread increases significantly, a recession tends to be in the making. Capacity utilization, changes in inventory stocks, and investment spending plans also prove useful in the forecasting game, offering somewhat less lead time. A change in the real exchange rate, if exogenously brought about, will tend to lead GDP; as an endogenous reaction to the economic situation, it will contain little new information at all. The very fact that the lead time of these indicators is frequently only a year to eighteen months suggests that Friedman's point about keeping ahead of the cycle must be taken seriously. At the same time, the problem may not always be as severe as supporters of laissez-faire would like us to think.

16.2.4 **The Costs of Inflation**

A frequent by-product of the Keynesian approach to demand management is higher inflation, as depicted in Figure 16.2. Unless contractionary policy is pursued with the same vigour as expansionary policy, there will be an upward bias or drift in the rate of inflation. This raises in turn the rather important question of priorities. Couldn't lower joblessness and higher output outweigh the

inconvenience of permanently higher inflation? The cost of inflation is another source of disagreement between Keynesians and monetarists. Inflation is undesirable, yet it is surprisingly difficult to explain why.

Income distribution

One commonly held fear is that inflation has important redistributive effects. First, inflation redistributes income by distorting relative prices. When prices rise rapidly, even small differences in rates of increase can lead to dramatic relative price changes. Typically, real wages stay ahead, which hurts firms' profitability, eventually deterring investment and harming growth. Those on fixed incomes and limited political clout, such as pensioners or dole recipients, do not keep up. Real exchange rates tend to swing widely in high inflation environments, shifting income between local and foreign producers, and between the local producers of traded and non-traded goods.

Second, inflation redistributes wealth. In contrast to real assets (real estate, durable goods, foreign exchange, precious metals), the value of nominal non-indexed assets is eroded if inflation comes as a surprise which is not factored into the agreed nominal rate of return. When real interest rates plunge to negative levels, wealth shifts from lenders to borrowers. Hyperinflations, in particular, can leave a legacy that survives many generations: 75 years on, Germans still consider inflation as an absolute evil.

The value of money

The answer to income and wealth redistribution is indexation. If all nominal values are indexed, the losers are simply those who hold money, which, by definition, is not indexed. As nominal interest rates rise, agents reduce their holdings of money balances. The losses suffered when the value of money declines steadily—more frequent trips to the bank—may seem trivial. Yet examples of hyperinflation in history show that the consequences can be extremely disruptive. Box 16.1 explains these costs and the concept of an ideal or 'optimal' rate of inflation.

Box 16.1 **Optimal Inflation**

Milton Friedman has argued that the optimal rate of inflation is negative and equal to minus the real interest rate, i.e. minus the marginal productivity of capital.[2] The nominal interest rate, the sum of the real interest rate and inflation, would then be zero. Friedman's argument rests on the principle that any good should be supplied up to the point where its marginal cost of production equals its price, itself equal to the marginal benefit to the consumer. For the public, the price of money is the opportunity cost of holding it, and in Chapter 8 that was shown to be the nominal interest rate. The cost of producing money turns out to be virtually nil (even a €100 banknote costs the central bank or printing office a couple of cents to produce). In theory, the state could make its citizens better off by providing them with a public good (money) which costs virtually nothing to make. To motivate people to hold this money in real terms, however, the opportunity costs must be driven as low as possible, i.e. the nominal interest rate must be close to zero.

While Friedman's point that households and firms use valuable resources for economizing on their holdings of money is certainly correct, these costs are most evident when inflation is so high that the demand for money all but vanishes, as was argued in Chapter 8. People spend an inordinate amount of time and energy in essentially unproductive activities, trying to avoid the inflation tax by speculating in foreign exchange, hoarding goods, and spending the pay cheque as quickly as possible. One problem with Friedman's prescription is that the relevance of these costs at low inflation rates are probably very small. Besides, inherent difficulties in measuring the rate of inflation—due to quality improvements, new products, and demand substitution—mean that there is a risk of erring and 'overdeflating' the economy, which would significantly stunt investment and consumer durable spending. If the true rate of deflation exceeds the rate of return on capital, agents have a powerful incentive to shift their assets into cash and bank deposits to ride the deflation wave. Why buy anything now when prices will be much lower next year? The recent experience of Japan, which has suffered a prolonged slump for the decade of the 1990s and endured declines in the GDP deflator in the period 1998–2000, is suggestive evidence that Friedman was off the mark on this issue.

Uncertainty and the value of price signals

Prices are essential signals in market economies: they tell producers what and how to produce, consumers what and how to consume, whether to save, etc. In all cases, what matters is not absolute but relative prices, that is, what one particular good costs in terms of others. A correct interpretation of (relative) price signals is crucial to the efficiency of a market economy. High inflation usually means more variable inflation. The more variable inflation is, the less confidence firms and households have that observed changes in money prices for goods and services represent relative price changes, rather than just inflation. Firms and households will tend to underreact to true relative price signals, confusing movements in the price level with changes in relative price. Evidence for the distortionary effect of inflation is given in Figure 16.5. Panel (a) documents the positive link between inflation level and variability. Panels (b) and (c) show that a more uncertain inflation is associated with more variable real wages and unemployment, an indication that nominal fluctuations may have real effects. When the efficient functioning of the price mechanism is attenuated, overall productivity declines, eventually resulting in lower growth and higher unemployment. Indexation may worsen the situation because it tends to freeze the hierarchy of all relative prices and to lock in real rigidities.

---

[2] The argument that the real interest rate should be equal to the marginal productivity of capital is presented in Ch. 6.

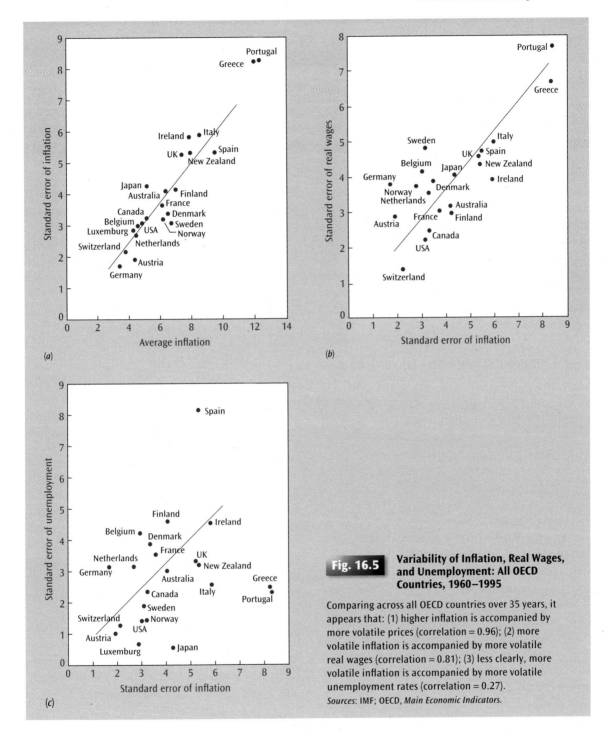

Fig. 16.5 Variability of Inflation, Real Wages, and Unemployment: All OECD Countries, 1960–1995

Comparing across all OECD countries over 35 years, it appears that: (1) higher inflation is accompanied by more volatile prices (correlation = 0.96); (2) more volatile inflation is accompanied by more volatile real wages (correlation = 0.81); (3) less clearly, more volatile inflation is accompanied by more volatile unemployment rates (correlation = 0.27).

Sources: IMF; OECD, *Main Economic Indicators*.

16.3 Expectations of Policy

The importance of expectations of the future on present decisions is stressed in Part II of this textbook. No important economic choice can ignore the impact of the future. Consumption and saving, investment, price- and wage-setting and asset allocation are all sensitive to agents' perceptions of the future. Among the many forces shaping the future are policy actions. Assessing the role and effectiveness of economic policies cannot, therefore, be conducted only by linking today's policies to today's outcomes. In fact, tomorrow's (expected) policies may be more important for today's outcome. This opens up a fascinating range of issues, including the puzzling recognition that current policy actions themselves may respond to agents' expectations of future policy actions.

16.3.1 Policy Regimes: The Lucas Critique

We know that current consumption is driven by wealth and current disposable income. Wealth, in turn, is the present value of future net incomes. Wealth is not observable because it depends on private expectations and because many of its components—chiefly human capital—are not explicitly valued by markets. In contrast, the link between consumption and disposable income discussed in Chapter 6 can be observed directly. This link takes wealth as given, and as long as wealth changes slowly is an acceptable approximation. If wealth were to change, however, previously established patterns linking current consumption and disposable income may cease to hold. Since wealth depends on agents' expectations, shifts in these expectations can have dramatic effects. For example, a temporary tax reduction affects current disposable income, but wealth hardly at all, with little effect on consumption. However, if believed to be permanent, the same tax reduction will increase wealth and boost consumption significantly. In the end, important policy changes that affect the future—called changes in the policy regime, because they correspond to lasting policy shifts—may break the pattern linking consumption and income observed over a previous regime.

The point is a general one. It underlies the **Lucas critique**, which asserts that past behaviour of economic actors can be a poor guide for assessing the effects of policy changes.[3] The actions of private agents are driven less by current behaviour of the government than by perceptions of their general rules of conduct, or the **policy regime**. For this reason, reactions of the public and financial markets to economic policy actions cannot necessarily be predicted by past behaviour.

One implication of the Lucas critique for policy is that governments are on safer grounds when planning small steps. Credible regime changes may trigger qualitatively different private reactions. This can be interpreted as yet another argument against activism, and in any case is a good reason for governments to be cautious. Another implication is that policy-making must combine current actions and binding commitments for the future. The following sections illustrate the Lucas critique in action.

Fiscal policy and regime change

One of the surprising implications of the Lucas critique is that a fiscal expansion—contrary to the usual expectation under a constant policy regime—might have *contractionary* effects. The case could arise if, for example, an increase in government purchases is perceived by households as permanent. The government budget constraint requires that higher public spending be matched in present value by higher taxes, which cut into private wealth.[4] Lower private wealth, in turn, leads to less private spending. If the reduction in private spending more than offsets the increase in public spending, it becomes possible that a fiscal expansion will be met by a negative effect on aggregate demand.[5] In effect, the private sector interprets the current increase in public spending as a first step towards fiscal relaxation which will, in

---

[3] This principle was first established in 1976 by Robert Lucas Jr, a leader of the Chicago school and Nobel Prize laureate. The Lucas critique has radically changed the way macroeconomists think about policy and its effects on the economy.

[4] This discussion is related to the Ricardian equivalence principle presented in Ch. 5.

[5] Graphically, the *IS* and *AD* curves shift to the left, not to the right.

the end, require severe future tax increases. The fall in perceived wealth, and in private spending, may be considerable, and can overwhelm the current expansionary effect of a fiscal policy change.

Conversely, a fiscal contraction could be expansionary if households, previously pessimistic about the government's ability to deal with its budget deficit and indebtedness, associate current spending cuts with a lasting policy of fiscal relief and infer a significant increase in their wealth. This intriguing possibility seems to characterize stabilization episodes in Germany, Denmark, and Ireland during the 1980s, in which fiscal contractions were accompanied by strong economic expansions. Box 16.2 presents the Danish case. A related example, that of France in the 1920s, is presented below in Box 16.5.

Box 16.2 **Denmark in the Mid-1980s**[6]

Over the period 1979–82, the Danish debt–GDP ratio rose at an unsustainable rate of 10% per year. In late 1982 the government adopted a tight debt stabilization package, cutting public spending and raising taxes. Table 16.1 shows how the deterioration of public finances was halted and reversed. Surprisingly, however, private consumption rose at the same time that tax increases cut into disposable income. Part of the explanation is that expected future tax liabilities of Danish households fell—while current taxes were raised—because the reduction in public spending was perceived as a serious policy regime change. A reduction in government spending believed to be permanent implies an increase in private wealth, increasing consumption spending, perhaps by enough to offset the effect of current tax increases.

Another, complementary interpretation of the Danish stabilization is that the government simultaneously changed its monetary policy regime: it abandoned its policy of accepting moderate inflation matched by crawling exchange rate devaluations within the EMS, and adopted a hard peg to the Deutschmark along the lines of the Netherlands (see Box 13.5). With an endogenous monetary policy determined by Germany, interest rates fell sharply. Wealth rose with the decline in interest rates, as witnessed by a bond and stock market boom during the period. As a result, consumption increased.

Table 16.1 **Fiscal Stabilization in Denmark, 1979–1986**

	1979–82	1983–6
Government		
Av. growth rate of public consumption (%)	4.0	0.9
Av. change (% of GDP) in cyclically adjusted:		
Net taxes	−0.3	1.3
Budget deficit	1.8	−1.8
Private sector		
Av. growth rate (%) of		
Disposable income	2.6	−0.3
Consumption	−0.8	3.7
Business investment	−2.9	12.7
Exports	6.0	3.2
GDP	1.3	3.6
Tangible Wealth	−4.2	7.7

Source: Giavazzi and Pagano (1990).

---

[6] This box draws on the study by Giavazzi and Pagano (1990).

Credible policy announcements

When the government announces a policy change, private agents tend to react with suspicion. This is not necessarily because governments are untrustworthy, but because they are political animals that react to short-run changes in their electoral prospects. Oftentimes the implementation of credible policy requires constant gentle reminders to both the public and policy-makers themselves of what was promised or expected in the past. For this reason, the UK government in the mid-1980s introduced the concept of medium-term financial strategy (MTFS). Each year, the government announces its fiscal policy intentions for the following three years. While not binding, the public nature of these announcements makes it costly to renege on them, since politicians do not like to lose face or have to apologize for departures from announced plans.

Another example of non-binding announcements can be found in the domain of monetary policy. It has become an increasingly popular practice among central banks not only to target inflation publicly, as discussed in Chapter 9, but also to publish public *forecasts* of inflation at periodic intervals. The most prominent of these are produced by the Bank of England. The ECB too publishes its own inflation forecasts. Since central banks have ultimate control over growth in the money supply and inflation, these

forecasts—to which they are held accountable by the public—reflect not only their available information, but also their own unobservable actions and deliberations. While it is clear that unanticipated supply or demand shocks may cause significant deviations from announced targets, the public announcement of central bank inflation forecasts makes it unlikely that central banks themselves will be a source of inflationary surprises.

Stabilizing hyperinflations

Hyperinflations—when the *monthly* rate of inflation exceeds 50%—are interesting because they can uncover economic mechanisms that are less easy to detect under normal conditions. A key aspect of hyperinflations is that core inflation becomes entirely forward-looking with an increasingly shorter time horizon. When prices rise at a rate of 50% or more per month, money-holders need to worry more about tomorrow's price level rather than today's.

Hyperinflations have been observed in a number of countries over the past century, and some of these cases are reported in Box 16.3. Sustained, significant surges in the inflation rate accompanied the end of central planning in Poland, Serbia, Russia, Ukraine, and Belorus. One of the best-known historical examples of hyperinflation is that of the Weimar Republic (Germany) in the period 1922–3. Table 16.2 shows

Table 16.2 German Hyperinflation: Money, Prices, and Inflation, January 1922–October 1923

	Currency (Jan. 1922 = 1)	Prices (Jan. 1922 = 1)	Inflation (% per month)
January 1922	1	1	1
January 1923	16	75	189
March 1923	45	132	−12
May 1923	70	221	157
July 1923	354	2,021	386
August 1923	5,394	25,515	1,262
September 1923	227,777	645,946	2,532
October 1923	20,201,256	191,891,890	29,720

Source: Holtfrerich (1986).

Box 16.3 **Fiscal Austerity and Stopping Hyperinflations**

Uncontrollable budget deficits are at the root of all hyperinflations. The basic linkage between budget deficits, public debt, and money growth was described in Chapter 15. When inflation rate rises to hyperinflation levels, the government finds it difficult to raise real resources via taxes, since taxpayers often intentionally postpone paying taxes and thereby reduce or eliminate their real tax burden. In the final stages of a hyperinflation, the entire deficit, and sometimes the entire budget, is financed by seigniorage, i.e. central bank credit. This new credit is matched by high-powered money growth and becomes the fuel for inflation, since monetary neutrality and $\mu = \pi$ will hold.[7] Formally, if the real budget deficit is $(G - T)$, then the nominal budget deficit is $P(G - T)$ and $\Delta M0 = G - T$, so the inflation rate in a hyperinflation is roughly given by

$$\pi = \mu = \frac{\Delta M0}{M0} = \frac{(G - T)P}{M0} = \frac{(G - T)/Y}{M0/PY}$$

which is just the ratio of the real deficit to real monetary base, both as fractions of real GDP. (Note that the denominator is endogenous and likely to *decline* as hyperinflations intensify.) Successful policies which ended hyperinflations share the feature that they credibly closed the budget deficit, even if in a number of creative ways:

Germany (1921–3): Monetary reform (the Rentenmark): 1 new Rentenmark = 10^{12} old paper marks; new central bank (Rentenbank) with binding limits on the volume of banknotes and lending to government; balanced government budget; dismissal of 25% of all government employees and 10% of civil servants discharged; a slight rise in unemployment in 1924.

Austria (1921–3): Establishment of an independent central bank forbidden to finance deficits with banknote advances; banknote issue backed by gold, foreign earnings assets, and commercial bills; currency reform, austerity budget, and new taxes; substantial increase in measured unemployment from September 1922 to March 1923.

Hungary (1922–4): New central bank prohibited from lending to government except on security of gold or foreign bills; gold reserves imposed; budget balanced by late 1924; less substantial increase in unemployment than in other episodes.

Poland (1922–3): New central bank; 30% reserve backing of notes (gold and foreign assets) beyond which backing of silver and bills of trade required; quick government moves to balance the budget; currency reform which imposed fixed gold content. Rise in unemployment by 50%; later loss of discipline by the central bank, deterioration of foreign exchange rate and price level.

Bolivia (1985–6): Exchange rate pegged by government using reserve loan from the IMF; nominal wage freeze; balanced budget; new valorized (inflation-proof) taxes introduced. Substantial increase in unemployment; output decline of 30%; real interest rates remained at double-digit levels for several years thereafter.

Israel (1985): Sharp cut in the budget deficit from 17% to 8% of GDP; US dollar exchange rate stabilized; new independence for the central bank, and a dramatic reduction in growth. Sharp rise in unemployment.

Poland (1990): Sharp cut in subsidies; sharp devaluation of currency followed by peg to US dollar; credit from central bank to government severely restricted. Unemployment rose from nil to 10%, output fell by some 10%, and real wages fell sharply.

Russia (1995): Move by the government to finance its deficit through borrowing directly from the markets (Treasury bills were created under the name of GKO) and the central bank committed the exchange rate to a crawling peg vis-à-vis the dollar with narrow bands of fluctuations, called the 'corridor'. GDP fell by about 10% between 1994 and 1997 while inflation declined from 130% to 11%.

Sources: Sargent (1982); Dornbusch and Fischer (1986); Berg and Sachs (1992).

---

[7] In hyperinflation episodes, bank deposits tend to disappear (why?), so the money multiplier tends to 1. Furthermore, rates of increase in money and prices dwarf that of the growth in real balances which accompany economic growth, so the latter can be ignored.

the price index and associated rate of inflation in Germany as well as the money stock during that period. In the single month of October 1923, the price index rose by 29,720%. This makes for a *daily* average increase of about 19%, and it could well have been double or triple that amount on some days. Failing to adjust wages or prices for just one day would have meant economic ruin. Under such conditions, nominal rigidities—which arise because it is costly to change prices too often—disappear entirely. Table 16.2 shows that money, prices, and the exchange rate in Germany moved tightly together during the hyperinflation, indicating that neutrality held on a monthly basis.

To defeat a hyperinflation, a lasting, credible reduction of money growth is required. There is no getting around this. The problem is that, if governments have gone down the route of hyper-inflation, it is probably for serious reasons. It is unlikely that mere announcements of lower monetary growth—or higher interest rates—will suffice to convince households and firms that the episode is over; rather, a policy regime change is necessary. First and foremost, stopping a hyperinfla-tion requires fiscal austerity. Several examples which confirm this conclusion are given in Box 16.3. Closing the budget deficit and bringing down the rate of money growth represent a dramatic com-bination of restrictive policies. The result is guaran-teed, eventually, as long as this policy is rigorously pursued.

The true challenge in the short run is to limit the output costs of the disinflation, and to make it politically acceptable and sustainable. The key to success is to affect expectations in the private sector. If the policy shift is convincing enough to shake the forward-looking component of core inflation, the costs can be contained. The necessary condition is that the monetary authorities be committed as clearly and unambiguously as possible to a new policy regime of non-monetary finance of budget deficits. Merely issuing a new currency—as in Argentina and Brazil in the 1980s—without any change in the policy regime is not enough. A better example is the end of the Weimar Republic hyperinflation. In January 1924, Germany created a new independent central bank which was prohibited from lending

to the Treasury. These features survive in modern Germany. In fact, inflation stopped in November 1923, when the new constitution of the bank was made public, and before it actually came into existence.

Because it is the sole determinant of inflation in the long run, a permanent reduction of monetary growth is clearly a necessary element of any success-ful stabilization policy. Policies which stop there are often known as 'orthodox' disinflation policies. Experience has shown that they run a significant risk of a protracted recession, since little is generally done to convince the public that the monetary authorities mean serious business. As a result, core inflation is slow to recognize or treat as credible the policy shift. Credibility is therefore essential for limiting the costs of disinflation. Quite often, the authorities attempt to supplement tight money by announcing a set of nominal 'anchors' designed to signal their determination. These 'heterodox strat-egies' were initially implemented in Bolivia and Israel in 1985, and success there led to the use of nominal anchors in other countries, for example Poland in 1990. Box 16.4 gives more details on heterodox policies.

16.3.2 Reputation and Credibility

If expectations of future policy actions affect private behaviour, governments may try to 'mani-pulate' expectations. This phenomenon is most apparent in the case of the Phillips curve: a promise of less inflation in the future, if believed, lowers both core and actual inflation now. Once this is achieved and inflation is low, will not the govern-ment be tempted to create an inflation surprise, for example to reduce the real value of its debt? Such attempts at manipulation may seem of little importance, because when the private sector dis-covers that promises are not upheld, it will simply revise its expectations and trust the government less.

In fact, the problem is more serious. How can a government that truly wants to keep inflation low convince the public of its intentions? If it reneges on its commitments, then the public will always want to be prepared for broken promises, and will

Box 16.4 Heterodox Disinflation Policies

The idea behind 'heterodox' strategies of announcing so-called nominal anchors is simultaneously to announce the new money growth targets and to fix some key nominal variables, like the exchange rate or wages. Those who depend on these prices naturally stand to lose. To assuage them, heterodox policies sometimes start by raising these prices, so as to provide an 'advance compensation', and then freezing them, or slowing them down by administrative rules. In Poland wages were increased by 30% before the programme was in place. They were then allowed to grow at only a fraction of the inflation rate (30% in January 1990, 20% from February to April, and 60% for the rest of the year except for a safety valve of 100% in July). The control mechanism was a tax of 200%–500% imposed on firms on wage growth in excess of the ceilings. The exchange rate was devalued by 31.6% on 1 January 1990 and held unchanged until May 1991. The path of inflation is shown in Figure 16.6. Real wages, which initially improved, went on declining, cumulating to an average loss of 31%. The initial undervaluation of the exchange rate allowed for a boost in exports, but then became progressively overvalued as inflation picked up. Nominal anchors are designed to buttress the credibility of the plan: by administratively controlling these anchors, the government makes the continuation of inflation painful and inconsistent with its own objectives. Sticking

to the anchors is a signal of a government's determination. Yet in the end they are a supplement, and no substitute, for the hard work of reducing the budget deficit which lies at the root of the hyperinflation problem.

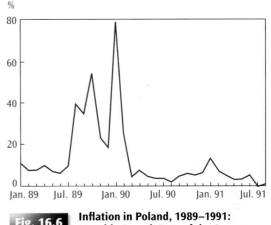

Fig. 16.6 Inflation in Poland, 1989–1991: Monthly Growth Rate of the Consumer Price Index

Inflation appeared towards the end of the Communist regime, peaked in January 1990 when prices were freed and subsidies cut, and then declined sharply.
Source: Berg and Sachs (1992).

conservatively assume a higher rate of inflation than the government intends to adopt. Core, and therefore actual, inflation will not decline. Reducing core inflation requires a period of recession (as at point *A* in Figure 16.2).

A similar example involves tax policy, in particular, the credibility of reductions in the corporate profits tax. Figure 16.7 reproduces the firm's investment decision.[8] A tax reduction shifts the ray describing the cost of capital from *OR* to *OR'*. This provides incentives for firms to accumulate more capital, from *K** to *K*'*. But firms must ask themselves how the government will meet its intertemporal budget

constraint once it has reduced corporate profit taxes. Could it be that the government will change its mind later on, when pressed to close the budget deficit, and tax already installed capital? If firms suspect such a policy, they will simply ignore the initial incentive. It is essential therefore for the government to promise that future taxes will not affect installed capital. This promise is not credible, however, for when the capital is in place the government's best course of action is to renege.

These are just two examples of a wider phenomenon. A broad range of policies are **time inconsistent**: policies that appear optimal today (low inflation, reduced taxes on corporate profits, and no taxation on installed capital) are not optimal later on, especially after agents have adjusted their

[8] Ch. 6 develops the principle of an optimal stock of capital.

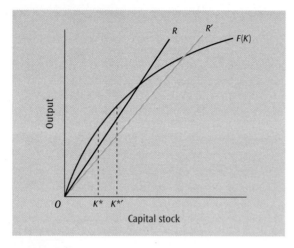

Fig. 16.7 The Effect of a Reduction in Corporate Taxes

A reduction of corporate profit taxation reduces the required pre-tax rate of profit. As the ray *OR* shifts to *OR'*, the optimal capital stock rises from *K** to *K*'*, with a corresponding increase in output.

behaviour accordingly.[9] If a course of action is time inconsistent, it is not credible, because the private sector will not consider it likely to be implemented. What is left is always less desirable: a higher rate of inflation than the government wishes, and less capital accumulation.

16.3.3 Rules versus Discretion

The phenomenon of time consistency is so conspicuous that societies have designed a number of ways of coping with it. The most obvious is the establishment of legal rules. For example, it is against the German Treaty of Rome for the ECB to lend money to Euroland governments. The second strategy is for the government to build up a **reputation**, i.e. the perception that it would never pursue such policies. To do so, it may impose rules upon itself to convince the public of its will to refrain

[9] Time inconsistency is a very general phenomenon, which applies to many fields besides economics. A son will promise to drive carefully if lent his parents' car; a person in prison always pledges not to engage in unlawful activity if released early; politicians promise the moon if elected. All of these promises are time inconsistent. The risk is that only time-consistent solutions, which are less desirable for all involved, are adopted: no son is lent a car, no inmate is released early, and politicians are never trusted.

from certain actions (like printing money), even if at some point such actions prove highly desirable.

Rules have the merit of preventing time-inconsistent actions. A vivid description of rules often refers to 'binding the hands' of the policy-maker. Rules, however, may also prevent governments from taking actions that are desirable. For example, it is often suggested that governments be forbidden from running budget deficits to avoid triggering the explosive debt process. A no-deficit rule, however, would block the automatic stabilizer mechanism. In the midst of a recession, when net taxes decline, such a rule imposes spending cuts or tax increases, i.e. contractionary policies which deepen the recession.

In the USA, budget rules exist in forty-nine of the fifty states (the exception being Vermont). (Similar, although less restrictive, rules exist for the German *Länder*.) No-deficit rules exist in thirty-six states. In nine states the automatic stabilizer is allowed to operate in that budgets are balanced on average, allowing deficits in bad years to be repaid in better times. Finally, more discretion is allowed in the remaining twenty states, where either the government or the legislature must adopt a budget balanced *ex ante*, not *ex post*. There is no binding rule at the federal level in the USA, nor has any sovereign state felt it necessary so far to adopt binding budgetary rules. Fiscal policy discretion is perceived as too important to be given up, or else it is felt that the time inconsistency problem can be dealt with by reputation instead of rules. The Growth and Stability Pact similarly contains escape clauses under hardship, allowing countries to run deficits greater than 2% of GDP in cases of severe recession. The role of credibility in episodes of debt is illustrated by the case of France in the 1920s in Box 16.5.

16.3.4 Central Bank Independence

Central banks face some of the most serious time-inconsistency problems. The value of money rests on the assumption that central banks will not create too much of it, despite strong incentives to do so. One incentive is the revenue from seigniorage. History shows that this temptation is often difficult to resist. Furthermore, surprise inflation reduces

Box 16.5 **High Debt in Inter-war France**[10]

France emerged from the First World War with a public debt of about 150% of GDP. Figure 16.8 shows the budget deficit, the wholesale price index, and an index representing the exchange rate (rising as the French franc depreciates). For a while, the French government financed huge deficits by borrowing against expected war reparations imposed upon Germany. When it became clear that Germany would not pay, sharp political disagreements made it impossible to close the deficit.[11] The alternatives under consideration were a tax on wealth ('the rich can pay' was a favourite slogan), inflation, or default. Inflation closely tracks debt stabilization attempts. The first surge in inflation (1919–20) corresponds to an early attempt at seigniorage finance. The second one (1923–4) followed the French occupation of the Ruhr in a last-ditch effort to extract war reparations. Inflation stopped in March 1924, when the parliament

adopted an across-the-board 20% tax increase. Soon afterwards, a left-wing coalition came to power. To improve its credibility, it adopted a rule establishing ceilings on central bank advances to the Treasury, but then secretly violated them. When the truth surfaced (April 1925), inflation shot up again. Each bout of nervousness was accompanied by massive capital flight and pressure on the exchange rate.

In July 1926 Raymond Poincaré, a conservative and highly respected politician, became prime minister. He promptly raised indirect and income taxes—but not taxes on wealth—and appointed as governor of the Bank of France a staunchly independent personality, Émile Moreau. The credibility of the Poincaré–Moreau team had a visibly powerful effect: from the brink of hyperinflation, prices stopped immediately and the franc even appreciated.

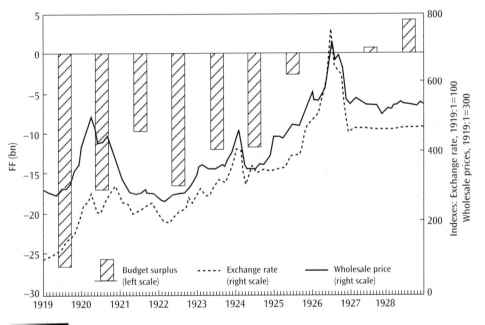

Fig. 16.8 **France in the 1920s**

Several partial attempts at solving the post-war debt and deficit problem brought temporary price and exchange rate relief. The mere appointment of a credible prime minister and a credible governor of the Banque de France brought price and exchange rate stability.

Source: Alesina (1988).

---

[10] This box draws on the study by Alesina (1988).   [11] The newborn Communist Party was rising, as were far-rightist movements.

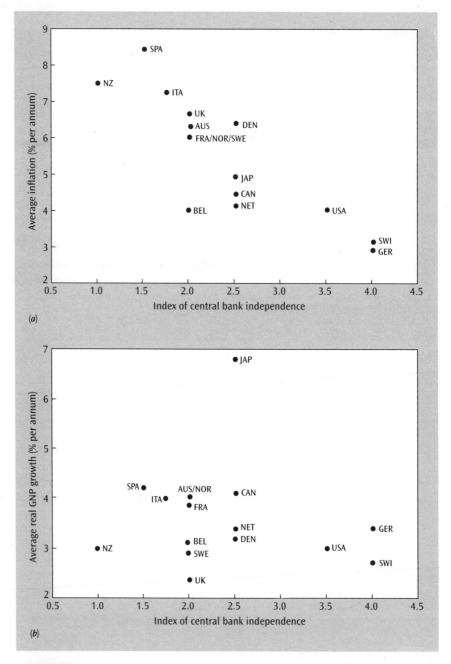

Fig. 16.9   **Inflation, Growth, and Central Bank Independence**

Both charts link an index of central bank independence to the inflation and GDP growth performance of OECD countries over the period 1955–88. Panel (*a*) exhibits a clear relationship: inflation is lower the more independent is the central bank. Panel (*b*) fails to reveal any link between independence and GDP growth: independence delivers low inflation at no cost.

Source: Alesina and Summers (1993).

the value of the public debt, and highly indebted treasuries often ask their central banks to help out.

Solutions to this problem are usually based on rules, or reputation, or both. *Rules* take several forms. The central bank may forfeit its power to impose reserve requirements (e.g. the UK and Switzerland); this reduces the demand for the monetary base which is the source of seigniorage. Another rule is to forbid the central bank from lending directly to the Treasury, and/or to limit its holdings of public debts (e.g. Germany). In general, central banks actively cultivate their reputations. One approach is publicly to adopt some explicit targets—money growth, inflation, a fixed exchange rate. Under conditions of high inflation, governments sometimes pre-announce a schedule of devaluations.[12]

In the end, however, the best way for a government to enhance its reputation is to grant its central bank independence from government influence and interference. Figure 16.9 relates the economic performance of the OECD countries to a measure of the degree of economic independence of central banks.[13] Panel (a) shows that where the central bank is more independent inflation tends to be lower. What about the output–inflation trade-off? From panel (b) it can be seen that there is no link between economic growth and the degree of central bank independence. The two panels together have a clear implication: by granting its central bank a large degree of independence, a country achieves low inflation at no cost in terms of long-run growth. This result is consistent with a vertical long-run *AS* curve. In the end, an independent central bank's main asset is its credibility. This provides a clear incentive for it to aim at a low inflation rate, and in the long run the economy will then settle in the lower portion of its *LAS* schedule. Some means of establishing central bank independence are presented in Box 16.6.

Box 16.6   The Nuts and Bolts of Central Bank Independence[14]

The autonomy of a central bank depends on its political independence and its economic freedom of manoeuvre. As a central bank is vested with important authority and serves the public interest, it must be subject to some measure of democratic control. The line between democratic control and political interference is a thin one, though. **Political independence** depends upon such aspects as the way in which central bank governors and boards are appointed. Long terms of appointment, with no possibility of early dismissal, offer more independence than terms with no set limit so that dismissal can occur at any time. Non-renewability of the term in office removes the incentive to please politicians. Current arrangements are described in Table 16.3. For example, the board members of the European Central Bank are appointed for eight years, non-renewable terms, while governors serve a minimum of five years with a renewal option; presidents of the National Central Banks are chosen according to national practice. Although governments often insist on being represented on the policy-making boards, they no longer exert direct influence on monetary policy decisions. When conflicts arise, precise procedures contribute to greater autonomy. In Denmark and the UK, there are no legal avenues for resolving disagreements between the central bank and the government, which effectively means that the government can impose its will. In Euroland, the European Central Bank is not obliged to obtain approval for policy decisions, although they must present their policies to the European Parliament at regular intervals and accept the non-voting presence of the Finance Ministry of the country which holds the EU presidency.

Economic independence depends on the practical aspects of daily operations. For example, the central bank may be able to restrict its lending to the Treasury. Yet, as open market operations can be the back-door for financing budget deficits, in Euroland, the central bank is not allowed to participate in auctions for Treasury bills or

---

[12] This strategy has been pursued in numerous Latin American countries, in Israel, and in Eastern and Central European countries.
[13] Ch. 9 presents an alternative measure of central bank independence.
[14] This box owes much to the work of Grilli et al. (1991).

Continued

Terms of Central Bank Governors and Boards

Canada
    Governor appointed by finance minister for 3-year term, renewable
    Board appointed by government for 3-year term, renewable

Germany
    President appointed by federal president for 8-year term, non-renewable
    Council members appointed by federal president for 8-year term, renewable

Netherlands
    President appointed by government for 7-year term, renewable
    Governing board appointed by government for 7-year term, renewable

UK
    Governor appointed by government for 5-year term, renewable

Switzerland
    Directorate of 3, appointed by council for 8-year term, renewable

USA
    President appointed by senate for 4-year term, renewable
    All board members (including president) appointed for 14-year term

European System of Central Banks (Maastricht Treaty)
    President appointed by EC Council for 8-year term, non-renewable
    Executive board members (up to 5 in addition to president) appointed by
        EC Council for 8-year term, non-renewable
    Council includes board members and governors of National Central Banks,
        each with terms of at least 5 years, renewable

Source: Roll et al. (1993), central bank communications.

to purchase new government debt. Of course, the ECB and all central banks will always be subject to pressure from finance ministries when interest rates are determined, since they help determine the financing costs of governments. Another important aspect is who decides on exchange rate policy, since money supply, interest, and exchange rates cannot be set independently. In Euroland, the exchange rate is decided by the council of ministers of the Euroland countries, but this rare limit on ECB's independence has yet to be tested.[15] Yet another distinction concerns the decision of the inflation target when its exists. The ECB enjoys **goal independence**: while its mandate is to achieve and maintain price stability, it is for the bank itself to decide what price stability exactly means. The ECB has announced that it aims at a 'positive rate of inflation that does not exceed 2% in the medium run'. Other central banks, e.g. the Bank of New Zealand and the Bank of England are given the inflation objective by the Minister of Finance. For example, the Bank of England has been instructed to aim at a rate of 2.5%, and must explain in writing any deviation of more than 1%. These banks are free to decide how to aim at the objective; they are **instrument independent**, not goal independent.

---

[15] It is interesting to note during the 1990s, the fiercely independent Deutsche Bundesbank, the German central bank, was 'trumped' twice by politicians: the first case was German economic and monetary union, and second, European Monetary Union. In 1990 it argued against a swift monetary unification with East Germany, then against the one-Deutschmark-for-one-Ostmark conversion rate. In the end, it bowed to the government's wishes. Thus, even the considerable freedom enjoyed by such institutions can be modified if public demand for such a change is sufficiently high.

Politics and Economics

Reputation is meaningful only when a long-term relationship is involved. When applied to governments and economic policy, this naturally implicates the political system. So far, governments have been described as well-meaning entities which care about the welfare of the country. A very different approach is to think of governments as being run by politicians who care about getting elected and staying in power. Policy then becomes endogenous to both economic and political circumstances, and, reciprocally, economic circumstances are partly shaped by policy actions. The loop is closed and provides interesting, if not always encouraging, insights into the role and function of demand management policies.

16.4.1 Electoral Business Cycles

It is risky for a government to approach an election with deteriorating economic conditions. The timing of elections often generates **political business cycles**. Simply put, governments attempt to manipulate the macroeconomic setting to improve their re-election chances. Table 16.4 shows that, indeed, during election years the budget tends to deteriorate relatively to the previous year and that growth is often higher, although the evidence is not particularly strong.[16]

Table 16.4   **Budgetary and Economic Conditions in Election Years, OECD Countries, 1972–1984**

	Does the budget deteriorate in election years?		Is output growth higher in election years?		Is unemployment lower in election years?	
	Yes	No	Yes	No	Yes	No
Austria	1	2	1	2	0	3
Belgium	4	0	3	1	0	3
Denmark	3	1	2	2	1	3
Finland	3	0	2	1	0	3
France	2	1	0	3	0	3
Germany	0	4	2	2	2	1
Netherlands	2	1	2	1	0	3
Norway	1	2	0	3	2	1
Sweden	2	2	3	1	3	1
UK	2	1	3	0	2	1
USA	2	2	3	1	3	1
Total	22	16	21	17	13	23

Note: Changes are measured as differences between election year and previous year (moved ahead one year if election is in Jan.–June). For unemployment, two cases are not classified because the rate did not change significantly.
Sources: Alesina (1989) and own calculations from OECD *National Accounts*.

---

[16] The fact that unemployment seems to worsen in election years in some countries is puzzling. One possibility is that randomly (exogenously) bad economic outcomes lead to the downfall of governments and premature elections. Another is that voters anticipated a pre-election inflation of demand and raise expectations of inflation, leading to a leftward shift of the *AS* curve and a recession. The most plausible is that policy-generated expansions in Europe have not been sufficient to stop the unrelenting increase in equilibrium unemployment during most of the period studied. See Ch. 4 for more details.

Table 16.5   Effects on Real Growth and Unemployment of a Change to the Left, OECD Countries, 1966–1986

	Growth	Unemployment		Growth	Unemployment
Australia	0.87	−0.29	Germany	0.39	−0.50
Austria	1.04	−0.24	Netherlands	0.67	0.36
Belgium	0.21	−0.53	Norway	1.04	0.01
Denmark	0.67	−0.42	Sweden	1.44	−0.16
Finland	2.32	−1.00	UK	1.51	−0.42
France	0.31	−0.67	USA	2.51	−0.66

Note: Each country's growth and unemployment are measured relatively to the average of the other countries listed in the table.
Source: Alesina (1989).

16.4.2 Partisan Business Cycles

In contrast to the political business cycle, which links economic swings to the efforts of politicians to remain in power, the partisan business cycle view claims that *changes* of governments generate business cycles. This section looks at the macroeconomic implications of the (cynical?) view that, when in power, a political party is interested only in pursuing policies that increase its chances of re-election. The first question is how to think about the election outcome. Suppose that the preferences of voters can be summarized in a single index, with low values corresponding to 'left' and high values to 'right'. The **median voter theorem** asserts the median voter of those voting—who has roughly half of the electorate to her left, and half of the electorate to her right is the decisive voter. A political party would maximize its election chances by advocating the policy mix most palatable to the median voter. Two strategies are possible.

In the first strategy, all political parties aim at the lucky median voter, and in this case the political parties are indistinguishable. Although this description does not accord too well with reality, it explains two important facts. First, in many countries the political arena is characterized by a two-party system with parties that offer very similar choices. Second, elections are often won by a very narrow margin. In

that case elections do not generate business cycles because the winner does not differ much from the loser and the public knows *ex ante* that each of them has a 50% chance of forming the government.

The other strategy is for a political party to aim decidedly at one end of the political spectrum but try to extend its appeal *up to* the median voter, thus catching just 50% of the electorate, plus one. This would describe fairly polarized political systems and would also explain the narrow margins of election outcomes. In this case, elections generate **partisan business cycles**, because policies change fairly sharply when a new party is elected.

It is customary to describe left-leaning governments as being Keynesian and right-leaning governments as being monetarist. Then, if a left-leaning government replaces a right-leaning government, we should expect to see GDP growth increase and unemployment decrease, possibly at the expense of rising inflation. Based on twenty years of observation, Table 16.5 confirms this presumption. The table can equally be read as indicating the effect of a shift to the right by merely changing the signs. In all cases, GDP growth picks up, and in all but two cases (the Netherlands and Norway[17]) unemployment declines.

---

[17] The estimated effects in these two cases are not statistically significant; i.e. they are not really different from zero.

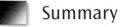

Summary

1. While demand management policies can in principle smooth business cycle fluctuations, recent experience and economic principles suggest caution.

2. Monetarists and Keynesians mostly disagree on the *degree* to which actual prices and markets achieve efficient allocation of resources and optimal satisfaction of individual needs. Monetarists contend that market-clearing is a good first-order approximation, and that markets are closer to perfection than governments. Keynesians consider that markets suffer from a host of imperfections and that economies can suffer from persistent underutilization of resources.

3. Uncertainty plays an important role in the debate. For Keynesians, it means that private decisions are taken with imperfect knowledge of future conditions. This results in wrong pricing and resource allocation decisions. For monetarists, uncertainty means that policy mistakes are as likely to make matters worse as they are to improve them. Keynesians want discretion in policy-making, whereas monetarists favour rules.

4. Because expectations crucially shape private behaviour, limited policy changes may not affect private behaviour patterns, while changes in regime policy may change them abruptly. The Lucas critique implies that policies that look good given the past may turn out to deliver very different outcomes from those desired.

5. Time inconsistency arises when the policy plans that are best today become less desirable at a later stage, possibly after the private sector has reacted. This represents a powerful incentive for governments to renege on promises once the private sector has acted in the belief that the promises will be carried out. Time-inconsistent policies are not credible.

6. There are two ways of making time-inconsistent policies credible: legally binding rules and reputation. Rules invariably restrict policy discretion and activism. Reputation requires that governments refrain from actions even if they are, at the time, desirable.

7. Monetary policy is a fragile instrument because of severe time-consistency problems. This has led central banks to seek rules (independence) and reputation. Independent central banks tend to be associated with lower inflation rates.

8. In reality, citizens have different interests and opinions. Real-life governments are not necessarily well-meaning, but instead care mainly about being re-elected. This may lead some governments to use economic policy in a politically opportunistic way.

9. Political business cycles may take the form of expansionary policies being introduced just before elections, to be followed by corrective contractionary policies after elections. Partisan business cycles may result from the alternation of governments that defend the interests of their constituencies.

Key Concepts

- monetarists, monetarism
- Keynesians, Keynesianism
- activist policies
- market-clearing
- recognition, decision, implementation, and effectiveness lags
- Lucas critique
- policy regime

- nominal anchors
- time inconsistency
- credibility
- reputation
- rules v. discretion
- median voter theorem
- political business cycles
- partisan business cycles

Exercises

1. It has been suggested that real interest rates on public debts are related to the size of the budget deficit, not to the size of the debt. Can you provide an explanation? (*Hint*: think about the long-term implications for the budget constraint.)

2. Imagine a sudden and unexpected wave of high wage settlements. What would be the likely solutions proposed (*a*) by a monetarist? (*b*) by a Keynesian? Argue their cases.

3. Explain why rising debts are sometimes accompanied by increasing inflation, even if money growth is held tight.

4. What are the costs of inflation? Are there any advantages of inflation? If so, what are they?

5. Monetary policy works through either the interest rate or the exchange rate. Do you think that the effectiveness lag differs according to the exchange rate regime? If so, explain why and how.

6. Why are large budget deficits often followed by exchange rate depreciations? Identify at least two channels.

7. Describe the lags that affect economic policy-making and their consequences for the effectiveness of: (*a*) fiscal policy; (*b*) monetary policy.

8. It has been proposed that central banks should set money growth and interest rates to fix the growth rate in the observed growth of nominal GDP. Others endorse fixing the inflation rate. Evaluate the rationale, advantages, and disadvantages of such proposals.

9. The following numbers have been taken from the International Monetary Fund's *International Financial Statistics* for the Republic of Bolivia:

	1984	1985	1986	1987
μ ($\Delta M/M$)	18900	58800	83.3	38.3
π ($\Delta P/P$)	13800	12100	376	10.6

A stringent disinflation programme was undertaken in 1986, successfully bringing inflation down to 10%. How can one explain the rapid increase in real money balances in 1987 (high money growth in 1987 despite the low inflation)? What additional evidence would you require to determine whether the Bolivian programme has collapsed or succeeded?

10. For more than two decades, European governments have severely regulated the ability of employers to dismiss workers for economic (business-cycle-related) reasons. In recent years some governments have announced that these regulations would be relaxed, with the hope of reducing the equilibrium unemployment rate. How might the time inconsistency argument be used to explain why employers have not created as many jobs as one might have hoped?

Suggested Further Reading

On the debate between Keynesians and monetarists, see the special issue of *Economic Policy*, 5 (1987) as well as the symposium on 'Keynesian Economics Today' in the *Journal of Economic Perspectives*, 7 (Winter 1993); also:

De Long, J. Bradford, and Summers, Lawrence H. (1988), 'How Does Macroeconomic Policy after Output?', *Brookings Papers on Economic Activity*, 2: 433–94.

Friedman, Milton (1953), 'The Effect of Full Employment Policy on Economic Stability: A Formal Analysis', in his *Essays in Positive Economics*, University of Chicago Press.

Lucas, R. E. Jr (1978), 'Unemployment Policy', *American Economic Review Papers and Proceedings*, 68: 353–7.

Recollections by leading economists involved in policy-making are presented in:

Tobin, James, and Weidenbaum, Murray (eds.) (1988), *Two Revolutions in Economic Policy: The First Economic Reports of Presidents Kennedy and Reagan*, MIT Press.

The original (and technical) exposition of the Lucas critique can be found in:

Lucas, R. E. Jr (1976), 'Economic Policy Evaluation: A Critique', in K. Brunner and A. Meltzer (eds.), *The Phillips Curve and Labor Markets*, Carnegie–Rochester Conference Series, North-Holland, Amsterdam.

On credibility, see:

Barro, Robert, and Gordon, Robert D. (1983), 'Rules, Discretion, and Reputation in a Model of Monetary Policy', *Journal of Monetary Economics*, 12: 101–22.

Cukierman, Alex (1992), *Central Bank Strategy, Credibility and Independence*, MIT Press.

Goodhart, Charles (1994), 'Game Theory for Central Bankers', *Journal of Economic Literature*, 32(1): 101–14.

On the cost of inflation, see:

Fischer, Stanley (1986), *Indexing, Inflation, and Economic Policy*, MIT Press.

On the link between politics and economics, see:

Alesina, Alberto (1988), 'Macroeconomics and Politics', *NBER Macroeconomics Annual*, 3: 13–62.

Alesina, Alberto (1989), 'Politics and Business Cycles in Industrial Democracies', *Economic Policy*, 8: 55–98.

Figure 16.9, showing the effect of central bank independence on inflation, is from:

Alesina, Alberto, and Summers, Lawrence (1993), 'Central Bank Independence and Macroeconomic Performance: Some Comparative Evidence', *Journal of Money, Credit, and Banking*, 25: 151–62.

This and other results on central bank independence can be found in:

Grilli, Vittorio, Masciandaro, Donato, and Tabellini, Guido (1991), 'Political and Monetary Institutions and Public Financial Policies in the Industrial Countries', *Economic Policy*, 13: 341–92.
Roll, Eric, et al. (1993), *Independent and Accountable: A New Mandate for the Bank of England*, CEPR.

On the different forms of central bank independence, see the debate between the ECB's Chief Economist Otmar Issing and the Bank of England's Willem Buiter:

Buiter, W. (1999), 'Alice in Euroland', CEPR Policy paper No. 1.
Issing, O. (1999), 'The Eurosystem: Independent and Accountable', CEPR Policy Paper No. 2.

as well as:

Eijffinger, S., and J. de Haan (1996), *The Political Economy of Central Bank Independence*, Special Paper in International Economics No. 19, Princeton University.

Supply-Side Policy

17

For almost twenty years now, European unemployment has been a major social problem and the sign of underutilized resources at a time of unfilled needs. [. . .] Faced with such a prospect, European economists cannot remain silent.

– Jacques Drèze and Edmond Malinvaud

17.1   Overview

In the last chapter, we explored the role of demand management in macroeconomic policy-making. Recessions are costly in terms of unemployment and lost output; recovery from these recessions can be accelerated by well-chosen activist policies. Yet, some have concluded that no policy is better than a misguided activist one. Since the economy returns to its long-run path anyway, they claim, demand policy can do more harm than good. All the same, most governments do make use of demand policy, and some rather frequently at that.

An alternative or even a complementary policy to demand-side management is to increase the productive potential of an economy, irrespective of the state of aggregate demand. Policy measures which raise the long-run or potential GDP ($\bar{Y}$) are known as **supply-side policies**. This is shown in Figure 17.1, which plots output itself, rather than its deviation from $\bar{Y}$, on the horizontal axis. Successful supply-side policies raise potential GDP from $\bar{Y}$ to $\bar{Y}'$ faster than if were it left to the normal process of economic growth. The attractiveness of such policies is that they bypass the uncomfortable trade-off between output and inflation. In the short run, more output and lower inflation are possible as the economy moves from A to A'.[1] Similarly, bad supply-side policies reduce $\bar{Y}$, causing higher inflation in the short run and higher unemployment in the long run.

This chapter surveys supply-side policies and assesses their effectiveness. One general conclusion

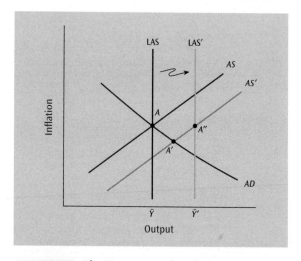

Fig. 17.1 **The Macroeconomics of Supply-Side Policies**

Supply-side policies aim at mobilizing productive resources to increase equilibrium output. Shifting the aggregate supply curve yields both more output and less inflation in the short run (point A'). In the longer run, inflation returns to its previous level but output is permanently higher.

is that, regardless of their effectiveness, supply-side policies do not produce immediate miracles. They may increase incentive to raise production; they may be aimed at improving general efficiency; they may require some sectors to decline and free resources for other, more valuable uses. All these measures take time to work, five to ten years, or even longer.

We examine three broad approaches to increasing the economy's long-run potential. First, good supply-side policy should aim to make markets as efficient as possible; and when markets fail that test, government intervention can improve matters. This was also the message of Chapter 15. Second, given

---

[1] Note that the short-run effect of the shift is a reduction in the rate of inflation, as the new short-run and long-run AS curves shift rightward. For a given rate of monetary growth the inflation rate returns to its previous level (point A''), although complicated dynamics may characterize this adjustment process, as Ch. 14 showed.

that governments are already interfering in the market place for both good and bad reasons, they should strive to minimize the negative impact of their intervention. One example is regulation; another is taxation; yet another is subsidy policy. Third, unemployment remains a deep concern in much of Europe where roughly 10% of the labour force is out of work. Yet in the most recent decade, the United Kingdom, the Netherlands, Denmark, Ireland, and more recently, Finland and Sweden have proved that unemployment need not be a curse. Even if the political resistance is strong, all of Europe can share in these successes, and we review how.

<table>
<tr><td>**17.2**</td><td>## Market Efficiency and Equilibrium Output</td></tr>
</table>

17.2.1 The Benchmark of Efficiency: Perfect Competition

Adam Smith (1723–90), perhaps the most famous economist of all time, claimed in his book *The Wealth of Nations* that efficient resource allocation was best left to the market system. One of the greatest achievements of modern economics has been to confirm that, under ideal conditions, market economies achieve optimal employment of resources.[2] What are those ideal conditions? Most importantly, markets must 'work', prices must be free to adjust, there must be sufficient competition, and 'externalities' identified in Chapter 15 must be absent. Not surprisingly, these ideal conditions are unlikely to be observed in practice. If this is the case, governments can intervene to produce better use of resources and thereby achieve a larger level of output in the economy.

An important example is the labour market, studied in Chapter 4. Consider Figure 4.7. Firms' demand for labour is described by the downward-sloping marginal product of labour (MPL); firms hire labour to the point at which its marginal productivity equals the real wage. Similarly, workers supply hours of work until their opportunity cost—leisure—outweighs the real wage. The market-clearing equilibrium point A can be seen as an ideal state. Increasing employment beyond point A in Figure 4.7 reduces the MPL below what workers are willing

to work for. Reducing employment below A would raise the MPL above the real wage necessary to motivate labourers to give up their free time. Put differently, if wages are above the market-clearing level, firms would restrict employment and workers would increase their supply, resulting in unemployment of labour. If real wages are too low, firms demand more man-hours than workers are willing to supply.

Why would the real wage ever move to its equilibrium or **market-clearing** level $\bar{w}$? The answer is: competition. Very unrealistically, imagine that hours of work are traded in a perfectly flexible market. If firms offer a lower wage than $\bar{w}$, they will not attract as many workers as they seek. Competition among firms will lead some to improve their offer. As they succeed in luring workers from their previous jobs, other firms will have to respond with yet a higher offer and competition will bid up wages until they reach the market-clearing level. Conversely, imagine that the workers initially ask for a wage above $\bar{w}$. Some will not find a job, or not be able to work as many hours as they wish. Forces of competition will trigger a decline in the wage as unemployed workers underbid those who have jobs, eventually driving wages to point A.

That point A represents an ideal state is a general principle: for an economy to achieve the optimum allocation of resources, all markets must clear. Either all prices are right and all productive resources are fully employed, or none of them is and underutilization and inefficiency spread throughout the economy. Economists tend to be split into two camps on this issue. Some are convinced that markets are naturally efficient, so there is no need for governments to interfere. This is the

---

[2] In the 1950s, Nobel laureates Kenneth Arrow of Stanford and Gerard Debreu of Berkeley showed how Adam Smith's intuition could be rigorously established. They identified the conditions under which a market economy delivers the socially optimal allocation of resources.

laissez-faire view. Others believe that few markets meet the high standards set forth by Adam Smith. The existence of **market failures**, when and where they can be identified, provides a justification for government intervention. Note, however, how cautiously this statement is worded. Interventions are only justified if two conditions are met: first, they should be limited to clearly identified market failures; second, they should be targeted directly at the market failure to avoid creating additional distortions of their own. We next identify several generic market failures and the associated range of interventions.

17.2.2 **Competition in Product Markets**

When several firms compete with each other in the same market, they are under constant pressure to adapt the price and design of their product to the desires of the consumer—otherwise they will disappear from the screen. They will try to operate as efficiently as possible, and in doing so perform the function society wants them to: allocate available resources to their most efficient uses. And that was what Adam Smith predicted.

Competition, however, can be painful. Every economic agent wants to protect herself from competition. Firms strive to acquire a premier position in the market at the expense of their rivals, thereby earning substantial profits aptly called **economic rents**. How do they do this? Firms normally strive to establish some monopoly power, or market dominance, by exploiting increasing returns or by differentiating their products. When production exhibits increasing returns to scale, larger firms can squeeze out smaller firms by producing more and thus reducing their costs; eventually a few of them survive and dominate the market (think of the market for automobiles). Firms can also try to stunt competition by preventing others from entering their markets. Most means of maintaining dominance in a market are prohibited; threats against competitors and extortion are illegal. Yet it is standard practice for producers to spend significant amounts of money creating brand names and convincing consumers that their products are different. If customers like consuming products which are different—or merely believe that they are—they will be willing to pay more for them. Firms use clever marketing as a means of obtaining and defending this monopoly power, and the amounts spent on product differentiation are evidently justified by the resulting profits. Product differentiation thrives on individuals' desire for variety in the market place.

Measures which increase competition and thereby economic output are generally referred to as **competition policy**. Competition policy can take a number of forms. In many countries, monopolies are regulated or supervised closely. Firms are seldom allowed to acquire excessive shares of their markets. Collusion in the form of cartels and price-fixing schemes are illegal. More recently, governments have also limited the ability of firms to dominate their input and output markets. The famous Microsoft court case is an attempt to limit the power of this firm. Similarly, the UK government has separated electricity generation from electricity distribution and the EU Commission has moved in this direction at the Community level with respect to both electricity and gas transmission. More generally, as European integration proceeds, antimonopoly powers are being transferred to Brussels, which now monitors market shares at the EU level. Some interesting cases of EU competition policy are discussed in Box 17.1.

17.2.3 **Competition in Labour Markets**

Workers also try to avoid competition, and labour markets are frequently characterized by non-competitive behaviour. For one, labour supply is intimately linked with the human condition, and competition among workers for jobs is often considered inappropriate, in bad taste, or even unethical. Second, wages are often set in bilateral negotiations, and trade unions are seen as protecting interests of employed workers in a vulnerable situation. An alternative perspective sees trade unions as monopolists with high real wages in mind.[3] With high real wages, labour demand is low and equilibrium unemployment high. If a majority of trade union members accept this trade-off, they will press for

---

[3] The analysis of trade unions is developed in Ch. 4.

Box 17.1   **EU Competition Policy and National Preferences**

Economists have a particular affinity for competition because it leads to efficiency in production. For obvious reasons, this enthusiasm is rarely shared by producers in non-competitive markets, where high profits may be at stake. Yet policy-makers and consumers may also be sceptical. Especially in the European Union, where cultures and traditions are defined by national boundaries, there may be reservations that unbridled competition might destroy or weaken national identities. It may be difficult indeed to discern the difference between respect for consumer preferences and restraint of trade. The latter means less competition, less efficiency, and lower output and employment.

Examples of this dilemma facing the EU abound. In a highly publicized case involving beer quality in the late 1980s, Germany was taken to the European Court of Justice, which has the final say in matters of competition policy. Since 1516, Germany had produced the golden beverage according to the *Reinheitsgebot* ('beer purity law'), which restricted the content of beer to four ingredients (water, yeast, barley, and malt). Such strict regulation of beer quality does not exist elsewhere in Europe.

This law was used to exclude 'impure' foreign beer which did not meet the exacting standards of the *Reinheitsgebot*. The European Court of Justice found that beer brewed using rice and other ingredients should be permitted, while allowing German brewers to market their beer as conforming to the previous regime. Ten years later and despite the new import rules, national tastes prevailed; most German beer drinkers continue to drink German beer. Similarly, Italians now must have a choice between *grani duro* pasta and that made with other wheat varieties; French cheese consumers can try Danish *blø* if they wish. The consumer, in theory, is better off.

Still, the *Reinheitsgebot* case raises a number of interesting questions. Should the EU forbid the import of beef from the USA, which may be treated with hormones or antibiotics? Should genetically modified plants be allowed? Should imports of foreign 'culture'—in particular, audio and video recordings—be limited? Should a minimum price of books in bookstores be guaranteed, as in France, Germany, or Austria? Such regulations are usually justified using non-economic arguments; the question remains whether these truly outweigh their economic costs.

an outcome that is not efficient. In a similar way, firms like to control or even reduce competition on labour costs, and firms are frequently organized in employers' associations. These associations take decisions that are usually binding also for members, and may be followed by non-members (usually smaller firms). If labour and management set wages in collective bargaining without considering the interest of non-member workers, typically the unemployed, and of non-member firms, the level of competition is reduced, and the economy is less efficient. This subject is picked up in Section 17.4.

Competition in labour markets is not limited to labour unions and management. A number of practices by professional associations—of lawyers, doctors, and architects for example—also restrict the supply of labour and raise wages. Limitations on international immigration can be interpreted as the ultimate restriction of competition for labour. Because so many political and sociological issues are

associated with immigration, it would be premature to advocate open borders for everyone on purely economic grounds. Yet it remains true that immigration is efficient, usually increasing GDP enough to compensate any losers in the receiving country. Box 17.2 gives more details.

17.2.4 Market Failures and Overall Market Efficiency

The goal of supply-side policy is to improve the functioning of markets. In general this means intervening where the market has failed. This was already the message of Chapter 15, which looked at—temporary—demand failures which call for demand-side policies that speed up the elimination of these failures. Here we look at structural failures, which call for supply-side policies that could aim at eliminating the failures. But many of these failures simply cannot be eliminated, they are in the nature

Box 17.2   **The Supply-Side Economics of Immigration**

Because labour is so abundant relative to capital in developing countries, many, many people there are very, very poor. In India, for example, annual GDP amounts to roughly €1–2 per day. Many Indians are highly educated and would readily migrate to Europe where the hourly wage might average €20–5 per *hour* or even more. Even those without exceptional skills but who are able-bodied and willing to work could compete with the less skilled. Almost on a weekly basis, we hear of Kurds, Chinese, Vietnamese, and Indians who are apprehended while trying to penetrate EU borders. Most of these people are not seeking political asylum as much as economic betterment; one can hardly blame them. Is it economically efficient to keep these people out?

The analysis of Chapter 4 suggests that it is not, and Figure 17.2 shows why. Two labour supply curves are drawn, one corresponding to that of the natives only, without the immigrants. The second curve to the right is the sum of the natives *plus* the newly arrived migrants. For the moment, the labour demand curve is assumed unchanged by migration; it represents the marginal product of labour. For a given wage level, the area under the curve and above that wage represents total profits earned by firms in the economy. In Figure 17.2, profits are thus *AWB* before the migrants arrive. When they do, the aggregate labour supply curve shifts outward, wages decline from *w* to *w'* and employment rises from *L* to *L'*. Total GDP rises by the amount *BLL'D*, the sum of the additional marginal products of the newly employed.

So if immigration is economically efficient, why all the fuss? First, the distribution of the increase in GDP is not shared by all: profits rise by *WBDW'* and the migrants earn *CDL'L"* but wages of native workers have declined from *WBLO* to *W'CL"O*. Only if the demand curve shifts

out—which may occur if there is new investment by natives, or if the immigrants themselves bring capital with them—is this situation likely to be remedied. Second, immigrants may place demands on infrastructure and the social safety net which they have not helped to pay for. Finally, although economists certainly understand the efficiency of immigration, other sociological aspects may be more important, mankind's complex tribal, if sometimes crude and primordial, instincts.

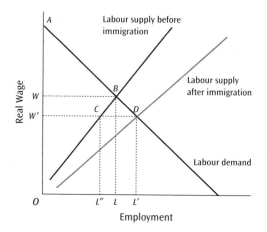

Fig. 17.2   **The Supply-Side Economics of Immigration**

The consequence of immigration is to shift total labour supply outward. In the new equilibrium, wages decline from *W* to *W'* and employment increases from *L* to *L'*. While GDP rises unambiguously by *BLL'D*, this gain is not evenly spread: the income of capitalists increases from *AWB* to *AW'D*, migrants now earn *CDL'L"*, while the income of natives declines from *WBLO* to *W'CL"O*.

of things. Supply-side policies may help by reducing the extent and the impact of these failures. We start by looking at the generic origins of 'natural' market failures, which we group in four categories.

Externalities

An externality occurs when someone's action inevitably affects others. A good example is pollution: when a firm dumps its waste in a river, those who live or work downstream suffer and may have

to spend resources to purify the water that they drink. The market alone apparently cannot redress the wrong. It turns out that it can, provided **property rights** are well defined and that it is not too costly to enforce these rights. If, for example, the law specifies that everyone has a right to clean water, it is the polluting firm that will have to spend resources to clean up the water. In facing this situation, the firm will adopt cleaner production processes. Alternatively, it will offer to indemnify those who live downstream to prevent them from taking the case to court (where it would probably lose anyway). Conversely, the law could specify a right to pollute. Then the costs would be borne by the people who live downstream, who would pay for cleaning the water, or offer money to the firm for it to reduce its disposal or adopt other production processes. The second solution may seem unfair, and it is. The point here is that, once property rights have been established, the market will deliver spontaneously the best possible outcome given the presumption that nature makes it impossible to produce without creating waste.

Externalities can be **positive**. This is the case when one's actions provide others with a better outcome. One example is putting flowers in your windows: you pay the price and passers-by enjoy the sight at no cost. A general conclusion is that not enough is produced when activities generate a positive externality. Since you bear the costs of putting flowers on your balcony, you balance the price and the benefit (your pleasure). Putting out even more flowers might actually raise society's pleasure, but you have no incentive to do so. Pollution is a good example of a **negative** externality. Market incentives are for producers of negative externalities to generate too much of these for the social optimum.

Any externality which is transmitted by market prices is called a **pecuniary externality**. Assigning property rights and creating a market is often enough to solve the problem. But other, inherently **non-pecuniary externalities** are more challenging. An example is training and education. Better trained people share their knowledge with co-workers and their own children. Thus their knowledge has a value for society at large and, if they are not compensated, they will not accumulate as much human capital as is optimal from the standpoint of the economy. For this reason, society has an interest in stepping in, and subsidizing education. In Chapter 18 we will see how externalities involving education, law and order, and health can influence long-run growth. We look at the policy implications in Section 17.3.1 below.

Public goods

Public goods like parks, clean air, or information are special: they are non-rival, meaning that con-sumption by one does not make them less available to others, and they are non-excludable, meaning that, when they are available, everyone can use them freely. As a consequence, no one can be charged for using them, and they must be provided by the state. Law and order is an externality, but it is also a public good. Just imagine a society where it is not provided, or insufficiently provided: economic activity collapses and poverty spreads, as has been the case in countries torn by civil wars, like Liberia or Somalia.

Increasing returns

Some industries are characterized by increasing returns to scale. We have excluded that possibility in earlier chapters because it creates new problems. A good example is railways. A railway that just serves two cities will only be used by people living in or going to these two cities. If it includes a vast network, the link between the same two cities will be used by many more people, many of whom will only pass through these two cities. The larger the network, the more valuable is each of its sections, and the larger the profits to be earned from each section. Left to the market, competition will lead to a **natural monopoly**, with just one company owning all of the network. But we know that, once it has established itself, a monopoly will tend to charge too much, resulting in the socially inefficient use of its product. There is a need for the state to intervene, in this case by granting monopoly rights to a company—which can be public—in exchange for a regulation which will prevent monopolistic pricing.

Information asymmetries

It is a simple observation that we know more about ourselves than others. This information asymmetry plays a pervasive role in all sort of markets. Traders often hide information that may reduce the price they can get for their goods; just think of the seller of a used car. Financial traders make profit by reacting faster than their competitors to new information, so they will naturally tend to hide their true motives. In the first case, the market can easily dry up. In the second case, one trader's move, if badly interpreted by the others, can trigger a stampede; this is what often lies at the root of financial crises. Here again, we face a fact of nature, with serious economic implications. The state has a role to play, for example by prescribing what information must be provided by sellers of used cars or by forcing financial firms to disclose much information that they would prefer to keep for themselves.

Even diehard free marketers recognize that markets are subject to failures, that these failures may have serious implications for economic performance, and that only the state can solve most of the associated difficulties. Should the state intervene and solve all market failures? Here economists disagree. Some, for example the public choice school led by Nobel Prize winners Friedrich Hayek and James Buchanan, maintain that, when it intervenes, the state does more harm than good. Others view state intervention as unavoidable, especially in modern societies where economic interactions can be quite complex and thus potential conduits for the diffusion of adverse effects of market failures. It is fair to say that in no country does the state completely refrain from intervening, for the right or wrong reasons. We look at supply-side policies directed at goods markets in Section 17.3, and at labour markets in Section 17.4. Many market failures not only affect the level of output, but also growth rate. In Chapter 18 we consider those policies that are mainly directed at enhancing growth. Similarly, we set aside for Chapter 19 those policies that deal with financial market failures.

17.3 Improving the Effectiveness of Goods Markets

17.3.1 Dealing with Externalities

The basic principle is to internalize the externalities, meaning make those that create an externality bear its costs or the benefits. In the pollution example above, this is achieved by making clean water a right. This principle is illustrated through a few important examples which have recently received prominent attention.

Human capital accumulation

The first example, also mentioned in Section 17.2.4, is investment in human capital. It is one of the most crucial factors of economic development. Human capital is acquired at school, of course, but also at work. In addition school years may well be spread over a lifetime to allow people to update their depreciating capital and learn about newly acquired knowledge. One person's knowledge benefits society in a myriad ways: it helps co-workers, of course, but better-educated people can make better decisions in everyday life—including to take better care of themselves and their children, or how to vote with a better understanding of what is at stake. An individual's return from human capital is believed to be significantly smaller for the individual than for society. If she invests with only her individual return in mind, she will underinvest regarding what is justified by the broader social return. This why society has a great interest in encouraging people to invest in more human capital than they would spontaneously. Free and compulsory education has been the first response to this externality. Subsidizing traineeship in firms or continuing education further the same goal. Further, unemployed people tend to see their human capital depreciate. This provides an additional justification for measures that reduce the duration of unemployment spells and for the active labour market policies described in Box 17.5 below.

Law and order

Law and order has all three characteristics of a market failure: it is an externality, it is subject to increasing returns to scale, and it is a public good. It is an externality since everyone benefits from others being honest. Investment in physical and human capital is threatened when crime robs people and firms of their assets, and will be less than desirable in the absence of law and order. It is subject to increasing returns to scale, since commonly accepted and enforced law works better than when everyone sets their rules and practises self-enforcement. Private protection, the spontaneous market response to the absence of law and order, is inefficient; it also accentuates the effect of inequality, as rich people can better defend themselves than poor people. Law and order is also a public good, since it is non-excludable and non-rival. Thus, on all three grounds, leaving law and order to the market results in a massive failure. Indeed, from time immemorial, one of the key attribute of any political power has always been the provision of law and order.

Health

Health is obviously a private 'good'. Everyone enjoys good health. It is also a source of externality. People with poor health do not work well and are often absent, so their productivity is reduced. If they are not paid while sick, they can become destitute, relying on society's generosity, or resorting to criminal activity to survive. Sicknesses can also be contagious, a vivid example of externality. Health can be provided privately, and it is so in many countries. Private health programmes generate inequalities, and most people think that it is unacceptable that rich people receive better treatment than poor ones. But, in addition, because of the externalities that it generates, privately provided health is inefficient, as everyone will only spend up to the point where their (marginal) benefit equals marginal cost. This is why most countries have established systems of social security and enforce compulsory medical examinations and vaccination. A healthy society is a rich society. Causality undoubtedly runs from wealth to health, but it also runs in the opposite direction.

17.3.2 Taxation and the Provision of Public Goods

The provision of public goods

Public goods are special because they naturally are non-rival and non-excludable. Being non-excludable, public goods cannot be charged to their users. A toll booth can be installed at a bridge's entrance, but what price should its owner charge? Non-rivalry means that the marginal cost of their use is very small; thus the price ought to be low. But fixed costs

can be large (a bridge is very expensive to build!), so how can the producer be compensated? In addition, a bridge is a natural monopoly if it is the only one in the vicinity. If the owner charges a high price and makes large profits, market competition will lead to the multiplication of bridges next to each other, a very inefficient outcome. Markets just cannot cope with such failures, public goods need to be provided collectively (free bridges), or their provision needs to regulated (privately built bridges are generally subject to strict regulations, including pricing and quality of service).

Public goods are pervasive: transportation and amenities, but also justice and police, passports, defence, and diplomacy, etc. In each case, there is a market solution, but it is inefficient as not enough —sometimes none at all—would be privately provided. And in each case, the insufficient provision of the public goods would greatly impair economic activity, possibly leading to the breakdown of other, well-functioning markets. This is why the provision of public goods is a fundamental supply-side policy. The more efficient the provision, the more productive the economy will be. Efficiency means that public goods are produced at the lowest possible cost—which also involves issues of corruption—as further discussed in Section 17.3.3. It also requires that resources be collected to finance the production of public services, an issue to which we now turn.

Taxation

Once a society has agreed to let government perform certain public functions, public resources need to be raised in order to pay for them. This is done through taxation of final goods and services, factors of production, and other activities. Taxation generally distorts markets by driving a wedge between the cost of producing goods and services and the price paid by the consumers. This effect is shown in Figure 17.3 for a tax paid as a percentage rate of the value of the activity (an *ad valorem* tax). Demand and supply of a given good or service depend on price. Under perfect competition, the demand curve describes the marginal utility of a representative consumer for the good, and the supply curve describes the marginal cost of producing it. At point E, where the two

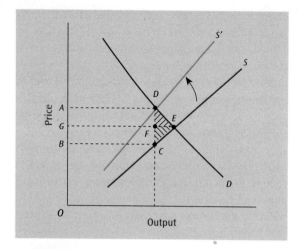

Taxes drive a wedge between the price faced by the buyer and the price charged by the seller. Here a sales tax (e.g. VAT) shifts the supply curve upward. The new equilibrium occurs at point *D*, with less output, a higher buying price (distance *OA*), and a lower selling price (*OB*) than at the tax-free equilibrium point *E*. Tax revenue for the government is measured by area *ABCD*, the quantity sold times the tax rate (the difference between the two prices). Consumers, who could buy quantity *GE* at price *OG*, suffer a 'welfare loss' measured by the area *ADEG*. Similarly, producers suffer a loss represented by the area *GECB*. Of these two losses—area *ADECB*—the government receives *ABCD*. What is left, the triangles *DEF* and *EFC*, represent, respectively, lost consumer and producer surpluses—deadweight losses—arising from the tax.

curves intersect, the consumer at the margin is willing to pay exactly what the producer requires; perfect competition achieves the social best. Taxes alter the situation: the price paid by the buyer must differ from the after-tax price received by the seller. The new supply curve *S'* shows that the producer receives only a fraction of the market (relative) price. At the new market equilibrium point *D* the price is higher and the amount consumed and produced is lower. Both consumers and producers are worse off. Box 17.3 provides more details on who loses and why.

Non-distortionary taxes do not affect economic behaviour. An example would be lump-sum taxes levied on individuals without any reference to incomes, wealth, or spending, or taxes levied unexpectedly on past incomes and wealth so that it is too late to react. For this reason, non-distortionary taxes are appealing to governments. In practice, however, retroactive taxation is considered unfair precisely because it takes people by surprise. Lump-sum taxes are also unpopular, as Mrs Thatcher's fateful experience with the poll tax in 1990 showed. As a result, nearly all taxes are distortionary.

Because distortionary taxes move the economy away from its first-best equilibrium, it is entirely conceivable that higher tax rates actually result in *lower* tax yields. This effect is sometimes called the

---

Box 17.3 **The Deadweight Loss from Taxation**

What are the losses to an economy from **distortionary taxation**? Figure 17.3 gives us the answer. The loss to consumers of not enjoying the price *OG* is given by *ADEG*. This can be thought of as consumers' willingness to pay above the market-clearing price, or **consumer surplus**. At the same time, the lower price (net of tax) to producing firms means that firms will lose profits on goods they would have sold at cost lower than the no-tax price. The existence of these profits is due to the fact that the supply curve is upward-sloping. This second area *BCEG* is known as **producer surplus**.

This consumer and producer surplus are not lost entirely. Despite the price rise, purchases of *AD* will still

occur. The tax income from an *ad valorem* tax is given by the rectangle *ABCD*. This leaves the two triangles, *DEF* and *CFE*, which represent lost consumer and producer surplus, or deadweight loss to society.

In raising a given amount of money, an objective of government should be to minimize the 'deadweight loss' arising from taxation, represented by the triangles of producer and consumer surplus in Figure 17.3. This can be achieved by taxing most heavily those goods with the most inelastic (i.e. steepest) demands and supplies. This is known as the **Ramsey principle of public finance**.

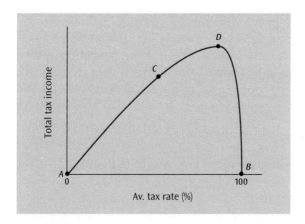

Fig. 17.4   **The Laffer Curve**

When the average tax rate is 0% there is no tax income (point A). When it is 100%, tax income is also likely to be zero (point B). At intermediate tax rates, there is some tax income, e.g. at point C. By continuity, the Laffer curve assumes a hump-shaped relationship between tax income and average tax rates. The maximum tax intake occurs at point D.

Laffer curve and is depicted in Figure 17.4.[4] This curve describes a theoretical relationship between *total* government tax revenues on the vertical axis and the *average* tax rate (the ratio of tax receipts to GDP) on the horizontal axis. The tax rate ranges from 0 to 100%; at a 0% rate, tax revenue is nil (point A); when the tax rate reaches 100%, no one is likely to work or produce at all so tax receipts are also nil (point B). At intermediate tax rates, tax receipts are positive, as at point C. The hump-shape of the curve indicates that the tax rate distorts the economy so much that beyond some tax rate, taxable income *declines* faster than the tax rate increases. The threshold point D corresponds to the average tax rate for which tax receipts are at a maximum. Any rate of taxation to the right of point D is inefficient because the same tax income can be raised with a lower tax rate, i.e. less distortion. The Laffer curve is not taken too seriously for policy purposes, since its most important detail is unknown: the location of point D. In the early 1980s, Laffer claimed

that the USA had passed this point; when the USA did cut tax rates, tax revenue actually declined.[5]

17.3.3 **Dealing with Malfunctioning Markets**

The solution to market failures is not always to produce public goods and services. In fact, it is increasingly being recognized that private producers tend to be more cost-efficient than publicly owned ones, provided that they be adequately regulated. In this section we look at monopolies and review some prominent examples of the privatization process and of how regulation operates.

Monopolies

Markets characterized by increasing returns tend to evolve to a situation where a very few firms buy out or eliminate the others. When only one firm survives, it is a monopoly. Once it has achieved that position, its incentive is to charge high prices, and possibly to stop innovating and letting its goods quality decline. When just two or three dominate, they have incentives to agree among themselves to raise prices and lower competition in terms of quality and innovation. This is called collusion. Thus, in the presence of increasing returns, markets evolve spontaneously to a situation where competition is insufficient to match the principles of market efficiency. Examples of industries prone to increasing returns include cars and airplanes, transports and telecommunications.

One response is to regulate these industries. Governments step in and either break down the monopolies (e.g. in the early 1980s, the USA broke down the dominance of ATT in the telephone industry), or prevent mergers, and to actively fight against collusion. Because competition increasingly takes place at the world level, such anti-trust and anti-collusion policies are often conducted at the supranational level. In Europe, the European Commission has been granted wide authority in that area.

---

[4] Economist Arthur Laffer, then from Chicago, is reported to have been influential in persuading President Reagan to cut taxes in the early 1980s.

[5] It is true that richer people in the USA ended up paying more taxes, since it made less sense to hire expensive lawyers to devise complicated tax breaks. Another important effect is that the underground economy tends to come out into the open when tax rates are lower. More recently, Professor Feldstein at Harvard University has argued that tax cuts in the USA will result in enough increased taxpaying to pay for a third—but by no means all—of the government revenue that would be lost.

Privatization

In many countries, the other response to market failures, especially the existence of natural monopolies, has been to set up state-owned companies that would not seek to exploit their monopolistic power. This has been the case of railways, electricity genera-

tion and distribution, water distribution, telecommunications, etc. Starting in the early 1980s in Europe, the performance of these state monopolies has been found wanting. The prices that they charged were regulated, and based on their costs, but who controlled the costs? Suspicion grew that, in the absence of

---

Box 17.4   **Privatization, Deregulation, and the European Telecommunications Boom**

In the early 1990s a number of European countries, led by the UK and later by Germany, began to privatize and deregulate their telecommunications industries. These had been the domain of the national postal systems, which had moved slowly to introduce new technologies and continued to charge high prices for services which cost little at the margin to produce. In effect, the Europeans were doing little more than recognizing the successes of the USA in the early 1980s after the break-up of the monopoly ATT (American Telephone and Telegraph) and the resulting deregulation of long distance telephone service. The Europeans went farther than the Americans, however, by agreeing on a pan-European standard for wireless technologies and wireless application protocols, they created a common market for an activity which obviously involves massive external

effects. They also intensified direct competition with local telecom service provision, which remains a local monopoly in most countries.

The deregulation of telecoms in Europe has led to visible positive supply-side economic effects. The telecom industry has not only been a source of value added and income growth for Europeans, but also hundreds of thousands of new jobs. Most importantly, consumers have benefited. Table 17.1 shows the extent to which prices for these telecommunications services have fallen in Germany. More recently, the public auction of third generation mobile communication radio frequencies heralds the combination of these technologies with the internet, and promises the introduction of new products and services that the old national postal services could never have offered.

Table 17.1   Telecommunications Prices in Germany, 1995–1999

	1995	1996	1997	1998	1999
All telephone services	127.1	128.9	124.0	122.4	108.4
All trunk line systems	117.1	120.9	118.2	117.4	104.6
by service:					
Fixed fees	90.5	99.5	99.2	99.8	100.0
Call-by-call fees	137.8	137.6	133.0	131.0	108.3
Local	80.3	93.1	93.1	93.6	99.4
National Long Distance	216.4	201.0	185.7	187.6	110.4
Internation Long Distance	236.3	212.8	212.2	188.8	159.4
All cell phone systems	236.0	201.3	157.9	144.0	114.4
by user type:					
Infrequent usage users	317.8	244.9	147.4	133.7	119.8
Low usage users	244.9	202.3	153.3	142.3	114.2
Average usage users	199.3	186.3	167.1	149.5	113.2

Source: German Federal Statistical Office.

competition, these firms were not particularly interested in producing at the lowest possible cost. The infamous monopolistic rent was not captured in the form of private profits, but in the form of slackness in production, poor quality of service, technological backwardness, and sometimes comfortable salaries and other advantages. The contrast between Europe and the USA, which relied to a much lesser extent on publicly owned companies, had become glaring.

The response has been a wave of privatization, still under way. Once a company had become private, it was interested in expanding across borders. The presence of state-owned monopolies in some countries prevented the entry of foreign competitors, while allowing the national company to expand abroad, clearly an unfair situation. This is why the Single Act of 1992 has given the European Commission the right to force national governments to privatize most of their state-owned monopolies and to open their markets to foreign competition. Ten years down the road, the process is still far from complete, a testimony of how entrenched the interests are. Box 17.4 recalls the successful privatization process in the telecommunications industry. This process has freed a dynamic force for economic growth and job creation.

Regulation

Regulation is often the best response when markets are not well behaved. Financial markets are essential for economic growth, since banks and financial intermediaries collect savings to finance investment by firms and public deficits. Yet financial markets are often considered with suspicion, partly because of markets' tendencies to undergo violent crises, a manifestation of the asymmetric information problem. In response, they are regulated. Banks are forbidden to take excessive risk, because depositors cannot effectively monitor their banks and stand to lose part of their savings if the bank collapses. Financial operators also face legal limit on the risk that they can take, in an effort to limit the occurrence of financial crises.

That regulation affects nearly every aspect of economic life reflects how widespread market failures are, but also a tendency of the state to do too much.

Asymmetric information explains why food labels, airline services, or driving licences are regulated. Yet, the regulation of store closing times in much of Europe, tree-felling in Germany, or chimney-sweeping in Switzerland might be a step too far, possibly protecting private interests at the expense of the public good.

Subsidies and industrial policy

For a variety of non-economic reasons, many countries operate elaborate systems of subsidies which shield certain firms and industries from the discipline of the market. Table 17.2 displays the evidence for some OECD countries. Subsidized firms can sustain losses and avoid adjusting to changing economic conditions. In doing so, they keep resources (e.g. labour) employed, but inefficiently. They do not face the full cost of their operations (part of the costs are charged to taxpayers), or else the factors of production are paid more than their true marginal productivity.[6] In fact, they may even keep factor prices artificially high and hurt productive activities that are not subsidized.

Table 17.2	Subsidies in Various Countries (% of GDP)		
	1975	**1990**	**1997**
Belgium	3.15	2.85	2.03
France	2.41	2.10	2.73
Germany	1.99	2.01	1.84
Italy	3.17	2.51	1.90
Netherlands	2.04	3.05	2.16
Spain	2.04	3.05	2.16
Sweden	3.05	4.65	4.28
USA	0.32	0.51	0.42

Source: OECD National Accounts.

---

[6] For example, after the oil shocks, a reduced world demand for tankers and the emergence of competitors in Asia (Japan, Korea) combined to create major difficulties for European shipyards. The UK, Germany, France, and many other countries reacted by subsidizing their shipbuilding companies. In the end, the costs became too large and the situation too hopeless for the subsidies to be maintained. While the subsidies did save jobs for a few years, they did so in a very inefficient way.

Public ownership of firms is another form of subsidization. Unlike private firms, state-owned enterprises (SOEs) rarely face demanding shareholders and are almost never shut down. When they lose money, they generally receive public resources. This may come either as an explicit subsidy from the government to cover the loss, or as a loan to the company at interest rates unavailable to other firms. SOEs operate in virtually every major industry in Western Europe.

Most countries regard certain economic activities as indispensable for strategic or political reasons. These include defence-related industries such as steel, energy, high technology, aircraft, and shipbuilding. As many of these activities exhibit increasing returns to scale, governments often try to guarantee that the firms are large enough. This is often the underlying logic behind **industrial policies**. Industrial policies amount to official backing of national corporations or whole industries. It takes the form of subsidies, public orders, and trade policies. **Trade policies** include tariffs on foreign goods, quotas on imports, export credits financed at concessionary rates, and procurement policies whereby domestically produced goods are chosen over cheaper foreign ones, not to mention 'buy domestic goods' campaigns.

The ultimate effect of these policies is to raise prices above competitive levels. Consumers or taxpayers make up the difference. Once again, the principle that prices reflect efficient production costs is violated. Supply-side considerations have led to a reassessment of strategic requirements. The European Single Act (1992) bans most trade policies mentioned above for intra-European trade. Yet industrial and trade policies survive, often conducted at the EU rather than national level, with such celebrated examples as Airbus and Ariane. More recently, private European banks have complained that state savings banks and their parent entities enjoy hidden subsidies in the form of government guarantees. EU competition authorities have demanded that these be privatized or at least set on equal footing, singling out the German *Sparkassen* and the *Landesbanken*. These institutions respond that they represent the only means of achieving blanket availability of banking services in remote, rural areas, and provide financing for projects that private banks generally shun. As the issue of state aids becomes increasingly political, it assumes the aspects of national preferences discussed in Box 17.1.

17.4 Improving the Efficiency of Labour Markets

The last section established that product markets can fail and require government action. The same applies to labour markets, but doubly so. Besides the obvious human dimension—that individuals and their well-being are associated with labour supply, wages, and unemployment—it turns out that a number of aspects of labour markets make them fundamentally different from markets for fish, steel, or tomatoes, even under ideal conditions. In this section a number of these differences will be explored. To the extent that policy-makers recognize these special aspects of labour markets, they can design policies which can keep the equilibrium rate of unemployment low and the level of output high.

17.4.1 Heterogeneity and Incomplete Information

One of the most striking facts about labour markets is its degree of turnover, or the rate of flow between the states of the labour force shown in Figure 4.14. For example, Chapter 4 noted that annual inflow into and outflows out of unemployment are frequently larger than the stocks of unemployment at any given point in time. The high rate of in- and outflow points to two important aspects of labour markets: heterogeneity of labour and incomplete information about its quality.

First, neither workers and the labour hours they supply nor the jobs at which they work are identical; we say that workers and jobs are heterogeneous. A trivial example of heterogeneity lies behind the turnover noted in Table 4.6, which is concentrated among young, female, and unskilled workers. Even in high labour turnover countries like the UK or USA, it turns out that most workers stay at a given job for a very long time. High turnover is frequently a transient phenomenon in the life cycle which is more characteristic of newcomers to the labour market, and reflects a complicated process of 'picking and choosing'.

Second, because workers and jobs can be so different, or heterogeneous, information is likely to be incomplete. Even with the help of modern technology such as the internet, it is still impossible to know about all jobs on offer at any point in time; it may be necessary to search harder to find the most attractive jobs. Some employers do not actively advertise job openings and may open a position only after meeting an acceptable candidate. Workers must decide on accepting a job or searching further without knowing what may lie ahead. Most likely, they will have had some employment experience in the past, which guides their expectations concerning pay and work conditions; the offers they can expect in the future may not always correspond to patterns in the past. For example, it is a fact that computer operators—workers who once programmed and serviced large mainframe computers—were highly trained and well-paid professionals in the 1970s and 1980s. As personal computer and networking technologies became dominant, the demand for this occupation shrank dramatically. Those who lost their job may have had difficulties finding a similar one at pay similar to that in the past. Similarly, a job and the employer who is deciding how to fill it has particular needs and expectations which may not be met by every applicant, but in times of tight labour markets it may not be easy to find the dream candidate.

It is for this reason that unemployment must be interpreted carefully. To the extent that the unemployed are really 'unemployed resources', they represent a lost opportunity and a reason that trend GDP is lower than it could be. Indeed, Chapter 4 gave a number of reasons why workers ready to work at current wages are unable to do so. Yet unemployment also contains some elements of efficiency. Those who have lost their jobs involuntarily through lay-off or plant closure frequently possess industry- or firm-specific human capital which would be wasted or unutilized were the worker forced to accept the first new job that came along. A crude indicator of the 'efficiency' of job matching in a given labour market is the extent to which jobs openings—called vacancies—and job-seeking, unemployed workers coexist at the same time in a labour market. Because job descriptions and worker qualifications are often specific, one can speak of a **job-matching** process. Forcing jobs and workers together indiscriminately would certainly not be efficient.

The extent of mismatch in the labour market is summarized by the **Beveridge curves** of Figure 17.5. Named to honour the work of British economist William Beveridge in the 1940s, Beveridge curves relate unemployment and vacancy rates in an economy over time. Movements in the north-west and south-east directions are associated with the business cycle: firms offer fewer jobs and unemployment is higher in recessions, while the vacancy rate declines and the unemployment rate rises in economic expansions. The *position* of the Beveridge curve, on the other hand, indicates the longer-run efficiency of job-matching in labour markets. The coincidence of a large number of vacancies with high unemployment—a Beveridge curve far away from the origin—suggests that workers are either badly informed, or unable to take up the offers for lack of mobility or adequate skills, or unwilling to change and adapt. The Beveridge curve seemed to shift away from the origin in the mid-1970s, suggesting increasingly inefficient or mismatched labour markets—in fact, a rise in the equilibrium rate of unemployment. In the USA, this shift was of temporary duration, while in the UK and Germany, the return to the earlier position has been very slow.

Shifting the Beveridge curve towards the origin—put differently, reducing the unemployment rate at any level of vacancies—can be good supply-side policy. For policy-makers, it simply means implementing measures which improve the job-matching process. One is to improve information on job openings by increasing the number and effectiveness of

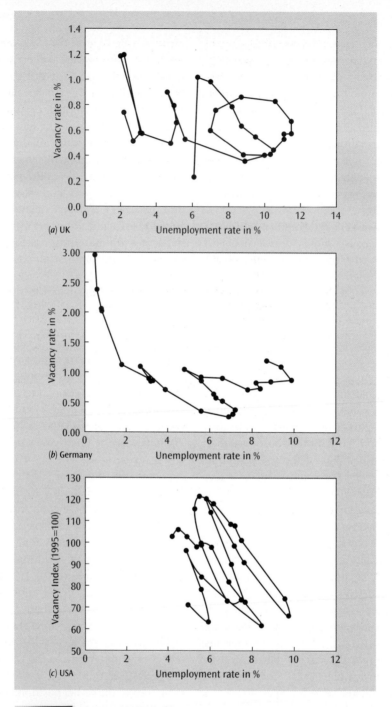

Fig. 17.5 **The Beveridge Curve**

The Beveridge curve is the empirical inverse relationship between vacancies and unemployment. In a recession vacancies tend to decline and unemployment increases. The more efficient is the job-matching process—the way unemployment workers and unfilled job vacancies are matched—the closer to the origin the Beveridge curve is. Over the past thirty years, the Beveridge curve seems to have shifted outward in several European economies, although not in the USA.

Sources: OECD; IMF.

job agencies. Recent advances in networking technology have made it possible for unemployed seeking work to know about job offers all over a country —as long as they are posted. Second, the adaptability of workers' skills may be enhanced via job retraining programmes. This means giving workers whose skills are unwanted or obsolete new ones which are in demand. Another possibility is to increase workers' and firms' geographical mobility, for example by making the housing market more efficient or providing subsidies to firms in search of new locations. In recent years, countries have begun to make more use of **active labour market policies**, which is nothing but the creative and flexible use of all of the measures already mentioned and more—as opposed to the passive policy of simply paying out unemployment benefits. Box 17.5 gives some details on the Nordic approach to labour market policy.

Box 17.5 **Active Versus Passive Labour Market Policies**

Despite a number of adverse shocks in the past decade, the Nordic countries continue to boast the world's lowest unemployment rates, proving that generous but strictly administered unemployment benefit programmes are consistent with 'European' solidarity with the unemployed. In Sweden, unemployed workers may claim benefits for roughly 300 days of unemployment. Unlike most countries, however, at the end of this period benefits are not renewed. Instead, a position in a job training programme is offered. Employment offices may even require that an unemployed person move to another city. Refusal can, and sometimes does, result in termination of benefits. As a result, the Scandinavian countries spend less on unemployment benefits and more on **active labour market policies**, i.e. programmes involving direct job creation, targeted job subsidies, retraining, relocation of families away from distressed regions, and special programmes to get young people started. In general, the unemployed are supervised more closely and kept in touch with the labour market. Table 17.3 gives details. In relative terms, Nordic countries spend more on active labour market policies than other Western European countries, while maintaining much lower long-term unemployment rates.[7]

Table 17.3 **Scandinavian Labour Market Programme Expenditure, 1998**

	Denmark	Finland	Norway	Sweden
Active measures				
Labour market training	1.07	0.41	0.1	0.48
Youth measures	0.08	0.16	0.02	0.03
Direct job creation	0.23	0.29	0.02	0.35
Total active programmes	1.89	1.23	0.91	2.01
Passive measures				
Unemployment compensation	1.86	2.35	0.49	1.91
Early retirements	1.88	0.45	—	—
Total passive programmes	3.74	2.79	0.49	1.91
Total	**5.63**	**4.02**	**1.4**	**3.92**
Long-term unemployment rate	1.4	3.2	n.a.	3.1

Source: OECD.

---

[7] More recently, aggressive implementation of active labour market policies in the Czech Republic, a formerly centrally planned economy, initially confirmed the Swedish success story in maintaining turnover among the unemployed. That other, more fundamental reforms were postponed meant that these gains were short-lived, and unemployment there has risen to levels typical for reforming planned economies.

17.4.2 **Imperfect Contracts and Labour Market Regulations**

Because of their social and political aspects, labour markets are often heavily regulated. Regulations cover a wide range of aspects: paid holidays, the length of working days and weeks, safety standards, works councils, union representation, and other facets of the employment relationship. These regulations may often have efficiency costs and sometimes seem only marginally motivated by good economic arguments. The columns of Table 17.4 report the relative severity of the most common types of labour market regulations in OECD Europe.

Besides the problem of imperfect information noted in the last section and that of imperfect competition discussed in Section 17.2, a number of economic factors have led governments to regulate labour markets, sometimes strictly. Again, most of them have to do with the special nature of the labour relationship, and are a response to the impossibility of writing and enforcing labour contracts which specify all possible events which could occur, as well as all responses to those events (nor is it particularly efficient, given what lawyers would charge to write such contracts!). The enormous complexity of the world of affairs and the inability or unwillingness of workers to deal with it may lead to exploitation; leaving the rest to the market may disadvantage workers in particular situations. For that reason, governments have often stepped in—although not always in the most appropriate way.

Imperfect mobility and regulation

One situation of possible exploitation relates to worker mobility. Mobility of demanders and suppliers is a central mechanism for correcting imbalances in a perfectly competitive market: if they feel they are getting a bad deal, they simply move elsewhere. In labour markets, things may not be so simple: the suppliers of labour are human beings. Mobility means changing jobs, an industry, occupation, or residential location, and people by their very nature tend to be immobile. Furthermore, they may even *value* their 'immobility', preferring to take a pay cut or even risk unemployment to stay put.

Under certain circumstances, an employer might try to exploit this immobility. For example, after the employment relationship has begun, employers may try to take advantage of the employed by lowering their real wages. In perfect market situations, the worker would simply leave the firm, and look elsewhere, incurring mobility costs. In advanced economies these costs may be rather significant, and this may not be a desirable mechanism. One way to prevent this is to impose minimum wages; another is to extend union contracts to uncovered workers and firms in the sector.[8] Similar arguments are often invoked to justify work week and work time regulations, job protection, and rules concerning job safety.

Regulation of dismissal

A related argument has been invoked for regulations of dismissal 'without cause', i.e. not due to malfeasance or misbehaviour on the part of the worker. Lay-offs for reasons related only to the business cycle are associated with uncertainty and economic dislocation. In many European countries, prior notice of termination of employment must be given to workers—during which time the employee remains on the payroll and represents a cost to the firm. 'Social plans' are often required for large-scale redundancies, in which the exact list of employees is decided using criteria like age, family status, and re-employability. Severance payments are often legally mandated for workers dismissed for economic reasons. While common in EU countries, job protection is by no means the norm in the OECD, with the USA and UK offering examples of countries where 'employment at will' contracts prevail.

While severance regulations make it difficult for firms to reduce employment in the short run, they also increase the effective cost of labour to firms. In doing so, they make firms more reluctant to hire in good times, precisely because they worry about consequences in bad times. Firms will tend to use the 'intensive' margin more often (overtime,

---

[8] Minimum wages are also imposed for reasons of income distribution. For example, if the elasticity of labour demand is thought to be low at low wages, then raising the minimum wage does little harm while increasing the income of the lowest-income working families, putting more value on employment.

Table 17.4	Measures of the Strictness of Labour Market Regulation (2 = most strict, 0 = least strict)

	Working time regulations	Regulation of limited-time contracts	Job protection legislation	Minimum wage regulation	Aggregate index
Euro area					
Austria	1	1	1	0	3
Belgium	0	1	1	1	3
Finland	1	1	1	1	4
France	1	1	1	2	5
Germany	1	1	1	1	4
Greece	2	1	2	2	7
Ireland	2	0	2	0	4
Italy	1	2	2	2	7
Netherlands	1	0	1	1	3
Portugal	1	1	1	1	4
Spain	2	1	2	2	7
Memo: Arithmetic Average	*1.1*	*0.9*	*1.3*	*1.1*	*4.4*
Other EU					
Denmark	0	0	0	0	0
Sweden	1	2	1	1	5
United Kingdom	0	0	0	0	0
Other OECD					
Norway	1	2	1	0	4
Switzerland	1	1	1	0	3
United States	0	0	0	0	0

Source: IMF *World Economic Outlook* May 1999.

conversion of part-time into full time) before hiring new individuals. The third column of Table 17.4 reports a ranking of the degree of 'job security' provisions provided in a number of industrial countries. It is noteworthy that countries in which youth unemployment rates are high tend to have the most restrictive dismissal laws.

As the economy becomes increasingly subject to global influences and technological advances, employment relationships have changed fundamentally in nature. They have become less likely to involve lifetime relationships, and are more likely at some point to be 'restructured' or reorientated towards fully new areas of activity. Severance rules of the type described inhibit the growth of new firms as well as the expansion of existing ones. As the pressures for more flexible employment grow, firms have become increasingly creative in finding ways to undo the intended effects of the legislation. For example, they may chain several short-term contracts together for the same employee, or hire workers from temporary help agencies, shifting the burden to others. In the end, it may be worth considering market solutions in which workers accept to work under 'employment at will' for a wage premium, allowing firms to pay for additional flexibility while preserving employment protection.

17.4.3 Incentives and Taxation

The social safety net

The social safety net refers to the system of transfers and benefits designed to help the disadvantaged and vulnerable in society. These include unemployment benefits, social welfare, old-age pensions, early retirement, health insurance, and disability benefits. A large gap divides European countries, which transfer between 20% and 30% of their national income to individuals or firms, from the USA, Japan, and Switzerland, which transfer only 10–15%. This might lead a casual observer to conclude that high European unemployment is a product of the 'social welfare state', which puts weight on solidarity but at the cost of productivity and economic efficiency. Yet it is too hasty to claim that Europeans have erred too far in the direction of social protection, in comparison to the rest of the OECD. The high level of transfers observed in Europe is to some extent a *response* to high unemployment, which may have other underlying causes. At the same time, these transfers—in the form of unemployment benefits, welfare, and premature retirement and disability pensions—take the pressure off workers and firms to adjust to a changing world economy. The greatest danger is that the safety net becomes a trap, leading to long-term unemployment.

Box 17.6   Crusoe Caught in the Safety Net

In Figure 17.6 Crusoe is faced with a time line (budget constraint), which is no longer strictly linear. This is because when not at work at all ($\ell = \bar{\ell}$), he receives a transfer of T from the government—unemployment benefits, welfare, or other payments associated with the social safety net. Moreover if Crusoe works a little bit, he loses benefits by exactly the amount of his additional income—an effective marginal tax rate of 100%. This is representative of the current situation in many European countries. Since Crusoe loses a euro of benefit for every euro he earns in work, the budget line is flat up to the point at which Crusoe receives T, whether he works or not. Crusoe values leisure, so it is hard to see why he would accept part-time work in this regime. Unless the after-tax wage is high enough, Crusoe is unlikely to work.

Figure 17.6 also shows the impact of reducing the effective marginal tax rate from 100% to some lower rate which is nevertheless higher than that for someone already in work and not receiving welfare payments, holding T constant. As the tax rate declines, the budget line for the household becomes steeper; at some point Crusoe can make himself even better off than he was at A, by choosing point B. In doing so his income is added to the tax base and contributes to higher GDP. The effect can be intensified if the carrot (the lower effective marginal tax rate) is combined with a stick (lowering T), although this type of reform is politically difficult to implement.

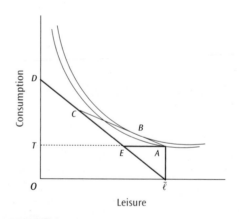

Fig. 17.6   Incentives and the Social Safety Net

In a social welfare system with benefit T when out of work but with 100% marginal tax rate, the individual depicted in this figure chooses not to work (point A), because no net additional income results from modest increases in labour supply, starting at zero. The budget constraint is $\bar{\ell}AED$. If the individual is allowed to keep some additional income (changing the budget constraint to $\bar{\ell}ACD$) the individual can improve her well-being by working (point B). The most important problem with lowering the effective marginal tax rate to unemployment benefit and welfare recipients is the cost to the state, which can be considerable.

It is useful to use the tools developed in Chapter 4 to help think about the adverse effects of the safety net on incentives. The social systems of most countries share two institutional features. First, poor or unemployed people receive transfers—income maintenance programmes or unemployment benefits —from the state. Second, income taxes are progressive: the rate of taxation increases as income rises. Taking up a job not only means receiving a salary, but also paying taxes if the salary is high enough, and thereby losing eligibility for income maintenance programmes. It is conceivable then that people can be financially worse off by taking a job, not to mention incurring a loss of leisure, and possibly some activity in the underground (shadow) economy. Implicitly, these people face an effective marginal tax rate—considering the overall effect of work on their income—in excess of 100%. Box 17.6 shows how safety net programmes may lead to a **welfare trap**, inducing people to remain unemployed or stay out of the labour force, thereby reducing the productive potential of the economy. Recent experience of 'work-to-welfare' in the USA indicates that the incentive aspect is important for bringing workers on social assistance back to work.

Labour taxation

Because labour is so important in any economy, it is natural to expect governments to tax it. Perhaps because the Ramsey principle of public finance (Section 17.3.2) is so compelling, labour is one of the most highly taxed 'commodities'. As Box 17.7 explains, not only is labour subject to income taxes paid by households, but also to a number of social security contributions by both employees and employers. It is also natural to expect that labour taxation might influence the demand for labour, with higher taxes raising the real cost of labour faced by firms, leading to lower employment in

---

Box 17.7 **Taxes and the Labour Market in Europe**

Labour taxes can be grouped into three classes: income taxes, social insurance charges paid by employers, and social security contributions by the employees. All three can be added up, as they either reduce the workers' net receipts and thus affect the supply of labour, or increase the cost of labour and reduce demand. They are usually not called taxes, but 'contributions' to funds for unemployment benefits, national health insurance, retirement and pension benefits, disability insurance, solidarity with various causes including low-cost housing and special retraining programmes, etc. Let τ_F be the employer's wage tax rate, let W be the wage of the employee before his own income taxes and employee social security contributions, let τ_W be the tax rate of contribution of the employee, and let τ_P be the personal income tax rate. The take-home pay for the worker after taxes will be $W_{\text{take home}}$ = $(1 - \tau_W)(1 - \tau_P)W$, while the cost of labour to the firm is given by $W_{\text{labour costs}} = (1 - \tau_F)W$. As a result, the effective labour cost is equal to the take-home pay multiplied by the factor $\dfrac{1 + \tau_F}{(1 - \tau_W)(1 - \tau_P)}$ which is often called the labour tax wedge. Holding $W_{\text{take home}}$ constant, increases in the tax wedge increase labour costs and reduce the demand for labour. In addition to all this, workers also pay income tax on their take-home salary, which may be progressive, or increase at the margin as taxable income itself rises.

Does high labour taxation necessarily lead to high unemployment? Not at all: it depends on how the supply of labour, or the collective bargaining system reacts. Equilibrium unemployment rate will remain unchanged only if after taxes wages fall by exactly the amount of tax—that is, if workers shoulder the entire burden. But the collective labour supply curve will not be vertical in general; households may find it attractive at high taxes to work less, work in the underground economy, or to take overtime pay in the form of a holiday (leisure), as is often done in Scandinavia. It is thus likely that such high taxes make hiring labour unattractive, and that a reduction of such taxes could increase employment. The problem for governments is how to replace the revenue that is lost.

the sector that pays the tax.[9] Table 17.5 shows the rate of taxation on labour in various countries in its various guises. Despite high unemployment, little effort has been made so far to alleviate the tax burden placed on the labour market.

Yet this net effect depends on the elasticity of labour demand and supply. If collective labour supply is relatively inelastic—perhaps reflecting the inelastic labour supply of households—the burden of the tax will fall primarily on workers, and employment will be relatively unaffected. In Europe, however, wages are set in collective bargaining,

leading in all likelihood to a flatter collective labour supply curve. Under these conditions, high labour taxes might reduce employment significantly, and be associated with a large loss of consumer and producer surplus.[10] In the very long run the elasticity of labour demand is likely to be very high, since firms may simply move to other locations where labour costs are lower. It is for this reason that the integration of European economies is forcing a harmonization of taxation across national boundaries, with or without explicit government coordination.

Table 17.5   **Labour Taxation in 1996**

Country	Total tax receipts (% of GDP)	Personal income tax	Social security contributions		Highest rate of personal income tax
			Employees	Employers	
Euro area					
Austria	44.0	20.9	14.0	0.0	47.0
Belgium	46.0	31.0	9.8	19.7	61.0
Finland	48.2	35.0	4.2	20.5	57.5
France	45.7	14.1	13.0	26.6	54.0
Germany	38.1	24.7	17.6	20.5	55.9
Greece	40.6	12.4	15.9	14.7	..
Ireland	33.7	31.3	4.5	8.2	48.0
Italy	43.2	25.1	6.8	23.7	46.0
Netherlands	43.3	17.5	25.0	6.8	60.0
Portugal	34.9	18.9	9.6	14.4	40.0
Spain	33.7	23.0	5.5	25.6	56.0
Arithmetic Average	**40.7**	**23.3**	**11.4**	**16.4**	**52.5**
Other EU					
Denmark	52.2	53.2	2.5	0.7	58.7
Sweden	52.0	35.3	4.5	24.9	59.6
United Kingdom	36.0	25.9	7.2	9.6	40.0
Other OECD					
Norway	41.1	26	8.2	13.6	41.7
Switzerland	34.7	32	11.9	11.3	43.9
United States	28.5	37.6	10.6	12.9	46.6

Source: OECD.

[9] This qualification is important. If some type of labour is untaxed, demand, employment, and wages may rise when labour taxes rise elsewhere. The obvious example is the underground economy, which always thrives when labour taxes are high.
[10] Ch. 4 provides more details on the collective labour supply curve; producer and consumer surplus are defined and discussed in S. 17.3.2.

17.4.4 The Political Economy of Labour Market Reform

Unemployment is generally regarded as a curse of modern market economies, and remains the subject of intense political discussion. In Europe, unemployment levels have been high for almost three decades. In addition, it was seen in Table 4.4 that, in contrast to the USA, European unemployment has risen steadily over successive business cycles. Unemployment represents underutilized labour resources; if this underutilization is not the conscious choice of households, it is involuntary and represents a supply-side problem. As the leading quote at the beginning of this chapter indicated, an important challenge for the nations of Europe is to address this issue, perhaps using the ideas and concepts developed here.

Suppose there is agreement—among policy-makers, at least—that labour markets should be reformed. How should a country go about it? Several problems arise with simply 'deregulating'. First, many companies that had wanted to reduce employment under the old regime will take advantage of deregulation, and lay-offs may actually increase in the short run. In most European countries, the political consequences of such a move are severe enough to make reform unthinkable. Second, an issue of *time consistency* arises.[11] Suppose a firm that would like to hire more employees expands its employment in response to deregulation. At this point, a government seeking approval with job-security-conscious voters may reimpose the dismissal regulations, 'trapping' such firms at higher employment levels. Firms will anticipate this, with the sad result that no new workers will be hired, despite deregulation! Governments will need to precommit themselves to a 'no-reregulate' regime before employers are convinced.

It is also true that an overwhelming majority (90–5%) of workers are employed, so that their domination over the unemployed might even be regarded as democratic, and is mitigated by unemployment benefits in any case. Governments frequently find it difficult to reform labour market institutions because their interventions are often regarded as interference in the collective bargaining process. One noteworthy approach is that followed by Spain, which

has a serious structural unemployment problem. Since the mid-1980s, temporary contracts for workers have been permitted, with some restrictions.[12] Such contracts allow firms to hire workers without restrictions on a limited-time, contractual basis. As a result, roughly four-fifths of all new employment in Spain since the late 1980s has been under such limited-time contracts. This response suggests that firms are willing to hire more workers when job security obligations are absent. Second, young people have been the primary beneficiary of such reforms, which has helped relieve the youth unemployment problem so acute in Spain. Finally, increasing the relative number of workers who have jobs with less protection seems to increase the consensus for broader reforms which followed. By increasing the power of the insiders, labour market reform became more palatable.

In general, the political economy of labour markets may be the most important element determining success or failure of reforms. Efforts to increase the attractiveness of part-time work have often been blocked by unions, who see their bargaining power diluted by new employees unlikely to be members. Work sharing proposals which increase the cost of labour are resisted fiercely by employer associations. Recent successful reforms in France have shown that management and labour often put many different elements on the negotiating table, trading reduced working time and relief on labour charges for flexibility, wage moderation, and reform of the unemployment benefits system.

Box 17.8 provides more detail on the extremes of labour market reform strategies. In rare cases, such as Britain under Margaret Thatcher, unions have been reformed against their will by democratically elected governments, with much social tension. The other extreme, in the Netherlands, was engineered in classic corporatist fashion, with the active involvement of unions, management, and the government. While both approaches involve radically different levels of social consensus and cohesion, they have one important aspect in common: they both required about a decade to bear fruit, as well as the patience of the electorate to stay the course until the benefits were realized.

---

[11] Time consistency is discussed in Ch. 16.

[12] For example, firms were not allowed to 'roll over' the same worker in a series of short-term contracts. Naturally, employers have devised numerous loopholes to deal with this restriction.

Box 17.8   **Bust 'em or Trust 'em? Trade Unions and Reform in the UK and the Netherlands**

At the end of the 1970s, both the United Kingdom and the Netherlands faced similarly distressing economic conditions. Both had high rates of unemployment and low growth in economic output. The root of the unemployment problem in both countries seemed to be that real wages had got out of hand, exceeding wage growth warranted by growth in total factor productivity. In the UK, a Tory government led by Prime Minister Margaret Thatcher took the position that the system needed to be changed. Her programme, which was passed by Parliament with much resistance, was a radical overhaul of the UK collective bargaining system. In a series of open confrontations, she limited trade unions' ability to disrupt the workings of the economy. New legislation limited wide immunity enjoyed by unions from civil suits to those directly involving industrial action, and forced unions to

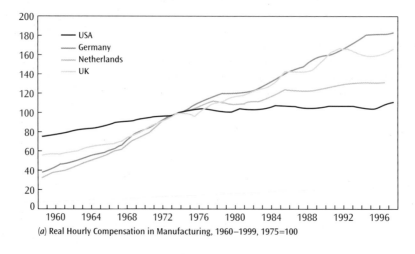

(a) Real Hourly Compensation in Manufacturing, 1960–1999, 1975=100

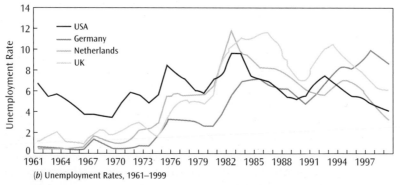

(b) Unemployment Rates, 1961–1999

Fig. 17.7   **Real Wages and Unemployment in the UK, the Netherlands, Germany, and the USA, 1960–1999**

The recent experience of the UK and the Netherlands strongly suggests that equilibrium unemployment declined in the late 1980 and early 1990s, in contrast to Germany. Much of this improvement can be linked to real wage moderation since the early 1980s. In the UK, this moderation was accomplished by reducing union power significantly. In the Netherlands, it was the outcome of a broad agreement between labour unions and employer associations, with the tacit and sometimes active support of government.
Sources: US Department of Labor; OECD.

Box 17.8 **Continued**

elect their officials in secret balloting. In the decade 1980–9, union membership in the UK declined by 21% and union density declined from 50.7% to 41.5%. Over the same period unemployment declined considerably, as seen in Figure 17.7. Although condemned at the time by many academic economists, Thatcher's reforms evidently did reduce equilibrium unemployment significantly in the UK in the years which followed.

In Holland, a radically different approach was chosen. In 1982, in a widely publicized agreement reached by labour and management at Wassenaar, unions consented to moderate real wage growth in both private and public sectors and management agreed to expand part-time employment. While not officially part of the agreement, the government followed with tax breaks for part-time

jobs as well as cuts in public sector employment and wages. Most important, tax rates on labour were reduced, blunting the net impact of real wage moderation on households' incomes. In the years that followed, real wages in the Netherlands grew much more slowly than in neighbouring EU economies, as Figure 17.7 indicates. In fact, Dutch real wage behaviour in the 1990s more closely resembles that of the United States than neighbouring Germany! The employment growth and decline in unemployment which later followed in the Netherlands seems to confirm that wage moderation is one important element of a successful labour market reform package, but need not require 'union busting', the radical dismantling of collective bargaining mechanisms.

Summary

1. Supply-side policies are appealing because, in contrast to demand-side policies, they do not imply a short-run trade-off between unemployment and inflation. They increase output permanently at any given level of inflation and economic growth, and may even increase the rate of growth itself.

2. One principle underlying supply-side policies is that markets do not function perfectly. By removing market imperfections, the economy's overall output and productivity can be enhanced.

3. There are three main sources of market failures: externalities, increasing returns to scale, and asymmetric information.

4. Externalities occur when someone's economic activity has an effect, positive or negative, on others. Positive externalities imply that one does not recognize the benefits to society of one's actions, and will undertake less than is socially desirable. Negative externalities imply that one does not recognize the costs to society of one's economic actions, and will undertake too much of them. Pecuniary externalities are solved once property rights are ascertained. Non-pecuniary externalities requires government interventions.

5. Increasing returns lead to monopolies. Some monopolies are natural, inherent to the task itself. The solution used to be state ownership. Increasingly, state monopolies are privatized and government interventions take the form of regulations.

6. Asymmetric information occurs when one's actions are not known to others. It may lead to inefficient outcomes. Regulation can be designed to alleviate this problem.

7. Public goods that are non-rival and non-excludable tend not be privately provided. Governments can and should step in, and provide these goods which can be highly productive.

8. Taxation is necessary to pay for the operation of government. It is also a source of inefficiency because it drives a wedge between the price paid by the consumer and the price received by the producer, reducing demand and supply.

9. Because the operation of governments requires resources with alternative uses in the private sector, supply-side considerations call for limiting public spending to the production of goods and services that cannot be produced by the private sector. There is much debate on the correct size of government.

10. Governments often subsidize firms and industries. Although the objective of subsidies is to protect firms, they remove the incentive to compete, and ultimately cost jobs. State ownership has similar effects. The supply-side response is to cut down on subsidies and to privatize.

11. High structural unemployment is a supply-side problem. It arises as a result of labour market distortions, some of which are due to private agents and others to interventions of government.

12. Eliminating structural unemployment is possible by better management of labour taxation, severance regulations, labour relations, and the social safety net. Active labour market policies can help prevent the emergence of long-term unemployment.

13. Labour market reforms are highly politicized and controversial. Because the beneficiaries of reform are usually in the minority, their interests may be difficult to protect. Broad-based reforms almost always require give and take of the involved parties. Whether conflictual or consensual, reforms require time—as long as a decade—to have a measurable effect.

Key Concepts

- supply-side policies
- market-clearing
- laissez-faire
- market failures
- economic rents
- competition policy
- property rights
- externalities, pecuniary and non-pecuniary, positive and negative
- human capital
- natural monopoly
- distortionary taxation

- consumer and producer surplus
- Ramsey principle of public finance
- Laffer curve
- privatization
- industrial policies
- trade policies
- job matching
- Beveridge curve
- active labour market policies
- welfare trap
- labour tax wedge

Exercises

1. Trace through the macroeconomic effects, in the short and long run, of a policy that reduces equilibrium output $\bar{Y}$ (for example, an increase in labour taxation). Under what conditions could this lead to a permanent increase in the rate of inflation? (*Hint*: Chapter 13.)

2. 'A cut in income taxes in Europe would have significant supply-side effects.' Comment.

3. Show diagramatically how shifting out the collective labour supply curve—using the six panel diagrams of Chapter 10—can lead to increased output.

4. Why does immigration policy represent supply-side policy? Why is it so controversial?

5. According to the Ramsey principle of public finance (see Box 17.3), on which would you levy higher taxes, jewellery or petrol? Labour income or capital income?

6. It is often alleged that the Laffer curve is more likely to be relevant in countries with a large underground economy. Explain. How might the underground economy contribute to the 'unemployment trap' described in Box 17.6?

7. Chapter 7 discussed the 'Dutch disease', the reaction of the real exchange rate to an increase in domestic wealth associated with a resource discovery. In the case of Britain and Norway, both countries enjoyed the benefits of the North Sea oil discoveries of the 1970s. Norway subsidized its exporting industries as a response, while Britain used the resources to help balance the budget and therefore pay for transfers and government spending. Why might a subsidy be good supply-side economics in this case?

8. It is sometimes claimed that overtime working contributes to the unemployment problem. In particular, hiring and firing costs make it more attractive to pay current workers to work more (the intensive margin) than to hire more workers (the extensive margin). Furthermore, tax provisions may shield overtime income from normal labour taxation. How might reform of overtime working be difficult under these conditions? Can you think of reform measures that might encourage fewer overtime hours?

9. It has been observed that the average wage of trade union members is higher than that of the population. How might this affect their attitudes to reforms and structural change?

10. Why do you suppose that unemployment is such an important factor in national politics—although the unemployment rate is rarely higher than 15% of the labour force, and 10% of the adult population of working age—in most industrial countries?

Suggested Further Reading

The classic statement of why markets achieve the social best is:
Smith, Adam (1776), *The Wealth of Nations*, London.

A modern 'classic' popular summary of the most important supply-side arguments is:
Friedman, Milton, and Friedman, Rose (1979), *Free to Choose*, Harcourt Brace Jovanovich.

Two views of the state's involvement in economic activity:
Against: Hayek, Friedrich von (1948), *Individualism and Economic Order*, University of Chicago Press.
Pro: Stiglitz, Joseph (1994), *Whither Socialism*, MIT Press.

For a detailed analysis of the political economy of labour market institutions:
St.-Paul, Gilles (1997), 'High Unemployment from a Political Economy Perspective', in de la Dehesa
  and Snower (eds.), *Unemployment Policy: Government Options for the Labour Market?*, Cambridge
  University Press.
St.-Paul, Gilles (2000), *The Political Economy of Labour Market Institutions*, Oxford University Press.

For evidence on minimum wages in Europe:
Dolado, J., et al. (1996), 'The Economic Impact of Minimum Wages in Europe', *Economic Policy*,
  23 October, 319–72.

For a study of the interactions of taxation and unemployment:
Daveri, F., and Tabellini, G., 'Unemployment, Growth and Taxation in the Industrial Countries',
  Economic Policy, 30 (April 2000), 47–104.

For an analysis of the reforms in the UK and the Netherlands:
Nickell, S., and Van Ours, J., 'The Netherlands and the United Kingdom: A European Unemployment Miracle?', *Economic Policy*, 30 (April 2000), 135–80.

For a theoretical analysis of the complementarities of labour market reforms, see:
Coe, D., and Snower, D. J. (1997), 'Policy Complementarities: The Case for Fundamental Labour
  Market Reform', *IMF Staff Papers*, 44(1): 1–35.

For an analysis of the European dilemma applied to Italy, see:
Bertola, Giuseppe, and Ichino, Andrea (1995), 'Crossing the River: A Comparative Perspective on
  Italian Employment Dynamics', *Economic Policy*, 21: 359–420.

Economic Growth: Theory and Policy

No one could have ever intended to deny that technological change is at least partially endogenous to the economy. Valuable resources are used in the pursuit of innovation, presumably with some rational hope of financial success. The patent system is intended to solidify that hope, and thus attract more resources into the search for new products and processes.

– Robert M. Solow

18.1 Overview

This chapter returns to long-run growth, the topic which motivated our first analysis of the macro-economy in Chapter 3. There, the Solow model identified three sources of economic growth: population growth, capital accumulation, and technological progress. An important conclusion of this analysis was that neither population growth nor capital accumulation can explain continuing advances in standards of living that have been observed in the past two centuries. Evidently, technological progress is the engine of growth. But what is technological progress? And can anything be done to harness or accelerate this formidable source of economic prosperity? This chapter delves more deeply into these fascinating issues which lie on the frontiers of economic research.

In the Solow model, population growth and capital accumulation cannot sustain economic growth on their own because both labour and capital are subject to diminishing marginal returns. Technological progress is the engine of growth because it is assumed never to exhaust itself: it increases exogenously irrespective of what happens. This assumption is unsatisfactory. Technological progress is the result of costly efforts at research—producing knowledge—and development—making that knowledge work for us. Research and development (R&D) in turn represents economic activity in its own right. So why doesn't R&D fall victim to decreasing returns? To answer that question, it helps to keep in mind how Chapter 3 concluded: it showed an example where growth perpetuates itself simply because marginal productivity of capital does not fall. This is our point of departure here: as we explore technological progress, we open up the hunt for possible sources of non-decreasing marginal productivities.

First, we extend our description of the productive system, captured by the aggregate production function, in three ways. To start with, labour is not homogeneous: some workers are highly skilled, others much less so. This leads us to introduce additional factors of production: human capital (skills acquired on the job or through investment in education, and kept in use through good health care) and public infrastructure. Section 18.2 explores the convergence hypothesis according to which poor countries eventually catch up with the richer ones.

Second, we recognize that technological progress is the outcome of costly efforts which must be rewarded in some way or another. Section 18.3 examines how knowledge can be thought of as an economic good, albeit with unique features. The analysis begins with the recognition that growth is a collective undertaking. Traditional economics assumes that the pursuit of self-interest is sufficient to promote the collective well-being. But introspection tells us this need not be the case. In many ways, we all depend on each other through channels which are not mediated by markets. In previous chapters, an externality was said to arise when one agent's actions have an implication, positive or negative, on other agents' well-being and behaviour, yet there can be no market price reward.

As Chapter 17 pointed out, externalities can be positive or negative: in either case, if left to themselves, markets may not lead to the optimal outcome. In the case of knowledge creation and related activities which have positive effects on growth, do we know whether these contributions to economic activity will be remunerated sufficiently? Will the inventor of the next wonder drug or telecommunications device reap some rewards for the hard work, or will copycats steal the idea? To this end, societies establish **property rights** over ideas for some limited time, enforce them with judicial systems, and generally seek to encourage entrepreneurial activity essential to research and development.

Finally, for some reasons, some people are excluded from this collective undertaking. Poverty exists everywhere in the midst of plenty. Does growth reduce poverty? And is poverty a threat to growth? More generally, the political system of a nation influences, and is influenced by economic growth. Especially for the poorest countries of the world these issues are of an existential nature and will be taken up in Section 18.4.

18.2 Growth and Complementary Inputs

18.2.1 Convergence and Complementary Inputs

In the Solow model, prosperity in the steady state is determined by two factors: (1) the saving rate and (2) the state of technology, which is represented by the production function. Low incomes per capita result from insufficient capital accumulation, presumably for lack of adequate saving, destruction by war or natural disaster, or the absence of a functioning market economy. Countries with similar technologies and savings rates should, however, have the same steady-state income per capita. Moreover, those starting from a low per capita GDP should accumulate capital per capita faster than wealthy economies and thereby eventually catch up. This is the **convergence hypothesis**.

The central prediction of the convergence hypothesis—that the poorer a country initially is, the faster it subsequently grows—can be tested. Figure 18.1 plots the average growth rate over the period 1960–97 of 102 countries against their per capita GDP in 1960. Panel (*a*) of the figure which looks at a large number of developed and developing countries, is not too encouraging. However, panel (*b*), which presents the same data for 23 advanced countries alone, offers more convincing support for the convergence hypothesis. While standards of living among the wealthier countries are converging, many poorer countries seem to be 'stuck' with low per capita GDP and low or even negative growth.

It is not easy to account for the continuing economic malaise of poor countries. Low savings alone

cannot explain the dramatic differences that we observe in reality. As long as state-of-the-art technology is available in all countries and if capital is free to move, investors (multinational firms, financiers) should move resources to countries where capital–labour ratios are low and, therefore, returns on investment ought to be high. As a result, capital–labour ratios (k) should be equalized across countries. This process may take some time, of course, but a process of convergence towards the similar capital–labour ratios, and therefore per capita GDPs should occur. Plainly, it hasn't.[1] The poorer countries' inability to close the income gap represents a massive challenge to the international community, and to economics as well. It questions the basic assumption that free markets benefit all. It also casts doubt on the validity of the Solow growth model. At the very least, it suggests that there is something systematic at work that the model does not take into account. Indeed, the two-factor production used in Chapter 3 may be too simple.

One strategy towards explaining persistent poverty in developing countries is to adapt the convergence

---

[1] Nobel Laureate Robert Lucas of Chicago has estimated that if India and the United States had the same production function, the marginal product of capital in the former should be about 58 times the marginal product in the latter! In his words, 'If this [Solow] model were anywhere close to being accurate, and if world capital markets were anywhere close to being free and complete, it is clear that, in the face of return differentials of this magnitude, investment goods would flow rapidly from the United States and other wealthy countries to India and other poor countries. Indeed, one would expect *no* investment to occur in the wealthy countries in the face of return differentials of this magnitude' (1990: 92).

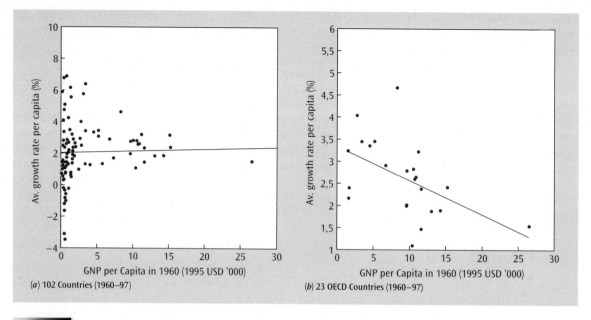

Fig. 18.1   **The Convergence Hypothesis in Reality**

Panel (*a*) shows no relationship between the per capita growth rate between 1960 and 1992 and initial per capita GNP, for a sample of 98 countries. Poor countries do not seem to catch up. However, when the sample is restricted to 23 OECD countries, as in panel (*b*), the convergence hypothesis is supported.
Sources: Barro (1991); Summers and Heston (1991).

hypothesis to include other influences—comple-mentary inputs—which are not explicit in the Solow model, in particular the education level of the population and the level of public infrastructure. When this is done, the convergence hypothesis tends to do better when confronted with the facts.

18.2.2 Human Capital

Just as firms acquire capital for producing goods and services, individuals can expend time, energy, and money to acquire knowledge. This activity ranges from going to school, learning a skill, or taking a training course. Acquisition of knowledge is an investment, and will be undertaken in general because it pays to do so. It is for this reason that one speaks of investment in **human capital**. Better-trained and educated workers tend to be more productive, and more productive workers can earn higher wages. Furthermore, more educated workers tend to enhance the productivity of other factors.

Skilled workers are better at operating complex machines, and may be used to manage other labourers and organize the production process. Thus, it makes sense to think of production as combining not only physical capital K and hours of work L, but also third input, human capital H. The economy's production function becomes:

(18.1) $$Y = A\,F(K, L, H)$$

Much of the reasoning of the Solow model in Chapter 3 can be repeated using this expanded version of the production function. Like physical capital, human capital can be accumulated and is subject to depreciation. Accounting for human capital yields non-trivial conclusions: human capital contributes to output per capita, so countries which invest more in education and training tend to be better off in the long run. Furthermore, as a com-plementary factor of production, human capital increases the marginal productivity of other factors. Yet this is not enough for our purposes: if the production function (18.1) is subject to constant returns to scale, so that the marginal product of human capital is decreasing,[2] long-run growth rates in economies with low and high 'savings' rates in human capital will still be the same.

While education is a key factor of growth, a number of puzzling issues remain which prevent drawing immediate conclusions. To start with, as any investment, education pays off later. Unlike many investments, human capital involves no collateral, or assets which can be pledged in case repayment of the loan is impossible. While firms can raise money from banks, stock markets or their owners to buy equipment, many people cannot pay for their own education, especially in poor countries. The usual response is that governments provide public education, along with scholarships for poorer students. Yet, if the returns from education come in the form of better salaries, should the state provide public money for private benefit? The answer may still be yes, if human capital creates externalities. It should be obvious that being the only one who knows how to read in a country is less useful, both privately and collectively, than if many other people also know how to read and write.

Externality thus explains why governments should provide resources for education, but it raises a new perplexing question: my education helps me get a better life through a better salary, but it also benefits my co-workers, so how do I get the incentive to invest enough to match their own interests as well? Free education is not enough, since years in school are years without any salary. Compulsory education is one answer. Social status, a non-pecuniary reward, is another one.

If externalities are present, human capital may no longer be subject to decreasing returns in the aggregate, even if any given individual perceives decreasing returns at the margin. At the individual level, there is only so much to be gained from another year at school. Collectively, the existence of an externality may alter this conclusion: if all citizens study longer and better, the marginal productivity of human capital overall may not decline. This would open up the possibility of self-sustaining growth described in Section 3.6.

It would also explain a key puzzle. Decreasing marginal productivity means that the reward to human capital should decline with its quantity.[3] Thus human capital should be better paid in less developed countries where it is less abundant. While it is true that elites in poor countries may enjoy a better relative position than in developed countries, educated people continue to migrate from poor to rich countries, not the other way round. The reason is that they benefit from the externality of human capital. At the collective level, human capital may not face diminishing marginal productivity.

18.2.3 Infrastructure

A second missing factor is public infrastructure, a type of public good already discussed in Chapter 15, which includes streets, public transport, telecommunication, postal service, airports, systems of water distribution, electricity provision, and sewage treatment etc. Public infrastructure contributes directly to production, much like any other form of capital. Firms use roads and telephone lines much as they use their own machines and lorries. At the aggregate level, the production function can be further augmented to include this stock of public capital K^G:

(18.2) $$Y = A \, F(K, L, H, K^G)$$

This obvious observation, however, raises a number of interesting questions. Public infrastructure is not free. While this is also true for private physical capital, there is a crucial difference. Firms carefully evaluate the balance of costs and benefits from acquiring more equipment. Because infrastructure is a public good paid with taxes, it is virtually impossible for the government to evaluate the benefits that accrue in millions of ways to millions of users. Moreover, policy-makers rarely reap the benefits

---

[2] If the production function is subject to constant returns to scale in all inputs, it must be the case that the marginal productivity of each input taken individually is decreasing. The reason is that otherwise, adding more of one input would keep production rising at least as fast. Then adding the other input at the same rate would have production rising even faster, i.e. increasing returns to scale.

[3] This is an implication of microeconomics principles: optimally, factors of production should be paid their marginal productivity.

of productive spending directly; at best, they will enhance tax revenues in the future, and they may not be in power to claim credit for the growth effects which accrue several years later.

A number of difficulties may arise in getting the level spending right. First, governments might underinvest because other uses of taxpayers' money are more politically rewarding, or because pressures to cut the budget force spending cuts. Second, the government might spend too much on infrastructure because political lobbies for public works defend this budgetary item. Growth may be held back for lack of adequate infrastructure in the first case, because of excessive taxation in the second case. In order to reduce the risk of such slippage, one solution is to privatize: over the last decade, the production of electricity, telephone, water, railways, etc. has been spun off to the private sector precisely for that reason.

Figure 18.2 shows the amounts that European governments spent on capital accumulation in 2000. Because much has been privatized in some countries such as the UK, these comparisons are difficult to interpret. In the European Monetary Union, annual budget deficits should not exceed 3% of GDP; this

rule seems based on the assumption that capital spending, which should pay for itself through later growth dividends, is of about that magnitude. In 2000, capital spending amounted to 3.7% of GDP for the Eurozone as a whole.

18.2.4 Is it Enough? A Sufficient Condition

If human capital and infrastructure are subject to the same decreasing returns as capital and labour, then there is little hope that differences in human capital and infrastructure investment could explain sustainable differences in growth rates across different economies. We just have a richer description of production, but the curse of the Solow model still applies: countries with the same savings rates and technology will converge to the same steady state.

This may be only partially true, however. The great English economist Alfred Marshall once hypothesized that what an individual perceives to be the effect of his or her actions may differ substantially from the realized aggregate outcome. In particular, while each individual experiences diminishing marginal returns to investment in his or her own factors of production, it could well be that when

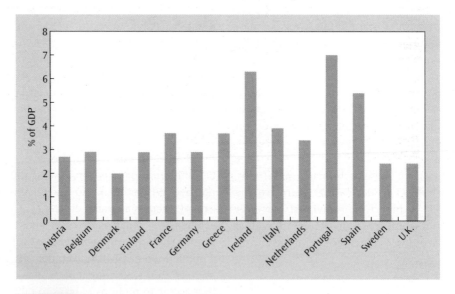

Fig. 18.2 **Public Capital Accumulation, 2000**

Public capital accumulation is shown as a percentage of GDP. Wide variations are visible across countries, partly reflecting privatization of infrastructures.
Source: OECD.

everyone engages in the activity, there are sufficient external effects on the productivity of others that effective productivity does not fall, but remains constant. This type of positive externality is called a **Marshallian externality**. Under certain conditions it could be a sufficient—but not necessary—condition for sustained growth. If the Marshallian externality creates conditions of constant returns to scale in production with respect to accumulable factors *only*—physical capital, human capital, and infrastructure—then growth does not necessarily imply that their marginal products decline, and endogenous growth is possible.[4] This was the message from Section 3.8.

18.3   Growth, Knowledge, and Innovation

18.3.1 Knowledge as a Public Good

We now confront the elusive subject of technological change, or growth in the factor represented by A in the production function.[5] Technological progress cannot really be assumed to be exogenous, as is done in Chapter 3. It comes as the result of the accumulation of knowledge, which is a very particular good indeed. Knowledge is a public good. In Chapter 15, public goods were identified as a justification for government intervention, and infrastructure and the education level of the population discussed in Section 18.2 also have public good aspects. Public goods are generally identifiable when they are either **non-excludable**, meaning that the consumer of a good cannot legally or physically prevent others from consuming it at the same time, or **non-rivalrous** when the consumption of a good by one person does not affect others' ability to enjoy it. Table 18.1 shows how different goods can be classified according to the extent to which they possess these two characteristics.

Knowledge is both non-excludable and non-rival. Knowledge is non-excludable because, once it has been produced, it tends to be freely available. Knowledge, like TV or radio programmes, is non-rival,

Table 18.1 Non-rivalrousness and Excludability: A Taxonomy of Goods		
	Rivalrous	Non-rivalrous
Excludable	Most conventionally marketed private goods	Police protection, patented Inventions, copyrighted material, subscription cable television programming
Non-excludable	Parking spaces, public tennis courts, beaches and park benches, congested highways	National defence, good weather, radio/television programming, internet, knowledge

---

[4] Marshall discussed external effects of one firm's investing in new capital equipment on other firms. He argued that while firms would never base their decision on their positive effects on competitors' productivity, it holds nevertheless that the social return from investment exceeds the private return. This argument applies with equal force to human capital and public infrastructure.

[5] More generally, technological progress can be represented in many forms. The standard production function can be generalized to $Y = A_1 F(A_2 K, A_3 L)$, with the terms A_1, A_2, and A_3 bearing the names 'Hicks-neutral', 'Solow-neutral', and 'Harrod-neutral technical change' respectively.

so that the consumption by one person does not preclude someone else from consuming (or using) it at the same time. But then, the producers of non-excludable goods will not generally be sufficiently compensated for their efforts. This is why street cleaning services and parks are supplied publicly. Does this apply to knowledge as well? Precisely because knowledge is non-excludable, a great deal of research—especially basic research—is funded by government or non-profit institutions. Yet the problem encountered with public infrastructure arises with knowledge: it is difficult if not impossible to determine the proper level of public financing of research. Since research is inherently uncertain and often entails very long gestation periods, it is a risky undertaking. It is possible that not enough will be spent on an activity which is obviously not politically attractive and yet over the long haul may be an essential source of increases in standards of living.

Non-rivalrousness further increases the risk that research activity will be lower than those levels which are best for society as a whole. Because knowledge can be used by all, it is a pure externality. Because it can be used over and over again, it will not reach diminishing returns for the same reasons that, say, increasing capital or labour inputs in production would. Mathematical results from ancient times (e.g. how to compute the area of a circle) have been put to such extensive use over the last 2000 years, that it could well be one of the most productive investments ever! Similarly, artistic works by Shakespeare, Baudelaire, or Goethe would have made their authors richer than their wildest dreams, had they been able to restrict and thus derive income from their commercial use.[6]

Three conclusions follow. First, knowledge is unlikely to face diminishing returns. It seems to be

one recipe for endless growth. Second, since it is impossible to imagine all the uses that can be made of any piece of knowledge, we will never be sure that we spend enough on its production. Third, if we want to encourage the privately funded supply of knowledge, we need to imagine ways of making it profitable, and that means reducing its non-excludability. The next section takes up this idea.

18.3.2 **Patents**

A **patent** is a legal right granted to exclusive commercial use of an invention, normally for a limited period of time. While not generally granted to ideas *per se*, patent protection is reserved for inventions which are sufficiently novel and wide-reaching, and thereby protects knowledge from imitators for a number of years. Similarly, **copyrights** safeguard artistic expression from plagiarism or outright duplication, and give their owners limited rights to some or all of the income derived from compositions, songs, music, pictures, and other forms of art. **Trademarks** recognize exclusive use of a name or symbol to distinguish a firm's product in the market place.

With the possibility of obtaining a patent, investing in R&D can pay off, since for some period the holder of the patent can charge prices which are at least high enough to cover the costs of the research and development of the product. But there is a side-effect: patents confer monopoly power to discoverers and thus allow them to charge much more than development costs. In one sense, monopoly is bad, since it allows the seller to set prices above the competitive level, and thus discourages demand. Patents indeed hinder the full exploitation of useful knowledge. The border between fair remuneration and

---

[6] Professor DeLong of Berkeley has described the fascinating example of the 'technology' of icons, cursors/pointers, double-clicking, and windows. This paradigm for working with information was developed by the Xerox Corporation in their Palo Alto research facility in the 1970s, before personal computers and the mouse were even invented. Apple was able to convert the technology into a usable system and Microsoft, Intel, and other companies were able to make enormous amounts of money on what was essentially a free technology. He writes: 'The net result? Large benefits to the economy and the society in terms of expanded productivity

growth from the work carried on at Xerox's Palo Alto Research Center in the 1970s. But barely a cent returned in revenues to Xerox from this particular drain on its cash flow. Companies that are in business to make money will not long spend a great time and effort on such research projects that do not boost productivity and revenues, even if they boost industry productivity and revenues manifold. Thus there is every reason to believe that the private sector tends to underinvest in research and development.' J. Bradford DeLong (1997), 'What Do We Really Know about Economic Growth?', http://www.j-bradford-delong.net

Box 18.1   **Protecting and Punishing Monopolists**

To many people, Bill Gates is a bad, mean monopolist. Monopoly rights belonging to the Microsoft Corporation have made him into one of the richest men in the world, since virtually every computer in the world is equipped with its computer software products. Perhaps this is why many cheered when the US Department of Justice initiated a lawsuit against Microsoft. The lawsuit, however, is not about monopoly power derived from legal patents and copyrights. It is related to Microsoft's heavy-handed efforts at stifling or even eliminating new competitor products and services. While Microsoft has made it possible for hundreds of millions of people to use computers for work and pleasure, history and innovations must continue. New innovators will continue to improve computers' software, and should be encouraged to do so. Herein lie the troubles of Bill Gates: his company is accused of using his monopoly power to stifle potential innovators.

Microsoft's encounter with justice is reminiscent of an equally famous trial pitting the US Justice Department against International Business Machines (IBM) in the late 1970s. At the time, IBM dominated the computer hardware industry: PCs didn't exist, and there was hardly a competitor which could produce powerful mainframe computers the way IBM did. The charge was very similar: IBM was accused of using its dominant position to eliminate new competitors. In the end, IBM argued that it retained its lead only thanks to its ability to innovate, and was hard-pressed to do so because of pressure from the competition. IBM won twice: the case against it was dismissed and its argument was soon proved correct as it lost ground to competition, especially with respect to small portable computers and networking machines. In relative terms, it is today a shadow of its former self.

exploitation of monopoly power is arbitrary and subject to considerable legal wrangling, as Box 18.1 reminds us.

Even if patent protection confers monopoly power on their inventors, however, it may be a necessary evil for promoting the production of knowledge and thus for economic growth. Since knowledge is non-rivalrous, it is likely to be exempt from the law of diminishing returns. If the widely shared benefits of knowledge production are not reflected in their compensation, researchers will not deliver as much innovation as is socially desirable, if only because too few bright students will choose this career. Viewed this way, it is perhaps less objectionable that successful innovators derive extra profits from their temporary monopoly power.

An altogether different story involves the pharmaceutical industry. Most wonder drugs are indeed patented, and their inventors reap massive profits. What makes the case different is that drugs are paid for by health insurance, private or public. Insurance agencies agree with the pharmaceutical industry on 'fair' prices, which exceed the marginal cost of producing the drugs by a factor commonly believed to be ten or more. Pharmaceutical firms claim that this

is the only way for them to recoup the huge costs of R&D. Critics call the industry's profits excessive, but find it difficult to find solid evidence to back their claim. They correctly note that a significant part of humanity cannot afford these drugs and die or are permanently incapacitated as a result, a fact most recently underlined by the global AIDS epidemic. Even more troubling is the absence of priority in the pharmaceutical research community to develop drugs which could eliminate tropical diseases, such as malaria, which kill or cripple hundreds of thousands. These diseases are ignored because they affect primarily poor people in poor countries with no ability to pay for the R&D costs.

It is worth noting that an example of the time inconsistency of optimal policy arises in this context, which was discussed extensively in Chapter 16. *Ex ante*, patent rights can tempt both entrepreneurs and researchers to create knowledge and to embed it in new applications. After an invention is patented however, the owner of the patent will charge a high price, possibly even higher than normal costs would warrant. From the perspective of the agreement, this is legitimate, of course, and tolerated for the most part. On the other hand, given that the invention has become public knowledge, it is easy to see why a government has an *ex post* incentive to abrogate the patent agreement. This would clearly make everyone better off.[7] While the treatment of Bill Gates in the USA might lead to a different conclusion, governments generally avoid reneging on their promise all the same: if they did, research and development would come to a standstill, since the promise of a patent would no longer be credible.

18.3.3 Technical Innovations

Long waves

Innovations add to our stock of knowledge but they come in many forms and shapes: new ideas (e.g. Newton's painful discovery of gravity), new techniques (electricity, the steam and combustion engines, computers), or new processes (float glass, household appliances, the internet). How do these major discoveries really occur?

One view is that discoveries appear more or less randomly. R&D produces innovations, some big, some small, continuously restarting growth by boosting the existing technology.[8] Another view, initially proposed by Joseph Schumpeter, is that big discoveries tend to be associated with waves. Figure 18.3 shows the average annual rate of increase in total factor productivity, the term A in (18.2). It shows a sharp acceleration in the UK and the USA early on in the twentieth century, which continues until the early 1970s. This wave is often associated with a succession of great inventions in the latter part of the nineteenth century: electricity, engines, petro-chemistry, pharmaceuticals, telephone, radio, etc. According to Schumpeter's vision of innovations, major innovations were bunched in their occurrence but diffused slowly over the following decades, rather than years. Figure 18.3 also shows

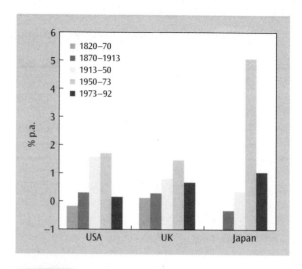

Fig. 18.3 **Long Waves in Technological Progress**

Sustained increases in technological changes seem to come in long-lasting waves.
Source: Maddison (1995).

that the wave did not hit Japan until much later, a question that we take up further in this chapter.

To explain why innovation came in long waves, Schumpeter put the entrepreneur at centre stage. When growth slows, profits decline and some enterprising managers react by investing more in risky R&D projects. More research effort eventually pays off, producing a number of innovations that emerge more or less simultaneously, all within a decade or two. What happens next is that, as profits rise spectacularly, fierce competition sets in. Competition takes two forms: improvements and **imitation**. Both chip at the monopoly power of the original innovators, eating into their profits and reducing their ability and desire to pursue vigorous R&D. Technological progress slows down, ending the big wave of accelerated growth. As profits gradually decline, a new generation of entrepreneurs emerge and prepare the next long wave.

This view claims to explain the pattern observed in the industrial revolution. The long cycles once observed and studied by Kondratieff (see Box 14.1) constitute an interesting interpretation, but one that cannot be taken as a well-established fact; there

---

[7] An excellent example is the growing number of anti-AIDS drugs, which have cost millions to develop but frequently considerably less to produce. Some developing countries have threatened or even started to manufacture and distribute these drugs, explicitly violating property rights. Recent concessions of pharmaceutical corporations (and the rich economies which host them) to supply drugs cheaply to developing countries can be seen as an attempt to regain control of their eroding intellectual property.

[8] This view is similar to that of the real business cycle theory of cyclical fluctuations discussed in Chapter 14.

haven't been enough of them to serve as convincing evidence. Yet some features of the long wave theory are attractive. The kind of competition that sets in following a wave of innovation explains both the long diffusion process and its eventual petering out. It is especially intriguing now that some claim that the information technology revolution is triggering a new wave of accelerated growth. Box 3.3 offers some commentary on this thesis. At any rate the long wave theory provides support for the view that innovations diffuse slowly; it takes time to challenge Ford or Microsoft, but the challenges do come and will ultimately be successful in eroding the market positions of the monopolists. It also illustrates the role patents can play in encouraging R&D and their tendency to create entrenched monopolistic powers.

Interaction with human capital

Innovations, almost by definition, involve new, advanced technologies. Transforming these innovations into production processes requires skills, often new skills. For this reason alone, it is to be expected that diffusion will be slowed by the necessity of building up new human capital. This process, in turn, depends on human capital already accumulated, the quality of the education system, and its ability to adopt and transmit new knowledge. For example, consider how much more difficult it would be to learn to create a homepage if an individual had never used a computer before.

Human capital is a linchpin for any theory of growth which is based on inventions and innovation. Not only does it raise current productivity, it also helps the diffusion of innovations. Figure 18.4

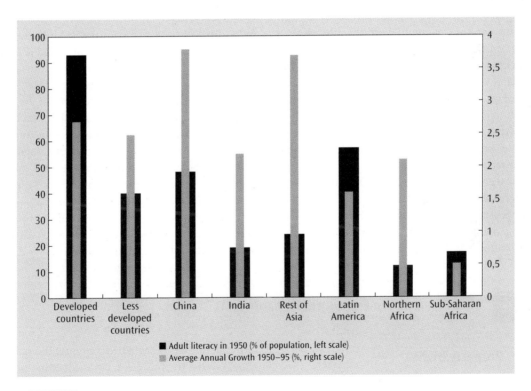

■ Adult literacy in 1950 (% of population, left scale)
▨ Average Annual Growth 1950–95 (%, right scale)

Fig. 18.4   **Human Capital and Growth, 1950–1995**

The figure displays average annual growth over the period 1950–95 and the literacy rate (percentage of adult population that is literate) in 1950. Extreme cases (developed countries vs. sub-Saharan countries) seem to indicate that low human capital is associated with faster growth. Causality could go both ways. One should not forget, however, that many factors other than human capital affect growth, so just looking at a figure like this one may make a link look weak while it is in fact quite strong.

shows that countries at each end of the spectrum of human capital (measured quite imperfectly by the literacy rate) achieve widely different performances. One interpretation is that a low stock of human capital hampers growth. Another interpretation is that causality runs the other way, that poor countries cannot afford accumulating much human capital, given the costs of education systems. We need not choose between these two interpretations, because they may *both* be correct at the same time. Taken together, they suggest the existence of **poverty traps**: poor countries cannot invest enough in human capital, which in turn hinders growth. For the same reasons, individuals too can be trapped in poverty, even in developed countries, which provides a justification for means-tested scholarships.

Multinationals and learning by doing

Finally, it is often believed that multinational corporations serve as a channel in the diffusion of innovations. This view is based on the phenomenon of **learning by doing**, whereby people and firms improve their knowledge on the job. When a multinational establishes a production unit in a developing country it usually brings with it a technology invented in its home country. Individuals who work in such establishments acquire the technology and can subsequently create their own firms based on the new technology, or migrate to other firms which can then tool up.

This possibility should be kept in mind when considering the controversies that surround multinational corporations. They are often criticized for shifting production to low-cost countries, thus taking away jobs from their home countries while offering much lower wages in the developing countries where they settle. The multinationals' response is that they create jobs in the developing countries, which means future customers for the goods produced elsewhere, and that their profits usually accrue to shareholders in the home country. An argument which they seldom make, which might be the most convincing from a *social* perspective, is that they contribute to convergence by accelerating the diffusion of innovations and thus the transfer of knowledge.

18.3.4 **Product Variety**

Another form of innovative activity arises when firms develop new variations of their products which are different from previously available ones, either for real or perceived reasons. Most but by no means all of these innovations are related to consumer goods. The introduction of a new automobile model or a grape varietal, a newly opened restaurant, or the annual waves of *prêt-à-porter* and *haute couture* all represent innovations for which consumers are willing to pay measurable amounts. In many cases, the increase in diversity makes the consumer better off, sometimes the new products themselves represent fundamental innovations for which needs still have to be developed or invented. To the extent that consumers are willing to pay an ever higher price, these types of innovation also represent growth potential for an economy.

18.4   Growth and the Economic Environment

18.4.1 **Property Rights**

A recurrent theme of growth theory is that it is driven by investment in both physical and human capital. As emphasized in Chapter 6, capital accumulation is a bet on the future: it requires spending now for future, uncertain returns. It is often taken for granted that firms' ownership of their equipment will be unquestioned both today and in the future, and that individuals will be able to use the skills that they acquire. In both cases, we assume that property rights exist, are clearly defined, and systematically enforced. This assumption is generally borne out in many countries, but not universally so, and probably not for most of humanity.

Property rights usually require precise legislation or constitutional provisions which guarantee that individuals and firms cannot be dispossessed of their belongings, except if they violate the law and even then, only after due process. The concept of property rights is not restricted to merely retaining one's belongings. In the extreme case, it would guarantee that one's possessions can always be used as intended and disposed of, under all circumstances. Such absolute property rights are rarely observed: landowners are rarely allowed to build 'the house of their dreams' without the implicit or explicit permission of their residential area. More relevant for economic growth, property rights are denied if a firm is taken over by the state, say, to produce weaponry against the will of its owners. Nationalizations, which occurred in France as recently as the early 1980s, similarly violate property rights, even if the owners are compensated, because they break the link between investment and its intended use. Nationalizations are an example of retroactive legislation, enacted after the original investment was carried out. They damage the fabric of trust between capital owners and the government, which depends on productive economic activity to finance its activities.

At the individual level, property rights should be extended to human rights. Being arbitrarily sent to jail, or being barred from some jobs, prevents one from using his human capital. Mere threats of imprisonment or assassination also deny property and human rights. As long as individuals are not guaranteed the freedom to exercise all (reasonable) activities as they wish, independently of their sex, race, political opinions, or religious beliefs, their property rights are not established.

It is easy to see why property rights are a precondition for long-run economic growth. If investors cannot be sure they will own their investments in a country, why bother to invest there? Even if the rate of return on capital in other, wealthier countries is lower, a lower risk of expropriation or arbitrary restriction of property rights may tip the balance in their favour. And if investment is held back, so will be future growth. This elementary proposition is far from being universally accepted. Box 18.2 briefly looks at the case of communist regimes which explicitly reject private ownership of means of production. More generally, property rights are routinely denied by arbitrary, undemocratic regimes and by wars, both civil and international.

The relationship between property rights, broadly defined, and growth is more complicated than meets the eye. There is powerful evidence that rich and fast-growing countries tend to be democratic, law-abiding, and peaceful, but it is not clear what comes first, economic well-being or property rights. One view is that property rights are a prerequisite for sustained economic growth, another view is that affluence makes basic freedoms and property rights more desirable. It could well be that each aspect strengthens the other, generating either virtuous circles of growth and better-established rights, or vicious circles leading to poverty traps which combine economic stagnation and the absence of property (and human) rights.

Indeed, there are cases of countries which embarked on a stable, often fast growth path while enjoying limited property and human rights: the communist countries, Pinochet's Chile, or some countries of South-East Asia. Conversely, it can be argued that some countries visibly fail to grow because property rights are non-existent. A sobering example is Sub-Saharan Africa, which has grown by a mere 1.5% (GNP per capita) over the years 1965–97, while the world's overall growth over the same period stood at 50.9%. This average performance conceals a wide disparity, depending on the policy regime as Figure 18.6 shows.

18.4.2 **Peace**

The other main threat against property rights is wars, which destroy both physical and human capital. If wars are occasional, the catch-up process sets in once they are over. The reason is clear: expected peace encourages investment. This was the experience of Europe after 1945, enjoying rapid growth while building supra-national institutions (the common market, the European Court of Justice, monetary union) and peace-enhancing mechanisms (NATO, the Organization for Security and Co-operation in Europe) to reduce the risk of renewed conflict.

On the other side, Africa has been devastated by wars, mostly civil wars as states inherited from colonial times have tried to come to grip with ethnic diversity. For example, the index of ethnic

Box 18.2 **Growth in Communist Countries**

In its unrecanted form, communism holds that private ownership of capital leads to never-ending concentration of wealth in a few hands, while workers are maintained at the subsistence level of existence. To avoid this, communism set about collectivizing ownership of production means, in effect by nationalizing large private firms, and in some countries even by banning small ones as well. In several countries, collective ownership was extended to land and housing.

What is left of incentives to work, invest, and innovate under such a system? In a system of central planning, communist regimes offered a combination of carrots (incentives) and sticks (penalties). Firm managers negotiated production plans with the central planning office, and were provided with the necessary means, equipment, and salaries. Both managers and workers were also offered various incentives to produce more: more

money, medals, better housing and honours. Under-performance was punished, sometimes harshly so.

How did it work? Figure 18.5 shows that, up until the early 1970s, the growth performance was good, certainly on a par with Western Europe. Part of the reason was catch-up after the war destruction, in the East as in the West. But then things turned sour, much worse than in Western Europe. Most countries experienced two decades of negative growth rates, an extraordinary failure. Central planning simply did not work, and brought the collapse of the communist regimes. The odd man out is China: a poor performance over the first period, followed by fast growth. Part of the story is the gradual relaxation of central planning, accompanied by the introduction of private ownership. But another part of the story seems to be the strict discipline imposed by the regime, a puzzling observation.

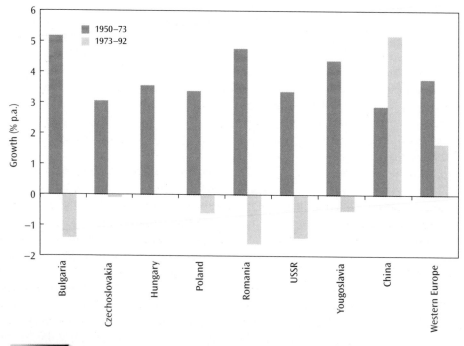

Fig. 18.5 **Growth Performance under Central Planning**

The good performance over the first 25 years has been followed by a catastrophic decline over the following until two decades. China stands out as a different and puzzling story.

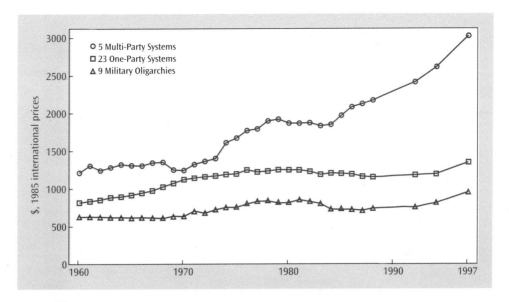

Fig. 18.6   **Real GDP per capita in Sub-Saharan Africa**

The five countries with democratic political regimes (Botswana, Gambia, Mauritius, Senegal, and Zimbabwe) displays a much better growth performance than countries with one-party systems. Countries with military regimes have stagnated.

Source: Benno Ndulu and Stephen O'Connell (1999), 'Governance and Growth in Sub-Saharan Africa', *Journal of Economic Perspectives*, 13(3).

fractionalization stands at 67.6% in Sub-Saharan Africa, and at 32.7% on average in the other developing countries.[9] Besides the obvious material destruction, investment is held back and human capital declines through the emigration of wealthy and powerful elites. Figure 18.7 establishes an unmistakable link between growth and property rights, where the latter is measured by a legal index of the rule of law prevailing in the country.

18.4.3 **Stable Economic Environment**

Individual property rights and peace are important aspects which can further economic development. They do not, however, represent the whole story. Other elements of the economic environment must also be right to attract investment, especially

foreign direct investment. Beyond property rights, the legitimate scope of government and its taxation behaviour should be directed towards establishing stability and continuity, rather than interrupting it. Even in democracies it is possible for governments to change frequently—with shifting coalitions of smaller parties, for example—and this may lead to constantly changing tax and expenditure policy. This type of uncertainty, especially if it applies to the taxation of physical or human capital, may deter longer-term projects from being undertaken.

The same applies to the inflation rate. It was shown in Chapter 16 that high and variable inflation rates tended to weaken the allocative function of prices and thus the efficiency of the economy. Since inflation is like a tax, it will tend to dull incentives to invest in productive activities and force firm owners to focus more on avoiding its effects.

Governments which understand this will take action to bind their successors to time-consistent policies. This may take the form of constitutional

[9] This index reports the probability that two people randomly chosen in a country belong to two different ethnic groups. Source: Paul Collier and Jan Willem Gunning (1999), 'Why Has Africa Grown Slowly?', *Journal of Economic Perspectives*, 13(3).

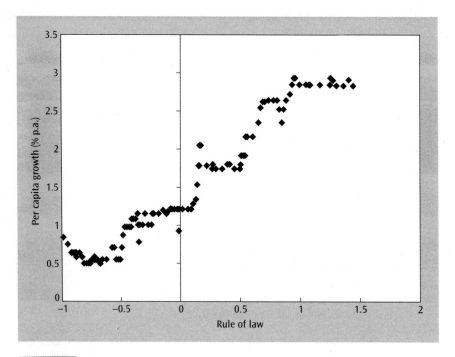

Fig. 18.7 **Rule of Law and Growth, 1960–1998**

Based on a large sample of countries, the figure relates average economic growth over nearly four decades with an index measuring how well the rule of law applies. The index ranges from –2.5 (complete breakdown) to +2.5 (perfect legal protection). It includes political corruption, likelihood of government repudiation of contracts, risk of government expropriation, quality of bureaucracy, and overall maintenance of law. The figure sends a very strong message: the better is the rule of law enforced, the faster a country grows. Note the beneficial effect only sets in after some minimal threshold.

Source: William Easterly (1999), 'On Good Politicians and Bad Policies: Social Cohesion, Institutions and Growth', The World Bank.

amendments, borrowing from abroad in foreign currency at long maturities, or the establishment of central bank independence. Currency boards and dollarization—representing the abdication of monetary policy in the most extreme way—are particularly striking examples of how countries have attempted to solve this problem.

18.4.4 **Openness to Trade**

Growth and openness to international commerce are known to be positively related. Countries which have large trade exposure—measured as the ratio of exports plus imports to GDP—tend to have faster GDP growth rates. The experience of more open

Western European countries, and especially the Asian Tigers of the last two decades suggest that open economies grow faster, all things considered. This faster growth can be attributed to a number of possible effects. First, closed economic systems can often impede the transfer of knowledge, effectively excluding some individuals from what should be a non-excludable good. Openness allows for ideas to flow more easily across national boundaries. Second, openness means increased competition from abroad. Domestic producers cannot rely on protection to shield their market positions from the threat of imports. They must constantly remain at the 'edge' of new developments. To use the terminology of Section 18.3, this requires either innovation or imitation; either will have positive effects on productivity and growth.

18.4.5 **Health**

An important aspect concerning human capital accumulation is health. Where health services are poor (or access is limited to the richest segment of the population), life expectancy is low. This obviously reduces incentives to invest in human capital, but also can affect the productivity of otherwise healthy individuals in a negative way, and even lead to outmigration of wealthy elites.

As with other issues the issue of causality arises immediately: does health cause income, does income cause health, or both? Figure 18.8 shows

that the relationship between income and life expectancy is positive, but by no means linear. The richest countries have achieved roughly equal life expectancies, but deep inequalities appear at lower income levels. In general, life expectancy declines dramatically with income. Not only is life expectancy shamefully low in the very poorest countries, but the growth benefits from improved human condition in these countries are likely to be shamefully high. In large parts of the world, existing medicines could cure endemic sicknesses, but people cannot afford them. The AIDS disaster in Africa is a tragic example of a vicious circle in which poverty shortens life expectancy, which further cripples incentives to invest in human capital and future growth.

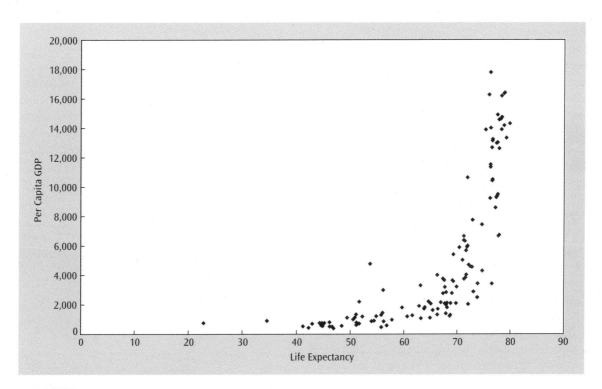

Fig. 18.8   **Life Expectancy and Income**

In a cross-section of nations, life expectancy declines dramatically at low to moderate income levels. It is difficult to believe that general health conditions do not influence investment decisions, especially in skills and education. At the same time, the demand for health depends on income.

Source: David Bloom, David Canning, Bryan Graham, and Jaypee Svilla, (2000), 'Out of Poverty: On the Feasibility of Halving Global Poverty by 2015', CAERE Discussion Paper No. 52, Harvard Institute for International Development, January.

18.5 Growth and Politics

18.5.1 Democracy and Growth

The relationship between democracy and economic growth is a controversial one. Democracy, we would presume, is conducive to a better growth performance, for all the reasons reviewed so far: property rights, economic and political stability, health, etc. Yet, democracies are not perfect institutions. The rule of majority does not preclude actions against minorities, including some that violate property and human rights. Such actions may include legal pressure on 'the rich', ranging from nationalizations to heavy taxation, both of which discourage investment. At the same time, well-organized lobbies in many democracies enable well-endowed minorities the ability to exert disproportionate influence on decision-making.

It is also frequently claimed that democracies are incapable of self-imposed current sacrifices necessary for sustained economic growth. Some salient examples are increasing the savings rate to accumulate capital for future generations, restructuring of economic activity which implies the painful decline of some sectors (farming and mining for example), reform of the social safety net and labour market regulations, and migration towards cities which is accompanied by some degree of social and family dislocation. The political difficulties faced by democracies to face up to such painful changes has fed claims that only dictatorships are capable of suppressing opposition to changing conditions long enough, for growth to take hold. In their view, democracy is a luxury that only rich societies can afford.

Yet this conclusion is certainly tenuous. Only democracies have the legitimacy to guarantee property rights essential for investment in human and physical capital (see Section 18.4). As the next section notes, inequality is harmful to growth, and inequality is better tolerated when the political regime receives legitimacy from a majority of citizens. It is even argued that such legitimacy is necessary to carry out the deep reforms that accompany sustained growth. Dictatorships can impose changes,

for a while; eventually the changes themselves—which may be desirable from an economic viewpoint—become as unacceptable as the dictatorship itself, and may be swept away in painful revolutions. Finally, democracies rarely go to war with each other.

Sadly enough, the evidence on democratic institutions and growth remains inconclusive. For every study that finds a positive role for democracy in fostering growth, another fails to detect such an effect. At least, there is no evidence that democracy harms growth. An interesting piece of evidence is Japan's performance as shown in Figure 18.3: Japan embarked on a high growth path in the second half of the 20th century, after it had adopted democratic institutions.

18.5.2 Inequality and Growth

A hump-shaped relationship between inequality of income and wealth was first reported by Nobel Laureate Simon Kuznets in 1955. The 'Kuznets Curve' depicted in Figure 18.9 states that, starting from an initially low level of development, higher

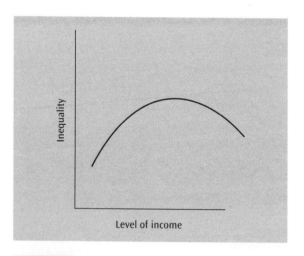

Fig. 18.9 The Kuznets Curve

Simon Kuznets observed in the 1950s that inequality first grows as country's average income rises, but then declines. This relationship is sometimes known as Kuznet's Law.

growth seems to proceed with increasing inequality and then the relationship reverses itself, and inequality declines.

Many theories have been put forward to explain the Kuznets curve. Some relate the creation of high productivity jobs to the transition from agriculture to industry. Early in that phase, industrial jobs are poorly paid, which is why inequality increases. Then, as industry matures it offers better salaries and then the development of the service sector further works toward more equality. Others assert that a low initial stock of physical and human capital inevitably provides large rewards to the happy few (i.e. the owners). As the stock of capital rises, its marginal productivity declines, and so do the rewards. In addition, better-off societies seem to be more concerned with equality than growth. As a result, taxation becomes more progressive and transfers explicitly aimed at reducing inequality become more widespread.

Over nearly five decades, the Kuznets curve has survived numerous statistical challenges and appears to be robust. Once again, as with property rights and democracy, we face the question of what comes first, the chicken or the egg: is it inequality that affects growth, or the other way round? Could there be too much insistence on inequality? One view is that fast growth requires sufficient incentives for would-be entrepreneurs: measures which compress income distribution, like redistributive taxation and social norms, dull these incentives and eventually hurt growth. On the other side, the accumulated evidence is clearly that inequality harms growth. Three main explanations have been advanced.

First, politics interacts with redistribution. While high inequality preserves incentives for entrepreneurs, it can backfire. When income is very unequally distributed, majorities will tend to vote for redistribution. In a democratic system, at least, it appears better to avoid severe inequalities. This seems to be the approach adopted in Northern Europe. Second, if credit markets do not function, then inequality will prevent a large fraction of the population from investing in human capital, which reduces if not eliminates their chances of becoming entrepreneurs, which has a cost to society as a whole. Finally, high levels of inequality tend to generate social unrest in the form of envy, self-arranged redress, and crime. As general insecurity rises, property rights decline. The standard response, to increase police and fill up jails, may alleviate the threat to property rights, but it represents spending that could be better used in a more peaceful society. It also requires taxation which, again, may hurt entrepreneurs.

Summary

Most of the arguments developed in this chapter are summarized and quantified in Table 18.2. The table presents estimates of the effect on average annual growth of a range of factors.

1. **Catch-up (convergence).** Starting below steady state in a Solow model, a country should be accumulating capital, both physical and human, more rapidly, as well as adopting new technologies. The table indicates that the economic backwardness is closed at a rate of about 2.5% per year (the higher is initial GDP, the less it subsequently grows).

2. **Human capital.** People's knowledge, ranging from basic literacy to sophisticated skills, represents an additional factor of production. Table 18.2 measures the effect of investment in education, the average number of years spent in secondary or higher education by males.[10]

---

[10] An important clarification: this does not mean that female schooling is unimportant, even if the study reported here does not detect any clear *direct* effect. Quite to the contrary, female schooling is usually found to be more socially productive than male schooling, but this effect is considerably more complex, and mostly *indirect*. In many developing countries, female school attendance is much lower than for males, so a little effort produces large effects. Also better-educated females make better mothers, with considerable impacts on children's education, health and, more widely, approach to life. Female education also affects fertility.

| Table 18.2 | What Drives Growth? Some Estimates |

Factor	Effect on average annual growth rate
Initial GDP	−2.5
Education	1.2
Life expectancy	4.2
Fertility rate	−1.6
Government consumption	−1.4
Rule of law	2.9

Source: Robert J. Barro (1997), *Determinants of Economic Growth*, MIT Press.

Raising the population's schooling by one year is found to speed up growth by a spectacular 1.2% per year.

3. **Health**. A one-year increase in life expectancy at birth raises average growth by a whopping 4.2%. The effect is likely to come through investment in human capital and, more generally, work effort. This effect is unlikely to be important in rich countries where it is retirement that limits the length of active lifetime. It may be crucial in the poorest countries where few people ever reach retirement age.

4. **Fertility**. The negative effect of the rate of fertility (the average number of children per woman) seems related to two main effects: capital widening as in the Solow model, and time spent by mothers in child rearing instead of economic production.

5. **Public consumption**. Reducing public consumption by 10% of GDP raises growth by 1.4%. This measure does not include productive spending, such as public infrastructure. The negative effect probably corresponds to the corresponding high public employment, which tends to be inefficient and invite corruption, as well as to the necessary tax collection, which acts as a disincentive to savings, investment, and innovative activity.

6. **Rule of law**. Lasting, credible property rights are a precondition for investment in both physical and human capital. Going the full way from the worst to the top ranking raises growth by 2.9% annually.

Key Concepts

- economic growth
- the convergence hypothesis
- conditional convergence
- Marshallian externality
- property rights
- non-excludable and non-rival
- patents, trademarks, copyrights
- long waves
- diffusion and imitation
- poverty traps
- learning-by-doing

Exercises

1. Define property rights and explain the link between property rights and investment in both physical and human capital.

2. 'Retroactive legislation raising income tax will have much worse adverse effects than retroactive legislation raising property taxation.' Comment.

3. Do you expect inflation to affect long-run growth? If so, how and why?

4. Like physical capital, knowledge and human capital depreciate. Explain.

5. Why is it generally the case that patents are granted for a limited period of time?

Suggested Further Reading

The 'new growth theory' was initially proposed in:

Lucas, Robert E. Jr. (1988), 'On the Mechanics of Economic Development', *Journal of Monetary Economics*, 22(1): 3–42.

Romer, Paul M. (1986), 'Increasing Returns and Long-Run Growth', *Journal of Political Economy* 94(5): 1002–37.

A popular advanced textbook is:

Barro, Robert, and Sala-i-Martin, Xavier (1997), *Economic Growth*, MIT Press.

Surveys are:

Symposium on New Growth Theory, *Journal of Economic Perspectives*, Winter 1994.

Barro, Robert J. (1997), *Determinants of Economic Growth*, MIT Press.

A collection of articles on European countries can be found in the following book:

Crafts, Nicholas, and Toniolo, Gianni (eds.) (1996), *Economic Growth in Europe Since 1945*, CPER.

A classic compendium of data and analyses is:

Maddison, Angus (1995), *Monitoring the World Economy*, Development Centre Studies, OECD.

A survey of Africa's growth tragedy is in: *Journal of Economic Perspectives* 13(3).

Studies on the relationship between growth, democracy and income equality:

Alesina, Alberto, and Perotti, Roberto (1994), 'The Political Economy of Growth: A Critical Survey of the Recent Literature', *World Bank Economic Review*, 8(3).

Aron, Janine (2000), 'Growth and Institutions: A Review of the Evidence', *World Bank Research Observer*, 15(1).

De Haan, Jakob, and Siermann, Clemens (1995), 'New Evidence on the Relationship between Democracy and Economic Growth', *Public Choice*, 86.

Goldsmith, Arthur (1995), 'Democracy, Property Rights and Economic Growth', *Journal of Development Studies*, 32(2).

Sachs, Jeffrey D. (1999), 'Helping the World's Poorest', *The Economist*, 14–20 August.

PART VII

Asset Markets and International Financial Architecture

Markets for financial instruments are a ubiquitous feature of economic life, but are they really important, or merely a distracting side-show? What function do these markets really have? How are they organized, both within and between nations? Is there a role for establishing rules of play, especially when troubles in the financial system of one country spill over to others? The concluding part of the textbook studies these issues and connects them with our primary interests, how economies grow and fluctuate over time.

Asset markets are important because they determine crucial variables: the interest rate, the valuation of firms big and small, the wealth of households, the price of risk, the relative value of national monies. Chapter 19 studies the principle characteristics of asset markets and how they relate to macroeconomic relationships explored up to this point. Special reference is made to the nominal exchange rate.

The globalization of financial relationships is here to stay; in principle this should make us all better off, but recurrent crises make us wonder about the net impact on our lives. Thus, financial markets are not allowed totally free reign, and are usually regulated. This is also why, as presented in the concluding chapter, the international monetary system is constantly being built and rebuilt. Its history is reviewed and the recent debate on the 'international architecture' summarized.

Asset Markets and Macroeconomics

19

19.1   Overview

From Tobin's q to interest and exchange rates, we have often encountered prices which are determined in financial markets. These prices share a number of unique features. They determine the value of **assets**, the various forms of wealth held by households and other agents. These prices are set in markets which seem fundamentally different from goods markets, not only because they are impersonal—transactions are almost never face to face—but also because they exhibit a high degree of volatility. They often appear driven by the whims of traders whose preoccupation is with very short-term gains, without much concern for the impact of their actions.

What distinguishes assets from other goods is that they are instruments for saving. Assets are durable; they are not consumed, but stored for later disposal. Their value is not in today's use, but in their resale price. For this reason, they are driven entirely by the future. Almost by definition, the future is uncertain, so assets are almost always risky. Precisely because they are standardized and risky, assets tend to be traded on large markets. Asset prices are of singularly common interest to all economic agents, and for this reason their impact on the macroeconomy is widespread and conspicuous.

This chapter offers a unified treatment of asset prices and markets, with some emphasis on exchange rates. We start by describing asset markets and explaining some of their key features. They are big because they deal in stocks, not flows. They are fast-moving because profit opportunities are huge, but dissipate in seconds. They put a price on a special economic factor, uncertainty. We then look at the asset prices encountered in many of the earlier chapters: bond prices, interest rates, stocks. We explore why markets sometimes embark on apparently senseless behaviour, producing successive phases of exuberance and bust. And we close the chapter with a more detailed treatment of exchange rates, the price of foreign exchange. The main aim is to solve a puzzle: exchange rates determine competitiveness in trade, but are driven by financial considerations. To that effect, we separate the short from the long run: the short run is financial, the long run is real.

19.2   How Asset Markets Work

19.2.1 Facts about Asset Markets

A number of aspects establish the fundamental uniqueness of asset markets. First, unlike goods and services which are bought for consumption and perishable in some sense (fruits don't last long, cars and computers get outdated, and services are produced while they are consumed) assets are **durable**. This distinguishing characteristic, plus the fact that they can be held with negligible storage costs, are two reasons that financial assets are a premier vehicle for saving. They can be bought now and sold later, either when the time comes to use savings for consumption or when they are exchanged against other assets to cash in profit or avoid a loss.

Second, in contrast with markets which trade in *flows* of goods or services, financial markets are markets for *stocks*. While trade on any given day involves only a fraction of existing assets, the whole stock of assets can be dumped on the market at very short notice, if the owners so desire. This explains the size and potential volatility of financial markets. For example, in September 2000 the stock of shares outstanding in DaimlerChrysler Corporation was about 1 billion shares. On an *average* day in the nine months preceding, about 3.5 million shares were traded, one-third of one per cent of the stock. Yet the number of shares transacted could vary from a few hundred thousand to potentially more than the entire stock outstanding—if stocks change hands

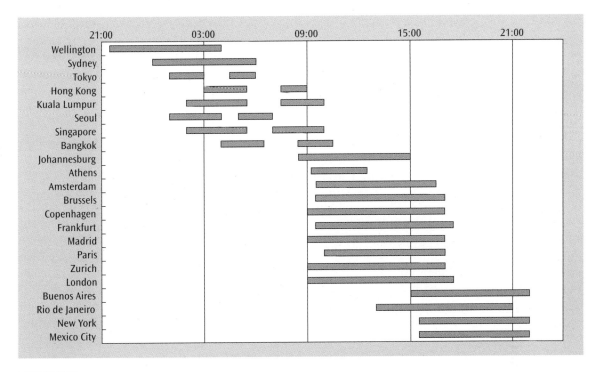

Fig. 19.1   **Trading Hours of Stock Markets around the World, Greenwich Mean Time**

Stock markets are located around the world. As the world turns, some market somewhere is open, processing new information and pricing assets accordingly.
Source: Deutsche Börse.

several times. Similarly, the market for foreign exchange involves daily volumes which stagger the imagination: on an average day, it is estimated that roughly 1.5 trillion dollars worth of foreign exchange is traded, mostly in dollars, euros, and yen. This represents about 15% of *annual* GDP of the United States or Europe!

Third, financial markets are typically well-organized trading systems dealing in standardized assets that can be traded in large quantities with ease. In earlier times, the markets were oriented around physical presence of market participants in a trading hall, or exchange. The action was dominated by shouting, gesticulating traders wading through seas of hastily scribbled papers. Today, most markets are computerized, and market participants are linked through telecommunication lines from terminal screens virtually anywhere in the world. The World Wide Web has created a single, global market in stocks and other financial instruments, with traders

constantly in touch with market activity. As Figure 19.1 shows, at any moment in time, twenty-four hours a day, some financial market is open somewhere in the world, and any individual in the world with access to a telephone may trade on it. This is perfect competition!

These characteristics require that the usual demand and supply analysis be adapted in two ways. First, durability means that looking at the flow of transactions can be misleading. The annual supply of savings by households represents a mere flow increment to their stock of wealth—their total demand for savings instruments. Similarly, borrowers issue a flow of new assets which adds to their stock of debt, which is the true supply of such instruments. In principle, the newly created assets are indistinguishable from existing ones. At any moment, trading involves both new and old assets, and the entire stock could be sold or purchased. Since the existing stock of assets dwarfs any flow increments, prices move to clear the demand for and supply of the whole stock. Second, durability—and the resulting use of assets for saving purposes—means that the primary concern of market participants is the future value of each asset that they hold. Thus, asset markets are necessarily **forward-looking** and involve considerable uncertainty.

The potential unloading of huge stocks on the market and the intrinsic presence of uncertainty explains why financial markets can be so very volatile. In a matter of minutes, changing expectations, or mere rumours, can radically alter demand and supply, swelling the volume of trade, or drying up markets. Prices, which equate demand and supply on a second by second basis, can therefore swing widely. This reasoning applies not just to strictly defined assets (stocks, bonds) but to any durable object that can be (relatively) easily stored and sold—artwork, commodities, or contracts for the delivery of goods which may not yet exist at some time in the future (such as oil, electricity, wheat, or pork bellies). In fact, all these durable goods are traded on markets (oil in Rotterdam, wheat and pork bellies in Chicago) which resemble those for financial assets.

19.2.2 **Functions of Asset Markets**

The intense activity associated with asset markets combined with the often phenomenal profits of market participants often create the impression that financial markets are gambling casinos with little economic purpose. Far from it, markets for financial assets perform three essential economic functions. The first is to bring together borrowers and lenders. The second is to put a price on the future and on uncertainty. The third is to allow participants to control the risk they are exposed to. In what follows these functions are explored in more detail.

Intermediation

Financial markets are the meeting place for millions of households and firms who want to shift resources intertemporally—either saving or borrowing —or intratemporally—from one form of asset or liability to another. But most individuals do not deal directly on asset markets. This is not only because

quantities they desire to trade are small, but also because transacting in asset markets requires a great deal of expertise. To avoid these problems, they can act indirectly through **financial intermediaries**. Financial intermediaries channel resources from savers to borrowers and investors, and help solve the 'double coincidence' problem that arose in Chapter 8 with respect to goods and services. Like money, financial intermediaries divorce the act of saving (deferred consumption) from the act of investment (creation of physical productive capacity).[1]

As a result, dealings in asset markets tend to resemble wholesale markets involving professional traders, who accept and execute large orders on the basis of mutual trust. As a result, they charge each other relatively small fees. For example on foreign exchange markets, an average trade is in the order of €5 million; going from pounds sterling to euro and back again involves a transaction cost of around 0.05% or about €2500. Similar fees are charged for large transactions involving stocks or bonds. In return for a fee, intermediaries place orders for several smaller customers at once, or may even 'make a market' by maintaining a large inventory which they can sell from or add to. In this way, intermediaries themselves become asset-holders.

Allocation of risk

The price of the future—or the rewards for waiting —is the interest paid by borrowers, as explained in Chapter 5. By setting interest rates, financial markets price the future. Bonds, which are loan contracts, represent fixed payment streams in the future; the price of these payment streams defines the relevant interest rate. Shares, which are partial ownership of companies, promise dividend payments which must be in line with interest rates, if they are to be sufficiently attractive to be held. But assets are inherently risky because they are held for future sale. Borrowers can default—totally or partially—on bonds, and dividends depend on firms' profitability, and firms can even go bankrupt. Asset-holders therefore look for ways to reduce their

---

[1] Put differently, financial intermediaries are responsible for achieving the outcome represented in Figure 10.7: the marginal rate of substitution of consumption tomorrow for consumption today is equal to the marginal product of capital.

exposure to risk. They are willing to accept some risk in exchange for better returns, but to some degree only, and they wish to protect themselves from catastrophic events such as a collapse of prices. Not all asset-holders are equally risk averse, and their horizons also differ. This leads us to another function of financial markets: to price risk and allocate it to those who are most willing to bear it.

Just as it is possible to protect ourselves against the costs of car accidents, house fire, unemployment, and death by purchasing insurance, it is possible to use asset markets to insure wealth against financial uncertainty. **Diversification**, the holding of wealth as a mix of several different assets, allows savers to reduce risk for any given expected rate of return. Box 19.1 explains in more detail why

holding a diversified set of assets is generally less risky than investing in any of its individual components. Diversification can also be supplied by the market in the form of new composite assets backed by a mix, or portfolio, of underlying risky assets. Intermediaries can vary the riskiness of these portfolios and accommodate different tastes of their customers.

Pricing of risk

Diversification reduces, but cannot eliminate, the riskiness of an economy's wealth. Some risk must be borne, and financial markets offer compensation to the bearers of that risk. Box 19.2 describes how and why. This compensation is called a **risk premium**. It means that the **rate of return**, or the total

---

Box 19.1 **Risk Diversification**

'Don't put all your eggs in one basket' is advice commonly given in all kinds of situations. The principle is remarkably simple: if you pool risky outcomes, the result is almost always less risky than any of the outcomes taken individually. In the language of statistics, we say that the variance of the sum of random variables is less than the sum of the variances of those same random variables taken individually: averaging removes variability. In a given year, some assets may pay off handsomely while others do badly. For this reason, investment counsellors advise their clients to diversify, or to invest their wealth in several different assets. The result is a composite rate of return which is less variable, sometimes much less so, and thus preferred by investors who are risk averse.

Consider the following, simple example. 'Investments' A and B both involve independent flips of a coin. In either case, 'heads' means receiving €100 euros, 'tails' means receiving nothing. On average, if repeated many times, either investment yields €50; we say that its expected value is €50. Now compare either of these two 'investments' with a new one, C, which is simply one-half of A plus one-half of B. The expected value of C remains €50 but its *variability* is lower. To see this, list the four possible outcomes: A=heads/B=heads, which pays €100, A=heads/B=tails and A=tails/B=heads which each pays €50, and A=tails/B=tails which pays nothing. Taken individually, A or B pay €100 or nothing; in the form of C, an

investor receives €50 with one chance out of two, leaving the probabilities of the extreme returns of €100 or nothing to just one chance in four. Diversifying A or B by holding a bit of each has reduced the risk. The diversification effect is even greater when the two investments tend to move in opposite directions (in the language of statistics: when they are negatively correlated). In the extreme case that the return from A and B were decided by the same flip of a coin, but 'heads' means A pays €100 and B nothing, while 'tails' means A pays nothing and B delivers €100. As before, A and B have the same expected value and same volatility, but now C pays €50 in *all* cases, diversification has eliminated risk completely. (On the other hand, if A and B are the same investment, there is no gain from diversification).

Diversification can reduce the riskiness of investors' portfolios, but it cannot eliminate it (because in reality risks are never perfectly negatively correlated). Insurance companies practise diversification by issuing a large number of policies to different individuals, but cannot avoid the 'big risks' such as crop blights, earthquakes, floods, or bad weather. Investment funds and unit trusts average out performance of individual investments, but cannot protect their clients from macroeconomic risks, which involve systematic shifts in monetary and fiscal policy, changes in technology, and shocks to terms of trade, as well as the business cycle.

Box 19.2 **The Price of Risk**

Return to the first example of Box 19.1. Investments A and B have the same expected value, €50. How much would you be willing to pay to acquire either investment? Most people are risk averse, and they would rather get €50 for sure than buy a risky investment with the same expected value. (Those who don't care and would pay €50 are said to be risk-neutral; risk lovers would pay even more than €50 for the thrill.) If you are willing to pay, say, €48 for A, the risk premium is €2 or 4% of the risk-free price. If total demand and supply of that asset are equated at €48, then the risk premium represents the market price of risk. Since B has the same characteristics, it should also be priced at €48. What about investment C? It has the same expected value as A and B, but is less risky. An investor would be willing to pay more for investment C than for either A or B. If the market price is, say, €49, the risk premium on the new asset is only €1 or 2%. Facing less risk, investors will prefer the new asset. The issuers of the assets A and B are also happy, as they pay a lower risk premium. This is why diversification is an efficient way of spreading the risks of individual assets in the market.

Now consider the second example of Box 19.1, when a single flip of a coin produces two opposite investments A and B. We found that the composite investment C is riskless, and it should sell for €50, with no risk premium. We say that all the risk has been diversified away, which

benefits both the sellers and the buyers of investments A and B. Finally, in the third example with a single flip of a coin when either A and B both yield €100 or nothing, the composite investment C does not reduce risk at all and it should sell for €48, with no reduction in the risk premium. Financial markets are at their best when they pool assets with very different risk characteristics. If much of the risk is macroeconomic (business cycles, policy actions), risk cannot be diversified much. Foreign assets, however, are likely to have different characteristics. This creates a strong incentive to pool markets across frontiers, a step in the direction of globalized financial markets.

Finally, for a more realistic example, suppose that you pay now, but the coin is flipped only in a year's time. Any investor will expect to receive interest for the time the money was parked in the investment above and beyond the risky gamble. Compensation for risk in this case can be expressed as a premium added to the risk-free interest rate available on say, a government bond. Suppose that, as before, the 'investment' has an expected value of €50 and the market currently prices it at €46 *today*; suppose further that the risk-free rate is 3%. Then the risk premium can be computed as 5.7%, (the total expected rate of return ((€50 − 46)/€46 = 0.08696 = 8.7%) minus the risk-free rate (3%).

payouts of an asset divided by its price, increases with the riskiness of assets.[2]

Both borrowers or issuers of stocks and bonds benefit from the existence of financial markets. Taken in isolation, each investment is risky and would have to pay a high yield to attract wary savers. Going through intermediaries who pool these individual risks, those using asset markets to raise funds will end up paying lower interest rates, while lenders or buyers of securities will face less risk for a given rate of return. Because clever rearrangement of assets can reduce a portfolio's overall riskiness, the best services tend to be offered by the major financial

centres dealing in stocks of companies from all over the world. This is precisely why asset trading tends to concentrate in few places and also why worldwide electronic trading is growing so fast. Stock market trading volume, or turnover, is often a sizeable portion of GDP. This is undoubtedly far beyond the average citizen's individual needs and leads to a frequent misperception of financial markets as a sophisticated version of Las Vegas. Yet it is the consequence of competition among intermediaries in providing fast and affordable services to their customers, whether they are lenders or borrowers.

19.2.3 **Information and Market Efficiency**

Because virtually anyone with wealth may trade in financial markets, asset prices reflect the collective

---

[2] More precisely, the theory of finance predicts that those assets with higher correlation with the average or 'market' rate of return will be compensated with higher expected rates of return. This is because they are those that can be less well diversified, see Box 19.1.

judgement of market participants. Given the relatively low cost of participating, asset prices should reflect all information relevant for assessing its underlying value or useful for predicting future performance. It is a hallmark of properly functioning financial markets that participants are engaged in a never-ending search for profit opportunities, either for their customers or for their own accounts. Both the amount of money at stake and the speed at which information flows makes it unlikely that opportunities not involving additional risk will be left unexploited for any significant period of time. Markets which satisfy this condition—that publicly available information cannot help but earn consistently above-average returns—are said to be efficient.

A more precise definition of **market efficiency** is that prices fully reflect all available information.[3] Market efficiency requires two things: that markets use all available information about the future, even at cost; and that they process information correctly, i.e. based on principles that are not systematically contradicted by the facts, nor do they make systematic mistakes. Efficiency in markets implies an absence of opportunities for easy profit—earning a profit by simultaneously purchasing and selling assets which are identical or with equivalent attributes. This **no-profit condition** implies a tight link between asset prices. Since risk is priced in financial markets, it makes sense to start with riskless arbitrage, and then consider the no-profit condition in the presence of risk.

Arbitrage

Arbitrage concerns operations which do not involve additional risk.[4] It is customary to distinguish three types of arbitrage: yield arbitrage, spatial arbitrage, and triangular arbitrage.

Yield arbitrage concerns two similar assets which happen to offer different returns. Strictly speaking, it

applies to riskless assets, like treasury bills, but it is sometimes applied to risky assets which bear similar risk (like assets A and B in Box 19.1). Consider the following example: two government bonds which otherwise have the same attributes offer different rates of interest, or yields. Holders of the less attractive bond will sell in favour of the one with the superior yield. In fact, the entire stock of the less attractive bond could be put up for sale. As the higher-yielding bond becomes more expensive and the lower-yielding bond becomes cheaper, the implied yields converge (recall the relationship between bond prices and bond yields from Chapter 5). Arbitrage prevents such pricing misalignment from occurring: yield arbitrage imposes identical returns for identical assets.

Spatial arbitrage concerns the same assets traded in different locations. For example, large commercial banks borrow from each other at the interbank interest rate. If the interbank rate in two cities were to diverge, enterprising banks present in both cities would immediately borrow in the cheaper market and lend in the dearer one. To see that spatial arbitrage forces the convergence of yields and prices, Figure 19.2 looks at three-month nominal interest rates on DM interbank deposits in Germany and in London's offshore market. One would expect that, with capital mobility and negligible risk differences, the yields should be virtually identical; in the past fifteen years this seems to be the case.

Triangular arbitrage applies mostly to foreign exchange markets and is possible when the relative prices of three—or more—currencies are not consistent with each other. If the euro costs one US dollar and one euro costs 8 Danish krone (DKR), then the DKR/$ rate must be (DKR8 /€)/($1/€) = 8 DKR/$. Otherwise limitless profit would be possible by buying the euro where it is cheap and selling it where it is more expensive. Figure 19.3 displays this example.

19.2.4 **The Interest Parity Conditions**

An important application of the notion of market efficiency is the interest parity conditions: covered interest parity, an example of riskless yield arbitrage, and the uncovered interest parity condition, which allows for risk.

---

[3] The idea of market efficiency is related to the rational expectations hypothesis introduced in Ch. 5. Rational expectations assume that agents do not make systematic forecasting errors. Market efficiency applies this concept to markets and price-setting.

[4] In financial market jargon, this distinction is not always so clear. For example, traders who search for information on corporate takeovers in order to take a position in the stock 'in play' are sometimes called risk arbitrageurs. Technically, this is a contradiction in terms: if a takeover is called off, the 'risk arbitrageur' may be left holding a great deal of stock and may suffer a large loss.

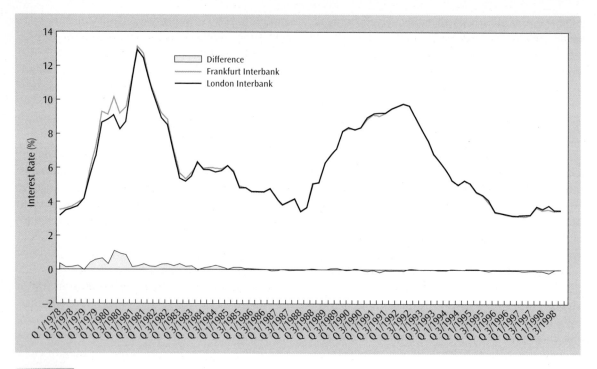

Fig. 19.2 **Spatial Arbitrage: DM Offshore and Onshore Three-Month Interest Rates, 1978–1998**

With a brief exception in the period 1979–81, when controls were operative, capital mobility seemed complete between offshore and onshore financial centres. Spatial arbitrage has been near-perfect, equalizing interbank interest rates on DM interbank transactions in Frankfurt and London.
Source: IMF.

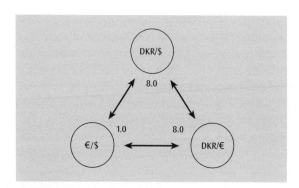

Fig. 19.3 **Triangular Arbitrage**

When two exchange rates among three currencies are known, the exchange rate between the remaining pair of currencies is given by triangular arbitrage. In the absence of transactions costs, any discrepancy between purchasing a currency directly and acquiring it using a third currency is eliminated.

Covered interest parity (CIP)

This arbitrage condition is based on the comparison of the return from a domestic asset with the return from a foreign asset with similar risk characteristics. For example, an investor in the UK can obtain an annual rate of interest i on riskless British Treasury bills issued in sterling at home and $i*$ on equally riskless bills issued in euros. The two investments are not equivalent, since the sterling value of the euro may change over the investment period, thereby altering the total return measured in sterling for the euro-denominated investment. Let the price of the pound in euros at the beginning of the year be S_t. By selling one pound at the beginning of the year, a British investor obtains S_t euros that she can invest for one year to receive $(1 + i*)S_t$ at the end of the year. This is a completely certain return, since both the interest $i*$ and exchange rate S_t are known at the beginning of the year, but it is in terms of euros, and the exchange rate in the next period is uncertain. The investor can eliminate all risk by signing a contract at the beginning of the year to sell $(1 + i^\star)S_t$ euros against pounds at the end of the year. Such a **forward contract** specifies the exchange rate at which this sum will be converted from euros to pounds: it is the one-year ahead **forward exchange rate**, denoted F_t. The forward exchange rate corresponds to a transaction which implies a delayed delivery of the currency; it is to be distinguished from the **spot exchange rate** S_t, which implies immediate delivery. Thus the British investor can be certain that for every pound invested this way, she will receive $(1 + i^\star)S_t/F_t$ pounds at the end of the year. Because all exchange risk is eliminated with the forward contract, the foreign investment is said to be **covered** or **hedged**. Now, she could instead have invested her money in the safe sterling asset and receive $(1 + i)$ at the end of the year. Both strategies are riskless, so arbitrage guarantees that the return must be equal (apart from minute transaction costs). This is the **covered interest parity condition**:

(19.1) $\qquad (1 + i^\star)S_t/F_t = (1 + i)$

A useful approximation of the CIP condition is:

$$i^\star = i + \frac{F_t - S_t}{S_t}$$

interest rate in Euroland = interest rate in UK + forward premium

which states that the foreign interest rate is equal to the domestic interest rate plus the **forward premium**, which is the percentage deviation that the forward exchange rate represents from the current spot rate. The Appendix further develops the concept of the forward premium.

Uncovered interest parity (UIP)

What happens when the investor does not eliminate exchange risk by engaging in a forward contract? Indeed, she could have sold sterling, invested in euros for a year, and waited until the end of the year to buy back sterling at the spot exchange rate. This is risky, though, because no one knows at the beginning of the year what the exchange rate will be by year's end. What appeared to be a good deal may turn out disappointing if the euro depreciates vis-à-vis sterling, leaving the investor with fewer pounds than expected. Of course, the euro can appreciate

unexpectedly, and the deal will turn out to be terrific. Leaving her foreign investment **open** or **unhedged**, the investor takes a risk, and this will involve a risk premium as explained in Box 19.2.

To examine the new situation, we start by assuming that the investor is risk neutral, so that the risk premium is zero. The strategy is the same as before, except that the euro investment will not be sold at the end of the year using the forward rate F_t agreed upon earlier, but at the prevailing spot exchange rate S_{t+1}. Going through the same reasoning, the expected return in pounds from one pound invested in euros is $(1 + i^\star)S_t/{}_tS_{t+1}$, where ${}_tS_{t+1}$ is the end-of-year exchange rate as expected at the beginning of the year. A one year investment in pounds still yields $(1 + i)$. The no-profit condition for a risk-neutral investor is the **uncovered interest parity (UIP) condition**:

(19.2) $\qquad (1 + i^\star)(S_t/{}_tS_{t+1}) = (1 + i)$

expected gross return in Euroland = certain gross return in UK

which can be approximated conveniently by:

(19.3) $\qquad i^\star = i + \dfrac{{}_tS_{t+1} - S_t}{S_t}$

interest rate = interest rate + expected appreciation
in Euroland   in UK   of sterling

The UIP simply asserts that rates of return are equalized across countries once expected exchange rate changes are taken into account. On the left-hand side of (19.3) we have the one-year euro interest rate; on the right-hand side we have the UK interest rate plus the expected capital gain or loss from changes in the sterling–euro exchange rate, expressed in percentage terms, for the same one-year maturity. Expectations cannot be observed directly, but the UIP implies that if rates in Britain are higher than those in Euroland $(i > i^\star)$, then the euro is expected to appreciate (i.e. sterling depreciates, or $({}_tS_{t+1} - S_t)/S_t < 0$. To be willing at all to hold euro-denominated assets with a lower interest than pound-denominated assets, investors will expect a capital gain as compensation. If euro-rates are higher, the UIP implies that sterling is expected to appreciate vis-à-vis the euro.

The uncovered interest parity condition can be modified to accommodate risk aversion by allowing for a risk premium ψ_t that the British investor will require to hold euro-denominated assets:

(19.4) $$i^* = i + \frac{_tS_{t+1} - S_t}{S_t} + \psi_t$$

interest rate = interest rate + expected appreciation + risk premium
in Euroland   in UK   of sterling   on euro

where ψ_t stands for the risk premium which makes a UK investor indifferent between investing in Euroland and staying at home. Turning things around, we can *define* the risk premium as the deviation from the uncovered interest parity condition, which can depend on time:

(19.5) $$\psi_t = (i^* - i) - \frac{_tS_{t+1} - S_t}{S_t}$$

RISK PREMIUM =   INTEREST   – EXPECTED APPRECIATION
                DIFFERENTIAL

We have looked at the situation from the point of view of a British investor who seeks to be compensated for the risk of holding euro-denominated assets. At the same time, European investors are likely to hold British assets; they face the same type of exchange risk the other way round: all things equal, they too would require a premium on euro-denominated assets, i.e. a negative ψ. The sign of the risk premium is thus not obvious. It will depend on the net bilateral asset position of Britain and Euroland, but also on the positions of third parties (e.g. US or Japanese investors) in each country's assets. The size of the premium or discount will also depend on the degree of risk—which can vary over time—and on traders' risk aversion. The risk premium is a complicated phenomenon whose full treatment is beyond the scope of this textbook.[5] All we need to understand is that the existence of a risk premium ψ_t (which can be positive or negative) means that we should not expect the uncovered parity condition to hold

exactly. It will be true up to a—generally volatile—risk premium.

Risk aversion, operating costs, and the bid–ask spread

The risk premium explains how assets which bear a rate of return can contain compensation for risk. How does this work for assets which bear no return at all? The most obvious example is foreign exchange, cash bought and sold by travellers, or bank deposits available for use on demand. Other examples include commodities such as gold, silver, and oil. In these cases, **market makers**, those who specialize in buying and selling them, hold the asset to meet customers' demand. As they are exposed to sometimes substantial fluctuations, they need to be compensated. The risk premium typically takes the form of a **bid–ask spread**.

The mechanism is familiar to anyone who has travelled abroad and has bought currency at an exchange booth. There, as on all foreign exchange markets, exchange rates are quoted in pairs: a lower 'bid' price for those who want to sell the foreign currency, and a higher 'ask' price for buyers. The difference is the market-maker's profit, in fact the risk premium. The bid–ask spread in wholesale foreign exchange trading is currently quite small—roughly 0.2% on a five-million euro transaction between euros and sterling. Yet it can be much higher for currencies which are inherently risky, or are thinly traded. Box 19.3 gives a nice example of how a bid–ask spread evolved over time for the *Ostmark*, the money of the German Democratic Republic, the communist German country which disappeared from the European map after German unification in 1990.

Box 19.3   **The Short-Lived Market for Ostmarks**

Even before the Berlin Wall fell on 9 November 1989, trade in the East German currency, the Ostmark (OM), was significant, and DM quotes for OM were published daily in major West German newspapers. After this historic date, volume increased by an order of magnitude as

East Germans tried to convert their savings into harder currency. It remained unclear until March 1990 that monetary unification would occur, implying automatic conversion of OM currency and bank deposits into DM. The conversion rate of one DM for one OM applying to

---

[5] In short, finance theory (the Capital Asset Pricing Model or CAPM) states that the risk premium is determined by the correlation between the asset's return and the return from the world portfolio. The reason for this result is provided in Box 19.2.

Box 19.3   **Continued**

a part of East Germany's holdings and one for two for the rest—resulting in an average estimated by the Bundesbank at 1.8—was first officially suggested in March. It was then formalized as part of the state treaty of monetary and economic union between the two German states in May 1990.

Considerable uncertainty characterized this period. Furthermore, before the Berlin Wall opened, the markets were relatively thin and trade was exclusively a Western business. This is reflected in the bid–ask spread which stood at more than 30% in early 1989, as seen in Figure 19.4. As the situation became clearer, trade moved to the streets of East and West Berlin and most banks entered the game. With the decision to establish a monetary union between West and East Germany by July 1990—in effect, replacing OMs with DMs—uncertainty declined, and so did the spread.

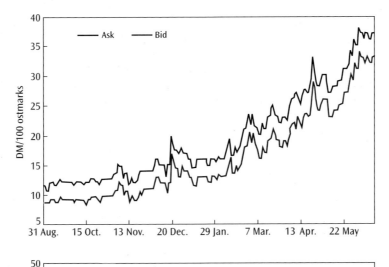

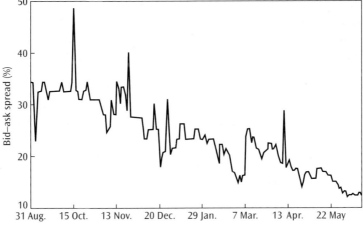

Fig. 19.4   **Ostmark–DM Rate and Bid–Ask Spread, August 1989–June 1990**

As monetary union approached, the risk involved in holding Ostmarks, the currency of the vanishing German Democratic Republic, declined. This is reflected in the bid–ask spread, which fell significantly.
Source: Burda and Gerlach (1993).

Linking Asset Markets and Macroeconomics

19.3.1 Bond Prices and Interest Rates

The term structure of nominal interest rates

The interest rate is the price of the future. In Chapter 9, we saw that the central bank determines the short-term nominal interest rate—for loans overnight up to one month duration—by altering the supply of liquidity to the economy. Yet, most borrowers are interested in the real interest rate and in longer maturities as most commercial loans range from one to ten or more years. To have an impact on economic conditions, monetary policy must also affect longer-term real interest rates. The other channels of monetary policy are the exchange rate, which affects external competitiveness, and asset prices which affect private wealth. We now examine the links between short-term nominal interest rates, the exchange rates, the long-term real interest rate, and the value of shares and bonds, all of which are determined in financial markets. Again, the central theme is the no-profit condition of efficient markets.

At any moment of time, financial markets offer loans of maturities ranging from the very short to the very long term. The associated rates on interest, converted at annual rates, map out what is called the **term structure of interest rates**. From the lender's perspective, a loan of longer maturity

means less liquidity, since repayment generally does not occur until the loan matures. Naturally, this is a riskier commitment. For the borrower, longer maturity is a longer-term commitment that the funds will remain at his disposal. To compensate the lender, interest rates bear a risk premium which increases in maturity, all other things equal. This is shown in Figure 19.5.

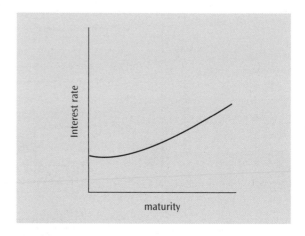

Fig. 19.5   **The Term Structure of Interest Rates**

Lenders require a higher return for committing their funds to long-term loans. Borrowers value long horizons for the use of their loans and are therefore willing to pay a higher interest rate as the maturity of the loan increases.

Box 19.4   **The Term Structure of Interest Rates**

The term structure of interest rates combines maturity and risk premia (which makes rates higher, the longer their maturity) with the **expectations hypothesis** which is based on the no-profit condition. Consider a long-term interest rate of L years' maturity. Ignoring the maturity and risk premia, it is equivalent to a succession of one-year loans which are 'rolled over'. If the annualized interest rate on the long-term loan is i^L, the return is $(1 + i^L)^L$ (by the rule of compounding annual rates). If the one-year interest rate expected to prevail t years from now is i_t^e,

where the superscript e denotes an expectation, the return from a succession of such loans is $(1 + i_1)(1 + i_2^e) \dots (1 + i_t^e) \dots (1 + i_t^e)$. The no-profit condition implies that these returns should be equal. As a first approximation, this equality states that the long rate at time t, i_t^L is an average of expected future short rates, possibly plus a risk premium ψ_t^L:

(19.6)
$$i_t^L = (1/L)\sum_{i=1}^{L} i_{t+i}^e + \Psi_t^L.$$

Table 19.1 Bond Prices and Yields

Description of the payment stream	Price in euros given yield i:	Yield given price P
A. One-year pure discount bond paying 1 euro:	$1/(1+i)$	$1/P-1$
B. Two-year pure discount paying 1 euro in 2nd year	$1/(1+i)^2$	$1/P^{1/2}-1$
C. Ten-year discount bond paying 1 euro in 10th year	$1/(1+i)^{10}$	$1/P^{1/10}-1$
D. Bond paying a coupon each year of C euro for		
2 years plus payment of 1 euro in 2nd year ($C<1$)	$X/(1+i)+(1+X)/(1+i)^2$	$[4P(C+1)+C^2]^{1/2}/2P-(1-C/2P)$
E. Consol paying 1 euro per annum, forever	$1/i$	$1/P$

Short-term interest rates change frequently, especially because monetary policy can change. If short-term interest rates are expected to increase over the next two years, for example, the longer-term rates will have to rise too. To see why, notice that a two-year loan can be arranged in a number of ways: one loan of two years maturity, or two successive one-year loans, or a series of twenty-four one-month loans, etc. The no-profit condition implies that these combinations are equivalent ways of borrowing money, and should impose the same cost to the borrower and the same reward to the lender, with due account for risk. If the interest rate is expected to increase next year, then the two-year rate must also increase, but today. The reasoning applies to all maturities, and Box 19.4 shows that long-term interest rates can be seen as averages of the current and expected future rates than can be chained to deliver an equivalent loan. Then the maturity and risk premia come on top. The result is that the central bank's actions, both current and anticipated, affect interest rates at all maturities. This explains why the bond markets are so intensely interested in what central banks are up to!

Bond prices

Lending is a job normally performed by banks, but loans can also be directly organized by large borrowers in financial markets. In that case, they take the form of bonds, i.e. a recognition of debt by the borrower along with a schedule of payments concerning both interest and the principal. Bonds can

then be traded like any other asset. But what determines the price at which bonds sell? The bond price represents the present discounted value of the payments agreed upon at the time when the bond was issued. The resulting inverse relationship between bond prices and interest rates was discussed already in Chapter 5, and is shown in Table 19.1 for some types of bonds. Bond A is the simplest case of a bond of one-year maturity. Its price is $P = 1/(1+i)$ and, with some manipulation, the interest rate can be expressed in terms of the price as $i = (1-P)/P$. More complicated bonds, involving coupons and longer yields to maturity cannot be expressed as neatly as Bonds B, C, and D (!), and require the use of a computer. The last example E is the 'ultimate bond' or consol: it exists forever, in principle, and is called for that reason a perpetuity. With few exceptions, only governments are in a position to make such a promise. But such debt has been issued in the past (and has existed for a long time!) in the United Kingdom. For consols, the interest rate and price move inversely and equiproportionately.[6] This is only approximately true for all other bonds.

Real interest rate arbitrage in the long run

The UIP conditions, with and without a risk premium, link nominal interest rate at home and

---

[6] The consol formula is: $P = 1/(1+i) + 1/(1+i)^2 + \ldots + 1/(1+i)^n + \ldots = [1/(1+i)][1 + 1/(1+i) + \ldots + 1/(1+i)^n + \ldots]$. The second term is the infinite sum of a geometric series. This implies that $P = 1/(1+i)\{1/[1-(1/1+i)]\}$ which can be simplified to the result in the table.

abroad and embody the tight linkages implied by international financial integration. Does the arbitrage argument extend to the *real* interest rate, which is decisive for intertemporal decisions? Intuitively, one might expect an arbitrage opportunity to arise if real interest rates across countries—with similar risk characteristics—differed significantly. It turns out that the purchasing power parity condition (PPP)[7] does imply that real interest rates at home and abroad will be equal although, like PPP, this is likely to hold only in the medium to long run.

This **real interest parity** condition follows from the UIP holds, e.g. in the form of (19.3). Rearranged, this means that the interest rate differential is equal to the expected exchange rate appreciation of the domestic currency. But in the medium to long term, relative PPP implies that the future rate of depreciation is equal to the future inflation differential:

(19.7) $$(S_{t+1} - S_t)/S_t = \pi^*_{t+1} - \pi_{t+1}.$$

If forecasts of inflation at home ${}_t\pi_{t+1}$ and abroad ${}_t\pi^*_{t+1}$ are consistent with PPP, the definition of the real interest rate[8] $r_t \equiv i - {}_t\pi_{t+1}$ and $r^*_t \equiv i^* - {}_t\pi^*_{t+1}$ along with (19.7) and (19.3) imply:

(19.8) $$r_t = r^*_t.$$

This relationship is called the **international Fisher equation**. As it is based on relative PPP, it is at best a medium- to long-run proposition. Nevertheless, it is a useful benchmark for evaluating long-term foreign investment strategies, as it implies that the real rate of interest should be largely the same in all countries and is independent of the evolution of exchange rates.

19.3.2 Stock Prices

Shares in firms, or stocks as they are often called, are held by households or their intermediaries, and are issued by firms to acquire resources for capital expenditure. Stocks are risky assets because they represent a claim to a share of profits in the issuing firm after costs—wages, interest payments, rent,

taxes, and other expenses—have been paid. How are stocks valued? Once again, we make use of the no-profit condition,[9] comparing now a riskless Treasury bill with a constant real yield r per annum and a traded share in a company which pays all its profits (in real terms) out at the end of each period as dividends d_t. The hitch is that, while the Treasury bill pays a fixed yield, the yield or rate of return on the stock investment consists of the dividend plus possible capital gains or losses when the share price changes. If q_t is the share price at the beginning of period t, the rate of return on the company share is the dividend yield, d_t/q_t, plus the anticipated capital gain, $(q_{t+1} - q_t)/q_t$ (a gain if $q_{t+1} > q_t$, a loss if $q_{t+1} < q_t$). The no-profit condition implies that both assets have the same yield over period t:

(19.9) $$\underset{\substack{\text{yield on} \\ \text{Treasury} \\ \text{bills}}}{r} = \underset{\substack{\text{dividend} \\ \text{yield}}}{d_t/q_t} + \underbrace{\underset{\substack{\text{capital} \\ \text{gain}}}{(q_{t+1} - q_t)/q_t}.}_{\text{total return on shares}}$$

which can be transformed into:

(19.10) $$q_t = \frac{d_t + q_{t+1}}{1 + r}$$

Today's stock price q_t is equal to the present discounted value of the dividend in the period, plus that of the next period's price q_{t+1}. A theme which recurs constantly in the study of financial markets, expectations of the future price drives today's stock price.

Can this be the end of the story? If q_{t+1} depends on q_{t+2} in the same way that q_t depends on q_{t+1}, we can substitute (19.10) for itself in an endless process of telescopic recursion. Will such an endless repetition converge to anything sensible? It turns out that, in the case studied, if the stock price doesn't grow faster than the real interest rate r, the current stock price is indeed well defined, and is given by:

(19.11) $$q_t = \sum_{i=0}^{\infty} \left(\frac{1}{1 + r} \right)^i d_{t+i}$$

which expresses the current stock price (in real terms) as the present discounted value of expected

---

[7] Purchasing power parity is presented in Ch. 8. The relative version is employed here.
[8] The Fisher equation is introduced in Ch. 8.

[9] Most of the assumptions regarding uncertainty, choice of dividend policy, payout in real terms, and risk neutrality are unnecessary, but simplify the example considerably.

future earnings only: the role of the future price disappears. The market values a company on the basis of what it is expected to earn, now and in the indefinite future.[10] The formula (19.11) is called the **fundamental valuation** of an asset, and can be found in many applications of financial economics, including the next one, the nominal exchange rate. It can rise suddenly when market expectations of future profits rise, for example, in times when new technologies are developed. Later in this chapter, we address the question whether stock prices always reflect rational pricing of future company profits.

19.3.3 Nominal Exchange Rates and National Money Markets

The nominal exchange rate and relative liquidity conditions in national money markets

The exchange rate can be thought as the relative price of national monies. Much as share price changes affect the return on stocks, the exchange rate affects the opportunity costs of holding various currencies, and assets denominated in these currencies. Indeed, we have already encountered the interest parity condition (19.2) which bears a telling resemblance to the share price equation (19.9). The interest parity condition builds a bridge between the exchange rate and liquidity conditions in domestic money markets, represented by their respective nominal interest rates.

This section extends the analysis of Chapter 11, in which the domestic nominal rate was compared by financial investors at home and abroad with some 'required foreign rate of return', designated by *i** but not described in much further detail. In this chapter, using the interest parity condition, we have already decomposed the 'required foreign rate of return' as the foreign nominal interest rate *i** less the expected rate of appreciation of our currency (equivalently, plus the expected rate of depreciation of the foreign currency). We now consider the consequences of that decomposition.

The UIP condition without risk aversion (19.2) can be rewritten as[11]

$$(19.12) \qquad S_t = \frac{(1 + i_t)}{(1 + i_t^\star)} [_t S_{t+1}]$$

The current spot exchange rate S_t is now determined by domestic and foreign interest rates and by the market's current *expectation* of next period's exchange rate $_t S_{t+1}$. Like all asset prices, the nominal exchange rate is *forward-looking*. What happened before is irrelevant: bygones are bygones and the exchange rate is not tied to its past. It is totally free to jump to any level warranted by current or expected future conditions. Especially important is the implication that an appreciation anticipated in the future shows up *immediately* in the current exchange rate.

As with stock pricing in the previous section, equation (19.12) determines the exchange rate in terms of itself in the subsequent period: S_t is driven by the expectation S_{t+1} which itself is driven by the expectation of S_{t+2}. To keep things simple, we now ignore uncertainty, and therefore the difference between actual and expected values of the exchange rate, as in the previous section. Inserting into (19.12) the similar expression linking S_{t+1} to S_{t+2}, we find:

$$S_t = \frac{(1 + i_t)}{(1 + i_t^\star)} \frac{(1 + i_{t+1})}{(1 + i_{t+1}^\star)} S_{t+2},$$

and, repeating the operation *n* times:

(19.13)

$$S_t = \frac{(1 + i_t)}{(1 + i_t^\star)} \frac{(1 + i_{t+1})}{(1 + i_{t+1}^\star)} \frac{(1 + i_{t+2})}{(1 + i_{t+2}^\star)} \cdots \cdot \frac{(1 + i_{t+n})}{(1 + i_{t+n}^\star)} S_{t+n+1}.$$

As with stock prices, the current exchange rate reflects all current and future interest rates at home and abroad, and its own long-run value. This expression shows just how important expectations of the future are for the present. Even events far into the future can have a large impact on today's exchange rate. This is why exchange markets—and asset markets in general—are so concerned with information. Even remote future events affect the present.

While not yet providing a complete theory of exchange rate determination, the discussion shows

---

[10] What is the relationship between this and Tobin's *q* used in Chapter 6? Tobin's *q* is the ratio of the share price (*q* here) to the replacement cost of installed capital.

[11] The derivation under the condition incorporating risk aversion (19.3) is given as an exercise at the end of this chapter.

that relative conditions in national money markets are essential for understanding how macroeconomic conditions influence nominal exchange rates. It shows how the anticipation of tight monetary policy at home in the future (i is expected to rise) can lead to an appreciation today (S increases).

An apparent contradiction resolved

There is a subtle question, however, which often trips up those trying to understand (19.13). Suppose interest rates at home rise unexpectedly. According to (19.13) an appreciation should result; yet we know from UIP that higher interest rates at home should be associated with a *depreciation* of our currency (S falling). The confusion may be further exaggerated if one explains the initial appreciation by capital inflows. Is this a contradiction?

The contradiction is only apparent, once we recognize that we implicitly assume that the exchange rate does not change in long-run (we hold S_{t+n+1} constant in (19.13)). The two ways of reasoning are reconciled in Figure 19.6. As the domestic interest rate rises i above the world rate i^*, the exchange rate appreciates temporarily, but is expected to depreciate back to its initial value. As required by UIP, an expected depreciation of the domestic currency (a capital loss) offsets the interest rate advantage at home. *Holding the future expected exchange rate constant*, the only way for the current exchange rate to depreciate in future periods is to appreciate *now*. Over time, the exchange rate will indeed depreciate back to its long-run level. Importantly, capital movements are not necessary as long as asset returns are equalized. All that is necessary is that markets change the price. In highly integrated and efficient financial markets, this happens almost instantaneously.

The fundamental determinants of the nominal exchange rate

The 'cumulated' interest parity condition (19.13) states that the exchange rate is determined by present and future interest rates and is anchored by its long-run value. The exchange rate **fundamentals**, therefore, are those variables that influence the current and future domestic and foreign exchange rates as well as the long-run exchange rate. Domestic and foreign

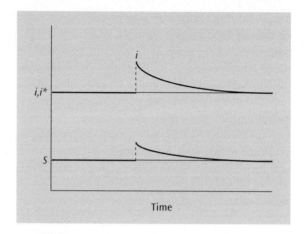

An Increase in the Domestic Interest Rate

When the domestic interest rate (i) rises above the world interest rate, uncovered interest rate parity requires that there be an expected exchange rate depreciation. Given an unchanged expected long-run nominal exchange rate, the exchange rate must appreciate now in order to generate that expected depreciation.

economic conditions—as captured by the *IS–LM* framework—drive domestic and foreign interest rates. The fundamentals thus include present and future monetary and fiscal policies at home and abroad.

We can now see the link between the present short-run 'financial market' view of the exchange rate and the long-run or 'relative price of goods' view elaborated in Chapter 7. There we saw that the nation's intertemporal budget constraint determines the long run value $\bar{\sigma}$ of the real exchange rate, defined as $\sigma = SP/P^*$. Given the price levels $\bar{P}$ at home and $\bar{P}^*$ abroad expected to prevail in the long run, the long-run value of the nominal exchange rate is

$\bar{S} = \dfrac{\bar{\sigma}\bar{P}^*}{\bar{P}}$. Now, in (19.13) we can always let the horizon extend far enough for S_{t+n+1} to correspond to $\bar{S}$, leaving us with the following expression:

(19.14)

$$S_t = \frac{(1 + i_t)}{(1 + i_t^*)} \frac{(1 + i_{t+1})}{(1 + i_{t+1}^*)} \frac{(1 + i_{t+2})}{(1 + i_{t+2}^*)} \cdots \frac{(1 + i_{t+n})}{(1 + i_{t+n}^*)} \bar{\sigma} \frac{\bar{P}^*}{\bar{P}}.$$

This expression indicates that the current nominal exchange S_t depends on three sets of fundamentals:

- the path of current and foreign interest rates, therefore all relevant economic conditions affecting the interest rate (as captured by the *IS–LM* framework): monetary and fiscal policies, foreign demand, etc.;

- the real exchange rate $\bar{\sigma}$ needed to meet the nation's intertemporal budget constraint, therefore the foreign debt and the country's competitive position;

- The level of prices $\bar{P}$ and $\bar{P}^*$ at home and abroad far into the future, therefore present and future inflation, both at home and abroad.

The list of fundamentals becomes long because of the ubiquitous role of the exchange rate in the relative price of goods and assets. In light of this, it is easy to understand why exchange markets react to a very broad range of indicators.

19.3.4 Market Efficiency or Speculative Manias? Implications for Macroeconomics

The efficient markets hypothesis poses something of a paradox: if markets are efficient, we shouldn't have to work very hard to obtain information on assets: the market has done it for us already! The current price of bonds, stocks, foreign exchange, and other financial instruments should represent a consensus based on information available to traders in the market. If stock prices decline today, we do not really need to find out why: the market has already processed the relevant information and drawn the correct implications. As a corollary, it is unlikely that anyone will outperform the market consistently. Reports of investors systematically beating the markets are more likely a sign of good luck than much else. For every winner we hear about, there are as many losers, who have disappeared from the market either because they ran out of money or because they were dismissed by their bosses. Using this line of argument, Nobel Laureate Milton Friedman argued that speculation cannot be destabilizing: those traders who are responsible for pushing asset prices away from their 'fundamental' prices given by equation (19.11) are those who buy high and sell low. If prices return to their fundamental values, these destabilizing traders

should consistently lose money and ultimately exit the market.

At the same time, some studies do turn up statistically measurable deviations from market efficiency. For example, if stock prices decline today, there is a tendency for them to revert over time to their previous values. This could imply that markets overreact to news, and that the markets may not be fully efficient. Yet why doesn't anyone buy these 'oversold' assets when it is profitable to do so? This would restore the price to its fundamental value immediately. The answer may lie in risk aversion, the fact that too few traders are willing to take positions and hold them long enough for this to occur. In this case, the deviation from the fundamental value may be consistent with the absence of profit opportunities, *given that the risk involved in correcting it has its own price*: the expected 'profits' are insufficient to compensate for the riskiness of betting against the irrational price. Betting against the market involves considerable risk, and deviations from fundamental values can get worse before they get better.

How and why might asset prices deviate from their fundamental values? It is always tempting to write off financial markets as irrational and prone to fads. But there are often more satisfying accounts which can be illustrated with two examples. One of them is the coexistence of professional traders and inexperienced amateurs. The other is the phenomenon of rational speculative bubbles.

Noise traders

In the first example, only a subset of traders are informed and have access to information about the true underlying value of assets, whereas the remainder are **noise traders** who act on limited 'noisy' information. These noise traders can be either irrational or simply misinformed, and they behave accordingly. The result is that they systematically lose money to the informed traders. Noise traders arrive continuously on the scene, with new ones replacing those who lose on average and quit in disgust, so that there are always some of them around. Despite perfectly efficient and rational behaviour on the part of the professionals, stock prices may again diverge from their fundamental value for long periods of time.

Bubbles

The second account of deviations from efficiency is the presence of **speculative bubbles**, persistent deviations of asset prices from their fundamental values. To see how bubbles may arise, consider the share valuation example from Section 19.3.2, which resulted from a no-profit condition (19.9) between the share and the real interest rate r. Let us assume for simplicity that the real dividend is fixed forever at d. The fundamental value is:

$$\bar{q} = \sum_{i=0}^{\infty} \left(\frac{1}{1+r} \right)^i d = \frac{d}{r}$$

It is constant and satisfies the no-profit condition equation (19.9), since $\Delta q = 0$. The puzzling observation is that an infinity of other paths of prices also satisfy (19.9). Consider the case where the stock price is higher than $\bar{q}$. With a constant dividend, the dividend/price ratio is now smaller than in the case of the fundamental value. For the no-profit condition to be satisfied, the right-hand side of (19.9) must remain equal to the real interest rate r. This is possible only if the share price is expected to rise tomorrow: the expected capital gain offsets the inferior rate of return provided by the dividend. Thus an overvalued share (when its price exceeds its fundamental value) calls for a continuing increase in price, further and further away from the fundamental. Any price today can thus be validated by its subsequent evolution. Figure 19.7 plots possible evolutions of the share price over time, for given r and d. Only one initial price does not 'explode', and it corresponds to the fundamental value.

The non-fundamental paths, which are exploding without any apparent fundamental justification, are self-fulfilling: prices rise because they are *expected* to, without violating any market efficiency condition. The apparently inexorable growth of the share price is called a **speculative bubble**: a bubble because it keeps growing until it bursts, speculative because its growth is due to the expectation of future capital gains. A bubble is rational in the sense that it will continue to grow as long as traders believe that the bubble will continue to grow, validate market expectations, and offer the 'normal' return.

There is a catch, however: bubbles eventually burst. Why? Because if an asset price were to grow

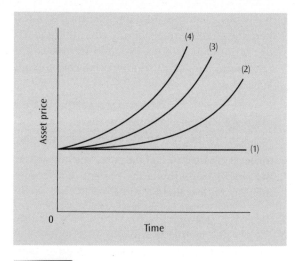

Fig. 19.7　**Possible Stock Price Paths**

Path (1) is the fundamental value of the asset. The price of the stock is equal to the present value of the dividend d, which is assumed constant, so it satisfies the arbitrage condition. Paths (2), (3), and (4) also satisfy the arbitrage condition, but are explosive bubbles.

indefinitely, it would eventually exceed the world's wealth, becoming too expensive for anyone. And if no one can afford it, its price must decline. But the logic of a bubble is that its price must be expected to grow for a very long time—in principle, forever. If there is a known date at which the price will stabilize, the situation will unravel. When the price stabilizes, (19.9) shows that, with $\Delta q/q = 0$, the asset price must be equal to its fundamental from that point on. In the period just before the price stabilizes, for it to be a bubble, the price must be expected to rise, and therefore to be below the fundamental value. This is a contradiction, however, with the earlier observation that the price of a bubble is always above its fundamental. So the period just before stabilization of the price cannot be *below* the fundamental, it can only be *at* the fundamental. Working backwards, it is easy to see that the same reasoning applies all the way to the present: there can be no bubble that is anticipated to stop growing. So bubbles grow for a while but rational traders know that it will eventually burst and they stand ready to jump. As in a game of musical chairs, someone eventually can't move fast enough, and gets burned.

Box 19.5 Tulipmania[12]

The bubble involved tulip bulbs with non-negligible fundamental value because they were of exotic varieties. Yet, they became exorbitantly expensive. Figure 19.8 displays the price of tulip bulbs in the first two months of 1637, when they increased by over 3000%, and then collapsed sharply. For example, the price of the Switser variety is reported to have fallen to one-twentieth of its 2 January 1637 price.

In one of the most authoritative accounts of the Tulipmania episode, Charles MacKay (1852) wrote:

The demand for tulips of a rare species increased so much in the year 1636, that regular marts for their sale were established on the Stock Exchange of Amsterdam, in Rotterdam, Harlem, Leyden, Alkmar, Hoorn, and other towns. Symptoms of gambling now became, for the first time, apparent. The stockjobbers, ever on the alert for a new speculation, dealt largely in tulips, making use of all the means they so well knew how to employ, to cause fluctuations in prices. At first, as in all these gambling mania, confidence was at its height, and everybody gained. The tulip-jobbers speculated in the rise and fall of the tulip stocks, and made large profits by buying when prices fell, and selling out when they rose. Many individuals grew suddenly rich. . . . Nobles, citizens, farmers, mechanics, seamen, footmen, maidservants, even chimney-sweeps and old clotheswomen, dabbled in tulips. People of all grades converted their property into cash, and invested it in flowers. Houses and lands were offered for sale at ruinously low prices, or assigned in payment of bargains made at the tulip-mart. Foreigners became smitten with the same frenzy, and money poured into Holland from all directions. The prices of the necessaries of life rose again by degrees; houses and lands, horses and carriages, and luxuries of every sort, rose in value with them, and for some months Holland seemed the very antechamber of Plutus.[13]

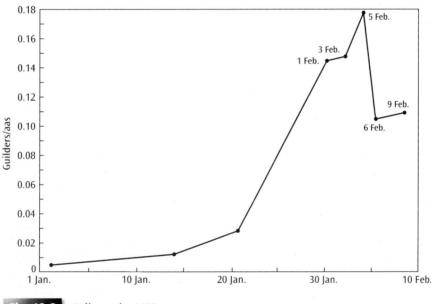

Fig. 19.8 Tulipmania, 1637

History has given us several instances of price behaviour that looks like speculative bubbles. In Holland, the price of rare tulip bulbs during the seventeenth century rose by extraordinary rates within a month's time, only to collapse thereafter.
Source: Garber (1990).

---

[12] Part of this description is taken from Peter Garber's (1990) survey of the Tulipmania boom.
[13] Plutus was the ancient Greek god of wealth.

Bubbles may appear bizarre, because they have all the features of economic rationality and market efficiency, save for the end. Economists still debate whether bubbles really exist; and some wonder if they do not have some subtly efficient aspect. Box 19.5 reviews a famous historical bubble-like episode in Holland's seventeenth century. One does not have to go that far back in history, however, to find suspicious episodes: the run-up of the world's stock markets before the crashes of 1929, 1987, and 1989, the explosion of property prices in the UK and Scandinavia in the late 1980s, and in Ireland in the late 1990s. In each of these instances, reports by contemporaries indicate that market participants were convinced that the boom would continue. In each case, the bursting of the bubble was followed by serious economic dislocation. Most recently, the advent of the 'new economy' ushered in by the information technology revolution was touted as the end of economics as we know it, a technological 'golden age'. For an impartial observer, however, it looks more like a confirmation of 'plus ça change . . .'. The breathtaking ascent of high-tech stock prices in the late 1990s, followed by an equally sharp decline which occurred in 2000–1, is reminiscent of a bubble (see Figure 19.9).

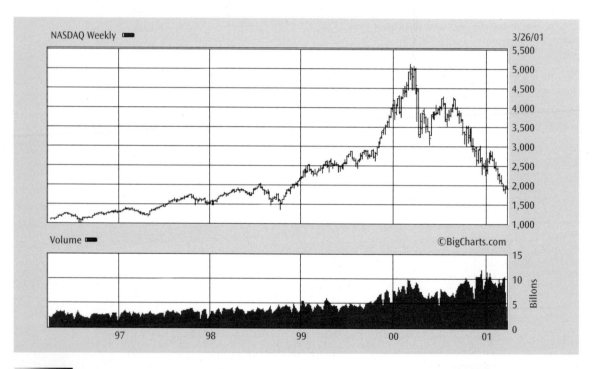

Fig. 19.9 **The Rise and Fall of the NASDAQ Stocks, 1996–2001**

NASDAQ stands for the National Association of Securities Dealers Automated Quotation (system). It is an over-the-counter stock exchange in the USA which has come to specialize in high-technology companies, especially those involving technologies such as personal computers, telecommunication, and the internet. After more than quadrupling in value over the period 1997–2000, the NASDAQ index collapsed just as spectacularly by more than 60% from its all-time peak.
Source: http://www.bigcharts.com

19.4 Exchange Rate Determination in the Short Run

19.4.1 The Exchange Rate as an Asset Price

Chapter 7 explained that, in the long run, the real exchange rate is determined by real forces: the country's net asset position and wealth, productivity in tradable goods, and world tastes. Ultimately, as a relative price of goods, the real exchange rate's role is to move the current account and to enforce the intertemporal budget constraint. This view does not, however, fit the short-run behaviour of exchange rates. Figure 19.10 presents day-to-day nominal changes of the $/€ rate. The variability of nominal

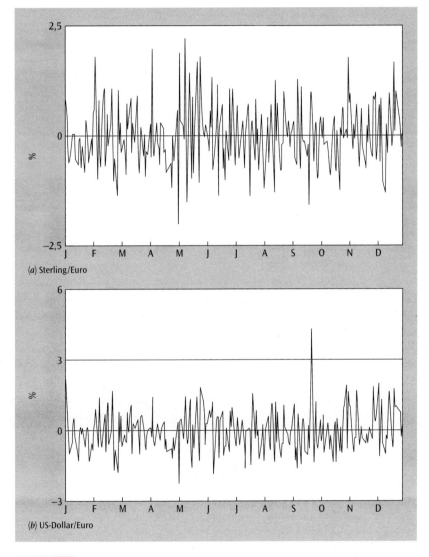

(a) Sterling/Euro

(b) US-Dollar/Euro

Fig. 19.10   **Daily Exchange Rate Changes in 2000**

Day-to-day variability of the nominal exchange rate is considerable. Sharp changes in one direction are frequently undone on the following day.
Source: Datastream.

Box 19.6   Mussa's Stylized Facts and the Asset Behaviour of Exchange Rates

In 1979, Michael Mussa, at the time professor at the University of Chicago and now Senior Economist at the International Monetary Fund, assessed the first half-decade of floating exchange rates after the end of the Bretton Woods system.[14] His observations, which remain true today, can be summarized in the following stylized facts:

1. On a daily basis, changes in floating foreign exchange rates are largely unpredictable.
2. On a month-to-month basis, over 90% of exchange rate movements are unexpected, and less than 10% are predictable.
3. Countries with high inflation rates have depreciating currencies, and over the long run the rate of depreciation of the exchange rate between two countries is approximately equal to the difference in national inflation rates.
4. Countries with rapidly expanding money supplies tend to have depreciating exchange rates vis-à-vis countries

with slowly expanding money supplies. Countries with rapidly expanding money demands tend to have appreciating exchange rates vis-à-vis countries with slowly expanding money demands.

5. In the longer run, the excess of domestic over foreign interest rates is roughly equal to the expected rate of appreciation of the foreign currency. On a day-to-day basis, however, the relationship is more tenuous.
6. Actual changes in the spot exchange rate will tend to overshoot any smoothly adjusting measure of the equilibrium exchange rate, the real exchange rate predicted by the analysis of Chapter 7.
7. The correlation between month-to-month changes in exchange rates and monthly trade balances is low. On the other hand, in the longer run, countries with persistent trade deficits tend to have depreciating currencies, whereas those with trade surpluses tend to have appreciating currencies.

---

exchange rates is often remarkably high, with daily changes of ±1% or more per day commonplace. (A daily change of 1% corresponds to an annual compounded return of more than 3000%.) These violent fluctuations, which are often followed by movements of similar magnitude in the opposite direction, do not match the behaviour of relative prices or price levels. This confirms the assertion of the previous section that in the short run, neither the nominal nor the real exchange rate can be thought of as the relative price of goods and services in different countries; rather, they should be regarded as an *asset* price—the price of national monies. This section provides a more explicit account of the short run—hour-by-hour or month-to-month—and then reconciles the interpretation of the exchange rate as the relative price of goods with that of the relative price of monies.

Because the exchange rate is a forward-looking variable, exchange markets are continuously absorbing and assessing news regarding political conditions, releases of economic data, and pronouncements by government ministers, analysts, prominent busi-

nessmen, gurus, etc. After the fact, much of this 'news' will be amended, made more precise, or disavowed if not actually proved wrong. In the meantime, however, it influences crucially the evolution of the exchange rate. This provides an explanation of the short-run exchange rate behaviour shown in Figure 19.10. News—both genuine facts and rumours—can move the exchange rate up one moment, and down the next. The fact that the 'news' component is so much more important than expected depreciation or appreciation deriving from UIP is consistent with the second stylized fact cited in Box 19.6. In practice, predictable trend changes—such as a return to PPP, a well-understood need to depart from PPP, or simply the changing profile of already expected interest rates—represent a relatively small part of short-term exchange rate movements.

When a variable changes randomly from period to period, it is said to follow a **random walk**.[15] In that case, the only change between its value today and

---

[14] Ch. 20 discusses briefly the Bretton Woods system in more detail.

[15] A variable x_t follows a random walk when it evolves as $x_t = x_{t-1} + u_t$ where u_t is a 'white noise', (i.e. with expected value of zero and serially uncorrelated). At time $t-1$, the best forecast of x_t is x_{t-1}.

its value tomorrow will be white noise, a random shock which can be as much positive as it can be negative and on average zero. Thus, the best next-period forecast of a variable that evolves as a random walk is simply its current value. Surprisingly, perhaps, this most naive forecast often turns out to be the best one, Mussa's first stylized fact. What about the fundamentals? The next section attempts to rehabilitate them.

19.4.2 Money and Goods Market Equilibrium

Returning to an old trick, let us collapse time into two periods, today (period 1), and the indefinite future when stationary equilibrium is reached (period 2). To further simplify matters, assume that output is constant at $\bar{Y}$. Recall the LM curve which describes the money market equilibrium condition in each period $t = 1$ and 2:

(19.15) $$\frac{M_t}{P_t} = \mathcal{L}(\bar{Y}, i_t).$$

The UIP condition links the domestic interest rate to the foreign rate and the expected change in the exchange rate. Inserting condition (19.3) in (19.15) gives, for period 1,

(19.16) $$\frac{M_1}{P_1} = \mathcal{L}(\bar{Y}, i^* - \frac{S_2 - S_1}{S_1})$$

Given the nominal money supply, the expected future exchange rate S_2, and the foreign interest rate i^*, money market equilibrium imposes a positive relationship between the current exchange rate and prices represented in Figure 19.11 by the upward-sloping MM schedule. To see why, imagine that the price level increases. This reduces the real money supply, so demand must decline too. This occurs when the opportunity cost of holding the domestic money, the nominal interest rate, rises. Since the foreign interest rate is taken as constant, UIP implies that the exchange rate must be expected to depreciate. Holding the future exchange rate S_2 constant, the current exchange rate must appreciate. This is quite sensible: the excess demand for money that follows a price increase prompts domestic residents to borrow abroad; the ensuing capital inflow leads to an appreciation.

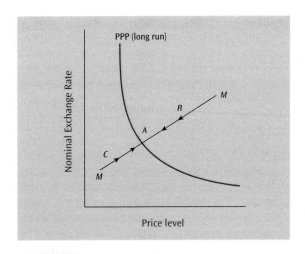

Fig. 19.11 General Equilibrium

Money market equilibrium implies a positive relationship between the exchange rate and the price level, the MM schedule. For a given nominal money stock, a price increase reduces the real money supply. Demand is equilibrated with supply by an increase in the interest rate which triggers an exchange rate appreciation. The long-run equilibrium in the goods market is characterized by PPP. This in turn implies an inverse relationship between the exchange rate and the price level, the PPP schedule. Equilibrium in the money market holds continuously, so positions off the MM schedule are not possible. In contrast, PPP is valid only in the long run—under some conditions—so in the short run, positions off the PPP schedule are possible. Long-run equilibrium occurs at point A, with equilibrium in both money and goods markets.

In the long run, goods market equilibrium is characterized by relative PPP, i.e. a stable real exchange rate. If prices abroad are constant, the real exchange rate remains unchanged as long as the exchange rate and the price level move in the opposite direction: an increase in the price level must be met by an equiproportional depreciation. This is represented by the PPP schedule in Figure 19.11.[16]

The money market is always in equilibrium: the interest rate and the exchange rate instantaneously jump to a level that guarantees equilibrium between money supply and demand. As a result, the economy is always located on the MM schedule of

---

[16] The PPP schedule corresponds to $S = \sigma P^*/P$ where σ is the real exchange rate, assumed to be constant in the long run. Formally, it is a hyperbola. If a shock causes the long-run equilibrium real exchange rate to change, the PPP schedule shifts: outward in the case of real appreciation, inward in the case of a real depreciation.

Figure 19.11. On the other hand, PPP is expected to hold only in the long run; because of price stickiness, the economy may well be away from the *PPP* schedule in the short run. In the long run, however, PPP reasserts itself and the economy must be at point *A*.

In the short run, point *C* below the *PPP* schedule corresponds to an undervalued exchange rate; more precisely, either the nominal exchange rate is undervalued, or the price level is too low and there is an excess demand for domestic goods. Over time, the price level must rise or the exchange rate must appreciate. The long-run equilibrium in the goods market is restored as the economy moves up along the *MM* schedule. Conversely, at point *B* above the *PPP* schedule, either the exchange rate is overvalued or prices are too high. Because they are too expensive relatively to foreign competitors, domestically produced goods are in excess supply and their prices tend to be falling. The return to equilibrium requires a combination of declining prices and exchange rate depreciation.

19.4.3 Exchange Rate Determination with Flexible Prices: The Monetary Approach

If prices are perfectly flexible, the goods market is always in equilibrium, and the economy can be characterized by the intersection of the *PPP* and *MM* schedules. Starting from long-run equilibrium at point *A* in Figure 19.12 (so that $S_1 = S_2$ and $i = i^*$), we consider a once-for-all unexpected 5% increase in the money supply. Long-run neutrality implies that the price level must increase and the exchange rate must depreciate, both by 5%, proportionately to the money supply. This is why the *MM* schedule shifts down and to the right to *M'M'*, and the long-run equilibrium is at point *C*. With fully flexible prices, neutrality occurs in the short run, and the economy immediately jumps from point *A* to point *C*.

It follows from this exercise that, when the equilibrium real exchange is stable, *all* long-run movements of the nominal exchange rate are due to changes in the nominal money supply. This is known as the **monetary approach** to exchange rate determination. If money increases by 5% more than the foreign money supply—and therefore the foreign

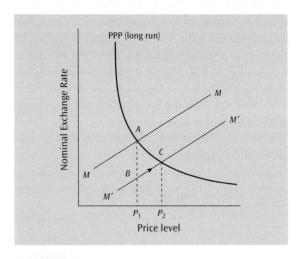

Fig. 19.12 **Overshooting**

An increase in the money supply shifts the money market equilibrium schedule down and to the right, from *MM* to *M'M'*. The new long-run equilibrium obtains at point *C*, the intersection of the *PPP* schedule (long-term goods market equilibrium) line and *M'M'*. In the short run, with sticky prices, only the exchange rate can move. The economy jumps to point *B* to maintain money market equilibrium. As point *B* lies below the *PPP* schedule, there is excess demand for domestic goods, and prices will start to rise. Over time, rising prices reduce the real money supply, pushing up the interest rate and therefore requiring an exchange rate appreciation as we move from *B* to *C*. As point *B* is below point *C*, the exchange rate initially overshoots its long-run level. This overshooting creates an excess demand for domestic goods and puts upward pressure on prices.

price level—both the price level and the exchange rate increase by 5% also. This provides an interpretation of stylized fact 3 in Box 19.6, which states that countries with high inflation rates have depreciating currencies. Yet if prices are sticky in the short run, the monetary approach will fall short of being a full explanation of nominal exchange rate behaviour.

19.4.4 Exchange Rate Determination with Rigid Prices: Overshooting[17]

In the short run (period 1) it is more realistic to think of the price level as rigid, moving only slowly to eliminate goods market imbalances and deviations

---

[17] The overshooting result was first established by Rudiger Dornbusch from MIT in 1976.

from the equilibrium real exchange rate. In the long run, prices recover flexibility and a 5% increase in the money supply remains described by point C. In period 1, however, the price level remains unchanged at P_1. At the same time, money market equilibrium requires the economy to jump instantaneously on to the new schedule $M'M'$ in Figure 19.12. With prices unable to move in the very short run, the task is performed by the nominal exchange rate which takes the economy immediately to point B. Over time, the price level adjusts and the economy will move up along MM from B to C.

A key feature of short-run point B is that it lies *below* long-run point C. The nominal exchange rate

overshoots its long-run level, depreciating by more than the 5% warranted by the money stock increase. From B to C, overshooting is eliminated as the exchange rate appreciates, while the price level rises to its new higher equilibrium level. That the exchange rate overshoots its equilibrium value is exactly what Mussa's stylized fact 6 asserts: actual changes in spot rates tend to overshoot any measure of the equilibrium exchange rate.

Box 19.7 provides an interpretation of overshooting using the IS–LM framework. Figure 19.14 shows the evolution over time of the interest and exchange rates and of the price level in the more general case when there are more than just two periods. Once

---

Box 19.7   **Overshooting and Undershooting in the *IS–LM* Framework**

The *IS–LM* framework allows us to consider the case—treated formally in the Appendix—where output varies. In Figure 19.13, we start from long-run equilibrium at point A (so $i = i^*$ and $S_t = {}_tS_{t+1}$). As in Section 19.3, we interpret i^* strictly as the foreign interest rate *only*. The increase in the money supply shifts the LM curve rightward to LM'. This depresses the domestic (nominal and real) interest rate and is met by a depreciation which shifts the IS curve to the right because of the gain in competitiveness. If spending is not too sensitive to the real interest rate (through investment) and to the exchange rate (through the current account), the IS curve shifts only to IS'. At point B, the domestic interest rate is below the world level and there must be a compensating expectation of exchange rate appreciation: the exchange rate overshoots. If spending is very sensitive to interest and exchange rates, the IS curve shifts further to IS'' and the economy is at point C. The interest rate is *above* the world level; the exchange rate is expected to depreciate afterwards so it jumps less than, rather than more than, its long-run change: now there is **undershooting**. In both cases, the interpretation is the same: with sticky prices, an increase in the money supply creates an excess supply of money, so that output must rise to restore equilibrium. (With flexible prices, the real money supply remains unchanged as the price level rises in the same proportion as the nominal money stock.) If demand does not rise enough (point B), the interest rate must decline on impact, and there is overshooting. If demand is very

responsive, it boosts output so much that the interest rate must rise, and there is undershooting.

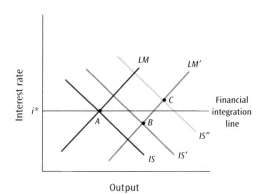

Fig. 19.13   **Overshooting and Undershooting in the *IS–LM* Framework**

Starting from full equilibrium at point A, an increase in the money stock brings the LM curve to LM'. As the nominal interest rate falls, the nominal exchange rate depreciates. With sticky prices, the real exchange rate depreciates, shifting the IS curve to the right. With a small shift (IS') at point B, the domestic interest rate is still lower than abroad: the exchange rate must be expected to appreciate, hence an overshooting depreciation. With a larger shift (IS'') at point C, the exchange rate undershoots: since the domestic interest rate exceeds the world level, the exchange rate is rationally expected to further depreciate and is therefore below its long-run level.

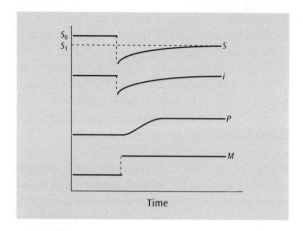

Fig. 19.14 **Overshooting over Time**

The nominal money increase eventually leads to an equiproportionate change in the price level—which rises—and in the exchange rate—which depreciates. Thus, we expect the nominal exchange rate to settle eventually at the level S_1, below its initial value S_0. Initially, with sticky prices, the money-supply increase pushes interest rates down. This requires that the exchange rate be expected to appreciate, hence an initial overshooting undervaluation, i.e. a jump below S_1.

the money supply has increased, initially the interest rate must decline to maintain equilibrium in the money market. This raises demand for domestic goods. In response, the price level rises gradually towards its higher long-run level. The lower exchange rate must be compensated by an expected appreciation. In the long run, the exchange rate will have moved from its initial value S_1 to S_2, which is 5% higher. In the short run, the exchange rate must jump below its long-run value: it *over*depreciates in order to appreciate thereafter. As the price level rises, the real money supply declines and the interest rate increases. A rising interest rate, in turn, coincides with an appreciating exchange rate. Figure 19.14 provides the background for Mussa's stylized fact 4, which links depreciation rates in the long run to monetary growth. Money increases 'tend' to lead to depreciations, but overshooting may blur the picture as the initial depreciation is followed by a partially offsetting appreciation.

Overshooting shows that persistent deviations of real exchange rates from their equilibrium values,

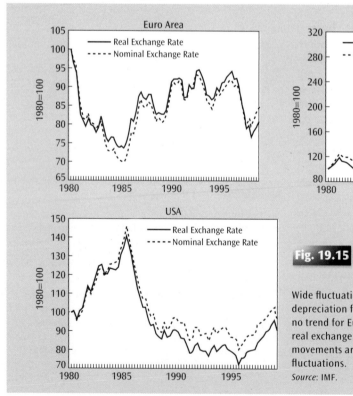

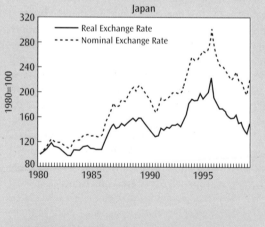

Fig. 19.15 **Nominal and Real Effective Exchange Rates: Euro Area, Japan, and USA, 1980–2000**

Wide fluctuations, around a stable PPP trend (real depreciation for the USA, real appreciation for Japan, no trend for Euroland), characterize the behaviour of real exchange rates. Most of the real exchange rate movements are linked to nominal exchange rate fluctuations.

Source: IMF.

or **misalignments**, are possible, even with rational expectations. This would be impossible if goods prices were perfectly flexible. The overshooting result implies that monetary disturbances can move the exchange rate away from PPP, *even in the absence of real disturbances*. This in turn affects consumption, the allocation of resources, firms' profitability, real wages, and the current account. Movements in the real exchange rate may also occur, of course, in response to real disturbances. Real disturbances, related to differences across countries in the rate of technological advances, tastes, or government

policies, might be judged to be less frequent. Figure 19.15 shows the effective nominal and real exchange rates for the three major currencies: the US dollar, the euro, and the Japanese yen. Fluctuations are sizeable (some 50% over periods of two to three years are not uncommon) but occur in the form of long swings around a fairly steady mean. Strikingly, nominal and real exchange rates move closely together, which is an indication that prices are sticky and that monetary forces play an important role in the short-run determination of the real exchange rate.

 ## Summary

1. Asset markets put a price tag on the future and on risk. They allow households and corporations to decide on saving and borrowing without themselves having to gather the whole array of uncertain information that affects their own future. They allow those savers who are most willing to bear risk to do so, at minimum cost.

2. While financial intermediaries can be thought of as intervening on financial markets on behalf of their customers, in fact most of the transactions correspond to trade among intermediaries.

3. Financial assets are traded with ease in large well-organized markets, they are durable, and they are cheap to store. This is why financial markets are understood as equating the demand and supply of asset stocks, rather than the flow increments to the stocks that are created each period. For these often very large stocks to be held voluntarily, returns among similar assets—similar in terms of risk and maturity—must be equalized.

4. The no-profit condition is a characteristic of efficient financial markets. In the absence of risk-taking, it takes the form of arbitrage. A good example of arbitrage is the covered interest parity condition: when capital is internationally mobile, a higher domestic interest rate is matched by a forward exchange rate premium.

5. In the presence of uncertainty and undiversifiable risk, the no-profit condition implies that expected returns are equalized up to a risk premium which rewards those risk-averse agents that accept to bear risk. A good example of the no-profit condition is the uncovered interest parity condition: when capital is internationally mobile, an expected exchange rate depreciation should be compensated by a higher domestic interest rate, and conversely.

6. Markets are efficient when they gather all the available information and treat it to the point where prices reflect fully what is known and the risks attached to any single asset. The evidence on market efficiency is mostly favourable, but some evidence suggests either that markets are not fully efficient or that efficiency is consistent with phenomena such as speculative bubbles or noise trading.

7. If both uncovered interest parity and purchasing power parity conditions hold, real interest rates are equalized worldwide. Since PPP holds at best in the long run, real interest rate equalization is only a medium- to long-run proposition.

8. Exchange rates are forward-looking variables, i.e. are free from the past and driven by the future. This is captured by uncovered interest parity condition—with or without a risk premium—interpreted as determining today's exchange rate as a function of today's interest rates and the expected exchange rate next period.

9. Today's exchange rate is linked, by a chain of uncovered interest parity conditions, to present and future interest rates at home and abroad, and to the spot exchange rate far along in the future. All that is presently known about the future is reflected in today's value of the exchange rate. Changes in the exchange rate occur primarily because new information arrives, including revisions of expectations about the future.

10. The long- and short-run views of the exchange rate are not inconsistent. Real factors that drive the long-run real exchange rate are present in today's nominal exchange rate. The long-run exchange rate is the *anchor* that guides the path of future expected exchange rates and relates it to the current value.

11. The forward-looking aspect of the exchange rate explains why its behaviour closely resembles a random walk, since new information arrives randomly. This makes it hard to see the link between the exchange rate and its fundamentals which are typically considerably less volatile. Yet, they are present via the market's expectations of their future expected values.

12. With prices sticky in the short run, an increase in the money stock leads to an exchange rate depreciation which overshoots its long-run value. All other things equal, an increase in the stock of money leads in the long run to increases of the same proportion in the exchange rate and price level.

Key Concepts

- assets
- fundamentals
- financial intermediaries
- rate of return
- risk premium
- no profit condition
- arbitrage, no-arbitrage condition
- risk aversion
- hedged
- covered interest parity (CIP)
- forward contract, forward exchange rate
- spot exchange rate
- uncovered interest parity (UIP)

- market maker
- bid–ask spread
- maturity
- term structure of interest rates
- consol, perpetuity
- international Fisher equation
- real interest parity
- noise traders
- speculative bubbles
- random walk
- monetary approach
- undervaluation, overvaluation
- misalignment

Exercises

1. Insider trading occurs when some traders have superior private information which they use to 'beat' the market. In most countries, insider trading is forbidden on stock markets but not in exchange markets.

   (*a*) Is it self-evident that insider trading on stocks should be banned? (*Hint*: think in terms of market efficiency.) Why do you think that insider trading is generally illegal?

   (*b*) Why do you think that insider trading is not prohibited in foreign exchange markets?

2. Explain why the bid–ask spread can be thought of as the price of risk.

3. Suppose that you could buy and sell US dollars for €1 and euros for ¥120, but that at the same time the dollar–Yen rate was ¥115.

   (*a*) What strategy would you pursue to take advantage of this 'money pump'? What would be the likely effect of the market's recognition of its existence?

   (*b*) The example given in the previous problem ignores the bid–ask spread. How would your answer change if the bid–ask spreads were: $0.99–1.01/€, ¥118–122/€, and ¥113–117/$?

4. (*formal*) Consider the example of a speculative bubble in the text (Section 19.3.4). Now imagine that while, as before, there are two assets, investors no longer have perfect foresight. The private asset can be purchased at variable real price q_t and pays a fixed real dividend d. Now, however, there is a probability s that in the following period $q_{t+1} = 0$ (i.e. the bubble will burst), and a probability $(1 - s)$ that it can be sold at $q_{t+1} > 0$. Investors are risk-neutral and equate the rate of return on the government 'safe' asset r with the expected rate of return on the private asset.

   (*a*) Write down the arbitrage condition.

   (*b*) Solve for the 'non-exploding' value of current q_t.

5. Derive an expression like (19.13) when risk aversion prevails; i.e. using the UIP condition modified for risk aversion (19.4).

6. Suppose the interest rate for one-year Treasury bond is 5% per annum, and for a Treasury Bond of two-year maturity, 7% per annum. By an arbitrage argument, at what rate could you lend in one year's time over a maturity of one year? Describe your trading strategy.

7. On 10 March 2000 the NASDAQ stock price index, which reflects to a large extent the market valuation of companies involved with telecommunciations, computer technologies, and especially the internet, had reached a value of 5133. By the end of March 2001 it had fallen to about 1800 or by more than 65% from its all-time peak, or to roughly its level of autumn 1998. Explain why the behaviour of the internet resembles a speculative bubble. Can you explain why this bubble could be 'rational' from the point of view of individual market participants? What is the potential damage for the macroeconomy of the bubble? Can you think of any benefits?

8. Assume prices are flexible. Using the apparatus introduced in Section 19.4, explore the implications for the short and long run for the exchange rate (British terms), prices, and interest rates of: (*a*) a permanent contraction of the money supply; (*b*) a permanent, exogenous increase in output; (*c*) a permanent, exogenous decline in the foreign price level.

9. A small open economy with perfect capital mobility is characterized by the following equations:

$$M_t/P_t = 0.5\bar{Y} - 30{,}000[i^* - (S_{t+1} - S_t)/S_t]$$
$$i_t = i^* - (S_{t+1} - S_t)/S_t,$$

with $\bar{Y} = 8000$ and $i^* = 0.04$.

(a) Draw the MM curve when $M_t = 2000$ and $S_{t+1} = 1$, limiting yourself to the cases where P_t and S_t are positive. Show what happens when M_t rises to 3000.

(b) In the long run, purchasing power parity holds so that $\sigma = SP/P^*$, with $\sigma = 1$ and $P^* = 0.5$. Show the PPP curve.

(c) What is the long-run price and exchange rate equilibrium when $M_t = 2000$? When $M_t = 3000$?

(d) Compute the short-term nominal exchange rate when M_t changes unexpectedly from 2000 to 3000, assuming that S was initially at its long-run equilibrium level.

10. In late January 2001 one could observe ten-year bond yields of roughly 5.2% in Denmark compared with 4.8% in Euroland. Yet Denmark currently fixes its exchange rate to the euro. Does this necessarily represent an opportunity for pure arbitrage or risky yield arbitrage? Why or why not?

Suggested Further Reading

A trader's inside view of how foreign exchange markets work can be found in the annual publication by Swiss Bank Corporation, *Foreign Exchange and Money Market Operations*, Zurich.

An entertaining survey of the arguments in favour of market efficiency which contains a large number of references is:
Burton, Malkiel (1999), *A Random Walk Down Wall Street*, W. W. Norton, 7th edition.

Contrary views are given by:
Shiller, Robert (2000), *Irrational Exuberance*, Princeton University Press.
Shleifer, Andrei (2000), *Inefficient Markets*, Oxford University Press.

A textbook introduction to the economics of finance is:
Sharpe, William (1990), *Investments*, Prentice-Hall.

A lively discussion of speculative bubbles in both technical and non-technical terms can be found in the Spring 1990 issue of the *Journal of Economic Perspectives*.

The classic description of exchange rate behaviour is:
Mussa, Michael (1979), 'Empirical Regularities in the Behavior of Exchange Rates and Theories of the Foreign Exchange Market', in K. Brunner and A. Meltzer (eds.), *Carnegie Rochester Conference Series*, 11: 9–58.

A recent survey of exchange rate behaviour is:
Froot, Kenneth, and Thaler, Jeffrey (1990), 'Anomalies: Foreign Exchange', *Journal of Economic Perspectives*, 4: 179–92.

The first derivation of the overshooting result can be found in:

Dornbusch, Rudiger (1976), 'Expectations and Exchange Rate Dynamics', *Journal of Political Economy*, 84: 1161–76.

Other useful, more technical, references include:

De Grauwe, Paul, Janssens, Marc, and Leliaert, Hilde (1989), 'Real Exchange Rate Variability from 1920–6 and 1973–82', *Princeton Studies in International Finance*, 56.

Dornbusch, Rudiger (1980), *Open Economy Macroeconomics*, Basic Books.

Gärtner, Manfred (1993), *Macroeconomics under Flexible Exchange Rates*, Harvester Wheatsheaf.

Meese, Richard (1990), 'Currency Fluctuations in the Post-Bretton Woods Era', *Journal of Economic Perspectives*, 4: 117–34.

Rogoff, Kenneth, and Obstfeld, Maurice (1995), 'Exchange Rate Dynamics Redux', *Journal of Political Economy*, 103: 624–60.

Probably the most extensive technical reference available to date on exchange rate models is:

Rogoff, Kenneth, and Obstfeld, Maurice (1996), *Foundations of International Macroeconomics*, MIT Press.

Appendix: The Forward Markets

The Table A19.1 shows forward rates as quoted in the *Financial Times*. Currencies are generally sold forward at standardized intervals (e.g. 1, 3, or 12 months), but in the retail market banks are willing to customize forward rates to the desires of their customers—within limits and always for a price, of course. The price for such a contract is usually stated as a **forward premium or discount** with respect to the spot price. A forward premium on the Danish krone vis-à-vis the US dollar exists when the forward price of dollars in krone is lower than the current spot price: the dollar is cheaper on the forward market or, equivalently, the krone is more expensive.

The forward premium or discount is usually expressed as a per-annum rate. If F_{t+1} is the forward rate agreed at time t for delivery at date $t + 1$ and S_t is the spot rate at date t, the forward premium is $(F_{t+1} - S_t)/S_t$; it is a discount if negative. $(F_{t+1} - S_t)/S_t$ is similar to a rate of interest over the period of the contract. To obtain its per-annum equivalent we compound it; for example, for a three-month contract we compute $(1 + r)^4$, which gives $(F_{t+1}/S_t)^4$ since $1 + (F_{t+1} - S_t)/S_t = F_{t+1}/S_t$. A premium of 2% per annum on the three-month Danish krone/US dollar forward rate means that $(F_{t+1}/S_t)^4 = 1.02$ so that $F_{t+1}/S_t = 1.00496$: F_{t+1} is 0.496% above S_t. This is the way forward rates are reported in Table A19.1. For each maturity (1, 3, and 12 months), the table reports the forward rate and then the annualized percentage deviation from the spot rate; a positive number corresponds to a premium, a negative number to a discount.

Table A19.1   Spot and Forward Exchange Rates, 4 May 1992

POUND SPOT—FORWARD AGAINST THE POUND

May 1	Day's spread	Close	One month	% p.a.	Three months	% p.a.
US..................	1.7785 - 1.7855	1.7845 - 1.7855	1.03-1.01cpm	6.86	2.78-2.75pm	6.20
Canada.............	2.1150 - 2.1225	2.1215 - 2.1225	0.70-0.66cpm	3.85	2.00-1.90pm	3.68
Netherlands.......	3.2900 - 3.3025	3.2925 - 3.3025	$3/8$ - $1/8$cpm	0.91	$1 1/8$-$1/4$pm	1.14
Belgium............	60.10 - 60.50	60.40 - 60.50	9-4cpm	1.29	14-5pm	0.63
Denmark..........	11.3275 - 11.3575	11.3425 - 11.3525	$3/4$ - $1/8$orepm	0.46	$1 3/8$-$1/8$pm	0.26
Ireland.............	1.0945 - 1.0995	1.0975 - 1.0985	0.01-0.04cdis	−0.27	0.01-0.08dis	−0.16
Germany...........	2.9275 - 2.9350	2.9275 - 2.9325	$3/8$ - $1/4$pfpm	1.28	$3/8$ - $1/8$pm	0.34
Portugal............	245.50 - 247.00	246.00 - 247.00	50-75cdis	−3.04	149-197dis	−2.81
Spain...............	183.60 - 184.10	183.75 - 184.05	19-26cdis	−1.47	88-101dis	−2.06
Italy.................	2196.00 - 2205.50	2202.25 - 2203.25	1-311redis	−1.09	9-12dis	−1.91
Norway.............	11.4300 - 11.4825	11.4725 - 11.4825	$5/8$ - $1/8$orepm	0.39	$1 1/8$ - parpm	0.20
France.............	9.8700 - 9.8875	9.8750 - 9.8850	1 - $1/2$cpm	0.91	$5/8$ - $1/8$ pm	0.15
Sweden............	10.5625 - 10.5900	10.5800 - 10.5900	$3/4$ - $1 3/8$ oredis	−1.20	$3 1/8$ - $4 3/8$dis	−1.42
Japan...............	236.25 - 237.25	236.25 - 237.25	$1 1/4$ - $1 1/8$ ypm	6.02	$3 3/8$ - $3 1/4$pm	5.60
Austria.............	20.57 - 20.65	20.59 - 20.62	$2 3/8$ - $1 1/4$gropm	1.06	$5 3/8$ - $2 3/4$pm	0.79
Switzerland.......	2.6725 - 2.6950	2.6725 - 2.6825	$5/8$ - $3/8$cpm	2.24	$1 1/4$ - 1pm	1.68
Ecu..................	1.4255 - 1.4285	1.4275 - 1.4285	0.09-0.03cpm	0.50	0.10-0.02pm	0.17

Commercial rates taken towards the end of London trading. Six-month forward dollar 5.17–5.12pm. 12 Month 8.85–8.75pm.

DOLLAR SPOT—FORWARD AGAINST THE DOLLAR

May 1	Day's spread	Close	One month	% p.a.	Three months	% p.a.
UK†..................	1.7785 - 1.7855	1.7845 - 1.7855	1.03-1.01cpm	6.86	2.78-2.75pm	6.28
Ireland†...........	1.6160 - 1.6265	1.6240 - 1.6250	0.87-0.84cpm	6.32	2.51-2.44pm	6.09
Canada.............	1.1880 - 1.1920	1.1890 - 1.1900	0.25-0.27cdis	−2.62	0.75-0.79dis	−2.59
Netherlands......	1.8450 - 1.8645	1.8470 - 1.8480	0.89-0.92cdis	−5.88	2.62-2.66dis	−5.72
Belgium............	33.80 - 34.00	33.80 - 33.90	16.00-18.00cdis	−6.03	46.00-50.00dis	−5.67
Denmark..........	6.3525 - 6.3925	6.3550 - 6.3600	3.55-3.95oredis	−7.08	9.40-10.10dis	−6.13
Germany...........	1.6395 - 1.6515	1.6405 - 1.6415	0.83-0.84pfdis	−0.611	2.43-2.45dis	−5.95
Portugal............	139.10 - 139.60	139.15 - 139.25	121-129cdis	−10.78	318-333dis	−9.35
SpainItaly..........	102.90 - 103.60	102.90 - 103.00	73-75cdis	−8.63	215-220dis	−8.45
	1232.00 - 1240.75	1233.75 - 1234.25	0.84-0.89llredis	−0.84	2.50-2.60dis	−0.83
Norway.............	6.4200 - 6.4450	6.4275 - 6.4325	3.40-3.80oredis	−6.72	10.00-10.60dis	−6.41
France..............	5.5300 - 5.5700	5.5325 - 5.5375	2.93-2.97cdis	−6.40	8.50-8.56dis	−6.16
Sweden.............	5.9225 - 5.9500	5.9275 - 5.9325	3.93-4.18oredis	−8.21	11.55-12.10dis	−7.98
Japan...............	132.50 - 133.35	132.65 - 132.75	0.08-0.09ydis	−0.77	0.20-0.22dis	−0.63
Austria.............	11.5650 - 11.6100	11.6050 - 11.6100	5.55-5.90grodis	−5.92	16.00-17.00dis	−5.69
Switzerland........	1.4980 - 1.5175	1.4995 - 1.5005	0.65-0.66cdis	−5.24	1.83-1.85dis	−4.91
Ecu†................	1.2420 - 1.2510	1.2475 - 1.2485	0.68-0.65cpm	6.39	1.94-1.87pm	6.11

Commercial rates taken towards the end of London trading. † UK, Ireland, and ECU are quoted in US currency. Forward premiums and discounts apply to the US dollar and not to the individual currency.

Source: Financial Times, 5 May 1992.

The Architecture of the International Monetary System

20

When we understand that Lombard Street is subject to severe alternations of opposite causes, we should cease to be surprised at its seeming cycles. We should cease too, to be surprised at the sudden panics. During the period of reaction and adversity, just even at the last instant of prosperity, the whole structure is delicate. The peculiar essence of our banking system is an unprecedented trust between man and man: and when that trust is much weakened by hidden causes, a small accident may greatly hurt it, and a great accident for a moment may almost destroy it.

– Walter Bagehot (1873)

20.1 Overview

The decade of the 1990s was the decade of currency and banking crises. The first outbreak was in Europe, when the Exchange Rate Mechanism of the European Monetary System fell victim to a speculative attack in the late summer of 1992, and all but collapsed in 1993. The spectre of financial crisis moved on to Mexico in late 1994. It reappeared in Thailand in mid-1997 and spread all over South-East Asia over the next six months, ravaging the area's banking systems. It returned to Russia and Brazil in 1998, leaving few countries untouched. Some leading banks and financial institutions in the USA, Japan, and Europe were badly shaken, some even went bankrupt. The international community did not stand idly by: tens of billions of US dollars were injected via the International Monetary Fund to put a stop to the crises, which spread like a modern-day plague. In the aftermath, the Fund faced fierce criticism, accused of being too harsh and intrusive by some, of perpetuating bad practices and lost causes by others. The international financial system was declared in need of a complete overhaul. The search for a new architecture has started in earnest, and it will take a long, long time to design a new one.

The world is changing. The emerging economies, formerly poor countries catching up with the developed world, are joining the bandwagon of globalization, a process both hailed and feared. And yet, many of the questions being debated are old ones. What exchange rate regime to adopt? Should capital movements be restrained? How to balance the relationship between the developed North and the poor South? What role for international financial institutions like the IMF and the World Bank? The present chapter revisits these old questions, and some new ones as well, with a fresh look. We have learned a great deal over the last decade, both about the theory of exchange rate crises and about the practice of exchange rate regimes.

Inevitably we must attribute a great deal of the present to history. Many long-standing international arrangements may be scrapped to solve the new problems of the world financial system. Accordingly, Section 20.2 provides a quick overview of the history of the international monetary system, if only to help us understand the current situation. Section 20.3 describes in some detail the role and structure of the IMF, the linchpin of the present system. The crises of the 1990s are presented and interpreted in Section 20.4, paving the way for a review in Section 20.5 of the state of play regarding the perennial question of choosing an exchange rate regime. The current debates are reviewed in Section 20.6.

History of Monetary Arrangements

20.2.1 The Gold Standard and How It Worked

For centuries, both domestic and international trade was carried out with gold and silver. Metallic monies were used for thousands of years because, as explained in Chapter 8, they were easily recognizable and acceptable by others. Being scarce, metal was a reasonably stable store of value; not easily subject to manipulation, it was a reliable medium of exchange. National currencies as we know them did not exist. Money was simply gold or silver weight, currencies were just particular denominations of metal, not necessarily one denomination per country. In fact, hundreds of denominations existed and circulated together. The responsibility of public authorities was to guarantee the precious metal content of their money. This role was taken over by issuing agencies, the mints, which were continuously melting coins —often produced abroad—and coining their own. In fact, national authorities sometimes coined foreign money as well.

Until the late 1870s, gold and silver coexisted as the main monetary metals. Progressively over the nineteenth century, banknotes started to circulate alongside gold and silver. These notes were a promise to pay the bearer in precious metal. They were as good as the name of the issuer, mostly his honesty in not issuing more notes than he had precious metal. Initially at least, the notes were issued by private bankers, who often failed to exercise adequate self-discipline. As a result the banknotes were not always fully backed by metallic reserves, which led to occasional banking crises. This is one reason why central banks were created, and why they displaced private banks as issuers of paper money. Central banks were formally required to hold close to 100% gold or silver to back their issues of banknotes. These notes were convertible into gold, coins, or bullion at the holder's request, and conversion was indeed routine. With close to 100% backing, banknotes simply represented another, more convenient way of holding gold or silver.

Box 20.1   **Bimetallism and Gresham's Law**

It was only at the end of the nineteenth century that gold became the premier international medium of exchange. For centuries, silver and gold had competed against each other. **Bimetallism**, as the system was called, established a fixed parity between gold and silver, and coins in both metals were usually accepted for all transactions, both nationally and internationally. The relative value of gold and silver was set by international agreements, which were occasionally called into question as new discoveries of either metal threatened to upset the parity. Troubled times then followed with the operation of **Gresham's Law**. This principle states that the currency (metal) that is more valuable (in non-monetary markets) than its official rate stops circulating: 'bad money chases out good'.[1]

Partly because silver became more plentiful, bimetallism ceased to exist in Europe in the 1870s. The last major countries to defend bimetallism formed the Latin Monetary Union in 1865, setting a parity of 15.5 ounces of silver for 1 ounce of gold. This union consisted of Belgium, France, Italy, and Switzerland. (For this reason all save Italy adopted the 'franc' as the name of their national money.) In the USA, where a central monetary authority was absent, bimetallism survived for a longer time. The final blow occurred when the newly created German state switched to gold and unloaded large amounts of silver on the free market. The risk of complete gold loss in a world under a gold standard forced the remaining countries to abandon bimetallism entirely.

---

[1] Living in the 16th century, Sir Thomas Gresham had been in charge of royal finances, then became a foreign exchange trader in Antwerp until he created the Royal Exchange, better known today as the London Stock Exchange. It is sometimes argued that the gold standard in the UK was an artefact of Isaac Newton's decision in 1717 to undervalue silver in terms of gold; within little time, Sir Isaac had only gold on his hands.

The **gold standard** lasted from 1879 to 1914, less than forty years. It emerged in the wake of the demise of bimetallism (see Box 20.1) and collapsed one month before the outbreak of the First World War. The gold standard era is sometimes nostalgically associated with the rapid industrialization of the time and is regarded as a great economic success story. This 'success' is often attributed to the gold standard's automatic adjustment mechanisms. In fact, the gold standard was not without problems, nor were these adjustment mechanisms as automatic as is often believed. But it remains a benchmark and, in many respects, new developments like monetary unions and currency boards (studied in Section 20.5.3) attempt to re-create some of its most desirable features.

Domestic operation of the gold standard

In principle, the gold standard was a simple affair. Gold was the sole (or main) form of money. Demand was stable (driven by the need to carry out everyday transactions). Dependent on mining successes, supply was also quite stable; even large discoveries amounted to small disturbances, for the amounts brought out (the flows of newly coined gold) were very small in comparison to existing stocks. The role of monetary authorities was merely to establish and guarantee the gold content of their own currencies, the gold exchange rate. Monetary policy is well described by the Mundell–Fleming model under fixed exchange rates of Chapter 11. It was entirely dedicated to the defence of the exchange rate, i.e. the gold value of the currency.

International operation of the gold standard

Fixed Exchange Rates. Pegging a currency's value to gold was sufficient to determine the exchange rates with other gold currencies. For instance, if the Dutch guilder was set at the price of 50 per ounce of pure gold (the usual weight reference) and sterling was set at £25 per ounce, the guilder was worth £0.5. If the exchange rate were to decline to £0.4 (a depreciation of the guilder relative to sterling), it would make sense to purchase gold in the Netherlands with guilders, ship it to the UK, tender it to the Bank of England in exchange for sterling, and, finally, convert sterling into guilders. For every 100 guilders tendered in the

Netherlands for gold, the transaction would yield 2 ounces of gold, sold in the UK to acquire £50. Selling these sterling balances against guilders at the 0.5 exchange rate would yield 125 guilders, a 25% profit! Such a prospect was sure to trigger large sales of sterling and large purchases of guilders in the exchange markets, promptly appreciating the guilder's value back to its only sustainable sterling value, £0.5. To be sure, the example ignores transaction costs, especially the cost of transporting the gold across the sea.[2] Once these are accounted for, the exchange rate can move a little bit from the gold-implied parity, leaving a band of fluctuation within which it is not worth undertaking the buying, selling, and shipping. These bands were known as 'gold points', and are similar to exchange rate intervention bands employed in modern fixed exchange rate systems. They implied margins of fluctuation of about 1%.

Endogenous money supply. Being the way to settle exchanges, nationally and internationally, gold was freely flowing as the counterpart of payment imbalances. A country running a trade deficit would lose gold to its trading partners; the metal was physically shipped abroad to pay for the excess of imports over exports. The exported gold coins were then minted and coined in the currency of the surplus country. Thus, a trade deficit implied a shrinking money supply, a surplus meant an expanding money supply. This had two consequences. First, the reduction of the money supply in the deficit country led to higher interest rates and to a capital inflow; a capital account surplus financed the trade deficit. Second, higher interest rates tended to slow down economic activity and to depress prices, which improved the country's competitiveness and restored the trade balance. In the surplus country the process went in the opposite direction: balance of payment surpluses led to gold inflows, which raised the money supply and depressed interest rates. In the medium run, higher inflation would tend to reduce the surplus, as competitiveness is eroded (the real exchange rate appreciates). This symmetric process is often called the **Hume mechanism**, after the

---

[2] These transport costs are unnecessary if the participating countries are willing to acquire foreign currencies and swap them back at regular intervals—as was often the case in the heyday of the gold standard period.

Table 20.1	Inflation Rates in Five Countries, 1900–1913 (annual average rate of increase in GDP deflator, %)			
France	**Japan**	**USA**	**Germany**	**UK**
0.9	2.8	1.3	1.3	0.9

Source: Maddison (1995).

Scottish economist and philosopher David Hume who first described it.

The main benefits of the gold standard

The world has never seen, and probably never will see, a true pure gold standard. As will be discussed below, this is not necessarily a regrettable circumstance! Still, some observers regret the passing of the gold standard. Why? First, the Hume mechanism had the virtue of credibility. Under a gold standard, monetary policy is entirely determined by the stock of gold. In principle, it is out of the politicians' hands. Second, with the money supply naturally constrained by the availability of a rare resource, inflation is not likely to emerge on any significant scale. This is documented in Table 20.1. Third, there is no need for a particular country to be at the centre of the world monetary system, avoiding conflicts on which country that should be.

Limits of automatism

Despite these appealing aspects, the gold standard had its limitations. Sterling was the main currency, backed by the most developed financial centre, London. Britain had been on the gold standard longer than other countries, since 1819 when the Bank of England received its key statutes (Peel's Act). Furthermore, as the largest creditor country, Britain provided the rest of the world with sterling balances which often ended up as reserve currency held by other central banks.[3] Three consequences followed from Britain's hegemonic position. First, the Bank of England was able to set the interest rate for the rest of the world, but with its eye on British eco-

nomic conditions. Second, the demand for sterling as a reserve currency allowed Britain to finance long-running balance of payments deficits, paid with sterling-denominated debt issued by the Bank of England. Put differently, Britain could escape the automaticity of the Hume mechanism: the money supply was not declining as gold was not shipped to cover the deficit. Third, the widespread acceptability of sterling balances allowed the Bank of England to maintain a ratio of reserves to deposits—known as 'the Proportion'—well below 100%; at the height of the gold standard late in the nineteenth century, the Proportion fluctuated between 30% and 50%. To the extent that its gold stock was shielded from the vagaries of the balance of payments and since the Proportion could vary, the Bank of England possessed considerable freedom to set its interest rate.

Britain was not the only country that tinkered with Hume's mechanism. Some countries actually imposed limits on gold exports and imports, as well as on minting and coinage. Many central banks accumulated sizeable reserves of foreign currencies, first and foremost in pounds sterling. Thus, the assumed link between metal and money supply was less than fully automatic. Furthermore, the gold reserves of the Bank of England eventually fell below the value of the Bank's liabilities towards other central banks, leading to an 'overhang' of unbacked British debt. It is something of a miracle that the overhang never threatened the credibility of external sterling liabilities.

The limits of a metallic standard

While the gold standard may have been mismanaged, there are a number of inherent problems with any metallic standard. The automatic mechanism that is often considered as the main advantage of the

[3] During the forty years preceding the First World War, some 20% of British savings were invested abroad.

gold standard does not come for free. It has a cost in terms of economic instability. And indeed the gold standard years typically display low inflation but greater output variability, in line with the trade-off between rules and discretion described in Chapter 16. If respected, the rules of the gold standard are very strict: the money supply is determined solely by the balance of payments, so macroeconomic adjustments must entirely be dealt with through wage and price changes. If wages and prices adjust slowly in a recession—that is a central message of Chapters 11 and 12—this adjustment process may take a long time. In the meantime, the economy 'goes through the wringer' of unemployment and recession.

Another problem is that the overall supply of gold depends on natural discoveries. Economic growth, on the other side, implies a continuously expanding demand for real balances. If gold discoveries do not match the demand needs, increases in the real money supply can occur only if the price level declines—i.e. the price of gold rises. Figure 20.1 shows that the gold supply has not been flowing

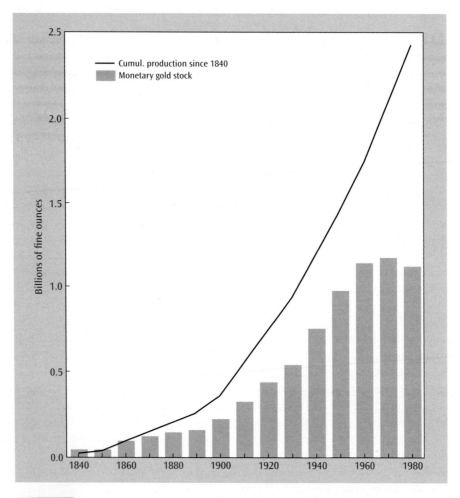

Fig. 20.1   **Monetary Gold Stock and Cumulative Gold Production, 1840–1980**

Although gold production has continued over time, its rate of increase has tapered off. At the same time, the demand for gold for industrial purposes has increased over the past hundred years. Perhaps not coincidentally, gold stocks held by central banks have remained flat for several decades.
Source: Cooper (1982).

regularly, with periods of scarcity coming on the footsteps of great discoveries in California, Alaska, and South Africa, as well as technological advances in mining and mineral processing. As these shocks were largely random, the money supply and the price level were hardly stable.

20.2.2 The Interwar Period

Interwar monetary arrangements can be conveniently arranged around three subperiods. The first ranges from the end of the First World War to the return to the gold standard in 1926. The gold standard was then maintained until 1931, and was followed by a period of managed float marked by competitive devaluations and a collapse of world trade as a consequence of the Great Depression.

The free float period (1919–1926)

In 1919 two countries, the UK and the USA, dominated the world monetary scene. Except for a gold embargo, the USA had never left the gold standard during the war. The UK, under the leadership of Chancellor of the Exchequer Winston Churchill, quickly pledged a return to the gold standard at the pre-war parity of $4.86.[4] In the aftermath of an expensive conflict financed by central bank credit and accompanied by high inflation, the pound had fallen by 30% in 1920, so returning to gold necessitated strongly deflationary policies. By 1921 the pound had been brought back to its pre-war parity, but was still significantly overvalued. Germany and a number of other Central European countries returned to the gold standard only after experiencing and vanquishing their celebrated hyperinflations. France devalued the franc immediately after the war but underwent rapid inflation in the years 1922–6. Its return to the gold standard in 1926 after the Poincaré stabilization marked the return to the pre-war situation, albeit at a devalued parity.

Ephemeral gold standard (1927–1931)

The newly restored gold standard had two competing centres, London and New York. It also had a number of badly misaligned currencies, some overvalued like sterling, others undervalued like the French franc. Gold holdings became an ever smaller part of foreign exchange reserves as most central banks were accumulating dollar and pound balances, while sterilizing at the same time. Free convertibility between banknotes and gold was suspended, and most central banks actively discouraged or prohibited the circulation of gold coins.[5] The Hume mechanism, the key automatism behind the success of the pre-war gold standard, was circumvented. The vestiges of the system were the principle of currency convertibility[6] and fixed exchange rates.

When the Great Depression hit the world after 1929, the gold standard was weak. With its overvalued currency, Britain was particularly vulnerable. Its gold reserves shrank quickly while France, with an undervalued currency, was accumulating gold and selling off its sterling balances. Soon Britain's official liabilities exceeded its gold reserves and it had to suspend convertibility in September 1931 and let sterling float. The gold standard was over.

The managed float (1931–1939)

After Britain allowed the pound to depreciate sharply to about $3.3/£, a number of countries holding large sterling balances followed suit (Table 20.2). Overnight, formerly overvalued currencies became undervalued. At a time when all countries were struggling against the Great Depression, these devaluations were a tempting means of exporting the recession to other countries by achieving a competitive trade advantage. A gold bloc, including France, Belgium, the Netherlands, Italy, Switzerland, and Poland, was established to resist the temptation of retaliatory depreciations. The situation worsened seriously in 1933 when the USA, the remaining centre of the gold standard, imposed an embargo on gold exports, introduced exchange controls, and depreciated the

---

[4] The USA had not changed its gold parity, so returning to a dollar price of $4.86 per pound was identical to restoring the old gold sterling parity.

[5] In some cases, e.g. Britain, convertibility was possible only for large denominations, since the Bank of England restricted its conversion to bullion (as opposed to coins). The system is sometimes referred to as the 'gold bullion standard'.

[6] A currency is convertible when holders, both private and official, may exchange it without restriction. Convertibility does not necessarily imply a fixed exchange rate, since a floating rate system also allows participants freely to purchase and sell foreign exchange.

Table 20.2	Beggar-thy-Neighbour Depreciations, Various Countries, 1931–1938 (value of currencies as a % of their 1929 gold parity)							
	1931	**1932**	**1933**	**1934**	**1935**	**1936**	**1937**	**1938**
Belgium	100.1	100.2	100.1	99.9	78.6	72.0	71.7	71.8
Denmark	93.5	70.3	55.8	50.0	48.5	49.0	48.6	48.1
France	100.1	100.3	100.0	100.0	100.0	92.4	61.0	43.4
Germany	99.2	99.7	99.6	98.6	100.3	100.1	99.7	99.6
Italy	98.9	97.4	99.0	97.0	93.0	82.0	59.0	59.0
Norway	93.5	67.2	62.7	56.3	54.5	55.2	54.7	54.1
Netherlands	100.1	100.3	100.1	100.0	100.0	94.9	80.9	88.8
Switzerland	100.6	100.6	100.2	100.1	100.0	92.6	70.2	70.0
UK	93.2	72.0	68.1	61.8	59.8	60.5	60.0	59.3
USA	100.0	100.0	80.7	59.6	59.4	59.2	59.1	59.1

Source: League of Nations, *Statistical Bulletins*.

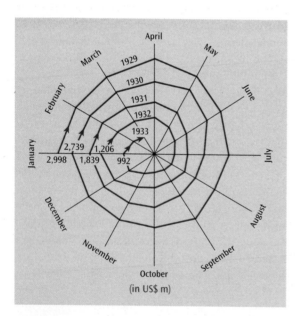

Fig. 20.2	The Decline of World Trade during the Great Depression

During the period 1929–33, the enormous increases in world trade that had been accomplished in the previous three decades were wiped out by a spiral of protectionist measures. This famous illustration by Professor Kindleberger of MIT shows just how quickly trade wars can get out of hand.
Source: Kindleberger (1973).

dollar from $20.67 to $35 per ounce of pure gold. The *coup de grâce* was the dissolution of the gold bloc following the devaluation of the Belgian franc in 1935. 'Beggar-thy-neighbour' policies (competitive devaluations) followed, but were self-defeating since each country attempted to devalue vis-à-vis all the others. The next step was a 'tariff war': each country raised its tariffs to restrict imports, thus encouraging the substitution of domestically produced products. Imports declined but so did exports, as other nations followed suit. While the aim of boosting output failed, international trade collapsed as shown in Figure 20.2.[7]

20.2.3 The Bretton Woods System of Fixed Exchange Rates

The principles

Preparations for the Bretton Woods conference of July 1944 started long before the end of the Second World War.[8] The conference led to the creation of the International Monetary Fund (IMF). The new

---

[7] Remember: $Y = C + I + G + X - Z$: *ceteris paribus*, reducing Z raises Y, but if X falls by the same amount, there is no net gain.
[8] Named after a small ski resort in the US state of New Hampshire. The conference considered two plans published in 1943, prepared for the USA by Treasury Secretary Harry White, and for the UK by John Maynard Keynes. The White plan eventually prevailed.

world monetary order was conceived as the antidote to the interwar situation:

- Exchange rates were to be fixed; realignments required prior IMF approval.
- The IMF could provide loans as an alternative to devaluation for countries facing balance of payments difficulties.
- The dollar was the centre of the system. All countries officially declared a fixed parity, called a **par** or **central value**, vis-à-vis the US dollar, which itself pegged to gold directly. Currencies were allowed to deviate by no more than 1% from the par value.
- Exchange controls and tariffs were allowed only as temporary measures for the immediate postwar period.[9] In the event, full currency convertibility was only achieved in Europe in 1958, and a number of developing countries still have non-convertible currencies and capital controls.

Gold and the dollar

Officially, all currencies were defined in terms of gold. Yet, at the end of the Second World War, the USA held about 70% of all gold reserves and was the only country credible enough to set a gold parity. With the US Marshall Plan providing them with dollar balances, the most obvious approach for the other countries was to declare a parity vis-à-vis the US currency.[10] The outcome was a *de facto* three-tier system, represented in Figure 20.3. Gold remained the fundamental standard of value, but for all currencies this was mediated by the dollar, hence the name **gold exchange standard** given to the Bretton Woods system. The system thus relied on the ability of the USA to maintain the declared parity of $35 per ounce of gold.

The International Monetary Fund

For a long while, the Bretton Woods system worked rather well. After a rash of post-war parity adjustments—including an unauthorized devaluation of the French franc in 1948—exchange rate stability prevailed. Trade expanded quickly and was easily financed by dollar balances, provided initially by the Marshall Plan, then by US trade deficits and the resulting capital flows. The IMF became the

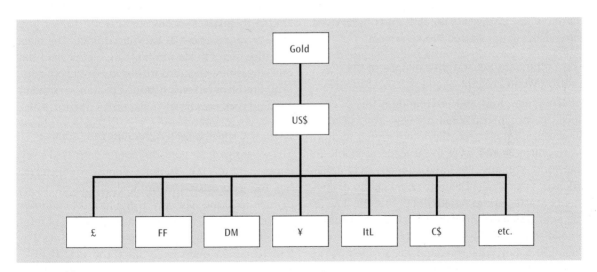

Fig. 20.3   **The Three Layers of Bretton Woods**

The three layers of the Bretton Woods system consisted of gold, the US dollar, and the other participating currencies. The USA declared a gold parity for the dollar, thereby pegging to gold. Intervention took place mostly in dollars, but implicit was the understanding that gold stood behind the dollars.

---

[9] Keynes was in favour of controls on short-term capital flows. The rolling back of tariffs was later entrusted to the GATT (General Agreement on Tariffs and Trade).

[10] The Marshall Plan was a massive aid programme for post-war Western Europe and Japan funded by the USA.

respected watchdog of the fixed exchange rate system. It developed an elaborate system of loans to countries suffering balance of payments difficulties. Its resources were provided by member-country deposits, 25% in gold or US dollars—depending on the country's gold stock—and 75% in the country's own currency. The size of a country's deposit, based on its size in international trade, determines its **quota**. Quotas determine each member country's voting weight and its borrowing rights, and are set anew every five years.

Devaluations were in principle restricted to cases of 'fundamental disequilibria', balance of payments deficits not of a temporary (cyclical) nature. In order to help member nations avoid devaluation, the IMF made, and still makes, resources available for immediate lending—called 'purchase agreements' when effected and 'repurchase' when reimbursed. Each member country is eligible for immediate lending for up to its quota. Beyond that, lending becomes conditional: the IMF requests a formal agreement on specific policy steps and results designed to solve the 'non-fundamental' part of external disequilibria. This **conditionality** has become the central source of power of the IMF, and has survived the collapse of the Bretton Woods system.

The Triffin paradox and the collapse of the Bretton Woods system

As economies grew and international trade developed, more 'international money' was needed. Since the US dollar was the international money, more dollars would have to be made available to the world economy. For internationally held dollar balances to grow, the USA must run balance of payments deficits, just as Britain did during the days of the gold standard. Inevitably, US official liabilities abroad must outgrow the country's gold reserves. Figure 20.4 shows that this happened in 1964. Yet at this point, the USA can no longer guarantee the gold value of the US dollar. This is the **Triffin paradox**,[11] a fatal weakness of the gold exchange standard.

A conjunction of economic and political events brought the situation to a climax. The Vietnam War and ambitious domestic social programmes (President Johnson's 'Great Society') led to increased public spending in the USA, which accelerated growth and inflation and deepened the current account deficit. At the same time, countries critical of the Bretton Woods arrangement began to protest loudly. The French President de Gaulle publicly complained about the 'privilège exorbitant', which allowed the USA to use seigniorage to finance its political activities (the Vietnam War) and economic power (the acquisition of European corporations by US companies at the time). In a dramatic gesture, France began to swap dollars for gold in the mid-1960s, increasing its precious metal stock from $3.7 to $5.2 billion between 1964 and 1966.

The markets took notice. Anticipating an increase in the price of gold, they sought to buy it as it was still cheap. The response of the monetary authorities was to form the Gold Pool (Belgium, Italy, the Netherlands, Switzerland, West Germany, the UK, and the USA, with France inactive after 1967), an agreement to sell gold to maintain the $35/ounce parity. As the drain on official gold holdings accelerated, the Pool pulled out of the gold market and declared that they would henceforth trade gold only among themselves—would neither sell to nor buy from private parties—at the official price. The market price of gold rose substantially higher than the official parities. Tensions within the Gold Pool grew until President Nixon's historic decision to suspend the gold parity of the US dollar on 15 August 1971.

From the Smithsonian Agreement to Jamaica

The severing of the gold–dollar link destroyed a key component of the Bretton Woods arrangement, but the gold crisis was not the sole factor in its demise. Inflation had been rising in most countries in the late 1960s, but at increasingly different rates (Figure 20.5), challenging exchange rate parities that had remained unchanged since the late 1940s.[12] Speculative capital movements followed. Britain and Italy came under IMF conditionality in 1969. The pound was devalued in 1967, followed by the French franc in 1969, while the Deutschmark was revalued. The delinking of the dollar from gold opened the Pandora's box for further realignments.

---

[11] It is named after the Belgian economist Robert Triffin who identified the 'fundamental flaw' of the Bretton Woods system.

[12] The French franc was devalued in 1958; the Deutschmark and Dutch guilder were revalued in 1961.

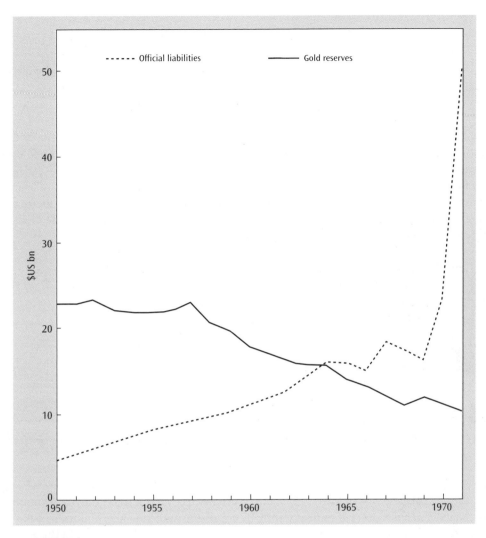

Official liabilities   Gold reserves

Fig. 20.4   **US Official Liabilities and Gold Reserves, 1950–1970**

As long as foreigners were willing to hold dollars, the USA could finance its large balance of payments deficits by increases in foreign holdings of official assets (dollars held by central banks). Yet the gold reserve of the USA declined over the entire period shown, as foreign central banks occasionally tendered their dollars for gold. Sometime in 1964, the stock of external official claims against the US gold exceeded the dollar's gold backing. At that moment, the credibility of the gold exchange standard was called into question.
Sources: Dam (1982); IMF.

The credibility of the exchange rate system was severely damaged.

The last major effort to save the sinking ship was an agreement reached in December 1971 during a conference at the Smithsonian Institution in Washington, DC. The dollar was devalued vis-à-vis gold to $38 per ounce, yet remained inconvertible into gold, even among central banks. Some currencies were revalued, others devalued; the margins of fluctuations were enlarged from 1% to 2.25% around par value, while the European countries maintained a reduced (half) margin: this was the '**Snake**' arrangement. By the end of 1972, the pound was floating, soon to be followed by the Swiss franc, the

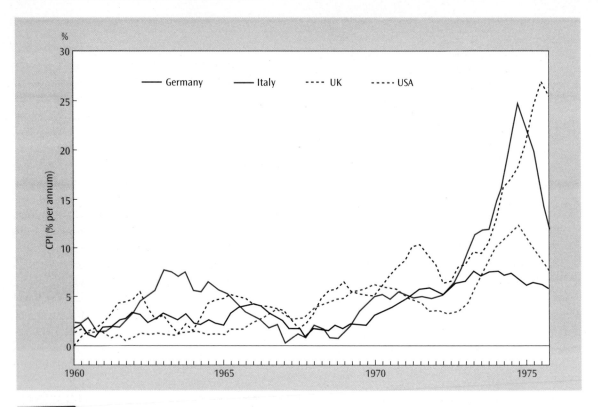

Fig. 20.5 **Inflation Rates: USA, UK, Germany, and Italy, 1960–1976**

Inflation rates during the Bretton Woods era moved closely together, which is characteristic of a fixed exchange rate regime. As soon as the system collapsed in 1971, inflation rates diverged sharply.
Source: IMF.

Italian lira, and the Japanese yen. In March 1973, the remaining 'Snake' members decided to float jointly vis-à-vis all other currencies including the dollar within a wider 2.25% margin. France left, then re-entered, as did Italy; then both left again. Sweden and Norway joined informally. By 1975 the principle of fixed exchange rates was more or less dead, at least for the convertible currencies of the industrialized countries. In January 1976, the Jamaica agreement made official the new role of the IMF: from then on, it would be in charge of overseeing a world monetary system of increasingly flexible exchange rates.

20.2.4 The European Monetary System

For Europe, the Bretton Woods system had offered a convenient, if indirect, way of pegging their currencies to each other, and this arrangement had deepened economic ties within the Common Market, consisting of the member countries of the European Community (EC).[13] The demise of the gold exchange standard posed a problem with both economic and political implications. The response was the establishment of the **European Monetary System (EMS)** which began operation in March 1979. All nine European Community (EC) members at the time formally joined the EMS, but the UK deferred participating in the **Exchange Rate Mechanism (ERM)**, the system of fixed exchange rates, until October 1990. With the exception of Sweden, all newer EC (henceforth EU) members (Greece, Spain, Portugal, Austria, and Finland) subsequently joined the ERM. After violent speculative attacks on the ERM parities

[13] The European Community is the predecessor of the European Union. The name change was officially decided in Maastricht in 1991.

in September 1992, Italy and the UK left the ERM; Italy rejoined in 1997. The ERM disappeared formally with the launch in 1999 of the European Monetary Union (EMU); a new EMS-II was established for EU member countries not part of EMU which nevertheless wanted to fix their exchange rates to the euro; its current member is Denmark.[14] It is expected that EMS-II will be used as the gateway to EMU for future EU members.

Key Features of the EMS

Three original features characterized the ERM:

- Bilateral Parities. Exchange rates were fixed but adjustable. In theory at least, there was no special-status currency, like the US dollar under Bretton Woods. Fixity was defined as an official central parity between any pair of member-currencies: a central rate, and a band of fluctuation initially set at ±2.25%, which was expanded to ±15% in August 1993, following a major exchange rate crisis.[15]

- Consensus decisions. A country could not alter its parity within the system unilaterally. Realignments had to be agreed upon by every member. Despite the apparent restrictiveness of this rule, realignments are not infrequent.

- Mutual Support. In order to defend the parities, member central banks were allowed to borrow virtually unlimited amounts from each other at very short notice. Prompt repayment was required —normally within forty-five days—but revolving credits were possible.

In practice, the German Mark emerged as the central currency. The Bundesbank intervened mostly in US dollars, whereas the other members used EMS currencies more frequently. Germany appeared to manage its exchange rate vis-à-vis the US dollar, leaving it to the other central banks to manage theirs vis-à-vis the Deutschmark.

The Four Phases of the EMS

During the first phase, from its establishment until the mid-1980s, the ERM operated as a fairly loose system which tolerated member countries' diverse tastes for inflation. Realignments were frequent and undramatic, aimed at correcting deviations from purchasing power parity (PPP) resulting from persistent differences in inflation rates between participating countries.

The second phase, from the mid-1980s to 1992, was marked by the gradual emergence of the Deutschmark as the system's anchor currency. Realignments were successfully avoided from January 1987 to September 1992. All countries tried to emulate the mark's strong currency status and identified low inflation as the main objective of monetary policy. During this period, the EMS came to be perceived as a major success: the absence of any realignment for nearly six years was attributed to adroit policy coordination. Emboldened by success, the authorities proceeded to prepare a shift to a single currency: the result was the Maastricht Treaty adopted by EU heads of states late in 1991.

This period of tranquillity and optimism came to an abrupt end in the summer of 1992. During the subsequent third phase of crisis and turbulence, continuous upheaval rocked the ERM ship, and it nearly sank. Not only did several realignments occur in quick succession, but two currencies actually left the ERM to float on their own. Roughly a year later, in August 1993, the margins of fluctuation were widened to ±15%, and the fixed exchange rate system hardly differed from free floating.

The fourth and last phase of the EMS, which represented two decades of European monetary history, an 'ERM without teeth', was hastily designed in the wake of speculative attacks. With 15% wide bands, the situation was stabilized, allowing an orderly transition to EMU.

The impossible trilogy

With hindsight it is easy to understand why the ERM was under duress. The globalization of international financial markets brought near-perfect capital mobility with it, allowing investors and speculators

---

[14] To date, Britain and Sweden have declined to participate in either the EMU or the EMS-II.

[15] Technically, the ERM parities were defined vis-à-vis the ECU, the forerunner to the euro, which was simply a basket of currencies of all EMS members. Bilateral parities were derived as cross rates implied by the central ECU parities. A special ±6% band was employed temporarily by Italy, the UK, Portugal, Spain, and Greece.

to swap billions of short-term assets at the push of a button. A central bank which commits to fixing an exchange rate in effect becomes the ultimate market maker in the money market, and is obliged to accommodate at the set parity all transactions that the market does not. This commitment, as was made clear in Chapter 9, is inconsistent with an independent monetary policy.

The coexistence of fixed exchange regimes and capital controls is thus more than coincidental. Capital controls enable countries participating in fixed exchange rate arrangements to preserve some monetary autonomy. The countries that use capital controls tend to have higher inflation. Indeed, controls may be essential to organize orderly realignments in the face of market attacks.

These policy conflicts and dilemmas are summarized neatly as the **impossible trilogy**. This principle states that the following three aspects of a monetary system are jointly incompatible:

(1) full capital mobility;

(2) fixed exchange rates;

(3) monetary policy independence.

They are, however, taken in pairs, feasible and have been observed throughout monetary history, and even today. The impossible trilogy is a direct implication of the Mundell–Fleming (*IS–LM*) framework: if capital is fully mobile, the interest rate is given exogenously by the foreign rate i^*, and the *LM* curve is given by cumulated net capital inflow.

This principle offers a powerful framework for reviewing the EMS experience. The early EMS was able to survive because of the presence of capital controls. During the first phase, it allowed for the coexistence of fixed exchange rates and some degree of monetary independence in the form of different inflation rates compensated for by periodic realignments. The second phase was an attempt to adopt the same monetary policy everywhere under German leadership. As long as economic conditions did not call for different policies, this was a relatively cost-less way to cope with the impossible trilogy. It is during that period that capital controls were dismantled. However, the shock of German unification and a worldwide recession in the early 1990s, which raised the costs of the loss of monetary policy independence, changed all that. The crises that followed correspond to the travails that go with ignoring the impossible trilogy. The solutions adopted—free floating in Italy and the UK, wide bands elsewhere —correspond to the abandonment of the fixed exchange rate.

Once capital controls are removed, the choice boils down to either a single monetary authority or a free float. The experience of 1992–3 shows that the temptation of monetary independence plays havoc with a fixed exchange rate arrangement. Politically, it was probably unavoidable that countries relinquishing monetary independence in a system of fixed exchange rates would challenge the Bundesbank's leadership, just as France challenged the American *privilège exorbitant* three decades previous. It is not surprising that the countries that pledged to abandon capital controls in the mid-1980s —Belgium, France, Italy, and Spain—soon thereafter proposed the creation of a European Monetary Union. Nor is it surprising that the Bundesbank initially expressed doubts about the urgency of taking a step which amounted to sharing its undisputed control over European monetary policy.

20.3 The International Monetary Fund

The influence of the IMF is probably stronger today than in the heyday of the Bretton Woods system, if only because it is now in charge of a system that is less internally inconsistent than before. In the post-Bretton Woods 'system', each country is free to choose its own exchange rate regime, and there is no agreed-upon international currency. Gold has long been 'demonetized', meaning that it is no longer a reference, and many countries have since sold large parts of their gold stocks.

Table 20.3	IMF Standby Loans: Number of Loans and Size (as a percentage of world exports)

	1970	1971	1972	1973	1974	1975	1976
Number	19	16	18	13	13	15	13
Average size	7.0	9.4	6.5	4.7	14.5	14.0	6.1
	1977	**1978**	**1979**	**1980**	**1981**	**1982**	**1983**
Number	19	12	20	22	22	21	30
Average size	26.6	8.9	5.2	10.4	14.1	7.0	12.8
	1984	**1985**	**1986**	**1987**	**1988**	**1989**	**1990**
Number	21	25	22	11	15	12	12
Average size	9.5	5.7	5.8	11.0	8.3	7.3	6.8
	1991	**1992**	**1993**	**1994**	**1995**	**1996**	**1997**
Number	20	16	13	18	21	13	10
Average size	11.5	7.6	4.5	4.8	25.7	7.1	64.5

Source: De Gregorio et al. (1999).

20.3.1 **IMF Assistance and Conditionality**

Countries continue to occasionally face balance of payment problems, although they are somewhat different from the Bretton Woods era. In principle, countries are now free to depreciate their currencies in response to adverse shocks, and over the longer haul, such policies can bring the current account back to levels consistent with an intertemporal budget constraint. Frequently, though, the authorities often prevent their exchange rate from adjusting to shocks by intervening in the foreign exchange markets, sometimes with borrowed foreign exchange. Eventually they may exhaust their foreign exchange reserves. What can they do then? An obvious answer is to treat the causes, and not the symptoms of the crisis. Taking remedial action, usually moving away from undisciplined monetary and fiscal policies, requires time, however, and the house is burning. The solution is to call the IMF, the international fire-fighter.

When called upon in an emergency, the IMF proceeds in three steps. It first assesses the situation and makes recommendations to the authorities. Then comes conditionality: an emergency loan is made available and the troubled country commits itself to a number of policy actions. Finally, as the loan is being disbursed, typically in several instalments, the IMF monitors the implementation of the agreement and may suspend further disbursements if the country in question is violating its commitments. Table 20.3 shows that in an average year, some 10 to 20 standby loans are arranged.[16] The average volume of loans outstanding represents about 12% of world exports. In 2000, 182 countries were members of the Fund.

It is important to stress that the Fund's assistance is not a gift, but a loan, generally with a maturity of 1–4 years. The interest rate charged is subsidized, but slightly above the market rate to discourage using the Fund as a cheap source of money. Most private financial institutions deal only with sovereign

[16] Standby loans are made in emergency cases; the IMF offers a large menu of lending facilities tailored after particular needs. They can be seen at the IMF website: http://www.imf.org/external/np/exr/facts/glance.htm.

borrowers in good standing with the IMF, so the Fund usually has a great deal of leverage over borrowing countries, which are generally excluded from the private capital market. This explains, of course, why countries in trouble turn to the IMF and are also willing to accept the conditions that it requests. Despite popular beliefs to the contrary, most countries actually pay back their loans. The reason is that the IMF has priority over all other creditors, and not repaying IMF lending means being excluded from all other sources of private international financing. Only a handful of 'pariah' countries have defaulted on IMF loans, and have to pay back when and if they want to re-enter the international financial arena. Most eventually do.

20.3.2 Special Drawing Rights

Despite having lost the official status it enjoyed in the Bretton Woods system, the US dollar remains the *de facto* means of payment for international trade and the foreign exchange reserve of choice at central banks. Although it is sometimes asked whether the euro might challenge or replace the US dollar, the more interesting question is why should the international means of payment be any particular country's currency? In the late 1960s, many countries lobbied for the creation of a new world currency, reviving an old idea which had been defeated at the Bretton Woods Conference in 1946.[17] If the IMF could be transformed into the world central bank, it was thought, it could issue its own currency for all central banks to settle their payments, borrow from each other, and intervene on exchange markets. Unsurprisingly the USA, the Fund's largest shareholder—with a veto right—objected.

With the objective of increasing and stabilizing the supply of international liquidity, it was decided at the Rio Conference in 1967 to create the **special drawing right (SDR)**. SDRs can be seen as a line of credit allocated by the IMF to each country in proportion to its quota defined above. Each member country can draw on its line of credit to obtain

convertible currencies from the Fund. At the time of its conception, the SDR was valued at the rate of SDR 35 per ounce of gold, thus making it worth exactly US$1. The SDRs were not however backed by gold or dollars; just like money created by banks, SDRs are valued simply because they are accepted.[18]

After gold convertibility was suspended, the SDR's value was redefined as a basket of four currencies.[19] SDRs yield an interest rate—the weighted average of interest available on the four underlying currencies. Symbolically, the SDR is the IMF's unit of account. As a basket, it is less volatile than any of its components, which has made it convenient for other purposes. Some countries peg their exchange rate to the SDR. Private debt issues have been denominated in SDRs, although technically they are just a basket of the constituent currencies. Some 9 billion SDRs were initially created in 1970, and more were subsequently added, the last time in 1981, to a cumulative total of 21.4 billion. A new allocation was decided in 1997.

20.3.3 Surveillance

The IMF is not just a fire-fighter, it is also a safety inspector. It continuously monitors the macro-economic scene in each member country in order to detect possible risks to its currency and to keep abreast of the local situation, should an emergency arise. Surveillance takes several forms:

- Annual visits and evaluations (called Article IV consultations). The IMF's economic assessments and recommendations, once highly confidential, are now posted on the Fund's website (each country has the right to refuse the release of this information, but that is considered a bad signal).

---

[17] The 'Keynes Plan' envisioned the creation of an international reserve currency, the bancor, which would play the role gold did in the old gold standard era, but which would be supplied by an international agency, i.e. not the United States.

[18] Hence the following quote by the economist Fritz Machlup: 'Now the forward-looking experts of the Fund and the negotiating governments have proved that their reputation for backwardness in economic thinking had been undeserved. All that matters for the acceptability of anything as a medium of exchange is the expectation that others will accept it. ... Money needs takers, not backers' (quoted by Dam 1989: 152).

[19] The four currencies, and their weights in the basket, are the US dollar (44%), the euro (25%), the yen (9%), and the pound (12%) reflecting their international use. The weights are revised every five years.

Box 20.2   How the IMF is Managed

The ultimate authority is exercised by the IMF's Board of Governors which meets, in principle, once a year. The governors are the finance ministers of all member countries. Voting is in proportion to each country's quota. The Board delegates managing authority to the Board of Executive Directors. There are twenty-four executive directors. The largest-quota countries (the USA, the UK, Germany, France, Japan, Russia, and Saudi Arabia) have one executive director each, while the other executive directors represent several countries, grouped along regional lines. The executive directors select the Managing Director to run the professional staff. All decisions are taken by the Board of Executive Directors who cast votes in the name of each country according to its quota. In this way the Executive Directors represent the interests of their countries, while the staff and the Managing Director represent the institution. Table 20.4 displays the voting rights of some countries.

Table 20.4   IMF Votes in 2001 (%)

	Votes
USA	17.30
UK	5.01
Germany	6.06
France	5.01
Japan	6.20
Saudi Arabia	3.26
Italy	3.29
Canada	2.97
Netherlands	2.41
Belgium	2.15
Spain	1.43
Sweden	1.13
Industrial Countries	59.77
Asia	9.48
Africa	8.59

Source: IMF.

- Twice a year, the IMF publishes the *World Economic Outlook* which outlines its views of the situation in member countries.

- For countries which are in difficult situations, the IMF conducts 'enhanced surveillance', which means more frequent evaluations and recommendations.

- For countries which have borrowed from the Fund, the so-called programme countries, the monitoring is more or less permanent, based on agreed-upon targets for policies and outcomes.

Each government knows that its policies are monitored and that the conclusions are presented to the Executive Board of the Fund in a procedure described in Box 20.2. Surveillance is justified as a preventative means of avoiding disruptive policies that wrecked the world economy during the interwar period. When countries pursue economic policies that are criticized by the IMF, this disapproval is noticed by the outside world and usually results in internal and external political and financial pressure, which can go far in correcting aberrant policies.

20.4   Currency Crises

20.4.1 Crises, Crises

Over the 1990s, the world has become globalized, meaning that trade and financial integration has accelerated, among other things. Long-standing trade barriers were brought down, as many countries (especially in Latin America and Asia) which had long protected themselves from international competition shifted gears and have become fierce competitors themselves. They also opened up their financial accounts, establishing full currency convertibility and allowing almost complete capital mobility. These liberalization moves were first met by successes: growth picked up, often led by exports and fed by very sizeable capital inflows. Figure 20.6 shows the case of Thailand, one of the East Asian tigers.

Then something very ugly happened in many emerging market economies. Capital flows reversed themselves, first slowly, then in a panic rush for exit. The authorities scrambled to defend their currencies, quickly exhausted initially plentiful reserves, and then threw in the towel. The result was a string of massive depreciations (some in the order of 50%). Indebted local firms and banks which had borrowed in foreign currency, mostly dollars, saw their debts double overnight, making them effectively bankrupt. Domestic and foreign speculators sold the shares of indebted companies on the local stock markets and parked the proceeds in foreign exchange, doubling the pressure on the beleaguered countries. Many economies have simply folded, plunging millions of bewildered people into unemployment and poverty.

Such **boom-and-bust** cycles are nothing terribly new. They have been observed in Chile in 1982, in Mexico in 1986 and again in 1995, in Thailand in 1997, from where it spread to Korea, Indonesia, and the Philippines, then on to Russia in 1998. It had also happened, in a milder way, in the UK in 1991 and in Finland and Sweden in 1992–3.

Boom-and-bust cycles share a number of common features. The boom starts with liberalization. It attracts foreign investment which feeds growth. Growth becomes too rapid to be sustainable, and soon inflationary pressures arise. The authorities, on the other hand, are so pleased that they overlook the growing overvaluation of the exchange rate; who wants to spoil the party with a devaluation? These easy years are usually characterized by unbounded optimism and laxity, and considerable risk-taking. Domestic banks have little trouble obtaining funds from abroad in foreign currencies and lend them on freely in domestic currency. Governments too often borrow abroad in foreign currency, getting better interest rates and betting on the continuation of the miracle. The IMF is either as optimistic as the local authorities, or is a voice in the wilderness as its

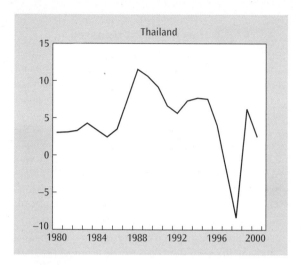

Fig. 20.6 **The Thai Boom and Bust**

Growth, already fast, picked up speed in the 1990s, spurred by massive capital inflows. When these flows reversed direction in 1997, the currency collapsed and the economy went into a tailspin.
Source: World Bank and Bank of Thailand.

danger warnings go unheeded. International investors marvel at their successes, but keep a critical eye on the situation.

Then something happens. The current account deficit deepens too much, or some miracle country elsewhere in the world stumbles. Then the investors move out faster than they came, accompanied if not preceded by local investors. The crisis erupts and output falls, often deeply. As Figure 20.6 illustrates, growth eventually returns, and often surprisingly fast. Yet confidence of citizens in free markets has been badly shaken, governments have fallen, things may never be the same again. The remarkable thing is that things can get so bad after having been so good.

Why do crises occur, then? Crises are like automobile accidents: they seem to happen randomly and unexpectedly, but this is generally not the case. A first class of explanations maintains that dangerous drivers are more likely to have more accidents. Not only can we see the accidents coming, but we can do something to prevent them, either by sending bad drivers to school or increasing the penalties for hazardous practices. This is the **first generation** theory of crises. The **second generation** theory is more subtle: it holds that crises can occur even among good drivers, merely because they are *expected* to occur. While impeccable drivers may be reasonably immune to such accidents, most of the average ones may not be.

20.4.2 First Generation Crises

The first generation theory sees crises as the outcome of a conflict between policies and a fixed exchange rate regime. We already know from Chapter 11 that, with perfect capital mobility, monetary policy must be fully dedicated to the fixed exchange rate if that is the chosen regime. Not all governments recognize this point, however. They may let the domestic supply of money grow too fast, perhaps because this looks like an easy way to finance a budget deficit. We know what happens next: interest rates decline and capital flows out. If the flow is not too large, because of limitations to capital mobility or because real-life markets are a bit more hesitant than theory claims, the authorities believe that they can have the cake and eat it too, expanding money domestically, buying it back on the foreign exchange markets to keep up the peg, and sterilizing to keep things going.

Figure 20.7 tells the story as it occurs over time. Recall from Chapter 8 that the asset side of the monetary base is the sum of the central bank's foreign exchange reserves and domestic credit ($M = R + D$). The central bank intervenes on the open market to increase the amount of domestic credit that it offers to commercial banks: this is the upward sloping trajectory of D. The derived demand for the monetary base is driven by the public's preferences, the now familiar *LM* condition:[20]

(20.1) $M = R + D = \mathcal{L}(i)$

where we ignore the evolution of output since it moves slowly over the horizon of interest here, which is measured in weeks or days. For the same reason we assume that the price level is constant and index it as $P = 1$. The nominal interest rate is driven

[20] For simplicity, we treat money and monetary base as the same, or equivalently, look at the derived demand for the monetary base M0.

by the interest parity condition, which sets the domestic interest rate equal to the foreign rate, after adding to the latter the capital gain to be had from holding foreign currency over the period:

(20.2) $i = i^* - \Delta S/S$

As long as markets believe that the fixed exchange rate will be upheld, if only for another day, the expected change in the exchange rate ($\Delta S/S$) is nil, and the domestic interest rate i is equal to the foreign rate i^*. This implies that the demand for money stays constant. But how can the money supply stay constant, when the monetary authority is increasing domestic credit at the same time? The answer is easily seen in (20.1): to keep the money supply M equal to the constant money demand $L(i)$, the central bank has to spend its reserves R at the same time as it expands domestic credit D. This is tracked in Figure 20.7 as the path of R over time. For a while,

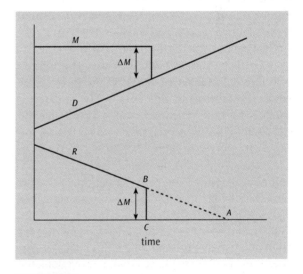

Fig. 20.7 **First Generation Crisis**

The central bank follows a policy of continuous expansion of the domestic component D of the money supply M. To keep the exchange rate constant it must intervene on the foreign exchange market and keep the money supply constant in face of a constant demand. Foreign exchange reserves R steadily decline, towards ultimate exhaustion. The attack occurs at point B, when reserves are just sufficient to absorb the sales of domestic money ΔM = BC induced by the expectation that after the crisis, the exchange rate will floats and depreciate continuously, raising the domestic interest rate and reduce money demand by ΔM.

foreign exchange reserves can be run gradually. Yet there is a natural lower bound to this process: either the reserves will be exhausted, or foreign central banks will turn off the flow of lent reserves. It is crucial to realize that if R reaches zero, the fixed exchange rate system must be abandoned. At this point at the very latest, the central bank is forced to abandon its peg for lack of ammunition. A naive extrapolation of this trend would point to point A as the 'day of reckoning'. After that day, one might reason, inflation will rise, as will nominal interest rates (if prices are flexible) and the exchange will plummet as will the demand for money, as investors stampede out the door.

This reasoning is flawed, however! Market traders will not wait idly by until the exchange rate collapses. Indeed, the message of Chapter 19 was that they attempt to anticipate this event, which in the end might lead to very large speculative profits. They understand that once the fixed exchange regime is abandoned—a certainty given the central bank's known determination to let D expand—the exchange rate will be floating, and depreciating, so ΔS will be negative. In this case, the interest rate i must increase (see (20.2)). If the interest rate increases, the demand for money will fall, and (20.1) tells us by how much, say ΔM.[21] This reduction occurs as agents simply sell their own money for foreign currency. Who buys the domestic currency? Only the central bank, to honour its standing commitment to defend the parity under attack. In the end, the fall in money demand ΔM must be matched by a fall in foreign exchange reserves ΔR.

But when? Buy foreign exchange too late, and the exchange rate has already depreciated. Buy foreign exchange too early, and miss out on the higher interest rates at home which will obtain as the money supply drops appreciably. It turns out that there is exactly one point in time represented by point B, when reserves reach the level ΔM, the correctly anticipated decline in the money supply post-attack. This is the last moment when everyone will be able to swap domestic for foreign money at the still fixed exchange rate. The crisis takes the form of a sudden sale of domestic money—a speculative attack

—which provokes a dramatic fall in central bank reserves from point B to point C, where the reserves have been exhausted. With no reserves left, $R = 0$, the parity must be abandoned. Thereafter, by (20.1) $M = D$, will continue to grow while the exchange rate, now floating, continues to depreciate.

This simple story captures the essence of an exchange crisis. Two aspects are quite striking. First, while it might appear that it is the attack that causes the collapse of the exchange rate regime, nothing could be further from the truth. The exchange rate regime was doomed long before the crisis, its day of reckoning only delayed by the existence of a large enough stock of foreign exchange rate reserves. The attack merely determines the timing of the collapse. Second, no one is surprised. All was quiet before the storm, but it was deceiving. Everyone saw it coming and was just waiting for the right time to act. The crisis was fully anticipated. In real life, of course, there is some uncertainty and things are not quite so clean—Figure 20.8 shows the evolution of British

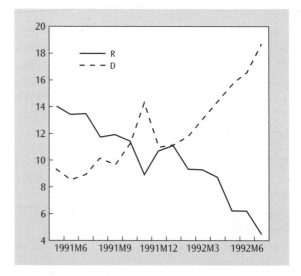

Fig. 20.8   **British Foreign Exchange Reserves and Domestic Credit: The 1992 Crisis (£ billion)**

The evolution of domestic credit and reserves in the months preceding the September 1992 crisis conforms well with the first generation theory of crises. Easy money (a rising volume of credit) made a crisis almost inevitable. As the Bank of England was maintained its ERM peg, foreign exchange reserves were declining. What the monthly data do not show is the precipitous fall on 12 September, estimated by some at £20 billion. *Source*: IMF.

---

[21] Precisely: $\Delta M = \mathcal{L}(i^*) - \mathcal{L}(i^* - \Delta S/S)$.

foreign exchange reserves and domestic credit in the run-up to the September 1992 exchange crisis—but the two conclusions remain valid.[22]

20.4.3 **Second Generation Crises**

First generation crises are the outcome of policies that are incompatible with a fixed exchange rate regime. Some might even say they are well deserved. In contrast, second generation crises are **self-fulfilling**, they do not have to occur, but do so, once it is expected that they will. The reasoning may sound circular, and it is. A simple variant of the previous example illustrates starkly how crises could be self-fulfilling. The central bank is now assumed to keep domestic credit D constant. Given a stable interest rate, the demand for money and foreign exchange reserves is also constant, all things equal. The situation appears perfectly stable and could go on forever, were it not for sudden losses of confidence in the domestic currency, for reasons which have nothing to do with current economic policy. If such an exogenous loss of confidence occurs, domestic money is sold and the central bank is forced to spend its foreign exchange reserves to uphold the exchange rate peg. In the two panels of Figure 20.9 we assume that the resulting attacks exhaust the remainder of the central bank's reserves.

The crucial link in the chain is the market's expectation of the central bank reaction to the exogenous attack. If market participants anticipate the central bank to maintain the money supply at its previous level by creating sufficient domestic credit, then the crisis will be vindicated *ex post*. This outcome is shown as in Panel (*a*). The money supply remains constant, but the central bank has lost its reserves

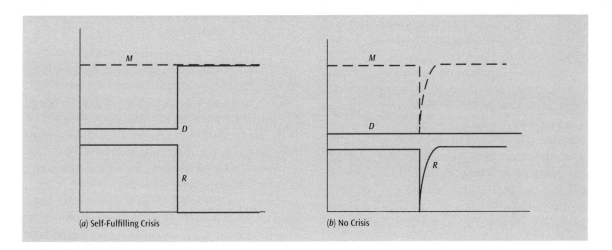

(a) Self-Fulfilling Crisis   (b) No Crisis

Fig. 20.9   **Second Generation Crisis**

The central bank has a policy fully compatible with the maintenance of a fixed exchange rate: domestic credit is kept constant. If a crisis suddenly occurs, it can behave roughly in two ways. In Panel (*a*), the market believes the central bank will attempt to offset losses of reserves in foreign exchange market interventions to keep the money supply, and the interest rate, unchanged. The attack and its consequences vindicate the markets' view that the central bank will cave in to pressure. In Panel (*b*) instead, the market believes that the central bank is much less likely to increase domestic credit, so the money supply falls by the full amount of foreign exchange market interventions. The interest rate increases, which attracts capital from abroad and replenishes the stock of reserves. The central bank proves its mettle, reserves are not exhausted, and the crisis does not occur. The aftermath for the real economy may, however, be quite painful.

[22] This highly stylized model neglects—intentionally—a number of aspects which are possibly more realistic, but don't help us to understand the underlying mechanism. Economic growth, asymmetric information among traders, and uncertainty about central bank policy could all in principle be introduced. That we don't means that the underlying intuition survives these modifications. That is what makes a good model!

and is unable to maintain a fixed exchange rate. There is, however, an alternative outcome. If the central bank does not increase domestic credit, however, the money supply contracts by the full amount of the attack, as seen in Panel (b). In that case, the interest rate increases sharply, which makes domestic assets attractive to international investors, and reserves are quickly replenished. The attack fails. If market participants are convinced that this is the case, an attack is pointless, and will not occur. Both outcomes are equally possible, both are an equilibrium.

Summarizing, if the market expects the central bank not to 'give in' to an attack by relaxing monetary conditions, it will expect the interest rate to rise after the attack, and there can be no attack.[23] If, on the other side, the market correctly anticipates that the central bank will not let the interest rate rise, or at least not sufficiently to attract a sufficient capital inflow, then any attack will be justified *ex post* by central bank behaviour. The attack is said to be *self-fulfilling*: it occurs because it is expected to succeed, even though pre-attack monetary policy was fully compatible with the fixed exchange rate regime. Reserves were not declining and the regime could have been maintained forever. The weakness does not lie in *observed* policies but in the *expected* central bank reaction.

Central to this story is the behaviour of the central bank when the attack takes place. Why should it ever behave as in Panel (a), a clearly less desirable reaction than the one depicted in Panel (b)? Herein lies the true explanation of self-fulfilling attacks. Raising the interest rate is not free, it carries several adverse consequences:

- High interest rates represent contractionary monetary policy. If the authorities do not want to allow unemployment to rise—because it is already too high, or because it is too politically damaging— they may prefer abandoning the exchange rate peg.

- High interest rates may create financial difficulties for short-term borrowers, and may lead to default. A sudden wave of defaults on loans can hurt the banking system. If banks are weak to start with, the result may be bank collapses, which would trigger a run on the money and further exchange attacks.

- High interest rates may also affect the finances of highly indebted governments. The solution would be to raise taxes or cut spending, but if the government is too weak to do so, the deficit will increase. This in turn may put pressure on the central bank to monetize the debt, which means an increase in domestic credit.

The upshot is that self-fulfilling attacks can only occur if some underlying vulnerability exists already. The vulnerability is not lethal, as in first generation crises, but combined with an attack it makes the cost of a defence of the exchange regime unacceptably high. The existence of a vulnerability is not a guarantee that an attack will occur; it may or it may not, and if it does, it will succeed.

Self-fulfilling crises underline the importance of central bank credibility, a concept studied in Chapter 16. Even in the pre-existence of a vulnerability, a central bank may decide to resist any challenge to the existing regime, as in Panel (b) of Figure 20.9. If its determination is known, then there will be no attack. On the other side, a decline in central bank credibility may trigger an attack. The attack may succeed if the central bank's resolve has indeed declined, but it may fail if the perception was erroneous.[24] What is not clear is what triggers the attack, why it occurs in some vulnerable countries and not in others. All that is needed, it seems, is for some smouldering embers to fall on the powder keg.

20.4.4 Contagion

The striking spread of exchange crises in 1997–8 has rekindled interest in the contagion phenomenon. A number of observers have rushed to the conclusion

---

[23] This is especially true when one considers that many 'one-way speculators' often operate with near zero capital: the speculator borrows domestic money at the domestic rate and purchases foreign exchange at the rate believed to be overvalued, and then invests it at the foreign interest rate. When the attack comes, the debt is paid off using part of the capital gain. Nothing scares such a speculator more than a sudden rise in domestic interest rates, since that means painfully higher refinancing costs and often financial ruin. *Sic semper mercatoribus!*

[24] Note that the reasoning assumes that markets are behaving rationally. This stands in contrast with frequent explanations that appeal to unspecified 'psychological factors', hinting that markets behave irrationally. While not ruling this out, we prefer as economists to avoid explanations which lie outside our purview, even if this has its costs.

Box 20.3 The South-East Asian Crisis of 1997–1998

In June 1997, pressure started to build on the baht, the Thai currency. On 2 July, the Bank of Thailand abandoned its peg, which was followed by an immediate 20% depreciation. Speculation immediately turned to the Philippines peso and to the Malaysian ringitt. The peso was allowed to float (within bands) on 11 July, the ringitt on 14 July. Next in the eye of the storm, the Indonesian rupiah too was left to float on August 14. By mid-October, bowing to months of pressure, Vietnam widened the band of fluctuation of the dong, and the Taiwan dollar was devalued. Brazil and Argentina started to feel the pressure at the end of October, while the Bank of Korea started to intervene heavily in defence of the won. When it had to give up on November 17, the won promptly fell by 10%, which triggered a new wave of attacks against the other currencies in the region (Figure 20.10). Stability finally returned when, following the other crisis countries, Korea reached an agreement with the IMF on 3 December, involving the largest ever loan. A conspicuous exception was Indonesia, where a political crisis was underway. The ringitt continued to collapse until President Suharto resigned in late May 1998; by then the ringitt had shed 75% of its initial value.

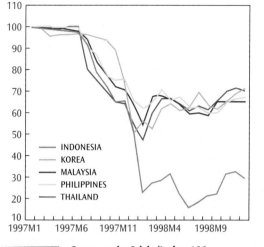

Fig. 20.10 **Currency in Crisis (Index 100 = January 1997)**

The Thai currency was the first to fall in June 1997. The other Asian currencies soon followed, a spectacular case of contagion. When the dust settled, most currencies had lost a third of their initial value, the Indonesia ringitt being down by 70%.

---

that markets are too erratic to be left on their own and ought to be regulated.[25] The principles developed above provide three reasons for contagion. A good illustration is offered by the Asian crisis of 1997–8 which is described in more detail in Box 20.3.

First generation contagion: competitiveness

The Asian tigers trade among themselves and export broadly similar goods to the developed countries. So, when the baht, the currency of Thailand, fell by 20%, the neighbouring tigers lost a few teeth and claws. To recover the earlier competitiveness, they would need a painful decline of local currency prices and compressed profits, or an exchange rate depreciation. Thus trade competition works as a natural channel for contagion. This story is remarkably similar to the interwar period described in Section 20.2.3.

[25] The issue of capital controls, and of the Tobin tax, is taken up in Section 20.5.2 below.

Second generation contagion: learning to know central banks and vulnerabilities

Self-fulfilling crises can occur if doubts persist about a central bank's resolve in the event of a crisis. The collapse of the baht and of the fixed exchange regime in Thailand made two points. First, it was readily apparent that banks and firms had borrowed huge sums of dollars, and that the banking system was weak. This made the country vulnerable to a depreciation, since many banks and firms would become bankrupt as dollar liabilities would sharply increase in local currency terms. Furthermore, the central bank was prevented from vigorously defending the baht, as high interest rates would induce loan defaults and similarly damage the banking system. Early reports indicated that the situation was similar elsewhere in the region.

Second, the Bank of Thailand was not in a position to resist the pressure. Having liberalized its financial account, it faced a massive exit of capital that had flowed in during the years of fast growth. Other countries in East Asia were in similar, if not identical positions. Thus a self-fulfilling crisis, long ruled out on the basis of the remarkable growth performance of the Asian tigers, became distinctly possible. The Thai crisis provided the trigger.

Three features of this process are remarkable:

- 'Cheap talk' and 'life as usual' before the crisis. Local and international investors who know the situation are aware of both the vulnerability and limited resolve of the central bank. They are concerned, but no one moves, since moving alone would achieve nothing.

- Herd behaviour when the crisis hits. When the first spark flies, previously concerned investors see their worst fears confirmed. They do not wait to see how events unfold, they make the event by withdrawing their funds in a state of panic.

- 'I told you so', after the crisis. Once the crisis has occurred, the vulnerability that seemed, and was, benign *ex ante* becomes conventional wisdom.

International investors' duress

Many international investors were clearly surprised by the Thai crisis, and suffered losses as they engaged in fire sales, selling their local assets at any price. For a number of reasons, their best next reaction is to move out of other similar countries, thus spreading the virus:

- Many financial institutions, like pension funds and insurance companies, are limited in their holdings of risky assets in their portfolios. When Thailand fell, Asian assets previously considered safe were suddenly considered riskier by rating agencies, and dumped *en masse* by institutional investors.[26]

- Individual asset managers are rewarded for doing better than the market. Most lost heavily in Thailand. Elementary prudence encouraged them to avoid the risk of future losses by promptly moving out of the region.

[26] The major rating agencies have been blamed for not foretelling the Asian crisis and hurriedly downgrading regional assets.

- The other investors, observing their colleagues' behaviour, come to suspect that they do not know the full story and that things are far worse than they thought. They too rush for the back door.

20.4.5 **Supervision**

One conclusion from our post-mortem of the Asian crisis is that where there is smoke there is fire, but that fire may range from an innocuous cigarette in an ashtray to the stove burning out of control. Do you call the fire department (the IMF) in every case? To extend this metaphor: in the former case, there is no 'fundamental' reason for a speculative attack, but under certain conditions, speculative attacks can still occur, and are a surprise (unlike crises of the first generation, which are bound to occur). Could more supervision have helped? One noteworthy and surprising aspect of the Asian crisis was the extent to which sovereign governments were *not* direct contributors to the crisis. A cursory examination of the Tiger economies confirms that fiscal policy was prudent if not tight, monetary policy was under control, and the IMF evidently shared this view.

The big mistake Asian governments and central banks seem to have made was to guarantee dollar loans made by foreign banks to local private sector entities. By doing this, governments reduced the true level of foreign exchange reserves available for intervention, and wrote a blank cheque for bad lending by international banks. This also rendered their pristine fiscal positions a poor indicator of their true financial strength in a crisis. In any case, the world financial system was sailing in uncharted waters, and it was not clear what kind of supervision, if any, could avoid similar problems in the future.

Lacking an international bank supervisory agency, it seems that the best stop-gap solution to problems of financial architecture is to open the door a little bit wider, publish even more information—and do it on the internet—making it a bit more difficult for such situations such as East Asia in the 1990s to arise. In any case, it is unreasonable to expect the private sector to help much in this regard. One characteristic of asset traders is their strategic disincentive to disclose bad news, especially if its truth is not 100% guaranteed. Better to sit on negative information and wait and see. Disclosing it can make one the laughing stock of the market. In contrast, disclosing good news can never hurt—after one has taken the positive position in the asset, of course.

20.5 The Choice of an Exchange Rate Regime

Ever since the end of the gold standard, policymakers and economists have debated the choice of an exchange rate regime. The choice was perceived to be between fixed-but-adjustable exchange rates Bretton Woods style, or more or less freely floating rates. Fashions have come and gone, from Bretton Woods to Jamaica. Nowadays the pendulum seems to have swung back to a revival of pseudo-gold standard arrangements (monetary unions, currency boards, dollarization) which rely largely on the Hume mechanism. Prompted by the globalization phenomenon and recent crises, the debate has also raised the old question of the desirability of capital liberalization. This section reviews the old debate and moves on to the more recent ideas.

20.5.1 The Old Debate: Fixed versus Flexible Exchange Rates

The case for flexible exchange rates

Two arguments favour flexible rates, and two criticize the case for fixed rates. They boil down to the view that it is better to leave the exchange rate to the markets than to the authorities.

- Exchange rate changes are needed to compensate for inflation differentials (the PPP principle). Fixed exchange rates can only be adjusted sporadically, which leaves long periods when they are misaligned. In addition, such realignments are easily predictable and lead to speculative attacks.

- Exchange rate changes are also needed to cope with shocks which alter external competitiveness, for example changing energy prices, the emergence of new competitors, etc. With a fixed exchange rate regime, either all prices have to adjust, or the exchange rate must be changed. With wage and price rigidity as a fact of life, the first solution can be protracted and painful, possibly requiring pressure on wages and prices to be brought about by the Phillips curve mechanism, i.e. unemployment.[27]

The case against fixed exchange rates is essentially that:

- We do not know with much precision what the equilibrium value of the exchange rate should be. Policy mistakes are likely to arise from ignorance, or from misguided political motivations.

- Fixed exchange rates are vulnerable to crises. As noted in Section 20.4.4, only those countries with impeccable credentials (no vulnerability, a highly credible central bank) may consider themselves immune to speculative attacks. All the others may be subject to a crisis, first or second generation, with devastating consequences.

The list of cases of exchange rate mismanagement is impressive. It starts with Britain's painful return to an obviously overvalued pre-First World War gold parity in 1925, to the dollar overvaluation that preceded the collapse of the Bretton Woods system, to numerous cases where thriving black markets indicate that the official parity is off the mark. More recent cases include the decisions of Italy and the UK to leave the European fixed exchange rate mechanism, the Asian crisis and several crises in Latin America.

---

[27] In a famous metaphor, a key proponent of flexible rates, Chicago economist and Nobel Prize winner Milton Friedman, noted that the shift to summer time can be achieved by having everyone adapt behaviour and do the same things an hour earlier, or by moving the clock ahead by one hour. The latter is much easier, he argued, than changing the habits of millions of people. Changing the exchange rate is easier than changing millions of prices.

The case for fixed exchange rates

This is really a case against flexible rates, and against the view that markets do a better job than the authorities. The case is built on the observation that flexible exchange rates tend to fluctuate widely, too widely to be explained by inflation differentials or real disturbances. Two explanations are usually offered, which are not mutually exclusive:

- Overshooting implies that the exchange rate tends to move away from its equilibrium level.

- Exchange markets deal with considerable uncertainty with large payoffs when betting right, and large losses when wrong. This leads markets to move in fits and starts, imparting additional uncertainty and instability to the economy.

For good or bad reasons, most European countries have demonstrated a keen attachment to exchange rate stability since 1945. The fear has always been that exchange rate volatility would hurt intra-European trade and threaten the Common Market. The decision to create a monetary union may be seen as the last step in continuous efforts at keeping intra-European exchange rates stable.

20.5.2 **The New Debate: Financial Liberalization**

Capital controls: the pros and the cons

The process of financial integration, which began in the 1980s and accelerated in the 1990s, has become controversial, if only because it has been linked to the wave of currency crises in the emerging markets. One after another, developed and then developing countries have dismantled capital controls which were put in place at the end of the Second World War, and sometimes long before. The restrictions can take a variety of forms: outright prohibitions of export or import of money and other financial instruments, limits on such transfers, dual exchange markets (one fixed, for commercial transactions, one flexible for financial transactions), and more recently, the Tobin tax which is described in Box 20.4. While capital controls are highly controversial, the principles involved are quite straightforward.

Critics of capital controls argue that restrictions to the free movement of capital prevent savers from getting the best available returns, and prevent firms from borrowing on the best possible terms. Saving and investment both suffer, with adverse effects on long-term growth. They further observe that, by isolating its domestic financial markets, a government can 'milk' them to finance its own budget deficits at costs lower than the international capital market would offer. Furthermore, when capital controls are effective, national interest rates cease to reflect the local economic situation. Since high and rising interest rates signal a worsening situation, they tend to discipline imprudent governments. Shutting down the signal offers relief to governments, but at the cost of a worsening situation in the future, possibly leading to a crisis on the way.

Those in favour of capital controls present three main arguments:

- First, following on an argument initially spelled out by Keynes, they claim that financial markets are unstable, prone to fads and panics. The result is volatility that is unjustified by underlying economic fundamentals, and is costly to firms and households.

- Second, following on the Mundell–Fleming result that full capital mobility prevents the use of monetary policy under fixed exchange rates, and makes fiscal policy impotent under flexible rates, they argue that restricting capital mobility restores the option of using demand management instruments. When applied to monetary policy, this principle is the **impossible trilogy** already discussed in Section 20.2.4.

- Third, saving is a source of growth if it is invested in productive uses like plants, machinery, schooling and training, etc. The proponents of capital controls note that the bulk of international capital movements are of a very short-term nature, aimed at even intraday trading opportunities, rather than long-term investment in human or physical capital.

The link with exchange rate regimes

The macroeconomic policy independence argument has a direct bearing on the debate on the choice of an exchange rate regime. The main weakness of fixed exchange rate regimes under full capital mobility is that in most cases they require the

Box 20.4 **The Tobin Tax**

Back in 1972 James Tobin, a Yale economist and Nobel Prize laureate, proposed to 'throw sand in the wheels of international finance'. He identified two main objectives, reducing exchange rate volatility and preserving the autonomy of macroeconomic policy (see the main text for the argument), and concluded that restraining capital movements was a worthy effort. The proposal was not well received; as Tobin recalls, 'It did not make much of a ripple. In fact, one might say that it sank. (. . .) I realize that I am opposed by a powerful tide. A widespread orthodoxy holds that financial markets know best, that the discipline they exert on central banks and governments is salubrious' (Tobin 1996).

Tobin claimed that capital movements ought to be slowed down. He was not in favour of the market-unfriendly, administrative restrictions in use at the time. He observed that the vast majority of foreign transactions involve round trips of seven days or less, speculative money which serves no investment or saving purpose. He argued that a single flat tax on every foreign exchange market transaction of very small size would deter the unproductive short-term trips without affecting much long-term capital movements which underlie productive foreign investment. Why? Investors compare the returns from any deal to the returns from holding safe assets, like government bonds. To do so, they compute profits and losses from any transaction in annualized terms. For example, a small tax of 0.1% per transaction implies a total cost of 0.2% for a round trip (invest, earn your profit, and bring it back). If the trip takes a year, it means an annualized cost of 0.2%. If the trip lasts less, say half a year, the annualized value of the tax about doubles. (The law of compounding applies, so it is a bit more but negligibly so.) As the horizon shortens, the annualized tax becomes very high, e.g. 10.9% on a week-long trip, see Table 20.5 below. Conversely, on very long-term investments, the tax becomes negligible.

Recently, the tax has undergone a revival both among serious economists and anti-globalization demonstrators. One of the new motivations is the tax revenue that its proponents expect, e.g. $300 billion annually with a 0.1% tax. Being an international tax, it could be used for international purposes: the UN and its agencies, NGOs, etc. It is felt, however, that should a Tobin tax be imposed, its yield would be many times smaller because the markets will organize themselves to minimize the volume of transactions, and also because they would migrate to safe havens—most likely a computer-laden ship in international waters.

Table 20.5 **The Impact of a 0.1% Tobin Tax and the Holding Period of Investments**

Holding period of investment:	1 day	2 days	1 week	1 month	6 months	1 year	5 years
Implicit tax (annualized basis)	55.2%	24.6%	10.9%	2.4%	0.4%	0.2%	0.04%

abandonment of an independent monetary policy. It requires some discipline for central bankers to give up any hope of influencing local monetary conditions, and few central banks have lived up to the requirement.[28] As a result, fixed exchange rate regimes are prone to speculative crises and have shown rather limited survival ability.

[28] One excellent example is the central bank of the Netherlands after the mid-1980s, which almost dogmatically tracked German monetary policy until monetary union was implemented.

The argument can be turned on its head, however. A direct implication of the impossible trilogy principle is that fixed exchange rate regimes are more likely to survive when capital controls are in place. A good example is Europe's EMS: it operated reasonably well in the 1980s until capital controls were removed, by 1990 at the latest; the system was badly shaken shortly thereafter in 1992. Thus the choice is not just between fixed and flexible exchange rates, but also involves the capital mobility regime.

> ### Box 20.5 Exchange Rate Regimes in the Transition Countries
>
> One of the many fascinating aspects of the transition process in Central and Eastern Europe is the diversity of exchange rate arrangements chosen. Here are countries which face the same fundamental challenge: move from central planning to a market-based economy and integrate with the rest of the world, mostly Western Europe, and yet they diverge on a central issue, and often change track. Initially, the absence of market prices meant that the true value of the currencies was completely unknown, which would have argued in favour of letting the exchange rate float and find its equilibrium. But the absence of financial markets, and lack of knowledge to set them up quickly, largely closed that option. Most countries elected to adopt a 'managed float' regime, which meant a floating exchange rate that was heavily controlled, fixed and adjustable rates in disguise. Some temporarily floated (Lithuania), others went to a currency board (Estonia and then Lithuania and Bulgaria), others fixed and then floated (Czech Republic, Poland, Russia) while others increasingly tightened up (Hungary). Similarly, capital liberalization has proceeded at different speeds, with a handful of countries moving quickly (Czech Republic, Poland). The diversity of solutions adopted is a testimony to the fundamental difficulty of choosing an exchange rate regime.
>
> An interesting issue is the future of these arrangements. Many transition countries will join the European Union in the mid-2000s. In principle they are first to become members of EMS-II, which means a fixed exchange rate to the euro. Then, if they satisfy a battery of criteria they are to be admitted in EMU. At the same time they are required to fully liberalize their capital account. The impossible trilogy principle and experience with fixed exchange rates in the presence of full capital mobility both suggest that this could be a dangerous gamble. Some countries may request to retain some capital controls, others may adopt a currency board link to the euro, still others could single-handedly euroize.

Countries which value exchange rate stability should not rule out restrictions on capital movements altogether. Similarly, countries which favour full capital mobility should not stick to a fixed exchange rate regime for too long. The question of fixed versus flexible exchange rates has become central to the accession process of transition countries, and it is reviewed in Box 20.5.

If full capital mobility is considered an inexorable evolution of economic relations, however, the fixed exchange rate option may be going the way of the hula hoop and bell-bottomed pants. The impossible trilogy means that monetary policy autonomy must be sacrificed, but few countries are prepared for such a step that may be difficult to defend on the domestic political front. Furthermore, the phenomenon of second generation crises suggests that it may take years, possibly decades, before the central bank has achieved a level of credibility which eliminates vulnerabilities. In the meantime, the threat of currency crises looms large. The **hollowing-out hypothesis** maintains that the choice of exchange rate regimes is no longer between floating rates and soft pegs—the traditional fixed-and-adjustable exchange rates—but between floating rates and hard pegs, regimes described in the next section. Critics of the hollowing-out hypothesis argue that soft pegs are still feasible, provided bands of fluctuations are large enough or the peg is allowed to vary (e.g. crawling pegs) to account for changing economic conditions.

Optimal sequencing

Back in the early 1950s, nearly all countries operated in strictly controlled environments. Many prices were fixed, some goods were even rationed, commercial banks were heavily regulated, and financial markets limited or non-existent. External controls regulated exports and imports, tariffs were heavy and capital flows essentially forbidden. What a difference half a century can make! Liberalization seems an inescapable trend, and basic economic principles support this trend. On the other hand, liberalization has not always been an easy journey. The Asian crisis once more showed that there can be serious setbacks on the way. Is there a better way of liberalizing? The response is to adopt a proper sequencing of liberalization. McKinnon[29] has proposed an optimal **order of sequencing**. It is based on two main ideas. First, liberalization should start with the restrictions that are costliest in terms of economic efficiency. Second, some steps need to be taken before others to avoid inconsistencies.

- The first step should be the creation of well-functioning domestic goods markets: free prices and abolish rationing. It makes little sense to have free external trade if domestic trade is heavily constrained.

- The second step should be the gradual liberalization of international trade, starting with administrative measures (quotas on exports and imports), moving on to eliminating export tariffs, and then finally reducing import tariffs to avoid shocks to domestic producers.

- Soon after the first step, the domestic financial sector should be liberalized, under competitive conditions. Banks should be allowed to freely set interest rates on deposits and loans, to open branches as they see fit, and choose the range of services that they offer their customers. Bank regulation and supervision should be developed in parallel to ensure the soundness of the banking system.

- Domestic financial markets come next. Bonds and stock markets are allowed to compete with the banking system to both collect savings and finance borrowing by firms and public entities. Here again, regulation and supervision must proceed in parallel to guarantee a proper functioning of naturally unstable markets.

- External financial liberalization comes next. The Asian crisis well illustrates the risks of full capital mobility when the domestic financial sector is not functioning properly. Furthermore, the exchange regime must be appropriately adapted to changing circumstances, as rigidly fixed exchange rates are unlikely to survive capital mobility when full capital mobility is established.

[29] Ronald McKinnon, a Stanford economist, has also contributed to the theory of optimum currency areas.

20.5.3 Monetary Unions, Currency Boards, and Dollarization

The menu of exchange rate regimes has recently been enlarged. A number of countries have adopted new arrangements which were once regarded as curiosities. These 'hard pegs' differ from the soft pegs by the fact that they do not allow margins of fluctuations and that they rule out realignments (devaluations or revaluations). Hume's mechanism has made a comeback by eliminating discretionary monetary policy entirely and reducing central banks to the role of passive *bureaux de change*. Three varieties of hard pegs have been observed which are worth noting.

Monetary unions

A monetary union involves the irrevocable fixing of exchange rates and the abandonment of margins of fluctuation among a number of countries. In fact it means that individual currencies are no longer distinguishable, a common currency may be substituted. The immediate implication is that individual central banks lose any remaining autonomy, although one central bank is needed to manage the common currency. This is a special case of the $N-1$ **problem** spelled out in Box 20.6. The union's central bank manages the overall money supply. Interest rates are the same across the union since money can flow freely. National money supplies are then determined entirely through the Hume mechanism.[30] If a country runs a balance of payments surplus, money is flowing in and the national money supply rises; a deficit results in loss of money supply.

It might seem strange for independent countries to give up their currencies. In fact, it is the logical consequence of the impossible trinity: with full capital mobility, fixed exchange rates imply the loss of monetary policy autonomy. Yet, the threat of currency crises remains: the only way to eliminate that threat is to eliminate the currencies themselves. Since there is no real policy autonomy to lose, the system can only be strengthened. At the same time,

[30] It should be noted that the mechanism described here is somewhat more general than Hume's in the following sense: an expansion of the money supply need not require a trade surplus, but could also be achieved with a capital account surplus (an excess of private capital flows).

Box 20.6   **The N − 1 Problem**

Take N countries with N currencies. There are $N − 1$ independent bilateral exchange rates, as Figure 20.11 illustrates: all the other bilateral rates can be retrieved from these $N − 1$ rates via triangular arbitrage. Now link these currencies together, either in a monetary union or just a system of fixed exchange rates. As $N − 1$ independent bilateral exchange rates are frozen, $N − 1$ central banks lose their independence, and the Nth remains free of policy constraints. In the Bretton Woods system, all central banks were pegging to the US dollar, leaving the Fed with the task of pegging the dollar to gold. In the EMS, no Nth country was designated, but the Bundesbank captured the Nth degree of freedom. In a monetary union, such as EMU, all N central banks lose their policy-making autonomy and a new central bank is created to manage the new currency.

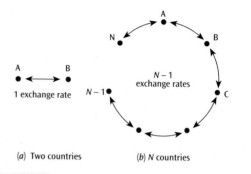

(a) Two countries   (b) N countries

Fig. 20.11   **The N − 1 Problem**

Two countries which decide to fix their exchange rate lose one degree of freedom. When N countries form a fixed exchange rate system, they commit $N − 1$ exchange rates, or $N − 1$ degrees of freedom. (All the bilateral exchange rates can be calculated from just the $N − 1$ rates shown in panel b: all the missing arrows can be drawn.)

Box 20.7   **Optimum Currency Area Theory**

A region constitutes an optimum currency area when its use of a common currency implies no loss of welfare.[31] The best way of thinking about it is to ask what is lost when the exchange rate instrument is abandoned. This becomes problematic when the union is buffeted by asymmetric shocks, i.e. shocks which hurt some members but not the others, for this is when the exchange rate is useful. Adjustment to asymmetric shocks must now take place through prices, which can be very painful. The theory looks for criteria which makes this adjustment unnecessary. Two main criteria have been suggested.

• Factor mobility. Consider the case when an adverse shock, for example a loss of competitiveness, hits a country. The country soon goes into a recession, and laments the loss of its exchange rate that could have been handy to restore its external competitiveness. If,

however, its factors of production could move out to more fortunate members of the monetary union, the pain would be spread out, and the common central bank could use the common external exchange rate to adjust optimally. If capital or labour or both are mobile there would be little cost in unemployment of factors, and the loss of internal (within the union) exchange rates would be trivial.

• No asymmetric shocks. Most of the shocks concern the world demand for and supply (competitiveness) of locally produced goods. If the members of the union produce a similar menu of goods, then the likelihood of asymmetric shocks diminishes. The same applies if the member countries produce a very diversified menu of goods; in that case a particular shock is likely to be of little import.

---

[31] The seminal work on optimum currency areas is by Robert Mundell, the same economist who shaped the Mundell–Fleming *IS–LM* framework presented in Ch. 11.

however, there are costs of a monetary union: giving up monetary or exchange rate policy has its own consequences. In the end, it depends on the company a country chooses. The theory of **optimum currency areas** spells out criteria for creating a monetary union and is presented in Box 20.7.

The wave of capital account liberalization, when combined with the attachment of some countries to exchange rate stability, makes it attractive to move from a soft peg to a hard peg, hence the renewed appeal of monetary unions. Europe has adopted this scheme, which is described in the book's website. Previously, monetary unions had been established in French-speaking Africa and in the Caribbean Islands. Some think that this is the world's future.

Dollarization (and euroization?)

Dollarization is the unilateral adoption by a country of the US dollar as sole legal tender, which can be thought of as a one-sided monetary union with the United States. It could involve the link to another currency, e.g. the euro, but that has not happened yet (it was rumoured that some Balkan countries were very close to adopting the Deutschmark as their currency). It is as close to the gold standard as a monetary system can be, without having gold itself circulate; it functions in the same way, including Hume's mechanism. It is another variety of hard pegs.

A number of countries never had their own currency: Panama and Liberia have been dollarized since their independence. Ecuador and El Salvador adopted the dollar in 2000 and 2001 respectively. Argentina flirted with the idea in 1999. One reason for dollarizing is the perception that a foreign central bank will do a better job at enforcing price stability than an indigenous one. Another reason is proven inability to come to grips with inflation, as in the case of Ecuador. If trade links with the country whose currency is adopted are intensive, it seems like a good idea. It remains, however, that the interest rate is driven by foreign economic conditions, which may be awkward.

Currency Boards

Currency boards used to be the arrangement of choice in the British Empire. They have made a comeback, starting with Hong Kong in 1983, followed by Argentina in 1991, Estonia in 1992, Lithuania in 1994, Bulgaria and Bosnia-Herzegovina in 1997. Currency boards resemble dollarization, except that the local currency is maintained. The three key features of a currency board are the following:

• A fixed exchange rate is established vis-à-vis an anchor currency. The local currency is fully convertible into the anchor currency at that rate, with no limit.

• The local currency is fully backed by reserves. This is required to ensure full and unlimited convertibility.

• Currency boards often hold reserves of 105% or 110% of their liabilities, a precaution since most of money is produced by commercial banks which are not restricted to 100% backing. In practice, it means that the high-powered money supply is entirely driven by the balance of payments via Hume's mechanism. Monetary authorities are completely passive.

With the exception of Hong Kong, currency boards have usually been adopted by countries which have long suffered high inflation and felt that there was no political will to establish a full-blown independent central bank dedicated to price stability. One transition country, Estonia, started off with a currency board, and its success at avoiding inflation has inspired many others.

Summary

1. International monetary arrangements initially arose from the need to provide international trade with easy means of settling transborder payments. For centuries, both domestic and international trade was carried out using gold and silver. On the other hand, the famed gold standard lasted less than forty years, from 1879 to 1914.

2. Taken literally, the gold standard implied a rigid monetary rule and a fixed exchange rate regime. By the Hume mechanism, a trade deficit caused a shrinking money supply, while a surplus meant an expanding money supply. Both processes act to equilibrate trade imbalances.

3. The evolution of the monetary system after the First World War can be seen as a series of *ad hoc* responses to international crises and system inadequacies. In particular, the Bretton Woods system was designed to avoid the competitive devaluations of the interwar period by establishing a system of fixed exchange rates based on the US dollar's link to gold. Nevertheless, this 'gold exchange standard' was not a gold standard in the strict sense.

4. The collapse of the Bretton Woods system was due to the internal inconsistencies of a system that required increasing amounts of international reserves to be provided by the USA, that were in theory convertible into gold. Large US balance of payment deficits in the late 1960s created a dollar overhang of official external liabilities which far exceeded the USA's gold assets.

5. The IMF fulfils two main roles. It exercises surveillance over member countries on a routine basis. It provides emergency assistance to countries which face balance of payments difficulties. Its loans are conditional on the adoption and implementation of programmes designed to cope with the source of payment imbalances.

6. Currency crises can be divided into two types. First generation crises occur when domestic policies are incompatible with the exchange rate peg. They are usually anticipated. Second generation crises are self-fulfilling. They afflict central banks which appear vulnerable or uncommitted to an exchange rate target, or which have not acquired sufficient credibility. They may occur under these conditions, but do not have to.

7. Currency crises seem to be contagious for three reasons: first generation contagion through loss of competitiveness; second generation contagion when markets discover similar vulnerabilities or lack of central bank commitment; and investors' contagion when losses in one country prompt international players to withdraw from other countries which suddenly appear risky.

8. Capital liberalization brings about long-term benefits. But financial markets are prone to bouts of instability which may result in currency crises. In addition, full capital mobility severely restricts the ability to carry out macroeconomic policies (Mundell–Fleming).

9. The choice of an exchange rate regime involves various trade-offs. In the end, small open economies may favour some degree of exchange rate stability while larger countries may prefer to integrate themselves in the world economy at fluctuating real exchange rates.

10. The widespread shift to capital account liberalization has had the effect of sharpening the choice between floating and fixed exchange rates. Soft pegs are increasingly seen as dangerous, hence the fashion for hard pegs: monetary unions, currency boards, and dollarization.

Key Concepts

- International Monetary Fund (IMF)
- gold standard
- Gresham's law
- bimetallism
- Hume mechanism
- band of fluctuation
- Bretton Woods conference
- quota
- gold exchange standard
- conditionality
- Triffin paradox
- special drawing rights (SDRs)
- central parity; parity
- band of fluctuation

- speculative attacks
- $N-1$ problem
- contagion
- self-fulfilling attacks
- impossible trilogy
- the hollowing-out hypothesis
- optimum currency area
- European Monetary Union (EMU)
- boom-and-bust cycles
- first generation, second generation theories of speculative attacks
- optimum currency area
- sequencing

Exercises

1. In Bretton Woods Keynes proposed a world currency, the bancor, and was rebuffed. Later on the IMF ended up issuing SDRs after all. Explain the difference between these two.

2. What did De Gaulle mean when he attacked the 'exorbitant privilege' of the USA?

3. Why can't beggar-thy-neighbour policies work? What is the difference with tariff wars?

4. The poorer countries regularly ask that the IMF issue more of its SDRs and distribute them to support their development. The richer countries refuse, contending that this would be inflationary. What do you think of this plan?

5. Argentina has adopted a currency board in 1991, tying its peso to the US dollar (1 peso = \$1). Inflation has quickly gone down, but Argentina has been struggling with low growth and high interest rates. Why? Critics claim that it needs an exit strategy. Discuss this issue.

Suggested Further Reading

Broad historical reviews:

Yeager, Leland B. (1976), *International Monetary Relations: Theory, History, and Policy*, Harper & Row (old, but encyclopaedic).

Aldcroft, Derek H., and Oliver, Michael J. (1998), *Exchange Rate Regimes in the Twentieth Century*, Edward Elgar.

For accounts of the gold standard see:

Bloomfield, Arthur (1959), *Monetary Policy under the International Gold Standard*, Federal Reserve Bank.

Cooper, Richard (1982), 'The Gold Standard: Historical Facts and Future Prospects', *Brookings Papers on Economic Activity*, 1: 1–56.

Dam, Kenneth D. (1982), *The Rules of the Game*, University of Chicago Press.

Eichengreen, B. (1992), *Golden Fetters: The Gold Standard and the Great Depression, 1919–39*, Oxford University Press.

The interwar experience is described in:

Cairncross, Alec, and Eichengreen, Barry (1983), *Sterling in Decline*, Basil Blackwell.

Kindleberger, Charles (1973), *The World in Depression*, University of California Press.

Robert Triffin's influential statement of the Bretton Woods dilemma is:

Triffin, Robert (1960), *Gold and the Dollar Crisis*, Yale University Press.

On the Bretton Woods system, see:

Bordo, Michael, and Eichengreen, Barry (eds.) (1993), *A Retrospective on the Bretton Woods System*, University of Chicago Press.

Horsefield, J. Keith (ed.) (1969), *The International Monetary Fund 1945–65: Twenty Years of International Monetary Cooperation*, IMF.

On the post-Bretton Woods era, see:

Eichengreen, Barry (1994), *International Monetary Arrangements for the 21st Century*, Brookings Institution.

McKinnon, Ronald (1993), 'The Rules of the Game: International Money in Historical Perspective', *Journal of Economic Literature*, 31: 1–44.

On the new architecture:

De Gregorio, José, Eichengreen, Barry, Ito, Takatoshi, and Wyplosz, Charles (1999), *An Independent and Accountable IMF*, Geneva Reports on the World Economy 1, CEPR.

Eichengreen, Barry (1999) *Toward a New Financial Architecture*, Institute for International Economics, Washington.

Kenen, Peter (ed.) (1998), *Should the IMF Pursue Capital Account Convertibility?*, Essays in International Finance No. 207, Princeton University.

On the Tobin tax, especially the introduction by Tobin in:

Ul Haq, Mabul, Kaul, Inge, and Grunberg, Isabelle (eds.) (1996), *The Tobin Tax*, Oxford University Press.

On currency boards and dollarization:

Ghosh, Atish, Gulde, Anne-Marie, and Wolf, Holger (2000), 'Currency Boards: More Than a Quick Fix?', *Economic Policy*, 31: 269–336.

The website of Professor Calvo: http://www.bsos.umd.edu/econ/ciecalvo.htm

A website dedicated to hard pegs: http://users.erols.com/kurrency/

On the subject matter of this chapter, massive and up-to-date information can be found on the website of Professor Nouriel Roubini: http://www.stern.nyu.edu/globalmacro/

The classic reference for the European Monetary Union is the Treaty of Maastricht itself, or the European Treaty, especially Title IV (http://europa.eu.int/en/record/mt/top.html). For analyses, see:

Bean, Charles (1992), 'Economic and Monetary Union in Europe', *Journal of Economic Perspectives*, 6(4): 31–52.

Wyplosz, Charles (1997), 'EMU: Why and How It Might Happen', *Journal of Economic Perspectives*, 11(4): 3–22.

References

Adelman, Irma, and Adelman, Frank (1959), 'The Dynamic Properties of the Klein-Goldberger Model', *Econometrica*, 27: 596–625.

Alesina, Alberto (1988), 'The End of Large Public Debts', in F. Giavazzi and L. Spaventa (eds.), *High Public Debt: The Italian Experience*, Cambridge University Press, pages 34–79.

—— (1989), 'Politics and Business Cycles in Industrial Democracies', *Economic Policy*, 8: 55–98.

—— and Summers, Lawrence (1993), 'Central Bank Independence and Macroeconomic Performance: Some Comparative Evidence', *Journal of Money, Credit, and Banking*, 25(2): 151–62.

Barro, Robert J. (1989), 'The Ricardian Approach to Budget Deficits', *Journal of Economic Perspectives*, 3(2): 37–54.

—— (1991), 'Economic Growth in a Cross Section of Countries', *Quarterly Journal of Economics*, 106(2): 407–43.

—— and Sala-i-Martin, Xavier (1995), *Economic Growth*, McGraw-Hill.

Baumol, William (1956), 'The Transactions Demand for Cash: An Inventory-Theoretic Approach', *Quarterly Journal of Economics*, 66: 545–56.

Berg, Andrew, and Sachs, Jeffrey (1992), 'Structural Adjustment and International Trade in Eastern Europe: The Case of Poland', *Economic Policy*, 14: 117–73.

Bloch, Laurence, and Coeuré, Benoit (1994), 'q de Tobin marginal et transmission des chocs financiers' ('Tobin's Marginal q and the Transmission of Monetary Shocks'), *Annales d'Économie et de Statistique*, 36: 133–67.

Booth, Alison (1995), *The Economics of Trade Unions*, Cambridge University Press.

Burda, Michael, and Gerlach, Stefan (1993), 'Exchange Rate Dynamics and Currency Unification: The Ostmark–DM Rate', *Empirical Economics*, 18: 417–29.

Chadha, Bankim, and Prasad, Eswar (1994), 'Are Prices Countercyclical? Evidence from the G-7', *Journal of Monetary Economics*, 34(2): 239–57.

Cooper, Richard (1982), 'The Gold Standard: Historical Facts and Future Prospects', *Brookings Papers on Economic Activity*, 1: 1–45.

Dam, Kenneth W. (1982), *The Rules of the Game*, University of Chicago Press.

—— (1989), *The Rules of the Game*, University of Chicago Press.

Danthine, Jean-Pierre, and Donaldson, John (1993), 'Methodological and Empirical Issues in Real Business Cycle Theory', *European Economic Review*, 37(1): 1–35.

De Gregorio, José, Eichengreen, Barry, Ito, Takatoshi, and Wyplosz, Charles (1999), 'An Independent and Accountable IMF', *Geneva Report 1*, CEPR.

Deutsche Bundesbank (2000), *Macro-Econometric Multi-Country Model: MEMMOD* Frankfurt Deutsche Bundesbank, June, p. 102.

Dolado, Juan, Kramarz, Francis, Machin, Stephen, Manning, Alan, Margolis, David, and Teulings, Coen (1996), 'The Economic Impact of Minimum Wages in Europe', *Economic Policy*, 23: 317–72.

Dornbusch, Rudiger, and Fischer, Stanley (1986), 'Stopping Hyperinflations Past and Present', *Weltwirtschaftliches Archiv*, 122(1): 1–47.

Ebbinghaus, Bernd, and Visser, Jelle (2000), *Trade Unions in Western Europe Since 1945*, Macmillan.

Fair, Ray C. (1987), 'International Evidence on the Demand for Money', *Review of Economics and Statistics*, 69(3): 473–80.

Friedman, Milton (1968), 'The Role of Monetary Policy', *American Economic Review*, 58: 1–17.

Garber, Peter (1990), 'Famous First Bubbles', *Journal of Economic Perspectives*, 4(2): 35–54.

Gerlach, Stefan, and Smets, Frank (1995), 'The Monetary Transmission Mechanism: Evidence from the G-7 Countries', Centre for Economic Policy Research, Discussion Paper 1219, July.

Giavazzi, Francesco, and Pagano, Marco (1990), 'Can Severe Fiscal Contractions Be Expansionary? Tales of Two Small European Countries', in O. J. Blanchard and S. Fischer (eds.), *NBER Macroeconomics Annual 1990*, MIT Press, pages 75–111.

Goodhart, Charles (1988), *The Evolution of Central Banks*, MIT Press.

Gordon, Robert (2000), 'Does the "New Economy" Measure up to the Great Inventions of the Past?', NBER Working Paper 7833, August.

Grilli, Vittorio, Masciandaro, Donato, and Tabellini, Guido (1991), 'Political and Monetary Institutions and Public Financial Policies in the Industrial Countries', *Economic Policy*, 6(2): 341–92.

Holtfrerich, Carl (1986), *The German Inflation 1914–1923: Causes and Effects in International Perspective*, Berlin/New York: De Gruyter.

Homer, Sydney (1963), *A History of Interest Rates*, Rutgers University Press.

Kaldor, Nicholas (1961), *The Theory of Capital*, Macmillan.

Keynes, J. M. (1930), *A Treatise on Money*, Macmillan.

Lucas, Robert E. Jr. (1990), 'Why Doesn't Capital Flow from Rich to Poor Countries?', *American Economic Revie*, 80(2): 92–6.

Maddison, Angus (1989), *The World Economy in the 20th Century*, OECD Development Centre.

—— (1991), *Dynamic Forces in Capitalist Development*, Oxford University Press.

—— (1995), *Monitoring the World Economy 1820–1992*, OECD Development Centre.

Marx, Karl (1867), *Das Kapital*, Vol. i, Dietz Verlag (1983).

Mitchell, Brian (1978), *European Historical Statistics*, Columbia University Press.

—— (1983), *International Historical Statistics*, Macmillan.

—— (1998), *International Historical Statistics*, Macmillan.

Rogoff, Kenneth (1998), 'Blessing or Curse? Foreign and Underground Demand for Euro Notes', *Economic Policy*, 26: 261–303.

Roll, Eric, Begg, David, Goodhart, Charles, and Wyplosz, Charles (1993), *Independent and Accountable: A New Mandate for the Bank of England*, Centre for Economic Policy Research.

Sahay, Ratna, and Végh, Carlos (1995), 'Dollarization in Transition Economies', *Finance and Development*, 32(1): 36–9.

Sargent, Thomas (1982), 'The End of Four Big Inflations', in R. Hall (ed.), *Inflation*, University of Chicago Press, pages 41–98.

Schneider, Friedrich, and Enste, Dominik (2000), 'Shadow Economies: Size, Causes, and Consequences', *Journal of Economic Literature*, 38: 77–114.

Summers, Robert, and Heston, Alan (1991), 'The Penn World Table (Mark 5): An Expanded Set of International Comparisons, 1950–1988', *Quarterly Journal of Economics*, 106(2): 327–68.

Tobin, James (1956), 'The Interest Elasticity of the Transactions Demand for Cash', *Review of Economics and Statistics*, 38: 241–7.

—— (1996), 'Prologue', in M. ul Haq, I. Kaul, and I. Grunberg (eds.), *The Tobin Tax*, Oxford University Press, pages ix–xvii.

Glossary

This glossary presents brief definitions of the key concepts listed at the end of each chapter. Numbers refer to the corresponding chapter(s).

absolute purchasing power parity (8)**:** theory asserting that price levels are equalized across countries once they are converted into a common currency

absorption (2)**:** total national (private and public) spending on goods and services

accelerator (6)**:** the positive effect of an increase in GDP on the rate of investment

accounting identities (2)**:** relationships linking macroeconomic magnitudes to each other by definition

active labour market policies (17)**:** programmes involving direct job creation, targeted job securities, retraining, relocation of families from distressed regions, or special programmes to get young people started in the job market

activist policies (16)**:** government policies which try to improve market outcomes by correcting market dysfunctions

acyclical (14)**:** an economic variable is acyclical when it does not move systematically with aggregate output over the business cycle

aggregate demand (1, 11, 12, 13)**:** the sum of planned consumption, investment, government purchases of goods and services, plus net export of goods and services (the primary current account)

aggregate demand curve (13)**:** downward-sloping curve relating aggregate demand negatively to the rate of inflation

aggregate production function (5)**:** a relationship linking total output to employed resources such as capital, labour, and other factors of production

aggregate supply (12)**:** total volume of goods and services brought to market by producers at a given price level

aggregate supply curve (12)**:** upward-sloping curve linking inflation to aggregate output supplied by firms

animal spirits (6)**:** term referring to entrepreneurs' optimism and willingness to undertake risky investment projects

appreciation (exchange rate) (7, 8, 13, 19)**:** a market-determined increase in the value of a currency (less of that currency must be relinquished to buy one unit of foreign currency); *see* depreciation; revaluation

arbitrage (11, 13, 15)**:** the simultaneous purchase and sale of assets of identical characteristics to earn a profit without risk-taking: **spatial arbitrage** responds to diverging asset prices across different market locations, **yield arbitrage** responds to differing asset returns, and **triangular arbitrage** to three asset prices that are not mutually consistent

augmented Phillips curve (12)**:** a Phillips curve incorporating core inflation and allowing for supply shocks

autarky (5)**:** the state in which a country operates when it does not trade with the rest of the world

automatic stabilizer (15)**:** the economic mechanism that automatically cushions the impact of exogenous changes in aggregate demand, via the effect of income on saving decisions

average or unit costs (12)**:** production costs per unit of output

balance of payments (2)**:** a summary of all real and financial transactions of a country with the rest of the world

balance sheet (8)**:** a statement of the financial position of a firm or other entity at a particular point in time, indicating its assets, liabilities, and net worth

balanced growth (3)**:** term describing a steadily growing economy where certain key ratios remain constant, for example the capital–output ratio

Balassa–Samuelson effect (7)**:** the observation that price levels in richer nations are systematically higher than in poor ones; attributed to higher non-traded goods price inflation in fast growing countries

band of fluctuation (20)**:** the range within which the market value of a national currency is permitted to fluctuate by international agreements, or by unilateral decision by the central bank

bank reserves (9)**:** the central bank liabilities (cash or central bank deposits) that commercial banks choose or are required to hold to meet demands of depositors and/or the requirements of regulators

beggar-thy-neighbour policies (11)**:** policies, especially exchange rate policies, designed to divert domestic demand away from foreign goods and towards domestically produced goods

Beveridge curve (17)**:** downward-sloping curve relating the unemployment rate to the vacancy rate; the position of this curve measures the efficiency of the job-matching process

bid–ask spread (9): in the foreign exchange market, the bid is the price at which one can sell foreign exchange (to some market maker); the ask is the price at which one can buy it on the market. The spread is the difference—usually quoted as a percentage—between the two prices

bimetallism (20): the use of both gold and silver as a commodity money standard

boom/recession (14): period of expanding/contracting aggregate economic activity

borrowing constraint (5): restrictions on borrowing arising from uncertainty about future incomes, which prevent agents from taking advantage of their intertemporal allocation of resources

Bretton Woods Conference (20): meeting held in 1944 and attended by officials from 45 nations to shape a new international money order after the Second World War

British terms (7): one of two ways of quoting the exchange rate, here in units of the foreign currency per one unit of domestic currency (e.g. US$1.52 for $1 for UK residents); *see also* European terms

bubbles (9): persistent deviations of asset prices from their fundamental values, or from widely held views about their fundamental values

Burns–Mitchell diagram (14): a diagram displaying the behaviour of macroeconomic variables over the typical business cycle as a deviation from their values at the cyclical peak

business cycles (1, 11, 12, 14): succession of periods of rapid growth and slowdown or decline in which output fluctuates around its long-run trend

capacity utilization (rate) (1): the proportion of installed equipment currently employed; higher rates occur during booms, lower rates correspond to recessions

capital (2): one of the factors of production; usually refers to plant, equipment, inventories, and structures

capital account (2): component of the balance of payments accounts that records financial transactions with the rest of the world

capital accumulation (3): the increase of the stock of capital, sometimes called net investment or net formation of capital. It differs from gross investment, which also includes the capital put in place to replace depreciated equipment

capital adequacy (9): minimum net worth banks are required to have as a fraction of total risky assets

capital control premium (19): the deviation from the covered interest parity arising from restrictions on capital movements

capital controls (11, 17, 20): restrictions on the movement of assets into and out of a country

capital–labour ratio (3): the ratio of the stock of capital to the use of labour

central bank (9): a public or quasi-public agency with an explicit legal mandate to issue banknotes and other liabilities as legal tender

classical dichotomy (10): the situation pertaining when equilibrium values of nominal variables can be determined independently of real variables; the real side of economic activity (growth, unemployment, etc.) is affected only by technology and tastes

closed economy (10): an economy that does not trade with, borrow from, or lend to other countries

Cobb–Douglas production function (3): a particular form of the general production function linking output Y to capital K and labour L: $Y = AK^\alpha L^{1-\alpha}$

coefficient of variation (1): a measure of variability expressed as the standard deviation divided by the mean

coincident indicator (14): a macroeconomic variable which coincides with aggregate output over the cycle

collective labour supply curve (4): the link between the amount of man-hours that workers supply collectively (via wage negotiations or through their unions) and the real wage

collectively voluntary/individually involuntary unemployment (4): unemployment that is undesirable from the point of view of individual workers but accepted by them collectively as they trade off higher wages for fewer jobs

commodity money (8): forms of money that have intrinsic value in other uses, or derive their value from the commodity out of which they are made, chiefly gold or silver

competition policy (16, 18): policies aimed at decreasing monopoly power and increasing rivalry among sellers in markets

conditionality (20): requirements imposed by the IMF on member-countries' macroeconomic policies for obtaining certain types of loans

constant returns to scale (3): term describing a production function in which simultaneous equiproportional increases in the factors of production result in an equiproportional increase in output

consumer price index (1, 2, 12): an index of prices of a basket of goods representative of the consumption pattern of the 'average consumer', using fixed quantity weights in some base year

consumer surplus (17): the difference between the maximum amount that a consumer would be willing to pay for a specified quantity of good and what she must actually pay for it

consumption (2): goods and services produced and sold to households for the satisfaction of wants

consumption function (6): a symbolic way of stating that the aggregate consumption is positively related to aggregate wealth and, if a significant proportion of households is constrained in credit markets, to disposable income

consumption–leisure trade-off (4): the fundamental determinant of the labour supply decision: in order to consume, we need income and therefore we need to work, which means giving up leisure time

consumption smoothing (6, 15): optimal choice by households to smooth out the impact of temporary disturbances to income on consumption plans by either borrowing (in the case of a negative shock) or saving (in the case of a positive shock)

contagion (20): situation arising when one country devalues in a fixed exchange rate system, causing others to lose competitiveness and become candidates for devaluation, even if this was not initially justified

convergence criteria (20): set of conditions that must be met by countries wishing to join the European Monetary Union

convergence hypothesis (5): the hypothesis of a negative association between per capita growth and initial per capita GDP

co-ordination failure (1): situation occuring when agents (households, firms) fail to realize that their actions are interdependent, and that acting jointly might benefit all

core or underlying inflation rate (12): the inflation rate taken into account during wage bargaining to anticipate future inflation or to recuperate losses from past inflation

corporatism (4): the degree to which trade unions, management, and governments work together to achieve macroeconomic objectives

correlation coefficient (1): a statistical measure, ranging from −1 to 1, which shows how closely two variables move together: a value of zero indicates the absence of correlation; a value of 1 indicates perfect positive correlation; a value of −1 indicates perfect negative correlation

countercyclical (14): term used to describe an economic variable when it is negatively correlated with the state of the economy; that is, it moves in the opposite direction to aggregate output over the business cycle

countercyclical fiscal policy (15): corrective device intended to keep the economy near its equilibrium level by increasing or decreasing aggregate demand via public spending or tax policies

covered interest parity (19): a no-arbitrage condition equating the difference between domestic and foreign interest rates to the forward exchange discount

credibility (16, 20): the degree to which authorities are believed by the public to take specific actions in response to disturbances; e.g. credible central bank is known not to tolerate inflation; *see* reputation

credit rationing (6): a condition in loan markets in which there is excess demand for loans at the market interest rate

crowding out (11): mechanism by which an expansionary fiscal policy may in the end have little, no, or even a negative effect on aggregate output and income because other components of demand decline

current account (2, 3, 7): the sum of a country's trade in goods, services, and unilateral transfers with the rest of the world

cyclically adjusted budgets (15): budgets adjusted for the effect of the business cycle on tax revenues

damped, explosive and oscillating cycles (14): a time series is denoted to be damped (explosive, oscillating) if it displays diminishing (increasing, steady) cycles

debt stabilization (15): the process of arresting explosive growth in the debt–GDP ratio, usually achieved by cutting government expenditures and raising taxes

decision lag (16): time lag in policy effectiveness needed by government to formulate policy

decreasing returns to scale (3): describes a production function for which an equiproportional increase in the factors of production results in a less than equiproportional increase in output; *see also* constant and increasing returns to scale

deflation (1, 13): a period of sustained decrease in the general price level, or more generally a sustained decline in the inflation rate

demand determined output (10): when suppliers produce whatever is demanded at a given price level

demand management (16): policy to keep the economy at its equilibrium level by correcting aggregate demand

demand shock (14): sudden increase or decrease in aggregate demand

demand side (1, 12): the analysis of spending decisions by economic agents

depreciation (capital) (2, 6): the loss of original value of a physical asset owing to use, age, and economic obsolescence

depreciation (exchange rate) (7, 8, 13, 19): a market-determined decrease in the value of a currency (more of that currency must be relinquished to buy one unit of foreign currency); *see* appreciation, devaluation, revaluation

derivatives (19): securities that derive their value from the behaviour of other underlying securities

desired demand function (10): total planned spending given the interest rate and real GDP

detrending (14): removing the trend in economic time series

devaluation (11, 13, 20): decision by the monetary authority to reduce the value of the currency; *see* appreciation, depreciation, revaluation

diffusion (18): the process through which discoveries are progressively adopted by various industries

diminishing marginal productivity (3, 5): the tendency that, as the inputs into production are increased, the increments of output will decline

discount lending or rediscounting (9): instrument of monetary control employed by the central bank when it lends reserves directly to commercial banks at the discount rate

discount rate (9): interest rate at which the central bank lends reserves to a commercial bank by discount lending or rediscounting

discounting (5): valuing future goods or money in terms of goods or money today; *see also* intertemporal price

disequilibrium (10): situation occuring when, at given output or interest levels, desired demand is not equal to supply

distortionary taxation (17, 18): *see* tax distortions

diversification (19): purchasing several different assets to reduce risk to wealth caused by fluctuations in the value of any single asset

dollar shortage (20): a situation that was feared within member-countries of the Bretton Woods system in the 1950s, because the USA ran current account surpluses

dominated asset (8): an asset that bears a lower rate of return than assets of comparable riskiness

double coincidence of wants (8): a condition required for barter to take place, in which the type and quantity of goods offered by one trader match those desired by the other

durable goods (6): goods that yield a flow of services into the future

Dutch disease (7): the loss of competitiveness arising from a real exchange appreciation as a result of the discovery of natural resources

dynamic inefficiency/efficiency (3): an economy is dynamically inefficient when a reduction of current savings can make all generations better off; it is dynamically efficient when future generations can be made better off only by reducing consumption (i.e. increasing savings) today

economic agents (1): term used to denote decision-makers in an economy

economic growth (1, 3): secular increases in the output of an economy, usually measured by the annual growth in GDP per capita

economic rents (17, 18): returns to factors of production that exceed the minimum amount necessary to keep those factors of production in operation

effective exchange rate (7): an index consisting of a weighted average of a country's exchange rates vis-à-vis its main trading partners

effectiveness lag (16): time lag resulting from a slow or delayed impact of economic policies on real activity

efficiency wages (4): wages paid in excess of the marginal productivity of labour in order to induce sufficient effort on the part of the workers

endogenous and exogenous variables (1): endogenous variables are explained by economic principles; exogenous variables, in contrast, are determined outside the system under study

endogenous growth (3, 18): an explanation of growth as the result of decisions taken by private agents in response to economic conditions, rather than in response to the exogenous evolution of technical progress

endowment (5, 6): the exogenous resources that economic agents expect to have in the present and in the future

equilibrium rate of unemployment (4, 11): the unemployment rate that occurs when employment and unemployment stabilize, i.e. when aggregate demand for labour is met by aggregate supply. Because labour supply may not perfectly reflect individuals' preferences, this unemployment may in part be involuntary (structural unemployment), but it may also reflect the efficiency of the labour market (frictional unemployment)

equity–efficiency trade-off (15): the fact that improving equity among society's members often has a negative impact on the economy's efficiency

European Central Bank (20): centre of a planned new European System of Central Banks

European Currency Unit (ECU) (20): the unit of account of the European Monetary System and the European Community, and the basis for defining the parities in the Exchange Rate Mechanism (ERM); consists of a basket of the EC currencies; *see* Exchange Rate Mechanism

European Monetary System (EMS) (20): international agreement set up in 1979 to stabilize the exchange rates between the currencies of some EC countries

European Monetary Union (EMU) (20): the planned-for achievement, by 1999 at the latest, of a single common currency for the European Community

European System of Central Banks (20): system including the European Central Bank and national subsidiaries in an integrated system of European central banks

European terms (7, 18): one of two ways of quoting the exchange rate, here in units of domestic currency per one unit of the foreign currency (e.g. DM1.5 for US$1 for German residents); *see also* British terms

excess supply (10): a market situation in which the quantity supplied exceeds desired demand at prevailing prices

Exchange Rate Mechanism (ERM) (20): the fixed exchange rate system of the European Monetary System

exchange rate regime (11): description of the exchange rate system adopted by a country: the exchange rate may be fixed, so that the central bank maintains the value of the domestic money in terms of another currency or group of currencies or it may be freely floating

export function (11): function representing part of a country's foreign spending and therefore following its fluctuations—the greater the foreign spending, the greater will be exports

externalities (5, 15, 18): activities that affect the welfare of economic agents not undertaking them directly

factors of production (1, 2): inputs in the production process, such as labour, capital, or land, which create value added (in contrast to intermediary inputs)

fiat money (8): money which the state declares to be legal tender although its intrinsic value may be little or nothing

final and intermediate sales (2): final sales refer to sales of goods and services to the consumer or firm that will ultimately use them; intermediate sales refer to producers who use and transform these goods or services as part of their own production of goods and services

financial integration line (19): the line in the *IS–LM* diagram defining the domestic interest rate level consistent with financial integration in the world economy with full capital mobility

financial intermediaries (9): economic entities that collect funds from depositors and lend them to borrowers

financial intermediation (2, 18): activity of bringing together borrowers and lenders; usually conducted by banks and other financial intermediaries, which collect savings and then lend them out to those willing to pay for their use

finding rate (4): the rate at which unemployed workers find a job, calculated as a ratio of job finds (per month or per year) to total unemployment

fiscal policy (13, 15, 16): the use of the government budget to affect the volume of national spending, or more generally to provide public goods and services, as well as to redistribute income

Fisher principle (8): the decomposition of the nominal interest rate (i) into the sum of the real interest rate (r) and the expected rate of inflation (π^e)

fixed capital formation (5): *see* investment

flows and stocks (2): a flow is an economic variable measured between two periods of time; a stock is a magnitude measured at a given time

foreign exchange interventions (2, 9): purchases and sales of foreign money in exchange for domestic money undertaken by monetary authorities

foreign exchange reserves (2): foreign currencies held by the monetary authority for the purpose of intervening in the exchange markets

forward bias (19): the difference between the expected future spot exchange rate and the corresponding forward rate

forward market (19): the market for foreign exchange delivered and paid for at some point in the future but at a price agreed upon today

forward forecast error (19): the deviation of the forward rate from the realized spot exchange rate

forward premium or discount (19): price of a forward contract with respect to the spot price

frictional unemployment (4): unemployment resulting from individuals' changing jobs or entering the labour force

fundamentals (7, 19): factors driving the exchange rate; the net external position, and determinants of the primary current account as well as monetary conditions and the degree of price rigidity: in general, the underlying real factors that determine the value of an asset

futures (19): contracts for future delivery of goods or financial assets, including **foreign exchange general equilibrium** (1, 4, 7, 10); a characterization of an economy that considers all markets and heirs impact on each other rather than a single market in isolation

general equilibrium (10, 11): condition of equilibrium applying simultaneously to several markets at the same time, recognizing the interdependencies between markets

GNP or GDP deflator (2): the ratio of nominal to real GNP or GDP, the rate of increase of which is a frequently used measure of inflation

gold exchange standard (20): the system established at the Bretton Woods conference in 1944 whereby gold was the fundamental standard of value, but for all currencies the gold parity was mediated by the dollar

gold standard (20): a system whereby a country defines its monetary unit in terms of gold

golden rule (3): proposition that per capita consumption is maximized in a growing economy at the point at which the marginal product of capital is equal to the growth rate

goods market equilibrium (10): is the situation in which the desired demand equals supply

Gresham's Law (20): the proposition that a money which is more valuable than its official exchange rate will disappear from circulation: 'bad money chases out the good'

gross domestic product (GDP) (1, 2): a location-based measure of a country's productive activity, corresponding to the value added generated by factors of production, both local and foreign-owned, within a country

gross national product (GNP) (2): a measure of the productive activity of a country computed on the basis of the ownership of the factors of production

hedging (19): techniques used to protect oneself against foreign exchange fluctuations; more generally, any trading techniques used to eliminate risk

human capital (5, 6, 17): the education, training, and work experience acquired by individuals

Hume mechanism (20): the process by which trade imbalances were equilibrated under the gold standard system: a trade deficit (surplus) implies a reduction (increase) in gold and money supply, which leads to higher (lower) interest rates, to capital inflows (outflows), and to falling (rising) prices improving (worsening) the country's competitiveness

hyperinflation (1, 8, 13, 16): term used to describe periods of extremely high inflation, usually when the monthly rate exceeds 50%

hysteresis (4): the failure of certain macroeconomic variables to return to their original values after the cause of the change is removed; temporary changes in certain variables lead to permanent changes in others

imitation (18): process whereby discoveries are copied by backward economies

implementation lag (16): time lag in policy effectiveness as a result of the time taken by parliaments and ministries to pass and originate legislation

import function (11): function representing part of domestic spending and therefore following its fluctuations: the greater domestic spending, the greater will be imports

impossible trilogy (20): principle stating that, while pairwise compatible, full capital mobility, fixed exchange rates, and monetary policy independence are jointly incompatible

impulse-propagation mechanism (14): mechanism that transforms shocks (impulses) into irregular oscillations like the business cycle

income effect (4, 6): the portion of change in quantity demanded which is attributed to the change in real income that results from the price change

increasing returns to scale (3): a characteristic of the production function which occurs when a simultaneous equiproportional increase in the factors of production results in a more than equiproportional increase in output.

index (1): a number that has no dimension (i.e. is not expressed in units such as DM, tons, hours, etc.); it is usually set to take a simple value like 1 or 100 at a specific date

indexation (12): a provision in wage or other contracts by which nominal values are adjusted frequently to reflect changes in some price index and to maintain the real value of the contract's provisions

indifference curves (3, 6): a graphic representation of all possible combinations of two items that will yield equivalent utility (satisfaction)

industrial policies (18): these amount to official backing of national corporations or whole industries, taking on the form of subsidies, public orders, or trade policies

inflation differential (8, 16): the difference between the domestic and foreign inflation rates

inflation rate (1, 8): the rate of change of the level of prices, measured by some price index or deflator

inflation tax (9, 15): real revenue that the government obtains by inflation. Inflation erodes the real value of nominal assets and therefore may improve financial condition of the government, reducing the value of its nominal liabilities

information asymmetry (8): a situation in which one party has better information than the other/s about the probability of an outcome, and all parties know it

installation costs (6): the costs of installing new productive equipment

interbank market (9): a wholesale market for money, which brings commercial banks together

interest rate (3, 5): payment for use of funds over a period of time; equivalently, the price of future income or goods in terms of present income or goods

interest rate parity (11, 13): the condition that interest rates are equalized across countries taking account of expected exchange rate changes

internal terms of trade (7): the ratio of traded to non-traded goods prices

international Fisher equation (19): uncovered interest parity and purchasing power parity imply that the real interest rates are equal across countries *ex ante*

International Monetary Fund (IMF) (20): an institution set up at the Bretton Woods conference in 1944 to promote international monetary co-operation and exchange rate stability, to establish a multilateral system of payments for current transactions, and to assist members facing balance of payments difficulties

intertemporal budget constraint (5): the relationship summarizing resources and opportunities available in the present and the future to a household for consumption; the present value of spending must be less than, or equal to, wealth

intertemporal price (5): the price of goods tomorrow in terms of goods today; how much we would be willing to pay for—or sell for—the good today for delivery at some future date

intertemporal trade (5): trade conducted by households and firms across time

interventionism (1): policy whereby a government supports, co-ordinates, and even controls certain aspects of private activity; *see* laissez-faire

intramarginal interventions (20): interventions by central banks within the bands of fluctuation to try to dissuade markets that a realignment is under consideration

investment (5): the acquisition of productive equipment for later use in production; also called fixed capital formation

investment function (6): relationship between investment and its fundamental determinants: aggregate investment depends positively upon Tobin's q and GDP growth, and negatively upon the real interest rate

investment, gross and net (1, 2, 3, 4, 5): the acquisition of new productive equipment: gross investment comprises the total expenditure on new capital goods, including replacement of worn-out equipment; net investment represents addition to the capital stock

invisibles (2): trade in services between a country and the rest of the world

involuntary unemployment (4): unemployment that occurs when individuals are willing and able to work at the going wage rates but cannot find a job

IS curve (10): for given values of exogenous variables, the combinations of nominal interest rate i and real output (GDP) that are consistent with goods market equilibrium

job finding rate (4): the rate at which workers move from the state of unemployment to that of employment; *see* separation rate

job matching (4, 17): the matching of job offers of firms' and unemployed workers

job separation rate (4): the rate at which workers move from being employed to being unemployed, because of quits, redundancies, or for other reasons

Keynesian assumption (10, 11): the assumption that the evolution of the price level is insensitive to aggregate demand in the short run

Keynesian model (11): model based on the assumption that prices are sticky, at least in the short run

Keynesian revolution (1): the development of ideas and policies to deal with situations where price and/or wage rigidities lead to recessions; these ideas stand in opposition to (neo)classical economics, which holds that markets are able to take care of themselves

(Keynesian) demand multiplier (11): a ratio indicating the effect of increases in exogenous components of aggregate demand on total aggregate demand

Keynesianism (10, 16): the view that government demand management policy should play a key role in macroeconomic policy: Keynesians hold that markets suffer from imperfections—for example slow clearing of labour and product markets—which are responsible for the occasional underutilization of resources

labour (1): factor of production, usually measured in man-hours, i.e. the total number of hours worked in a firm, an industry, or a country

labour and profit shares (1, 3): the labour or wage share is the fraction of total income paid to workers; the profit share is that going to the owners of capital

labour demand (4): the relationship linking the number of man-hours that firms wish to hire and the cost of labour

labour force (4): the total number of individuals who are either working or actively looking for a job

labour force participation (1, 4): the proportion of working-age people who are in the labour force

labour supply, individual and aggregate (4): the relationship linking the wage rate and the number of hours that employees are ready to work: aggregate supply refers to the overall behaviour of the labour force, while establishing that workers are interested in providing more working hours, and firms will want to use fewer man-hours, when the real hourly wage rate increases

labour tax wedge (17): the difference between labour's cost to firms and wages actually received by workers

Laffer curve (17, 18): the relationship between government tax revenues and the average tax rate: beyond some point, increases in tax rates are associated with decreases in tax revenues, because the distortionary effects outweigh the revenue gained

laissez-faire (1): term used to describe the view that properly functioning markets will deliver the best possible social outcome, and that intervention by the government in economic affairs should be rejected; *see* interventionism

leading and lagging indicator (14): a macroeconomic variable which systematically leads (lags) aggregate output over the cycle

leakages (11): part of income not respent in the circular flow of income and expenditure, either as private savings, taxes, or imports

learning-by-doing (18): the on-the-job adoption of new technologies

legal tender (8, 9): money that is mandated by law to be accepted in the payment for goods and services

leisure (4): time spent not working

lender of last resort (9): the central bank, in its implicit commitment to protect bank customers by providing failing banks with sufficient monetary base to prevent collapse

life-cycle theory (6): theory that consumption choices are made with a planning horizon equal to the individual's expected remaining lifetime; that an individual will build up savings during working years and exhaust them during retirement years

LM curve (10): for given values of the exogenous variables and the price level, the combinations of real output (GDP) and interest rates for which the money market is in equilibrium

long-run aggregate supply (12): the vertical line in inflation–output space, showing that real and nominal variables do not influence each other in the long run

long waves (18): theories that identify the existence of very long cycles in economic growth, largely based on technological discoveries and their slow diffusion

Lucas critique (16): the hypothesis that households and firms incorporate perceptions of the policy regime in their behaviour; as a result, shifts in the policy regime can have fundamental effects on behaviour

Lundberg lag (14): assumption that output responds to spending with a lag, on the hypothesis that firms react initially to sudden changes in demand not by changing production, but by running down inventories

man-hours (4): a measure of labour input which is equal to the number of people employed times the average number of hours spent working

marginal cost of capital (6): the cost of an additional increment to productive capacity

marginal productivity of capital (6): additional output produced by employing an additional unit of capital in the production process

marginal productivity of labour (4, 12): additional output produced by employing an additional unit of labour in the production process

marginal rate of substitution (6): the rate at which one commodity can be substituted for another without changing the level of utility

market-clearing (16): term describing a market that works perfectly by equalling demand and supply at every instant

market efficiency (19): the property that asset prices reflect all the available information and risks attached to any single asset

market maker (19): traders or institutions that stand ready to deal in a particular asset

markup pricing (12): the percentage by which a firm increases the selling price of goods above the average or unit costs of production

mathematical model (1): a list of equations formalizing postulated linkages between exogenous and endogenous variables

median voter theorem (16): if voters' preferences are evenly spread along some dimension, then a political party's maximizing election strategy is to advocate policies that are most favoured by the median ('middle') voter

medium of exchange (8): currency or other objects used to pay for goods

menu costs (10, 11, 12): lump-sum costs incurred when adjusting a nominal price or wage

merchandise trade balance (2): the sum of exports less imports of merchandise goods for a country vis-à-vis the rest of the world over some time period

minimum wages (4): the lower bound set on wage rates that may be paid to workers, usually but not always by law

misalignment (19): a persistent deviation of the real exchange rates from its equilibrium value

misery index (1): the sum of the unemployment and inflation rates

mismatch (4, 18): situation arising when the labour market doesn't clear because workers and vacancies are of such different industrial, occupational, or location nature that not enough job matches can take place

model (1): a set of economic linkages, including the assumptions made in drawing up the list of endogenous and exogenous variables

monetarism (16): ranging from the view that the quantity of money has the major influence on economic activity and the price level to the view that money affects only nominal—not real—variables, this multi-faceted school of thought concludes that monetary policy is best used by targeting the rate of growth of the money supply; monetarists reject activist policies because of uncertainty, lags, and government incompetence

monetary aggregates (8): various definitions of the money stock, differing largely by their degree of liquidity

monetary approach (19): the view that, under stable-equilibrium exchange rates, all long-run movements of the nominal exchange rate are due to changes in the nominal money supply

monetary base (9): the sum of currency in the hands of the public and bank reserves

monetary economy (1, 10, 11, 12, 13): the part of the economy dealing with monetary and financial, nominal phenomena

monetary interdependence (11): term referring to the fact that, under fixed exchange rates, foreign monetary policy changes impact on domestic monetary conditions

monetary neutrality (8, 10): term used to describe the fact that money does not affect the real side of the economy

monetary policy (9): actions taken by central banks to affect monetary and financial conditions in an economy

monetary union (20): an agreement among sovereign countries to use a common currency

monetization (9, 15): open market purchases of Treasury bills by the central bank, or, more generally, the lending of the central bank to the government to cover its deficit

money demand function (9): the relationship between real money demand and its determinants: real GNP, the nominal interest rate, and the cost of bank transactions

money growth line (13): is a horizontal line corresponding to the rate of inflation controlled by the domestic monetary authorities under flexible exchange rates

money illusion (12): term used to describe the failure to distinguish monetary from real magnitudes

money market equilibrium (10): equality of the exogenous and the central-bank-controlled money supply and the money demand that corresponds to a particular output level and exogenous transaction costs

money multiplier (9): the link between the monetary base and wider monetary aggregates

multiplier-accelerator model (14): model of the business cycle developed by Paul Samuelson in which the interaction of the accelerator principle of investment and the multiplier leads to cyclical behaviour

Mundell–Fleming model (11): the open economy version of the IS–LM model

N – 1 problem (20): in a fixed exchange rate system with N countries, the fact that $N - 1$ bilateral rates can be sufficient to determine all, leaving one degree of (monetary) independence

natural monopoly (17): occurs in industries exhibiting increasing returns (telecommunications, transport, etc. . . .)

neoclassical assumptions (10): the view that prices adjust even in the short run, so that the economy is always dichotomized

neoclassical approach (10): model claiming that flexible prices clear all markets even in the short run

net exports (2): difference between the flow of domestic goods and services sold to foreigners and the flow of imported goods and services

net national product (2): a measure of national output which nets out the depreciation of productive equipment

net taxes (2): the government's tax income from households and firms after transfers have been subtracted

net worth (8): the difference between assets and liabilities listed in an institution's balance sheet, representing its value to the owners

neutrality of money/monetary neutrality (8, 10): the principle that the money supply does not affect real variables such as real output or unemployment, but rather the price level

no-arbitrage condition (19): the condition imposed on a model that arbitrage profits must be absent

noise traders (19): irrational or misinformed traders who cause deviations of stock prices from their fundamental value for a long time

nominal (1): a variable expressed in value or money terms, as opposed to 'real' terms (i.e. terms of goods)

nominal anchors (16): in stabilization programmes, the practice of setting or targeting one or more nominal variable—such as the exchange rate or nominal wages —in order to hasten return to the equilibrium level of output and to influence expectations

nominal exchange rate (7): the value of foreign currency in terms of domestic money

nominal interest rate (8): the interest rate as quoted on financial markets or by banks

nominal wage and price rigidity (12): the fact that, owing to menu costs, contracts, or customer relations, prices denominated in money do not react immediately to changes in demand, and thereby prevent output and employment from reaching their equilibrium levels in the short run

non-traded goods (7): goods that are not easily traded

normative economics (1): economics that passes judgement or provides advice on policy actions; *see* positive economics

numeraire (7): a benchmark good in terms of which all other goods are priced

offshore markets (19): markets for assets denominated in a country's currency but located outside that country

Okun's Law (1, 12, 13): the observed inverse relationship between fluctuations of real GDP around its trend growth path and fluctuations of the unemployment rate around its equilibrium level

open market operations (9): transactions undertaken by a central bank which exchanges securities for its own liabilities; these operations have the effect of supplying reserves to, or draining them from, the banking system

opportunity cost (5, 6, 8): the value of a resource in its best alternative use

optimal capital stock (6): the stock of physical capital that maximizes the value of the firm, for which the marginal productivity of capital is equal to the marginal cost of investment

optimal currency area (20): a region for which no welfare loss is implied by the use of a common currency

option (call and put) (18): a contract that allows the owner to purchase (call) or sell (put) an asset at some predetermined price at or before some specified point in time

out-of-equilibrium conditions (3): conditions when a market is not equilibrium

output cost of disinflation (13): the sacrifice ratio, which compares the cumulated increase in the rate of unemployment with the reduction in inflation achieved over some period of time

output gap (12): temporary deviations of GDP from its trend or equilibrium level

output–labour ratio (3): the ratio of output to the labour used to produce that output

overshooting (17): situation arising when, in response to a disturbance that modifies its long-run level, the nominal exchange rate moves in the short run in the same direction but by a larger amount, to be eventually reversed

par or central value (20): the fixed official exchange rate declared by the monetary authority of a country

parallel currencies (8): currencies issued by private institutions or foreign countries that are used alongside domestic money

parity/central parity (20): defined as a fixed but adjustable exchange rate between any pair of countries; *see also* par or central value

parity grid (20): the complete set of central parities and margins of fluctuation in the EMS

partial equilibrium (3): the analysis of the determinants of equilibrium in a particular market, ignoring whether other markets are in simultaneous equilibrium

partial market equilibrium condition (1, 4): the equality of demand and supply in a particular market under study

partisan business cycles (16): business cycles resulting from the succession in power of parties with different economic priorities and preferred policies; *see* political business cycles

PCA function (11): function given by the difference between exports and imports and determined by domestic spending, foreign spending, and the real exchange rate

peak/trough (14): upper/lower turning point of a cyclical economic time series

pecuniary/non-pecuniary externalities (17): externalities that are/are not transmitted by the market's price mechanism

permanent income (6): the flow of income which, if constant, would deliver the same present value as the actual expected income path

persistence (14): long-lasting effect of a shock hitting the economy

personal income/personal disposable income (2): total household income after income taxes and fines and fees have been paid; the amount that can be used for consumption or savings

Phillips curve (12): an empirical relationship linking the inflation rate negatively to the unemployment rate

Plaza and Louvre Accords (20): agreements from the mid-1980s between industrial countries on limiting exchange rate fluctuations

policy lags (16): the delays (recognition, decision, implementation, and effectiveness) between the occurrence of a situation calling for policy action and the ultimate effect of that action; may actually exacerbate rather than smooth economic fluctuations

policy mix (11): the joint use of monetary and fiscal policies

policy regime (11, 16): explicitly or implicitly established set of rules of governments

political business cycles (16): business cycles resulting from the use of macroeconomic policies to improve the state of the economy just before elections; *see* partisan business cycles

position (long or short) (19): a trader is long in a given currency when she owns, or has contracted to receive, that currency in the future; similarly, a trader is short when she has contracted to make payment in a foreign currency at some future time

positive economics (1): the description and explanation of economic phenomena; *see* normative economics

poverty trap (3): a situation where a country cannot enter a phase of sustained growth

PPP (purchasing power parity) line (13): a horizontal line corresponding to the foreign inflation rate, because at fixed exchange rates purchasing power parity rules out permanent differences between domestic and foreign inflation

preferences (3): the way we describe an individual's behaviour when faced with alternative spending opportunities

present discounted value (5): the value of a stream of income or spending spread over time and valued at today's price; *see also* intertemporal price

price level (1): the average level of prices in an economy

price line (7): graphic description of the relative price of two goods

primary budget deficit (5): the budget deficit net of debt service (i.e. net of the payment of interest on the public debt)

primary current account (5): the current account less net interest payments (net investment income); alternatively, the difference between gross domestic product output and aggregate domestic spending when unilateral transfers are equal to zero

primary current account function (6, 7): the relationship linking the primary current account positively to the real exchange rate and negatively to the level of GDP or income

primary government budget surplus (5): the excess of government tax revenues over non-interest expenditures, or, equivalently, the excess of net taxes plus interest payments over government purchases of goods and services

privatization (1, 17): the sale or transfer of part or all of state-owned enterprises to the private sector

procyclical (14): an economic variable that it is positively correlated with the state of the economy; that is, it moves in the same direction as aggregate output

producer surplus (17): difference between the price that a producer actually receives for a given quantity of goods and the amount corresponding to the minimum price at which he would be willing to supply the same quantity

production function (3, 4, 5): theoretical relationship linking aggregate output to inputs of factors of production

productive efficiency (15): the optimal use of available productive resources

productivity growth slow-down (3): the downturn of total factor productivity growth observed since the mid-1970s despite the developments of new technologies

profit share (4): the proportion of GDP paid out to shareholders

progressive tax (17): tax system in which the tax rate is increasing with the (pre-tax) income level

property rights (18): rights to private ownership. The absence of effective enforcement of property rights stunts economic growth

public goods (8, 15, 18): goods and services that are provided free of charge and the consumption of which by one person does not prevent the consumption by another person (characterized by non-excludability and non-rivalry)

purchasing power parity (PPP) (7, 8, 13): principle asserting that the rate of nominal exchange rate depreciation is equal to the difference between the domestic and foreign inflation rates; a stronger (and less plausible) absolute form of PPP equates price levels across countries when expressed in a common currency

q-theory of investment (6): theory linking investment to Tobin's q, the ratio of firms' market value to the replacement cost of installed capital

quits (4): voluntary separations from jobs on the part of the employee

quota (IMF) (20): a country's voting and borrowing rights in the IMF, based on its initial deposit upon joining

Ramsey principle of public finance (17): principle that, for a given amount of revenue to be raised, goods with the most inelastic demands and supplies should be taxed most heavily in order to minimize overall loss of consumer and producer surplus in an economy

random walk (19): a variable that changes randomly from period to period, where the only change between its value today and its value tomorrow will be white noise and can be positive or negative

rate of capacity utilization (1): measure of the degree to which firms employ their plants and equipment; one indicator of cyclical conditions

rational expectations hypothesis (5): hypothesis asserting that agents evaluate future events using all available information efficiently so that they do not make systematic forecasting errors

real (1): a variable expressed in volume, adjusted from its nominal counterpart to take account of inflation

real business cycle theory (14): theory of the business cycle which explains economic fluctuations primarily as a consequence of technology shocks assuming price flexibility

real consumption wage (4): the ratio of nominal wages to the consumer price index; a measure of the price of leisure (or the return to work) in terms of consumption goods

real economy (1, 10, 11, 12, 13): term referring to the production and consumption of goods and services, and the incomes associated with productive activities; *see* monetary economy

real exchange rate (7): the cost of foreign goods in terms of domestic goods, defined as the nominal exchange rate adjusted by prices at home and abroad

real interest parity (19): the difference between domestic and foreign real interest rates, which is equal to the corresponding nominal differential less the expected inflation differential

real interest rate (8): the difference between the nominal interest rate and the expected rate of inflation

real wage rigidity (4, 12): rigidity arising when unemployment fails to cause real wages to decline

recognition lag (16): time lag in discovering that policy intervention is called for

relative price (7): the price of one good in terms of another, usually computed as the ratio of two nominal prices

relative purchasing power parity (8): situation occurring when the cost of the same basket of goods in different countries increases at the same rate once converted into a common currency

reputation (16): the effect on the public of self-imposed rules by the government to refrain from some actions, even if at some point such actions are highly desirable

reserves ratio (9): the ratio of a commercial bank's reserves (vault cash or deposits at the central bank) to the total demand deposits it has issued

returns to scale (3): the impact on output of an increase in all inputs by the same proportion: if output increases equiproportionally, the production function is said to exhibit constant returns to scale; if output increases more or less than proportionally, we have respectively increasing or decreasing returns to scale

revaluation (11, 13, 20): decision by the monetary authority to increase the value of the currency; *see* appreciation, depreciation, devaluation

Ricardian equivalence (5): hypothesis that the time profile of taxes needed to finance a given stream of government purchases has no effect on agents' intertemporal budget constraint and therefore on real spending and saving decisions; then public debt is not considered as private wealth

risk averse (19): behaviour characterized by a preference to avoid risk

risk neutral (19): behaviour characterized by an indifference to risk

risk premium (18, 19): compensation above and beyond the expected rate of return on an asset required by agents to hold it

Robertson lag (14): assumption that current spending is related to past income

rules vs. discretion (16): legal rules are established to rule out time-inconsistent discretionary government policies

saving (2): postponement of consumption using some part of disposable personal income

seigniorage (9, 15, 20): exploitation by the government of the monopoly power of the central bank to create money as a means of raising real resources

self-fulfilling attacks (20): exchange rate attacks that are not justified by the exchange rate fundamentals, but occur because, if they succeed, the authorities will relax monetary policy, proving the attack to be rational *ex post*

separation rate (4): the rate at which employed workers become unemployed per unit of time; *see*: job-finding rate

severance payments (4): compensation, usually in the form of lump-sum cash payments, paid by employers to workers who are made redundant for economic reasons

small-country assumption (11): working assumption that real and financial conditions abroad are unaffected by domestic economic developments and that the 'foreign' rate of return is exogenous

'Snake' (20): arrangement between EC countries during the final years of the Bretton Woods System to stick to a reduced (half) margin

soft budget constraint (15): expression used to describe the situation of state-owned firms whose losses are automatically covered by the government budget

Solow decomposition (3): the three-way decomposition of the sources of economic growth into capital accumulation, increase in labour utilization, and the Solow residual capturing technological progress

Solow growth model (3): a theory that analyses growth as being driven by exogenous technological change and the accumulation of factors of production

Solow residual (3): the part of GDP growth unexplained by the increase in factors of production and conventionally ascribed to technological progress

spatial arbitrage (19): arbitrage that occurs when investors identify a divergence of prices of identical assets in different market locations; *see* arbitrage

special drawing rights (SDRs) (20): a reserve money created by the IMF in 1967 and allocated on the basis of quotas; used among central banks as an additional source of liquidity

speculative attacks (20): sudden loss of foreign exchange reserves of central banks, arising when exchange market participants anticipate an imminent devaluation

speculative bubbles (19): persistent deviations of market prices from their fundamental values

spot market (19): market in which transactions are for immediate delivery of good or asset purchased

stabilization policies (15): policies designed to stabilize aggregate income and spending as well as unemployment

stagflation (12, 13): periods when both inflation and unemployment increase

stationary GDP (14): the level of GDP that would in theory result after full adjustment occurs, in the absence of further shocks to the economy

steady state (4): a hypothetical state in which all variables have responded fully to exogenous changes in the environment

sterilization (9): actions undertaken by central banks to offset the impact of a foreign exchange intervention on the domestic money supply, usually a money market purchase or sale of securities in the same amount as the foreign exchange market intervention

sticky price business cycle theory (14): class of theories of the business cycle in which the rigidity of prices are of central importance

structural unemployment (4): unemployment arising as the result of a mismatch of demand and supply of labour; *see* mismatch

substitution effect (4, 6): the component of the total change in quantity demanded that is attributable to the change in relative prices

supply determined output (10): when the price level adjusts freely, so that general equilibrium is always found at the intersection of the *IS* and the goods supply schedule, then output is supply determined

supply shocks (12, 13, 14, 17): exogenous increases in non-labour production costs

supply side (1, 12, 17): the productive potential of an economy and the factors that determine its overall efficiency

swap transactions (19): exchange of sums of money of the same currency but on different terms, for instance selling francs for delivery now while simultaneously buying them back for delivery in three months' time

systemic risk (9): the risk of a generalized collapse of the banking system, arising because banks and financial institutions hold large amounts of each other's liabilities

tax distortions (15): effects on real behaviour arising from the wedge that taxes introduce between the price received by the provider of a good or service and the price paid by its consumer

tax smoothing (15): the proposition that a government should not change tax rates in response to temporary causes of budget deficits, but should borrow instead

technological progress (3): the contribution to economic growth of technological change, usually captured by the rate of increase of total factor productivity

terms of trade (7): the ratio between the price of exportables and the price of imports; measures how many foreign goods can be purchased with one unit of domestic output

time inconsistency (16): characterizes policies which, although optimal today, become less desirable at a later stage, especially after agents have adjusted their behaviour accordingly

Tobin's *q* (6): the ratio of the present value of the return from new investment to the cost of installed capital; often approximated as the ratio of share prices to the replacement price of equipment

total factor productivity (7): productivity in the production process that is attributable not to any particular factor of production, but to all; growth in total factor productivity is often measured as a weighted average of growth in average productivities of all factors of production

tradable goods (7): goods actually traded or potentially tradable with foreign countries

trade policies (17): policies designed to support a domestic product's sales through tariffs on foreign goods, or quotas on imports

trade union voluntary/involuntary unemployment (4): unemployment resulting from the fact that trade unions ask for higher real wages than if the market were perfectly competitive, which may be involuntary from the perspective of individuals

trade unions (4): organizations of workers formed for the purpose of taking collective action against their employers to obtain improvements of pay and other working conditions

transaction costs (8, 17): costs arising from transactions, especially financial transactions

transfers (2): direct payments by the government to individuals or firms not related to the provision of goods and services, e.g. subsidies, unemployment benefits, pensions

trend (1, 13): long-term tendency in a time series

triangular arbitrage (19): arbitrage requiring that the relative prices of three or more assets are consistent with each other; *see* arbitrage

Triffin paradox (20): the inconsistency of the US dollar (a national currency) as a world reserve currency with its gold backing: in order for internationally held dollar balances to grow with the world economy, the USA had to run balance of payment deficits over time which eventually outstripped its gold reserves

turning points (14): times when economic cycles reach a peak or a trough

uncovered interest parity (UIP) (19): the condition that rates of return on assets of comparable risk are equalized across countries once expected exchange rate changes are taken into account

underground economy (2): economic activities from which income earned is not reported and therefore is untaxed

undervaluation/overvaluation (7, 19): a currency is undervalued/overvalued when its exchange is below/above its long-run equilibrium value, or the level consistent with its long-run fundamentals

undiversifiable risk (19): a risk that cannot be reduced by holding a mix of several different assets

unemployment (4): individuals without a job who are actively seeking work

unemployment benefit (4): financial assistance to those seeking a job but unable to find suitable employment

unemployment rate (4): the ratio of the number of unemployed workers to total labour force

unemployment stocks and flows (4): the stock of unemployment is the number of people willing to work but unemployed at a moment in time; flows refer to workers coming into unemployment (inflows) or to previously unemployed workers finding a job or leaving the labour force (outflows)

unpaid work (2): economic activity that is not paid for and is not accounted for in GDP

utility (6): the satisfaction that a consumer derives from the consumption of goods and services

value added (2): increase in the market value of a product at a particular stage of production; calculated by subtracting the value of all inputs bought from other firms from the value of the firm's output

velocity of money (8): the number of times on average that a unit of money is spent during the measurement period (usually a year)

voluntary unemployment (4): the difference between total labour availability and the employment that would result from labour market equilibrium; reflects the fact that some people who are in the labour force do not wish to work at the current wage level

wage inflation (12): the annual rate of growth of nominal wages

wage share (4): the proportion of GDP paid out as wages

wealth (2, 5, 6): the sum of inherited assets or debts and the present value of current and future incomes

welfare traps (17): situations where public subsidies—part of the welfare state—discourage private activities and keep recipients dependent on welfare payments

yield arbitrage (19): arbitrage which applies to assets that are equivalent in terms of their risk characteristics; *see* arbitrage

Solutions to even-numbered exercises

Chapter 2

2. The GDP declines as her work becomes unpaid.

4. The GDP increases by €11,000, 10% of the sale, which is the remuneration of the real estate agent. She performs a service, and adds value. The capital gain on the house (€30,000) is not part of GDP.

6. Disposable income is after-tax income, here 40% of GDP *plus* transfers received from the government, which must therefore represent 20% of GDP. Net taxes, gross taxes less transfers are 60 – 20%, i.e. 40%, another way of finding disposable income: GDP *less* net taxes.

8. It is true that GDP would be higher if these people were staying and spending their income in the country. On the other side, if there is a shortage of manpower, they contribute to GDP (profits, taxes) by creating some value added that could not be produced without them.

Chapter 3

2. Yes, but only in the absence of depreciation, population growth, and technological progress. Each of these requires capital widening to reach a steady state.

4. In all cases, GDP per capita does not grow in the steady state since there is no technological progress.

6. Imagine that we are to the left of $\bar{k}'$ and consider raising the capital–labour ratio. Because the production function is steeper than the depreciation line, moving right raises output more than investment, so consumption rises. It means that we move in the direction of the golden rule. Conversely, starting to the right of $\bar{k}'$, the production function is less steep than the depreciation line, so moving rightwards raises output less than investment, and consumption declines. It means that we move away from the golden rule. Starting from $\bar{k}'$, wherever we move, consumption falls. This is why $\bar{k}'$ is the position where consumption is highest.

8. As workers become more effective (A increases) to keep K/AL constant along the steady state.

Chapter 4

2. (*a*) From eight to sixteen hours of leisure, the budget constraint is as in Figure 4.2; from zero to eight, it has a slope equal to minus the higher overtime wage. The two segments intersect at eight hours of leisure. The budget line is no longer a simple straight line, but piecewise and convex (bowed in towards the origin). (*b*) Overtime makes him better off in the weak sense, that is, he can always choose to ignore it, but can potentially use it to increase his level of utility—note that the crucial element is not his consumption or income, but how happy he is. (*c*) Crusoe will choose overtime if he can reach a higher indifference curve at the point where his marginal rate of substitution of consumption for leisure —given the extra hours worked—equals the real wage. Since the overtime wage is paid only for the additional hours, there will generally be two points of tangency and thus the crucial criterion is the level of utility corresponding to the indifference curves.

4. Linking unemployment benefits to labour taxes, if effectively perceived by each individual firm, has the effect of shifting back the labour demand curve (approximately by a factor of t, the wage tax paid by the firms[1]). In addition, the wage offer curve is likely to shift up, worsening unemployment. In the presence of real wage rigidity due to labour supply mediated by unions, unemployment will increase.

6. Migration exerts pressure towards real wage equalization between both countries. If we assume full wage flexibility, (*a*) real wages must fall in West Germany and (*b*) rise in East Germany. In (*c*), migration triggers an increase in employment in West Germany. The effect on East German employment is not obvious: with real wages increasing faster than marginal productivity (as has probably been the case) employment falls. However, as investment increases in Eastern Germany, employment should also rise. If the East German workers

---

[1] Mathematically minded students may wish to derive the exact extent to which the labour demand curve shifts back. Consider the inverse labour demand curve, which is identical to the marginal product of labour: $MPL(L)$. The marginal product to the firm is reduced now by its marginal tax liability, which is $d(t \cdot MPL(L))/dL = t(MPL + dMPL/dL)$, where t is the fixed tax rate on the wage bill. Thus the net of tax marginal product to the firm is $MPL(L) - t(MPL + dMPL/dL) = (1 - t)MPL(L) + t\, dMPL/dL$. Only if $dMPL/dL = 0$ (linear labour demand curves) will the approximation be correct. Otherwise the actual net MPL will less, especially for high values of L (large firms).

organize themselves into unions, they will demand higher wages, hence alleviating the downward pressure on West German real wages. Note that this will tend to worsen unemployment in East Germany.

8. Bonus or profit-sharing schemes such as those found in Japan increase the flexibility of real wages, since some of the uncertainty over the business cycle is passed on to employees. When a shock occurs, total wage costs to the firm are immediately reduced through the bonus system and employment is stabilized. On the other hand, risk-averse workers may demand higher average wages to compensate them for fluctuations in income, which may have adverse effects on employment.

10. Using the flow approach, we see that $u = s/(s + f)$ in the steady state. Severance regulations make it difficult to fire, so s will be lower. This will reduce the unemployment rate. Yet, if firms associate the regulation with a risk of not being able to fire in bad times, and if bad times are coming, the hiring rate, or the exit rate out of unemployment f may decline as well. Without further information about the relative magnitude of the effects, net impact is ambiguous.

Chapter 5

2. If dividends are kept to be reinvested in the company, they will bring profits in the future. These profits must be discounted at the going interest rate, which represents other opportunities, e.g. Treasury bills. If, and only if, the expected return on investment in the firm exceeds the interest rate, the investment adds value to the firm and its share price should increase, making the shareholder wealthier.

4. In period 2, Crusoe leaves a bequest B_2:

$$C_2 + B_2 = Y_2 + (Y_1 - C_1)(1 + r)$$

His intertemporal budget constraint is.

$$C_1 + C_2/(1 + r) + B_2/(1 + r) = Y_1 + Y_2/(1 + r)$$

6. Interest rate: 5% $PV = 100 (1 + 0.05) = 95.24$
                  10% $PV = 100 (1 + 0.1) = 90.91$

Chapter 6

2. If Ricardian equivalence holds, the path of taxes does not matter. An unexpected transitory increase in public spending leads the private sector to cut spending, but less than the needed tax increase (consumption smoothing), so aggregate spending temporarily rises and the current account worsens. When public spending goes back to normal, private consumption remains depressed, overall spending is down, and the current account improves.

If the increase is permanent, private spending falls one for one and the current account is unaffected.

4. (a) In terms of today's consumption:

$$\Omega = 1000 + (1500/1.05) = 2428.57$$

In terms of tomorrow's consumption:

$$\Omega' = 1000*(1.05) + 1500 = 2550$$

Permanent income Y^p is such that $\Omega = Y^p + (Y^p/1.05)$, i.e. $Y^p = 1243.9$

(b) $Y^p = 1346.3$
(c) $Y^p = 1442.9$
(d) $\Omega = 2363.64$; $\Omega' = 2600$; $Y^p = 1238.1$

6. Since purchasing durables resembles saving (buying a washing machine which you can use tomorrow instead of buying it tomorrow), it should go up when facing a temporary increase in income, and down in the opposite case.

8. Unification requires a temporary, unexpected increase in public spending. Its financing should therefore be spread over many generations. Hence the recommendation: run a budget deficit.

Chapter 7

2. With fixed nominal exchange rate and foreign prices, a doubling of the domestic price level results in the doubling (appreciation) of real exchange rate (as P increases to $2P$, $\sigma = SP/P^*$ increases to $2SP/P^* = 2\sigma$). Similarly, all other things given, a doubling in foreign prices leads to a 100% depreciation and a doubling in the nominal exchange rate also means a doubling of the real exchange rate.

4. Demand for non-tradables declines in the country paying reparation, so its real exchange rate depreciates, with the opposite effect in the victor-country. The first country produces more traded goods and a primary current account surplus, with the opposite result in the victor-country. (After the First World War, Keynes warned that the victor countries would face an external deficit if Germany were to be forced to pay large reparations. His view was not taken seriously, until he was proved right.)

6. The Balassa–Samuelson principle predicts that non-traded prices will grow faster in the poorer member countries which catch up with the richer countries. If traded goods prices are the same, this means that inflation will be higher in the poorer countries.

8. The Balassa–Samuelson effect. The real appreciation is an equilibrium phenomenon, so no overvaluation.

Chapter 8

2. True. As long as the nominal money supply is constant, a positive inflation rate implies that the real money supply is declining.

4. (*a*) Using the Fisher principle, the nominal interest rate remains unchanged if expected inflation declines by 2%.

(*b*) Demand for money doesn't change if the nominal interest rate remains constant.

6. The real demand for money changes, in percentage terms, as:

$$\Delta(M/P)/(M/P) = 0.8\Delta Y/Y - 0.1\Delta i$$

To keep it constant we want, therefore, $0.8\Delta Y/Y - 0.1\Delta i = 0$

So $\Delta Y/Y = 1\%$ requires $\Delta i = 8\%$;
and $\Delta Y/Y = 2\%$ requires $\Delta i = 16\%$;
and $\Delta Y/Y = 5\%$ requires $\Delta i = 40\%$.

8. As people become richer, the value of leisure time rises and they dislike going to the bank to take out cash. Instead they are willing to pay for the opportunity cost of holding more cash.

Chapter 9

2. Direct lending finances part of the budget deficit, thus reducing the government's need to borrow: if the lending is €100 million, the debt is that much lower than it would have been otherwise. Buying back €100 million of public debt from the market has the same effect since the debt is now owed by one branch of the government (the Treasury) to another branch (the central bank) and not to the public. In both cases, the central bank creates €100 million worth of monetary base.

4. The monetary base is the sum of currency in circulation and bank reserves. When the central bank intervenes in the open market it increases the monetary base by increasing reserves. Then commercial banks use their additional reserves to make loans to their customers. The customers may decide to keep the newly created money as bank deposits, in which case there is no increase in currency in circulation, or to fully withdraw their money from the banks, in which case all of the newly created reserves are turned into currency, and there is no increase in bank reserves. Most likely they will withdraw part of their borrowed money, so that there will be an increase in both currency in circulation and bank reserves, at the discretion of the customers.

6. This can lead to instability of the money multiplier m, which links the chosen monetary aggregate M to the monetary base: $M = m$M0. In that case controlling M0 will not allow a precise control of M.

8. Rework the box with $CU = \alpha D$. (9.5) becomes M0 = $CU + R = (\alpha + rr)D$ and (9.6) becomes M1 = $CU + D = (1 + \alpha)D$ and $m = $M1/M0.

10. Money creation *per se* is costless, it only involves (computer) bookkeeping. The costs are partly administrative: dealing with the customer (including marketing efforts), following up repayment, possibly taking bad-payers to court and even suffering default. The costs are also financial as some portion of the loan must be deposited as reserves with the central bank at an unattractive rate.

Chapter 10

2. (*a*) 5000, 6200, 3800; $Y = 7000 - 400i$; (*b*) 4000, 5200, 2800; (*c*) 3000, 5400, 600; $Y = 7000 - 800i$.

4. (*a*) 5000, 6200, 3800; $Y = 7000 - 400i$; (*b*) 4000, 5200, 2800; (*c*) 3000, 5400, 600; $Y = 7000 - 800i$.

6. (*a*) $\bar{Y} = 10000$; $\bar{w} = \frac{1}{2}\sqrt{40} = \sqrt{10}$; $r = i = 2.5$; (*b*) $P = 2$.

8. $Y = 9500$ to 9750; $i = 3.75$ to 3.125; $L = 4512.5$ to 4753.125. Assumption: firms supply output, and workers supply labour at given fixed nominal wages and prices.

10. Taking Figure 10.7 as the starting point, the current endowment decreases, so that for a given production function and tastes, the marginal rate of substitution of goods tomorrow for today will exceed their rate of transformation via planting and harvesting. Crusoe will plant less and eat more today, the marginal productivity of planting rises until he is content with his saving/investment plants. In a market economy, the (gross) real interest rate is equal to this rate of substitution, and rises in equilibrium.

Applied to the six-panel diagram, current output declines for any given labour input, so the S curve shifts back and $\bar{Y}$ declines. The labour market is unchanged, as is the IS curve. The rise in the real interest rate reduces money demand, as does the decrease in equilibrium output/income. This means that money market equilibrium obtains with unambiguously lower real balances, lower than that associated with the decline in output alone. For a given nominal money supply, prices will rise. For details see the website.

Chapter 11

2. (*a*) GDP falls by 2000, from 13000 to 11000. The answer can either be derived directly by plugging in values of exogenous variables and solving for $\bar{T} = 3000$ and $\bar{T} = 3500$, or using the lump-sum tax multiplier of 4 as follows: $4 \times \Delta\bar{T} = 4 \times 500 = 2000$.

(b) GDP rises by 2500, from 13000 to 15500. The answer can either be derived directly by plugging in values of exogenous variables and solving for $\bar{G} = 3000$ and $\bar{G} = 3500$, or using the government spending multiplier of 5 as follows: $5 \times \Delta \bar{G} = 5 \times 500 = 2500$.

(c) GDP rises by 500, from 13000 to 13500. The answer can be derived directly or as the net effect of both previous multipliers, the spending multiplier (5) positively, less the tax multiplier, since taxes were raised to pay for the spending: the net effect is $5 \times \Delta \bar{G} - 4 \times \Delta \bar{T} = (5 - 4) \times 500 = 500$.

4. The LM curve is given by the equality of real money supply and real money demand: $\bar{M} / \bar{P} = \mathcal{L}(Y, i, c)$ or 2500 $= 0.5Y - 300i + 50c$. Increasing c (an exogenous increase in the demand for real balances) from 10 to 20 shifts the LM curve up and leftwards from $2000 = 0.5Y - 300i$ to $1500 = 0.5Y - 300i$. This can be seen by plotting this curve in (i, Y) space (the IS–LM diagram). Similarly, doubling the price level at a given nominal money supply moves the LM curve up and leftwards from $2000 = 0.5Y - 300i$ to $750 = 0.5Y - 300i$. In contrast, increasing the money supply from 2500 to 3000 shifts the LM curve down and rightwards to $2500 = 0.5Y - 300i$.

6. (a) The LM curve is $2000 = 0.5Y - 300i$. For $\bar{S} = 1$ and $\bar{G} = \bar{T} = 3000$, the IS curve is $Y = 15500 - 500i$. But in a fixed exchange rate regime $i = i^* = 10$, so the equilibrium interest rate must also be 10; Y can be thus read from the IS curve: $Y = 15500 - 5000 = 10500$. The money supply is endogenous, since the central bank is obligated to intervene to maintain $S = 1$. Using the demand for money function, we find $\mathcal{L}(Y, i, c) = 0.5(10500) - 300(10) + 500 = 5250 - 3000 + 500 = 2750$, which at $P = 1$ corresponds to a nominal money demand $M = 2750$. Higher interest rates imposed on the domestic economy by foreign financial conditions reduced domestic money demand, which would normally be accommodated by central bank sales of foreign exchange, with the effect of retiring high-powered money, and, via the money multiplier, reducing the money supply.

(b) Under fixed exchange rates, the full government spending multiplier will apply, since interest rates do not rise. GDP rises by 2500, from 13000 to 15500. Fiscal policy is potent under fixed exchange rates. The interest rate remains at 10, so the demand for money rises by $(0.5) \times 2500 = 1250$, and supply is accommodated in the process of central bank interventions to prevent an appreciation.

8. (a) The LM curve is $2000 = 0.5Y - 300i$. As before $\bar{G} = \bar{T} = 3000$, but now S is endogenous. The LM curve, combined with the condition $i = i^* = 10$, determines the value of GDP: $2000 = 0.5Y - 300(10) \Rightarrow Y = 10000$. The exchange rate must adjust until $Y = 10000$. The IS curve

is $Y = 18000 - 500i - 2500S$, so at $i = 10$, $10000 = 18000 - 5000 - 2500S$, or $S = 3000/2500 = 1.2$. The exchange rate appreciates above its original value, to make aggregate demand consistent with the given international interest rate. Compared with Problem 4, output is lower.

(b) The IS curve shifts from $Y = 18000 - 500i - 2500S$ to $Y = 20500 - 500i - 2500S$, and with $i = i^* = 10$, $Y = 15500 - 2500S$. Since the real money supply remains constant, the LM curve $2000 = 0.5Y - 300i$ is unchanged, so $Y = 10000$. For the IS to intersect the LM at $i = 10$ we require a value of S such that $10000 = 15500 - 2500S$, or $S = 5500/2500 = 2.2$. If the money supply increases, of course, the answer changes: the relevant LM curve becomes $2500 = 0.5Y - 300i$, and $Y = 13000$. This confirms that when exchange rates are flexible, monetary policy is potent, while fiscal policy is crowded out. In the end the increase in government spending implies an appreciated exchange rate relative to the case without: the equilibrium value of S in this case is 1.

(c) In the case of flexible exchange rates, the IS curve shifts from $Y = 18000 - 500i - 2500S$ to $Y = 16000 - 500i - 2500S$, and with $i = i^* = 10$, $Y = 11000 - 2500S$. The LM curve $2000 = 0.5Y - 300i$ continues to be valid, so $Y = 10000 = 11000 - 2500S$, or $S = 1000/2500 = 0.4$. The exchange rate depreciates to crowd in spending so that Y is unchanged. In the fixed rate case, GDP falls from 13000 to 11000.

10. A fixed exchange rate in a booming economy like Poland's, driven by disturbances to the IS curve, will put upward pressure on the demand for money, leading to tighter monetary conditions and rising interest rates. Foreign capital inflows keep interest rates from rising too much, since they are purchased by the central bank and 'monetized', but this implies a rapidly growing money supply. Because income is growing fast—and presumably faster than in neighbouring countries—imports will be growing faster than exports and the current account will deteriorate.

Chapter 12

2. Think of a one-off supply shock $s > 0$ in Figure 12.6: the Phillips curve and short-run aggregate supply curves shift upwards, but only for one period only. If core inflation does not rise, in the following periods the curve will shift down again. Workers in an oil-importing economy may face a larger supply shock, if domestic energy suppliers are more likely to be involved in long-term contracts and would not follow suit.

4. The idea that the new technologies of internet, telecommunications, and personal computing all make us more productive could permanently increase the level and perhaps even the growth of equilibrium output. If equilibrium unemployment is structural, it might decline if more jobs are created at given wages that didn't exist earlier. New technologies which improve job search and matching might reduce frictional unemployment and thereby depress the equilibrium rate of unemployment. If it takes off, the internet might lead to a permanent decline in the mark-up of prices on wages, which would mean a one-off shift in the Phillips curve and short-term aggregate supply.

6. Increasing the VAT is like a supply shock, and is very likely to be felt by all, and have an effect on wage negotiations. Workers will want an increase in nominal wages to compensate them for this increase in the price level; firms may not be able to afford it. The winner of the battle of the mark-ups is not clear. Thus it may affect the equilibrium rate of unemployment as well, if workers are able to protect their real wages. The same applies to other taxes, with varying degrees of intensity: firms with market power will try to pass on corporate profits tax on their customers, depending on the competitive situation in product markets. Workers will resist the loss of purchasing power and demand higher wages. Income tax rises may also give rise to worker demands for increased real wages.

8. These taxes can act as supply shocks if they are included in the headline measure of inflation used in determining pay changes. In the case of RPIY, a restrictive monetary policy by definition raises interest rates. In Britain most homes are financed at variable rates, meaning that an increase in rates leads to an immediate increase in the cost of owning a home. Because so many Britons own homes, it was felt by policy-makers to be reasonable to include this in the index of the cost of living. Yet, if workers measure their nominal pay by the RPIY, they will demand higher wages whenever monetary policy is tight, leading to a one-off shift in the supply curve to the left. Similarly, a contractionary fiscal policy consisting of a tax hike (VAT or excise taxes) will increase prices for any given rate of core inflation, shifting the AS curve to the left.

10. The long-run effect should be easiest: the equilibrium unemployment rate $\bar{U}$ shifts to the left and the equilibrium level of output $\bar{Y}$ to the right, and inflation is independent of the two. If the reforms take hold immediately, the economy will find itself at an unemployment rate which exceeds $\bar{U}$; at the old inflation rate, this will correspond to a different downward-sloping Phillips curve and upward-sloping aggregate supply curve. The result—holding everything else constant—is deflation, as nominal wages and prices rise more slowly than they would at the equilibrium rate. Later we will see that the path to the steady state can be made less painful if demand is 'supportive' during this phase.

Chapter 13

2. A one-off expansion of the money supply (interpreted as a temporary increase in the growth *rate* of the money supply) will move the LM curve out, lower interest rates, and induce a depreciation at given i*. An increase in monetary growth which is believed to be permanent, in contrast, will additionally create the expectation of higher inflation and, via PPP and eq. (13.7) will raise the expected depreciation rate $(-\Delta S/S)$ and in turn cause an even greater depreciation and output expansion.

4. First, the demand shift which is associated with bringing down the rate of monetary growth is negative and will cause output loss for any given position of the supply curve. Second, the inflation rate which lies behind wage and price settlements (core inflation) may not fall rapidly, leading to further output loss. This second reason need not obtain, if expectations of inflation decline and the policy is believed to be permanent.

6. With rational expectations, a fiscal expansion under fixed exchange rates will be accompanied by more rapid wage and price increases, leading to the same real appreciation that occurs when core inflation and inflation itself are sluggish, but without any significant delay. Consider, in the opposite direction, a contraction of the money supply under flexible rates. For any given shape of the AS curve, the contractionary effect (on prices) will be anticipated and incorporated into expectations. The only point at which the expectations are correct is when output equals the equilibrium level. This would lead to immediate declines in nominal wages and prices, followed by increases when the contraction is relaxed.

8. This represents a leftward shift to the AS curve under fixed rates yet is nevertheless temporary, since the foreign rate of inflation (other Euroland countries) remains constant. A recession is likely, which could be ameliorated with expansionary fiscal policy, but this would depend on the policy coordination of the governments involved. Recovery will be associated with an endogenous depreciation (domestic prices rise less fast) and current account improvement.

10. First and foremost, prices of basic products were deregulated leading to a supply-shock-like disturbance (a leftward shift of AS). At the same time firms were exposed as being technologically backward and unable to compete in worlds markets. In total this is like a backward shift of LAS, at least for many years until new capital can be invested.

Chapter 14

2. The parameters a_0 and b_0 are exogenous or autonomous components of consumption and investment expenditures, respectively. From the expression for the steady state of Y, $\bar{Y}$, it is clear that the sum of the two autonomous expenditures is multiplied up by $1/(1 - a_1)$. Since a_1 is the marginal propensity to consume out of income, the result is very similar to the multiplier derived in Chapter 11.

4. If supply shocks predominate, the correlation between inflation and output should be negative, as a shifting AS curve traces out outcomes along a given AD curve. If demand shocks are more important, inflation and output will be positively correlated. In reality, over long periods of time the correlation may not be constant: in periods of severe supply shocks (e.g. the stagflation of the 1970s) a negative correlation result might be expected, while in other periods demand shocks may have predominated. On average, the correlation may well be zero.

6. (i) Since investment expenditures (Figure 14.4 panel (b)) are strongly cyclical and peak before GDP in a fashion similar to the primary current account, it is tempting to conclude that they are driving the primary current account. This is also consistent with the fact that investment goods are often imported from abroad, and that capacity constraints are usually operative in that sector before the peak. On the other hand, if all countries were synchronized, it would be difficult for all to behave in this fashion, since all countries cannot run a trade deficit (naturally, there may be other countries in play here besides the five considered in Figure 14.4!).

(ii) Since Germany is indeed a leading exporter of investment goods, its leading PCA surplus may be the mirror image of counter-cyclical primary current account surpluses observed elsewhere. It may also reflect a fundamental reluctance on the part of German monetary and fiscal authorities to inflate domestic demand in recessions, preferring to rely on external stimuli. An RBC explanation would need to rely on the behaviour of relative *prices*, in this case, the real exchange rate or the relative price of investment goods, as opposed to quantities in the sticky price case. It might also argue that, if Germany is specialized in investment goods, the implementation of technology innovations involves an increase in exports from Germany to the rest of the world.

8. Reviewing the *IS–LM* analysis, procyclical interest rates occur if shifts in the *IS* curve are primarily responsible for output fluctuations. If monetary shifts predominate, interest rates should be countercyclical. Furthermore, if nominal interest rates are strongly procyclical, it is likely that the inflation rate is at least mildly procyclical (Figure 14.3). Thus, shifts in the *AS–AD* model seem to predominate with the *AD* curve, and these seem to be coming from the *IS* curve, and probably from a regime of fixed or managed exchange rates.

10. If demand (marginal product of labour) is constantly equal to supply (the value of leisure) then flat real wages can only be explained by a flat labour demand or supply curve. A flat labour demand curve can be ruled out *a priori*, so some justification must be brought forward for why workers supply much additional labour voluntarily for little current monetary compensation. Since individual households do not exhibit highly elastic labour supply, the RBC theory must appeal to heterogeneity (different agents) and/or fixed costs of going to work which lead to 'all-or-nothing' behaviour. The sticky price view of the cycle assumes wage and price rigidity, which gives the answer immediately. In addition, efficiency wages, labour contracts, and other institutions can help explain real wage rigidity.

Chapter 15

2. It diminishes the incentive for inflationary finance, since higher expectations of inflation will be reflected in higher nominal interest rates and a depreciating currency. The end result is a higher financing burden. Furthermore, a devaluation increases the debt burden by revaluing the debt stock and increasing the amount of produced resources that must be transferred to service this debt.

4. Perfectly anticipated increases in inflation will be reflected in nominal interest rates, so it will be impossible for the government to gain, except from pure seigniorage —that is, the real resources acquired by the government via creation of real means of payment, which remains even when inflation is anticipated. During hyperinflations, the real value of tax revenues declines as a consequence of delays in payment and assessment. The first term on the right-hand side (the primary budget surplus) falls. It makes it more difficult for the government to stop monetization of the public debt (the second term on the left-hand side) as debt issue becomes increasingly difficult. One solution is to raise taxes and cut government spending in order to reduce the primary budget deficit at the time money growth is brought under control. This kind of stabilization policy was implemented successfully in Bolivia (1985–6) for instance. However, it involves major political risks, as such policies are very costly and unpopular. Another solution is to invest in tax assessment and collection.

6. Ignoring seigniorage, the necessary primary budget surplus must keep the debt GDP ratio constant, that is, a surplus as high as $(2 - 3.5) \times 0.40 = -0.6\%$ of GDP (a deficit). In contrast, if the interest rate is 6% then we have $(6 - 3.5) \times 0.40 = 1.0\%$ of GDP.

8. (*a*) Primary budget surplus (PBS) = $(r - g) B/Y = 2\%$ (for details see solution to Problem 6 above). (*b*) With $r = 2\%$

any primary budget surplus is sustainable. With $g = 1\%$, $PBS = 4\%$.

10. When $\pi = \mu$, seigniorage (s) is equal to the inflation tax $\pi(M0/P)$, i.e. the inflation tax when the Fisher effect holds for interest bearing assets:

$$\pi = 0\% \quad \Rightarrow \quad s = 0$$
$$\pi = 1\% \quad \Rightarrow \quad s = 9$$
$$\pi = 2\% \quad \Rightarrow \quad s = 16.4$$
$$\pi = 5\% \quad \Rightarrow \quad s = 30.3$$
$$\pi = 10\% \quad \Rightarrow \quad s = 36.8$$
$$\pi = 20\% \quad \Rightarrow \quad s = 27$$
$$\pi = 25\% \quad \Rightarrow \quad s = 20.5$$
$$\pi = 50\% \quad \Rightarrow \quad s = 3.5$$

Seigniorage follows a hump-shaped pattern when inflation rises because, as inflation increases, people will tend to hold fewer real money balances, which reduces the tax base on which seigniorage is set. For the values of inflation given, a 10% rate maximizes seigniorage.

Chapter 16

2. Using the framework of Chapter 13, the outcome is likely to be stagflation: a leftward shift in the AS curve, leading to higher inflation and declining output or growth rates. The monetarist would be likely to argue that the wage settlements reflect underlying microeconomic phenomena that must be worked out by the markets.

4. See Section 16.2.4. Advantages to higher inflation might be to shift the tax burden on money and other nominal assets which do not pay the nominal interest rate. This is less likely to be convincing nowadays. If carried out as a surprise, this could also be used to tax other nominal interest-bearing assets. It has also been argued that inflation may help ease the real adjustment of real wages if workers suffer from 'money illusion', resisting for example a nominal wage cut of 2% at zero inflation more than zero nominal wage growth with 2% inflation.

6. Financial markets may expect the central bank to monetize the deficits (seigniorage financing) which would possibly reduce interest rates and create capital outflows. Another is the mechanism outlined in Chapter 7: suppose a large budget deficit is associated with current account deficits. In order to meet the intertemporal budget constraint, a depreciation will be necessary. If future exchange rates are expected to depreciate then the interest rate parity condition implies that the exchange rate today should decline too. Finally, it could well be that the response is endogenous: current tax shortfalls signal a severe recession looming, which the exchange markets interpret as times of lower interest rates, capital outflow, and depreciating currency.

8. The rationale of either proposal is to set a rule which eliminates the discretion in demand management and makes policy easy to understand, and to anticipate. Monetary neutrality implies that in the long run, real growth is invariant to growth in money, and that money growth will be related to growth in prices. This means that a rate of growth in money is equivalent to fixing growth in nominal GDP. The disadvantage is that perverse policy reactions may occur if money demand shifts, or more generally velocity changes in an unpredictable way. The advantage of inflation targeting vis-à-vis nominal GDP targeting is that there are fewer sources of disturbances which could cause problems. But both will be vulnerable to supply shocks that raise inflation and contract output.

10. Restriction of dismissal rights is a limitation on the freedom of managers to employ factors of production as they wish. It turns out to be a costly one, if necessary employment reductions are not possible in times of severe economic downturn or structural change. While firms may not be able to reduce employment directly, they will certainly lose workers over time due to quits, retirements, and other forms of mobility. The jobs thus vacated are less likely to be replaced if they impose further costs on employment, and are likely to be the victims of capital–labour substitution. When governments announce a relaxation of the rules, the time inconsistency is transparent: if the firm hires new workers, employment rises, and the government has an incentive to reimpose the restrictions. Once the line has been crossed, it may even be difficult for a 'conservative' government to convince firms with deregulation, since it can always be reversed by future governments.

Chapter 17

2. Besides demand side effects which are known from Part IV and V, a cut in taxes is likely to affect the supply side, to the extent that the supply of production factors to the market depends on income taxation. The effect will depend on the relative supply and demand elasticities. If labour supply is inelastic, large output effects in the short run are unlikely, however. Similarly, in the medium to long run, capital is likely to move out of a small open economy which has high rates of income taxation, leading to reduced output and employment.

4. Clearly, immigration policy means regulation of labour supply and in many European countries the most important source of new labourers. By increasing aggregate labour supply, policy-makers can increase aggregate supply; further, by influencing the *composition*

of immigration, the relative abundance of the scarcest (and at the margin, the most productive) productive factors can be increased. The controversy surrounding migration is certainly not only economic, but disparities resulting in the distribution of the increased output leads the disadvantaged to oppose migration.

6. If rates of taxation are very high, the importance of tax evasion and the underground economy increases, depressing government revenue and leading to effects associated with the Laffer curve. (The difference is that the economy activity still takes place; it is simply untaxed.) Presumably, this effect is stronger in countries where the underground economy is already sizeable. For low-wage workers, the probability of being 'trapped' in the welfare system is higher, and the more attractive it is to work in the underground economy and escape being in the tax base.

8. Hiring costs can create a group of insiders who have jobs and are insulated from market pressures. It may pay to use overtime at the margin, especially if there is favourable treatment of overtime bonuses. Since the employed are in a majority, they are most likely to resist efforts to redistribute working hours. Reform measures might include a statutory binding overtime premium or a more equitable tax treatment of overtime hours. Going directly to the source, one might abolish the underlying distortions.

10. It is a mystery that unemployment ranges from 5% to 15% presently and yet remains a political issue. There are several possible explanations for this fact. First, it is usually the change in unemployment and not the level which triggers the most political discomfort. This is probably due to the fact that rising unemployment reinforces the perceived risk of becoming unemployed. Another is that the fiscal burden of supporting even a modest fraction of the labour force means higher taxes and lower labour demand for those already in employment.

Chapter 18

2. Income is a flow, so a retroactive tax does not prevent people from reacting to future incomes (by working less, migrating, etc.). It is much less confiscatory than a tax on a stock, which has been accumulated over many years and cannot be easily moved.

4. Old truths may not hold forever! Great effort has gone into making cartwheels run smoothly, but this know-how may be of little value nowadays. Similarly, people age, and what they learnt when they were young may become irrelevant or simply forgotten.

Chapter 19

2. The holder of assets bears price risk. The best example is foreign exchange, although this is only one of many assets which bear two prices. At any given point in time there are traders, or even market makers, who have indicated a willingness to meet random buyers and sellers of foreign exchange. To do this, they must maintain an inventory of foreign exchange on hand. Exchange rate fluctuations thus expose the market maker to risk. To compensate for that risk, the market maker charges a price (ask) which is higher, sometimes considerably higher than the one she is willing to pay when buying (bid). With every euro of foreign exchange purchased at bid and sold at ask price, the dealer or market maker earns the difference; this can be thought of as compensation for risk-bearing. The riskier the price, the larger the bid–ask spread.

4. (a) A version of (19.9) which equates expected values is $r = d/q_t + (_t q_{t+1} - q_t)/q_t$. Using the given probabilities, $_t q_{t+1} = s q_{t+1}$. Given the current value q_t, the arbitrage condition now reads $r = d/q_t + [(1 - s)q_{t+1} - q_t]/q_t$; the total asset yield for the private asset (dividend yield plus expected capital gain) is set equal to the certain rate r. In general q_t is not constant along the path defined by that equation.

(b) The previous solution holds for all value of q_t; the question is, which value is consistent with $q_t = {}^t q_{t+1} = \bar{q}$. Now substitute $\bar{q}$ for all values of q in the equation: $r = d/q_t + [(1 - s)q_{t+1} - q_t]/q_t$ and solve to obtain $\bar{q} = d/(r + s)$. The probability of a bust depresses the fundamental value of the asset just like the interest rate used in discounting.

6. An arbitrage relationship would imply that the 7% yield on the two-year bond should be equal to that obtained by investing for at the one-year rate at 5% for one year and then reinvesting the proceeds at the one-year rate in the second period. Denote that one-period rate in the second periods as $i_{1,2}$. Then the arbitrage condition is $(1 + 7/100)^2 = (1 + 5/100)(1 + i_{1,2})$, so solving for $i_{1,2}$ we obtain $i_{1,2} = (1 + 7/100)^2/(1 + 5/100) - 1 = 0.09038 \approx 9\%$. This is the answer that would have resulted from the approximation given in equation (19.6) of Box 19.4: $0.07 = 0.5(0.05 + i_{1,2})$ implies $i_{1,2} = 0.09 = 9\%$.

(8) (a) a permanent appreciation (S rises); (b) a permanent appreciation (S rises); (c) a permanent appreciation (S rises). Because prices are flexible, long and short run are identical.

10. Certainly not! The interest differential has several interpretations. Despite the fixing of the exchange rate in the 'EMS-II' system, Denmark is not a participant in the European Monetary Union, so it is relatively easy

to imagine how the parity could change over the next decade. In its history, Denmark has devalued before and almost by definition has more political influence over monetary policy than is the case in Euroland. Market participants may expect a devaluation with some probability, even though this has not occurred in the recent past. (This is known, incidentally, as the 'peso problem', after a similar observation on Mexican–US interest rate spreads in fixed exchange rate regimes). A second possibility is that no devaluation is expected, but precisely because of these factors, the markets demand a risk premium for Danish Krone-denominated investments. In the first case, even risk-neutral participants would admit the 40 basis point (5.2–4.8) spread; in the latter case the spread could only exist if the marginal trader is risk averse.

Chapter 20

2. Since the dollar is the world currency, it is held worldwide. By issuing dollars, the Federal Reserve reaps seigniorage profits. Since about two-thirds of all dollars issued by the Fed are held overseas, half of the Fed's seigniorage tax is levied on foreigners.

4. It is true that every injection of liquidity is inflationary but: (1) there would be less need for dollars, hence US balance of payments deficits, which would exert a counter-inflationary influence; (2) relatively small amounts of SDRs could make a big difference for the poorest countries with a negligible effect on the world money supply. Of course, the true reason for opposing this move is the belief that this money might be misused by the recipients.

Index